MAKING CHOICES, TAKING CHANCES

NURSE LEADERS TELL THEIR STORIES

Birch Trees at Dawn on Lake George
Georgia O'Keeffe
(oil on canvas, 36 × 30″)

The Saint Louis Art Museum
Gift of Mrs. Ernest Stix

Miss Georgia O'Keeffe and her work
epitomize the spirit of dedication, individualism,
and successful achievement in one's chosen field.

MAKING CHOICES TAKING CHANCES

NURSE LEADERS TELL THEIR STORIES

THELMA M. SCHORR, R.N.

President and Publisher,
The American Journal of Nursing Company,
New York, New York

ANNE ZIMMERMAN, R.N., F.A.A.N.

Formerly Executive Administrator,
Illinois Nurses Association,
Chicago, Illinois

The C. V. Mosby Company

St. Louis ♦ Washington, D.C. ♦ Toronto   1988

MOSBY

A TRADITION OF PUBLISHING EXCELLENCE

Editor: Thomas Lochhaas
Assistant editor: Linda Hart
Production editor: Russell L. Hughes
Designer: Susan E. Lane

Printed in the United States of America

The C.V. Mosby Company
11830 Westline Industrial Drive, St. Louis, Missouri 63146

Library of Congress Cataloging-in-Publication Data

Schorr, Thelma M.
  Making choices, taking chances.

  Includes bibliographies and index.
  1.   Nurses—United States—Biography.   I.   Zimmerman,
Anne.   II.   Title.   [DNLM: 1.   Career Choice.   2.   Nurses—
United States—biography.   WZ 112.5.N8 S372m]
RT34.S36   1988   610.73′092′2   87-34968
ISBN 0-8016-4611-1

GW/VH/VH   9   8   7   6   5   4   3   2   1

*To the nurses in this book
who made choices, took chances,
and generously told about them*

Preface

Making choices, taking chances—that's what this book is about. It came into being when a graduate student, out of frustration, asked, "How do I find out about the nursing leaders whose articles, books, and speeches appear on all of my bibliographies?"

It was her inquiry that channeled our thoughts into what we believe is a one-of-a-kind book. We searched and could find no contemporary biographies. There are a few oral histories, some compilations of interviews, some dissertations about individuals, and the short biographies that accompany articles and books. However, nowhere could we locate a primary source of stories that would detail the growth and development of a nursing leader.

So we decided to solicit first-person stories from nurses whose careers had taken a path for which they were well known. We expected that we would be able to organize the stories around particular subjects. As the manuscripts came in, we realized that this was not possible—for a variety of reasons. Among these is that our view of what each person's major contribution to nursing has been and the writers' beliefs about these contributions did not necessarily coincide. Consequently, we backed away from the subject-matter idea and chose instead to focus on the people themselves, hence the alphabetical order of the table of contents.

Our selection of contributors was intended to be representative and not all-inclusive. Undoubtedly, every reader will question our choices—why this person was chosen rather than that one. Every nurse will have his or her own list of great nurse leaders. The people in this book come from *our* lists, and originally our lists were much longer—but we had to make choices. In the end, the process of honing our huge combined list of contemporary leaders became almost random, and we now have an abundant selection of names from which to choose—enough for a second edition or even a series.

Not every reader will agree with the track chosen by some of these nurses—nor do we. Nevertheless, the consequences of decisions of those leaders in pursuing their ideas markedly influenced the future of nursing. In some instances, their ideas continue to do so.

Where we found different points of view on an issue, every attempt was made to represent each position. There may be different versions of a single incident, but what is presented here comes from the eyes of the beholders. There was no effort made to alter or challenge any writer's perception. We were careful in the editing process not to alter any writer's style or personality. The subject headings within the chapters are the writers' own.

We found these very personal stories to be rich in knowledge, history, and inspiration, and we expect that you too will find them a source for all of this and much more.

The commonalities in the lives of these leaders, as well as the differences, are apparent. Many of these nurses excelled academically from the beginning—for others, it was an uphill struggle to get into and stay in nursing school. No one found the going easy, and for some it took extraordinary effort and perseverance. Fortunately, timidity was no handicap in any instance.

Most of these leaders are goal oriented, but the element of good luck cannot be ignored. Being in the right place at the right time in relation to choices and career changes is expressed over and over again in these pages, as is the willingness to seize opportunities.

Not all of them chose nursing initially, but every contributor expressed satisfaction and having no regrets with his or her final decision.

You will find remarkable accounts of career choices and chances. For instance: dreaming of being a cowboy and ending up as an expert on death and dying; choosing between a safe, secure job in an institution and venturing into independent practice as an entrepreneur; leaving a promising job with AT&T at age 29 to enter nursing, and later becoming an outstanding clinical nurse specialist; and moving one's worksite from a New York City tenement to a Navajo hogan in the Southwest.

There are common threads in these stories. Many wrote of the influence of nurses they had known, some through childhood illnesses, some in other ways. They tell of strong support from parents, spouses, other family members, and close friends. These leaders are remarkably open in sharing their personal joys and heartaches, as well as their professional successes and failures. Many are widely published but had to work at acquiring effective speaking skills. They write about their active participation and investment in professional nursing organizations and interdisciplinary activities, as well as about their involvement in research and their commitment to advance it. The similarity is striking among those for whom financial support from scholarships, the U.S. Cadet Nurse Corps, and government traineeships and loans was crucial to their education. Many lived by these fundamentals: taking responsibility for one's own acts, having respect for learning, doggedly pursuing goals and visions, developing a strong sense of advocacy, and having a sense of self-worth.

Outstanding mentors had a strong impact on the professional and personal lives of many. You will find in these pages the grace of Katherine J. Densford (Dreves), the expectations of Katharine Faville, and the determination of R. Louise McManus. The writings of Virginia Henderson are referred to with respect for her wisdom and authority.

It is not our expectation that you will read this book from front to back. Rather, there are stories you will savor and reread—some you may skim and return to later, perhaps following an encounter with the person or with his or her works. With some, it may be the relevance of the professional content that draws your attention; with others, it may not be the issue itself but the person's approach to it; for some it will be the actual prescription that is suggested; for many, it will be a sheer delight with the prose.

For students, the trials and travails these leaders overcome will be encouraging. Moreover, the content will augment knowledge and stimulate further research. Many of these stories of success will be of interest to both women and men who may be seeking new directions in their careers.

We anticipate that these autobiographies will be a rich resource for those writing term papers, making speeches, and needing encouragement. Those whose sense of well-being is sagging or whose sense of direction is hazy may be heartened by the fortitude and pioneering of some of these nurses. When nursing is going through one of its periodic shortages, we hope that some of this material will be used to attract people into the profession and to guide them into leadership roles.

These stories reflect nursing's splendor and frailties. We hope the book will spark debate, stimulate awareness, nudge introspection, and evoke pride. Above all, we think it will bring to life the character and the humanness, the intellect and the modesty, the reality and the vision of these leaders.

One last word. We thank our families for their patience and encouragement, our friends for their suggestions and admonitions, and at Mosby, Tom Lochhaas for his enthusiasm and Russell Hughes for his meticulous copy editing.

Most of all we thank the nurses who searched their memories and shared them with us.

Thelma M. Schorr
Anne Zimmerman

ABOUT US . . .

Thelma Schorr

I was born in New Haven, Connecticut, the only child of Simon and Rebecca Mermelstein. My mother was hospitalized many times when I was a child. She died when I was 14. Whether I was drawn to nursing because of my mother's illness, by the sensitivity of a nurse who let me see my mother's body when I wouldn't believe she was dead, or whether I just wanted to get away from New Haven, I'll never know.

In June 1942 I entered the Bellevue School of Nursing in New York City. I graduated in 1945 and immediately became charge nurse of a "male medicine" ward at Bellevue. We had some marvelous patients, and conversations with them whetted my intellectual appetite. So I went to Columbia University's School of General Studies at night, taking subjects like philosophy, French, and history.

In 1949 I wrote a petition protesting the "dumping" of tuberculosis patients on open wards with no equipment for isolation precautions—a practice hazardous for patients and for staff as well. All 45 of the nurses working in medicine signed the petition, but it received no attention when we sent it to the hospital administration and to the city's commissioner of hospitals. So we went to the newspapers, where it received front page treatment and banner headlines, culminating in the hospital commissioner's acceptance of all our suggestions and his admonition that I'd be a troublemaker all my life.

Because the *American Journal of Nursing* wanted to do a story about the successful collective action at Bellevue, the editors invited me to lunch, and, the next day, called to offer me a job. I worked part time there while I attended Teachers College full time to get my BS. I had always liked to write, and at *AJN* I learned to edit from Nell Beeby and Edith (Pat) Lewis.

In 1954 I met Norman Schorr, a public relations professional with a newspaper background who has always been supportive and encouraging, even though he has raged at my writing everything in longhand. I never learned to type. In 1955 we were married. In 1957 Susan was born, in 1958 Marjorie, and in 1962 Elizabeth. After the birth of each child, I was able to return to work because at home we had a capable, intelligent housekeeper, Lena Mae Shaw.

In 1959 Barbara Schutt became editor of *AJN* and brought to it a crusading pen. She wrote provocative editorials that challenged staff nurses to focus their collective power on improving their own and nursing's status. In 1970 she had a myocardial infarction. After she recovered she resigned, and I became editor of *AJN*.

What a heady time those next 11 years were. Except for the unique satisfaction of direct patient care that I had known at Bellevue, I thought that being editor of *AJN* was the most exciting job in nursing. Being tuned in to all that was happening in the field, deciding on the presentation of content, working with authors and bright, challenging staff, writing editorials each month, working with the ANA leadership, being in close touch with nurses throughout the country, speaking on issues or on writing—all marvelous experiences.

In 1981 I became president and publisher of the American Journal of Nursing Company and am responsible now for the total publishing operations of *AJN*, as well as for *Nursing Outlook, Nursing Research, MCN, Geriatric Nursing,* the *International Nursing Index,* the *AJN Guide,* the AJN Nursing Boards Review, and the Educational Services Division.

Setting policy for the AJN Company and providing strong support for me have been the members of the Company's board of directors and particularly the chairs—Mary Woody, Anne Zimmerman, Ora Strickland, and Barbara Nichols. To them, my thanks, and to nursing, my love.

Anne Zimmerman

The first of five children, I was born in the mining town of Marysville, Montana. It was my mother's long illness and my hospitalization with a fractured femur that attracted me to nursing. It was the Great Depression that propelled me into it.

In Helena, Montana, I graduated from the St. Johns Unit of the Sisters of Charity of Leavenworth School of Nursing in 1935. Though my parents originally thought that I was too strong willed to succeed in nursing, I loved it.

I had a superb instructor, Margaret Bottinelli (Troxel), from whom I learned the true meaning of social justice. Her teaching that the right to a just wage need not be at the expense of patient care stayed with me all my life.

I was married in 1936, and four years later I faced raising my 18-month-old daughter, Nancy, as a single parent. Always my pride and challenge and now an adult companion, Nancy has continued to encourage me to do more than I think I can. She is a psychiatric clinical nurse specialist.

Organizing people, events, and things interested me from the beginning. (My siblings would have said I was plain bossy.) I liked pediatric nursing, but I knew that working conditions could be better than they were, and I vowed to do what I could to make improvements. Active at every level of the American Nurses' Association, I have attended every meeting of the ANA House of Delegates since 1945. I went from being a volunteer to becoming the executive director of the Montana Nurses Association in 1945, and two years later I joined the staff of the California Nurses Association (CNA) to work on the economic and general welfare program.

To me, my seven years with CNA were the equivalent of graduate education. Shirley C. Titus, the executive director, was a visionary, a champion of nurses' rights, and a scholar. From that experience I learned every facet of organization work. I also learned how to convert the ideas of a genius into solutions to burning problems. From 1951 to 1952 I lived in New York City, directing the ANA economic and general welfare program.

I moved to Chicago in 1954 to become the executive director of the Illinois Nurses Association, a position I resigned in 1981. My commitment to help nurses act collectively to achieve a decent salary and gain some measure of control over the environment in which they practice never faltered. For this I received the ANA Shirley Titus Award in 1980. In 1976 I was elected ANA president. Being elected to this coveted office represented the epitome of recognition by my peers and underscored for me the goals I had for nursing.

Time came to take leave of the rigors of organizational life and to heed the admonishment of my grandchildren to "lighten up, Grama." What could have been a harsh transition into oblivion became instead an exciting new experience when Julia Lane, dean of the Niehoff School of Nursing, Loyola University, invited me to teach a course in contemporary health issues to the graduate nursing students. Those four years matched the rest of my career as far as absorption in one's work and satisfaction are concerned. While some would call it a late-life career change, I thought of it as the recycling of an executive.

As for now, I have my "consolation hot line," which my friends keep busy with accounts of their heroics, their laments, and their requests for advice (freely given). Having no constituency, and consequently being accountable only to myself, is a freedom that I savor. Meanwhile, my optimism and hope for the future of nursing continue unabashedly.

Contributors

Linda H. Aiken, *PhD, RN, FAAN*
Vice President
Robert Wood Johnson Foundation
Princeton, New Jersey

Myrtle K. Aydelotte, *PhD, RN, FAAN*
Professor of Nursing & Dean Emeritus
College of Nursing
University of Iowa
Iowa City, Iowa

Jeanne Quint Benoliel, *DNSc, RN, FAAN*
Elizabeth Sterling Soule Distinguished Professor
Nursing and Health Promotion
University of Washington
Seattle, Washington

Hattie Bessent, *EdD, RN*
Director, Minority Fellowship Program
American Nurses' Association
Washington, District of Columbia

M. Elizabeth Carnegie, *DPA, RN, FAAN*
Visiting Professor, Vera E. Bender Endowed
Chair in Nursing
Adelphi University
Garden City, New York

Luther Christman, *PhD, RN, FAAN*
Dean Emeritus
College of Nursing
Rush University
Chicago, Illinois

Maureen Cushing, *JD, RN*
Attorney at Law
Mooney, Mahoney and Cushing
Boston, Massachusetts

Anne Davis, *PhD, RN, FAAN*
Professor
Mental Health and Community Nursing
University of California
San Francisco, California

Rheba de Tornyay, *EdD, RN, FAAN*
Professor, Department of Community Health
  Care Systems
Dean Emeritus, School of Nursing
University of Washington
Seattle, Washington

Donna Diers, *MSN, RN, FAAN*
Professor and Former Dean
Yale University
School of Nursing
New Haven, Connecticut

Eileen McQuaid Dvorak, *PhD, RN*
Executive Director
National Council of State Boards of Nursing
Chicago, Illinois

Claire Fagin, *PhD, RN, FAAN*
Margaret Bond Simon Dean & Professor
School of Nursing
University of Pennsylvania
Philadelphia, Pennsylvania

Martha H. Hill, *PhD, RN*
Robert Wood Johnson Clinical Nurse Scholar
School of Nursing
University of Pennsylvania
Philadelphia, Pennsylvania

Constance Holleran, *MSN, RN, FAAN*
Executive Director
International Council of Nurses
Geneva, Switzerland

Judith Bellaire Igoe, *MPHN, RN*
Associate Professor and Director, School Health
  Programs
Health Sciences Center School of Nursing
Executive Director, Center for Human Caring
University of Colorado
Denver, Colorado
William S. Perry Chair in Health Promotion
Texas Woman's University
Denton, Texas

Beatrice Kalisch, PhD, RN, FAAN
Director
Nursing Consultation Services
Arthur Young & Company
Detroit, Michigan

Lucie S. Kelly, PhD, RN, FAAN
Editor, *Nursing Outlook*
Professor, Public Health and Nursing
Columbia University
New York, New York

Imogene M. King, EdD, RN
Professor of Nursing
University of South Florida
Tampa, Florida

Marguerite R. Kinney, DNSc, RN, FAAN
Professor, School of Nursing
University of Alabama
Birmingham, Alabama

Karren Kowalski, PhD, RN, FAAN
Director
Women's Hospital
AMI St. Luke's
Denver, Colorado

Marlene F. Kramer, PhD, RN, FAAN
Professor of Nursing
Orvis School of Nursing
University of Nevada
Reno, Nevada

Eleanor C. Lambertsen, EdD, RN, FAAN
Formerly Director of Nursing
The New York Hospital
Cornell Medical Center
New York, New York

Madeleine M. Leininger, PhD, LhD, RN, FAAN
Professor, Nursing and Anthropology
Wayne State University
Detroit, Michigan

Carrie B. Lenburg, EdD, RN, FAAN
Coordinator, External Degrees in Nursing
Regents College Degrees Program
Slingerlands, New York

Lucile Petry Leone, MPHN, RN
Formerly Chief Nurse Officer
U.S. Public Health Service
Assistant Surgeon General
PHS Commissioned Officer Corps
San Francisco, California

Myra Levine, MSN, RN, FAAN
Professor Emerita
University of Illinois
College of Nursing
Chicago, Illinois

Ruth Watson Lubic, EdD, RN, CNM, FAAN
General Director
Maternity Center Association
New York, New York

Marie Manthey, MNA, RN
President
Creative Nursing Management
Minneapolis, Minnesota

Ida M. Martinson, PhD, RN, FAAN
Professor and Chair
Department of Family Health Care Nursing
School of Nursing
University of California
San Francisco, California

Ingeborg Grosser Mauksch, PhD, RN, FAAN
Associate Executive Director
Redi-Care, Incorporated
Fort Meyers, Florida

Angela Barron McBride, PhD, RN, FAAN
Professor and Associate Dean
School of Nursing
University of Indiana
Indianapolis, Indiana

Margo McCaffery, MS, RN, FAAN
Consultant
Santa Monica, California

Mildred Montag, EdD, RN, FAAN
Professor Emerita, Teachers College
Columbia University
New York, New York

Virginia M. Ohlson, PhD, RN, FAAN
Professor Emerita
College of Nursing
University of Illinois
Chicago, Illinois

Sister Callista Roy, PhD, RN, FAAN
Professor and Nurse Theorist
School of Nursing
Boston College
Boston, Massachusetts

Rozella M. Schlotfeldt, PhD, RN, FAAN
Professor and Dean Emerita
Case Western Reserve University
Cleveland, Ohio

Doris R. Schwartz, MA, RN, FAAN
Senior Fellow
School of Nursing
University of Pennsylvania
Gwynedd, Pennsylvania

Gloria R. Smith, PhD, MPH, RN, FAAN
Director
Department of Public Health
Detroit, Michigan

Margaret Stafford, MSN, RN, FAAN
Clinical Nurse Specialist
Hines Veterans Administration Hospital
Northlake, Illinois

Jean E. Steel, MS, RN
Assistant Professor and Consultant
Graduate Program
School of Nursing
Boston University
Wellesley, Massachusetts

Virginia Stone, PhD, RN, FAAN
Consultant
Durham, North Carolina

Margretta M. Styles, EdD, RN, FAAN
Professor and Livingston Chair in Nursing
School of Nursing
University of California
San Francisco, California

Joy K. Ufema, RN
Thanatologist
Airville, Pennsylvania

Harriet H. Werley, PhD, RN, FAAN
Distinguished Professor
School of Nursing
University of Wisconsin
Milwaukee, Wisconsin

June Werner, MSN, RN
Chairman
Department of Nursing
Evanston Hospital Corporation
Evanston, Illinois

Virginia T. Williams, MS, RN
Family Nursing Practice
McHenry, Illinois

Contents

Aiken, Linda H.	1		Lenburg, Carrie B.	193
Aydelotte, Myrtle K.	7		Leone, Lucile Petry	206
Benoliel, Jeanne Quint	15		Levine, Myra	215
Bessent, Hattie	23		Lubic, Ruth Watson	229
Carnegie, M. Elizabeth	27		Manthey, Marie	236
Christman, Luther	43		Martinson, Ida M.	246
Cushing, Maureen	53		Mauksch, Ingeborg Grosser	251
Davis, Anne	61		McBride, Angela Barron	261
De Tornyay, Rheba	70		McCaffery, Margo	267
Diers, Donna	77		Montag, Mildred	274
Dvorak, Eileen McQuaid	85		Ohlson, Virginia M.	281
Fagin, Claire	94		Roy, Sister Callista	291
Hill, Martha H.	105		Schlotfeldt, Rozella M.	299
Holleran, Constance	115		Schwartz, Doris R.	311
Igoe, Judith Bellaire	123		Smith, Gloria R.	321
Kalisch, Beatrice	129		Stafford, Margaret	327
Kelly, Lucie S.	136		Steel, Jean E.	337
King, Imogene M.	146		Stone, Virginia	343
Kinney, Marguerite R.	154		Styles, Margretta M.	349
Kowalski, Karren	160		Ufema, Joy K.	356
Kramer, Marlene F.	171		Werley, Harriet H.	364
Lambertsen, Eleanor C.	175		Werner, June	379
Leininger, Madeleine M.	187		Williams, Virginia T.	394

Linda H. Aiken

Linda H. Aiken, PhD, RN, FAAN, is Vice President
of the Robert Wood Johnson Foundation

❖

*As a program officer at the largest health philanthropy in the
United States, Linda Aiken exerts major influences on health policy
research. But she always maintains her strong nursing identity. Out of
the wisdom developed in her rich experience, she offers career guidance
about seeking mentors, taking risks, maintaining a willingness to relocate,
getting into a professional network, and using every aspect of one's life
experiences "to build a repertoire of talents and expertise that is unique
in its breadth and scope."*

*"Do not abandon your heritage as a nurse," she writes, "no
matter where your career path might lead."*

*H*ealth policy research and the promotion of innovations in health services delivery are the focus of my professional career in 1987. I have a strong identity as a nurse and remain actively involved in policy research in nursing. My interests and activities, however, span a broad spectrum of health and human services issues, and the trajectory of my career has been somewhat nontraditional. This essay traces the key factors, people, and events that have shaped my professional life and provides some personal perspectives on careers that might be useful to others.

My professional career and accomplishments have been strongly influenced by several extraordinary individuals who took a special interest in my growth and development. The first was my mother who, as a college graduate and a career teacher, was unusual for her generation. She believed strongly that women as well as men should be prepared in an occupation that would provide the means for independent economic support.

Teaching and nursing were the only two occupations that my mother and I ever considered. I had a preference for nursing at a young age and spent much of my time reading books like the *Cherry Ames Nurse* series and Frank Slaughter's novels about medicine. My mother and I both look back in wonderment that we never considered other options like medicine, law, or engineering. At that time, my mother, at least, did not consider business a discipline worth studying in college. Women of today, of course, have many more choices of occupations than I thought I did in 1961 when I graduated from high school.

I spent my early years in Gainesville, Florida, a small community then dominated by the University of Florida. The University of Florida was *the* place to go to college among my peers and family. By the time I graduated from high school, the university had just opened its new health sciences center and launched a new baccalaureate nursing program. My desire to go to the university was stronger than my choice of nursing as a career. If the school had not had a nursing program, I probably would not have become a nurse. I believe this preference among students for a good university is stronger now than ever. Nursing will lose some bright, talented potential recruits if universities close their nursing schools, as seems to be a trend of late.

The University of Florida College of Nursing was a very special place in the early 1960s. Its founding dean, Dorothy Smith, was a charismatic visionary who created an imaginative and intellectually stimulating environment for nursing. All of us who were students in that era knew that we were part of an exciting experiment to produce a new breed of nurse. Visitors came from around the world to see what Dorothy Smith had created. Despite the fact that she was in great demand as a national speaker, Dean Smith taught in the undergraduate program and practiced in the hospital. As a result, I had enough close contact with her in class and in other school-related functions as an undergraduate to be forever influenced by her vision of nursing.

After graduation I stayed on at Florida for three years as a staff nurse, a graduate student in the medical-surgical clinical nurse specialist program, and a junior faculty member. My appreciation of Dorothy Smith deepened as I grew older, and we have remained close friends and confidantes. Dorothy has been a mentor to me for 20 years in all senses of the word. Her confidence in me, and her expectations, kept me going over the trouble spots, especially in my early career.

My initiation into the real world of nursing came when I took a position as the first clinical nurse specialist ever employed by a midwestern university hospital. Nurses' attitudes were my greatest problem there, particularly those of administrative level nurses and the faculty, who were threatened by a nurse who did not want to punch a time clock in the hospital or be a traditional faculty member. Those were difficult years, but I had learned well at the University of Florida what a clinical nurse specialist should be and I went about becoming one. I became clinically expert in the care of critically ill patients. This offered many rewards and bolstered my self-confidence. I also tried my hand at clinical research. The interdisciplinary education I received at Florida gave me good instincts, and I sought out a senior clinical psychologist in the medical school to help me design a study of post-open-heart surgery psychosis, which affected many of my patients at the time. The study was an excellent learning experience and produced my first research publication in *Nursing Research*.

During those bleak years, I again found mentors who helped me both to endure the backward environment of nursing and to continue to grow. Ingeborg Mauksch and Hans Mauksch served as important mentors to me during this period in separate ways.

Ingeborg, one of the few doctorally prepared nurses at the university, was dynamic, enthusiastic, and willing to invest her energies in others. She gave me perspective during a period when only patients and students clearly valued my work. It was during this time that I chose to pursue, under Ingeborg's influence, a doctoral degree. The degree would give me clout enough to influence the course of hospital nursing, which was my major interest. My goal was to follow in Dorothy Smith's footsteps and serve simultaneously as dean of a school of nursing and director of nursing in an affiliated teaching hospital.

Hans Mauksch, a well-known medical sociologist who had worked on nursing issues, encouraged me to consider sociology, and in 1970 I began doctoral studies in sociology at the University of Texas at Austin. I was fortunate to receive a federal Nurse Scientist Award, which financed my graduate studies at the institution and in the discipline of my choice. I researched a number of universities that had outstanding medical sociology faculties but in the end went to Austin, where my husband found a good job.

The sociology department at Texas was nationally renowned, but its medical sociology program turned out to be less well developed than I had hoped. The strength of the department was demography and population studies. The demography program focused on pragmatic issues and used sophisticated multivariate statistics and computers. Since I lacked skills in those areas, I decided to major in demography. In retrospect, that was a good decision because the skills I learned in the management of large data sets have been useful throughout my career.

At the end of my PhD program, I negotiated a joint appointment in sociology and nursing. The university, however, did not have a medical school and teaching hospital. That limited my ability to pursue my interests in hospital nursing. I also knew that my education in medical sociology was incomplete. While in graduate school, I had learned from faculty and from reading that the nation's most outstanding medical sociologist, David Mechanic, was at the University of Wisconsin. On impulse, I wrote to see if he had a position for me. I was accepted into the postdoctoral program in medical sociology and decided to go. This was a difficult decision because I had a husband and two school-aged children who were happily situated in Austin. I decided to commute between Madison, Wisconsin, and Austin for a year; the children stayed in Texas.

Opting to commute turned out to be a major decision in my career. At every professional crossroad I have chosen the less conventional path. While these choices have created some personal havoc in the short term, they have always paid off over time. In the case of the Wisconsin choice, I had read and was impressed by Mechanic's work. As director of the medical sociology program, he conveyed through his work an understanding of clinical medicine and the complexities of health services delivery. His research seemed applicable to the kinds of problems that interested me.

The year in Wisconsin was painful because of my concern about my children. I would have had an easier year if I had taken my younger child, a first-grader, with me. But that year of study changed my whole career. Through David Mechanic, I met many of the nation's top health services researchers. My year at Wisconsin put me into the orbit of the Robert Wood Johnson Foundation, which sponsored my postdoctoral fellowship there.

The foundation had just been launched as the largest national philanthropy in health, and foundation executives asked Mechanic to recommend candidates for a research position. I was hired as a program officer in research just two years after the foundation began its national program.

Three career-related issues are worth noting here. First, taking risks and moving around, especially early on, often pays off. I think this is one reason men often progress faster than women. Second, one of the major values of graduate education is to get into a professional network that offers good career options. In choosing a graduate program, find faculty members with professional contacts. Third, employers consider the combination of clinical nursing and strong research preparation a unique and valuable asset. Many nurses with graduate preparation in nonnursing disciplines do not effectively use their nursing expertise, and some even perceive their nursing background as a detriment to their career advancement. My philosophy, which has always served me well, is to use every aspect of one's educational and personal background and set of life experiences to build a repertoire of talents and expertise that is unique in its breadth and scope. Many people work well in a narrow range of activities. Few are competent in wider ranges.

The decision to join the Robert Wood Johnson Foundation was a professional risk. Having spent four tough years becoming a researcher, I was going to work at an institution that could derail me from an academic career and a career in clinical nursing. David Mechanic, who had become an important mentor and career counselor for me, thought it was worth the risk. Also, the foundation had a special feeling about it—a feeling I had once experienced when taking part in the educational experiment at the University of Florida.

Again I was fortunate that my immediate supervisor at the foundation, Robert Blendon, took me under his wing from day one and invested a great deal in my development. Blendon was an exceptionally talented and creative policy analyst. The president of the foundation, David Rogers, also placed a high priority on "growing young people." The three of us developed a stimulating intellectual relationship that resulted in a number of research papers published in major journals and a close personal bond that made working fun.

Publishing was not part of my assignment at the foundation. In fact, most foundation executives do not publish at all, much less write scientific papers. Early in my career, Dorothy Smith impressed upon me the importance of writing and conducting research. I have found over time that writing sharpens thinking skills in general. I do not find it particularly easy; in fact, it is often agonizing. But I always learn something by trying to write a paper.

The pressures on nurses to publish have increased substantially in recent years. Since I have a reasonable publication record, I am often asked for tips. Here are some that I have found useful. First, you have to choose a research question or topic of importance and interest to others. Identifying the topic of a paper is often the hardest part. I have found three approaches to be useful.

Look first to what you do on a daily basis for possible subject matter and research opportunities. Trying to identify a research problem without ever having experienced that problem is difficult. (Personal and professional experiences are rich in potential opportunities for writing and research. This is especially true for nurses.) Second, build a research team to collaborate with and to have critique your work. Make the team as heterogeneous as possible while maintaining a commonality of interests. This strategy is always useful to young investigators and to seasoned researchers as well. Third, always write a preliminary draft of a paper. It is easier to motivate yourself and others to give serious thought to an idea if you have something concrete to work with. Often, I write a number of drafts before I reach something that begins to take shape. No matter what colleagues think of the first draft, it helps to break the inertia and moves the project forward.

My work at the foundation has required that I work closely with people from a wide range of backgrounds and disciplinary interests. I have had an opportunity to see firsthand the value of interdisciplinary collaboration and perspectives. I believe that, in general, nursing is far too isolated from the rest of the health services world and from the broader university, business, and political communities. Much can be gained from deliberately establishing an active commitment to groups and issues that extend beyond nursing. I strongly urge every nurse to participate in interdisciplinary groups like the American Public Health Association or local community volunteer service agencies. These activities enhance our effectiveness as nurses.

As I look back on my career, I am convinced that mentors are critical. Try to find them for yourselves, and become mentors to others. Take risks. Be willing to relocate when a move might enhance your professional life, even if some roots must be pulled. Make an effort to become involved in interdisciplinary activities. Speak out at meetings even if you have to prepare your remarks ahead of time. Many of us feel inhibited in public speaking situations; this can be remedied through practice.

Do not abandon your heritage as a nurse no matter where your career path might lead. Nursing is a profession that is held in high regard. There is nothing to be gained and much to be lost by leaving the field. Nursing is a perspective that can only enhance a career.

Myrtle K. Aydelotte

Myrtle K. Aydelotte, PhD, RN, FAAN,
is Professor of Nursing and Dean Emeritus
at the College of Nursing, University of Iowa

Myrtle Kitchell Aydelotte — "Kitch" to her many friends throughout the country — is an expert in organizational arrangements, which she demonstrated in three major positions during her career. She was concerned with the perception of nursing as a profession and the self-image of staff, both inside and outside the organization itself.

From her early years, Kitch lived by a strong set of personal beliefs: cultivation of independent thought, the assumption of responsibility for one's own acts, high personal standards, and a sense of responsibility for others.

A woman who has combined marriage, family, and an administrative career, she writes about male and female professional relationships and maintaining femininity while pressing an argument or proving a point. How physicians and nurses relate is critical to patient welfare, she points out, and the success of their collaboration depends on their respect for each other's knowledge and skills.

*R*eflection on one's career and the motivation to choose that career leads one to review events and relationships that helped to mold character and shape decisions.

My childhood was filled with influential people and events. Independence in thoughts and acts, responsibility to myself and to others, and the establishment of high personal standards were introduced to me at an early age. The people who nurtured these qualities were members of my own family and a few fine teachers with whom I studied during my high school and college years.

I was born at home, delivered by a physician who had been trained at a university. As the youngest of a large clan of stepbrothers, stepsisters, and full siblings, I was coddled and cherished by my family, especially my two stepsisters who were in their teens when I was born. In a sense, I had three mothers.

My early home environment was simple and rural. We were poor during the Depression years, as were many others. Our family life, however, was rich in affection, understanding, and appreciation for one another. Tolerance and humor characterized our lives together as we supported each other's aspirations.

My father was a widower with four young children when he married my mother. She had been married previously, had borne one child by that marriage, and had divorced before the age of 20, which was unusual for the time. My father was a handsome man, tall, somewhat vain, intelligent, and keen in human relations. My mother was strong. Before her marriage to my father, she had supported herself and her son for over 10 years, working as a housekeeper. She had met adversity but had a sense of humor and was pragmatic, financially astute, and industrious. She was the planner, the organizer, and the driving force in our family. Her emotional makeup gave rise to times of playfulness as well as moments of moodiness and discouragement. She held strong convictions regarding women and their need to care for themselves. She nurtured ambition in the two youngest children in the family, my brother and me.

I cannot remember when I did not want to be a nurse. I also wanted a college education. My stepsisters had completed some college work and I admired them. Learning was exciting to me. I was promoted two grades in elementary school and graduated from high school as valedictorian just before my sixteenth birthday. In high school, I had some excellent teachers. A Mr. Lindquist made the sciences exciting. Ms. Vannier presented the logic of mathematics in such a way that its form became beautiful. Ms. Stege introduced me to the richness of drama. Four years of Latin taught by the school superintendent provided an understanding of the structure of the English language, which I value highly.

The high school library, though not large, contained writings by Hawthorne, Scott, Poe, Stevenson, Shakespeare, and other classical writers. I read them all.

I decided to enter a university program of nursing the year after my high school graduation. I had no money and was struggling to find a way to go to college. Because I was bored, I enrolled in high school for another year, taking the science courses again as well as typing and shorthand.

The local physician and his daughter were advising me about hospital schools of nursing, but I wanted a fuller education. No member of my family was a college graduate, but I wanted to be one. I felt that I lacked knowledge in literature, music, and the visual arts. Two events happened that helped me to choose nursing as a career.

My mother's first child, 19 years older than I, was a World War I veteran who developed Parkinson's disease following the influenza epidemic of 1918. A public health nurse from the Veterans Administration visited our home in the spring of 1934. When she learned of my interest in nursing and college, she told me about the five-year baccalaureate nursing program at the University of Minnesota. I applied and was accepted. I do not remember that nurse's name or what happened to her, but I am deeply indebted to her.

The second event was a visit from my older stepsister. She was employed as a secretary at a business school in Des Moines, Iowa. She was earning a modest salary, and she offered to loan me money for tuition. My other stepsister, a statistical assistant at the University of Minnesota, suggested that I earn my board and room as a maid or "student girl." She fixed lunch for me during the week and helped me through the complexities of university registration, the purchase of books, and other problems students face. The two of them made my career possible.

My family (especially my mother) supported my decision, but it was a decision I made myself. It reflected my upbringing to be responsible and resourceful. My family believed in me.

Life at the university opened new vistas for me, although the first two years were difficult. The transition from a small high school to a large university was not easy, and I was pressed working for my board and room, but I learned a great deal. I still recall with a thrill my English professor's readings of poetry, essays, and plays. Hearing classical music was a new experience.

The two families with whom I lived introduced me to Jewish culture. They were charming, warm, and affectionate people who approved of my work and ambition, and they respected my need to study. They enriched my life by helping me through a difficult time and giving me a taste of a different way of life. They were all professionals. The women were fully employed and served as examples of how women can be feminine and competent. These women and their husbands gave me moral support, enabling me to face the academic challenges and the physical and psychological work needed to succeed. More than anyone else, they taught me the value of endorsing and supporting young people who wish to succeed and how to offer them support.

The next two-and-a-half years were spent in the School of Nursing itself. Those years gave me the opportunity to develop three sets of beliefs: a belief in the value of clinical nursing practice ably performed, a belief in the value of the collaboration of work by physicians and nurses, and a belief in the necessity of research and scholarship. My greatest gain in the School of Nursing was the development of the base for clinical nursing practice.

During that time, the University of Minnesota nursing faculty was highly distinguished: Katherine Densford, Irene Beland, Ida McDonald, Myrtle Coe, Lucile Petry, Ruth Harrington, and Margaret Arnstein, to name only a few. The class work was extensive. Physicians delivered some of the lectures. Practice assignments were particularly exciting. We were expected to make observations, plan, predict results, and report results of our actions. Basic to all of this was the theory we had been taught. Autonomy was emphasized. I well remember "reporting off" to the head nurse of each nursing unit. We gave a full report of the conditions of patients, what we observed when we came on duty, the medical regimens and changes thereof, the rationale for our planning, the problems of execution, the predicted results, and the documentation. We each waited our turn to report. Our findings were thorough and included scientific explanations when necessary. Patients' psychological reactions to therapy were as important as their physiological responses. Time was not the major element—thoroughness was.

Our relationship with physicians was close but not patriarchal. Relationships were formal and respectful. Though we were students, our information was valued. The physicians we dealt with later gained fine reputations as clinical investigators. We students stood in awe of the physicians, but they treated us with respect, with courtesy, and as people of value. Two interns, Drs. Textor and Rawson, alternated nights with me when I was on night duty. They believed the assignment was too difficult for me alone. There were no romantic attachments in our arrangement. We three had gone through a series of clinical assignments together, and that experience had built strong bonds. Our respect for one another's knowledge and skills persisted; we learned that an interdependence existed among us. As a result of this relationship, I learned how physicians and nurses collaborate, each providing an essential but different aspect of care. The relationship also taught me self-confidence and to value myself. Physicians have never intimidated me. I learned that what I had to offer to a clinical situation—my knowledge, decision-making skills, and intuition—was valuable. Without those, a physician was handicapped.

In my undergraduate years I was introduced to research. As a senior, under the tutelage of Lucile Petry, I carried out my first research project, an experiment using control and experimental groups. The effect of sterilization on the absorption of purulent drainage by earwicks interested me, and I examined it. The experiment took me on an adventure involving the structure of cotton fiber, the chemical and physical composition of purulent drainage from ear infections in pediatric patients, and the physical effect of sterilization by dry heat on the cotton. I remember going to various campus libraries and making appointments with a number of faculty members in a variety of departments, who referred me to useful sources. I had a wonderful time with my small research project. It taught me the need for thorough study, how to set up standard procedures, the necessity of controlling variables, how to measure results, and how to use statistics. Most important, it infected me with the excitement and satisfaction of conducting research.

At the end of my undergraduate studies, two significant events occurred. Katherine

Densford, the director of the school, called me to her office, which was an unusual practice. To my knowledge, she did not hold conferences with graduating students. "When are you going on to graduate school?" she asked. I was flabbergasted. Although I wanted to go on to graduate school, I had no idea that anyone else had thought of such a future for me. "You must do it as soon as possible, and you must earn a doctoral degree. A master's degree was sufficient for my generation, but not for yours." I left her office after promising that I would continue my studies.

The second event led to my career in nursing administration. Thelma Dodds, Director of Nursing at the Charles T. Miller Hospital in St. Paul asked me to consider the position of head nurse on a medical-surgical nursing unit. I accepted. I was younger than anyone else assigned to that unit. I did not deem it a problem that I was filling a position left open by the resignation of a very popular head nurse, or that I had acquired no staff nurse experience. With Ms. Dodds' guidance, including the advice that I establish my own administrative style and be myself, and with the remarkable support of the nurses themselves, especially the assistant head nurse, Ms. Cheney, I succeeded. I had a happy, satisfactory experience in first-level administrative nursing. The position provided me the opportunity to supervise and manage a group effort and gave me deeper knowledge of clinical nursing practice. The quality of nursing care at the Miller Hospital was excellent.

With this beginning, my career in nursing administration continued and expanded to encompass teaching and research. I developed the belief that administrators should become scholars in their discipline. A number of people and events contributed to the development of that belief.

During World War II, I served as an assistant to Cecilia Hauge, Chief Nurse of the 26th General Hospital. She taught me many valuable lessons. Her knowledge of administration and her political skill were remarkable. Her sense of humor sparked the learning. After World War II, a short-term assignment as Ms. Densford's assistant gave me an overview of educational administration. Her confidence in the faculty, her establishment of priorities, her broad view of issues, and her sense of timing were evident. She believed in young people and allowed them freedom to develop, providing them with opportunities for study and experimentation.

As I matured, I observed that the faculty's motivation to reach goals was essential. Ms. Densford taught me how to avoid indolence and how to make use of my time. Each week she regularly devoted two or three mornings to library study. I also set aside periods of time for professional reading, although my graduate studies demanded much more time than a few morning hours each week.

Doctoral study introduced me to two people who influenced my later career, Dr. Ruth Eckert and Dr. Melvin Neale. Research papers that I prepared for Dr. Eckert provided a rich background for teaching and curriculum development. Dr. Neale, who directed my doctoral work, advised me to select courses across a wide spectrum of subjects. He believed that as an administrator, I would need to draw on many different content areas. Both Eckert and Neale emphasized scholarship, and both taught me to make good use of what I knew. They taught me to recognize that most often one works with incomplete data, but that the data should be as representative as possible and should focus on the various dimensions of the problem to be solved.

Dr. Eckert served as a model of a woman faculty member who combined marriage, career, and community leadership. Dr. Neale coached me, both as a student and later as a dean, on how to handle male-female relationships. He said that I would not be accepted as "one of the boys," but that my relationships would evolve out of the quality of my ideas and the skill with which I presented them. He emphasized the need for logic, rationality, and reason in presenting my positions. More than anyone else, he urged me to maintain my femininity while pressing an argument or inviting discourse on the matter to be considered. He perceived femininity in a positive sense, not as something cute, coy, or emotional. He taught me to respect my abilities and to forecast what could happen in various situations. He proposed that I practice examining and describing a situation, then analyze, evaluate, and project results. His emphasis on forecasting situations led me to develop a practice that has served me well.

My career during and following graduate school slowly unfolded and expanded. The nature of the problems and the kinds of people with whom I worked changed in complexity and number. The three major positions I held in my career dealt with building nursing organizations. The work settings and the maturity of the nursing organizations varied.

Structuring the College of Nursing at the University of Iowa involved the transition of a school of nursing once operated by a hospital and medical school to an autonomous entity within the larger university. Developing a department of nursing within a university hospital and health center involved the transformation of a service unit to a professional clinical department. Staff arrangements within a professional association involved the redesigning of a staff structure and the development of coalitions in national and international settings.

In all three positions I was concerned with the self-image of staff and with the perception of nursing as a profession both inside and outside the organization itself. All three situations required the restructuring of working relationships. In each case it was necessary to clarify lines of accountability and responsibility and to set new expectations of performance of staff. The work was intellectual and political.

In each of these executive positions, my role involved three major functions: providing leadership to carry out the objectives of the organization; writing and research; and building a solid intellectual foundation among staff members to ensure continuity in the organization after I left. My length of service in the positions varied from a little over four years to nine. The length of tenure for each position was based on a variety of factors, including the development of other interests, the accomplishment of goals, or an intuitive sense that I should move on.

My functions were carried out with the help of many individuals. I depended on consultants, mentors, friends, and staff. I learned to value others' ideas, to seek advice on problems, to invite review of plans, and to change my mind. The people who contributed to my success are too numerous to list in full, but I will mention a few. Margaret Arnstein and Wellborn Hudson launched me on a research course that brought me national recognition. Among those advising me on other matters were Margaret Bridgman, Hildegard Peplau, Marjorie Cantor, Hattie Bessent, Florence Erickson, Margaret Carroll, Lutie Leavell, Harvey Davis, Grayce Sills, and Anne Zimmerman. If I were to provide a full list, I would need pages of paper. Many people with diverse backgrounds advised me along the way, and my work successes reflect their wisdom and advice.

My work was fairly successful. The College of Nursing has undergone curriculum changes. Its mission has expanded as deans have come and gone and as the faculty has enlarged and improved educationally. The structure I designed has been responsive to growth. The autonomy of the college, a building block which I put in place, continues. The department of nursing has likewise grown, but the characteristics of professionalism, self-direction, and autonomy that I fostered persist.

The impact of my presence as the executive director of the American Nurses' Association is more difficult to assess. Major changes external to staff itself have taken place, but the support role of staff remains.

The forces that propelled me along the way in my professional life were early teachings I received from my family. Independent thought, responsibility to myself and to others, and high personal standards have certainly guided me. In addition, I believe that as I matured professionally, I developed a set of beliefs about the profession and my role in it. A restlessness and curiosity about nursing and its discipline have resulted. These forces drive me on.

My beliefs are these:

- I strongly believe in the value of education as a foundation for nursing practice, research, and lifelong study.
- I believe in nursing's value to society and believe nurses have a moral contract with society to provide nursing care of the highest quality. Clinical nursing practice must be exquisite and administrative nursing practice must be imaginative, sound, and supportive of practitioners, patients, and clients.
- I deeply believe in people and the early socialization of the student into the profession. Older nurses have an obligation to nurture, sponsor, and serve as mentors to the younger generation.
- I believe nursing will evolve into a profession and that the evolution can be accelerated through study of the discipline, greater education of the practitioner of nursing, and the provision of expert nursing practice. An occupational group, aspiring to become professional, determines its own destiny by its behavior. Therefore the performance of each practitioner is critical. The image of nurses and nursing is cast by the quality of the professional practice provided and the personal behavior of the individual practitioner.

Now, what has almost 50 years of practice in the profession taught me? What have I gained through my efforts? I have received personal satisfaction and a modicum of recognition from my peers, and I have also learned a great deal. Some of my lessons have been pleasant; others have been bittersweet. I have learned:

- To examine questions from many angles and to examine the history of the matter under review. I have learned to consult with individuals who have had prior experience with the subject.
- To look forward, to dream of what may be possible while keeping in mind the events that have gone before and the current environmental forces that will play on the realization of that dream.

- To change my ideas as new knowledge is gained but always to keep in mind the object of my work and the moral code under which I operate. The end does not always justify the means.
- To discuss issues and present my point of view. Failure to state a position adds to the ambiguity of an issue and limits argument. An individual with knowledge has an obligation to share it so that it can be examined in relation to the question. To present issues and points of view requires courage.
- To accept differing opinions and rebuffs of my own point of view or proposal. Leadership and popularity are two different entities. One may be wrong sometimes or out of step, but there is always that opportunity to learn more.

Basically, I have learned that life is an adventure and that people are good. To me, my investment in nursing has paid off. I like myself and what I have done. But, since my work represents the investment of many others, I hope they, too, believe that the knowledge, time, and energy they have given to me has yielded high returns.

Jeanne Quint Benoliel

Jeanne Quint Benoliel, DNSc, RN, FAAN,
is Elizabeth Sterling Soule Distinguished Professor
of Nursing and Health Promotion
at the University of Washington

❖

In 1962 Jeanne Quint Benoliel joined a research team in a sociological study of hospital personnel and dying patients. She found that attitudes and behaviors that had created problems for her in nursing were the traits that were valued in the culture of social science. She learned a great deal in her five years on that study, not only about the dying, but also about the competitive masculine world of social science and the marginal position of women in the male-oriented world of academia.

*W*hen asked to describe how I happened to make death and dying a central concern in my professional life as a nurse, I was stimulated to contemplate the events, happenings, people, and places that had influenced my choices in living along the way. In retrospect, they seem to fall into four areas: childhood influences, early experiences in nursing, critical personal life events, and significant professional contacts and experiences.

CHILDHOOD INFLUENCES

Born near the end of World War I, I grew up in a period in which girls were socialized to believe that their primary roles in life were to be wives and mothers. Career expectations for women were generally traditional, such as nursing or teaching. Being a nurse was often presented as good preparation for marriage and motherhood. I did not have the urge to become a nurse until late in high school, and the decision to enter a hospital school of nursing was influenced as much by economic realities as by career goals.

My father was in the U.S. Navy and did not see me until I was 18 months old. I was the oldest of three girls in a family in which my mother dominated. She had been a nurse, and I grew up learning about nursing as she had experienced it. I think the atmosphere of my early family life was overly protective yet aided in developing my sense of responsibility. I was not aware of this at the time but came to understand it much later.

My family emphasized doing well in school. Reading and music were highly valued, and I grew up with a fondness for books. I was a bright kid who always got good grades; in high school I took an academic program with mathematics as my major. I was overweight, however, a loner, and felt that I was an outsider. This feeling of being marginal made me sensitive to other marginal people. Later in life, I was concerned with the welfare and well-being of people who were "have-nots" in the human community.

During my childhood there were a number of deaths in my family. Dying was treated as a part of ongoing life experience. My aunt died when I was 7 and my grandfather when I was 13, and both were at home, with my mother heavily involved in the care-giving. All of the children participated in the funerals and other services as though these were normal activities, and I suspect that these experiences influenced my ideas about the meaning of death and dying.

EARLY EXPERIENCES IN NURSING

At the age of 18, I enrolled in the School of Nursing at St. Luke's Hospital in San Francisco. The experience of hospital training was a curious mixture of life in a cloistered residence with bed checks and tight rules combined with the responsibility of being on night duty in charge of a ward six months after entry into school. In those days we stood up in class when the physician/lecturer walked into the room, and we gave up our seats at the nursing station whenever a physician came onto the ward. If anything, that socialization encouraged a belief that physicians were superior beings and nurses were expected to be deferential. It is worth noting that when people died, there was no mad rush to initiate cardiopulmonary resuscitation. More commonly, dying people were simply allowed to die.

I graduated in 1941 and took the California licensing examination in November of that year. My first job was as a staff nurse at the San Diego County Hospital, where I worked in the tuberculosis pavilion. Shortly after I took that position, the country was shaken by the bombings at Pearl Harbor. In the following weeks, cities on the West Coast were blacked out at night as a precaution against Japanese air attacks. I can remember being on night duty and looking at the sky, wondering what I would do if such an event took place.

In June 1943 I left San Diego and enrolled at the University of California in Berkeley to use a scholarship I had received when I graduated from St. Luke's as top student in my class. After three months in school, during which I worked part time at Alta Bates Hospital, I joined the Army Nurse Corps in response to the great pressures on nurses my age to do their patriotic duty. By the end of October, I was on my way to Camp White, Oregon, for basic training. In March of 1944 I boarded the *S.S. Lurline* (a honeymoon cruiser converted to a troop transport) bound for Milne Bay, New Guinea. We did not know that was our destination at the time.

I spent the next 21 months in various parts of New Guinea and the Philippines with the 80th General Hospital. It is an experience that I am glad to have had, but one I would not wish to live over. In the war in the South Pacific, not all of the casualties resulted from battle. Many soldiers were hospitalized with malaria, dengue fever, and tsutsugamushi fever (also known as scrub typhus), which caused prolonged debilitation and sometimes ended in death. My memories of that time are full of images of 18- and 19-year-old kids with psychiatric breakdowns and other emotional problems resulting from soldiering in a jungle where the enemy could not be seen.

At the end of 1945 we returned to the United States, and I can remember the great thrill of passing under the Golden Gate Bridge into San Francisco Bay and seeing the wonderful signs of welcome and appreciation for a job well done. Readjusting to civilian life was not exactly a picnic, however. For the first time in my life, I could not sit still. I took up knitting to relieve tension.

In 1946 I moved to Oregon to join Phyllis Moore, with whom I had undergone basic training in the army. Under the GI Bill, we went to school at Oregon State University in the fall of 1946, and I was awarded a baccalaureate degree with a major in nursing education in 1948. With my new degree in hand I returned to California to teach at the

Fresno General Hospital School of Nursing, where I remained for five years. I am still in contact with some of the women who were my students during that time.

CRITICAL LIFE EVENTS

I first married in 1949 when I was 29. When I look back on that marriage now, I realize that we were a couple of mixed-up people each searching for an answer. It was destined not to work out. In the week of our second anniversary, my husband became acutely disturbed. I was forced to place him in a local psychiatric hospital, where he was diagnosed as having paranoid schizophrenia. Not having funds enough to support his care in a private hospital, I faced the traumatic experience of having him committed to a state institution where (without any consent from him or me) he underwent electric shock therapy.

That period of my life was perhaps the most difficult I have ever known. I can remember the terrible feeling of trying to communicate with someone who was not the person I had married, in manner or behavior. I remember the terrible helplessness I felt, knowing that institutional commitment was my only option. I recall feeling responsible and not being able to talk about what had happened. Over the next two years, my husband was in and out of the hospital several times, and I felt myself moving toward some kind of emotional crisis. I realized that I was being destroyed by the experience, and I made the decision to leave the marriage and Fresno.

After leaving Fresno, I worked in one of the state mental hospitals for six months because I needed to know what went on behind those walls. I knew from personal experience what it was like to be a family member who was told very little. In the fall of 1954, I enrolled for graduate study at the University of California—Los Angeles in a nursing program leading to the master of science degree. That year in school brought about changes that gave new direction to my life.

Shortly after enrolling at UCLA, I became deeply depressed, although I was not really aware of it at the time. I found myself thinking about suicide but I received no support from the nursing faculty when I tried to talk about it. Fortunately for me, I reached out for help to Bob Tannenbaum, my teacher in a group dynamics course. Through him I came to realize that I had serious problems and the need for some kind of formal therapy. At his counsel, I entered into a contract with a therapist whom I consulted for five years.

Being in school again was also important—but not particularly because of the courses that I took. During those years I found the library and returned once more to my love of books. Particularly influential to my thinking during this period were the writings of Karen Horney, *The Way Things Are* by Percy Bridgman, and *The Plague* by Albert Camus. I became aware of the activities of the American Civil Liberties Union and developed interest in the civil rights movement and social injustices.

After graduation in 1955, I took a position as instructor on the faculty of the School of Nursing, UCLA. I was the first graduate of the program to be so appointed and was told by Lulu Wolf Hassenplug that other faculty members had high expectations for me. The events of the next few years were to alter the direction of my professional career in profound ways.

On April 8, 1956 (in my first year on the faculty), I learned that my sister, who was in her eighth month of pregnancy with her fourth child, had experienced a cerebral hemorrhage and was being kept alive on a respirator. The baby had been delivered by cesarean section.

The next morning I drove to the hospital in El Cajon, California. When I walked into her room, her physician turned to me and said, "She'll never breathe on her own. What should we do?" Together, we decided to disconnect the machine. My brother-in-law and his best friend and I sat for eight hours waiting for her heart to stop beating. The baby was in a nursery across the hall.

This experience had a powerful effect on me. I remember walking into the room, looking at Patricia and thinking, "This could be me." At the gut-level of my being, I knew then that death could come at any time—that any day could be one's last. Because of that experience I developed a renewed sense of what was important in life.

My sister's sudden death was a critical event in my family's life, and I have written about some of the immediate and long-term consequences of that crisis elsewhere (Benoliel, 1979). It was only the beginning of a series of family crises. My mother had major surgery in 1957, and my father died of cancer in July 1958. Just prior to my father's death—in May of that year—I had a breast biopsy. I was fortunate to be in therapy during those crucial years and was thankful that I had supporting relationships with my good friends from the Berkeley days, Ellen Stephenson and Sylvia Hartman.

SIGNIFICANT PROFESSIONAL EXPERIENCES

Although the period in Fresno between 1948 and 1953 was one marked by major personal difficulties, it was also a time during which I became active in professional nursing organizations, notably the American Nurses' Association and the National League for Nursing Education, through my work in the local and state units. I remember being thrilled to meet Lucille Petry (not yet Leone) at one of the meetings. An important professional contact for me came when Alice Schindel became director of the Fresno General Hospital School of Nursing in 1950. Perhaps 10 years older than I, Alice came into nursing with a background in creative writing, and her area of clinical specialization was pediatric nursing. She was a creative person who recognized my unused talents and encouraged me to develop them. Alice was the first nurse in an authority position with whom I enjoyed a positive relationship.

The four years on the faculty at UCLA between 1955 and 1959 found me learning what it was to be an academic, in great measure because of the strategies of Lulu Hassenplug. My involvement in teaching in a new experimental baccalaureate program in nursing was exciting. My colleagues included Dorothy Johnson, Harriet Coston, Jo Eleanor Elliott, and Helen Nakagawa. By 1959 I was ready for a change, and I enrolled in an experimental research training program for nurses headed by Eleanor Sheldon, the sociologist, and Dorothy Johnson.

Although the program was designed to prepare nurses for research in the behavioral sciences, I was permitted to set up a special program for study in physiology and statistics because of my interests. My preceptor was Margaret Slusher, a research anatomist. Her area of interest was physical and biochemical responses to stress and the interrelated influences of the endocrine and nervous systems on these responses. I spent a lot of time observing research experiments in different laboratories in addition to taking courses in physiology and statistics. I also came to realize that the combined use of physiological and behavioral indicators in research on human beings was not a simple matter.

This period of introduction to research had several important consequences. I began to undergo a critical shift in thinking about the differences in perspective of practitioners and investigators. I learned that methods of research are directly tied to the problem identified for study, as well as the current state of knowledge and observational technology in that field. I questioned whether I wanted to remain in nursing, consider working for a PhD in neurophysiology, or move into a new career in statistics with Frank Massey. I also wrote a proposal then for the study of women's adaptations after mastectomy with Harold Garfinkel, a sociologist, who served as consultant during its development. The completed proposal was submitted to the National Institute of Mental Health through the School of Nursing, which funded the study in 1961.

In the meantime, I had taken a position in statistics in the School of Public Health. When news of the grant award came through, Lulu Hassenplug persuaded me to return to research by reminding me that it is important. Through a series of negotiations, I was appointed to a joint position as junior research nurse in the School of Nursing and junior research statistician in the School of Public Health.

The mastectomy study was conducted over a two-year period beginning in the fall of 1961. A surgeon in the School of Medicine served as coinvestigator, which helped to facilitate the implementation of the study. Although I had limited prior research experience, I knew by intuition that it was important to have support for the study from someone in the medical school. The year 1961 was one of tremendous learning. It required putting a research plan into motion, hiring staff members, negotiating with physicians for their support, contacting potential women subjects, and covering all of the details that go into initiating a research project. It was hard work, and I was doing it essentially on a half-time basis.

That study served as a turning point in my professional career. The data we collected helped me to understand women's death-related fears and concerns prompted by the diagnosis of cancer. It also helped me to understand the problems of learning to live with an uncertain future and the difficulties that nurses have in talking with women about these concerns. I learned what problems nurses have with their own feelings of helplessness and hopelessness.

Much of this learning was translated into publications so that others might read and understand. Because of the study, I met Anselm Strauss, who was searching for a nurse to join a research team in a sociological study of hospital personnel and dying patients at the University of California in San Francisco.

In 1962 I left Los Angeles to join the research team in San Francisco, but I continued to manage the mastectomy study through to its completion in 1963. I was introduced to the concepts and ideas of symbolic interactionism, a theoretical perspective that became very influential in later analyses of the mastectomy data. The travel and phone calls that became necessary in my new-found dual role proved to be difficult and exhaustive. But, more important, tremendous amounts of energy were required to counteract the efforts of powerful faculty at UCLA to influence my research associate into changing the direction of the study.

In San Francisco I was being socialized into the strange new world of sociology with its different language, values, and expectations. At first I felt rather overwhelmed by the new jargon, but in time, I came to fit in very well with the group. I found that the attitudes and behaviors that had always created problems for me in nursing were the traits that were valued in the culture of social science.

The five years on the dying patient study were important to my professional development. Not only did I learn a great deal about the complexities of field research, I read widely in the social and behavioral sciences and met many interesting people. I began to be known for my research through journal articles and presentations across the country. I also became active in the American Nurses' Association through an appointment to the Committee on Research and Studies from 1966 to 1968. I remember some of those meetings well because Martha Rogers and I continually argued about whether a doctoral degree was essential in order to do research.

Between 1962 and 1967, I had two encounters that were critical to my full development as a professional nurse and as an autonomous person. In 1964 I gave a presentation based on the mastectomy data at a special session at the annual convention of the American Medical Association. The focus of the presentation was on the organizational features that interfered with communication among patients, physicians, and nurses in teaching hospitals. I sent a copy of the paper to my surgeon coinvestigator at UCLA indicating that it had been accepted for publication. Within a week, I had received a carbon copy of letters to the chancellors of both campuses, the deans of both medical schools, and the dean of the school of nursing in San Francisco that in effect said of course I could publish what I wished, but that the paper would do a gross disservice to UCLA.

Needless to say, I was very upset. At their request, copies of the paper were made available to the chancellor on the UCSF campus and to the dean of the medical school. When I met with the chancellor (a former surgeon), he said, "My, my. Whatever did you do to that surgeon?" He supported my efforts. The dean of the medical school was also encouraging. In fact, he gave me a message that I have never forgotten: "If you are going to be in this competitive game, you need to develop iron guts."

This experience was another turning point. It forced me to face the reality that my primary commitment was to patients, not to physicians. It was a powerful experience, and not altogether painless. It served as a reminder that what is significant in human experience is not learned without a certain amount of agony.

A second confrontation with the male world took place when I became aware that I was not to be one of the authors of the major publications resulting from the dying patient study. To this day, I am not completely sure when and where the decision was made, but I was not party to it. I confronted Anselm and asked him whether my position on the project was simply to be a data collector. Although that confrontation did nothing to change the decision, it was important in my working relationships with him. Publishing my analysis of the data on student nurses as a single author was one means by which I learned to cope with the situation.

Those five years of experience as a "minority" member on a research project with two men more than adequately introduced me to the competitive world of men in social science. It also increased my awareness of the "marginal" position of women in the male-oriented world of academia and the many problems that women face in the rough-and-tumble marketplace of ideas.

CONCLUSION

Living in San Francisco in the 1960s was an exciting experience. This was the period of flower children and the Jefferson Airplane. Esalen Institute at Big Sur was just beginning to develop programs to foster human growth and development. My experience during this time included contacts with Ken Kesey and the Merry Pranksters, Sidney Jourard, Abraham Maslow, Joan Baez, Paul Tillich, and Abraham Kaplan. All of them contributed to my life in important ways. As the dying patient study grew to a close, I realized that to stay in academia I needed a doctoral degree, and I entered the doctoral program in nursing science in 1967. By this time, however, the direction of my professional interests had been charted, and getting the degree in 1969 was almost anticlimactic—except for my mother standing up and cheering when I walked onto the stage to receive the diploma. Being my mother's "golden egg" wasn't always easy.

REFERENCE

Benoliel, J.Q. (1979). Dying is a family affair. In E.R. Prichard et al. (Eds.), *Home care: living with dying* (pp. 17-34). New York: Columbia University Press.

Hattie Bessent

Hattie Bessent, EdD, RN, is Director of
the Minority Fellowship Programs of the
American Nurses' Association

❖

Hattie Bessent's grandmother taught her to be first, and so she was: the first black nurse in the state of Florida to receive a doctoral degree; the first black woman faculty member at the University of Florida; the first black dean of the Graduate School of Nursing at Vanderbilt University.

In the course of a career as a nurse, researcher, professor, and administrator that has taken Dr. Bessent from Hong Kong to Harvard, there is no forgetting the beginning: Jacksonville, Florida, in the 1930s, where she and her little sister were learning to be what they already were in their grandmother's eyes — the best.

On Saturdays, our chore was to take the bus into town and buy the *New York Times*. We were little girls of 8 and 10. We caught the bus on the side of the road, even though there was no real stop there, because the driver knew my grandmother, which meant he knew enough not to argue with her. We would read the paper when we got home. We talked about current events, and my sister and I had to give presentations about the things we read. I am still a news freak.

We grew up in a black community where my grandfather was the Baptist minister. We were expected to be good examples. We were, though we had our share of fun— like eating dill pickles in church. Of course, if our grandmother were to fix us with her stern eye, we straightened up more than just our posture.

As a Girl Scout, I used to be in charge of first aid on camping trips. That was my earliest venture into nursing. I was also exposed early on to what it is to need, and I learned how to give comfort to people in pain. I made the rounds with my grandfather when he visited the sick and the elderly, and I saw him healing in his own way.

When I was 12 or 13, I started working as a volunteer at a nursing home. I remember one day overhearing a physician saying that someone at the home had just died of loneliness. That kind of desolation has haunted me, and in a way I've never left that place. I still visit there when I'm in Jacksonville.

My grandmother is over 100 now, and, when I call her, I always ask if she is alone or if the woman who takes care of her is nearby. If she is alone, I make sure it's because she wants it that way. My parents died when I was nine and my sister was six. I believe that may have something to do with my feeling haunted by loneliness and also with my belief that one of the greatest accomplishments in life is to ease another's pain. Of course, that is what nursing is about.

My grandmother had an unusual aptitude for motherhood. She raised us with a combination of strict standards and sincere affection, and she gave us that stern eye, but she also gave us lots of kisses. Grandmother let us see ourselves in the best light possible because that was the light she saw us in. She was blessed with the gift of being able to show a child how to succeed.

We were rewarded for A's on our report cards. We didn't get anything for B's, so we didn't bring home B's. And girls like us *didn't* get pregnant. That was all my grandmother had to say on the subject of sex. When I began to menstruate, she took me and my sister to the doctor, who showed us anatomical charts and explained everything to us as if we were a couple of precocious premed students. My grandmother didn't go in with us, but sat outside in the waiting room. It *was* the 1940s, after all.

The most influential thing about my grandmother was that the word "impossible" wasn't in her vocabulary. Over the years, in various circumstances, people have said to me, "That hasn't been done before," or "That isn't the way things are done." My reply has always been, "Let's do it then. Let's be the first."

When I graduated from high school, I didn't go right into nursing. I studied to become an x-ray technician, earned my license, but wasn't satisfied. So I became a licensed lab technician. Still something was missing. I missed making people feel good, just telling them "good morning," and listening to them. Self-expression is important to me. I like to be a sounding board for others because I know how much I need one myself. My call to nursing was the same call to fight loneliness that has beckoned me back time and time again to that hometown nursing home.

I earned a BS in nursing education at Florida A&M University, and then my MS in psychiatric nursing at the University of Indiana, Bloomington. I grew up in a black world, and because I was a minister's granddaughter, I was a role model to my peers. I was expected to be a leader. At the University of Indiana, I plunged into the white world, butting up against racial hostility and ignorance. I was prepared for this and had lots of support. My grandparents, my old schoolteachers, the church, and my community were with me. To use the parlance of psychology, I had internalized that combination of self-discipline and self-esteem that my grandmother had mined so industriously. I had a bedrock.

I was interested in the effects of illness on the mind and spirit, so I specialized in psychiatric nursing. I went home to Florida after I finished my master's degree in 1962 and was soon working as a nurse in charge of a psychiatric unit at one of the hospitals in Jacksonville. I was the first black nurse in the city to hold such a position.

A few years later, I joined the faculty at the University of Florida in Gainesville, where I taught courses in psychiatric nursing. I received a Career Teacher's Grant from the National Institute of Mental Health in 1969. Once again, these were breakthroughs—I was the first black woman and nurse to hold a faculty position at the University of Florida, and I was the first black in the state to receive the Federal Career Teacher's Grant.

One of the toughest challenges for me was in the person of Dr. Ira Gordon, who directed the Institute of Human Resources at the University of Florida. I tried calling him to see about gaining admission to his doctoral program in education. He didn't return my calls, so I sent him some writing samples. Finally, I got a call from him. He asked me to come to his office. I was happy. At last, I was going to have a chance to talk to him at length.

When I went in to see him, he told me that he was going on vacation the following day, and that he wanted to have done with me. "I don't work with special cases," he said. "Get your GRE [Graduate Record Examination] scores to me today. If they're not good enough, I'm not going to let you into the program and that's final."

I hadn't received my scores yet. I called Princeton, and the man who took my call said, "Madam, if you were the mayor of Miami I couldn't tell you what your scores are. You'll have to wait until we mail the results to you."

I relayed that information to Dr. Gordon, whose only response was that I should call back and tell them *he* wanted to know my scores that day. So I called and told the man I had spoken to earlier that I was one of Dr. Gordon's students. He said, "Why didn't you tell me that in the first place?" That was when I knew for sure that Ira Gordon's name carried some weight. I got my scores over the phone and they were very good. I was thrilled. Dr. Gordon accepted me into his program, and I went on to collaborate with him on research on intellectual stimulation.

My grandmother wasn't surprised by my scores. She expected as much from me. "You're on your way," she said.

It has always been my style to act behind the scenes, rather than carry a banner and march in protest. Wherever I've been hired first or invited first, it has always been made clear that other blacks would follow—that if you bring in Hattie Bessent, she'll bring other blacks in with her.

I was never directly involved in the civil rights movement, though I strongly supported Dr. Martin Luther King, Jr. I contribute financially to organizations like Coretta Scott King's center for education.

My style is subtle. I finesse the changes necessary in policy and attitudes, persuade funding sources that their money will be well spent, play down discord, and play up mutual advantage.

Over the last decade, I've devoted most of my time to these efforts as director of the American Nurses' Association Minority Fellowship Programs (MFP). To maintain funding for the five programs that the ANA sponsors for minority nurse education is a big job, particularly in light of current cutbacks in the federal budget. The MFP has to prove its case over and over again to get federal funding renewed. Fortunately, the programs are successful. They are enabling ethnic minorities who couldn't otherwise afford to advance their nursing education to move ahead.

This success doesn't speak for itself. As MFP director, part of my job is to advertise the success and another part is to make sure it doesn't slip away. I'm making a case on Capitol Hill to maintain federal funds for MFP and at the same time am trying to convince private foundations to become new funding sources.

My role is as an enabler. I encourage students to excel and to enjoy the pleasure of professional competence. I then present these students to those who will hire them because of their abilities.

I visit academic departments around the country to make sure our Fellows are getting good educations and to troubleshoot when there are problems. I talk to Fellows every day. I tell them they have to work hard to prove themselves. We talk about the stresses of combining a career and motherhood and about how a husband can feel threatened by a wife's PhD.

We have constant interaction. I share my experience with them. They share new ideas with me. The fight against loneliness connects like a thread my first afternoons at the nursing home in Jacksonville and my role today as an MFP director in Washington.

M. Elizabeth Carnegie

M. Elizabeth Carnegie, DPA, RN, FAAN,
is Visiting Professor, Vera E. Bender Endowed Chair in Nursing
at Adelphi University, Garden City, New York

Elizabeth Carnegie was born with the strength to succeed and with the determination to make the world of nursing a better place for minorities. Always with the love and support of family members and against great odds, she doggedly and courageously pursued her education and career goals. Without rancor, she tells of the humiliating indignities she endured as a black in the North as well as in the South, and from nurses as well as from the larger community. Her commitment to upgrading the status of black nurses led to many personal triumphs, including the much heralded publication of her history of black nurses, The Path We Tread.

*T*he story of the achievements of black nurses in the United States has been one of faith, ambition, preparation, perseverance, aggressiveness, courage, conviction, and the unwavering belief in the integrity of human beings. My story is of just one black nurse who managed to overcome many obstacles on the way to realizing her professional goals.

I was born on April 19, 1916, the fourth child of John Oliver Lancaster (a musician) and Adeline Beatrice (nee Swann) in Baltimore. When I was two years old, my parents divorced. To help my mother care for her children, her sister Rosa, a housewife, and Rosa's husband, Thomas Robinson, a tinner with his own business who lived in Washington, D.C., took me to rear. This left my mother to care for my sisters Myrtle and Beatrice. (One child, a boy, had died shortly after birth.)

Aunt Rosa's daughter by a previous marriage, Iola, was married and living away from home by the time of my "adoption," so I was the only child in the Robinson household. On major holidays my mother would bring my sisters to visit us, and Aunt Rosa or Iola on occasion would take me to visit them in Baltimore, just 40 miles away.

During her frequent visits to our home, Iola would teach me to read, to write, and even to speak a little French, which she had learned in high school. When I was four years old, Aunt Rosa enrolled me in kindergarten. It was exciting for me, having the companionship of other children. When the school year ended, I was the only child not promoted to the first grade. The reason was my age—I was too young. A law had just been passed requiring that a child be at least six years old before entering the first grade. In response to my tears, Aunt Rosa went to see the principal. Since no birth certificate was required to prove my age, she probably told him that I was old enough. At any rate, the next day I joyously joined my classmates in the first grade.

When I was eight years old and in the fourth grade, my mother decided that she could support all three of her children, so I went to Baltimore to live with her and my sisters. I was enrolled in Public School 112 in the first semester of the fourth grade. While I was living in Baltimore, a cousin from New York visited us and asked to take me back with him to spend the summer with his family. For the next few years, that was an annual summer vacation for me.

When I had been in Baltimore for two years, my mother became seriously ill. Aunt Rosa moved my family to Washington, rented an apartment across the street from her house for my sisters, enrolled them in public school, moved me and my mother into her home, and nursed my mother back to health. I was again in school in Washington but was six months ahead of my former classmates.

One year after my mother had recovered from her illness, she married Edward Davis and later gave birth to my brother, Roland. She died in 1928, three months after Roland was born. Here again, my extended family stepped in. My aunt Mamie and her husband, Daniel Sears, had no children and so "adopted" Roland.

Born and reared a Catholic, I was active in the church as a child, playing the organ for the children's Mass, and singing in the choir at high Mass. Those of us in the parish who attended public schools were required to attend classes conducted by the Oblate Sisters of Providence, an all-black order. I idolized these beautiful nuns and wanted to be one of them when I finished high school.

All schools in Washington were then segregated, and I went to an all-black high school. It was during the height of the Great Depression. My uncle could get little work as a tinner. To get through high school, which I was determined to do, I worked after school and on weekends preparing fruits and vegetables at the Allies Inn, a cafeteria that hired black help but catered to whites only. Many blacks who worked there did so while attending either high school or college.

I graduated from high school at 16 and decided to spend some time with my relatives in New York. I had the idea of possibly furthering my education there. Reluctantly, Aunt Rosa permitted me to go. Once I was there, it was a matter of survival. The only job that I could get was as a domestic. Not having had such responsibilities at home, I was neither prepared for nor equipped to accept this position. Having lost the desire to become a nun, I was undecided on a career goal. I had no money, and no one in my family could finance my education.

One of my cousins had attended Lincoln School for Nurses, one of the two schools of nursing for blacks in New York at that time, and suggested that I consider nursing as a career. Another cousin scheduled an interview for me with the superintendent of nurses at Lincoln and took me there. The minimum age required for admittance was 18, but no birth certificate was required, so I put my age down as 18, completed the application, took the aptitude test, and promptly forgot about it.

I went back to Washington that summer of 1934 to live with Aunt Rosa. I also went back to work at the Allies Inn, this time at the steam table. In July, I was notified by Lincoln that I had been accepted to the school and that I was to report on September 4. I had not really thought about a career in nursing, but I was happy to have been selected and went back to New York with the savings from my summer job.

I learned to like nursing and I particularly enjoyed being able to stay out until 10 PM on most nights and until midnight once a week. That was a freedom to which I had not been accustomed at home. I also participated in extracurricular activities such as the glee club and dance classes and was active in tennis, basketball, swimming, ice skating, and horseback riding. At Lincoln I was nicknamed "Lanky," which was not only short for "Lancaster" but described my long, lean frame. The name has stuck with me through the years, although I would say my description has changed.

For one of our classes at Lincoln, Mabel K. Staupers, executive secretary of the National Association of Colored Graduate Nurses (NACGN) was invited as a guest lecturer. NACGN was an organization founded in 1908 to fight discrimination against blacks in education, employment, and organized nursing. As black students in a black school founded in 1898 by white philanthropists, we found that Mrs. Staupers's message had real meaning for us. She told us of the struggle black nurses were engaging in to gain recognition as full-fledged members of the American Nurses' Association, of the problems they were having in gaining admission to schools of nursing in both the North and South, and of the discrimination they faced when seeking employment in hospitals, public health agencies, and the like. This information was new to us because, even though we had taken a course in history of nursing, our instructor was white and had made no mention of the contributions of black nurses to the profession, nor had she mentioned the racial problems that existed.

Shortly after Mrs. Staupers spoke to our class, NACGN held its annual convention in New York in 1936 and used our school as convention headquarters. Because I was active in student affairs I was selected to serve as one of the hostesses to the student delegates, which gave me the opportunity to attend the program sessions and to participate in the social events. The student delegates were from other black nursing schools—Mercy in Philadelphia, Freedmen's in Washington, D.C., and St. Philip in Richmond, Va., to name a few. Lincoln was located in the Bronx in a Jewish area, but to show that I was knowledgeable about black Harlem, I took the student delegates to the Savoy Ballroom. When we told the manager that we were students attending the NACGN convention, he let us in free. We danced for a while, then left in time to get back to Lincoln by midnight.

At this NACGN convention, I learned about the problems faced by black nurses and made a solemn pledge to myself that when I graduated, I would do all within my power to help change the system and break down the barriers that were keeping black nurses out of the mainstream of professional nursing.

When my class was graduated in 1937, the Great Depression was not yet over and we were faced with finding employment. Only 4 of the 200 hospitals in New York City employed black nurses—Lincoln, Harlem, Seaview, and Riverside. The last two were hospitals for tuberculosis patients. I was fortunate enough to be employed almost immediately as a staff nurse at Lincoln, where I earned $75 per month plus maintenance.

Two weeks after taking my state board examination, I took the federal civil service examination for "junior graduate nurse." There were only two federal hospitals at that time where black nurses could be assigned—the all-black Veterans Hospital in Tuskegee, Alabama, and Freedmen's, a general hospital, also all black, in Washington, D.C. Assignment to Freedmen's depended on successful completion of a one-year probation period at the VA hospital in Tuskegee.

While waiting for the results of the civil service examination, a few classmates and I decided to further our education and enrolled at New York University (NYU) on a part-time basis. Having enjoyed a student experience at the Henry Street Visiting Nurse Service in Harlem, I decided to get a bachelor's degree, with a major in public health nursing. After I had attended classes for about a month, my civil service appointment came through for Tuskegee. I resigned from Lincoln, withdrew from my two courses at NYU, and took off for the Deep South.

Having been reared in Washington, D.C., I had been exposed to racial discrimination in schools, hospitals, churches, and many stores, but until I went to Alabama, I had not been segregated on a train. On the train I took south, the small coach reserved for blacks was up front next to the engine where soot was a problem. After a two-day trip, I arrived at Chehaw, Alabama, and rode the five miles on a special train to Tuskegee. I reported for duty that same day, wearing a borrowed uniform because my trunk had not yet arrived.

Most of the nurses at the hospital had been on the staff since it opened in 1923, and they had to get accustomed to our group of young graduates from various schools. Except for social affairs at the nearby Tuskegee Institute, a black school founded by Booker T. Washington in 1881, there was little to do for entertainment in town. As a 21-year-old woman, I had no problem getting dates, which gave me entree to social activities at the institute. I even became engaged to be married while in Tuskegee.

Macon County, where Tuskegee is located, had a health department that employed two nurses—one white and one black. I was anxious to do my share in contributing to the health and welfare of this rural community, so, when I was assigned to work nights at the hospital, I volunteered my services to the health department during the day.

Having been accepted by the county health officer, I bought a car, had some uniforms made (at my own expense), and went into the county to work with black families, the vast majority of whom were very poor. This experience included supervising untrained midwives who delivered the babies of almost all of the black mothers in their own homes.

After a year in Tuskegee, I was eligible to apply for a transfer to Freedmen's Hospital in Washington, D.C., which I did. I also broke my engagement to be married. My stay at Freedmen's was short lived. While working nights there, I had enrolled in two courses at Howard University, a black university in Washington. I knew that attending school full-time would get me closer to my goal, a baccalaureate, so in February 1940 I enrolled at West Virginia State College, a black school.

I provided nursing service to the students in exchange for my tuition, room, and board. I also received a stipend of $10 per month from the National Youth Administration. To earn additional money, I worked one summer as a staff nurse at Homer G. Phillips Hospital in St. Louis and another summer as a combined counselor, nurse, and business manager at Clifftop, a Girl Scout camp in West Virginia. During the Christmas holidays, I did private duty at Lincoln Hospital in New York.

West Virginia State College was located in a rural area 12 miles from the nearest town. With no physician in the area, the nurses at the college answered emergency calls on campus and in the village. Because I had a car, I responded to the night calls. For some reason babies seem to be born more often at night than in the daytime, and I delivered more than my share of them. My only compensation for this was the privilege of registering the birth certificates and giving all of the female babies my name—Mary Elizabeth.

In June 1942 I was awarded the Bachelor of Arts degree from West Virginia State College, with a major in sociology and minors in psychology and history.

In 1941 (the year before I finished college) the Medical College of Virginia in Richmond, which operated two nursing programs—one for blacks and one for whites, with separate clinical facilities for each—started hiring black faculty for St. Philip, the black nursing program. I joined the faculty in 1942 as clinical instructor and supervisor of obstetric nursing. There were four other black nurses on the faculty; we taught the black nursing students, lived in the dormitory for blacks, ate in a separate dining room from the whites, and supervised black extracurricular activities. I coached the basketball team and the drama club. Ironically both black and white faculty, although working separately, met together regularly on a nonsegregated basis as one faculty.

Although I had worked in the South before, it had been at all-black institutions where respect was not confused with race. Working at the Medical College of Virginia was different. White personnel followed the southern custom of not addressing black nurses by the title of "Miss" or "Mrs." To them, I was "Nurse Lancaster." However, we black faculty addressed our students, each other, and our black patients as "Miss," "Mrs.," or "Mr." and insisted that the black students do likewise. A newly employed white director of nursing service at St. Philip, Alda Ditchfield, upheld blacks and had the courage to use proper titles for the black nurses, black students, and black patients.

During my employment at St. Philip, our country was engaged in World War II, and nurses were being recruited for the Armed Forces. With persistence from the NACGN and other black leaders, doors to the Army Nurse Corps had finally been opened to blacks in 1941, although on a segregated basis and by quota. Those of us who applied for admission to the Navy Nurse Corps were told, "Colored nurses are not being assigned to the Navy."

After I had been denied admission to the Navy Nurse Corps, I decided to seek federal funds that were made possible by the Bolton Bill to begin pursuing a master's degree. During the summer of 1943 I attended Teachers College, Columbia, in New York.

While I was in New York, I visited Estelle Massey Riddle (Osborne) whom I had worked under when she was the director of nursing at Homer G. Phillips Hospital. She was then a consultant on the staff of the National Nursing Council for War Service. It was she who told me that black nurse leaders were eager to have more young black nurses trained for leadership positions, especially in nursing education, in order to head schools for blacks that were then directed by whites. She indicated that she thought I had the potential to become a dean of a baccalaureate nursing program.

That opportunity came for me in 1943 when Hampton Institute, a black college in Virginia, at the encouragement of the National Nursing Council for War Service, agreed to establish a baccalaureate program in nursing. At that time, very few black nurses had master's degrees, which would have qualified them for a deanship. So those of us who had bachelor's degrees and the potential for leadership had to be groomed until we could be further educated.

Through the efforts of the NNCWS and the NACGN, I was released from St. Philip and joined Hampton's faculty as assistant dean of the baccalaureate nursing program. Because it took them more than a semester to find me, it became my lot to do the groundwork in establishing the program. The graduate courses that I had just completed at Teachers College gave me some orientation to principles of education. That bit of knowledge, limited as it was, enabled me to get the program started. Estelle Riddle of NNCWS and Rita Miller, Chairperson of the Division of Nursing at Dillard University in New Orleans, were instrumental in helping me launch the program.

When I went to the Virginia State Board of Nurse Examiners to get approval for the program, the executive secretary, without greeting, asked "How old are you?" I told her that I was old enough (I was 27). She said, "You look mighty young to be running that school of nursing." Before our conference was over, however, I think she was convinced that I could manage the program.

The first students were admitted in February 1944. Shortly thereafter, a white dean took my place and I continued as assistant dean while carrying a teaching load. The current faculty at Hampton University give me credit for having initiated the nursing program there, which was the first baccalaureate nursing program in the state of Virginia. (In 1977 the faculty named the college's nursing archives in my honor.)

Near the end of my first year at Hampton, the college president was instrumental in securing for me a fellowship from the General Education Board of the Rockefeller Foundation. I enrolled as a postgraduate student at the University of Toronto in Canada with a major in administration of schools of nursing—a one-year program that led to a certificate. I had wanted to continue my pursuit of a master's degree at Teachers College, but who was I to look a gift horse in the mouth?

One of my former St. Philip students, Bernice Carnegie, was a native of Toronto and was at that time pursuing a postgraduate certificate in public health nursing at St. Philip. She had gone to St. Philip for her basic nursing education because blacks were not accepted in any nursing program in Toronto. Having not been assured of living accommodations at the University of Toronto, I contacted Bernice, who secured housing for me at her sister's home in Toronto. While living there, I met her brother Eric. After a short courtship, we were married in December of 1944.

By the time I had completed the course at the University of Toronto in 1945, the General Education Board had become interested in the program in nursing at Florida A&M College in Tallahassee. It needed to be reorganized, with a nurse as head of the program instead of the medical director of the hospital. I accepted the position as the first dean of the school of nursing.

Florida A&M College had one of the two schools of nursing for blacks in the state, and the only one that was administered by blacks. Until 1950 it was the only baccalaureate nursing program in the state. My first responsibility there was to develop a sound educational program in professional nursing.

Florida proved a challenge to me in many respects. I had the job of reorganizing the school of nursing, of getting it nationally accredited, and of making it an integral part of the college. At A&M I also had the opportunity to help black nurses gain the respect of the public in general, and also the respect of other nurses. Both of these tasks were accomplished, but not without problems.

I was invited to present my clinical rotation plan to a meeting of the directors of all nursing programs in the state by the Florida State Board of Nurse Examiners. I gladly did this and was highly praised for it. However, when lunch was served at the hotel where we met, I was relegated to a table in a far corner of the room where I was to eat alone. My first impulse was to leave, but I was afraid such action would lead to sanctions against my program and my students. I sat through the luncheon, but could not eat, nor could I bring myself to join in the afternoon deliberations after that humiliating experience.

Because the hospital had only 40 beds (with an average daily census of 25 patients) the students had to get most of their clinical experience elsewhere. For 10 years A&M students had been affiliating at Provident Hospital, a black facility in Baltimore, which was nearly 1,000 miles away. The college had no control over this affiliation. Because I knew that clinical facilities closer to home had to be found, in the spring of 1946 I requested permission to visit large hospitals in nearby states. All of these hospitals, some with nursing programs for blacks, had white directors of nursing. The response to my mailed queries was cordial enough, but when I, a black woman, arrived and extended my hand in greeting, it was left dangling in every instance. This alone made me decide that I could not, in good conscience, have my students subjected to such indignities.

On my way back to Tallahassee from these visits, I changed trains in Jacksonville and spent the night with a friend who was a public health nurse. After hearing my story, she suggested that I see the director of nursing at Duval Medical Center, a large county hospital in the city. I went there the next day.

The director, who was white, accepted my extended hand. After a tour of the hospital, I asked about using the facilities for Florida A&M students. When she said that the hospital had no funds for an educational program, I promised that the school would provide faculty, housing, and board, and she said she would take it up with the hospital administrator. I left with the feeling that there was hope, not only for the future of our school, but for the human race.

It was not difficult to convince the college president, Dr. William H. Gray, that we needed to have full control over the nursing program, and that since the hospital in Jacksonville had no housing facilities, it would be our responsibility to provide them. Jacksonville was 169 miles from Tallahassee.

Together we made plans for what we called the "Jacksonville unit" and arranged for a conference between the board of directors of the hospital, the board of control of the college, and the Florida State Board of Nurse Examiners. The plan was approved by all bodies and, with a grant from the GEB, we purchased a house near the hospital that was large enough to accommodate 12 to 16 students. The grant also enabled us to employ faculty, a dietician and a cook, to furnish an office in the space provided at the hospital, and to stock a room adjoining the office with books for a library and classroom. We signed a contract and were on our way.

During many planning conferences that were held, a few problems arose. Prejudice again reared its ugly head. At one of the early conferences, I introduced the faculty member who was to be in charge of the unit. As dean of the school of nursing, I was addressed as "Dean" Carnegie. I could not object to that. However, my instructor was addressed and referred to as "Nurse" Mack instead of "Miss" Mack. Having experienced this indignity at St. Philip in Virginia, I could no longer accept it.

The hospital director noticed that I insisted on addressing my instructor as "Miss" and decided that we should have a frank discussion of the issues. She, a Northerner, began by informing me that the white nurses would not address our students as "Miss" because it was a Southern custom not to address blacks in that manner. "What will they be called?" I asked. "They'll be called 'Nurse'," she said.

In utter amazement, I replied, "But you can't call them nurse, because they are not nurses. You'll flatter them. They are students studying to become nurses." "Gee," she gasped, "what will we call them?"

"Why not 'Miss?' " I asked, adding that they had been taught to respect themselves and others, and that I was sure they expected to be treated in a like manner.

I asked her how she felt about it personally. She said that she did not mind addressing our students and faculty as "Miss." I assured her that if she set the example, others on her staff would follow. She complied with my wishes and they followed her lead. How easily old customs can yield to right and courageous examples.

Of course, there were other obstacles. About a week before the students were to leave the Tallahassee campus, the Jacksonville newspaper ran an article about our plans, along with another story that said that the white nurses had threatened to walk out of Duval Medical Center en masse if our students were placed there. This alarmed the students, but I assured them that we had a contract with the hospital and that we were going there regardless of what might happen. With courage, the students left on schedule and conducted themselves with dignity and fortitude. There was no general strike.

For about a year, we were permitted to staff only the wards on which all patients were black. After that year the barriers were dropped, and the entire hospital was made available to our students for clinical experience. In the meantime, President Gray had applied to GEB for funds to build a new hospital on campus to serve as a clinical facility for the nursing students that would also meet the needs of the community. GEB granted the first $50,000 for construction of the hospital; the rest had to be raised by a special fund-raising committee of the college. Ground was broken a few years later, and a beautiful modern hospital was constructed.

On another front in 1946 in Florida, black nurses were fighting for full-fledged membership in the Florida State Nurses Association, the only avenue to membership in the American Nurses' Association. Eleven years before, in 1935, the Florida Association of Colored Graduate Nurses had been organized as a constituent unit of NACGN. I was personally committed to join in the black nurses' efforts to gain recognition as professionals.

The FSNA had voted in 1942 to admit black nurses into the organization but did not permit any type of participation by blacks other than the payment of dues—a clear case of taxation without representation. (Ironically FSNA started returning a portion of our dues at one point to help us run a separate association.)

I remember my first convention in 1946 in Miami. The white nurses (FSNA) met on Miami Beach; we black nurses (FACGN) met in the basement of a black church in the black section of town. Our president was permitted to attend one program session of the FSNA convention, and she reported on it to us. Returning the courtesy, we invited the president of FSNA to attend one of our sessions. We made use of the occasion to protest our exclusion from the FSNA meetings, which we had partially financed with our dues. The wheels of progress were set in motion—slowly.

In 1947 the two organizations met at the same time at Daytona Beach, again in different sections of the city—FSNA at a white hotel and FACGN at a black college. This time, all of the black members were permitted to attend one program session of the FSNA convention. We were also invited to attend the joint program meeting of FSNA and the Florida State League of Nursing Education. The meeting was devoted to a discussion of collegiate education for nurses, and the guest speaker was Dorothy Rogers Williams, executive secretary of the Association of Collegiate Schools of Nursing. Since I was the dean of the only collegiate school in the state, answers to the questions raised from the floor were obvious to me and to my faculty, so I became very vocal from the back of the room, where we had been ushered to sit.

Three years later, Florida State University in Tallahassee established a nursing program. Still later, another program was established at the University of Florida in Gainesville. When the University of Florida's program marked its twenty-fifth anniversary in 1981, I was invited as a guest and was cited for having pioneered baccalaureate nursing education in the State of Florida. Times and people do change.

It was also at the 1947 FSNA convention that the president of FACGN, Grace Higgs, was made a courtesy member of the FSNA board. She had no voice or vote. The following year, 1948, I was invited to speak at the FSNA convention in West Palm Beach at the program meeting titled, "Florida's Future As It Affects the Negro Nurse." This session was open to all nurses. I learned months later that some of the white nurses had planned to walk out if I spoke from the platform. I did speak, the ovation was overwhelming, and no one walked out. I presented facts that no one could deny and painted a picture of optimism for both black and white nurses in the state of Florida.

FACGN met at the Colored Women's Clubhouse, where I was elected president. That automatically made me a courtesy member of the FSNA board.

The next FSNA board meeting was held at a hotel in Jacksonville. I attended and took an active part in the deliberations, forgetting (or maybe not forgetting) that I was not supposed to do so. About midway into the meeting, the president asked me to leave the room for a few minutes. When I returned, the board had voted me a full-fledged member with all rights and privileges.

All board meetings were held at white hotels where I could not be housed or fed. However, there was always a black nurse in town who would provide housing for me. For food, I would have to drive to the black side of town. A car was a necessity because it was against the law for white taxis to carry blacks, and there were no black cab drivers on the white side of town.

I recall meeting one time with the board at the palatial home of a white person (I believe she was an honorary member of FSNA) in Palm Beach. I did not know that lunch was to be served. To everyone's chagrin but my own, I appeared during the dessert course. The hostess graciously made room for me at the table and served me dessert.

During my term as president of FACGN, the 1949 International Congress of Nurses was scheduled to meet in Stockholm. The FACGN members voted that I should attend. Various units of the organization raised money to defray my expenses. The Miami black nurses raised $500 by selling fish dinners in the basement of a Baptist church. Fish fries have been the butt of many a black joke, but I'll bless them forever. They sent me on my first trip to Europe.

The board of directors of FSNA contributed money for my trip, as did several of the white FSNA districts. The students and faculty of Florida A&M College also made donations. When enough money had been raised, I went to New York to board a converted troop ship destined for Stockholm. The send-off was tremendous. Flowers, baskets of fruit, and other gifts were showered on me. I slept in a top bunk, and my cabin mates thought I was a celebrity but couldn't understand why I was not traveling first class.

In Sweden I received extraordinary attention from the press because I was an oddity—the Swedes probably had not seen many black people before. I was featured in all of the local newspapers, to the envy of my white colleagues.

When I returned from Europe, having participated in a study/tour through eight countries, I was again invited to be on the program of the FSNA convention, this time to give a report on the ICN meeting and to show movies that I had taken while on tour. The FSNA again met at a first-class hotel; we blacks were housed in private homes and met at a place called "Jones's Barbecue Stand." After careful deliberation and with the knowledge that the NACGN had voted for dissolution a few months before, we members of FACGN voted our black organization out of existence. After all, we had been accepted as members of FSNA, which gave us membership in the American Nurses' Association, and all of the districts had accepted us, although some limited our attendance at meetings. Since we were not incorporated, it was not difficult for us to dissolve. We allowed ourselves a few months to wind up business, so the official date of dissolution was May 1, 1950— a full 15 years after the group was formed. We presented certificates of appreciation to the organization's charter members and to a few white nurses for their efforts on our behalf. One white nurse, for example, had supported our admission to the FSNA but had said, "Let them in. After all, no black nurse will ever be president of the American Nurses' Association." Little did she know that a black nurse, Barbara Nichols, would be elected president of ANA in 1978.

In 1949 I was placed on the ballot of FSNA as a candidate for election to the board of directors for the first time, and I won. It was the first time a black had run for office in a southern state association.

At the last business session of FSNA before the FACGN dissolved, I announced to the convention the action taken by FACGN. The dissolution had some ramifications: part of our dues could no longer be returned to help us run a separate association; with no local units, black nurses expected to be able to attend all district meetings and all sessions of the state conventions as equal members. Those problems were eventually solved, but they seemed insurmountable then. I recall one white nurse suggesting that a Negro section of the FSNA be formed on the state level (one had already been formed in one district). My reply, which was supported by several white members, was that if a Negro section was formed, then a Chinese section would have to be formed. (I don't think we had any Chinese members, but we were fighting for a principle.) We pounced on every absurdity thrown at us until all efforts at segregation were quashed.

The most difficult task in the move toward integration was finding meeting places that would accommodate both races without violating the state's segregation laws. In Tallahassee, we started by meeting at the Leon County Court House. With the exception of the three black nurses on the staff of the county health department, all of the black nurses in Tallahassee were on the faculty or staff of Florida A&M College. This made it easy for us to go to meetings together.

For many months in Tallahassee, we played a game of musical chairs. The white nurses would wait outside the building for us to arrive and take our seats, then they would proceed to sit on the opposite side of the room. If we sat in the back, they would sit in the front; if we sat in the front, they would sit in the back. We black nurses began waiting for them to arrive first, then we would enter and scatter ourselves to ensure integration in the seating arrangement, at least. After the novelty wore off, no one paid any attention to who sat where. Before long, we were all participating on a democratic basis, working on committees together.

At the next state convention in 1950, I was reelected to the board of FSNA, this time for a three-year term. At this meeting, for the first time, black nurses attended all business and program meetings, but were barred from the luncheon. This worked more of a hardship on the speaker, Marian Sheahan, than it did on us because we blacks demanded that Miss Sheahan attend our luncheon and give the same speech to us that she gave to our white colleagues. Moreover, our luncheon was held in a black restaurant on the black side of town.

I took an educational leave from Florida A&M College in 1951 and went to Syracuse University on another GEB fellowship to pursue a master's degree in educational administration. As a graduate student at Syracuse, I could not resist getting involved in community and school affairs. In the community, I helped to organize the Syracuse chapter of the National Council of Negro Women and, at the request of the students, I served as advisor to the undergraduate chapter of the National Association for the Advancement of Colored People.

In 1952 I was back in Florida when the FSNA convention was held in Daytona Beach. There was integration in every respect, except for housing and those events that were strictly social. The luncheon meeting at the hotel included all members on an equal basis.

Also in 1952, an extension program for registered nurses was started by the faculty of Florida State University in Tallahassee. This program was designed to meet the needs of white nurses in the state and was closed to black nurses. We made an attempt to have black nurses included in the extension program by arguing that the two groups attended professional meetings together on a nonsegregated basis, but the Attorney General for the state of Florida ruled (and told me personally on the telephone) that it was against the law for this to happen in the classroom.

In order to meet the needs of the black nurses, we had no choice but to start an extension program for them at Florida A&M. This was done in 1952 in Jacksonville, where a black public school was used to hold classes. In Miami, we used the facilities of the school of nursing for white students from Jackson Memorial Hospital for a summer term in 1953.

It was in 1952 that the National League for Nursing came into being, with constituent state units. I was elected secretary of the Florida League for Nursing and chairman of two local committees. I had also been active in FLN's predecessor organization, the Florida State League of Nursing Education.

During my eight years in Florida, my activities were not limited to nursing. In 1949 the governor of Florida appointed me to the Commission on Human Medicine and Health Care of the Southern Regional Education Board (SREB), which led to the establishment of the nursing education program at SREB. The academic deans at the college elected me to chair the Deans' Council, I was a frequent speaker at capping and graduation exercises at black schools throughout the South, and I also spoke at functions for other health-related programs in black institutions. In my spare time I served as president of the Tallahassee alumnae chapter of Delta Sigma Theta sorority, a public service organization.

I remained a practicing Catholic while in Tallahassee. When I first went there in 1945, there was only one Catholic church. The back pew was reserved for blacks. Of course, we resented this type of discrimination in the Church, of all places. A group of us decided to defy our relegation to the rear of the church.

One Sunday, we deliberately sat up front. The usher insisted that we move, but we were so engrossed in prayer that we could not possibly hear him. Our "kneel-in" shook up the priest and other church officials, and it had some impact on the system, although not immediately. A few years later, when a new church was constructed, Catholics of all races were accepted as parishioners on an equal basis and could sit anywhere in the church.

The year 1953 ended one era in my life—an exciting one which gave me many rewards in spite of immense difficulties. I had achieved my goal at Florida A&M College (now University), which was to upgrade the school of nursing so as to meet national standards and to offer a curriculum that would compare with the best in the country. This was accomplished in 1952 when the program was accredited by the National League for Nursing. These achievements cost me my marriage, however, because my husband Eric refused to leave Canada to join me. He did not want to face Florida's segregation laws. Each year I had promised that I would return to him, but there was always another major project to better the nursing program that I had to complete before leaving.

I also saw complete acceptance of the black nurse in the Florida State Nurses Association. In 1984 the FSNA invited me to be a guest of honor at its Diamond Jubilee convention in Jacksonville and cited me for having made the school of nursing at Florida A&M a "showcase."

After I left Florida, I learned that whenever I had left the campus to attend board meetings of the FSNA, which were always held at a white hotel, the entire college faculty would pray for my safe return. They knew that I would refuse to ride freight elevators in hotels while there on business. They also knew that my life had once been threatened in Alabama for trying to use the restroom at a service station where I had just bought gas. When I go back to Florida now, those who lived through that era with me always reflect on those days.

In July 1953 I was offered and accepted employment as assistant editor of the *American Journal of Nursing* (AJN), the professional journal of the American Nurses' Association.

Having just left the Deep South with its blatant racial discrimination, I did not believe that I would face the same problems in New York City, but I did. For months I tried to rent an apartment in downtown New York near my office, only to be told by white landlords, "We do not rent to colored." With financial help from my aunt Iola I bought a house in the borough of Queens.

Nell Beeby, chief editor of the *AJN,* was at first concerned about my being discriminated against while representing the company in the field. I assured her that I could take care of myself, and that I hoped she would not hesitate to send my anywhere in the country. In my travels I had some unpleasant encounters, but they were minor compared to what I had experienced in the past.

In 1953 the American Journal of Nursing Company was publishing only three magazines—*AJN, Nursing Outlook,* and *Nursing Research.* Because *Nursing Outlook* had a small staff, I was assigned to handle education material for that publication, although I was on the staff of *AJN.* After three years I was promoted to associate editor of *Nursing Outlook,* with education content as my responsibility. In 1970 I became senior editor of *Outlook.*

In December 1959 I received an invitation to attend the inauguration of President William Tubman of Liberia, West Africa. I went at the expense of the company, with the charge to write an article about nursing in Liberia, Ghana, and Nigeria (Carnegie, 1960). I was serving on the national board of Delta Sigma Theta then. As a national officer, I was authorized to set up a chapter of Delta in Monrovia, Liberia, which I did.

In Ghana I was privileged to address the nursing students at the College of Nursing in Accra. My next stop, in Nigeria, was interesting. I had arrived in Ibadan, the only passenger leaving the plane, to find waiting crowds of chiefs in their tribal robes, the military, photographers, television cameramen, and squads of police officers. My feeling of being overwhelmed by such a reception was short lived—the turnout was for England's Prime Minister Harold Macmillan, who was touring Africa and whose plane arrived five minutes after mine. My press card was honored, and I was permitted to remain on the field and to take pictures of the prime minister and his party when they arrived.

In 1964 I again went to Africa. For a few years, I had been on the board of Women's Africa Committee of the African-American Institute. One of our projects, funded by the U.S. Department of State, was to host a leadership training program each summer for women of Africa. Each year, a board member would go to a selected area of the African continent to interview women leaders and seek participants for the program. I was elected to go. Before traveling to central and southern Africa (Nyasaland, Southern Rhodesia, and Northern Rhodesia) to interview the program finalists, many of whom were nurses, I attended the East African Women's International Seminar in Nairobi, Kenya (Carnegie, 1964).

In 1967 I decided that I wanted to earn a doctoral degree, although it was not required for my position with *Nursing Outlook.* I enrolled in the Graduate School of Public Administration at New York University, first part time and later full time. I completed my doctorate in 1972, and my dissertation was published as a book by the National League for Nursing under the title, *Disadvantaged Students in RN Programs* (Carnegie, 1974).

In 1973 I was named chief editor of *Nursing Research.* My first editorial was titled "ANF Directory Identifies Minorities with Doctoral Degrees" (Carnegie, 1973). This editorial drew attention to the fact that there were few minorities so prepared. Shortly thereafter, in 1974, ANA applied for and received a grant from the National Institute of Mental Health to help minority nurses earn PhDs. The board of directors of ANA appointed me to the advisory committee for the minority program, and since 1980, I have chaired that committee. Since our first fellowships were given in 1975, about 80 minority nurses have earned doctorates through this program.

It was also during my tenure with *Nursing Research* that I was inducted into the American Academy of Nursing, which had been created by the ANA board in 1973. In 1977 I was elected treasurer of the academy, and in 1978 I was elected president. The academy is composed of a cadre of scholars in the profession and numbers nearly 500 today.

Nursing Research, which was first published in 1952, had never had a large circulation because of its specialization in research. In 1978, because of cost constraints and new competition, the AJN Company could no longer support a full-time paid editor and decided to go with a part-time volunteer editor, as is the custom with many other professional research periodicals. I was at an age where I could take early retirement from the company and not lose certain benefits, so I did. At my retirement party, the board commended me for meritorious service and for a quarter of a century of accomplishments.

While I was editor of *Nursing Research,* I served on the board of Nurses' Educational Funds, an independent, nonprofit organization that grants and administers scholarships to registered nurses for study on the master and doctoral levels. I still serve on the organization's interracial board, which consists of leaders in nursing and business. NEF is supported by contributions from the business community, foundations, nurses, and from individuals interested in the advancement of nursing.

After I had served on the NEF board for about 10 years, I wanted to encourage black nurses to apply for scholarship awards, so I made a commitment to provide money on an annual basis that was earmarked for a black doctoral student. This became known as the Carnegie Scholarship. In addition, because Estelle Massey Osborne was the first black nurse in this country to have earned a master's degree, I initiated a scholarship in her memory.

As editor of *Nursing Research,* I had been invited to speak, to conduct workshops, and to write about research in nursing. So when I retired in 1978, I got the idea to start my own business as a consultant on scientific writing. Schools of nursing and other organizations throughout the country invited me not only to lecture, but to help with writing research for publication. I did this for two years until Hampton University in Virginia invited me to be a Distinguished Visiting Professor to teach research in the master's program. This I did for three years, commuting from New York every two weeks. I served as Distinguished Visiting Professor in 1984 at the University of North Carolina at Greensboro; in 1986 at Pennsylvania State University; and in 1987 at the University of Michigan, Ann Arbor.

After I left Hampton in 1983, I knew that I had to write the history of blacks in nursing. An account of the personal histories of some black nurses had been written in 1929 (Thoms, 1929), and the story of the National Association of Colored Graduate Nurses had been written by Mabel K. Staupers (Staupers, 1961), but no comprehensive history of blacks in nursing had been recorded under one cover.

For 25 years as an editor of major nursing periodicals, I had noticed that black nurses had been left out of the history books in America, with the exception of one or two sentences alluding to the first black nurse, Mary Mahoney, and NACGN's existence from 1908 to 1951. I believed that it was up to me to fill this void with my book, *The Path We Tread: Blacks in Nursing, 1854-1984* (Carnegie, 1986). This, I think, has been my greatest contribution to nursing.

Response to the book has been tremendous. I have made television and radio appearances and have been asked to appear at book receptions all over the country. The book has been reviewed in the leading nursing journals, and I have given formal speeches on its content.

My most cherished honor for the book came as a legislative resolution made by the

New York State Senate on May 22, 1986: "Resolved, that this legislative body pause in its deliberations to honor Mary Elizabeth Carnegie for her contributions to the field of nursing as a nurse practitioner, educator, and author; and be it further resolved that this legislative body congratulate Mary Elizabeth Carnegie on her new book, *The Path We Tread: Blacks in Nursing, 1854-1984. . . .*"

All over the United States, black nurses, many unknown to each other, have always fought for a common cause. There were many, of whom we can be rightly proud, who lived through the same era as I. They were fighting on the same front in schools of nursing and professional organizations in other states, and on other fronts—in public health, hospital nursing service, industry, private duty, and in the military.

Black nurses, with the cooperation and support of liberal white nurses and others, have cleared innumerable hurdles. There is still some catching up to be done, but the trail has been blazed for a swifter run.

REFERENCES

Carnegie, M.E. Nurse training becomes nursing education at Florida A & M College, *Journal of Negro Education,* Spring, 1948.

_____. Using the nursing abilities study in curriculum planning, *Am. J. Nurs.,* Dec., 1952.

_____. Flying trip to West Africa, *Nurs. Outlook,* Mar. 1960.

_____. East African women's international seminar, *Nurs. Outlook,* July, 1964.

_____. ANF directory identifies minority nurses with doctoral degrees (editorial), *Nurs. Res.,* Nov.-Dec., 1973.

_____. *Disadvantaged Students in RN Programs,* New York, National League for Nursing, 1974.

_____. *Historical Perspectives of Nursing Research,* Boston, Mugar Library, Boston University, 1976.

_____. *The Path We Tread: Blacks in Nursing, 1854-1984,* Philadelphia, J.B. Lippincott, 1986.

Lancaster (Carnegie), M.E. How a nursing program was developed in a Negro college, *Am. J. Nurs.,* Feb., 1945.

Staupers, M.K. *No Time for Prejudice,* New York, Macmillan, 1961.

Thoms, A.B. *Pathfinders: The Progress of Colored Graduate Nurses,* New York, Kay Printing House, 1929.

Luther Christman

Luther Christman, PhD, RN, FAAN, is
Dean Emeritus, College of Nursing,
Rush University

❖

Luther Christman recounts the rich resources he enjoyed while growing up in a small town, where he learned to take advantage of his environment and to cultivate interests in nature, poetry, and art. He describes here the strategies he has used to overcome the discrimination he believes he suffered during his career as a male in a predominantly female profession. He set high career goals and reached them and has been widely recognized for his achievements in nursing. A longtime advocate of advanced education for nurses, Christman believes it must parallel the education of other professional disciplines, and he continues to lament the discrimination he sees in the profession. The recognition he has with other groups as well as in nursing circles attests to his wide range of activities and accomplishments.

My early life in small-town America before radio and television helped me to develop a keen awareness of others. I learned that getting ahead did not have to come at the expense of others. One could experience being different, being self-directed, without creating controversy. Living on the plateau of a mountain gave me a sense of vision and filled me with curiosity. I could see the sweep of rolling hills with their many peaks and valleys. The horizon always seemed to be expanding.

Each family in my hometown was a beehive of activity. Every child had many chores. Mine included making sure we always had fuel, feeding and caring for the chickens we raised, weeding the garden, and performing handyman tasks around the house. Whatever time I had left, I devoted to reading and to ideating about the future of science. I read every book in the Tom Swift series. Horatio Alger's novels had a big impact on me and stimulated within me a sense that success was within anyone's reach. The school librarian noted my insatiable appetite for reading and carefully guided me to the classics. The literature and poetry I read set off many flights of fancy and stimulated my imagination. When not reading, I roamed the mountains with my dog. Nature offered a continuous variation on a theme. Each tree, each wildflower, each animal, seemed to have something to say. I was active in the Boy Scouts in our town. I became the senior patrol leader and tried to have my fellow scouts see nature in this interesting way.

I remain a committed conservationist to this day. One can but wonder why the beauty, symmetry, and harmony of nature does not cross into the world of humans. Roaming the hills helped me to develop serenity, to organize my thoughts, and to see that each variation on the theme of nature was beauty in itself. Change was interesting and stimulating. Dorothy, my wife, claims that everything I have done and everything I have written was first considered while I worked in my garden.

Those regular outings resulted in some aesthetic urgings. I began to write poetry, to sketch, and to draw. I mused over becoming a poet or an artist and over writing or drawing the unusual. I was discouraged by everyone. The depression was on, and mine was a blue collar environment. Everyone said that poets and artists could barely support themselves. I was brought sharply down to earth but never lost the desire to be creative in whatever I did. My grandmother was a wonderful person with whom I had many lively discussions. She was wise, philosophical, and without prejudice. She encouraged me to be expressive, to develop aspirations, to achieve goals, and to live a productive life. She gave me vision and hope.

My teenage years were relatively untroubled. I had a wide circle of friends, both boys and girls. Because of the depression, play was limited to walks, hikes, doggie roasts, and small parties. Camaraderie, wit, and what is now called interpersonal competence were the order of the day. Acceptance by others was based primarily on these criteria.

I have often been asked why I became a nurse. The answer is, I stumbled into the profession. A clergyman counseled me into becoming a nursing student. My wife and I had been high school sweethearts, and we wanted to do something together. The pastor was a Philadelphian and knew about the Pennyslvania Hospital School of Nursing for Men. He wrote for an application to the school, helped me fill it out, and filled out a separate application to the Pennsylvania Hospital School of Nursing for Women for Dorothy. He was a Methodist and had contacts in the Methodist Hospital in Philadelphia. Both of us were admitted to schools of nursing. We were grateful because job opportunities were scarce. The nursing profession offered more opportunities for employment then than any other profession. My parents neither supported nor opposed my choice of career. They said I would have to earn my way on my own. I survived.

It did not take me long to realize that men were a minority in the profession and were viewed with suspicion by female nurses. The segregated (male/female) nursing schools at Pennsylvania Hospital had a similarly segregated faculty. Although there was much accord, underlying tensions existed.

One day, while I was scrubbing in the operating room, a young woman needing a cholestectomy was brought into the room. The surgeon discovered that she had a full bladder and ordered a catheterization. The operating room supervisor told me to leave. She said I could not stay because I was a man. When I mentioned that the surgeons were men and that the surgery would be further delayed were I forced to leave and then to rescrub, she stomped off. After the surgery the supervisor told me that I did not understand the role of men in nursing.

On another occasion, I was called a pervert for answering a urologist's request to examine a specimen under a cystoscope while in the presence of a fully draped female patient and female nurse. A similar reaction occurred when I requested a maternity experience. I submitted a request to the members of the faculty of the school for women asking to be assigned a maternity rotation so that I could be prepared in a manner akin to that of most nurses in the country. I was denied because of my gender. I questioned that because all of the obstetricians were men. Even policemen and taxicab drivers were being trained to handle emergency deliveries. "That's different," they said. I tried to persuade them that a male nurse would be more helpful in an emergency delivery than a policeman, but they were steadfast in their decision. They said that if I was ever seen anywhere near the delivery room, I would be dismissed immediately. Discretion became the better part of valor and I retreated.

Shortly before I graduated, a position as a night supervisor in one of the smaller hospitals was advertised. I responded and they were interested. When I asked how long I would have to work nights and when I could be considered for day shifts, I was told, "Never, we would not allow our patients to know that we had a male nurse on the staff." I lost interest immediately.

Dorothy and I graduated in 1939 and we were married in December of that year. I thought hospital schools were not useful and decided to go to college immediately. I took a job in Pittsburgh that paid twice what nursing paid for only 40 hours of work per week. The job would do well to support me through college, I thought, since the hours were flexible. I applied to Duquesne University because it was only a few miles from our apartment. The admissions officer seemed pleased with my transcripts from high school and the hospital. He took me to the dean of nursing who refused to interview me. She and the admissions officer argued. She won. She thought that men should never be allowed to earn a degree in nursing.

Pearl Harbor put a damper on my burning ambition. I was eligible for the draft. The armed forces had a taboo on men serving in the nurse corps. I considered this an injustice more to the men who were wounded in battle activity than to male nurses. Male nurses were not able to function as corpsmen because to do so they had to go to corps school, but they were too qualified to enter that training, so they were assigned duties outside of health care. I transferred to Philadelphia so that Dorothy and our infant son would be near relatives if I were drafted. The United States Maritime Service needed corpsmen, and I knew that the whole service was draft exempt. I applied with a strategy in mind, was processed almost immediately, and received a permanent assignment to a training base in St. Petersburg, Florida.

Shortly after I arrived, I wrote a letter to the Surgeon General of the United States in response to his call for registered nurses. I wrote that I knew female nurses were not permitted in battle areas, and that I wanted an immediate and permanent assignment to the battle zone for the duration. After receiving what I considered a snide reply I sent copies of my letter and his response to every U.S. senator and about three fourths of the members of Congress. The responses were interesting. Both Democrats and Republicans agreed that men should be commissioned. Republican senators wrote to say this was how the New Deal wasted everything. Democratic senators claimed it was the Pentagon that wasted everything. The Surgeon General was called before several committees relating to the war effort. He was annoyed. He had a nurse draft bill introduced because of the nurse shortage. I discovered that approximately 1,200 male nurses had been drafted and that none were functioning as nurses. The *Saturday Evening Post* wrote an editorial questioning the policy of not using male nurses. A column questioning that policy also appeared in the *Christian Science Monitor*. The *St. Petersburg Times* likewise ran an article that raised questions about the services' refusal to use male nurses. When the Pinnella County District Nurses Association endorsed my position, a nurse from the Army Nurse Corps subsequently appeared at one of their meetings to chide them about that move. Her position was that if men were commissioned, all the senior women nurse officers would immediately be demoted and replaced by men. I received a letter from Colonel Mayo, who was stationed in the Pacific area, endorsing my stand. He said the only way he saw male nurses getting an opportunity to serve would be in activities related to hospital administration.

The pressure to commission men was beginning to mount. Secretaries who worked at the base offered their services after normal work hours to help me answer all the mail I received. They wondered how a corpsman could do so much to stir up the system. After the Battle of the Bulge, the Surgeon General withdrew his request to draft women nurses, and the whole issue died. Many senators had assured me that no women would be drafted until all qualified men were commissioned. It was not until the Korean War that men were accepted into the nurse corps.

After the war I returned to Philadelphia to pursue a degree. I was told by many women nurses to apply at the University of Pennsylvania. I sent my transcripts and was interviewed. A faculty member who conducted the interview said, "If you present these credentials to our admissions office you will be admitted immediately. We also know what grades you will have if you do." I asked what they would be. She said, "You will get an 'A' in all of your courses outside of nursing and an 'F' in every nursing course because you are a man." She said the nursing faculty did not believe that any man should get a degree in nursing. I recalled an earlier experience and said, "I do not agree." I wondered how widespread this attitude was. She said, "Why don't you apply to some kind of field where you could use your intelligence instead of wasting it on nursing?" I excused myself. I left the Penn campus and went across the city to Temple where no gender questions were asked and I was admitted without incident. In order to support my growing family, I worked full time while going to school full time. Many years after that incident I was asked by a search committee if I wanted to become a candidate for the deanship at Penn. I declined, not because of the past but because I was very happy with what I was doing.

After I graduated from Temple, I accepted a faculty position at the Cooper Hospital School of Nursing. In addition to teaching, I was asked by the hospital administrator to work on nurse productivity and organizational effectiveness. Practices were introduced, some that had been tried before and some brand new. These included the use of ward clerks, the establishment of an expanded central supply station, automatic replenishment of drugs, a messenger service, and removal of nonclinical activities from the nurses. The plan was a success, but one day all of the head nurses demanded to meet with me. They were angry because all they had to do was to take care of patients. I learned an important lesson of participatory management. No matter where I worked after that, I always involved the whole staff in decision making. I gained insight into how doggedly nurses resist change. Later I was offered the position of associate administrator of that hospital, but I turned it down. Even though the salary was greater than that of the director of nursing, I declined because I wanted a career in the nursing profession.

During those few years at Cooper Hospital I served on the economic security committee of the state nurses' association with Dr. Ella Stonesby and Alice Clarke. Dr. Stonesby was taciturn in our meetings and rarely spoke. Alice and I were young and eager. We visited several editors of large newspapers to secure their support for a scheme we had in mind. In those days nursing salaries were very low. We approached the various groups of private duty nurses in the state and asked them to raise their rates by approximately $1.50 per day. They were perturbed but acted on our suggestion. Hospital administrators called us and threatened to stop our actions, but we replied that it was a private contract between patients and nurses. Just as we anticipated, the marginal difference in salary was sufficiently attractive that staff nurses began to resign to enter private duty. Hospital administrators had to raise salaries sufficiently high to retain the staff nurses. A year or two later we repeated the manuever with the same result. I was asked to present a paper to a meeting of hospital administrators, who offered to place me as one of their own. I understood their motives and refused their offer, saying that I preferred to develop a career in the nursing profession. I left the state and Alice became a publisher. We both deplored the use of conventional bargaining tactics, which tended to be confrontational rather than productive. We apparently had little or no effect on nurses' bargaining tactics. We know of no actions similar to ours.

I was offered a position as assistant dean in the school of nursing at the University of Pittsburgh as soon as I earned my master's degree. Ruth Keuhn was the most dynamic person I had encountered in nursing. We discussed the role I would have as assistant dean. The world seemed to open up. However, I was reluctant to accept the position without a doctoral degree because all of the major figures I had encountered in academia had doctorates. I turned it down for that reason. In reflection, my professional career probably would have been greatly enhanced had I taken that position.

Instead of university life, I accepted a position at Yankton State Hospital in Yankton, South Dakota. I became one of a small group charged with reorganizing the state mental health program. In those times hospital attendants served in primary care roles because they were entrenched in their positions. Not long after my arrival, I circulated a questionnaire to the attendants asking them to list their most preferred assignments. I also asked them to list their least preferred assignments. After the data were analyzed, the attendants were moved to their least preferred assignment on the same day. Early on that day, two male attendants came into my office and tossed their keys at me. In resigning they said that before the end of the day most of the other attendants would do likewise and that I would be held in public disgrace because the hospital would be without enough staff to stay open. I looked at my watch and said, "Gentlemen, this is an important issue. However, I have a meeting to attend that will last at least 30 minutes. If you will be kind enough to wait until my return, I will discuss it with you." I hurried to the personnel department and asked them to get final checks in the hands of these two men. Because I said I would be tied up for 30 minutes, I did not return until then. Neither attendant was there. So much confusion, chaos, chagrin, and anger existed among the attendants that the nurses, physicians, and professional staff in general were able to move in and take over so that reform could begin. Education and service were unified under a practitioner-teacher model. Students and faculty members both supported this endeavor and accepted that it was the model used to strengthen the major clinical professions. I was appointed to the state board of nursing.

Nurse-physician team management of patients was established. This meant that nurses had the same rules of accountability as physicians. They were as responsible for the quality of nursing care as physicians were for the quality of medical care. This model was used a number of years later by other nurses and was called primary nursing. The difference in semantics was important because it caused resistance from physicians in some settings. The physicians cooperated wholeheartedly in a nurse-physician team concept. We studied ways to reduce the team nursing emphasis that had been in place, and we supported the nurse-physician concept by using nurses' aides as assistants to the nurses instead of as care-givers. This was done to strengthen the clinical structure for nurses.

I became active in promoting clinical master's degree preparation. I was appointed to the first national committee to examine this concept and to make recommendations. Eventually, a document was published by the National League for Nursing (NLN) regarding this preparation.

After I left South Dakota, I went to Michigan to take on the task of changing the mental health system of that state. Organizational change was brought about in a steady and deliberate manner. A number of nationally known educators and clinicians were brought in to offer regular workshops for nurses. One university school of nursing was supported to develop the unified model in psychiatric nursing. A group of nurses in the state, outside the mental health system, lobbied to have psychiatric aides licensed and prepared in a fashion similar to licensed practical nurses. I wanted scholarships for professional nurses. The legislators were caught in the middle of it all and discussed it with me. I suggested they pass the aide bill without the funding to implement it. They did this and the appropriation to fund professional nurse scholarships won out, even though it seemed unrelated to the other bill.

I became active in both the NLN and in the American Nurses' Association. I enrolled in the doctoral program in sociology and anthropology at Michigan State University and was elected president of the Michigan Nurses' Association (MNA). I was busy with my job, school, and association office during the next four years. One of my first acts as president of the MNA was to convene a representative group from both the MNA and the Michigan Hospital Association to examine the economic status of nurses. The meeting was long and the groups were at odds. During a break in the meeting, I went to the men's room. In that confine an animated conversation was under way. I listened for a while, then said, "If salaries are not increased by 10%, I am calling a press conference to accuse the hospital administrators of this state of being responsible for the nurse shortage. There is little or no difference in staff salaries from hospital to hospital. I am going to accuse you folks of restraint of trade." An argument ensued, and I stuck to my guns. They agreed to the increase when I suggested we measure the success of the pay hike against the number of nurses with active licenses. The state board of nursing said then that 14,000 out of about 42,000 nurses had active licenses. One year later, over 16,000 nurses were working. After a second increase about 19,000 nurses held active licenses. That number increased to 21,000 after a third increase.

While attending the 1964 ANA convention, I introduced the resolution that established the American Academy of Nursing. My purpose was to try to gain the same visibility and recognition for nurses that other organizations had granted scientists and physicians. The resolution passed overwhelmingly.

My next position was as associate professor at the University of Michigan. I had appointments in the School of Nursing, the Institute for Social Research, and the Bureau of Hospital Administration. It was through the aegis of the Institute for Social Research that Basil Georgopoulos and I did a controlled field experiment to study the role of the nurse specialist. Although unpublished, those data remain current and useful. I have used that work consistently in attempting to innovate care and educational programs. I also gained insight into how clumsily hospitals are organized. The science editor of the *Saturday Review of Literature* requested that I write an article on what was wrong with American hospitals. I took the position that if airlines were staffed the way hospitals were staffed, there would be no room for passengers. I suggested changes.

It was while at Ann Arbor that I wrote Christman's Laws of Behavior. I developed these laws to help me view serious matters from a lighter perspective. They are:

1. We all want the world to be in our own image.

2. People cannot use knowledge they do not have.
3. In every instance, given the choice between rationality and irrationality, people opt for irrationality and are rational only when forced to be.
4. Most people under most circumstances will generally do what is right if they know what is right and if the temptation to err is not too great.

My doctoral dissertation had been on selective perceptions and predispositions to act, so the connection to the laws is obvious.

These laws have enabled me to roll with the punches and to see humor in the behavior I have observed in the profession. They explain everything from reluctance to establish an educational entry level into practice to the unwillingness to respond to the affirmative action mandate that was designed to democratize the profession.

I was appointed Dean of Nursing at Vanderbilt University. Concurrently, I was appointed Director of Nursing at Vanderbilt Hospital. The unification model was strengthened. This appointment marked the first time a man was named dean in the profession.

During my years at Vanderbilt, the practitioner-teacher model was refined and strengthened, a grant was secured to develop nursing practice as an applied science, another grant was obtained for the purpose of teaching the behavioral sciences in a more meaningful way, money was obtained to substantially increase the efficacy of learning labs, and the number of students was greatly increased.

An incident that indicates the attitudes of some members of the establishment toward men in the profession occurred after I had been at Vanderbilt for about two years. At a meeting of deans of the Southern Regional Education Board, a dean of one of the major schools stood at a floor microphone and said, "All those great things you hear that are happening at Vanderbilt have nothing to do with Luther Christman's competence because he doesn't have any. The only reason he is successful is that all the male faculty members in the entire university automatically give in to him every time he makes a request." A dead silence ensued. As everyone knows, that is the way men always behave with each other. I used the closest floor microphone to say, "She just says so because it is true!" After some tittering everyone left the room. It was interesting to me that not one woman attending the conference suggested that the comments may have been out of line. One has to be hopeful that prejudice will eventually diminish.

It was during my Vanderbilt years that I was nominated for the presidency of the American Nurses' Association. Before anyone knew who the candidates might be, there was conversation among the board members that the time might be right to have a person elected who was a scholar, had a doctorate, had done research, was recognized clinically, and had published. When the nominations were announced, one candidate had none of the credentials, and I had most of them. The majority of the board members campaigned at the election convention for the one with the least qualifications because she had been "on the board longer."

At the onset of the convention a number of newspaper reporters met with me. They sensed a story because I was the first man to be nominated for the presidency of the association. The reporters thought that I had an excellent chance of being elected. Later in the convention they called for another meeting where they told me my chances of being elected were slim. The chief turning point in their opinion was the buzzing at the convention that "no man should ever be elected president of the ANA." Imagine how some nurses encouraging this attitude would have reacted if that statement had been made in reverse at male-dominated organizations. Women had little cause to belabor male-dominated professions when they set such a bad example themselves.

In 1972 I was recruited by Rush University to help launch the school and develop dynamic nursing programs. The recently reopened Rush Medical College was the keystone around which a university was to be constructed. We were able to open the College of Nursing and Allied Health Sciences within one year at the undergraduate and graduate levels. Faculty and students were recruited (most transferred from other schools), degree-granting authority was obtained, and approval of the board of nursing was received. The framework for the Rush Model of Nursing was laid. The college grew so rapidly that it became free standing. Two other colleges, a College of Health Sciences and a Graduate College were established soon thereafter. A complete school of nursing, from undergraduate to doctoral studies, supplied the impetus for other developments.

Primary nursing, levels of practice, quality assessment, workload indices, clinical research, and contacts with many foreign countries were indicative of the kind of effervescence that was taking place among faculty, students, and staff. The nursing staff was organized into a self-governance model similar in its bylaws to those of the medical staff. The levels of practice design made it theoretically possible for each nurse to set her/his own salary. Through the structure of the professional staff organization, it is possible for the nursing staff to have a major influence on the decision-making process within the nursing division. Generous donations from John and Helen Kellogg made possible the Center of Excellence in Nursing. This is a dynamic concept with strong potential.

The clinical doctoral program enhanced the level of clinical practice, stimulated research, acted as a prod to develop postdoctoral programs, and spurred the development of the combined doctoral program—the DNSc/PhD, an analogue of the MD/PhD program—as a valuable means of developing strong scholars.

The matrix form of management for the medical center facilitated cooperation between administrators, physicians, and nurses. A basis for interprofessional cooperation was set in place to develop working relationships with patient care as the central focus rather than any one profession. The formation of over 30 associated practice groups of nurses and physicians was one outcome of these improved relationships.

In 1974, with the support of management, the faculty of the college of nursing started a community nursing service in order to provide continuity of care to medical center patients. Last year they served over 30,000 patients and provided a good milieu for student experience. One of the great satisfactions that the staff and faculty enjoy is the large number of foreign nurses who are interested in the Rush model. The regular stream of visitors is a source of strong stimulation.

One of the outcomes of this regular contact with foreign nurses has led us to perceive the nursing profession in a larger context. For the past few years we have held a retreat at a conference center in rural Wisconsin owned by Rush. In these workshops, leading nurses from many foreign countries explore the theme that the nursing profession can never be strong in any one country until it is strong in all countries. Strategies for strengthening the profession are explored. The biggest achievements gained in the workshops have been to bring more objectivity to issues and to question time-worn traditions. Although these workshops are not doing much by way of bringing on necessary changes in the profession, they may ultimately be of some value because of the caliber of the nurses involved.

One of the reasons that I sometimes seem to diverge from the mainstream of the profession is that I have not functioned exclusively in nursing organizations. I belong to more professional and scientific organizations outside the profession than inside. These contacts have enabled me to make transitions in thought from the outside world to the world of nurses. They may have enabled me to be more objective.

More as a matter of explanation than as a litany of self-indulgence, I have been honored by invitation to the National Institute of Medicine and the Chicago Institute of Medicine. I have been made a fellow in applied anthropology in the American Association for the Advancement of Science. I am a member of Alpha Kappa Delta, the American Sociological Association, a founding member of the National Academies of Practice, one of the few people and the only nurse to be made an honorary member of Alpha Omega Alpha (the physician honor society), and was named an Old Master by Purdue University. In addition, I have received an honorary Doctor of Humane Letters degree from Jefferson University and the Founder's Award for Creativity by Sigma Theta Tau, nursing's honor society. These experiences told me that the world can be a pleasant place.

My career is mostly behind me. If any of the endeavors in which I have been involved have been of assistance in making the nursing profession stronger and better than it was when I found it, I am satisfied. As is the case for most people, I have 20/20 hindsight. If time could be rolled back, I would certainly do some things differently. However, on the whole, I am reconciled to the reality of the path I have taken.

Maureen Cushing

Maureen Cushing, JD, RN, is an
attorney specializing in trial law. She is
with the Boston firm Mooney,
Mahoney and Cushing

An exquisite sense of caring is the essence of nursing that Maureen Cushing carries into her practice of law. She practices with one foot in each profession — which keeps her interest so keen that she is an effective resource for answers to legal questions posed by nurses. She says that contrary to some people, she has never left nursing but has taken on a second career. She enjoys identifying the parallels between the disciplines of nursing and law. "I understand a client's suffering and anxiety in much the same way I understood a patient's pain and suffering. In nursing I knew I could always do something."

It was her love for the dramatic that took her into nursing in the first place. Today, she says, when she sees lawyers who seem impressed with their own dramatic courtroom skills, she thinks, "You want drama? Watch a nurse working to save a patient in septic shock, or listen to her talking to a patient who has just been told there is no treatment because the cancer is too far advanced."

*I*t is now nearly 10 years since I last stood at the foot of a post-op patient's bed and tried to decide whether the patient's latest clinical signs would require potential life-saving intervention or were simply insignificant fluctuations. I frequently find myself trying to identify some of the parallels between the disciplines of nursing and law. For me there are many, and rarely does a day go by that I have not thought about some aspect of my other life. It substantially influences how I view clients and opposing parties, how I evaluate and prepare cases, and, to a lesser extent, how I conduct a trial. This may not be true for any other nurse attorney, but it is strikingly apparent to me. I have thought more about the essence of nursing since leaving it than I ever did when I was actively practicing it. I anticipated that the distinctions between the two careers would be dramatic, and it surprises me to be using so much of my nursing experiences and values in my present practice. I brought a great deal of my nursing mindset to the practice of law, and it has served me quite well.

There are some nurse attorneys who have intentionally distanced themselves from the nurse image, but for me that would be completely wrong and would not be in my best interests. I like to challenge myself by singling out one word to describe something. I guess it is the concept approach to life. Thus, drama is why I went into nursing in the first place; joy is what I got from nursing; and service is what I owe to any profession.

I was the third child of Irish immigrants and grew up in a small New England town. The ethnic mix of residents was diverse, and there was a feeling that your neighbors would rally round whenever you needed them. I remember one Easter when my brother, who had scarlet fever, caused everyone in my family except my father to be quarantined. The neighbors left groceries and hot meals at our front door, and most of the time we did not know whom to thank. Births, deaths, and illnesses were a community affair. It was a proud working class community that influenced me almost as much as my parents' philosophy that the measure of a person was how much that person helped those in need. Both my parents had an exceptionally strong work ethic and, by example, instilled this same ethic in their children.

My mother's greatest wish was that her children would go to college. Two of her three children did so. I have vivid memories of my mother bringing food to my older brother's room late at night while he studied. Although I did not know it at the time, my parents were also setting me up to think in terms of another American dream—being my own boss. When I left nursing, I did not seek a job but rather struck out on my own. On hindsight, it would have been a lot easier to have worked for someone for a while.

Most of the children who were my age were schoolmates who lived in the more rural part of my town, and I biked to their homes after school. This exposed me to many different ethnic groups and family customs. In most of these homes both parents worked to make ends meet. As children I think we fed off each other's imagination. When we had to play alone we relied on our own creative talents. Later, in both nursing and the law, I found it necessary to tap into this creative ability.

As a child I read two or three books at one time and, like most children, I read under the covers with a flashlight. I liked to test myself by trying to keep the various plots and characters straight in my mind. This was good discipline for the amount of professional reading and sorting out of information which was to be required in both nursing and law. As a nursing instructor I spent many long hours with textbooks spread across my living room floor tenaciously trying to master an elusive bit of theory and break it down so that I could remember it. Then I had to teach it with simple words so that students could understand and remember it. Today I use the same dynamics when trying to get a complex medical point across to a lay jury as I did in teaching students and patients. It took me a long time to learn that simple language is as much an art form as is eloquent speech. There are many ways that the arts of nursing and law are as alike as they are dissimilar. When I left one career for another, I thought I had to start from scratch and I lacked the vision to see what could be readily transferred from past experiences.

My first memory of the world of hospitals was when my 12-year-old brother, who was a Down's child, broke his hip. I recall that he was hospitalized a very long time and my mother had to work two jobs in order to pay the hospital bill. I vividly remember being allowed to climb the back stairs to the hospital's pediatric ward, where I stood on the screened-in porch and talked with him through the screen. I was five years old, and I liked the drama of a hospital. It was not the memory of the ward itself or even the uniforms as much as it was the people in a place where exciting things happened that appealed to me. The ward was open and filled with dozens of cribs and a few beds. I could see that order reigned in that seemingly chaotic world. I went to that same hospital to receive my diploma and worked on that ward before it was finally torn down. I never viewed my work with patients as anything less than dramatic. For me, there is far less drama in the law. Sometimes when I see lawyers acting impressed with their dramatic courtroom skills, I have to keep myself from saying, "You want drama? Watch a nurse working to save a patient in septic shock, or listen to her talking to a patient who has just been told there is no treatment because the cancer is too far advanced." Nursing can be a very humbling experience. The highs in nursing are frequently of a personal nature and are not subject to display as an attorney's work is.

Other than drama, I do not know what I expected from nursing. I knew that I always wanted to be a nurse and I knew I always wanted to work in an acute care hospital setting. It was no mistake to become a nurse, and I would do it again so long as I could do bedside nursing. I have always loved the fact that the nursing discipline is both an art and a science. It took me quite a long time to become comfortable with practicing law because it draws much more heavily on the art aspect. The reasoned analysis of nursing was easier for me than the reasoned analysis of legal problems.

Growing up with my brother, Jackie, made me more patient than I would otherwise be. While Jackie was just one of the kids to everyone in our school, my other brother and I would become very protective of his feelings when we left that secure environment. He is a very sensitive person, and even today it hurts me to hear him say, "I know I am different from others." My biggest regret is that he was born before it was learned how much can be taught to Down's children. Jackie is the most gentle person I have ever met.

I think that my studying law was inevitable. From young adulthood on I liked to argue, although not with any degree of skilled persuasion. As a family, we were comfortable with heated discussions. There were some guidelines, like having to know something about the subject being discussed and not just shooting from the hip. We had ways of putting hip shooters down.

My decision to enter law was a simple one. I always loved bedside nursing, but I believed that I would not be physically able to do this kind of work after a period of time. When I decided it was time for me to pursue graduate work, I was drawn to law and to journalism. I quickly ruled out journalism because I did not think I had the creative talent for it. Sometime before my decision to enter law school a colleague in the nursing school where I taught asked some of the faculty to be her sample test takers for a tests-and-measurements graduate course she was taking. This all happened before the women's rights movement and, oddly, she gave us a motivation test for males. There was no nurse category on the test. In one series of motivation tests I scored very high in the areas of persuasion and salesmanship and seemed more inclined toward becoming a judge than a health care provider. Then, as now, I had no more desire to be a judge than I had to be a doctor. I took great exception when she attributed my testing high in these areas to the fact that I frequently dated law students.

I have spoken with a number of nurse attorneys who have more dramatic reasons for going into law. Although I had seen my share of hospital errors and injuries by the time I left nursing in 1978, I still believed that patients were in good hands when they entered hospitals. However, by that time I had heard some distressing tales from nurses in a variety of practice settings when I gave nursing and health law lectures across the country. While I was troubled by the positions in which nurses were being placed, I felt a kindred pride with those nurses whose high standards frequently put them at risk of losing their jobs. Often when I returned to Boston from giving a lecture, I would throw a nurse's question at other litigators to see how they would have answered it. I sometimes did it to shock them with the dilemma but more often to see if there was more to be said on the subject.

I did not begin to practice law in earnest until a number of years after I had completed law school. I had been a bedside nurse for exactly 20 years, and I loved hospital work. Also, I was not eager to face the hardship of making the transition from nursing to law. I think people who went into second careers then were somewhat of an oddity, and the doors of the legal profession were not open to attorneys with a nursing background. This has changed to some extent today. Although I had no idea about the kind of law I wanted to practice, I did not want all the nursing years to be locked in a trunk. I wanted to use both the knowledge and skills I had acquired as a nurse in my second career. To a large extent I have been able to do that.

One of the first things I did after leaving nursing was to join a nursing practice committee of my state nurses' association. I always want to touch base with clinical nursing on some level, and, besides, joining the committee was a nice way to ease out of nursing. Prior to that time I never had the time to attend meetings during the workday, and night school had pretty much precluded participation in professional committee work. I knew there were some able nurse educators in my state, and I wanted the opportunity to talk nursing with them. Being on that committee taught me more about professionalism in nursing than any other single experience because it exposed me to scholarly, concerned nurses who articulated and dealt with nursing issues in a no-nonsense manner.

While my route to becoming a litigation attorney was very circuitous and fraught with worry about whether I would ever again make a living, it had very definite benefits. I became exposed to many areas of law practice and lawyering styles. The first year after I left nursing I spent the entire year giving nursing malpractice and health law lectures. I had closely followed the negligence cases since starting law school but did not have any particular affinity for this type of practice.

Today it amazes me that I did not know from the very beginning that I would like trial work because the stress and demands of bedside nursing are not unlike the demands and occasional glimpses of drama of trial work. I should have reflected on what kept me in nursing for 20 years. It was not until I began working with a trial attorney that everything started to fall into place, although the craft of lawyering was not learned overnight.

I became involved in bar association meetings while I was still practicing nursing and joined every committee that dealt with anything remotely connected to health law issues. This, more than anything, helped me weed out areas of law I was not interested in and also showed me the realistic possibilities of integrating my nursing background with law.

Around that time, Massachusetts was dealing with the Chad Green cancer treatment case, developmental disability laws, and hospital payment systems. I became involved in medical treatment cases and began to represent both hospitals and families in these matters. Dealing with these cases kept me in touch with hospital nursing and gave me a perspective about patient care issues I wish I had had while actively practicing nursing. In one case I was appointed guardian to an incompetent woman and, while reviewing her nursing home medical progress notes, I discovered that the physician had inadvertently written that, in addition to other severe medical problems, she had multiple sclerosis and Parkinson's disease. This incorrect medical history could have influenced the court in deciding for or against a surgical procedure which I knew the woman would have to eventually have. My nursing need to know details dictated that I review her medical records frequently.

Emergency medical treatment court cases can be very demanding because by their nature many require an immediate decision, and when the telephone call comes into the lawyer's office, everything else must be relegated to the back burner until the facts are gathered and the court is petitioned. Shortly after I left nursing I served as guardian to an elderly Italian woman who was completely alone. She had been in a Boston hospital for six months after suffering a stroke in a nursing home, and one of my chores was to "spend-down" her accumulated funds so that she would be eligible for financial assistance. My biggest problem turned out to be that I was unable to prove her citizenship, which was a threshold requirement for assistance.

The nursing home where she had previously lived did not have a record of her social history, which would have been a starting point in my search for documentation of her citizenship. The woman was from a remote area in Sicily and had spoken only a Sicilian dialect before becoming incompetent. I was able to construct some kind of history from her own and her deceased spouse's medical records and other government information. I was surprised by the amount of detective work I had to do to supply that woman with a history. I wrote to consulates, told my story to immigration departments, and went back to her old neighborhood, in an attempt to recreate her past. I stared at her wedding picture, which was one of the few possessions she owned, and I tried to gain some inspiration into her past. I was finally able to comply with the requirements, and after my guardianship term expired the nurse who had been her primary nurse while she was hospitalized volunteered to assume permanent guardianship. During the transfer phase we worked closely together, and we both agreed it was one of our special nursing memories.

Later the nurse told me that she and some of the other nurses had a birthday party for that woman. I had uncovered the name of one of the woman's old Italian neighbors and tracked her down, even though she had moved to another town. The primary nurse brought the two women together, and after about one-half hour the patient began to talk to the woman in her native dialect. Everyone had thought previously that the woman was aphasic because no one had been able to understand her even when an interpreter had been used. Handling this kind of treatment case has taught me about a kind of human suffering I had not experienced in hospital work. Because my perspective was different I was sometimes more affected by a client's medical condition. I think that was true mostly because so many of the people I represented were alone in the world.

I think nursing is set apart from other disciplines because nurses as a group consistently perform tasks in an above-average manner and they are honest in accounting for the care that they render. It took me a long time to realize that to be happy in practicing law I had to surround myself with attorneys who placed the same value on high standards as I did. In nursing I loved the responsibility, the challenge of making decisions, and the people. I also loved the camaraderie and teamwork associated with hospital work. I liked walking into a hospital and saying "Good morning" 50 times before 8 o'clock. There were values in nursing which I wanted to transfer to my law practice. These included attention to detail, honesty, compassion, and, particularly, the need to work with people who would not level off professionally. I am still looking for the science part of law, and initially I was uncomfortable with not knowing what I was doing before I plunged into something, since that approach is seldom used in bedside nursing.

There were and are so many extraordinary role models for nurses to follow that the new nurse fits into her role with more ease and confidence than beginners in most other professions. I do not have a keen sense that I had any single nursing mentor when I began to practice, but I certainly leaned heavily on more experienced nurses. Back then, you learned how to operate a respirator by having the resident teach you during your shift. Nurses relied on the expertise of nurses on the earlier shift, who showed them which tubes to irrigate and how new machines worked. All of this fitted into the "needs to know now" concept. Nurses are intuitive and know when trial and error is not the route to be taken. I learned to teach my students by trial and error because teaching did not come naturally to me. It was something to be worked on by breaking down the parts of teaching and becoming skilled in each part. I've had to approach litigation in much the same way. Teaching made me a better nurse because I was forced to do more in-depth studying than I would have done otherwise.

I simply could not have survived in law without my mentors. While there are many areas of the law in which a beginner can quickly become competent, trial litigation is not one of them. One night at a law program, the registrar, who knew I had been a nurse because we had a mutual friend, introduced me to the man who registered just in front of me. She said that he and his brother each had 50 years of trial experience and frequently argued cases before the state high court. I later prevailed upon him to take me under his wing, and over the next several years I learned the basics of trial litigation from the two brothers. In addition to learning that the hallmark of a trial attorney is in-depth preparation, I learned that high standards were an asset and that a lawyer with a creative bent comes out ahead more often than not. To read that pretrial preparation is the top priority is one thing, but to spend one day with telephone directories and writing letters to locate missing witnesses is another thing. How often I heard, "I would rather have tried and failed, than never have tried at all." In one case an important out-of-state missing witness called late on a Friday. The case had been scheduled for trial on the following Monday. We had been searching for over six months for the witness, and he had no way of knowing when the trial would start. He helped us prove an important factual element in the case.

As I sat across from their desks I saw moral attorneys at work and got a clear sense of why and how the practice of law changed over the years. They showed me by example that the door should always be open to legal brethren in need of advice and counsel and that help and direction should always be given to a client in need of legal services. I was taught to respect the courts and my adversaries but not to waver in my advocacy role. Without these lessons I would not have been able to reconcile the values of my first career with the practice of the law.

One thing I have found in law that I did not see enough of in nursing is the ability of a colleague to take delight in and publicly praise another lawyer's skill in a particular area. It is not uncommon to hear one lawyer praise another when there is nothing to be gained by doing so. I recently heard a plaintiff's lawyer say that his adversary's ability to create a visual picture of events for the jury was masterful and poetic.

I have always subscribed to the principle that when a unique opportunity comes your way you must act upon it because it may never come your way again. I have some wonderful life vignettes because of this philosophy. Some are worth more than others in the scheme of things, but few turned out to be wrong for me. Opportunity may come in the form of a challenge, or it might be just plain luck that directs it to your door. I have found that it has rarely come when I wanted it to come, and I have had a tendency to use that fact as an excuse for not becoming involved in some endeavors. In nursing and law I have tried to take advantage of every bit of good luck that has passed my way. In law we say that we learn by our mistakes. In nursing we seldom have that latitude, but that shouldn't deter us from accepting the minichallenges.

When someone asks you to review a manuscript, give a legal lecture to 3,000 nurses, talk about something on television, or write, do it. Do your best and ability will develop. Make your mistakes, then go back and study. Your next effort in that area will be better. If you over-prepare yourself, you will do fine.

I enjoy writing for publication and find the finished product gives me great satisfaction. Nurses should not be reluctant to write because they possess the most important element necessary to be able to do so—a wealth of experience, both scientific and personal. With respect to writing, the three best pieces of advice I have received are: one word follows another; keep it simple; and learn by doing. Editors are used to hearing, "But, I've never written a single word." If others can see things in us that we cannot see, perhaps we should put our trust in them. Although I was pushed toward trial work, I would frequently ask my mentors how they knew I would be suited for it. They would respond, "Give us our due."

I consider myself extremely fortunate to have been a nurse. For me, nursing and the law have been very passionate careers, and my personality was suited for both, although with the law it was not as comfortable a fit as it was with nursing. The law consumes much of my time, and a client's problem becomes my own. I understand a client's suffering and anxiety in much the same way that I understood a patient's pain and suffering. Only by giving some of it away are they able to get through a difficult time. In nursing I often saw nurses willing their courage to patients. A lawyer does much the same when she says, "Let me do the worrying from now on." I have talked with a number of nurse attorneys who say that the desire to relieve a client's suffering and anguish is a prime factor in their law practice. It bothers me when I am unable to help a client who is suffering. In nursing I knew I could always do something.

On prominent display in my law office I have two statues. One is Lladro's nurse and the other is a Hummel of St. George slaying the dragon. I have special affection for the statue of the nurse because a patient on one of the floors I was assigned to gave one just like it to the floor nurses, and it was one of the first things I saw as I barrelled through the swinging doors of the ward. It had a commanding presence, and the nurses became quite attached to it. After leaving nursing I bought a copy of the statue even though it was during the lean time of my transition. I bought the Hummel during a more flush time after deciding on trial work.

Although I got that statue because sometimes there are real dragons to contend with in trial work, I have come to look at it in a different light. As it stands side by side with the nurse, I've come to see the dragon as a symbol of all the suffering I saw in hospital work. I often look up at these two figures and think that among the many things a nurse does, slaying bad dragons is surely one of her functions. For one reason or another, I guess I will always be comparing what I do now with what I did then.

Anne Davis

Anne Davis, PhD, RN, FAAN, is
Professor of Mental Health and
Community Nursing at the University
of California, San Francisco

"Seize the opportunity" has been Anne Davis's motto, which has taken her far in nursing and on travels all over the world. She writes of two overriding and interacting professional interests in her life: ethics and international nursing. Blessed with an adventurous spirit, an inquiring mind, and a family who valued both, she was fearless in undertaking new things and persisted to overcome barriers that were put in her way.

She describes her own philosophy: "There is no way that I can ever repay all of these people who have been a part of my life, so the best that I can do is to give whatever I can give back into the common pot."

Since I have been asked to write an autobiography, these comments reveal something of me as a person and as a nurse, but more important, they say much about our profession. Two ideas form my theme here. First, nursing, a complex and broadly based profession, has the ability and the vision to make good use of someone like me. Second, nursing has provided me with opportunities that I might not have had in another discipline.

I have developed two overriding and interacting professional interests: ethics and international nursing. Recently they have come closer together in my work focus, but I am getting ahead of my story, and as someone once wisely said, the best place to begin is at the beginning.

The beginning for me was my family. I grew up as a cherished and only child, arriving 16 years after my parents had taken their vows. My family fostered not only a great deal of love, but also a great deal of discussion. We discussed what I refer to as "big ideas," and I was expected to have not only an opinion, but an informed opinion. At the very least I was expected to produce a thoughtful comment on the issue that was under discussion. In these talks there were several major themes, many of which would fall into the category of values or ethics. I didn't know that then, of course. Then it was simply the three of us sitting around discussing these ideas. We didn't have serious discussions all of the time because we liked to have fun, too. But we did discuss inequality, freedom, social justice, and the ethics of war, since I grew up during World War II. Much of our focus was on the European scene, since living on the East Coast made us feel closer to Europe than to Asia. I had an uncle who had worked in Japan, and it was through him that I came to appreciate aspects of Japanese and Chinese culture.

As I entered my teens, we began to discuss what I might choose to do with my life. I had always had an interest in literature. I loved reading anything that I could get my hands on, and while that was of very high value in my family, my parents did, on occasion, worry that I spent too much time alone. That concern coupled with my being an only child led my parents to do such things as send me off to summer camp. I reluctantly went—mainly to please them. It was a bit of a mixed bag. I was used to having my privacy and my own room. Suddenly I was off to summer camp, where I had to share psychological and physical space. It was a good experience, I suppose, but I didn't want to do it again.

I read a great deal of poetry, fiction, and biography. Poetry was important to me, and there was much talk about my going to college and getting an advanced degree in the humanities. What that put in my mind was that a baccalaureate degree was not going to be the end of my education. One should go on; one had to go on. Along with reading poetry, I read many books having to do with values. I didn't think of it in that way then, but when I look at my library, which began to form when I was in high school, I realized how many of my books raise questions about the meaning of life, the values of a good life, and the meaning of friendships.

I was a very good student in high school, and I was a loner. Already I had staked out a pattern for myself that I have had to work at changing over my lifetime. I've been a loner because so many of the things that I like to do are solitary pursuits—reading books, writing poetry, playing the piano, and listening to music. I have never been troubled by going out to dinner or to a concert or even around the world by myself.

Owing to certain personal changes in my life, I enrolled in nursing school rather than in the humanities. I had enough sense to know that I should go to a National League for Nursing (NLN)–accredited school. I was young and naive in many ways, but I did know the importance of this. I enrolled at Emory University in Atlanta. I was mediocre as a student. I think that my youth and naivete about certain things plus a lack of help to integrate much of the knowledge I was being given led me to be just average. I was fairly good clinically, but in the classroom I was inconsistent. I flunked nursing arts, which was the first class that we had to get through, and I didn't do well in neurological nursing either. I had a classmate who was compulsive, and while I don't think she really understood a lot of what she was learning since she simply memorized everything, she made very good grades. She would take me aside and drill me the night before an exam until I could get through it.

I was very busy exploring other aspects of life at that point in my youth and doing all kinds of things that were considered appropriate for the young to do. I found that some aspects of nursing school were difficult to cope with, especially the suffering that patients experienced. My role of intimate stranger brought me into another person's life in ways that I really didn't feel comfortable with. I often tried to help, but I think it is questionable just how helpful I really could have been because those were things that you could not learn from a book. You had to learn them from life. You can develop compassion and learn how to care for and about a suffering person, but I don't think you learn that in an academic setting.

While I was a student at Emory, I went to New York for my pediatric affiliation at Babies Hospital, Columbia Presbyterian Medical Center. I liked pediatrics very much in the classroom, but I found that with very, very sick children it was extremely difficult to practice. I had never seen so much suffering, and at times I became really physically ill from the experience. I became very attached to many of the children, just as I had become attached to many of the adults while I was at Emory. After having been through most of the clinical experiences in nursing, I still didn't find anything I wanted to do until I found psychiatric and community health nursing.

I went to St. Louis, and there I began to learn psychiatric nursing. It was mostly descriptive psychiatry that I learned, but it opened up a whole new world to me. On my own in the library, I discovered Freud's writings and began to read them. While I didn't understand everything he wrote, I did understand enough to realize that his theories presented different ways of thinking about people and relationships from those to which I had been accustomed. The most important thing that happened while I was in St. Louis was that one of my professors, who had worked at McLean Hospital outside of Boston, read poetry. She would often begin classes with a poem, and while I didn't always like her taste in poetry, I liked the idea that she read it in class. The fact that she thought poetry had something to say to people in nursing pleased me. I decided to look into psychiatric nursing in more detail.

I went to McLean Hospital as a staff nurse when I finished my baccalaureate degree at Emory. While I was at McLean, I heard about a master's degree program at Boston University from my head nurse. The head nurse, who was a man, asked me if I would like to go to Boston University with him to look into this master's program and into the university's National Institute of Mental Health stipends for graduate students. I had not heard of these stipends before, and I was very interested to learn that there was money somewhere out there that could help me get through school. Off we went to his interview, where I just sat and listened. At the end of the interview I asked for an application. I went home and completed it and mailed it in the next day. I received the last stipend for the next academic year and he didn't get one, which didn't make me very popular with him. The lesson here is that I recognized an opportunity and seized upon it. I have had many opportunities in my career, and though I may have missed a few along the way, I haven't missed many. First you have to recognize that you have an opportunity, and then you must pounce on it with a vengeance. It may be that nothing will result, but if you don't ask, it is a foregone conclusion that nothing will.

I had a wonderful year at Boston University. I believe I was the youngest and most academically naive person in the class. At the end of that master's program I really wasn't satisfied with my level of knowledge. I'd been working at McLean part time then to gain more clinical experience, and I knew a great deal more than I had known prior to my time in Boston, but there were so many things I didn't understand and hadn't experienced. I remember saying to my major professor in the school of nursing at the end of the master's program, "I feel I am just beginning and that I have just scratched the surface, and I don't want it to end." I suppose it was a good way to end a master's program— wanting more.

I wanted to know that all I had learned would really work in the clinical world, so I applied for a job at a Veterans Administration hospital in the Boston area. Numerous people told me that I'd never get a job there, but I did. I worked in a large building where there were 300 men patients including World War I veterans who had been gassed and World War II veterans who had had lobotomies. I learned a great deal about psychiatric nursing there and I worked with a wonderful psychiatric technician. I still believed that I needed to learn more from the academic setting to gain a better understanding of what I was doing clinically. I wasn't satisfied with my ways of conceptualizing what I was experiencing. I applied for another stipend from the National Institute of Mental Health and for doctoral study at Teachers College, Columbia (TC), in New York City. When I learned that I had been accepted to TC, I put my few worldly possessions in my old second-hand blue car and drove to New York City. There I lived in the international house and continued to read poetry and books about values and issues. Early that year two members of the nursing faculty met with me and told me that because I had not done well on the entrance examination I could not continue in the doctoral program. I was told I was not doctor material. They said I could stay for the remainder of the year and take classes since I had the stipend.

I was upset about this. It was the first time I had ever been told that I wasn't capable of doing something. When I got myself pulled together and my initial shock wore off, I decided I was going to make the best of things and concentrate on post-master's study in the social sciences. I took many courses in social psychology, comparative religion, literature, and nursing. Living at the international house was a great experience. Even though the stipend I received really was enough to live on, I believed that I should work. The world of clinical nursing had me in its gravity. By the time I had moved to New York, I had experience working in a small-town general hospital, an operating room, a physician's office, a psychiatric hospital, and a VA hospital. Next, I worked as a staff nurse at the Women's Hospital in Spanish Harlem. The only other experience that I'd ever had similar to my experience in Harlem was the summer in Boston when I had worked at McLean all day on the disturbed female unit and worked another 8 hours at Boston City Hospital during an epidemic with polio patients. I remember going home and falling into my bed and sleeping 19 hours when the crisis was over. For this second tour of duty we were paid with a late dinner of hospital food. Events at Women's Hospital had some similarities to those events in that they presented a face of life to me that I had rarely seen before. In Boston I had never before worked in a city hospital and I had never been involved with an epidemic. At Women's Hospital I was thrown into what was a typical large-city hospital. It was there that I had my first experience of not being trusted by my nursing administration, and it was profoundly disturbing. At the international house I made a friend who lived in San Francisco. Her father had established the Psychoanalytic Institute there, and she told me what it was like to live in that city. I had never been west of St. Louis, where, as a typical Easterner, I thought the earth ended. In my mind there was simply nothing out West, or if there was anything out there it was cowboys and Indians. Obviously, I had seen too many stereotypic films.

This friend invited me to visit her in San Francisco, and I did. I packed my things and drove down the East Coast and across the southern United States. I took eight weeks to travel across the country on my own. I camped and I visited all of the national parks, as well as Colorado, Mexico, and the Grand Canyon. It was a time for much reflection.

When I arrived in San Francisco, I decided that I would return to the East Coast after 10 months. I planned to go back by way of Oregon and Washington through the northern parts of the United States. In San Francisco I worked as a staff nurse at Langley Porter Psychiatric Institute. One day over lunch, I met with Marion Kalkman, who was in charge of psychiatric nursing education at the University of California, San Francisco. She asked me many questions because I was a nurse with a master's degree and this was 1958. There weren't too many of us around in those days. Not only did I have a master's degree, but I had a wealth of clinical experience. A few days after our luncheon, Marion called me at work and asked me to come down and see her. She offered me a teaching position that had opened up when one of the faculty members left to get her doctorate. I was dubious about accepting this offer because I was going to return to the East Coast. Both Marion Kalkman and Helen Nahm, the dean at UCSF, said that I could leave after 10 months; they simply needed an instructor until the end of the academic year.

I joined the UCSF faculty on December 1, 1958, and a whole new world opened up to me. Like many new teachers, I should have paid the university during my first year there because I was learning more than I was teaching. Marion had an enormous influence on me. She was one of the most cultivated and educated persons that I had ever met in nursing. She was well read, and she read poetry. We had a strong relationship with some big differences of opinion, and occasionally we had heated debates on aspects of psychiatric nursing. Our relationship was based on a mutual love of books and poetry and on our interest and involvement in psychiatric nursing.

I taught for three years, during which time I had begun to think seriously about going overseas. I wanted to have the experience of living abroad. I remember talking on my thirtieth birthday with a student who was about to marry a man who had received a Fulbright scholarship for study in India. I told her I thought she was going to have a wonderful experience. When she left my office, I wondered why I was sitting there telling her how wonderful it was all going to be. Why didn't I go myself? I gave notice to the university and took out my retirement fund savings, which amounted to $3,000, to embark on a two-year adventure overseas. I sailed to Egypt on a Dutch freighter and then went to Jordan, Syria, and Lebanon. Finally I went into Israel by way of Cyprus.

I worked for a time on a kibbutz in northern Galilee near the Lebanese border. The area was quiet in those days. Next I worked on an archeological dig at Hamat on the Sea of Galilee near Tiberius. After that, I did some teaching for the Ministry of Health. Through the teaching position I met many wonderful colleagues and friends. After one remarkable year, I left the Middle East and went to Europe. I was ahead of my time, a 30-year-old hippie in an age when "hippie" had yet to be coined. I traveled alone in Europe during 1963, living inexpensively and meeting nursing colleagues from all parts of the world. Looking back now at this and other rich experiences, I realize that I am very proud of the camaraderie among nurses at the international level. Many people were wonderfully kind to me. My philosophy is: There is no way that I can ever repay all of these people who have been a part of my life, so the best that I can do is to give whatever I can give back into the common pot. This is the idea of the great chain of being in transcendentalism, and I believe in that very strongly. We all have the obligation to give back into the chain of being, and I particularly am obligated to do so because I have been blessed and have received much from people who have enriched my life.

I worked for a time as a staff nurse at a state mental hospital in Copenhagen, where I also visited the home of Isak Dinesen, who has become popular since her memoir has been made into a film, *Out of Africa*. After a few months in Copenhagen, I met a colleague in Denmark and we traveled to the Soviet Union. That was a very interesting experience, even though we were there as tourists and not as professionals.

The end of my two years of travel was a difficult time for me for several reasons. I realized that I probably would never again have such a long period of time when I wasn't answerable to anybody for anything. I had been my own person in every sense of that word, free to come and to go, to do or not to do. It was a luxury few people can ever afford. Those of us who have had it haven't had it for very long, but then it's not something that many people would want to continue forever. I had some concerns about coming back to the United States. It is complicated, but let me just say that I wasn't sure I wanted to come back. I was staying with a friend in London when President John F. Kennedy was assassinated. When I fully grasped the implications of that event, my trip was over. My time abroad was forever over.

I had been writing to people at the University of California, San Francisco, while I was away and had decided to return to that institution. I had also decided that I would again apply for doctoral studies, even though I had been told before that I wasn't doctoral material. I wasn't going to let anyone define me as a second-class person. I know from this and other experiences that exams and tests can never fully measure a person or predict the future. Such devices are necessary, but they cannot be taken as gospel, nor can they predetermine one's abilities. The sum of any human is always greater than the sum of his or her parts.

I entered the doctoral program at Berkeley in the year of the free speech movement, and although it was very difficult to concentrate on my studies, I enjoyed being a student. I found the issues of the free speech movement and of the Southeast Asian war to be complex but worthy of my attention.

One of my first classes was a philosophy course in which I was the only student not majoring in the discipline. I worked hard just to keep up with the other students. When a general strike was called, I found myself in an ethical dilemma. I didn't want to break the strike because I thought there were compelling reasons for it. On the other hand, I didn't feel that I could miss a class in philosophy and still pass the course. The campus was in chaos, but I found my philosophy professor and asked him if he was going to hold the class that week. He had a wonderful response: "We will meet again when we can meet with honor." I thought, "Thank all the gods, I don't have to break the strike and I don't have to miss a class." My dilemma was solved.

At Berkeley, we studied, we marched to protest the war, and we discussed the larger questions of life. It was a good four years. I did very well as a student because it was an environment in which I thrived personally and intellectually. During each summer, I taught a continuing education program in psychiatric nursing in San Francisco to stay active in nursing. In addition, during two of those summers I went abroad.

All through those years of work and study, value questions kept coming to my mind. Psychiatric nursing certainly was a fertile field in which to raise many of these questions. While many people did not seem interested in discussing values then, occasionally I did meet someone (usually a psychiatrist or another nurse) who was interested in discussing such concerns. In the course that I taught each summer to prepare nurses to teach psychiatric nursing, I raised some value issues. I finished my doctorate and went back to UCSF to teach psychiatric nursing.

In 1975 a notice came out that the Kennedy Foundation in Washington had fellowships available for nurse educators who wanted to study ethics. It sounded like something I would like to do. There's nothing more practical than developing conceptual ways of thinking about the world. Otherwise, life is like walking through a museum filled with unlabeled artifacts. I needed more systematic conceptual ways of thinking about ethics. Several hundred people applied for the fellowship. Twelve of us were invited to Washington at the Kennedy Institute's expense for interviews. Of the dozen interviewed, four received fellowships, and I was one of them. I spent a remarkable year (including one of the coldest winters ever) at Harvard. This fellowship was the key to opening all of Harvard's doors. The philosophy department, the law school, the medical school, and the school of public health all offered courses of interest to me. It was a wonderful, wonderful year.

In the meantime I had been working at the Stanford Research Institute on a project to establish a school of nursing in Jiddah, Saudi Arabia. At the end of my academic year at Harvard, I was invited to work further on this project in Jiddah. Even though I had been to the Middle East before, traveling in Saudi Arabia was a very different experience. I returned to Harvard, completed my work there, and then flew to the International Council of Nurses meeting in Japan where I toured the country alone for five weeks.

When I returned to UCSF, I began to teach a class in ethics. Before I left Harvard, I had written to the director of nursing service in the hospital on the UCSF campus to say that I wanted to do some clinical ethics consultation there on my return. I have both taught in the classroom and done these consultations in the hospital ever since my return. I think it is important to have some grounding in the clinical world as well as in the theoretical world.

Since I finished the Harvard postdoctoral studies in 1977, I have had opportunities to do more things than I could ever have imagined. I have been a visiting professor in numerous universities both in the United States and abroad. I have been asked to write many chapters for books and many articles for journals. I'm involved in several international research projects, including a joint project between Japan, Israel, Sweden, and the United States. Another project with which I am involved is being conducted in Australia and the United States. A few years ago, along with some colleagues, I was instrumental in establishing the international cross-cultural health and nursing specialty at our school of nursing. This development and my background in ethics have allowed me to bring together two long-standing professional interests.

I am told that when I was very small we had a travel book with many pictures that we kept on a coffee table. I used to drag this book around and announce to one and all, as I pointed to pictures of various places in the world, that I was going to each place someday. And so I have. I have met some of the most remarkable human beings imaginable. I have friends and colleagues in Southeast Asia, Europe, the Middle East, Africa, and South America. I've done a great deal of traveling and thinking about what I have learned at home and overseas from a value and ethics perspective. There are still many places I want to visit, many people I want to meet, many experiences I want to have, and many ethical issues I want to ponder.

Not only has nursing permitted me to do all of these things, it has also encouraged and helped me to pursue and combine my interests. There are times when I get tired of being dumped on as a woman and as a nurse. One of the things I have come to realize (and this does not make it right) is that my women colleagues in other fields are also dumped on. Sometimes the double dose I receive because of my gender and profession makes me angry, but I have come to realize that being dumped on says less about me, my reality, and who and what I am, than it does about the person who is doing the dumping. That doesn't mean I like it, but it means that I am much more apt to challenge people and tell them what I think.

Sometimes I wonder what my life would have been like had I gone into literature or taught poetry. It probably would have been a good life because I grew up in a family that encouraged me, provided for me, and loved me. I grew up in a simpler world than that of today, where things were not so complicated and where there were fewer choices. No matter what I could have done in my life, I cannot imagine that I would have had as many rewards, opportunities, and adventures in any other profession as I have had in nursing. I do not think of myself in any other way, nor would I want to.

One of the rewarding aspects of teaching ethics within nursing is the opportunity I have had to work with other nurses as well as with people in other disciplines. People in philosophy, theology, the humanities, medicine, and the social sciences have come together to raise questions, to analyze issues, and to evaluate possible solutions to some of the most profound ethical issues confronting us as health professionals. These issues that health professionals must face are wide ranging.

Nuclear war, the AIDS epidemic, the lack of health care for certain people in this country and other countries, political oppression (which lends itself to psychological and physical abuse), and the clinical problems of nursing are just a few of the problems we must deal with in our professional lives.

It really is remarkable that a discipline such as nursing can accommodate so many people with so many different talents. We are all needed—those of us who work in critical care units of large hospitals or in long-term care facilities, those who work in the inner city and those who work in rural areas, those who are administrators, teachers, and policy makers, those of us who conduct research, and those who raise some of the basic questions about our values, obligations, and duties to others. It has been said that an unexamined life is not worth living. The same could be said of professions.

For those of us who know something of nursing's history, we can be proud that, as a profession, we have supported legislation over the years that has enabled many people to live better lives, to work in safer environments, and to receive adequate health care, even when they cannot afford it. We have a proud history in nursing, and I for one am very happy to be a part of that. I take my motto from a colleague who lives in Beijing, People's Republic of China: "I am but a small, infinitesimal drop of water in a large surging sea, but I must use that drop with everything that is in me to make the best and most use of it."

Rheba de Tornyay

Rheba de Tornyay, EdD, RN, FAAN, is
Professor of the Department of
Community Health Care Systems and
Dean Emeritus in the School of Nursing
at the University of Washington

Rheba de Tornyay decided in nursing school that she wanted to help make changes in nursing education that would attract and retain bright students who would learn to solve problems for themselves rather than have to be told what to do. Branded a troublemaker, she was elected student body president as an undergraduate and proceeded to organize what would become the Student Nurses' Association of California.

All her life, Rheba has worked successfully to improve nursing education. As a faculty member and dean at San Francisco State University, the University of California at Los Angeles, and the University of Washington, her commitment and stamina have focused on teaching faculty and staff how to solve their own problems. Her epitaph, she says, should read, "She loved to teach nurses."

I did not always want to be a nurse. In fact, as I look back from this vantage point at the end of my career in nursing, I wonder why I did not always know that a nurse was what I should be. As a child growing up on a chicken ranch in the small town of Petaluma, California (about 40 miles north of San Francisco), I was always nursing my pet dogs and cats. In high school my favorite subjects were the sciences, and I remember telling a teacher that I wanted to be a veterinarian. He told me that girls did not become veterinarians but said if I really tried hard, I could probably become a physician and take care of humans. I never wanted to become a physician, and unfortunately neither he nor my other teachers ever talked about nursing as a field to pursue. Because we had no nurses in the family and because I was healthy as a young person, I had virtually no contact with nurses until I entered college at the University of California, Berkeley.

It was a far cry from Petaluma High School (with its 200 pupils) to Berkeley. I flailed about, not knowing what I wanted to major in while continuing to enjoy the biological sciences, as well as psychology and sociology. I took a vocational aptitude test and scored highest in nursing. Still it didn't sink in that I should pursue nursing as a career, mainly because I would have had to leave the Berkeley campus. World War II was on, and the campus was filled with young men who were enrolled in Armed Forces training programs. Civilian students were required to take what was called a National Service Requirement, and that resulted in the luckiest break of my life. I chose to take a course to prepare to be a Red Cross nurse's aide. The classroom activities fascinated me, and I found myself wanting to know more and more about caring for the sick. Finally, outfitted in my blue pinafore with the arm emblem of the Red Cross, I began my clinical experiences at Peralta Hospital in Berkeley in the maternity wards. I absolutely loved it! One day, as I was helping to make a bed, the nurse whom I was assisting asked me if I had ever thought of becoming a nurse. My life's ambition at last became clear.

I wanted to begin my nursing education immediately. It never occurred to me after two years of college that I should go to a baccalaureate school, particularly since I did not have all of the prerequisites for nursing study at the University of California, San Francisco. I set out to visit all of the three-year diploma schools in San Francisco and chose Mount Zion Hospital School of Nursing because I liked the nurses' residence and because they seemed eager to have me. We were a class of 10, the first class after the U.S. Nurse Cadet Corps had ended, when recruitment into nursing schools was at an all-time low.

Nursing school challenged my abilities to retain my personal integrity while succumbing to the required subservience of hospital nursing of that era. I am convinced that the roots of my desire to become a nurse educator were formed at that time. I wanted to help make changes in nursing education that would attract and retain bright students who would learn to solve problems for themselves rather than be told what to do. I was considered a troublemaker throughout my three years as a nursing student, not in the clinical setting, but in the nurses' home. I was elected student body president and organized the other student body presidents of schools in the area to form the Bay Area Student Nurses Association, the precursor to the Student Nurses' Association of California. I wrote a letter of complaint to the California Board of Nursing Education and Nurse Registration about the working conditions of nursing students. Because of that and other such activities I lost my privileges (such as staying out until 10 PM) and was grounded to my room each evening for the purpose of reflecting on my attitude (which hardly improved).

I knew this was not the way to develop young nurses, and I decided that I wanted to go into nursing education to help bring about necessary reforms. Because my nursing program had emphasized the physical care of patients, I wanted a more extensive background in the emotional aspects of patient care. I elected to become what was called a junior psychiatric nurse at Langley Porter Neuropsychiatric Hospital at the University of California, San Francisco, for a year. I worked the following year in a convalescent hospital while I completed the requirements for the baccalaureate degree at San Francisco State College (later to become San Francisco State University).

After completing my degree, I was invited to teach at Mount Zion Hospital School of Nursing. I was thrilled to be going back to my home school, with the opportunity to make some of the curriculum and teaching changes that I knew were needed. In my naivete, I thought I would be listened to as a young instructor. I enjoyed the students and studied hard to keep up with them. However, it was soon apparent that I needed advanced education in order to become a master teacher.

I met Rudy, who later became my husband, just when I was beginning to look into graduate schools. He became an important consideration because I was unwilling to leave him or the San Francisco area. I returned to San Francisco State to study for my master's degree in education and married Rudy the day it was completed.

San Francisco State was planning to develop a baccalaureate program in nursing that would emphasize liberal arts as well as nursing throughout the four-year program. The first department chairperson, Evelyn Pederson, had distinct views that the nursing major should be identical to other college majors, with the clinical nursing courses considered equivalent to laboratory courses in other disciplines. I took some courses with Dr. Pederson and used the educational principles I was learning for nursing course and curriculum development. Her beliefs pointed the way for a modern nursing education that would develop the student as a professional nurse and also as a well-rounded individual. I thought the opportunity for nursing faculty and students to mingle within the academic community was a positive move toward helping nursing to become a mainstream academic discipline.

For a second time, I was invited to become a member of the faculty in the school from which I had recently graduated. Because I needed to find a position for one year while I was waiting for San Francisco State to begin its nursing program, I spent that year teaching in a vocational nursing program. (California calls practical nurses "vocational" nurses.) This became one of my richest teaching experiences. It was during that year that I learned to teach a diverse student group. My students ranged in education from one student who tested at a tenth grade equivalency to one who held a master's degree. Routinely, I gave extra examples to those students who had difficulty grasping the principles and offered more enriching experiences to the advanced students.

I remained at San Francisco State University for 12 years. The program began in 1955, and during the first year the faculty consisted of the chairperson of the department and myself. The next three years we recruited additional faculty, and I began climbing the academic ladder as an assistant professor. The program thrived, and we felt like pioneers in this new approach to nursing education. It was symbolic of our new approach that our students were allowed to choose their own nursing uniform and did not wear a nursing cap or white hose.

I continued to feel the need for additional education, and San Francisco State University required the doctorate for progression in the tenure track. I was deeply committed to the new nursing program and wanted to work toward my doctorate while continuing to teach. I began taking courses in the school of education at Stanford University in the summer of 1957 and was admitted into the doctoral program in 1958. I took my education courses seriously, trying to apply everything I learned to my own teaching.

Four years after I had joined the faculty at San Francisco State, the chairperson of the nursing department became ill, and the dean of the school of education (of which the nursing program was a part) asked me to chair the department. I was not prepared for the job (it seemed to be the story of my life—although not prepared I was the best prepared of the faculty at the time) but agreed to be the administrator of the unit while a search was made for a qualified chairperson. That time kept stretching out, and eight years later, when I finally completed my doctorate in education at Stanford, I left San Francisco State. Those 12 years with a program that ushered in the modern age of nursing education were exciting ones, and I have always been proud to have been a part of it all.

Completing my doctorate was a turning point in my career. It gave me the ego strength to know that I could be a scholar. I acquired a desire to write that continued throughout the rest of my career. Perhaps it was a compulsion, perhaps a habit, but it became part of my self-image, and I wanted to share my views with others.

One of the most influential persons during my doctoral study years was Fred McDonald, the chairman of my dissertation committee, who advised me to change positions when I completed my doctorate. He told me that I was different, and that unless I moved on to a different position, I would not grow professionally. He discussed me with Helen Nahm, dean of the School of Nursing at the University of California, San Francisco (UCSF), who invited me to come to UCSF as a visiting professor. She needed someone to head up a program to prepare graduate students to teach nursing, and I regarded this as an opportunity to put into action the principles and commitment I had for nursing education.

I had become increasingly convinced that students learned best when they could try new experiences in safe and supportive environments, and so I adapted Stanford University's "microteaching" techniques for the purpose of preparing nursing instructors. Microteaching consists of short (five-minute) teaching segments by student teachers to practice one specific instruction technique on other nursing students paid to act as teaching subjects. The students were required to give written feedback to the student teacher. Each segment was videotaped, thus allowing student teachers to validate the student-subjects' comments and to receive immediate feedback about their own teaching performance. During my four years at UCSF, a total of 360 graduate students elected to receive their initial experience in nursing education through this technique. I incorporated materials and strategies developed in this course into my book *Strategies for Teaching Nursing,* which was first published in 1971, has undergone three editions, and has been translated into Japanese and Spanish. I regard this small volume as one of my major contributions to nursing education and hope it has been useful in improving the teaching of nursing students.

Although I had decided to leave nursing education administration forever, after four years of teaching and continuing to develop the microteaching method for preparing nursing faculty, I accepted the invitation of the search committee at the University of California, Los Angeles (UCLA), to interview for the deanship of the School of Nursing. I had missed the workings of a general campus during my years at UCSF, and although I knew that the UCLA School of Nursing had a troubled recent past and that it was possible that the school might be closed, I felt welcomed by the faculty and believed that the administration would now support the school. I was looking for a new challenge, and UCLA seemed to be it. So in July 1971, Rudy and I and our two geriatric Siamese cats became Southern Californians.

The UCLA years were indeed challenging. I have concluded that nursing has a difficult time on a campus that views itself as a strong academic center, and where the applied fields are generally not perceived as central to a university's mission. UCLA was the second of the campuses in the University of California system and in some respects, at least at that time, was competing with sister campus Berkeley. The UCLA School of Nursing had lost ground over a years-long struggle to stay open. Other major schools of nursing were constructing new buildings with matching federal funding, while UCLA's School of Nursing was inadequately housed with one multipurpose classroom and no research laboratories. Finding space and funding for the school was my primary goal. We succeeded in floating a major bond issue that would provide matching funds for the School of Nursing building, but when it finally seemed assured fate intervened and it appeared that construction would not come to pass. Eventually the school did receive its building, but this was after I made the decision to leave for the University of Washington to accept a deanship in the School of Nursing there.

The environment at the University of Washington seemed perfect for a nursing program. The university was a first-rate state-supported institution like the University of California. However, it was on a single campus, it had nurtured professional schools, and it touted distinguished schools in the health sciences specifically of interest to me. There was a vice-president for health sciences who orchestrated the coordination of the health science disciplines, and a group of health science deans who obviously respected and enjoyed one another. Communications were open between the deans, the vice-president, and the new president of the university. The nursing faculty was first-rate, and I was given the opportunity to continue to recruit additional gifted faculty. I felt then, and events proved my intuition to be correct, that the University of Washington had all of the elements necessary to continue to be an extraordinary school of nursing.

My interest in teaching skills continued throughout my deanships. In 1983 I was asked by Slack Publishing Company to become the editor of *The Journal of Nursing Education.*

My aspiration for this journal, the oldest journal in the field devoted exclusively to nursing education matters, was to increase the publication of scholarly articles while at the same time publishing helpful articles for nursing faculty involved in creative teaching endeavors. When I became editor, the time lapse from acceptance of a manuscript to publication was three years—an obviously unacceptable length of time. I decided to take a bold step and returned all accepted manuscripts to the authors if the manuscripts were longer than what was considered to be acceptable. I also published page restrictions for new submissions. Within three years we had reduced the time from acceptance to publication to one year. Furthermore, the type of articles published became more scholarly. I believe this journal continues to serve the nursing community through its publication of research in nursing education.

From my earliest years in nursing education, I have always been a strong proponent of nursing organizations. I served as commissioner of the American Nurses' Association Commission on Nursing Education from 1968 to 1972 and as the president of the California Nurses' Association from 1971 to 1973. I enjoyed these activities, and they further developed my commitment to and philosophy about the major issues of the profession. Debates about entering the field, receiving credentials, and professionalization of nursing continued and were refined as the years went on.

I was thrilled and proud when I received a telegram from the president of the American Nurses' Association, notifying me that I had been appointed a charter fellow in the American Academy of Nursing. I was asked to be the chairperson pro tem of this newly formed body, which was designed to advance new concepts of nursing and health care as well as to identify and explore issues in health as they relate to nursing's role. There must be something special about being among a small, chosen group, because the 36 charter fellows turned our first meeting into an effective working seminar. Our first tasks were to develop by-laws and plan for others to enter the academy as quickly as possible. I was elected as the first president of the American Academy of Nursing, and I claim this as the single event in my career of which I am most proud.

Being the third nurse elected to the Institute of Medicine, National Academy of Sciences, in 1972 was also a major influence on my career. I have always believed that the health science disciplines benefit from close collaboration, and this organization provided rich experiences (as well as professional and personal contacts) that changed my views of health care in general and nursing and nursing education in particular. I know that I, as well as the other nurses elected, positively influenced the deliberations of the Institute of Medicine through our nursing perspective. Serving on the institute's governing council and its executive committee gave me invaluable insights that helped me to break away from some of my more parochial nursing views.

David Frost, the British commentator and interviewer, has often asked his guests what they would like to have someone write as their epitaph. For me it would be "She loved to teach nurses." My greatest sources of satisfaction have been my students, many of whom have gone forward to become major nursing leaders. I felt during my years as an educational administrator that my major contribution was through teaching faculty and staff to solve their own problems. I did not have the advantage of having major nursing mentors in my formative nursing days because I did not develop my nursing background through the traditional route of graduate nursing education. Moreover, the people who believed most strongly in me—my dissertation advisor at Stanford University and my husband—were neither nurses nor women. I lacked nursing mentors and, as a result, have tried to meet the needs of my students and younger faculty who have chosen me to help them with their careers. Although the development of nursing education has at times been slower than my patience could tolerate, when I look back to 1946 (when I chose to enter a diploma nursing program where all personal decisions were made for me at the same time that I was required to make professional decisions I was not prepared to make) and compare those times with today's, I am heartened by the great strides we have made. I believe my own commitment, stamina, and belief in the value of our profession are the common elements that have sustained me during my career as a nurse educator.

Donna Diers

Donna Diers, MSN, RN, FAAN, is
Professor and former Dean at Yale
University School of Nursing

❖

> *"Once upon a time," begins Donna Diers, who from childhood*
> *grew up telling stories. And now this gifted storyteller—longtime dean*
> *at the school of nursing at Yale and currently the editor of Sigma Theta*
> *Tau's* Image: Journal of Nursing Scholarship*—spellbinds us again,*
> *talking about research, theory, analytical thinking, autonomy, and the*
> *filthy windows behind Yale University president Kingman Brewster's head*
> *as he offered her the deanship.*
>
> *There is no doubt in her mind, she writes, that nursing is*
> *powerful, central, and less in need of defending than of defining and*
> *publicizing. These are her goals, and she lives by one unbendable rule:*
> *never badmouth nursing in public.*

Once upon a time, I got on an elevator in Texas to get to an amphitheater where I was going to give a speech. There was a poster on the back wall of the elevator advertising my appearance. Someone had written next to my name, "Who she?" And somebody else had written, "Flamboyant! Controversial!"

Who, me?

This shy person from Wyoming, flamboyant? Controversial?

The speech was not one of my great triumphs. If one is advertised as flamboyant and actually is, the audience thinks one is trivial. If one isn't flamboyant, they're disappointed. I am shy, but I'm not so sure that I am controversial. My reputation for personal autonomy and my articulation of it professionally are what people are talking about when they call me flamboyant, I suspect.

If personal autonomy is defined by a certain sense of independence, then I came by that honestly. The family legend is that my first word was "Dutch" (or maybe it was "Deutsch"—my grandfather spoke German to me). I'm a typical Taurus, slow to rile but stubborn. Another family legend (which I remember to be true) is that I refused to eat the last four peas on my plate at lunch one day and sat there all afternoon until dinner, stonewalling by unsuccessfully trying to hide the peas under my knife. My mother finally gave up.

Wyoming is not irrelevant here. We lived in a town, not on a ranch, and while I did walk three miles to high school in the snow on occasion, that's about it for my pioneer spirit. But Wyoming is a place that values independence (autonomy) and self-sufficiency. When I first met theorist Ida Orlando, she charmed me by saying she felt that people from those states out there with lots of sky were more clearheaded than others. True or not, I spent a lot of time outdoors as a child, in the mountains on back roads where one never saw another person.

I come from a family of independent people, some of whom actually *were* pioneers. Everyone in the family had and still has personal talents and interests, some shared, some not. When I was a child, my thing was reading, which I could do alone. I had read all of the Oz books the library had by age 10 and started to read books in other series. Eventually, I began to tell stories to my younger brother and his friends. Using words—writing, telling stories—was something I got into early that turned out to be useful later.

Wyoming puts a good deal of the state and county taxes and the royalties from minerals into the schools, and it has an unusually good public school system. I had three years of Latin and three years of journalism in high school and received excellent instruction overall. That too was useful, because when I was about 12 years old, I shot up 12 inches to my present height of nearly 6 feet, found that I needed glasses, and had to wear braces on my teeth. I turned from a kind of sharp but ordinary kid into a bookish nerd.

I never seriously wanted to be anything but a nurse. There are no nurses in my family, but I knew early on that I liked the notion of becoming one. And that's mostly what it was, a notion, founded on white caps (which I used to make out of typing paper and then try on in front of a mirror) and on a neighbor up the street who wore stiffly starched, long-sleeved white uniforms and looked like everything I wasn't: clean, disciplined, competent.

I was recruited into the University of Denver School of Nursing, which had just opened; I was in the first (and next to the last) class. It was a chance for me to live in the big city and to go to a school where I didn't know anybody and where I would not be burdened by my history (I had a fantasy of changing my name, so my personality would change, too).

I liked college, but what I really liked was nursing. The DU program started as a preexisting diploma program was being phased out; there were two classes of the hospital school students still there. I thought they were fabulous. They seemed at ease in patient care and with the residents, and they were so efficient. In those days (late 1950s) it was legal for student nurses to work as student nurses rather than as aides, and I did so, beginning in my sophomore year. Sometimes I would do special duty for a patient who needed a private duty nurse but whose family could not afford one; in such cases the hospital paid for my services. More often, I worked one or two evenings or nights a week at the hospital. That experience, even more than the supervised clinical experience the university provided, turned me into a nurse, and I have believed ever since that it ought to be possible to combine the best of the clinical experience of a diploma program with the best of the intellectual experience of a university program.

I found my nursing heart in psychiatric nursing. The town where I grew up in Wyoming had a large Veterans Administration facility that focused on the treatment of psychiatric patients, so I was not unfamiliar with what psychiatric patients were like. I gained wonderful experience at Colorado State Hospital. Psychiatric nursing allowed me to use everything I had—not just physical energy or thought, but also my emotions and analytical capabilities. It felt as if the difference one could occasionally make was so much more a personal difference than relieving pain with a medication, or making someone comfortable with a backrub, change of linen, and cup of milk.

When I graduated, I knew that I wanted to work in psychiatric nursing and also that the opportunities for that in Colorado were not great. One boring evening in the spring of my senior year, I wandered into the school of nursing library (where there was a secret cache of fiction books that I knew how to find) and began reading the bulletin board. There, among the changes in course schedules, random announcements, and rules, was the letter that more than anything else has changed my personal and professional life.

The letter was from Anna T. Baziak (now Dugan), then director of nursing at the Yale Psychiatric Institute (YPI). She had written to all the deans of BSN programs. My dean, who was new and did not know (or like) us seniors, simply posted the letter. Anna was recruiting newly minted BSNs for the YPI, under what later became an official grant-supported program to test the effect of hiring new graduates whom the institution could shape. I thought this sounded neat. In the first place, I'd never been east of Indianapolis, and this was Yale, for heaven's sake. Anna described the YPI (accurately, as it turned out) as a small, psychoanalytically oriented inpatient facility that treated mainly young adults. I knew by then that I was better with people my own age than with children or the elderly, and while I didn't know Freud from Maxwell Jones, the notion of an institution that encouraged the kind of in-depth introspection I was given to anyway sounded ideal. I applied, got the job, and eventually flew off all by myself to Idlewild in New York. I left Denver the night John Kennedy was nominated for President, and I watched Wyoming put him over the top on TV in the Denver airport. It was just all too symbolic.

The two years at the YPI were very special, and so was Anna. There were four recent graduates hired at about the same time, and we all became fast friends. Anna personally supervised us, in both formal and informal sessions, and if there was one belief she instilled in us, it was that nurses have an autonomous role. She was not interested in debating conflicts with medicine, and she believed that in a therapeutic community, the role of nursing was mostly independent. Oh, we got the usual stuff about "interfering with the transference" from residents, but in general the work of nursing was appreciated, supported, and made public in patient-staff meetings, and that was the most uncomfortable part of all. Nurses participated in the teaching rounds, with the entire world-famous department of psychiatry faculty. We, or at least I, got the feeling I could do anything. Part of that came from watching Anna, who was only 27 at the time.

I was introduced not only into the world of psychoanalytic psychiatry, but the world of a medical center, and the world of professional nursing as well. I had never known anybody who actually wrote articles before—Anna did. There were graduate nursing students who did summer placements at YPI whom I grew to know and admire, and I decided to go back to school. Anna was a close friend of Ida Orlando, and she taught us Orlando's approach to the nurse-patient relationship (the first autographed book I ever owned was Ida's).

I went to graduate school at Yale to learn to be Anna Baziak, but I emerged with a passion for research, something I had never even known about. Robert Leonard caused that change. He was a sociologist who simply believed that nursing made a difference because the nurses he knew, especially Rhetaugh Dumas, told him so. Thus there simply was no defensiveness about nursing with Leonard. His feeling was that it was fine as a discipline and that it was important to study the effect of nursing practice in order to understand it better.

Florence Wald was then dean, and the Yale School of Nursing bore her stamp (as it still does). She envisioned nurses as what we now understand to be primary care practitioners, or case managers. She believed that clinical research and scholarship were essential to the development of the field. Since I loved nursing already, it was no big deal to expand that love to include the methods and scholarship to provide order to the ideas.

Those were heady days. Rhetaugh Dumas had just joined the faculty and was continuing her research in preoperative preparation. Ernestine Wiedenbach was in charge of the nurse-midwifery program, and the attitudes of that specialty pervaded the place. The philosophers Bill Dickoff and Pat James joined the faculty the year I became a graduate student (only I didn't take their logic course, to my eternal regret). John Thompson was teaching nursing administration, and I didn't take his course either. The whole school believed that there were no limits to what nurses could learn and use in practice or research.

Virginia Henderson and Leo Simmons had just finished their monumental review of nursing research, and Virginia was deep into production of the *Nursing Studies Index*. Clinical research was being born as was clinical experimentation, and it was all so logical that when I later learned how controversial it was, the controversy seemed silly. Virginia's notion that we should study "the work rather than the workers" made utter sense.

Professor Leonard took me to a nursing research conference in New York City that year, where Jeanne Quint (now Benoliel) first presented her research on death and dying. (Jeanne and I giggled in the front row, inventing a study that correlated the height of an investigator's heels and whether she had stockings with seams in them to the quality of the presentation.) Leonard also worked with his graduate students on publishing, and by the time I graduated, I had three articles in print and was hooked on it forever.

President Kennedy spoke at Yale's commencement exercises at the end of my first year in graduate school (where he uttered the memorable line that now he had the best of both worlds, a Harvard education and a Yale degree), and Martin Luther King received an honorary degree the year I graduated, both to standing ovations.

I was invited to join the faculty at Yale to teach psychiatric nursing and research methods. Professor Leonard left the university that year, and his junior colleague, Powhatan Wooldridge, and I took over his research methods course. Pow was finishing his doctoral dissertation then, and so I fell into teaching the same course I had just taken. It was not a splendid course that year, but it got better.

Those were also the days of the first nursing research funding from the federal government and the American Nurses' Foundation, and a number of us applied for those early grants. A number of us got them, too. I spent the next several years of my life discovering that the analysis of nurse-patient interaction loses its fascination rapidly and poses inquiries that never quite go anywhere.

Faculty research development efforts were flourishing then nationwide, and Yale had one of the first grants. Under that mechanism, faculty got involved in various activities, including released time, writing workshops, using seed money for pilot studies, and so on. The activity that counted the most for me was what we called the nursing theory seminar. It was, at first, a faculty group (later we let students in) who met weekly with Professors Dickoff and James to *develop nursing theory*. It never occurred to me that this was kind of an outlandish activity. It seemed completely natural, and Dickoff and James, like Leonard, believed that nursing did operate with theory and that our task in the seminar was to pull that theory out of unstated assumptions, traditions, or observations. We had grand intellectual arguments; tempers ran high.

I do not recall a single conversation during the theory seminar years about what the distinction might be between medicine and nursing. Under Leonard, Wooldridge, and their sociologist colleague, Jim Skipper, we had disposed of the arguments about how much of nursing was sociology. Nursing was simply (and complexly) nursing, and the first article I ever wrote entirely by myself was about that distinction.

Those were also the early days of expanding nursing roles, a process in which

Margaret Arnstein, who succeeded Florence Wald as dean at Yale, played a huge part. We had nurse-midwives and psychiatric nurses, the latter moving increasingly into autonomous practice roles, sometimes even into office practice. Primary care and clinical specialization in acute and critical care soon followed. The Yale School of Nursing in those days (1958-1974) consisted entirely of a graduate program for people who were already nurses. (It is still entirely a graduate program.) All members of the faculty were specialists, faculty practice was an explicit value and requirement, and the entire faculty taught and did research. It was an intensely rich atmosphere where nurses were proud.

I know now that the deans and others protected us junior faculty from the slings and arrows of others, particularly in national nursing politics. The Yale School of Nursing was small (at one point we had 17 faculty and 13 students) and conspicuous, questioning mainstream notions. Virginia Henderson's impassioned statement at a National League for Nursing meeting, arguing against the necessity for accreditation of master's degree programs, comes to mind. We were deliberately inbred because the faculty were creating new practice roles and new research strategies, and for some time there weren't people to do what we were doing.

I did have a master career plan when I finished my basic program. I was going to work for two years in psychiatric nursing, then return to school and get a master's in that specialty, then work for two more years after that (there the details of the plan got a bit vague), then return for a doctorate in something. But my time on the faculty was so absorbing—what with the research, the theory work, and the new programs—that the years just rolled by. The faculty development days served as my doctorate. I've been asked repeatedly why I never got a PhD. (Many people think I have one.) In the early years, when I was actually more flamboyant than I am now, I used to snarl, "Because I don't need one." What that really meant was that I had already done what the degree is supposed to equip one to do—research, publish, and eventually get tenure. It didn't matter at Yale that I didn't have a PhD, so I stayed.

In 1972 Yale President Kingman Brewster asked me to succeed Miss Arnstein as dean of the school of nursing. Next to coming to New Haven in the first place, that decision changed my life more than anything.

I had negotiated my way onto the search committee for the dean and at some point in the search process, the chairman of the committee and provost, Charles Taylor, asked us all for confidential letters addressing the possibility of inside candidates. I wrote one, not naming myself. But the more I thought about it, the more I thought, "Hell, I could do this." After a search committee meeting one day, I asked to see Taylor and told him I would like to be considered. He said, "How old are you?" I said, "Thirty-three." He said, "Well, that's not too young; I was only thirty-six when I was appointed provost." Then he grilled me about what I thought about the school, about nursing, and what I would do if I were dean. Afterward, I felt that I had flunked.

That was a freeing feeling, however, and so I went forward with plans for a sabbatical in Canada the next year. But that interview started a six-week-long process of thinking about what I *would* have done as dean, what I believed in, and how I would handle various problems. It was clear to me that since I didn't know how to be a dean, I needed to examine the principles and values on which a dean might operate, figuring that the actions themselves would then follow.

Out of those sleepless midnight conversations with myself came the following: I have an unshaking belief in nursing; I have a genuine respect for nurses and our work; and I have some notions about equity and fairness and rewards for the quality of one's work. Those nights of introspection also led me to an intense examination of leadership and loneliness.

When President Brewster called, I knew I was not his first choice as dean, and that he was taking a risk in appointing me (which he later told me, flat out). That day is still fresh in my mind. It was foggy, and I walked from my apartment to the president's house for the appointment, worrying mostly about how to introduce myself to his butler. The carillon on the Old Campus was playing Bach. I rang the doorbell and was greeted not by a butler, but by Mr. Brewster (who was a stunningly handsome, patrician man) and two huge retrievers. I thought, "Okay, this is the first test," and enthusiastically petted the dogs—"Good doggie, good doggie."

Mr. Brewster laid the question on me and then nattered for a while about why he was asking me to be dean. I remember staring at him and being acutely conscious of the windows behind his head, which were filthy. I thought, "Can't the president of Yale University get his windows cleaned?" At the end of the nattering (a very useful strategy, by the way, when one has to give out bad or good news) he said, "And now I have to ask you, Donna, is this something you want to do?" And I said, "Very much."

We negotiated some, he called Miss Arnstein to tell her, he poured me a huge and welcome drink, his wife wandered through in a sweatshirt to walk the dogs, and he introduced Mary Louise to me. I left his house to walk to Miss Arnstein's, knowing that I was forever changed.

If there is anything that teaches one both personal and professional autonomy, it is being a dean. Speaking for superb, talented, professional nurses and having to articulate issues in all kinds of forums makes one dig deep into what nursing is, so one can express it to lay people or colleagues. Since I did not practice, I had to know practitioners whose issues I could serve. There was simply no doubt in my mind, as I listened to an oncology nurse clinical specialist talk about DNR orders, or to a nurse practitioner talk about scope of practice, or to a nurse-midwife talk about competition with physicians, or to a psychiatric nurse talk about the strange intergroup phenomena a mental health facility fostered, or to a pediatric nurse practitioner talk about her caseload of abused children—that nursing was powerful, central, and less in need of defending than defining and publicizing. I set that as my goal and lived by an unbendable rule: never badmouth nursing in public.

And so, we created new programs in specialty practice, and we reopened an entry into practice option for college graduates. We caused much local trouble and some trouble in other places too, not because our programs or activities were bad, but because they were unusual. They didn't fit the rules or regulations. I had the courage of the faculty and students behind me, however, and that probably made me more outrageous than I would have been if alone. I learned to dicker, to talk about nursing so that it made sense, to take tough stands and negotiate from strength, to compromise, and to give up when a battle was truly lost. I learned offense (and probably offensiveness too). The emperor, after all, had no clothes.

It was 12½ hard, satisfying years, and I grew up.

Many years ago, when I was a young faculty member, the psychiatric nursing students invited Helen Mannock, then a faculty member at Boston College, to visit. Helen was a real original, a tiny, outspoken, eccentric woman, utterly sure of herself. Her motto was "Make the decision, take the risk, pay the price," and when I first heard it, at a time when I was thinking of some important decision or other, it knifed straight through me. Not a bad way to live, really, implying as it does, accepting the consequences for one's own actions. That's all that autonomy really is. One learns the mature judgment to predict the consequences, which makes taking positions much easier. And one learns that one cannot be universally loved and adored, that one is fallible, but also that one can survive.

One learns also that nursing is so incredibly complex and rich a field that one can move widely within it to do whatever one is committed to doing. Doing a deanship is wonderful experience and quite a lot of fun, but it burns out eventually. Returning to teaching and research, and to a newfound interest in carrying nursing into the policy arenas, is just another way of doing the same thing. And always, always, writing about it.

There are some colleagues and companions and other like-minded thinkers who will help because they too believe in nursing and in our efforts to push nurses forward.

Examples? Look through this book, and join us.

Eileen McQuaid Dvorak

Eileen McQuaid Dvorak, PhD, RN, is
Executive Director of the National
Council of State Boards of Nursing

❖

Three basic beliefs have governed the choices Eileen McQuaid Dvorak has made in her professional life. The first is that everyone must make a difference in this life. The second is that a high value should be placed on intellectual development. And the third is that opportunities should be taken as they arise.

Incremental experiences, she says, have shaped her life and have prepared her for pioneering achievements. In 1979 she organized the present National Council of State Boards of Nursing. That was a year of major personal and professional changes, but her experiences had prepared her for success.

*B*eing invited to submit an autobiography raises a dilemma. I have a sense of wanting to share the humorous aspects of my life and not to appear sanctimonious or to appear to be delivering a homily. However, the audience reading this chapter may not be able to distinguish humor from flippancy, or to differentiate what I mean to be humorous from what is intended to be quite earnest. For that reason I present this brief autobiography from my serious side, incorporating only a few of what I consider to be humorous incidents.

Incremental decisions can shape one's life in either a negative or a positive way. In preparing this article, I had to look back on my life and think about why I chose a certain path and what incremental decisions led me to my previous and current positions in nursing. Rather than reciting what I did chronologically, I share with the reader why I did things and, to a limited extent, the people and situations important to the "why."

BELIEF: CONTRIBUTION

There are three beliefs that have governed choices I have made in my professional life. These beliefs are interrelated and sequential. The one that has been basic is the belief that people must make a difference or their existence is pointless. Because I cannot accept the premise that anyone's existence is pointless, I believe that everyone is meant to make a difference in this life.

I wanted the difference I made to be a contribution to others. I selected a career in nursing after considering careers in mathematics, medicine, and music. In nursing, I perceived that I might have the ability to make the greatest contribution. So I entered the College of St. Rose in Albany, New York, to major in nursing.

My father and mother were amazed at my choice because they had expected I would major in music. I had graduated from a conservatory of music at the same time that I graduated from high school. However, support for my decision was consistent with my family's philosophy. The only person in my family who was in a health-related field was an uncle who was a physician; he was married to a nurse. They later supported my entry into nursing but did question my selection of a baccalaureate nursing program. As a matter of fact, Uncle Earl and I continued a friendly debate about the education of nurses through my master's degree program as well.

Making a contribution was the major basis for my work in practice, in teaching, and in regulation. My first contributions as a young nurse graduate were made in clinical practice in the care of children. I practiced at St. Mary's Hospital in Troy, New York, Carney Hospital in Dorchester, Massachusetts, and Children's Hospital in Chicago.

I believe that teaching is a contribution to humankind. After an early venture into teaching at A.N. Brady Maternity Hospital in Albany, New York, I decided that I could make a greater contribution by influencing others to accept a philosophy of caring than I could by administering care outside of teaching. The contribution expands geometrically in teaching.

After completing my master's degree in nursing, I decided to accept a position of teaching maternity nursing at Boston College School of Nursing in Chestnut Hill, Massachusetts. I perceived that working with bright, capable young women would be a contribution. I still take satisfaction in meeting a former Boston College student and learning about her contributions to nursing and to people.

Why did I join the New York State Education Department (NYSED) as supervisor of nursing education? What form of contribution could I make in that position? Many saw it as a regulatory position, and they emphasized that in a negative sense. I saw it as an extension of teaching, as a position that would enable me to work with faculty members in all types of nursing programs in New York State. The position would allow me to contribute to the public health cause in a different manner than nursing practice could, but it would allow me to contribute, nonetheless.

Mildred S. Schmidt, executive secretary of the New York State Board of Nursing, was also the administrator of the nursing education unit in the NYSED. Mildred has been a mentor to me since the early 1970s. She was able to impart a philosophy of service to me and to other staff members in the unit. We served as consultants who helped the exceptionally talented nursing education community in New York meet the regulatory guidelines within state law.

BELIEF: PURSUIT OF KNOWLEDGE

The second belief that has been instrumental in my life is the value I attach to intellectual development. "Ex nihilo, nihil fit," or, "From nothing, nothing is provided." This belief is concomitant with my belief that everyone needs to make a contribution. To contribute, one must develop one's talents and abilities to the utmost so that one has the background, knowledge, and comprehension necessary to make the greatest gift.

Knowledge is most easily acquired through formal study, but it can be gained in informal settings and through self-study, too. The quest for knowledge guided me from undergraduate work through graduate work on master's degree and doctoral degree levels. Throughout my life, I have sought knowledge and intellectual stimulation. My parents instilled this desire in me, and my early teachers nurtured it.

Father T. Gerald Mulqueen, high school principal at Catholic Central High School, devoted his life and energies to helping young people learn and to encouraging them to discover and use their full potential. For example, by the end of my junior year in high school, I had completed all requirements for graduation except one semester of English. Therefore, I had selected nonstrenuous courses like typing, beginning foreign languages, and home economics when I registered for my senior year. Father Mulqueen called me to his office, handed me my "revised" schedule, and said, "You can keep typing—you'll need it in college." My revised schedule did include typing. It also included

Latin 4, calculus, physics, and solid geometry. Social events became secondary to me that year.

My belief about the need for knowledge has led me to pursue formal education with both serious and pleasurable intentions. Almost immediately after completing undergraduate study, I enrolled in graduate school at Boston College part time to study education. The college's reputation for its scholarly faculty attracted me there.

A few years later, I changed my course of study to maternal-child nursing at Boston College Graduate School when that major was first introduced there. I was able to study full time because I received a federal traineeship. One of my undergraduate classmates went to work in Boston at the same time, and we shared an apartment. Fortunately, her weekly pay sustained us when my monthly stipend ran out before the end of each month. I met and made friends in Boston who have remained with me over the years. Ann Tierney shared these early Boston experiences in education with me. Our ongoing relationship is the quintessence of friendship. I earned my MS degree with a major in maternal-child nursing and a minor in education. Working on my master's thesis introduced me to the world of research, and I gained admission to world-renowned libraries in both Boston and Cambridge. To this day, I am awed at the magnitude of knowledge lying in libraries that I will never have time enough to read, much less learn.

Years after completing my master's degree, while I was teaching and administering at Hudson Valley Community College (HVCC) in Troy, New York, I felt the need for further formal study. It happened to me after the school's first nursing class graduated. I decided to study part-time at New York University, a large, private university located in Greenwich Village in New York City. I was accepted into the doctoral program in higher education administration.

Over the course of several years, I became very knowledgeable about bus routes and time schedules. I commuted back and forth between Albany and New York City once or twice a week. Later, when I was working on my dissertation, I drove the 150 miles from Albany to New York every Sunday morning, then returned in the evening after doing computer runs of data and working with a member of my committee, Dr. Nathan Jaspen, on analysis of that data. Nathan taught me more about statistics in working on the dissertation than I had ever learned in classes. I thought that working on my dissertation was fun. It was a culminating and creative experience. When it wasn't that way, I vented my frustrations by playing the piano. The "Sabre Dance" by Khachaturian was my favorite vehicle for venting.

The faculty and administration at HVCC helped me in my doctoral study efforts by lending me verbal support and by putting up with my schedule adjustments. This support was an extension of the college's commitment to education for all.. All of the nursing faculty at HVCC had made commitments to help one another bear the burden created by working and pursuing advanced degrees at the same time. I remember holding departmental meetings in the evenings to accommodate all full-time and part-time faculty. We all did it without complaint. One semester, several of us would go to a nearby restaurant and order for ourselves and for two other faculty members who were taking classes. They would rush in and eat, and then we would all rush out to the departmental meeting.

Applying ideas to generate new programs or to solve problems is enjoyable, particularly when it is a group endeavor. My time of study at New York University contributed to a generation of ideas that led to innovations both at HVCC and at the New York State Education Department, where I worked as supervisor of nursing education after leaving Hudson Valley. Patricia Beck, a faculty member there and a good friend then and now, used to groan when I would announce the day after my class in New York, "I got this great idea riding back on the bus last night."

Since receiving my PhD from New York University, I have studied piano (again), sculpting, oriental brush painting, German, ethics, and other "fun" subjects. Most of these subjects I studied along with my husband. Last year, I enrolled at the University of Chicago to study psychometrics with Benjamin Wright. My two courses with Dr. Wright resulted in two research studies, one of which was selected for presentation at the American Educational Research Association's annual meeting in 1987.

Doing research, although still a major interest, has had to be an avocation for me because the nature of my commitment to the National Council of State Boards of Nursing precludes devoting large blocks of time to research.

Pursuit of knowledge on an individual basis and with my husband continues, with no abatement of intensity. One of the greatest gifts I have received in my adult life is the support in my belief about the value of intellectual stimulation from my best friend, my husband. Together we study the classics, spiritual works, music, art, photography, poetry, ethics, leadership, management, or whatever subject might interest either or both of us. During our 60-minute commutes to and from our respective offices in Chicago, we discuss our latest subject of interest, read poetry, or read a book about management style.

BELIEF: OPPORTUNITIES

The third belief that governed choices I made is that one must say yes to opportunities as they arise. Back in my teaching days in Boston, a faculty colleague who taught mental health and nursing of psychiatric clients often said, "Making a choice, taking a chance, and paying the price is a sign of maturity."

Accepting my first teaching position, learning about associate degree nursing education, and becoming an administrator and a consultant have been opportunities in my life that I have said yes to. Helping my friends and working with people who shared my basic beliefs helped me to accept positions. A predilection for taking chances permeates much of my professional life.

I started teaching nursing because a hospital administrator I had known asked me to help her when her agency needed an instructor in maternity nursing for St. Peter's Hospital School of Nursing, a diploma program in nursing in Albany, New York. I had never taught before and had only been involved in pediatric nursing for two years. There was a slight element of risk involved in accepting the position, but I did accept it. The students affiliated at A.N. Brady Maternity Hospital in Albany. In my position there, I learned to study on my own. I also learned from the resource people on the hospital staff. Hugh Foley and Mac MacDowell were the chief obstetric residents there. Our friendly relationship in working together and learning together served as a basis for my future collegial relationships with physicians and other health professionals.

After two years of teaching, I decided I needed more background in education than I could achieve by independent study. That decision led me to pursue a master's degree in Boston.

When my father died unexpectedly, I returned to Watervliet, New York, to be with and take care of my mother. At that point, Margaret (Peggy) Collins, who was a classmate and friend from the College of St. Rose, contacted me. Peggy was the chairperson developing the new Adirondack Community College (ACC) nursing program. I had acquired teaching experience by then in diploma, baccalaureate, and master's degree programs, but not in associate degree programs. Therein lay my next opportunity.

I joined the faculty of ACC and worked—with Peggy's direction—to help her establish the program. The college was based in Hudson Falls, New York, which is 50 miles north of my home in Watervliet. I have fond memories of beautiful mountain scenery and rural vistas from that time, and not-so-fond memories of early morning snowfalls on clinical days. Most important, I have very fond memories of the students. This was my first experience in teaching older adult undergraduates; they taught *me* a great deal. The first day in a fundamentals of nursing clinical laboratory, one student asked if she could leave 15 minutes early for that one day only to pick up her child from a day nursery. I knew then that I was in a different world. I remember another young student asking me seriously in class when I was teaching stages of labor, "Is it like birthing a calf?" I honestly didn't know if it was or not.

After one year of teaching in and learning about associate degree nursing programs, I became chair of a new associate degree nursing program back at HVCC. Peggy Collins was instrumental in supporting that decision to accept a new opportunity. In administering an associate degree nursing program then, it was expected that the administrator would continue to teach.

On a September morning that was the first day of registration for Hudson Valley students, the three new nursing faculty members and I stood at the registration tables waiting for the doors to open. At that point I can remember thinking, "What am I doing here?" From then until that first class graduated and even thereafter, I did not have time to think or voice that question again.

It was while I was on the staff of the New York State Nursing Education unit that we drafted a proposal for the Regents External Degree Program in Nursing. Weathering reactions of the major New York nursing leaders about instituting such a program was no easy task. At the risk of our psychological well-being, we, the staff who believed that learning, no matter where it occurred, could be assessed and recognized in nursing as well as in other disciplines, presented our concepts one stormy February evening at a meeting of the state's nursing leaders in Albany. The consensus of the attendees shifted from "What do they think they're up to?" to "We ought to explore this some more" by the end of that first full meeting. As most people in the profession know, those nursing leaders, with the coordination first of Dolores Wozniak and then of Carrie Lenburg and Marianne Lettus, took that idea in the early 1970s and generated a testing model product that has served a population of nursing candidates who were previously ignored.

In fulfillment of one of my responsibilities as nursing supervisor, I served as member and then chairperson of what was then called the Blueprint of Examinations Committee of the American Nurses' Association Council of State Boards of Nursing. I accepted the appointment at the request of the council's executive committee and at the behest of Mildred S. Schmidt and Peggy Collins. Peggy was then a fellow staff member at the NYSED nursing education unit. By serving on this committee, I was exposed to the Council of State Boards of Nursing. While serving on that committee, I met many people with whom I am still in contact. Among the friends I made through my committee work is Michael Kane, who was then at the National League for Nursing Department of Test Construction. Mike has remained a good friend who can be called on, one who can blunt the serious edge of problems with his sense of humor (as befits an Irishman).

Mike Kane and Lee Laskevich, another friend from the National League for Nursing who met with the blueprint committee, joined us in the late 1970s to revise the test plan for the licensure examination for registered nurses. The committee recommended taking this revision to the Council of State Boards of Nursing. Tackling the first revision of the test plan for registered nursing examinations since the 1950s was quite an opportunity. The council supported the extra meetings, and New York State supported my expenditure of time over the development period. It was a fascinating time—a period of learning, of interpretation, of being responsive to fears and concerns of nursing students and faculty members, and of being responsive to members of various nursing organizations.

During that time of working on the revision of the test plan, the council became a freestanding not-for-profit organization. The first board of directors managed the new organization; it set up a search committee for the executive director position, as well as a site committee for the organization's headquarters. I was invited to submit an application for the position of executive director. I hesitated in doing so because my mother was seriously ill at that time. I did submit one but then had to cancel interviews with the search committee because my mother was too ill for me to leave her. The committee rescheduled what was to be a final interview because it had to submit recommendations to the board of directors. My mother died four days before that meeting date.

When the board offered me the position of executive director of the National Council of State Boards of Nursing, it meant another major change in a year full of major personal changes. My close friends, Ann and Frank Reed, urged me to accept the offer. I can remember, too, Peggy Collins's comment, "How many people have the opportunity to start an organization?" After pondering this opportunity for a short time, I accepted the offer in May 1979.

Chicago had been selected as the organization's headquarters. I began organizing there in August 1979. I hired an administrative assistant, and we established the office base and began operations. The two of us continued to operate the new organization headquarters for four months. During that time, I traveled extensively. On one of my return trips to Chicago, I met my husband-to-be at O'Hare International Airport. Members of the council's board of directors who have known my husband and me and of our beginning jokingly say they keep an eye out every time they walk through O'Hare for a comparable opportunity. So, Chicago has been an important site for me, both personally and professionally.

Mildred Schmidt was serving her first term as president of the board and she continued, along with other board members, to be a major information resource as we opened new doors, continued to work on revisions of the test plan, and recruited a deputy. Ray Showalter took the position of assistant executive director in January 1980. Ray and I shared joys, sorrows, ideas, defeats, affirmations, and all of the other trials associated with operating a business.

This is not the story of the National Council of State Boards of Nursing, so I shall drop here the details of organizational development. Let me say only that working in the position of executive director has been one of the greatest (if not the greatest) opportunities I have had. It presents an opportunity to work—with the direction of committed persons and with committed staff—to become a builder, to create new systems, to teach others, to learn new things on a daily basis, and to contribute to the understanding of the public health and safety mission of the nursing regulatory boards and agencies.

The corollary of accepting opportunities when they arise is setting goals and knowing when they have been achieved; or knowing when there is no hope to achieve them and when they should be left to a person better able to see them achieved. The most concrete example of this corollary in my life was when I helped in initiating the associate degree nursing program at HVCC.

The goal I had at Hudson Valley, which was shared by the college faculty and administration, was to establish an excellent program that produced competent practitioners in nursing. One means of ensuring that goal was to receive accreditation from the National League for Nursing. As in all accreditation processes, this was not a simple task.

To accomplish the goal of achieving accreditation, we began a concerted effort to have all nursing faculty members educated at the master's level in nursing. I described earlier how we achieved this end. In the meantime the nursing department became especially active in helping the college to receive Middle States Regional Accreditation, a necessary step before any specialized accrediting body can evaluate a program. Nursing faculty served on a variety of college committees; I was on the steering committee for the regional accreditation. It took several years of effort, but the college was granted that accreditation.

The following year, NLN was invited to review and evaluate our nursing program. I was enrolled in doctoral study then, and all nursing faculty had earned master's degrees in nursing. Notice of receiving NLN accreditation precipitated a celebration of all faculty and administrators of the college. A close-knit group, the team had accomplished its goal.

Throughout my administrative experience, I was working with faculty to help the college identify potential nursing department administrators for the future. By the time I decided to accept the position with the New York State Education Department, I had three faculty members that I could recommend to fill my position. Patricia Beck was named chairperson of the nursing department; she and the faculty brought the program to even higher standards.

CONCLUSION

The major thrust of this article is to share some of my background and, more important, the basis for what I have done. Through it all, the impact of family, friends, and colleagues is apparent. I rely on persons who share the same belief system I have. I said at the beginning that incremental decisions can shape one's life in either a positive or a negative way. I believe the decisions in my life have had positive results.

Philosophical concepts that can be difficult for less-than-gifted writers to express often appear in classical writings. And so I borrow this quote from literature, as it seems to have particular relevance here:

> Perhaps man's sole purpose in this world consists in this uninterrupted process of attainment, or in other words in living, and not specifically in the goal, which of course must be something like twice two is four, that is, a formula; but after all, twice two is four is not life, gentlemen, but the beginning of death.
>
> Fyodor Dostoyevsky, *Notes From the Underground*

Claire Fagin

Claire Fagin, PhD, RN, FAAN, is
Margaret Bond Simon Dean and
Professor of the School of Nursing at
the University of Pennsylvania

Claire Fagin is a scrapper, a builder—someone who gets the best out of people she works with and then revels in their successes. She attributes her own successful leadership to four constants that have played a part in her work at all levels.

First, she believes in democratic participation and is most comfortable when there is shared decision making.

Second, she values the empathy that was developed in her childhood and later honed by her experience in psychiatry.

Third, she enjoys peer relationships. If people are smarter than she is, she wants to learn from them. If they are learning, she loves helping them to realize their potential.

Fourth, she is an activist, willing to battle for what she believes in.

And what she believes in is this wonderful field of nursing.

Until I was in high school, my stated ambition was to be a physician—to follow in the footsteps of an extremely successful aunt. I had some inkling by that time that I did not want to be a physician but had not gotten around to breaking the news to my family, whose goals for me had been clear from early childhood. By the end of high school I had become convinced that medicine was not of interest to me, but I had no idea what I would find interesting. I graduated from high school at 16 and enrolled at Hunter College in New York City (still quiet about my rebellion from the family's professional dreams for me) in a rigorous program that would keep my options open. That first semester was wonderful, and my enjoyment of math and languages led me to consider adopting one or the other as a possible major. By the summer of my freshman year, the battlefront news of World War II had become an extremely important part of life, and thoughts of how to serve our country were shared by young men and women. The boys would either enlist or be drafted, while most girls would sit at home and write letters. My need to participate in some way was met in part by active political participation, but that wasn't enough for me. I was not quite 17, and there were not many direct-action opportunities at that age.

I started noticing billboard pictures of gorgeous women in the uniform of the U.S. Cadet Nurse Corps. I thought, "Why not?" This would meet my need to serve, and it might even interest me. I had by then had some contact with nurses in public health, since my next door neighbor was a public health nurse, and my father had been visited by a public health nurse after suffering a myocardial infarction. While not inspiring me in any overt way, they certainly provided a positive image, and I was able to recall that image when I started to consider nursing as a career. A friend and I began to investigate local hospital schools, but before we did anything serious, we happened on the office of the New York City Nursing Council for War Service. The name alone grabbed us, and we went in to see what it was all about. This was my first important career-shaping event, and I will always be grateful to the woman we met that day. Her name was Dorothy Wheeler. (She later became the director of nursing for the Veterans Administration system and was written up in the *New York Times* as the highest paid nurse in the country.)

Miss Wheeler was an inspiration to me and influenced substantially the subsequent course of my career. She was a petite, attractive woman who was extremely alert, perceptive, and vivacious. Her interview with us was sharp and revealing, and her advice was convincing. She told us that under no circumstances should we consider a hospital school of nursing. "The wave of the future is baccalaureate education," she said, adding that no person already in college should dream of going to a hospital school. She sat with us and wrote down three schools she thought we should look into based on the information she had gleaned from the interview. They were Adelphi University, Skidmore College, and Wagner College. We followed Miss Wheeler's advice and interviewed at these schools. For a variety of reasons, we both chose Wagner College. Not the least of those reasons was the fact that Mary Burr, the dean at that time, was a warm, motherly, accepting person who did not question our leaving college at the end of our freshman year.

My experience with Miss Wheeler was the first of many such experiences that I have had in nursing that have directly influenced my future. This type of experience has led me to believe we place too much emphasis on mentoring, that is, the long-term continuing relationship with an influential, and too little on the ad hoc brief counseling experience that many of us have been lucky enough to have. As I look from the present back to that fortunate walk on Lexington Avenue in New York, where I met Miss Wheeler, I can identify many other colleagues, teachers, friends, and family members who have contributed in various ways to my development.

Before I expound on the many experiences I have had in this wonderful profession, here are several constants that have influenced all my work at different levels of leadership:

1. I believe in democratic participation and am most comfortable when there is shared decision making. This belief was fostered by my family. It was reinforced during my time at Wagner College and came into full bloom in my experience and graduate work in psychiatric nursing.

2. The quality of empathy was developed in me by very early experiences in my home, and then later was honed to a great extent by my personal and professional experience with and in psychiatry. My mother's enormous asset (and weakness) was her ability to see the other person's view no matter what her child said. If she couldn't see it immediately, she would ask probing questions that forced me to recognize that I might have had a part in a given situation, whether I was bloodied or not. I hated it, but I know that this interaction taught me empathy. Through this kind of learning, one can build one's inter-personal competence at many points in life. I have built on this personally and have used my mother's technique, with intellectual addendums, in both teaching and administration.

3. The relationships I enjoy most are peer relationships. If people are smarter than I or better at something than I am, I don't feel competitive with them. Rather, I feel inspired to try to learn more, or to copy, or to follow. I have no problem sitting at the feet of experts, if they are truly expert. When people are in the learning stages of life, it is my pleasure to help them realize themselves and their potential. I have no need for nor do I take much pleasure in a superordinate role. As an administrator, this plays out in the standard I use to measure myself: the extent to which I have built leaders around me dictates my success.

4. I am an activist. I have never been able to sit back when faced with real or perceived unfairness. I fight in skirmishes, battles, and wars. Little did I know when I chose this provocative profession that this characteristic would be exercised so often.

Does it seem strange that these four constants have played a major part at every crossroad in my work life? Perhaps it explains to some extent why the nursing profession, which was such an accidental career choice for me, has met my personal and professional needs and goals better than any other profession I can imagine. In a career spanning more than 30 years, there has been plenty of time for such reflection. It has been said that many nurses do not have a dream of how their careers will unfold. That certainly is true for me, yet the progression of my career has logical steps in it and more similarity than difference.

I am the dean of the School of Nursing at the University of Pennsylvania. The program is among the most highly rated nursing programs in the country, and the university is one of the most prestigious in the world. When I came to this position some 10 years ago, the faculty and the administration, in keeping with the reputation of the university, knew they wanted the school to become one of the leaders in the nursing world. Before I came to the university, I was able to assess the problems and potential of the school and to establish goals. The goals were widely discussed with the faculty because I believed it important for them to understand and commit to the achievement of these goals. Major achievements are difficult for an individual to accomplish, but a concerted effort can see substantial achievements made. All of the goals that we set at that time were met in a five-year period, and over the next five years many other goals were set and for the most part accomplished through the efforts of an extraordinary faculty (whose work ethic and quality are without peer) and a talented and committed support staff. Students at Penn are very special. They are among the most select in the country, and they have chosen, and in the case of the graduate students rechosen, nursing with extreme clarity. It is a challenge to teach them and to provide an experience for them that equals their quality.

That this has been a rewarding experience for me should go without saying. Given the constants I stated earlier, it should be clear that working with a faculty of peers, fighting our way up in this environment, meeting extremely challenging goals, and sharing in the building of leadership among colleagues and students, all come naturally to me.

I came to Penn after an extremely fulfilling experience at a unit of City University of New York. Assuming that position was a major turning point, since it constituted a change in direction and specialization for me. I regret that I am not able here to mention all of the names of the many special people who have contributed in small and large ways to my work.

I was in the second class of nursing students at Wagner College. The college was welcoming to us, and the student group was diverse and not much different from any other college group. The program was interesting in its plan. The first year was spent on the Wagner campus in Staten Island, New York. During that year we took the requisite sciences, liberal arts, and some nursing courses. The following two years we affiliated in various hospitals, living in nurses' residences and returning to campus one day each week. At the end of the three-year program, we received a diploma in nursing and were eligible to take the state board examinations. A fourth year to complete the liberal arts and science requirements for the BS degree was optional. Because of the war and the number of young men being drafted, Wagner had an innovative program of study with courses offered in one-month blocks. This meant that if a male student was drafted, he would be able to complete the courses in which he had enrolled.

I had no idea how I would fare in the science component of the program, nor did I have the vaguest idea of whether or not I would succeed in or enjoy the nursing courses. As it turned out, I disliked but excelled in the sciences, and I did well in and loved every nursing course. At the end of each specialty component—surgical nursing, medical nursing, pediatric nursing, and operating room nursing—I felt I might choose that particular concentration for my future work role. After a few of these experiences, my confusion was rampant, since it was obvious that I couldn't prefer everything. However, my learning experiences at Creedmoor State Hospital soon solved the dilemma. It became clear very rapidly that I would choose psychiatric nursing for my option during my senior cadet experience and that I would seek a position in that field upon graduation.

Pursuing psychiatric nursing did not turn out to be so easy, since I had to complete my last year at Wagner and since there was no psychiatric hospital nearby. Instead, I worked at Seaview, a long-term tuberculosis hospital, in pediatrics as a staff nurse and later as a clinical instructor. The psychological needs of these children were staggering, given the severity of their illnesses and the long-term separation from their families. Certainly, this experience helped to further my interests in psychiatric nursing (particularly in child psychiatric nursing) and led me to a glimmer of interest in the subject of separation. Some of the colleagues I had at Seaview were friends I had made at Wagner, and others I had met during my affiliation there earlier. So, additional building blocks began to set a foundation for my future. Because this was an understaffed public hospital in a rather remote location (at that time), there was a lot of opportunity for innovation and experimentation in testing the system, in doing as much with patients as we were capable of, and in leadership. I received my BSN in May 1948. By the time I left Seaview in October 1948 (for a system transfer to Bellevue Hospital and adolescent psychiatry), I had tested all of these parameters and felt quite confident in my nursing skills and in my ability to do for patients what was "right" without worrying about bureaucratic restraints. Another turning point was negotiated as I entered a new and, as it turned out, critical, formative experience.

Bellevue was different from Seaview in every way, shape, and form. While also a city hospital, it was reasonably well staffed with nurses, was extremely well staffed with physicians, residents, and interns from prestigious medical schools, and was dominated by the Bellevue mystique. The Bellevue cap was powerful, and at times I thought I would do almost anything to have one. However, I learned again that an eye on the patient and on his needs helps you accomplish your major goals, providing you can tell people what you want and the reason why—even without the Bellevue cap or the MD degree. Leadership can't help but thrive after you have had enough successful experiences of that type and have learned what does and does not work.

On my first morning at Bellevue, I met my future supervisor, Mildred Gottdank, the director of education. She was a tiny person with piercing eyes, and she was very verbal, intimidating, tough, challenging, and smart. It was obvious that she knew more about psychiatry than I knew existed, and she had a master's degree. A friend and I had left Seaview together, and we were fortunately together for this first interview with the indomitable Miss Gottdank. We could see at a glance that as she took her long look at us she was thinking, "What on earth do I need you two for?" She said, "Miss Mintzer, you are going to PQ 5. That's our adolescent unit, and you have all this pediatric experience." My friend was assigned to 0 7, the unit for disturbed women. Miss Gottdank then walked out of her office with us to deliver us to our assignments. PQ 5 came first. She walked to the door, rang the bell, and opened the door with her key. I walked in, and as she closed the door, I could hear the key turning in the lock. There I stood, terror-struck, surrounded by a mob of adolescent boys who were staring me up and down.

This unit's population was boys between 12 and 16 years old, most of whom had come in from the courts with records ranging from truancy to murder. They were tough in appearance, and many were also tough in behavior. I stood transfixed at the locked door. That was the first test of whether or not I would make it there. Initially, the boys tried to provoke me by flirting and pulling my hair, and they watched to see how I would handle the leaders. It was all hazy to me, but I stood my ground, got through the first day, and went on to what proved to be one of the most satisfying and influential experiences of my life. I worked at Bellevue for two years, loved every minute of it, and could not wait to get out of bed in the morning to rush there. I visited patients and families with other colleagues in my off time and made more lasting relationships than I can recount in this short sketch.

I loved working with adolescents and was always good with them. I worked with a team of psychiatrists, residents, teachers, and psychologists, which taught me what successful colleagueship and interdependence were all about and filled me with a sense of my own worth and the worth of psychiatric nursing. Three of us—one psychiatrist, one vocational psychologist, and I—worked particularly well together. We followed youngsters from the ward to their homes on our own time and worked with their families in prototypic ways that were extremely rewarding to us and very helpful to them. I worked with students from a number of schools, and while the course content was far from sophisticated, I was learning all the time and was a good instructor (according to later reports).

I had some difficulties there with nurses and residents who were more tradition and position bound than quality oriented, but whenever called to explain my behavior to Miss Gottdank, I managed to explain the theory behind my intervention, and she was satisfied and went to bat for me. When the residents complained, it was to the chief psychiatrist, Dr. Paul Zimmering. He was equally supportive of my work and made sure his support of me and of psychiatric nursing was extremely visible at group meetings when new residents were present. So, with all of these good things happening (at $2,400 a year), why did I leave Bellevue?

In May 1949 one of my close nursing colleagues decided to get a master's degree, and she left for Smith College School of Social Work. That gave me some pause to think, since I was education oriented and it was obvious that I could use more grounding in theory to explain what I was doing and what I believed. I talked a great deal in the intuitive mode rather than in the intellectual mode, and that bothered me. Miss Gottdank could interview a patient for 5 minutes and get more information than I could in 45 minutes. That bothered me, too.

In July a new ward instructor joined our group. She had just completed a master's degree at Teachers College and had been in the first class in psychiatric nursing directed by Hildegard Peplau (not yet known by a wide nursing public). This nurse, Gertrude Stokes, was different. When she spoke at our meetings, her comments were more theoretical and intellectual than mine. Naturally, given what I have said earlier, I admired this and wanted to be like her. Until then, I had thought that I was a really terrific speaker. I decided that if I was to stay in this field, I needed to be able to talk the way she and

Miss Gottdank did. So, I applied to Teachers College and was awarded a National Institute of Mental Health (NIMH) fellowship to study full-time for my master's degree with Hildegard Peplau. I took a leave of absence from Bellevue, fully expecting to return. This was another major turning point in my life and certainly a building block in my career.

Times were really different then for graduate study in nursing. The student body was extremely diverse with a range in age from me at 23 to men and women in their middle to late forties. The courses during that year were superb, and, again, the opportunities for making lasting friendships and colleagueships abounded. In addition to the special experience of learning from Hilda, we met Esther Garrison during that year. Esther was the chief nurse in the training branch at NIMH and was responsible for the development of support for nursing within NIMH. She had a unique way of spotting and encouraging talent and did so with many people, including Hilda Peplau and Gwen Tudor Will, a classmate in my program and already a nursing leader.

Lest anyone get the impression that I was a bold and assertive person at that time, let me dispel that notion. I was rather shy, and asserting myself did not come easily. However, I was a doer and a fighter, so I managed to speak up for issues I believed in, and since I never suffered as much from doing that as from not doing it, eventually I built enough confidence to have such behaviors become part of my persona.

Hilda Peplau and many of my classmates were very affirming and supportive. There was a sense among all of us that we were future leaders, and everything necessary to make this happen was available to us. Some were already in leadership positions, and others were about to be placed in established roles. It was a heady atmosphere, indeed. In addition to Hilda, I had several memorable professors at Teachers College, including Goodwin Watson, Lyman Bryson, Emma Spaney, and others.

When I visited Bellevue to plan for my return, I was told that I would now be a supervisor, since I was overprepared for my previous position. I was crushed because a supervisor at that time was a very traditional role, was unconnected with patient care, and was characterized by the figure of a crisply uniformed nurse going from floor to floor with a clipboard. There was no way that I was going to be a supervisor at Bellevue. And so, another turning point was forced on me. Hilda had developed an outline for a study of the functions and qualifications of psychiatric nurses for the National League for Nursing (which was then the National League of Nursing Education). She decided that I should be the director of that study and convinced the executive director of the League to interview me. This was an interesting experience. I had been told that the job paid $6,000 per year. During the interview, the executive director asked me how old I was. I told her that I was 24, and she said the job would pay $4,200 per year. When I said I had been told the salary was $6,000, she said that was true, but that I was too young for that salary. I carried on for a good bit about the unfairness of this arrangement, and she said that in six months, if I proved myself, she would give me a raise, which she did—but not up to $6,000. I lost a boyfriend over that, since he was clearly after my money.

I assumed the title of psychiatric nurse consultant and directed a study that was to be the first of my publications that I never could have completed without Hilda and a few other colleagues. I was not a researcher, nor was I a writer. It took many near misses before that document was completed. The term "consultant" was something of a misnomer, and as I traveled all over the United States to gather data for the study, it really got in my way. All the people I interviewed were older and more experienced than I was, and their greetings were often colored by their preconceptions about this young New Yorker with a high falutin' title. It took me a while to get through that, and in some cases I didn't. In a few cities there were nurse educators serving on the planning committee for the study who were extremely warm and welcoming. One of these women was Tirzah Morgan, then at the University of Washington. She was an original who was wonderful to me during my League year, and she became a good friend in later years.

One month after I had accepted the job with the League, I met Sam Fagin, an electrical engineer working in the Washington area. We married in February 1952, midway through my contract year. We bought a house in suburban Maryland, and I commuted on weekends. Sam was more than accepting about my work. He understood perfectly that I could not leave the position before it was finished, and we managed quite well during the commuting period. I was already known to a minor extent as Claire Mintzer, but I wanted very much to assume his name as my own feminist statement. All of my married nursing and nonnursing professional acquaintances of the previous era had used their maiden names (including my aunt and all her friends), and I felt I was making a new statement as a married professional woman. So it goes.

During the first months of my new position and before my marriage, Gwen Tudor came to see me in New York. She was preparing for a major new position as chief nurse at the Clinical Center, National Institutes of Health, which was still under construction. She asked me to consider becoming her assistant. She wanted me to develop the psychiatric children's unit and be responsible for in-service education. I hesitated, but it became obvious that this was a fabulous opportunity, and I took it. There were several turning points that year—a new marriage with a move to Maryland, and 6 months to get ready for a new position just 15 minutes away from my new home. Serendipity!

An entire chapter could be spent on my Clinical Center experience. The people I met, worked with, and became friendly with were at the leading edge of psychiatric work. Relationships I formed there served me well in later professional experiences. The opportunities to expand my skills in leadership and staff development as well as clinical skills in working with patients and families were without limit. Because we were brand new, I was able to help Gwen develop a staff for each unit, equip the units, set policies, plan educational programs, work with members of other disciplines to establish norms, and get to know everyone who came to look, to stay, or to show new products, films, and treatment strategies. We thought we were great and ahead of our time in all dimensions. Indeed, we were in many, and at least trendy in others.

Another opportunity came my way in 1956. I was asked to be a member of the department of psychiatry (led by the renowned Reginald Lourie) at Children's Hospital in Washington, D.C., to serve as psychiatric liaison to the staff in the hospital. We had developed similar roles in nursing at NIH, but I had not worked with all disciplines while there. At Children's, I was to be a participant observer and work with members of all disciplines in a consultative role. It was a terrific job, and again I met outstanding people and formed lasting relationships. I also learned how to develop a grant application that focused on this work. The application was approved and funded, but Sam and I returned to New York, where he did some post-master's work in math at Courant Institute, New York University. That was another turning point for me and a major change in the direction of my career.

Until that point I was involved in clinical practice and was quite convinced that it was my destiny. I loved every minute of it, had no interest in formal teaching, and had no desire to pursue a position in education. However, I had come to know many nurse educators during my job at the League, and some of these people had visited the Clinical Center during my time there. One of these people, Dorothy Mereness, was completing her doctorate at Teachers College and planned to take a position at New York University to develop a graduate program there. After her visit to NIH, she wrote to me and invited me to contact her if I ever returned to New York. I did so, and this proved to be another major decision leading to my current position.

It was exciting to be part of a new program and to know that we were at the leading edge of developments in the field. We were the first to focus an entire semester of study on community mental health and on family therapy. Our graduates joined organizations that advanced nursing in these movements. All of the contacts that Dorothy and I had made earlier in our careers were extremely useful as we planned innovative field placements. Martha Rogers was the head of the Division of Nursing at NYU, and she was extremely supportive of Dorothy's efforts.

I was an instructor at NYU from 1956 to 1958 when Sam and I adopted a baby boy, Joshua, and I decided to stay home and devote myself to (almost) full-time motherhood. For the next two years I worked as a mental health consultant at a visiting nurse organization for one day every two weeks and was on call for Dorothy at NYU whenever she needed a fill-in. In 1960 I decided that I was tired of sitting in a Manhattan playground with child caretakers while the mothers were out shopping (not one of my minor vices or pleasures) and that I would get my PhD if I could meet all requirements for a doctoral program. I did qualify, and I completed work for the degree in 1964. In 1963 Sam and I adopted our second child, Charlie.

My dissertation, "The Effects of Maternal Attendance During Hospitalization on the Behavior of Young Children," had been stimulated by my earlier interest in childhood separation, which was strengthened by Joshua's two hospitalizations. The dissertation, which was published by F.A. Davis, received a great deal of national attention from the media and was credited for contributing to the change in hospital visiting privileges for young children in this country.

Dorothy invited me to return to NYU to plan and direct a new program in child psychiatric nursing. The program was funded, and the first class consisted of six students. Dorothy Mereness left NYU in 1965 to become dean of the school of nursing at the University of Pennsylvania, and I became the director of graduate programs in psychiatric nursing at NYU, a position I held until 1969. When I assumed the position, there were 6 faculty members in my group and we had a total of 22 students in the programs. When I left, there were 13 faculty members and some 42 students in the master's programs. The programs were superb, as was evidenced by the accomplishments of the graduates in later years.

I left NYU to become chair of a new department of nursing at Herbert H. Lehman

College, a unit of City University of New York. I had become convinced that the way to really influence the profession was through the professional socialization of students who could deal with the system effectively. The small number of nurses with master's degrees would never be able to achieve the changes that were necessary, and if baccalaureate graduates did not demonstrate differences in their practice from other nurses, I believed that advancement of the profession was in jeopardy.

I knew next to nothing about undergraduate education and set about to study the nursing and health literature and to recruit faculty who could help me in developing a truly innovative undergraduate program. Almost simultaneously, because of my own social interests and because City University had introduced open admissions, I developed a program to recruit and maintain minority students in the new program and to tailor our program for RN transfers.

The baccalaureate program at Lehman was designed to prepare nurses as primary care practitioners. The faculty was committed to this goal, and the program that resulted was cited throughout the nursing and health literature as a model. We were very proud of our accomplishments and of the success of our graduates. Many positions were created for them, and a mark of confidence was the development of new positions within the ambulatory care clinics of the Health and Hospitals Department of the City of New York.

The "team" movement was at its height during this period, and Lehman and Montefiore Hospital, our major affiliate and the instigator of the nursing program, decided to mount other health programs and organize them in the form of a Health Professions Institute. Committees worked on programs in administration, social work, and nursing, and later I became the head of the institute, remaining as chair of the Department of Nursing.

The faculty at Lehman was organized in groups, each with a leader. Decision making was decentralized wherever possible, with strong subgroup and faculty participation in all relevant matters. My style of leadership had become clear to me and to others by this time, and the faculty developed at Lehman was memorable. They were splendid people with extraordinary theoretical and clinical skills, were extremely enthusiastic about what we were doing, and were inspiring to each other and to students. I saw our group as a jewel and we were extremely respected on the Lehman campus and at Montefiore.

So, after seven years, why did I leave my beloved group and my beloved city? The answer is easy. We had accomplished extraordinary things at Lehman for our students and for nursing. Lehman was a liberal arts college without a medical school or hospital of its own. I had concluded that I wanted to test my skills in a larger universe—that of a nursing school in a major university that had a medical school and hospital.

Clearly, the University of Pennsylvania fit the bill. However, I was not too interested in Penn after I received answers to questions I had about university support, salaries of faculty, size of the student body, and other vital matters. Barbara Lowery (whom I've come to call the queen of search committees since she always gets her woman), university administrators such as Thomas Langfitt, Vice President for Health Affairs, and Edward Stemmler, dean of the medical school, and a faculty eager for and committed to change were all too persuasive for me to reject.

They were all correct. Penn was right for me, and I was right for Penn. The university had the combination of factors I was seeking, with so many hurdles for achievement that the challenge for all of us was immense. We had committed to meeting quality goals, and the next few years were full of enormous joint accomplishments. Clearly, the recruitment of faculty and the development of existing faculty within the school were the crucial elements of these accomplishments.

Strategic planning was put to explicit use at Penn. All of the goals that had been established had steps and timetables for their accomplishment. Most were achieved according to the timetable, but some preceded our expectations while others were slightly delayed. Nothing was left to chance or hopes. Faculty members were mutually stimulating, enforced group goals, and supported each other. They pushed, pulled, and bolstered each other in varied experiences and have reached professional heights I could only have dreamed of in my previous experiences. The present faculty includes clinicians from our university hospital and other clinical settings, and the achievement of excellence and status within a university such as Penn is an affirmation for us and for the profession. As far as nursing is concerned, I have felt that if we can do it here, it can be done anywhere.

When I came to Penn, the school was ready for movement and it had already developed a core of strong, independent thinkers among the faculty. They were ready for the recruitment of outstanding outsiders—Diane McGivern and Florence Downs were crucial initial appointments—and those who were not ready for movement left. My style is not for everyone. The expectations engendered are high, and while my leadership is sometimes considered ambiguous, my expectations for myself and for others are clear.

I feel lucky to be in a fantastic university with the most wonderful faculty and staff that I have ever worked with anywhere. At every turning point, nurses are free to choose to stay in the field in any of the myriad varieties of opportunities available to us or to leave that field for another. This is certainly true at times of educational decisions. I feel I have given a lot to the profession, but I am not even near to repaying what it has given me. I shall always be grateful for the stroke of fortune which brought me to choose this wonderful field.

Martha H. Hill

Martha H. Hill, PhD, RN, is a Robert Wood Johnson
Clinical Nurse Scholar at the School of Nursing,
University of Pennsylvania, while on leave from
the School of Nursing, Johns Hopkins University

Martha Hill was influenced (but not coerced) by her nurse mother and physician father to choose nursing as a career. Her vivid description of the excellence in education and practice that she experienced at Johns Hopkins reflects her continuing enthusiasm and focus on high-quality care.

Her research in hypertension is well known, and the role she envisions for nurses in interdisciplinary investigation is fostered by her love for the profession and her concern about how nursing care is delivered, as well as by her splendid interpersonal relationships with coworkers.

She is able to combine family and career and to make the most of every opportunity which presents itself when circumstances necessitate a change of environment. Martha is an avid learner and teacher, and she shares generously the knowledge and energy that bring about close ties within the many groups she works with.

My choice of nursing as a career was made, I now think, by exclusion. In the spring of my senior year in high school, I decided that I did not want to attend the women's college where I had planned to go the next fall. I changed my mind because I was certain that I did not want ever again to conjugate French verbs, write English term papers, or perform laboratory experiments. Never questioning that I would leave home and study something, I began a private search for an acceptable alternative education to pursue.

In addition to rejecting a four-year liberal arts college as "too boring," I eliminated music conservatories because I wasn't talented enough. I wanted desperately to *do* something, to learn skills that directly benefited others, and to keep out of the traditional classroom and library.

My family clearly played a part in my deciding to go into nursing. My mother had been a nurse, and she and all of our neighbors were frequently grateful for her practical knowledge and skills. My father, a Harvard and Massachusetts General Hospital (MGH) orthopedic surgeon, always had great respect for "a damn good nurse." Perhaps by osmosis, I absorbed and came to share their values. Once I got the idea, however, I was clear not only about what my goal was, but also about where I was going to go to achieve it. I decided to go to the best place I knew of that met the geographic requirement, had the excellent educational reputation I sought, and would be acceptable to my parents—Johns Hopkins. My application was readily accepted, and my course was set.

From the very first day, I was greatly impressed with Hopkins. Dr. Margaret Courtney, who was the coordinator of the first-year program, was tall, straight, stiffly starched, and intimidating. I had never met a nurse quite like her without the protection of my father on Sunday morning rounds at MGH, and certainly I had never met one with a doctorate. Margaret Courtney represented for me the best qualities of a Hopkins nurse: intelligence, competence, curiosity, compassion, candor, commitment, integrity, and a terrific sense of humor. I never imagined that she would be instrumental in my beginning doctoral study while I coordinated an educational program under her leadership 20 years later.

The legendary Hopkins "tradition of excellence" in education, patient care, and research was evident everywhere in the school of nursing and hospital environment. I never regretted the three years I spent there as a student in the diploma program. I was challenged as never before, and as I have been challenged only once since—while completing my dissertation requirements at the Johns Hopkins University School of Hygiene and Public Health. I loved the challenges (particularly of working nights on the Osler wards) and the collegiality that was essential for everyone to do her or his job. Professional values of caring, searching for better ways to deliver patient care, and seeking to understand how to prevent and treat disease permeated all aspects of the Hopkins environment. The lasting friendships I formed then with classmates, faculty, medical students, and residents have been an invaluable source of richness in my life.

As I neared the end of the curriculum, I had only an idea of what I was going to do next—go to college, work, travel to Europe with friends, get married at 25, have four children, and live happily ever after. I have no memory of then planning a career in professional nursing. Yet, I decided to pursue my BSN at Georgetown directly after graduation and live with Jane Mylander, a good friend who was a computer programmer. We rented a town house in the Foggy Bottom neighborhood of Washington.

Another important crossroads was arrived at when I realized that Georgetown would not exempt me from senior medical-surgical and public health, nor would they be persuaded by my tales of single-handedly providing care for an Osler ward with 32 patients while on night duty, or carrying a large caseload in a census tract in East Baltimore for three months. While I knew that I did not know all there was to know about nursing, I was certain that I did not then want to study *more* nursing. What I wanted to study was liberal arts: music, literature, art history, and yes, even French. I was extremely fortunate in that my father still was able and willing to provide me with this opportunity, and I knew I had better not delay. After deciding that I could return to study nursing at a later time if I wished to, I enrolled at George Washington University, where I spent a happy year studying liberal arts full-time, exploring Washington, D.C., as a single young woman, and falling in love with Gary Hill, a Hopkins graduate student.

At the end of that year I returned to Baltimore. I worked part-time evenings at Hopkins on medical-surgical units while finishing my degree under the advisement of Margaret Courtney. In June of 1966, a week after I received my BS degree from Hopkins, Gary and I were married. While we were on our honeymoon in Europe, he presented his research at an international conference, and we began our continuing passionate interests in travel and things French—Romanesque churches, Gothic cathedrals, food, wine, museums, and friends.

With marriage to a medical student came harsh economic realities and a need to maximize my income. I've been lucky. For the first (and only) time, I felt I had to choose the available position that paid the highest salary. Rather than work full-time as a staff nurse, I became an instructor in the first-year program in the Hopkins three-year nursing program. By this time Margaret Courtney was the director of the school, and she and Anne Hewitt McKewen, the coordinator of the first-year program, were excellent role models for faculty. From them, and from fellow faculty who were superior teachers and clinicians, I learned how to plan curriculum, prepare and deliver a lecture, write exam questions, and motivate, guide, and evaluate students.

I loved the interaction with the students and patients. I was sufficiently dependent on the stimulation and challenges of daily contact in this exciting environment that the births of our sons, Paul in 1969 and Justin in 1972, did not keep me at home for long. Moreover, my salary was an important component of our life-style, one on which Gary and I worked very hard and actively pursued our interests. We chose to live next to the hospital, which meant close proximity to work, stable child care, and low rent. For me, a supportive husband, a caring housekeeper who came to our home, and walking to work in five minutes made it possible to continue to work and still have some time and energy for life at home.

The closing of the Hopkins diploma program in 1973 was difficult for many reasons, including tradition and the adverse impact it had on patient care and education of all disciplines in the hospital. I chose (out of loyalty and commitment to the students and the diploma school) to remain on the faculty, teaching in whatever courses I was needed until the very end. Thus, after five years of teaching at the first-year level, I found myself teaching second-year medical-surgical nursing, and then third-year community health and outpatient nursing.

My decision to remain on the faculty was a good one, for this experience provided me with the opportunity to demonstrate to myself (as well as to the students) that I could be competent in a variety of areas. Perhaps more important, I was able to observe nurses practicing in many settings. In the adult outpatient clinics, I was greatly impressed with the attention the nurses gave to the appointment book, the telephone, the utility room, and the break schedule. I rarely saw a nurse talking with a patient. The patients' needs and problems that the students and I identified were enormous and needed good nursing assessment and intervention. I decided after that firsthand experience that real opportunities existed for nursing in the ambulatory care area, if the traditional "get the right chart, the right doctor, and the right patient in the same room, at any time" approach were discarded for the more contempory "nurse the patient" movement of the nurse practitioner.

When the director of outpatient nursing asked me one day how things were going and what I thought about nursing in her department, I mustered all of the tact I could while being honest. In response to her acknowledgment of the problems and the lack of solutions, I offered to write a report summarizing my observations and suggestions for how nursing might improve its contribution to patient care. Fortunately, I had learned somewhere to keep good notes of factual events on the chance that I might in the future need to document performance, whatever the quality. At the end of the report, I concluded that money could be saved by replacing several of the nurses with unit clerks (from whom they were largely indistinguishable), and that better patient care by nurses could be provided by upgrading all but one of the staff nurse positions to nurse practitioner positions.

The decision to speak up about the poor quality of the nursing care that I had observed and to come forward with constructive suggestions about how to implement responsible changes in the care delivery system brought another major opportunity in my career. I was offered a position as staff assistant to the director of ambulatory nursing with responsibility for evaluating and changing nursing practice. I grabbed this chance to play a part in the decentralization of Johns Hopkins Hospital and thoroughly enjoyed being a part of the triad formed by medicine, nursing, and administration. This was my first experience since my student days to be part of an interdisciplinary team, and I loved the shared learning, mutual respect, and collegiality that developed.

In order to integrate the changes in nursing practice and the learning needs of the adult nurse practitioner program students, I became the clinical coordinator of the nurse practitioner program. I then decided to take the year-long course along with the outpatient department staff nurses I would be supervising, so that I would know well what they had been taught and so I would be able to develop reasonable job productivity criteria. To complete course requirements, I needed to practice patient assessments and to provide primary care to a caseload of patients two days each week. I chose to practice in the medical clinic, where I found Mike Moore, a moonlighting nephrology fellow. I asked him if he would have the time to act as my preceptor while I refined my skills. He was delighted to have some help, and after a few weeks I was seeing most of the patients while Mike got many other things done, including getting caught up with his journal reading. He was a superb teacher, a splendid physician, and a delightful person. He respected the perspective of a nurse and felt strongly that the primary care needs of the majority of the patients (older women with obesity, hypertension, and miscellaneous minor but chronic problems) could be met most satisfactorily by a well-qualified nurse.

The time I spent with Mike Moore was my real introduction to the enormous and deceptively simple-sounding problem of uncontrolled high blood pressure. The opportunities for nurses to influence patient care and outcomes were unlimited. I learned everything I could about the pathophysiology, pharmacology, and patient and provider behaviors that were necessary to achieve the outcomes desired by both. I wrote an algorithm and designed a system to establish a nurse-run clinic. The days I was in clinic were my happiest, despite all of the problems associated with getting the right patient, myself, and the patient's chart in any room at some time proximate to the appointment time. At times I longed for a nurse to direct traffic in the clinic and to coordinate the logistics for me. But those days were gone. Part of the price of the changes in nursing roles and responsibilities was a certain amount of "do-it-yourself."

In addition to the excitement I felt from being in practice again, I continued to enjoy being a part of the interdisciplinary triad administering the ambulatory care department and related programs. I worked hard to increase my effectiveness as a collaborator in an interdisciplinary setting. The skills that were most valuable were the abilities to analyze the problems and needs of nurses as integral components of the system within which they practice, to identify the mutual goals of all of the participants in the system, and to focus discussions and planning on achievement of improved patient care outcomes. I had found my niche.

The nirvana lasted but a year, for in the meantime Gary had completed his residency and military service. It was time for us to leave Hopkins and to venture out into the world where he would have his first "real" job. Although I was sorry to leave Hopkins and all of our friends, I was ready to move to Philadelphia, where Gary had accepted a faculty position in pathology at the University of Pennsylvania. It was time for me to tackle the next phase of my life, for the first time buying a house and starting children in school.

While I was searching for a position as a nurse practitioner with experience in hypertension, several physician friends gave me the name of Dr. Karl Engleman, a hypertension specialist at the Hospital of the University of Pennsylvania in Philadelphia. When I went there to look for a job, I soon learned that the department of nursing was not prepared to make a commitment in the philosophy and management of the system to use nurse practitioners, much less hire an experienced nurse practitioner who had organized her own clinic. Karl Engleman, a man of quick, incisive intelligence and blunt conversation, was not interested in semantics. He said, "I don't care what you're called. I need someone who can go down to the clinic and take care of patients." "Good," I replied, "that is what I want to do. I need an office, a telephone, access to a clinic secretary, and your support in the hospital system." In response to his asking me how much money I wanted, I told him how much I was then making. He whistled and said, "That's a lot of money." (It wasn't, and I refused to be intimidated.) I replied, "Would you like the names of some references?" and gave him the names of several Hopkins physicians with whom I had been working. When I sat next to the physician director of the Hopkins Hospital Outpatient Department the next afternoon at a meeting, he smiled widely and whispered, "Karl Engelman called this morning and asked if you were worth it."

Thus began one of the best experiences of my career. I was in a situation where my talents and skills were needed, and the basic resources necessary for me to do the job were provided. Earning the respect of polite (but distant) nurses and physicians required demonstrating that I knew what nursing could offer in this setting. The challenge was to repeat my experience at Hopkins. The necessity of developing effective working relationships in an academic teaching environment that was new to me gave me the opportunity to select and apply principles of nursing and change theory on behalf of patients with high blood pressure.

From 1974 to 1980, my primary appointment was at the Hospital of the University of Pennsylvania in the Section of Hypertension and Clinical Pharmacology. I planned, implemented, and evaluated nursing care for people with possible or diagnosed high blood pressure. The opportunities for nursing were many: case finding, referral, patient teaching, follow-up, diagnosis and treatment using protocol guidelines, monitoring progress toward goals, and research.

My goal in all activities was to identify or create situations in which I, and later other nurses, could practice in an innovative and professional manner. The primary nursing objectives were to provide high-quality patient care and to serve as patient advocates. In response to recognized need and as a result of my activities, several specific hypertension-related nursing programs were developed: the screening and nurse management clinics at the Hospital of the University of Pennsylvania, a hypertension outreach program in West Philadelphia, and the "Nurses Do Make a Difference" program of the State of Pennsylvania.

The screening clinic was not difficult to establish within the system and was successful very quickly. The nurse management clinic, or long-term follow-up program, however, required all of the skills I had acquired in patient assessment, in understanding of "medical" management, and in presenting the special values of nursing in a decisive and nonthreatening manner. At my insistence a jointly developed protocol of patient management was established. The physicians and I achieved mutual understanding and respect of what we wished to accomplish through discussions of how we wished to improve patient care.

These two clinics formed the structure within which nurses, physicians, graduate nursing students, medical students, and fellows could provide interventions for people seeking or enrolled in care. In addition to my patient care responsibilities, I participated in the clinical research activities in the section. I helped to recruit patients for studies, to collect data, and to interpret findings. I learned a great deal about experimental design and the difficulties and excitement of clinical research. I also learned that I would never become a coinvestigator or principal investigator of a major study until I had a doctorate.

In the meantime I was taking courses in the master's degree program in the school of nursing at Penn. I was stimulated by the mixture of required courses and opportunities for independent study. I am grateful still to faculty members Barbara Jacobson, who challenged my ability to master biostatistics and research design, and Anne Keane, who was the first person to encourage me to submit my written work for publication. I was tremendously gratified when the National High Blood Pressure Education Program selected my articles "Helping the Hypertensive Patient Control Sodium Intake" and "What Can Go Wrong When You Measure Blood Pressure" for national distribution through the High Blood Pressure Information Center.

My career as an independent investigator began with my master's thesis, "The Quality of Follow-Up Care Provided by Physicians and Nurse Practitioners in a Hypertension Clinic." Publication of this study and the research and publication of a subsequent one that examined the complexity of illness of hypertensive patients were collaborative efforts with Mike Reichgott, a physician colleague in the section.

The hypertension outreach program was the first extramural program developed and delivered by a nurse at the Hospital of the University of Pennsylvania to be funded by the United Way of Southeastern Pennsylvania. I wrote the application, with Karl's and Mike's support, in an attempt to find salary support while extending my expertise in high blood pressure detection and control out of the academic teaching center and into the community. Established in 1978, the program was launched to increase community awareness of hypertension and to increase the effectiveness of treatment efforts in West Philadelphia. This target area was 53% black—a group with a particularly high prevalence of severe hypertension. The hypertension outreach program coordinated existing hypertension-related resources to increase the proportion of hypertensive individuals whose conditions had been diagnosed and controlled.

The nurse coordinator position in the outreach program was primarily consultative. It provided a challenging opportunity to merge public health nursing and clinical specialty skills and roles. The position required skills in health education and health promotion, community resource coordination, and the ability to serve as a liaison between intramural and extramural hypertension-related activities. Additionally, it offered the opportunity for nursing to initiate and develop a community leadership role in attacking a major public health problem that had been viewed almost exclusively in terms of the traditional medical model.

As the nurse coordinator of the outreach program, I spent most of my time and effort identifying continuing, viable, and appropriate community programs with which to work. One successful effort was the West Philadelphia Local Coordinating Council, which supported the development of local screening sites, training volunteer screeners, and providing public education programs. Another success was the formation of an informal coalition of ambulatory care nurses at five West Philadelphia hospitals. I provided catalytic leadership in helping these institutions and nurses develop community screenings, nurse-run high blood pressure clinics at the hospitals, and satellite care clinics in the community.

As a result of volunteer activities with the American Heart Association–Pennsylvania Affiliate, I became involved in developing the "Nurses Do Make a Difference" program, a statewide continuing education program for nurses that was concerned with high blood pressure. Support was obtained from the Heart Association, the Pennsylvania Nurses' Association, and the Pennsylvania Department of Health. The committee of five nurses included two nurse practitioners from the Veterans Administration in Pittsburgh, the PNA staff person for continuing education, a Philadelphia nurse with expertise in health education, and myself. We had a grand time developing and providing educational materials for nurses, including curriculum modules and skill-building continuing education programs. The sponsors of the committee cosponsored the programs with schools of nursing, hospitals, and health departments at multiple sites across the state. This program provided an opportunity to accelerate the dissemination of up-to-date scientific information and related implications for nursing practice in a wide variety of settings.

I think that all of the programs developed during these formative years in my career integrated my generic interests, which I value enormously: interdisciplinary health care delivery where nursing plays a prominent role, demonstration of improvement in health care delivery, innovation in nursing practice, reaching into an underserved population, and combining nursing practice with community effort and clinical research.

These experiences led to other opportunities and responsibilities, including a joint appointment in the graduate program at the School of Nursing at Penn and serving with Susanna Cunningham, of the University of Washington School of Nursing, as the liaison representatives of the American Nurses' Association on the coordinating committe of the National High Blood Pressure Education Program at the National Institutes of Health. I credit these accomplishments in large part to the environment at Penn, which encouraged individuals with creativity, competence, and commitment to achieve at a very high level. The example set by Claire Fagin, the dean, and her encouragement, helped create a climate in which almost everything was possible. If something was not possible, one asked, "Why not?"

The years from 1974 to 1980 were challenging. Our 1975 sabbatical in Paris afforded time to really learn basic conversational French, to travel, to improve my cooking, to meet people, and to discover the demands of being a full-time mother away from home. After our return, as we grew to love our home, neighbors, and housekeeper, Elise Love (who really was a love, as well as the keeper of the house and the mother of us all), we resisted having our lives dominated by the needs presented to us by our sons' learning disabilities. We were fortunate to find excellent help, especially at the Benchmark School in Media, Pennsylvania, but there always were compromises and associated pains as one learned to accept what was best for one's individual child. The parent group at Benchmark, of which we were members, was an important source of support, especially in maintaining our senses of humor.

Another concern was Gary's not finding the professional opportunities at Penn that I had. In 1978 he accepted the position of chief of pathology at Baltimore City Hospital. Because the boys were not ready to be mainstreamed into a regular classroom and because I had just received the United Way grant, we decided that we would continue to live in Philadelphia, and that Gary would commute.

And so began the next chapter in the lives of this two-career couple—two years of every other weekend as a family in a Baltimore bachelor apartment, alternate weekends in our Philadelphia home, and Gary's return home on Wednesday nights. As a life-style, it had advantages. Both of us were productively pursuing our careers, and the boys were doing well in school. But it was expensive, and we were concerned about the consequences of adjusting too well to the psychological, as well as to the physical, distance. As the move back to Baltimore approached, I grieved deeply for our Philadelphia home, our neighbors there, Elise (who made it possible for me to do so much of what I was able to do professionally), and my colleagues and patients at Penn.

Finding an unusually attractive, conveniently located house that needed lots of tender, loving care was the critical step in my becoming enthusiastic about going to Baltimore. The second thing that changed my attitude was the realization that, since this was the time for me to pursue a doctorate, the place where I could most imagine pursuing it was at the Hopkins School of Hygiene and Public Health. I turned down several job offers, for I knew then what I didn't want to do and what I needed more time to investigate. I was looking for a position that would require me to continue to question, analyze, and produce, within an academic setting that insisted on practice, teaching, research, community service, and working as part of an interdisciplinary team while balancing the conflicting obligations of family (now without Elise) and career.

Several weeks after the move, while I was painting the ceiling of a closet, Margaret Courtney called to offer me a position assisting her in developing and implementing a revised curriculum for the BS degree for the RN part-time study program at Hopkins. The opportunity to work with Margaret, as well as her enthusiastic support for my practicing a half day per week in the Hopkins hypertension clinic and for my beginning doctoral study, sold me on the position. Of course, the tuition remuneration was a critical factor as well. After Margaret's retirement, Carol Gray, her successor and the first dean of the new Hopkins University School of Nursing, gave me her unqualified support as I continued to meet professional demands as a full-time faculty member, a full-time student, and a national committee member. The professional and personal responsibilities were almost unbearable at times, but I pushed myself hard, knowing that I was in the right place, doing what I wanted and needed to do in the only way that I could afford.

The doctoral program in behavioral sciences was the perfect place for me to build on my primary clinical interests—cardiovascular disorders (particularly high blood pressure) and their behavioral aspects. I was able to study topics that had been of clinical and research interest: patient and provider behavior, clinical epidemiology, health care evaluation, efficacy of new treatment interventions, and societal influences on health and illness. The faculty, many of whom were internationally known in their areas of expertise, were accessible and collegial. The most valuable mentoring was provided by David Levine, a physician and behavioral scientist, who was during my doctoral program my original advisor, unofficial therapist, and dissertation committee chairman. I thrived because of the rigorous curriculum, the interdisciplinary and international student body, and the challenge of being a student again.

One of the best parts of the doctoral experience was membership in a group of six nurses who had elected to go to the school of hygiene for doctoral study in different programs. We bonded and helped each other in turn to recover from divorce, to adjust to the diagnosis of multiple sclerosis, to adapt to unexpected pregnancy after a decade of infertility, and to cope with terminally ill siblings and parents (my situation). We were professional nurses supporting each other through the best and the worst of times, with great respect and affection for each other.

At one point in my doctoral study years, I had 18 ideas on my list of "Possible Dissertation Topics." I used the independent study option to explore the literature about several of these. One of the many questions I had, after serving on several national task forces to develop consensus guidelines for hypertension policy, was "What difference do these reports make?" When I learned that this question had not been studied, I elected to investigate the dissemination and influence of consensus reports in changing practice behavior.

During these years I was assimilated into the group regularly attending the Hopkins High Blood Pressure Conference Series and Hypertension Journal Club by Paul Whelton. It was in this group of people, who respected and appreciated the perspective that a nurse with my background and interests could bring, that I found an interdisciplinary group from whom I learned a great deal. The friendships that developed were and are very important to me, and the promise of collaborative research already is a reality.

In my last year of doctoral study, I decided to apply for a postdoctoral fellowship in order to reduce the number and complexity of roles in my life. I wanted very much to begin another research study in a situation where my time would be protected. Now, as a Robert Wood Johnson Clinical Nurse Scholar for two years at the University of Pennsylvania, I am having another extraordinary experience. My objectives are to continue to develop as a scientist/researcher, to examine important clinical issues and research questions, and to continue to develop as a clinician. I feel very fortunate to have this chance to further develop my research skills and professional growth. I am delighted with the example and guidance of my preceptor, Barbara Lowery, who is thoughtful, creative, pragmatic, and unfailingly positive in her leadership.

After this fellowship, my major goal is to ensure an effective leadership role for nursing in collaborative research, patient care, and policy efforts. I expect to return to Hopkins and be a more active, better-qualified investigator in interdisciplinary research. I also look forward to teaching nursing and to starting an interdisciplinary clinic with nurse colleagues, such as Diane Becker, who are interested in cardiovascular risk reduction.

I have been pleased that I decided years ago not to go directly to college, and that I have played a part at institutions as outstanding as Hopkins and Penn. Nursing has provided me with unlimited opportunities to develop and practice a wide variety of skills in all kinds of settings and to influence any number of people and systems. Nursing calls for curiosity, imagination, creativity, interest in others, analytical and communication abilities, independent thinking, energy, and organization. I have learned and grown a great deal.

It has been gratifying and stimulating to become a writer, speaker, and consultant. I have always enjoyed asking and answering questions and learning from others by sharing some of the things I've learned. For me, and for many others from different disciplines, high blood pressure control became an area where people with different skills and perspectives could come together to address a common goal: to reduce morbidity and mortality. It was the perfect setting for nursing to contribute collaboratively and to serve all interests, including its own. And for me, it has been a great deal of fun.

Constance Holleran

Constance Holleran, MSN, RN, FAAN,
is Executive Director of the
International Council of Nurses,
headquartered in Geneva, Switzerland

❖

Connie Holleran has always had the good sense and the guts to take advantage of opportunities whenever and wherever they presented themselves. She built on her early interests and ever-increasing talents as she advanced through unusual paths in her career. Obstacles never daunted her. She faced the embarrassment of returning home after failing anatomy and physiology as a freshman in nursing school, was readmitted, and graduated near the top of her class.

Testifying to her conscious political know-how are her achievements both in the legislative arena and on the international scene.

How do you develop political skills? Connie believes that interest, awareness, being informed, and learning to return to fight another day are key factors. She has an insatiable appetite for news and knowledge, and she talks about how crucial it is to know the rules if you are to play the political game successfully. And her stories show that she makes the most of every chance to enjoy some pleasure along the way.

*R*esponding to a request to tell all about one's career, particularly as it relates to politics, is a bit difficult. I will use a variety of approaches just to get the facts of my life down on paper.

First of all, I think of my work as more public policy-making than political, although politics is a big part of it all and I do love politics.

I am the second of four children and grew up in Manchester, New Hampshire, then a city of 80,000 people, located 52 miles from Boston. In my young years a trip to Boston took two hours by car.

It is hard to say what really influenced me to become a nurse. I am sure it was a combination of things. I had a cousin who served in the army during World War II, and I had visited her at the hospital in Boston when she was a cadet nurse. Also, in grade school we had a very nice public health nurse, Miss Dolan, whom we had to see whenever we, or others in our families, had diseases like scarlet fever or measles. That was pretty often. I remember one day Miss Dolan and my first-grade teacher, a nun, asked what I wanted to be when I grew up. I said either a nurse or a nun. After much laughter, they said I could be both. I think that for me, half was enough.

At age 10 I became ill, and while I was in the hospital, decided some nurses were not really nice to kids. They were more interested in the physicians than in us, and if you repeatedly vomited the thick, awful medicine they gave us every morning, you were not the nurses' favorite! Also they would ask you to bring them things from across the room when you had a johnny on—also not a nice thing to do to a 10-year-old. So, I decided I would change things, become a nurse, and be good to the kids.

In high school I was editor of the school paper and worked on the magazine editorial staff. The faculty advisor suggested I would like journalism. Later he said there were few opportunities for girls in that field. I was interested in English, history, journalism, and nursing. My parents did not favor a college education for girls (we could not learn to drive, either) and nursing did have lots of appeal, so off I went to Massachusetts General Hospital (MGH), which was known as the having the best nursing school around. I had studiously reviewed catalogues and written for information for several years. I even asked one school if having flat feet would keep me out of their program. (I remembered that later when I was on an admissions committee.)

In September 1952 I went to Boston to start my auspicious career, only to be home again in January after having failed anatomy and physiology. Having to face the neighbors changed my whole outlook. Having been told that MGH would allow me to reenter in March (a great privilege, I was advised), I decided it was serious business, and I returned not only to study harder, but to scare all of the new students into doing the same. My parents came again to the welcoming tea because if I could do it, so could they. I came out near the top of the class, having proved that repeating everything from the probation period does not kill you. A strong hand (or a knee in the back) was rather steadily applied by Ruth Sleeper (Director of School and Service at MGH) at many points in my early career. When I was a staff nurse, she asked me to participate in something for television. I demurred, but that did not fly. I did it. (I was very shy and hated to be noticed.) Later I taught at the school and was asked to make a presentation to a nursing service group. My shaking so distracted them that they were happy when I raced through it in 3 minutes instead of 15. Still later, Miss Sleeper provided me with more opportunities that I did not fully recognize as such at the time.

I went to Teachers College, Columbia, a year after graduation from MGH because TC required a year of experience for admission. By now, I wanted to be a teacher and to be a better one than some I had had. (I wouldn't scare kids to death.)

New York was a wonderful experience. On arrival, I found out that they had no dormitory room for me (a frequent TC trick), no apartment, no nothing. I had almost no money and was hardly a worldly sophisticate, so I found a cheap hotel in Times Square (not so bad then, really fun) and began to pray for luck. I finally connected with a good person, a nurse whose roommate was getting married, and it worked out fine. I worked nights and summers and finished in a year and a half because TC has some outstanding and flexible teachers who made it possible.

Back I went to Boston and MGH to be a teacher. I worked hard to be a good one. The students said, "Well, you are always fair—tough, but fair."

I delayed going to graduate school for one year because I had a chance to go to Europe with friends. I worked out a deal with Miss Sleeper. I would postpone leaving the faculty if she would give me a month's leave of absence to go with my four weeks of vacation, and if I could go with my two faculty buddies. She agreed. She and others there all encouraged travel and new experiences for all of us. We had a good time on a budget of $60 per week.

I was determined to go to graduate school in September of the following year. Miss Sleeper called me in before Thanksgiving to ask if I would postpone school so that I could do a year as an exchange teacher in Belfast, Northern Ireland. The person they had planned to have go had died the previous year. I had to agree to return to the school for an additional year. I thought, "Two whole years of my life. How can I?" I asked if I could think it over during the holiday. That really was to give me time to see if a certain man would call. If he did, no deal. If not . . . . Well, he did not call, and the next August off I left on an Italian ship, violins playing and all at the sailing. One of my friends who was seeing me off somehow got me entangled with a nun who pleaded with me to share a table for two with her. My friend apologized profusely. I had been at a table with six men and two women! The Berlin Wall had just gone up, and no one knew if war would break out. The ship had many cancellations, and I had a good time. (All of this really does relate to my later work. Courage and political skills need to be developed.)

My time in Belfast proved to be a wonderful career opportunity. I was 27 years old.

The Irish believed that Sister Tutors should be older. I learned a lot, met many people, and toured health facilities in the United Kingdom and Scandinavia (on my vacation and with my money).

During that year I visited the International Council of Nurses (ICN) Headquarters in London, and staff members Ellen Broe and Ingrid Hämelin helped me plan my visits to Denmark, Sweden, and Finland. Little did I imagine that 20 years later, one of the board members present during my interview for the ICN executive director position would be Ingrid.

In 1963 I went to Washington, D.C., to attend Catholic University (CU). When I went to look the place over, my friends and I met the Speaker of the House of Representatives and had a private tour of the Capitol. It was a good time to be in Washington and to be from Boston. There were parties galore until November 22 of that year, when President Kennedy was assassinated. Then it became a place of sadness.

I was the only one in my class to finish CU on time. It tells you something about CU and my social life.

In selecting my master's thesis topic I was very careful. It had to be interesting to me. It had to be done on a very tight budget (no computers, mass mailings, etc.) and I could not be dependent on waiting for others to get their replies in to me. Having all that for a start, I selected the roles of the Department of Health, Education and Welfare (HEW, now the Department of Health and Human Services) and the American Nurses' Association (ANA) in the enactment of the (first) Nurse Training Act of 1964 as my thesis topic.

One aspect of my study required me to interview Jessie Scott. I'd never heard of the Division of Nursing or much about the U.S. Public Health Service. In fact when I was asked by Jessie's deputy what I knew about the USPHS, I said I know you take care of the Indians. In spite of that, Jessie saw me. During the interview she asked if I would like to work with the division. By then I had an idea of what they did, so I said I was nowhere near ready for anything like that. She said no one ever was, and that it would all be new, so why not think about it, and, if the Nurse Training Act was passed, come to see her? I wrote and told Miss Sleeper of the offer. The law was passed on September 4, 1964. In October I went to talk to Jessie. She casually mentioned that she had seen Ruth Sleeper and that they had talked about me. She offered me a job. I accepted the appointment for the first of February. Now you know why I finished at CU on time.

I went home and told an old friend what I'd done and what salary had been discussed, and she found it "thoroughly disgusting." She said, "They must be hard up." (Her university salary was much lower.) With help from Dorothea Omen, who made herself available to me over the Christmas holidays that year, I did finish and take comprehensive examinations on January 30, so that I could start work on Monday, February 1, 1965. That date happened to be the first day of the first National Advisory Council of Nurse Training. The U.S. Surgeon General, the Chief Nurse, and many of the top names in nursing were there. There was a cocktail party that evening, and I thought it was not going to be a bad job at all.

My five years as a nurse consultant in the division were tremendous in terms of job satisfaction and learning. There were some frustrations, of course. It was like being in a good university all of the time. We had staff development opportunities and seminars, and Jessie did let people grow as fast as they wanted to. She also promoted me rapidly, and I never felt quite ready when she gave me the opportunities. I remember telling her that she must be able to find someone better at one point. She looked shocked. She used to tell staff before council and review committee meetings that we could not show our feelings on our faces about various applications because they had to be judged on their merit and had to stand on their own. Anyway, she showed a little shock that one time, but I got the promotion.

Through all those years there were no eight-hour days. I wore out briefcases carrying things home and back. The more speeches I gave, the more requests seemed to come in. By that time I could stand before a group without shaking, but I did not really enjoy it. Preparing a speech is a lot of work.

After five years of working with schools, universities, and health agencies on projects to improve nursing, I was ready for a change. The ANA's Washington office was appealing to me, but the organization was in a real financial bind. Hildegard Peplau interviewed me (she was acting executive director) in the north terminal waiting room at National Airport. Side by side, in uncomfortable seats, we talked. She asked me to consider coming on staff at the ANA, if the dues increase was approved to help develop projects to get outside funding. I agreed, but that meant no job for a few months, so I had a lovely trip to Portugal, Spain, and Morocco on my own. I spent my retirement money to survive.

In May I attended the ANA convention in Miami, and the dues increase passed. (I did not lobby or participate at all.)

Poor Eileen Jacobi. She took over as executive director of the ANA right after the convention, and Hildegard was elected president. I called to say, "When should I come to work?" and "I assume ANA will pay all moving expenses." I think it was all a big surprise to her. In mid-June I moved to New York. Again panic—panic to find an affordable place. And again, as if from heaven, I found an apartment facing the Hudson River, and I could easily walk to work. (That's why I never understand those who don't love New York. I always walked, poked, browsed, and learned. I didn't have to use subways or get caught in traffic.)

In terms of projects, we started slowly. Our first one was to do a nationwide survey to identify needs, and then to develop an ANA plan for continuing education. Another project had to do with mental health. After about four months, Eileen asked me if I would move back to Washington to head ANA's office there because she was making some administrative changes and because Julia Thompson was to retire very soon. (Julia had established the Washington office of the ANA and had run it for over 20 years.) I agreed to the move, so in December I gave up the gorgeous apartment and moved back to Washington. There were two nurses, one secretary, a few gray metal desks, no carpets, and a duplicator that was so slow you hated to use it. After a few months we moved next door. It wasn't an elaborate location, but we had carpets we inherited, some wood paneling, and a very small conference room. It was only after I left ANA in 1981 that additional space and a large conference room were obtained.

The years that I was in the ANA Washington office were hectic. It was during the Nixon and Carter administrations. Cut, cut. We established the Nurses' Coalition for

Action in Politics (N-CAP) in 1974. (We had tried earlier but people were not ready for it then.) We sued President Nixon for release of impounded funds. (The NLN finally brought the suit, but I did all the work with the lawyers, got ANA agreement on the last day possible, and then, because it seemed wise, got NLN to carry it on.) I worked extremely hard to keep nursing united on legislative issues. It took a lot of effort to communicate, educate, and coordinate all along the way, but it did pay off. There are many things I could have done better, but I was learning on the run. Mary Mullane was in Washington then, retired from her deanship at the University of Illinois. She was a great help to me in my early days, and the staff was very committed and involved.

I saw the job as having several parts—communicating nursing's interest to policy-makers (Congress and Executive Branch), communicating our needs for their help, and communicating the ANA's legislative plans and goals to the nursing community. (That is why we started sending memos to every school of nursing in the country. It really helped to build up ANA's visibility and its strength in Washington.) The work also required strategy planning with a number of groups within the ANA, as well as others. As hard as it was and as understaffed as we were, we never lost a real legislative issue in 10 years. We won every veto override and every budget amendment that reached the floor.

People used to ask me where I acquired my political skills. Actually, I was never aware of having any. Rather than political skills, I think interest, awareness, and being informed are the key factors to developing political savvy. I grew up in a family where we had at least two and often three daily papers, and all conversation stopped for the evening news, which was then discussed. My dad had served in the state legislature in the 1930s, and he was always active in his union. He had great respect for the government and for the country, and we grew up always hearing that we didn't know how lucky we were. Dad was an orphan who was earning his own way by age 9, and he came alone to relatives in the United States at age 14. He was wounded while in France in World War I, and I found out years later he was cared for by the MGH medical unit. My mother died of pneumonia when I was three and a half, leaving Dad with three daughters. He later remarried and they had a son. Dad lived to be 71, and always, despite his losses, he considered himself to have been very fortunate.

All I can say for developing political skills is be alert, listen carefully, be interested, learn as much as you can about both the political process and the issues, and work hard. The process and the rules are very important because you can miss just one little step and lose the whole ballgame. Many times, I called the House or Senate parliamentarian to be sure I knew exactly what maneuvers would be possible to use, then I prepared just in case. You must be set to go well in advance because schedules change. Always be ready also to cancel vacations, dinners, and other personal matters. Congress won't wait.

For example, one time we were waiting for a veto. At least there was a pretty good chance that there would be one. I visited the Senate staff at 6 PM on a Friday to give them our estimated count, should an override vote be needed. They told me they were busy on another bill. There would be time later for ours. It wouldn't happen until the following week. I convinced one of them to take my vote count list (which I had put on pink paper so they couldn't lose it) just in case. On Saturday morning I went shopping to get a bathing suit. When I got home around noon, Ginny Bauknecht, our very good public relations staff member, called me and said, "Where have you been? They announced the veto this morning." She was already working on a press release. I called the "Hill" and found out the override vote was scheduled in about an hour and a half—on a Saturday afternoon. The bill did not involve only nursing concerns, but a lot of health issues as well. I called the chair of the Coalition for Health Funding, and fortunately he was home. He picked me up within 10 minutes, and off we went. We could not believe it was going so fast. I knew from our count that we should, on an ordinary day, be able to win that vote, but on a summer Saturday? The chair and I decided all we could do in the short time available was to split up. One of us went to the Republican Lobby and one went to the Democrat Lobby to speak to every senator we could find. I waited for Senator Mansfield to finish talking to friends, then asked him how it looked. He answered in his usual brief way. "OK." Then as he walked away he said over his shoulder, "Otherwise, I wouldn't have scheduled it today."

I sent a note in to the floor to the committee staff director, informing him that I was outside if he needed anything. His note out was, "What is your count? Is everyone here?" The next note from me was, "Jay has the pink paper with the count. I don't know who is there." In any event, we won. But the point is: be prepared, triple-check details, and be ready to drop everything and run. Our staff had done good work, as had our members, and it all came out well.

In 1978 I was invited to submit an application for the position of ICN executive director. However—because under *great* pressure from the then ANA president, Anne Zimmerman, I had only a few weeks before withdrawn my resignation from ANA and agreed to stay on—I had to decline. Again in 1980 I was asked, this time by the ICN president Olive Anstey of Australia (whom I knew from having visited Australia when she was president there). She asked if I would please consider sending in an application for the ICN position because they really needed a person with association experience who could strengthen the ICN's relationships with the World Health Organization and other United Nations agencies. I was on my way to Maine (where I had recently purchased a vacation cottage), so I said if she would send me the ICN budget, position description, and staff regulations, I would consider it. She would not send the budget (unlike the ANA, evidently the ICN's budget was not published or distributed other than to their member associations), but eventually the other documents came.

I asked others about the status of the organization's finances because I did not want to take on a red bottom line operation where I would have to cut staff. It was in pretty good shape. I was interviewed by ICN board members Hildegard Peplau (this time in a Statler Hilton Hotel guest room) and Beccy Bergman of Israel. My previous employers, Eileen Jacobi (then an ICN board member) and Jessie Scott (then chairman of the ICN's Professional Services Committee) were among my references. On a Saturday in early February 1981 at 7:30 AM, a call came from Geneva. Could I travel on Sunday to be interviewed by the full board of directors on Monday? There were no banks open, so I called my brother Pete. I bought the plane ticket on my credit card, and with the cash from Pete, off I went. Needless to say, I was hired and moved to Switzerland in mid-March of 1981.

My previous experience seemed to be ideal for the work to be done here. I manage an office and staff the same size as in Washington, plan programs, raise money for projects, work with Amelia Maglacas (nursing's liaison at WHO), lobby the International Labor Organization, help WHO develop materials for ICN priorities, and focus on policy planning skills needed to help national nursing associations.

I have not done career planning, yet each step in my career has led to a next. It has been a combination of opportunities offered, opportunities taken, very hard work, and heading in a direction where, because I like it, I have been willing to put a lot into it. As a result I have had great job satisfaction, lots of reinforcement, and support from coworkers and peers and perhaps an unusual nursing career. I have loved every job and still enjoy it all.

Judith Bellaire Igoe

Judith Bellaire Igoe, MPHN, RN, is Associate
Professor and Director of School Health Programs at
the University of Colorado Health Sciences Center
School of Nursing and is Executive Director of the
University's Center for Human Caring

*Over the past 20 years, Judith Igoe has devoted her energies
to the advancement of improved community health programs for school-
age youth. The School Nurse Practitioner program was her first project,
followed by the School Nurse Achievement Programs, Health PACT, and
most recently, a new graduate degree plan for a community health nurse
for school-age youth. She is now focused on developing school-based
clinics and achieving third party reimbursement for nurses. Though most
optimistic about the eventual outcomes, Ms. Igoe, in her pragmatic way,
anticipates that these may be her most complex efforts to date.*

*In the fall of 1987, Ms. Igoe assumed the William S. Perry
Endowed Chair in Health Promotion at Texas Woman's University and
now commutes between Colorado and Texas.*

*Some of her early ideas, she says, now "seem presump-
tuous . . . but I have always felt a sense of entitlement."*

*A*n interesting assortment of ancestors, a wonderful mother with limitless imagination and physical energy, the right mentors, a firm sense of entitlement, and the good fortune of having an inquisitive mind: these are the gifts of my life for which I am especially grateful. They've helped me with my nursing career, and they've helped me personally.

My generation of nurses was raised on Cherry Ames novels and on the "Ben Casey" television series. My father was a professional writer, so my earliest years were spent in close proximity to typewriters—this conditioning had its own special influence on my approach to nursing. When I was eight or nine years old, for example, my original compositions went off regularly to *Reader's Digest* and other popular magazines—and came back pink-slipped (rejected), just as systematically. Nevertheless, I realized early the importance of persistence and the benefit of putting one's ideas and plans in writing. Eventually this awareness, coupled with an aptitude for report writing, would motivate me to direct my work toward worldwide consultation and grant-writing assignments. These are the affairs that fascinate me now, along with the formulation of health care policies for community health programs for school-age youth. However, the forces driving me toward nursing were entirely different and yet not at all inconsistent with society's expectations for women at that time—1957.

In an era when adolescents defined who they were by what they did (or intended to do), I was fortunate. I knew that I wanted to be a nurse even before I got to high school. What a relief. Nursing held a special appeal for me for several reasons. Helping people was one primary reason, and job security was a second. With the death of my father several years before, I'd had the unpleasant experience of watching my mother struggle to make ends meet and still have enough insurance money left to pay for the college educations of my brothers and myself. Mother had no career, and it didn't take me long to figure out that I needed to protect myself, just in case history was to be repeated. Interestingly, as I write this now, it strikes me that I've always hedged my bets with a variety of options, just in case plan A or plan B didn't quite work out.

Down deep my real career aspiration was acting. This was a logical choice, given the number of Saturday afternoons my friends and I spent with our eyes glued to the screen at the Capital Theatre, barely conscious of anything else except the taste of our salty popcorn. In high school I transferred my interests in the movies to drama classes, and fortunately this experience helped me to overcome my shyness and natural desire for distance and to deal with the social requirements of adolescence. I suspect this initial inclination to the performing arts eventually led to my attraction to teaching, conducting workshops, and making speeches. I found a stage, but a very special one, where the audience is there to learn and not necessarily to be entertained.

Had it not been for my favorite relative, Uncle Jim, my nursing education would have started out much differently than it did. Uncle Jim was a prominent ophthalmologist who on occasion taught in the diploma program associated with his hospital. He believed a college education would eventually become the only legitimate means of entry into the nursing field and convinced me to go to college instead of to the hospital school of nursing. How hard I fought this decision. Fortunately, I lost that fight.

I attended Loretto Heights College in Denver. One year later, I transferred to the University of Iowa College of Nursing. Looking back, I can see that this mix of private and public schooling was most fortunate. At Loretto there were only a dozen of us in the nursing major, and we learned basic sciences in almost tutorial fashion. That learning experience fostered curiosity and creativity. At Iowa the clinical opportunities were far superior to what the smaller Loretto could offer at the time. This was particularly true in the areas that would later become my specialties, pediatric and public health nursing. So I was lucky enough to begin my nursing education with a sense of curiosity mixed with creativity. That was followed with strong clinical experience.

From 1958 to 1961 at Iowa I received an excellent foundation in nursing within a nurturing and positive environment. Nurses were then expected to assume considerable responsibility for patient care. As a result, medical and nursing students frequently found themselves sharing learning experiences. The faculty were expert clinicians who role-modeled nursing at its best. They expected our best.

I remember how proud we were to be nursing students. We were bound to one another with a warm esprit de corps. We were eager to learn it all and to graduate to positions that would bestow on us even more authority and responsibility for patients. I longed for the day when I could finally add RN to my name. In my mind it symbolized my entry into adulthood and a chance to experience all of the wonderful opportunities therein.

While I was in college, Uncle Jim was even more of an influence. During my school vacations he frequently invited me to accompany him on hospital rounds. When he had a particularly interesting case, he invited me to join him in the operating room. This was at the same hospital where I had worked as an aide in high school and college. Inevitably, this created unrest among the other nurses, who complained about this kind of special treatment. However, following Uncle Jim's example, I learned to ignore it. Going along with Uncle Jim was such fun that I was determined that nothing would keep me from it.

My determination, and the ability to withstand criticism, became an important asset later on in my nursing career.

When I at last could add RN to my name, I went to Hawaii to start my nursing career. This was an unusual move in 1961, only a few years after the islands had gained statehood. A friend and I had no difficulty finding positions at Queen's Hospital. I had wanted a job in public health nursing, but I easily settled for my second choice, pediatrics.

Over the next year, while practicing pediatric nursing in an acute care setting, I learned a great deal from the more experienced nurses. They answered my unending stream of questions and helped me improve my clinical skills. Open heart surgery was still a novelty at that time, and I can vividly remember learning how to special the post-op pediatric patients when there was little technology available.

It was during this time that I discovered I could also learn a great deal from patients and their families. My observations of Japanese mothers caring for their children eventually enabled me to learn new and improved ways of dealing with children. Their gentle ways of discovering their children's individual responses to hospitalization and their comforting customs are special memories for me now.

While in Hawaii, I began to realize how important it was for patients to be active participants in their own care. Later I would translate this belief into a consumer health affairs program called Health PACT.

After a few years in pediatrics, I still wanted to try public health nursing, so I returned to the mainland to work as a county public health nurse in Woodbury County, Iowa. In the course of this work, I had my first taste of school nursing and loved it. My entrepreneurial spirit soared as I looked around those school clinics. The potential for independent nursing practice was obvious.

I was also awed to discover that my assignment had once been held by Ann Magnussen, RN, a leader known for her contribution in directing the nursing services for the American Red Cross. I often heard the elderly women from my caseload reminisce about Ms. Magnussen, and I became determined to carry on with the high quality of nursing services for which she was so well remembered. This was at least part of the reason I began devoting time to devising new and different ways to deliver my community health nursing services. While I no longer consciously compete with the memory of Ann Magnussen, I do continue to schedule time for this type of creative planning.

Some of my earlier ideas now seem presumptuous to me, but I must admit that I have always felt a sense of entitlement. I have always felt that I was entitled—no, expected—to invent innovative ways to manage new situations without giving thought to the consequences.

As a public health nurse in a small midwestern community, I learned of a family that was living in two old cars on the outskirts of town. I worked with other community members to move this family into a house with modern conveniences. At the time I knew little about community organization and even less about changing people's life-styles and habits. I helped spread the word about this family who needed help, and donations came from all around. They moved into a nice house, and it was furnished with extravagant and inappropriate gifts.

Within a short time the house began to deteriorate because the family had no idea how to maintain it. The townspeople became disgruntled with me because the family had failed to make major changes in their life-style. I could have retreated in shame, vowing never to tackle a similar situation again, but that wasn't my style.

I looked at the situation and figured out what had worked and what hadn't. Then I applied this new knowledge to another situation and then another, learning more each time. More favorable outcomes emerged every time.

I'm glad I've never been overly concerned with failure. It has kept me going, made me persistent. How did that attitude come about?

My mother taught me not to fear failure. Mona Marie Badgerow Bellaire Kellen is a bona fide risk taker. In 1937, at 21, she convinced her upper-middle-class parents to allow her to follow her husband, a neophyte war correspondent, to China. The two of them made a strikingly handsome couple, and they rose to prominence among the Shanghai international set.

Younger than their associates by 10 to 15 years, they were enthusiastic and explored the Far East with vigor. They regularly sent well-written news stories back to the news service in New York and did radio broadcasts about the Sino-Japanese War. They shot numerous reels of film recording the war-torn parts of Shanghai, disregarding the dangers involved.

My mother was eventually forced to leave China because of the war (and 18-month-old me), but she characteristically waited for the last ship out and filed a thrilling account of the departure. Just as the gangplank was to be raised, Japanese soldiers came on board and arrested many unsuspecting individuals. My mother still recalls that she wondered what to do if the soldiers discovered the false bottom in her carry-on luggage that concealed the information she was smuggling out.

Mother's courage and determination were put to the real test four years later. My father, who had established a fine reputation for himself as a war correspondent, magazine writer, and news reporter for ABC, was killed. The adventurous, glamorous life-style came to an end.

Mother moved my two younger brothers and me back to Iowa, where she had been raised. Despite the absence of excitement, she managed to instill in all three of us a thrill for the environment in which we found ourselves. Daily, we were encouraged to think up wonderful, crazy approaches to living. We learned to think big and to dismiss failure rather than dwell on it, once we had figured out what went wrong. That's how I learned not to be afraid of failure.

It didn't take me long as a public health nurse to realize that I needed more education. I attended graduate school at the University of Minnesota School of Public Health in 1967, and again I had an extremely positive learning experience. There were extraordinary opportunities for interdisciplinary education. I learned to hold my own in discussions and arguments with my colleagues in nursing and with others as well. My coping skills expanded considerably this time. Daily, I stretched myself intellectually and emotionally to develop new concepts, write papers, take tests, and achieve goals that formerly had not even entered my consciousness, and at the end of graduate school I headed west. The pediatric nurse practitioner program at the University of Colorado was just beginning, and I was eager to combine this role with my graduate degree in public health nursing.

Soon after my arrival in Denver, I met two mentors who would help me shape my career in primary care. Loretta Ford taught me to think, value, and question nursing in ways I hadn't thought possible—and in the end I emerged from the process loyal to my field. Henry Silver contributed to my knowledge of business, grant writing, and politics.

I must admit that I did not always agree with my self-designated mentors, but I will always appreciate the time they spent with me and the doors of opportunity each one opened for me. They taught me endurance, a quality both of them possessed in abundance. For those two, 10- and 12-hour days were customary. To my knowledge, they never turned down new projects because energy stores were lacking.

Five of us graduated in the Spring, 1968, class of Pediatric Nurse Practitioner School. Several of us have maintained our friendships over the years, including two of my close associates at the University of Colorado today. Together, we learned to perform a number of tasks people customarily expected physicians to perform in those days: physical examinations, well baby care, care of common childhood illness and injuries, simple lab work. I was grateful that I had the graduate public health nursing background and role in which I could fit this new knowledge.

At Colorado, I found myself linked to a movement that I knew would be historically relevant. The nurse practitioner role made sense to me. I knew that, in time, it would revolutionize practice. Maybe I had gained some of Uncle Jim's talent for looking into the future of nursing. At the time, though, it appeared to me that the role might not survive. Time and time again, I saw and heard the strong criticism that organized nursing had for the role. Medicine was less vocal then, but as soon as they discovered that the nurse practitioners refused to relinquish their nursing functions for an assistant role, they became just as belligerent.

I ignored the criticism, just as I had learned to do years earlier in the hospital with Uncle Jim. I found a focus, and I clung to it. The health needs of school-age children and their families became my special commitment.

I embarked on a career with the Tricounty Health Department in an office just north of Denver. Subsequently, I worked briefly at a private group practice in Denver and then began working back at the University of Colorado with the School Nurse Practitioner Program. My job was to develop the curriculum and act as den mother for the first group of nurses that came into the program. That was 34 classes ago, and I've been there ever since.

It was the perfect opportunity.

Beatrice Kalisch

Beatrice Kalisch, PhD, RN, FAAN, is
Director, Nursing Consultation Services,
Arthur Young & Company

❖

Beatrice Kalisch says that the most important professional decision she ever made was to become a nurse. Famous for the nursing image study that she and her historian husband Philip Kalisch did in the late 1970s, she spent the first half of the 1980s building on it, writing about it, and speaking in almost every state and in many countries abroad. She was also then chair of the Parent-Child Nursing Program at the University of Michigan, including graduate programs in maternity nursing and nursing of children, as well as a pediatric nurse practitioner program.

Finally, with two children giving her pleasure and sapping her energy, Bea gave up her work at the university and agreed to join a team of health professionals at one of the Big Eight accounting firms, helping providers cope with the new competitive business environment of health care.

I was born in Tullahoma, Tennessee, in October 1943, the first child of Peter and Margaret Peterson. My father, who was serving in the military then, was stationed at the air base there. He had emigrated from Denmark several years before and had recently married my mother, who had grown up in Tennessee. Once World War II was over, we moved to Omaha, where my father worked for the utilities district and my mother stayed at home in the traditional role of wife and mother. I had two younger siblings, a sister and a brother.

When I think back on the events in my childhood that might have led me to choose nursing as a career, one key event was that I served as a candy striper when I was about 11 years old. Every other day I would walk to the hospital, which was probably a mile and a half away, and spend several hours there. I loved it! At first I worked with an occupational therapist who was assisting polio victims, and later I got involved in feeding those patients. I felt so good (and a little scared) sitting on my stool by their beds. They seemed happy to have me there, too.

It was the experience of sitting on a bus next to a nurse in full uniform, cape and all, that really finalized my decision to become a nurse. Also, I had admired the nurses who took care of me when I had an appendectomy, and of course, I collected every one of the Cherry Ames books and read each of them several times.

I never really swayed from my decision to choose nursing as an occupation, even though my dad really wanted me to be a teacher. He had always wanted to be a teacher himself and had never achieved that goal. In the end, he wasn't overly disappointed. His biggest concern was that I go to college, and he pushed higher education on me all my life. (He thought it was great when I got my master's degree, but when I started working on a doctoral degree and he still had no grandchildren, I think he thought he had maybe pushed a bit too hard.) When it came time to go to high school, for example, I had the choice of going to the school that almost everybody else from my grade school went to, or to another one that better prepared students for college. My father pushed me to go to the school with the tougher standards, even though it meant leaving all of my friends behind. I fought the whole idea until one day when my father said, "Just try it for a year, and if you aren't happy, then you can transfer." I thought so much of him and I so appreciated the fact that he did seem to understand how I felt that I went along with his urging. Once there, I made new friends and liked it. My father always fostered a strong belief in my capabilities and encouraged me to do whatever it was I wanted to do.

In high school I belonged to the Future Nurses of America and took numerous courses in math, chemistry, and biology. I also enrolled in several Spanish courses (anything to avoid Latin, even though everyone seemed to think a nurse would need it). I went steady with one boy all through high school and therefore was never without a date for the school dances. I remember collecting stickers for each dance and plastering them all over my notebooks and wearing lots of crinolines.

I was full of energy and ambition as a child. I started working when I was nine doing odd jobs around a nearby ice-cream shop, and as soon as I was old enough, they hired me to work inside. I always had a part-time job after that. I think my parents encouraged it, but it also seemed like the right thing to do. I needed ways to use my energy, and I loved the spending money.

I went to camp for a couple of weeks almost every summer. One summer, I told the camp nurse I had chosen nursing as my career, and she asked, "Well, where are you going to go to school?" I listed several diploma schools and she responded, "Have you considered the University of Nebraska?" In the face of my blank stare, she proceeded to explain why I should choose the baccalaureate program. I accepted her offer to take me to meet the director of the school. I am grateful for that because I do not think I would have enrolled in a generic BSN program without her encouragement.

When I finished high school, I immediately enrolled at the university and took summer courses. I thought the curriculum was going to be so difficult that I would need a head start. I took courses in history and English. Since I had received advanced placement for the English course, my professor took a special interest in me. She tried to get me to switch majors from nursing to English. The thought intrigued me, but I was determined to stick with nursing. A much more monumental event occurred in the history class—I met my future husband, Phil, who assisted and tutored me. That was the beginning of a four-year courtship and now a 22-year marriage.

In terms of my nursing education, the first year was spent at the university campus, and the following three years in the school of nursing on the medical campus. I still remember being afraid that I would not be able to pass all those chemistry courses, but it really wasn't that difficult. My first clinical experience is permanently etched in my memory. I had an instructor who could have given the word hyperactive a new meaning. Around her, I did everything wrong. I became convinced that I wouldn't make it as a nurse, but once I advanced to another instructor, things changed. My new instructor sat me down and said, "What are you afraid of?" After that, my confidence steadily grew. My entire class lived on one floor of the dorm; I think there were around 37 of us, and we got to know each other extremely well, which had both advantages and disadvantages. Certainly, by the end of three years, we were ready to graduate and get away from one another. Yet we had developed some meaningful relationships that still flourish.

Phil and I got married in April 1965, just before I graduated. He had been teaching at Northwest Missouri State University in Maryville, Missouri, about 90 miles from Omaha. Once I graduated, I spent the summer there, and then we moved back to Pennsylvania where he started working on his doctoral degree. While he was in school, I worked as a staff nurse in the pediatric unit in a local hospital. I hated that job, not because of the work, but because my philosophy of care did not mesh with the head nurse's philosophy. The first thing she told me during my orientation (which basically consisted of a walk around the unit) was that the hospitalized children were always better off without their parents around. Having no political skills at all, I agreed with her. I also remember the

LPNs. They managed me, not the other way around. I did struggle to implement the things I had learned in school. I enjoyed being with the patients rather than sitting in the back room having coffee. One day, I was playing with a nine-year-old boy who had just learned he would miss a year of school because of illness. In walked the head nurse, who said, "Nurses aren't for play." This led me to look for another job, and I wound up teaching in a three-year diploma program in Philipsburg, Pennsylvania.

We then moved to Baltimore so that I could pursue my master's degree at the University of Maryland. Phil continued to work on his doctoral degree and on his dissertation. Once I completed my master's degree, I went to work at American University in Washington, D.C., and developed the first pediatric nursing course for them. I would have been happy to stay in that position, but Phil kept pushing me to go back to school. "You had better do it now while you have the chance," he insisted, thinking we might move to some place where it would not be possible for me to continue in school (and we did). So, I was grateful that I did go ahead and enroll again at the University of Maryland on the College Park campus to study human development. (There were only a couple of doctoral programs in nursing then.)

My major advisor, Hugh Perkins, seemed to take a special interest in me. He was the closest thing to a mentor I ever had. I had just completed all of my course work when Phil got an offer to teach at West Texas State University in Canyon, Texas. I wound up doing my dissertation research long distance. One of my committee members (male) predicted, "You'll probably never finish your doctoral program now." That statement only made me more resolved to reach my goal. I worked night and day on my dissertation, and one year later I was back for my oral defense.

After that, I remember thinking, "Now what?" In fact, I felt a little let down, wondering, "Is this all there is?" So I went to work as a clinical specialist at a hospital in Amarillo, Texas. Later I taught and was curriculum coordinator in an associate degree nursing program for a year in the same city. Subsequently, we moved to the University of Southern Mississippi in Hattiesburg, where I first was a member of the nursing faculty and later chaired the baccalaureate program in nursing. We moved north to the University of Michigan three years later, where I became chair of the Parent-Child Nursing Department. During those years, work was everything to us. Phil and I went for six years without taking a single vacation.

During that period, Phil and I launched our first major joint research project, which was a study of the impact of the U.S. Cadet Nurse Corps on American nursing. We were happy when we were awarded our first grant, couldn't believe our good fortune, and talked of nothing else for a week. Of course, we had severely underestimated the budgetary demands. Not only did we put in 80 to 90 hours a week to get the work done, but we also applied for and received a supplemental grant about the same size as our original award. We were on our way as funded researchers.

The Cadet Corps study led to some contract research we completed for the Division of Nursing of the U.S. Public Health Service on the impact of federal funds on nursing education and practice. Interestingly enough, that study in turn led to our nursing image and nursing news research. We had interviewed many senators and congressmen as a part of the data collection process for the contract study. Many of their comments led us to conclude that the stereotypical views of nursing were largely based on mass media–generated images. In fact, many of those interviewed referred to nurses who were popular in the media at that period of time, particularly on television. As we tried to convince them that nursing needed research dollars, they would indicate that, by their perceptions, nurses' logical involvement in biomedical research would be in supportive roles such as collecting data for biomedical investigations. Why would nurses need their own research money? "What are nursing research questions?" they would ask. Similarly, when we talked about demonstration projects for nursing practice, they questioned how nurses could be in charge of the delivery of any important health care services. "What do nurses do— don't they basically follow physicians' orders?" And so the conversations went. At that time we were also experiencing a shortage of nurses.

All of this led us to think about the importance of the image of the nurse. It became apparent to us that our first challenge was to document the image of nurses over time. We had a hunch that the image had been more positive in earlier decades, so we developed another research grant application. We based part of the content analysis methodology on a study that had been funded by the U.S. Office of Education concerning the image of schoolteachers in the mass media. We submitted our application and soon got a call from the Division of Nursing saying that grant officials were going to make a site visit. In the intervening weeks before the visit, we worked hard to refine our approach, to develop some of our research tools, and to refine some of our measurement tools.

The site visit was key to our getting the grant, and we have always been grateful to those people who had a broad enough perspective of nursing to see the importance of this particular line of inquiry. Nurses did not consider image to be important back then. In fact, many viewed image and nursing as if the two terms were like oil and water— what did they have to do with each other? That was before most leaders in the profession recognized the significance of the issue. However, we were able to convince the site visit team that this was a worthwhile research problem and that we had the skills and abilities to conduct the study. Not only did they approve the grant, but they suggested we double our budget.

That study turned out to be exhaustive; it took us months just to collect data from various novels, films, and television programs that contained nurse characters and themes about nursing. We worked exceedingly hard and uncovered vast amounts of data—more than we ever expected when we initiated the study. Each of the novels had to be read and coded. Each of the films had to be rented or purchased, then viewed and coded. The same was true for television programs. We received about 10,000 clippings of newspaper articles about nurses and nursing each year, and they had to be analyzed in a similar fashion. The staff had to be trained to code data, and their reliability had to be checked. It was an extremely ambitious study, but one that we felt was worth all of the effort we put into it.

It was also during those years that we wrote many journal articles and several books reporting the results of our research. Our first major book was *The Advance of American Nursing,* published in 1978 by Little Brown, Inc. Even though designated as a history of nursing text, it was incredible how much primary source material was required for the book because the field was so underdeveloped. In other fields there are commonly many studies already published on which to build such a survey.

Again, many nights, days, weekends, and lots of energy and commitment made it possible to complete that work and those works that followed: *Politics of Nursing, Nursing Involvement in Health Planning, Images of Nurses on Television, The Changing Image of the Nurse,* and over 80 journal articles. We also edited a series of a dozen books titled *Studies in Nursing Management,* and I completed an extensive annotated bibliography and a couple of studies on child abuse during those years. The work became easier, but it still required time and effort. Phil and I did manage to collect enough antiques to fill a house and donated quite a lot of time to political matters, however. Most of my time was spent teaching, administering the department, working on research, writing, and making speeches all over the country. Although we had been giving speeches for years, around 1980 it seemed like all of a sudden we were being asked to speak a lot more often than ever before. This took us to almost every state and several countries and allowed us the good fortune to meet many excellent nurses.

I was thrilled in 1977 to learn that the executive committee and the dean had selected me to be appointed to the newly established Shirley Titus Distinguished Professor of Nursing chair. Frankly, I wasn't expecting it. It was one of the first chairs in nursing, and I felt honored.

It was also during those years in my role as chair of Parent-Child Nursing that I developed, with the faculty, a master's degree program first in maternity nursing, and then in nursing of children. We wrote and received funding for both programs from the Division of Nursing under the Advanced Nurse Training Grant Program. I also ran a pediatric nurse practitioner program for a time, and I went to Case Western Reserve University to get postdoctoral preparation as a nurse practitioner, since that content had not been offered in my previous educational programs. In addition, I participated in the development and refinement of the PhD in nursing program at the University of Michigan. It was tough to get it approved by our graduate school, but we made it.

Another significant event occurred in 1979, when a large number of the students and faculty became concerned about rescission of federal nursing education funds (that the Carter Administration had proposed) and succeeded in obtaining the support of the House Appropriations Committee in a quest to restore this money for expenditures on nursing. As a result, our students decided to go to Washington and lobby Congress. We developed materials for them to use in meeting with the congressmen, senators, and their staffs. We rented a bus and contacted nurses in other states as well as in Michigan. In March 1979, we all met on Capitol Hill at a designated location. I still don't believe it worked out as well as it did. It was a wonderful experience, and at the end, we were all able to sit in the House chamber and watch the rescission bill fail before the 435-member House. Several nurses of political consequence today received their political initiation in this group effort.

Once we completed the initial image study, we moved into using newspaper articles to forecast nursing trends. This is basically the approach used by John Naisbitt in his book *Megatrends.* That practice led us to get involved in futures research, which has been very exciting because the evolution of the nation's health care system promises to provide many innovative roles for nurses.

With such heavy involvement in our careers during our research period, the decision to become parents had been pushed aside. As we grew older, we realized we very much wanted children. Philip (now three years old) and Melanie (two years old) are truly the joys of our lives. They certainly require a lot of our energy, but they give me more pleasure than anything else has in my entire life.

In the spring of 1986, I was approached by Arthur Young, one of the Big Eight accounting firms, and was asked to consider a newly created position as a principal in the firm, in charge of nursing consultation services. After many interviews with key Arthur Young partners, I decided this opportunity represented a once-in-a-lifetime chance to move into a new arena and to make a positive impact on nursing in an entirely new and different way. As a member of a team of health professionals (hospital administrator, marketer, finance specialist, strategic planner, hospital industrial engineer, and hospital information specialist), I work closely with nurses, chief executive officers, and boards of governance in many hospitals across the nation. Providers need a great deal of assistance in coping with the new competitive business environment of health care and also with the numerous issues that are creating the nurse shortage.

In looking back, I would say there are several people who have had a profound impact on my life. First, there were my parents, particularly my father, who had high expectations of me and didn't let the fact that I was a female limit my aspirations. Second, there was my husband, Phil, who departed from the stereotype of the 1960s male in that he actively encouraged and fully supported me to pursue a true career, and who always has and still does carry his share of the ever-present household and child care responsibilities. My major advisor in my doctoral program, Hugh Perkins, was also key to my success. In the final analysis, the most important professional decision I made was to become a nurse. I love nursing and have never regretted my decision.

Lucie S. Kelly

Lucie S. Kelly, PhD, RN, FAAN, is
Editor of *Nursing Outlook* and Professor
of Public Health and Nursing in the
Schools of Public Health and Nursing,
Columbia University

Lucie Kelly's bright intellect and her sparkling, brashly attractive personality have been a part of her being from childhood. The daughter of immigrant parents, she came to America from Germany at the age of four, and she hit the ground running. As an avid reader and eager learner, she was an A student who took advantage of every scholarship or grant available. She even persuaded her initially reluctant father that she was a worthy educational investment. Combining communication skills—writing, speaking, and acting—with the courage to tackle anything and everything that came her way, she moved quickly up the educational ladder and into a variety of leadership roles. Recognizing that nursing isn't an easy career but cherishing her successes, she reached the pinnacle of her career when her granddaughter said proudly, "I want to go to college and be a nurse like you."

My mother tells me that when we were emigrating from Germany to America, I repeatedly escaped her watchful eye to climb the steps to the first-class section of the passenger ship *Bremen*. There she would find me chatting with the passengers with all the insouciance of a four-year-old who didn't know she didn't belong. I liked to tell the passengers of this wonderful adventure to join my father who, after repaying his fare to the distant cousins who sponsored him, had sent for us. I could hardly wait to get to America because I adored my father and it had been six long months since we had last seen him.

I'm sure I didn't think about the fact that I couldn't speak English, and that my parents could barely manage the language. Nor did I know that we had arrived at the start of the Great Depression and that the job my father had to take was a lowly one in a small factory. I did realize early on and into my adolescence that my parents were haunted by the devastating inflation in Germany that they had fled, and while we never lacked necessities, the purchase of luxuries of any kind was debated seriously and often rejected. It was important in my family to work hard, be thrifty, and never fail. I was held to those standards from childhood, and I was embarrassed (and sometimes punished) if I did not achieve as expected.

I was eager to go to school, and I loved it. I was also lucky to have a caring first-grade teacher who took an interest in me, the little immigrant kid. There were no second-language classes, and although I spoke some English by then, I learned the language correctly from her, being careful all through school years to make sure that my spelling and grammar were perfect. My special joy was reading, and it was a wonderful surprise to be told by a teacher that there was actually a library outside the school where I could take home books free. My mother and I walked three miles or so to the library in all kinds of weather, she to choose her German books, and I, anything that caught my fancy. By then, I wouldn't speak German except when I had to at home; I was a little ashamed. (I relearned it in college and later took my doctoral language exam in German.)

Overall, I liked school a lot. I had my share of indifferent, perhaps incompetent, teachers, but mostly I remember those who broadened my horizons and probably helped form my future interests. I enjoyed art and music and became a fairly decent cellist. The ancient world was made real to me, and I enjoyed six years of Latin. There were teachers who nurtured my writing skills, which somehow evolved with no conscious effort on my part. I even liked most of my math and science teachers, although I hated those subjects, with the exception of the social sciences.

Was I a teacher's pet? Of course. What else could be expected from a student who was smart, was eager to learn, always did her homework, was never disobedient, and rarely broke the rules? I enjoyed reciting and made presentations in assemblies, debates, and other school activities. While for many years I was nervous before a big group, I always prepared carefully and seemed able to reach an audience. I also had some skill in presenting material in a different way, always with a catchy beginning. I could think on my feet, and in debates I could anticipate the opponents' points and counter them.

I don't know where all that came from. Perhaps one factor was my love of language and words and my vivid imagination, all encouraged by my early teachers. Not long ago, I found a copy of the high school graduation speech I gave and it was good, even by my current standards. I also found notebooks with essays, poems, and stories, mostly hopelessly romantic, and not bad efforts for grade school. In junior high, I wrote for and then was editor of the school paper, and in high school I edited the school magazine. In an unsophisticated way, I understood even then how I could influence others—although I like to think I persuaded for good causes. (I was also very idealistic.) I wanted to be at the top. In my high school yearbook, I wrote about myself, "I'll get there, somehow."

The "there" was college, a remote possibility given the fact that my father couldn't see spending money for that kind of education. (Later, he took complete credit for my PhD. Who knows, perhaps he earned it.) He had little real notion of what college was all about. Our family in Europe were working-class people. Attuned as my father was to the general impossibility of the times for any of them to be admitted to the German "gymnasium" or academic high school, my desire seemed unrealistic to him, particularly since I had it in my mind to study law or journalism. My father was willing to pay for some further education, but it had to be practical and affordable. He took great pride in the fact that he had completed a difficult apprenticeship in Germany and that he designed and made beautiful things in metal. I never could get interested in learning to type, and somehow I found nursing. I don't know how—friends, the family doctor, an early hospitalization—who knows? Ignorance about nursing schools in those days must have been universal. I applied at the hospital used by our well-respected family doctor—a school so inadequate that, as I discovered later, it was on the verge of losing its state approval. No one guided me elsewhere, not even my admired school counselor, who encouraged my dream of going to college. However, with her help, and without my parents' knowledge, I applied for a scholarship at the University of Pittsburgh. For program choice, I wrote down nursing, figuring that if I did succeed in getting a scholarship, this choice would mollify my father. It never occurred to me to apply to another college. Ever since I had walked up the path to Pitt's soaring Cathedral of Learning, I was fixed on being a part of that environment.

Miracle of miracles (or perhaps not, with my straight A average, my career choice during those war years, and my heartfelt statement), I received what was then called the senatorial scholarship, which gave me half-tuition. But what of the rest? I prepared a speech for my father—if he would just let me live at home, I would work part-time to pay the rest of the tuition. Just let me go to college! Whether my speaking skills were honed by desperation or whether my father was, after all, proud and bemused by my accomplishment and determination, he agreed to my plan. In fact, although I did work and paid for my books and other expenses, he covered the balance of my tuition until I later received another scholarship.

College was not easy, especially since I worked as a department store clerk almost every day and had to study at odd times. Moreover, I was now with intellectual peers. When I was taken on as a student assistant by an English professor, I had to give up my position as reporter for the college newspaper. I had already bypassed the sorority scene—no time and no money. On the other hand, I took pride in having the English professor gradually entrust to me the responsibility of correcting the required essays of the Air Cadets. I was excited when the most esteemed freshman English professor said that I was a talented writer and spent time helping me to improve. I thought our writing assignments were fun; almost everyone else viewed them with horror. I even managed good grades with the next English professor, who graded me down when he disagreed with what I said, although he begrudgingly approved of how I said it. (Today, sometimes when I say or write something controversial, I think of him, but it merely stops the pen for a reflective moment.)

I loved college just as I'd loved school before, although the commuting by streetcar, the time pressure, the outside job that I tolerated, and the inability to participate in all the extras that were a part of college life deflated my dream balloon a little. Yet, the prenursing group—idealistic and excited about "nurse training" and relieved at being part of the Nurse Cadet Corps with all tuition, books, housing, and uniforms paid, along with a stipend—made it almost worthwhile to be rushed through what I considered the college part of my education.

What was nursing like in a collegiate school from 1944 to 1947? Perhaps not terribly different from the best diploma schools. Our theory courses were rigorous, but we never worked nights, and our clinical hours (often split) were planned around our class hours. I was not particularly happy or unhappy in my classes, although I still didn't like the sciences. (I made Sigma Theta Tau, nursing's honor society, but didn't accept the invitation.) Like most of my classmates, I liked working with patients, but was often afraid of the head nurses and sometimes the teachers. I always looked forward to the next rotation, but I had no favorite clinical specialty. I can't say that that part of my education enhanced either my writing or speaking skills. Yet, one teacher (we didn't think of them as professors) persuaded me to take a speech course instead of abnormal psychology, a course which I thought would show seriousness of purpose. It was fun, and I was a sensation, especially when I demonstrated how to use a gun (with live ammunition) after lessons from a boyfriend who had returned from the war. I always did like doing the unusual, and for the first time in a long time, I was rewarded for doing so with an A+.

Good and bad memories from those years are mixed. I remember my last day "on duty." I was married and pregnant, and with rare exception my head nurses and supervisors, almost all single women, repeatedly chastised me for that unheard-of condition for a student nurse. I was frequently given the most difficult and demanding patients and was criticized constantly. If it had not been for my husband (who kept reminding me that I had only a little time left to finish) and my own will to prove to my father that I *would* finish, although married, I would have left. On that last day at 11 PM I finished my charting, picked up my bag, and said, "I'm never coming back."

Famous last words! When my daughter Gay was three months old, my husband had an accident, and off to work I went. (After all, wasn't that one of the lures of nursing—

always a job available?) I chose psychiatric nursing in the university hospital, primarily because it paid the munificent salary of $201.50 per month, considerably more than what the other hospitals were paying. It was the day of electric shock and diabetic coma therapy, of prefrontal lobotomies and long drug-induced sleeps to quiet patients, as well as psychotherapy. Violence among patients was frequent, and it was not unusual to go home physically bruised. Moreover, even in this model hospital, control (much less care) of mental illness was elusive, and it was depressing to see the endless cycle of discharge and readmission. Still, I might have stayed, except that the unmarried ex-military director of nursing recanted her promise that I need not work nights because of my baby. So after six months there, I left and began a four-year cycle as the classic "appliance nurse"— working when we needed additional funds for an appliance, a car, a house.

Professionally, those were dormant years—a little part-time staff nursing, occupational health, and private duty. There was the same bureaucracy I had resisted as a student—continual nursing shortages with no time to care for patients as I would have liked. Private duty nursing was little more rewarding, and the system was repressive. The "best" patients were assigned to the single nurses from that hospital's school, then in descending order, to the married "inside" nurses, to the single "outside" graduates, and finally to the married "outside" graduates. I usually got the patients with entire body burns from steel mill accidents, communicable diseases, or other "undesirable" conditions. Oh, yes, joining the ANA was a requirement, but to most it was just one more price to pay rather than a professional responsibility. I was not happy with my choice of career.

The turning point for me came in 1953 when a night supervisor at McKeesport Hospital suggested to the director that I might make a good faculty member. I was a "good" nurse and had a baccalaureate besides. It looked like a great opportunity and a step up. Preparing for teaching the first class on short notice was the first intellectual challenge I'd had in nursing for some time, and I enjoyed it—every bit of it.

I worked hard to be a good teacher, studying ways to improve. Best of all, I seemed to have a talent for teaching in the clinical area and in the classroom. I liked the students; they liked and trusted me. I spent extra time with them, advising, counseling, nurturing the brightest (the beginning of my mentoring pattern). Most of all, it was heady to feel that I was developing, yes, molding, these young women into the "right" kind of nurses with high standards of care. I was soon in charge of the first-year program and found that I also liked (and was good at) being an administrator, selecting, supervising, and evaluating faculty, and working with others in the faculty and hospital to strengthen the program. I started to take a few classes at Pitt again and found that the local nurses' association meetings actually had something to offer (especially contacts). Those were generally happy years of professional growth and satisfaction that culminated in my returning to Pitt full-time in 1956 for graduate study, thanks to new federal legislation that provided nurse traineeships.

Graduate school was—well—different. There was a greater degree of collegiality between teachers and students, and generally, more self-direction was required. Once more, my desire to do well, the ease with which I was able to write and speak, and my excitement about learning paid off. Although I'd started with the recognition that even though I'd been teaching, I needed the degree (or would eventually), being in the classroom was generally stimulating and rewarding. Nevertheless, I looked forward to returning to McKeesport Hospital School of Nursing as educational director. It wasn't easy to go to school, manage a home, fulfill my responsibilities to husband and child, and overcome the feeling of being different in suburbia. I was certainly the only wife going to college for anything, much less a master's. Doctoral study later (while working) really put me beyond the pale.

As my program was ending, Dr. Ruth Kuehn, the nursing dean, invited (summoned?) me to lunch at the prestigious University Club. Once more, my life was changed. With her usual charm, but in short order, she informed me that she had selected me out of that graduate class as someone with the ability to become a leader in nursing and to do doctoral work, and eventually to become a dean. She said she would take me under her wing, beginning with an appointment on the faculty as assistant professor and later as chair of surgical nursing. I was to start within a month. The elegant luncheon was wasted on me as my head whirled; none of this had ever entered my mind. I knew it would mean a lot of hard work, but somehow I also knew that I had to do it. My very supportive husband was pleased for me, and I entered a new career phase.

University teaching returned me to earth rather quickly. This new world was not consistently wonderful. Yet Dr. Kuehn was the classic mentor, and I never lost my respect, admiration, and affection for her. A respected national nursing leader, she groomed me, trained me, opened doors for me, challenged me, tested me, supported me, and protected me. She gave me unheard-of opportunities to mingle with and relate to her peers and to move into situations that tested my mettle; then she critiqued what I did. She helped me to select my first research project and guided me to the right journal for publication, *Nursing Outlook,* where it was published with almost no editing. It is a wonder I didn't frame that article! Another senior faculty member put me on the local NLN speakers' bureau after pressing me none too gently to become a member, while still another pushed me into more local and state ANA activities. I did all of this, along with post-master's classes in the School of Nursing and Education, while adjusting to teaching and, a little later, to educational administration at a middle level.

It was a juggling act, especially as I became much more involved in the Pennsylvania Nurses Association on a state level. But it was finally necessary to choose a doctoral program, and that was difficult. Dr. Kuehn and I went through the program potentials. Without enthusiasm, I finally decided on educational psychology and set off to see the department head in the School of Education.

Once more, luck, fate, or timing dealt me a good hand. Dr. George Fahey had just been given approval to start a new master's and PhD program in higher education. As he described it, we both realized that it was made to order for me. With my academic record, experience and education in teaching and nursing, and the intent to prepare for educational administering, I was the kind of student he wanted. He became my advisor and secondary mentor. Again, a nurse traineeship allowed me to become a full-time student, and Dr. Kuehn readily gave me a leave of absence.

It was an exciting year. The teachers of this select first group were the top university administrators, including the chancellor. We were treated more like colleagues than students. Before long, I had developed a dissertation proposal based on the research needs cited in the 1963 Surgeon General's report on nursing. Consequently, I received a research grant from the Department of Health, Education and Welfare (DHEW, now the Department of Health and Human Services) that enabled me to finish my dissertation during the grant year. It was a lengthy descriptive study on nursing education, resulting in the prediction that the nurses of the future would be educated at two levels, associate and baccalaureate, and would be licensed as practical nurse and professional nurse. I completed this in 1965, just before the ANA position paper on nursing education.

By this time Dr. Kuehn had retired to Wisconsin, although she had stayed on my committee until I successfully defended and became the first PhD graduate of the higher education program. (I stayed in touch with her until she died in 1986; she told me after she retired how proud she was of her protégé.)

Pitt now had a series of acting deans. Returning from my leave, I served as assistant dean, but within six months I had an offer from the board of McKeesport Hospital to become the director of nursing. The enticement was strong. I got what I wanted—in writing. Although I'd never even been a head nurse, I believed my own propaganda that a nurse administrator was a powerful influence in changing nursing care. Therefore, I didn't know what couldn't be done, and so did it: flexible schedules; self-governance; tuition reimbursement (with key college classes brought on site); nurse participation on medical committees; nurse decision making on equipment and other purchases and in design and functions of new units; the first clinical specialist in the area; and 24-hour in-service education by a full-time staff. In the school of nursing we brought back all the good students who hadn't been allowed to complete their schooling because of marriage, discontinued the age limits and the live-in requirements, and recruited the first male students. That meant having a good administrative team and good communication with the board, the community, and the alumni. It was particularly important when I was able to gain acceptance of closing this accredited diploma school as the good community college associate degree program began. I felt strongly that the move to higher education was inevitable.

At the same time, as the only PhD nurse to head a community hospital nursing service, I found myself in demand as a speaker nationally and became president of PNA and a member or chair of community, interprofessional, and other committees and groups. The experience I gained equalled another PhD. It was a generally satisfying situation, but I became restless. When I was offered the position of professor and chair of the nursing department at California State College, Los Angeles, then identified as the largest baccalaureate nursing program in the United States, I accepted. Now I had the "dean-type" position Dr. Kuehn had wanted for me.

I stayed for three years that were just as stimulating and rewarding as those at McKeesport, with more emphasis on political activities. I was appointed by Governor Ronald Reagan to the Medical Board's committee on physicians' assistants. I became even more involved in professional groups, and I continued to do considerable speaking. In addition, I became a strong advocate of the nurse practitioner role and, at Cal State, was responsible for initiating one of the first nurse practitioner master's programs. The reason for my departure was romantic, not professional. I had been divorced for several years when I met and later married a New Yorker, so I said good-bye to California and prepared to resume a career in the East.

When my new husband asked me not to take a full-time position for a while, I was a little nonplussed. I filled the next two "nonworking" years by writing a third edition of *Dimensions of Professional Nursing,* teaching several classes at Teachers College and one at Russell Sage, becoming a part-time staff member at the NLN in the research department (which included making site visits for the NLN for the open curriculum project), and becoming involved in the New Jersey State Nurses' Association. When I attended one of the NJSNA meetings, I introduced myself to Anne Somers, a health economist, who promptly recruited me for her Office of Consumer Health Education (OCHE) at the College of Medicine and Dentistry of New Jersey. I also became an adjunct associate professor of community medicine at Rutgers Medical School. My vacation had ended.

Being "out of nursing" brought some criticism from my nursing colleagues who said nurses with doctorates, then numbering only a few thousand, were needed on the nursing scene. I must say that that annoyed me. I hadn't lost touch with nursing. I taught seminars on nursing and patient education to medical students and worked with a variety of hospitals and other agencies to integrate, sometimes introduce, health education for patients and the public. It gave me the opportunity to interact closely with individuals in other fields, to testify before a Congressional committee (I'd already had experience with state legislative committees), and generally to have nursing seen in a different light in a different setting. Before the year was out, I was offered the position of Director of OCHE when Anne Somers resigned; yet I could not overlook another opportunity that came my way at the same time.

The dean of Columbia University's School of Public Health invited me to join the faculty as the school's "presence in nursing." Other than my undergraduate study, I had no public health nursing training, but that was not what this dean was looking for. He wanted a nationally recognized nurse to represent the school and wanted her to have an impact on the public health faculty. It was an intriguing offer, particularly since my desire for a joint appointment in the School of Nursing was agreed to.

Even before the appointment was firmed up, I was asked to join a Columbia team advising the Shah of Iran on education and administration in his developing medical center in Tehran. That was probably the deciding factor, since I found working in this international environment to be very exciting. (It was the beginning of professional visits, consultations, and lectures in Lebanon, Egypt, Israel, Ireland, Scotland, Spain, the Soviet Union, Kenya, Thailand, Taiwan, Japan, Korea, China, and Brazil.)

So, in the fall of 1975, I became a professor of public health and nursing. Although my primary appointment (and office) was in the School of Public Health, I taught and participated actively in both programs. After a year, my proposal for a nurse administrator program, including the option of a joint degree with nursing, was funded by the W.K. Kellogg Foundation. Developing that interdisciplinary program, with its year-long residencies with top nurse administrators all over the country, and watching the graduates successfully assume responsible positions was probably one of the most satisfactory professional experiences I've had. I like to think that I brought back into nursing nurses who were ready to turn away and look at other career options. As role models, they now had four strong nurse faculty with doctorates in the program—nurses who had broad professional interests and who were bright, attractive, and articulate—good teachers who could write, do research, and maintain a deep interest in the students while managing families and a career. It seemed to make a difference to the nurses—and others.

The years at Columbia have been interrupted only by a leave during which I became the first executive director of the Mid-Atlantic Regional Nursing Association (MARNA), in its developmental year. This too was a rewarding and challenging period, again providing opportunities to expand the influence of nursing and to meet key individuals in government and organizations.

In addition, upon request of the dean and the faculty of the Division of Health Administration, I twice stepped into the position of Acting Head during periods of crisis and helped put the division back on an even keel. (Neither of those times did I want that position permanently, although I've always said that health administration needed to be controlled more by humanistic nurses. It's more fun at this stage in my career to have the freedom of a tenured professor without the restraints of being an administrator.)

During all those years, I found satisfaction in continued participation in professional activities, including election to the ANA Board of Directors. Most exciting of all was being elected president of Sigma Theta Tau, which at the end of my term became international. Conventions, workshops, speeches, visiting professorships, and TV and radio presentations became an even bigger part of my life, and I missed only South Dakota in my professional treks.

Another highlight was the opportunity to write a monthly column for *Nursing Outlook*. I called it End Paper, and as editor Pat Lewis said, "Now the readers have two editorials, one in the front and one in the back." I had free rein to say what I wanted, a privilege I cherished. What I wrote drew accolades and anger, but always comments like, "You sure say it like it is." When *Nursing Outlook* became bi-monthly in 1982, I was asked to become editor. For all of its complexities, that appointment is something I value highly—professionally and personally.

The third edition of *Dimensions of Professional Nursing,* my first plunge into book publication, went very well and was followed by a fourth and fifth edition, also successful. The need for a less detailed, less complex version of that content became apparent so *The Nursing Experience: Trends, Challenges and Transitions* followed in 1986. The environment at Columbia, where these kinds of activities are expected, encouraged this professional lifestyle.

An autobiography, however short, tends to encourage reflection as well as remembrance. That somewhat disillusioned baccalaureate nursing graduate certainly did an about-face. And why shouldn't I have? Nursing has given me opportunities, diversity, rewards, and honors that are not easily matched in other fields. I haven't regretted any of the career choices I made, although sometimes I'm amazed at my nerve in having accepted them. Of course, I'm glad that I succeeded. I'm proud of the four honorary doctorates, various citations, medallions, and other honors that came to me because of my role in nursing. I'm pleased that two surveys have named me as one of the 50 most influential nurses in the United States. I like being recognized, and most of all, being told by nurses that I have influenced their careers, their feelings about nursing, and commitment to the profession. I have mentored young nurses since I was in a position to do so and have endless pride in them and in their accomplishments. I have touched the lives of thousands of students, not all nurses, and have given them my best. When young nurses ask, "How can you manage all that—career and family?" I must answer, "Tain't easy. You pay a price. In terms of personal time, you sometimes have to give up something you want to do."

Is it worth it? Is nursing a career for tomorrow? With all its problems, is it worth fighting for and working for? I say yes, without question, although with no illusions. My daughter chose another career route, but my granddaughter says, "I want to go to college and be a nurse like you."

Imogene M. King

Imogene King, EdD, RN,
is Professor of Nursing at the
University of South Florida, Tampa

❖

Pondering the question of what led to her transactional theory prompted Imogene King to reflect on what stimulated her formulation of goals. She did not want to be a nurse. She always wanted to be a teacher. She talks of her loving and supportive family, her love for the English language, her excellent grammar school education, and her high achievement in high school. A nurse aunt and surgeon uncle, together with the call for nurses for World War II, influenced her decision to enter nursing. But she soon went on from her diploma program to get a degree in nursing with a minor in nursing education. In her work for her master's degree, she studied various curricula. Through her doctoral studies, her research, and her creative career, she has always looked for better ways to organize knowledge and facilitate learning.

Here, she discusses her work on transactional theory as well as courses she initiated for both undergraduate and graduate students. She feels her work in theory development complements her larger contribution to nursing education, her first love.

My formative years as the youngest of three children were spent in a loving and joyful family in a small midwestern community. Honesty, open communication, and respect for each individual were behaviors we learned as children in our family. While we were still quite young, we learned reasoning and decision making in problem identification and resolution. We were taught to look at alternatives before making decisions. These behaviors were reinforced throughout my formal educational programs.

When I received a letter from Thelma Schorr in which she asked me to write an autobiographical sketch, I was shocked, overwhelmed, and honored. Thelma asked me to do a "This Is Your Life" in 15 pages or less. So, sit back, relax, and think of storytellers who always start by saying, "Have you heard this one?"

One of the questions in Thelma's letter, among other helpful suggestions on how to begin this chapter, was, "What led you to conceive and develop your transactional theory?" This was her question to me about my theory of goal attainment, in which transactions are operationally defined within a process of human interactions. The question aroused my curiosity. I had never thought about the factors that influenced my career. While reflecting on why and how I became involved in what many call the scientific movement in nursing—theory development and testing the ideas in research in nursing practice—some interesting thoughts emerged from that elusive thing called memory. As I curled up in my reclining chair, I pondered the question of what led me to develop a theory for nursing.

I never wanted to be a nurse; I always wanted to be a teacher. I am revealing this because events conjured up from my reflections will indicate this to be true. My professional career in nursing has spanned more than 40 years, during which I have been actively involved in nursing practice and nursing organizations, in teaching nursing to many students in basic and graduate programs, and in continuing education for nurses. I have always been a teacher whose subject matter has been nursing and its practice.

EDUCATIONAL EXPERIENCES
Elementary

In the elementary school experience, I was fortunate to have had excellent teachers, the School Sisters of Notre Dame from St. Louis. They taught us the three R's, which gave us basic knowledge and skills. In addition, we were given roles and performed in plays. We were taught the art of debate. In the fourth grade, circa 1932, a topic of debate was, "Should there be an international language and if yes, should it be Esperanto?" I debated in favor of Esperanto as the international language of the future.

One major event will remain with me for a lifetime. In the seventh and eighth grades, one of the most demanding courses I had was called orthography. The teacher tested us every week. We had to pronounce words, spell them, hyphenate them, tell their derivation, define them, and give at least one synonym and antonym for each one. Now I know why I have this thing about words and their meaning. This is how we begin to develop concepts. Concepts represent the knowledge we have about our world. So now you and I both know that my cognitive skills developed early in childhood with reasoning, problem solving, and decision making and continued in formal educational experiences. It is amazing how much past experiences really influence future events in one's life.

Secondary

In the 1930s the United States and the rest of the world had not yet envisioned the explosion of knowledge that we are witnessing today. Automobiles had only begun to change mass transportation models. In high school education, one could choose between a commercial program or the classical college preparatory program. Remember my secret? I wanted to be a teacher, so I selected the college preparatory program, which required four years of language. Latin was the only language taught in our school at that time. Instead of wasting time in study periods, I selected electives of shorthand and typing and therefore had the best of both programs. As I recall, I was on the honor roll throughout high school with a grade point average of 3.8 or thereabouts on a 4.0 scale.

In the late 1930s and early 1940s, the United States was coming out of the Great Depression. The role of women in higher education was almost nonexistent, except for "finishing schools" for the wealthy. Young girls were recruited for nursing and for teaching. Both fields offered primarily apprenticeship-type programs. A college for women offered me a four-year scholarship, but I do not remember why I refused it.

After graduation from high school, I worked as a secretary for two years. When the United States entered World War II in 1942, a call for nurses was heard across the country. My aunt was an older nurse working in St. Louis at that time. My uncle, a surgeon, suggested I give some thought to entering a nursing program in St. Louis. He suggested two excellent programs, St. Louis University's five-year program leading to a BS degree and St. John's Hospital School of Nursing, which offered a three-year program leading to a diploma. I was in a hurry and selected St. John's. At the completion of the diploma program and after passing the examination for the registered nurse license, I enrolled in Maryville College in St. Louis to pursue liberal arts and science subjects. After completing freshman courses at Maryville, I transferred to St. Louis University to complete a program leading to a BS in nursing. In the 1940s one could major in nursing and choose either nursing education or public health nursing as a second major. I selected nursing education, since my goal was to become a teacher. From the time I graduated from St. John's and passed the licensing examination in 1945 until I completed my BS in 1948, I worked part-time as a staff nurse, a private duty nurse, and a school nurse. I also worked in a physician's office. That was called working your way through college.

Undergraduate Study

The period immediately after the end of World War II was an exciting time to study at St. Louis University. The story was told to us that the Jesuits of the St. Louis Province selected their best teachers to teach these "serious college students," the veterans of World War II. I believed the story because some of the greatest teachers in the liberal arts courses were Jesuits. Education in a Jesuit university in the 1940s and 1950s was truly "liberal" education combined with professional studies. Would you believe that when I met the requirements for the BS degree, I had a major in nursing and in nursing education with prerequisites in educational psychology, history of education, and philosophy of education? I had a minor in chemistry (a minor in a science was required), a minor in philosophy, and an additional prerequisite of logic. I selected three additional credit hours in philosophy as an elective. We had two semesters of world history, four semesters of English (including two in literature), and introductory courses in the behavioral sciences. We were also required to study one year of a foreign language, and I chose French. World history and history of education courses provided the background for my current avocation, history of nursing in the context of society. The educational psychology and philosophy of education courses motivated me to begin to develop a concept of learning that has been published recently (King, 1986). My concept of learning formed the theoretical basis for my own learning as well as for my teaching. Incidentally, a thesis was required in this undergraduate program. My thesis was qualitative in nature and related to a new idea in nursing education, that of planned clinical instruction as part of the formal education for nursing students. I developed such a program as part of the thesis. I was employed by St. John's Hospital School of Nursing to implement the clinical instruction program. The idea of planned educational learning experiences was new in the late 1940s. A study by Christy and West (1950), *Nursing at the Midcentury,* provided facts used to begin a voluntary national accreditation of schools of nursing. St. John's was on the first published list of accredited schools. We had a planned clinical instruction program for students implemented in which classroom experiences were related to students' clinical experiences. My bachelor's thesis was used to plan change in one diploma school curriculum.

Within a year following attainment of my bachelor's degree, I found myself taking one course per semester beginning with psychology of learning, tests and measurements, and educational guidance and counseling. I had an insatiable desire for knowledge that continues to the present day.

Graduate Study

At the time I decided to pursue work toward a master of science degree in nursing, information was being disseminated in nursing journals about the beginning of the community college movement in the United States and their experimental programs in nursing.

I attained my master's in two years (1955-1957) as a part-time student at St. Louis University. My program was designed to give me knowledge of nursing administration with a practicum in administration in nursing in higher education. A master's thesis was required, and again I elected to conduct a qualitative study to compare the curricula in the experimental programs with the curricula in selected diploma programs that were shortened to two years and a summer session. I used content analysis to compare philosophy, program objectives, and courses offered in the different programs. From the findings, I proposed a program that called for the closing of one specific hospital school and the opening of an associate degree program in an accredited junior college conducted by the Sisters of Mercy in St. Louis. About seven years later, the Sisters of Mercy initiated an associate degree program and closed their diploma program. Eventually, the Sisters of Mercy stopped conducting a formal program and provided a rich clinical environment for experiences for students from other programs. My master's thesis was useful in suggesting change.

Many changes were taking place in society and in nursing and the health field. The explosion of knowledge had begun to emerge. Since my goal was to teach nursing students at the undergraduate and graduate level in a university, I had to get a doctorate. Reports of exciting events in nursing education were being published by faculty members at Teachers College, Columbia University, New York. I was admitted to the doctoral program at Teachers College and chose Dr. Mildred Montag as my advisor. Since I had informed her I had only two years to complete my program, she facilitated my movement through it. Actually I completed the doctoral program in one calendar and one academic year (1959-1961).

To review my educational experiences:

1. My bachelor's thesis topic was a planned teaching program called Clinical Instruction in Nursing, a new idea in its time.
2. My master's thesis compared selected hospital school programs of two to two and one-half years and the experimental associate degree programs of two to two and one-half years in length in the Montag study. I constructed a curriculum that called for a specific hospital program to be closed and an associate degree program to be opened.
3. My doctoral dissertation was qualitative in nature. In that dissertation I developed a curriculum for a master of science degree program that would prepare teachers of nursing practice. Everything I studied recommended implementation of teaching programs for the practice of nursing.

A pattern in the above list is evident. It shows that I have consistently looked for ways to organize knowledge and programs to facilitate learning and application to practice throughout my career.

My theory of goal attainment (King, 1981) is a result of years of experience in nursing practice and nursing education and of thinking about the nature of nursing. My theory is composed of a theoretical basis for nursing process that results in goal attainment. Analysis of my reflections on my educational background has shown my desire to be a teacher of the subject I call nursing practice. My recent publication, *Curriculum and Instruction in Nursing* (1986), indicates my synthesis of multiple experiences related to teaching and learning.

The explosion of knowledge in the early 1960s and the development of a new master's program in nursing led me to a conceptualization of nursing that was published in a book titled *Toward a Theory for Nursing* (1971). From this conceptual framework, one theory has been developed and is being tested currently in several areas of practice. I have identified a second theory from my conceptual framework, and it is a theory of nursing administration.

When I became involved in theory development, I realized I had to increase my knowledge in statistics and in research methods. Most of my research in the 1960s had been qualitative. It was difficult to get qualitative research published and also to get funds to conduct qualitative studies then. Fortunately, nursing has matured as a science, and nurses have accepted the fact that knowledge can be discovered through methods of inquiry other than the experimental, two-variable, cause and effect design.

I returned to classes for normal course work in systems research, advanced statistics, experimental research design, and some short computer courses. In 1985 I completed a two-year continuing education program in measurement in nursing research sponsored by the University of Maryland. That program increased my knowledge of major concepts in measurement and resulted in the development of an instrument that measures goal attainment and activities of daily living.

EXPERIENCE IN PRACTICE AND EDUCATION

My practice experiences for the first 10 to 12 years of my career were in medical-surgical nursing of adults. I worked in a physician's office, as a staff nurse, as a head nurse, as a private duty nurse, as a school nurse, and as a teacher-practitioner. I spent a year as an occupational health nurse in industry.

My first teaching experience was as a faculty member in the hospital school of nursing where I had received my basic nursing education. My responsibilities included teaching medical-surgical nursing and communicable disease nursing courses. I was responsible for the planned clinical experiences and instruction in the hospital for students in those courses. At the same time, I practiced nursing in a hospital.

When a history of nursing course was required, I had the good fortune to teach it. Even today, I enjoy teaching a course titled "Nursing Education in Institutions of Higher Education," which includes historical events. In the early 1960s I taught a course in "Leadership and Management" in the senior year in a baccalaureate program. During this period separate baccalaureate programs existed for RNs in the university. My experiences included teaching such courses as "Roles and Responsibilities of Professional Nurses" and "Health Teaching and Patient Education." I initiated a course in theory development in nursing in a graduate program in 1969 and have been teaching a course of this type for master's and doctoral students all through the years. Additional experiences in teaching graduate students included courses in research, curriculum and instruction, adult health nursing, and practicums in adult health nursing. I have served as a lecturer in philosophy of science and theory courses for doctoral students.

My graduate teaching experiences included being a chairperson and a member of many thesis committees in several universities. I planned and implemented an area of concentration in nursing theory for a doctoral student in educational research in a school of education in one university. I have served as a member of dissertation committees in at least four universities. These experiences included writing comprehensive examination questions for master's and doctoral students.

The highlights of my professional career have been presented here. My reflections have indicated some of the reasons for my involvement in concepts, in theory development, in research, and in curriculum and instruction. My goal as a teacher, which can be seen throughout my professional career, culminated in a book, *Curriculum and Instruction in Nursing* (1986). Nurses have told me that my articles and books have made real contributions to the advancement of nursing as a profession and as a discipline. It is my hope that the theoretical ideas I espouse will be tested in research and will continue to expand the scope of knowledge in nursing.

PERSONALLY SPEAKING

What about Imogene King, the person? I mentioned my growth and development in a loving and joyful family. Would you believe that I was sometimes called a tomboy as a child? I often could be found playing basketball, tennis, or golf. Yes, I played with my dolls, too. Little girls in the 1930s played jacks and watched the little boys play marbles and baseball. I am still playing, but since breaking a couple of bones recently in a fall on the tennis court, I have given up tennis. My golf game is on hold, but my three partners are waiting for me to return to complete our foursome. Swimming and walking are the other forms of exercise I engage in, since Florida weather permits this many months out of each year.

In the late 1930s and 1940s, the dance craze was "jitterbugging." We considered this a type of competitive sport, and we practiced new and old steps for hours before each dance. I have always been healthy and seem to have twice the energy of most people.

I have always been goal-oriented and thank my parents and sister and brother for guiding me in positive and constructive activities throughout my life. I have been extremely grateful for the good fortune of growing up in a wonderful family. My extended family was a mainstay in my early years, with cousins, aunts, uncles, and one grandfather visiting us frequently. I am grateful for the wonderful teachers I had throughout my educational experiences.

Two wishes that I have had since childhood have been to be able to play the piano for my own enjoyment and to be able to paint. Art has been an avocation of mine, along with history. As a young adult, I had an excellent piano teacher and learned to play just a little. As I became mobile in the profession, I made a decision to give up piano, since I couldn't take it with me. I have attained my goal of becoming an artist and look forward to having more time to paint as I move into retirement—from a salaried position, but not from the joys that life has brought my way.

The only way to complete this autobiography is to say thanks to my family, my friends, and to nursing. I have achieved many goals, both personal and profession-al, and have also learned from supportive family and friends how to cope with some failures. I hope that in my desire to be a teacher, and in teaching many students at every level of nursing education, I have in some small way helped others learn. I hope that my contributions to nursing serve as a small payment for the many joys (and a few frustrations) and wonderful moments nursing has brought to my life and career.

Marguerite R. Kinney

Marguerite R. Kinney, DNSc, RN, FAAN,
is Professor, School of Nursing,
University of Alabama at Birmingham

Marguerite Kinney found her nursing identity in critical care early in her career. Her focus has been steadfast ever since—throughout her entire educational program and into her present academic appointment. She has always wanted to know all there is to know about the acutely ill patient and has fostered this inquiry in the American Association of Critical Care Nurses (AACN) and on the international scene. It was during her presidency that AACN's first research committee was appointed, leading to activities that have become a major program of that organization. As editor of Focus on Critical Care *and the author of a major textbook on critical care, she has put to good use her love of English and writing. Her career, her travels, and her ability to enjoy and respect her family provide a model for any woman juggling the demands and the delights of personal and professional success.*

Like many young girls who grew up in the 1940s and 1950s, I thought nursing was an attractive career choice. Many of my friends were choosing to pursue careers as nurses, teachers, and social workers. Those choices probably represented influences of our earlier days. I know that I was very much influenced by my aunt (for whom I was named) who was a nurse. I can recall as a small child visiting my grandmother in Vermont, standing on the kitchen table, wearing my aunt's nurse's cap and cape and listening to her talk about her nursing career. I remember movies of World War II (which were plentiful in the late 1940s and 1950s) that depicted nurses as heroines caring for the wounded. They were always portrayed as caring human beings who took care of people and made them better just by being there. The movies made it all very romantic.

There was really nothing in my early experiences to deter me from a career in nursing. I grew up in a college town where an academic program with a major in nursing was available at the university. I always knew that I would go to college. My father emphasized education for his daughters and valued it highly. I was fortunate that I could combine a college education and a career in nursing.

When I studied nursing as an undergraduate student, there was almost no such thing as intensive care. Although there were postanesthesia recovery rooms where I did work some, there was nothing like what we know today as intensive care or coronary care units.

I remember one experience I had caring for a boy who was about 15. He had been shot in the abdomen in a hunting accident and was very ill with peritonitis. What we had to offer him at that major university hospital was a private room and someone (it happened to be me) to take care of him. I had a blood pressure cuff, a stethoscope, a watch to check his pulse, and a thermometer to measure his temperature. That, essentially, was it—this young boy and me in a room together, with me praying that he wouldn't die. I recall it now because I am so grateful for information that is available to us today in critical care to indicate the condition of a patient. I didn't really know what to expect from that young man, but I did know that he could die, and I didn't want him to do it with just me there in the room. I wanted to be able to do something, but I could only watch and wait. That made a big impression on me. I had heard that good nurses were able to feel when things were not right, and I thought I should be able to feel things about this young man. I felt very inadequate. I think I was only a junior nursing student at the time.

There was a four-year interim between the completion of my baccalaureate degree and the beginning of my graduate study. I spent that time in teaching fundamentals of nursing and worked for a brief time as a staff nurse at a community hospital in the outpatient clinic. By the time I returned to graduate school, open-heart surgery was in full swing at the university hospital. Patients young and old were going for surgery and then being sent back to a special room near the operating room. I did have an observation experience there. Observation was all that was allowed because there were 15 or 20 people with responsibilities for caring for this patient—interns, residents, fellows, anesthesia personnel. The room was full of people, and I could see that surveillance was going on. There was not much to do in terms of intervention, however, and I remember that a good many of those patients died.

When I completed graduate school, I again took a teaching position in a diploma program associated with a private hospital, and while I was there the coronary care unit was opened. Prior to that time, there was no special area in the hospital for patients with myocardial infarctions. Opening that unit was a big event. The fact that nurses were to intervene with preestablished protocols was an exciting thing at that time. Nurses received instruction on the electrocardiogram, treatment with lidocaine, and so on.

Shortly thereafter, I left that position and moved to an area where a cardiovascular surgeon was in the process of setting up an open-heart surgery program. Although my plan at the time had been to return to clinical practice as a staff nurse, I felt the need to refine my clinical skills. Someone in the nursing administration there asked me to help him establish the nursing part of the program. As we talked, I became excited about the possibility of taking care of or being involved with patients who were having their hearts operated on. There was no coronary care unit or post-open-heart care unit at that hospital at the time, although there was a large critical care unit for patients who had had major surgery and trauma.

I think the time that I spent as a member of this open-heart surgery team probably was a pivotal point in my career and ensured that critical care would remain my primary interest for the rest of my professional life. What I experienced there was a sense of commitment to the task at hand, a real team effort, and a sense of identity as a nurse. I was clear about what I had to offer these patients and knew that some of those things were different from what physicians had to offer. It really was a holistic experience. I saw patients with the surgeon at the time of consultation. I sometimes saw them even before the surgeon did, at the time of cardiac catheterization in conjunction with the cardiologist. We then prepared them for admission for the surgery. I did all of the preoperative teaching, met with the family, went to the operating room, and very often had some opportunity to assist in the surgery. That enhanced my appreciation for anatomy and physiology a great deal. When the patient was taken from the heart-lung machine, I returned to the unit, reported to the family, answered their questions, addressed their concerns, and assisted the staff in making preparations to admit the patient. Then I would go back to the operating room and accompany the operative team and the patient to the critical care unit, where I stayed to assist the nurses with postoperative care. I often had the opportunity to see patients throughout the recovery period and again in their postoperative visits to the surgeon, both in the immediate convalescent period and in the months afterward. It was a rewarding experience, and I learned a great deal.

It was then that I developed an interest in preoperative teaching from a research point of view, and, as I moved on to doctoral study, that was the area I pursued for my dissertation. It was clear to me that patients reacted individually to the preoperative teaching, but I did not know what variables played into each individual's reaction. As I was able to look into it further, it seemed to me that there were some possible theoretical explanations for the variation in individual reactions. Research in my clinical area of interest began in my doctoral study years and has been something that I have continued to do.

I like knowing a great deal about acutely ill patients. I have occasionally worked on a general nursing unit since being introduced to critical care and find it very frustrating to have a large number of patients about whom I know very little. Knowing a great deal about the patients is one variable that I like about intensive care. I also like the action. It seems to me that it is an area where one sees nursing at its finest. I don't say this with any sense of elitism; it just seems to me the opportunities for nursing's contributions are very great in this unit. I have often said that I would like to experiment with undergraduate nursing education by taking nursing students into the critical care unit for their first clinical nursing experience. People look at me as if I were crazy when I say that. I certainly don't mean to give them a bigger burden than they can handle, but I think in the right circumstance, working with knowledgeable faculty, this would be an opportunity for students to see nursing at its best, to see the decision making that comes from a data base that is purposely acquired and gives direction for intervention. The critical care unit would be a place where nursing students could begin to make some sense out of the anatomy and physiology they learned in a classroom or laboratory. Most often, the concepts learned in a classroom are difficult to apply without being able to see the variables and interaction. So I think this is a place where students could be excited about nursing and what nursing has to offer, and I think we would do well to pay attention to that rather than putting students in their first experiences into situations that are perhaps boring, where nursing's role is more limited than in critical care. I don't know that I will ever have the opportunity to try this out, but I would surely like to.

As for my role in the AACN, we did have a small chapter in the city where the open-heart surgery program was located, and the nurses in that unit, along with those in the general intensive care unit there and in other hospitals in the city, banded together and formed a small chapter. I suppose we did it out of self-defense, because I do remember this period as a time when there seemed to be some resentment on the part of other nurses toward those of us who were in critical care. I am sure there were some reasons for that. They saw us as feeling elite, as being granted special considerations that they did not feel they had. In our estimation, we felt closer to one another. In chapter work, I came to realize how much we needed to learn. Our primary motivation was to learn more about caring for the critically ill. Through the national organization we came to receive more and more educational support—the publication of *Heart & Lung* and critical care newsletters and, in 1974, the first National Teaching Institute (NTI)—all helpful to us in satisfying our thirst for knowledge. As I moved on to teaching in a university, I remember that when my first class of graduate students had completed their degrees, I received a nomination from one of them for the national board of directors of the AACN. I was flattered, but I never dreamed that I would actually be elected. When I was elected, I quickly came to realize the importance of this group in terms of critical care nursing and developed an appreciation for their potential. That experience is one I would wish for everyone.

Having been elected to lead the organization, I became acutely aware of the state of critical care nursing in this country. I had many opportunities to travel internationally and to meet with physicians and nurses from other countries to share with them both what we were doing and also what our vision was for the future. My term as president gave me the opportunity to help determine a direction for the organization. One of the programs that I had the experience necessary to try to influence was that of research. Although now it may seem strange to think of the AACN as ever having been without a research thrust, it simply was not a part of the organization's overall goals then. The AACN came into being primarily to meet educational needs of nurses, so the resources and energies of the association had gone in that direction. I am sure it was my preparation and experience (although minimal at the time) that led me to question why we should not have a major goal statement that related to research. My suggestion that we establish such a goal was enthusiastically received. AACN's first research committee was appointed and turned out to be a marvelous group. We had nurses with both master's and doctoral degrees, and essentially we were writing on a clean slate as far as the suggested activities of the committee were concerned. We met several times and found it to be an exhilarating experience. We planned research presentations in conjunction with the NTI and then held our collective breath, hoping we would get abstracts submitted and that registrants of the NTI would go to those sessions. Our worries were groundless. At the NTI, there is standing room only for the research presentations.

One of the issues that I remember being concerned about during my period of leadership with AACN was the image of specialty nursing organizations within nursing in general. I remember being very committed through the Federation of Specialty Nursing Organizations and ANA to try to bring about harmony and cooperation, particularly between AACN and ANA. This task was made easier by the ANA leadership who had come to recognize the place of specialty nursing organizations within nursing. I believe everyone in that period of time worked hard to address issues in a cooperative, collaborative manner and not to foster a divisiveness within nursing.

As I reflect back on those years, I am acutely aware that opportunities that opened up to me resulted from my being in the right place at the right time. I certainly didn't aspire to ever being an author or an editor of a textbook or of a journal, but I did always like writing and English. If I had not been a nurse, I probably would have been a high school English teacher somewhere. As opportunities to participate in publication projects presented themselves, I found myself enjoying those experiences more and more, even though I would not have sought them out. They came to my doorstep by virtue of my AACN activities. Editing a major comprehensive nursing text was a big learning experience, and as we are now in the first revision of that text, I am amazed to learn how much there is to know about revising texts. I also know that my nomination as editor of *Focus on Critical Care* came about as a direct result of my AACN board activities and through people I came to know during that time. This editorship has been a rewarding experience. While I recognize the responsibility that being an editor involves, I also recognize the opportunities that it presents. I am struck with the talent and the willingness of critical care nurses to participate in publication projects. They often don't know how much they have to share, and with encouragement and some help, the outcome is often very satisfactory.

Another conclusion that I could draw from this reminiscence is that one's colleagues influence what one does and the direction one might take. I have been privileged to work with and come to know well some bright, talented, and visionary people who are committed to nursing. I know that these associations have shaped my thinking and my doing. I am grateful for those opportunities. It is fun to think about what my career would have been if I had not become so intensely involved in AACN and hence had gone in some other direction. I think my interest in critical care nursing would not have changed, but some of my horizons would be narrower.

I suppose I should comment on how one maintains an active professional life while being a wife, mother, daughter, church member, community member, and the like. People often ask me, "How are you able to do so many things and keep it all together?" I am not sure that I do always keep it together, but I know that I have work habits that are sufficient for me. I don't work an eight-hour day. It is my custom to take work back and forth from home to the office and pretty much work all day. However, I do play. My husband and I like to camp, and Alabama has some lovely state parks. One or two are just a few miles from our home. Once I get on the campground it's as if I were a thousand miles from home. It's a very relaxing way to get away from the pressures and demands of work. I realize my good fortune in having a husband who recognizes and adjusts to my work habits. He is busy and travels, and we don't have a division of roles in our house that places every caretaking responsibility on me. More than that, he has encouraged me and has always seemed to take great pride in my accomplishments. I can truthfully say that I have never felt that I was hindered by his demands in any way.

My faculty colleagues as well as the administrators to whom I report have supported me in my professional activities in more ways than I can tell. The School of Nursing was generous with allowing me the time required away during my periods of intense leadership, and they continue to be generous, giving me opportunities to travel and to participate in professional activities. The people with whom I work most closely have shown their support in many ways, and students have been supportive as well. They seem to benefit from the experiences that I bring back to them, in terms of both timely information and analysis of current issues.

I am well pleased with my choice of a career. Critical care continues to offer exciting new developments and opportunities, and it certainly isn't dull.

Karren Kowalski

Karren Kowalski, PhD, RN, FAAN,
is Director of Women's Hospital
at AMI St. Luke's in Denver

❖

From ordinariness to mastery of women's health care, Karren Kowalski tells her moving story — sometimes painful, sometimes glorious. But always, she knew that the essence of living was in the journey, and the lives she has touched are her reward. Never losing her early flair for the dramatic, she finally chose to be a nurse because she could get a scholarship in nursing. She graciously credits her mentors with helping her make choices in her life and work experiences and thus spurring her on to high personal and professional achievements, one of which has become a national model for women's health care. Another achievement has been her work with bereaved parents. Her courage and her aptitude for answering challenges shine through her description of joys and sorrows. She is now pursuing her goals for nurses and for women in a humanistic business environment that she finds exhilarating. She has developed a new leadership style and enjoys sharing her power with the nurses with whom she works, secure in the belief that the more power she gives away, the more she has.

*M*astery of knowledge and skills, whether they are in leadership, photography, ice skating, or women's health care, begins with ordinariness. The nurses in this book began as students, and they were quite ordinary. Prior to traveling my road to mastery of women's health care, I was an ordinary graduate nurse working in labor and delivery. I was incredibly naive, had very little idea of what labor and delivery care was about, thought physicians were gods of a higher order, believed "natural childbirth" was a curse and saddle blocks were salvation, and never imagined that two-bed labor rooms with white ceramic tile and a curtain down the middle were anything less than perfect.

The next few pages will show my 20-year metamorphosis from ordinariness to mastery in the health care of women and their families. This journey has been intermittently exciting, delightful, sad, and painful, and it has been filled with learning experiences and long days of just plain hard work. There are many roads from ordinariness to mastery, and the road I chose is but one of them. However, I believe each of these roads requires a passion, a commitment—a willingness to do whatever it takes to reach desired goals. Early nursing leaders such as Dorothea Dix, Linda Richards, and Mary Breckenridge loved what they did. Their work was a passion, a mission. Ansel Adams loved photography; skating champions love skating; I love creating women's health care the way women want it.

Hand in hand with the passion comes the knowledge that the "essence" of life is not the mission. Regardless of the nobility of that mission, the ends never justify the means. What keeps life in perspective for me is knowing that the essence of living is the process or the journey—it is the lives that I have touched, the people I have helped along the way, and knowing that I have made a difference.

THE EARLY YEARS

I have always been dramatic. When my father came home at the end of World War II and first saw me, a super-charged two-and-a-half-year-old, he called me "Hotrod." I often wonder if that influenced my speeding through life, burning rubber and creating as much dust and noise as possible. I often have those kinds of days, and Dad still calls me Hotrod.

I grew up knowing that I was special; everyone noticed my curly red hair. Children can cope with considerable adversity if they believe they are special and know they are loved. My parents were divorced when I was five. My father gained custody of me, and for the next three years I lived on a farm with my aunt and uncle and rarely saw either of my parents. When I was nearly nine, I returned to my father and new stepmother. This early experience of loss and separation helped shape one of my missions.

I can remember wanting to be an airline stewardess. In those days, they liked to hire nurses as stewardesses, and thus I considered nursing. I volunteered at the county hospital and did well. However, in my junior year of high school, I discovered theater. All thoughts of a career in nursing faded from my mind, but my parents held out hope. I chose Indiana University because I could go to Bloomington and try my wings at theater. There was never a conscious choice to attend a baccalaureate nursing program. I had no great passion for nursing except to play the part of Florence Nightingale in the Crimea. However, a career in theater was viewed by my father as being too racy; I had a scholarship in nursing, not acting. Because there has always been a strong pragmatic aspect to my nature, I decided to pursue my nursing major. After all I had consistently been told, "You can always get a job."

I spent those school years figuring out who I was and getting my life straightened out. I was more interested in relationships than studies. I loved the clinical components of school and did well in them, but the theoretical components were decidedly boring. Consequently, I was thankful for 30 hours of A in history, and when I graduated, I swore I would never go back to school again.

My stepmother, who came from a traditional background, believed that a woman's identity and happiness were dependent on whom she married. She encouraged me to go to nursing school and marry a doctor, so I married the first one who asked me. He happened to be a budding neurosurgeon—a brilliant clinician with the interpersonal skills of a doorknob. However, I was going to save him. After two years, I realized that he didn't want to be saved; he wanted a housekeeper and cook rather than a partner. Worse yet, he did not love me, and even being Mrs. Dr. X wasn't worth the loveless existence. We divorced.

I was on the rebound when I enlisted in the Army Nurse Corps with a guaranteed assignment to Vietnam. I had been out of school for 10 months, working in labor and delivery. In retrospect my decision to enlist was the solution to some of my problems. It was an easy way to leave Indiana and escape the pain of a failed marriage, and it was patriotic and exciting. I was assigned to the 3rd Surgical Hospital in the middle of the 173rd Airborne Brigade at the Bien Hoa Air Base, just north of Saigon. The hospital was a Mobile Army Surgical Hospital (MASH) unit, not unlike the television series. We received only battle casualties. Now, 20 years later, I cannot watch Vietnam movies, nor have I been able to visit the Vietnam memorial. The pain would be overwhelming. In my efforts to repress memories of the maimed and the dying, I tell funny stories about our "Major Burns" and about running the venereal disease clinic for the 173rd Airborne. After Vietnam I was only too glad to return to labor and delivery—to a happy working environment.

MENTORS

Mentors are like gifts to our lives: they challenge, question, and support us when our days seem darkest. I have been blessed with several, and will discuss the influences of four of them. After Vietnam I went to Germany where I met Walt. He was an Army Signal Corps officer. We were married there; our wedding present from the Department of the Army was his orders for Vietnam, so we decided to get out of the Army. We moved to Denver, and I returned to working nights—for the third year. I decided to break my vow and go back to school so I could demand more money and better hours. My undergraduate grade point average was so low the University of Colorado could admit me only on probational status. My first mentor, Ingeborg Mauksch, taught me in graduate school. Meeting her was like running into a brick wall—she stopped me in my tracks. She taught the first course I took, and I was in awe of her. I had never before met a nurse who had a doctorate *and* was married *and* had children. It was the first time I saw these combined goals as possibilities. In the early 1970s, Inge taught us—in addition to "Trends in Nursing"—that it was great to wear $100 dresses. I had never heard nurses utter monetary concepts (other than poverty and self-sacrifice). It was wonderful! Then at a fireside chat one evening, she asked me why I was in graduate school and I told her the truth—for more money and better hours. Inge suggested I had better reevaluate my goals or choose another discipline because nursing needed leaders, "and leaders are motivated by values over and above money and hours." I spent the next 15 months figuring out what I could contribute.

What was my mission? My purpose? What could I lead? My experience in university teaching hospitals had given me a somewhat jaded perspective of OB care. Patients rarely saw the same care provider more than once and could consider it a miracle if the person doing the delivery had a familiar face. Some interns and residents would examine a woman in labor whom they had never seen before and say, "Spread your legs, honey." I was incensed at that treatment of women. Rather than change specialties, I decided to change OB practice, at least within my sphere of control. When I completed graduate school, this sphere became the labor and delivery unit at Colorado General Hospital, the teaching hospital of the university, where I was the new head nurse. It was my first mission.

To address these concerns, I decided to create a system in which indigent patients could get continuity of care from a provider who was warm, caring, and an advocate for the woman. I believed that approach would afford the best possible beginning for those families. Nurse-midwifery seemed the perfect model to provide that care, but unfortunately, it was an illegal practice in Colorado. I was told it would take eight to ten years to change the legislation. It was actually six years later, when I was president of the state nurses' association, that we succeeded in getting enabling legislation passed for nurse-midwifery practice.

I could have given up and stuck with the old system, but I chose to search for additional alternatives. I began by asking questions. Could nurses provide continuity of care without being nurse-midwives? Could other models work, such as nurse practitioners? In the end I used labor and delivery nurses, expanded their antepartum assessment skills, and assigned them to a caseload of patients in the antepartum clinic. The nurses saw these patients all through their antepartum course and were on call when their patients were admitted in labor. The nurses and the patients loved the system. Although I did not realize it at the time, what I had done was to change the entire environment. I had made nurses responsible—to their patients rather than to the system. Nurses truly became patient advocates and were willing to change whatever did not work for their patients. We initiated peer review projects and patient education projects. We confronted physicians about how patients were treated, and we showed parents their babies who had died.

My mentor throughout the development of this concept was a physician, Dr. Watson Bowes. He encouraged me, helped with problem solving, ran interference for me with his medical colleagues as well as with the administration, and then introduced me to the national OB speaking circuit to share what we were doing in Colorado. Any time another physician would call and ask Watie to talk about the program, he would claim he didn't know enough about it and refer the call to me. Watie's support was even more meaningful, considering my attitude then. It was the era of my life in which I discovered the feminist movement, or what I now refer to as my "rage phase." It was another mission.

One of the keys to my success has been that I have consistently surrounded myself with people who expected more from me than I did. I was not terribly popular in the head nurse group, partly because I was so rebellious and outspoken. Consequently, I stumbled onto the state nurses' association. My support developed from a group of "young Turks" like myself who were all from different organizations in the metropolitan Denver area. My initial contact with this group was when someone called to ask if I would run for chair of the Maternal-Child Nursing Conference Group. I accepted, thinking that I would never win, but I did. The chairperson position introduced me to Virginia Ward Paulson, executive director of the Colorado Nurses' Association, and thus to the "young Turks" she sponsored.

Ginny encouraged me, supported me, put challenges in my way, and pushed me to my limits, encouraging me to be more and to do more than I ever thought I could. Through her love and nurturing, I entered the organization hierarchy and eventually became state president. I reconnected with Inge, and Ginny encouraged me to write. When times looked the bleakest, she would say, "I know it doesn't feel like it right now, but this happened for the best. It is really an opportunity." Even when she retired, she continued to mentor me. As she was dying of breast cancer, I ran for first vice-president of the American Nurses' Association because I knew how much she wanted me to do it. I was in the middle of my doctoral program, and it was not the best timing. I lost by 19 votes. She said what she always had, "This happened for the best." It is an attitude I have continued to hold about most everything in my life. I have consistently found that it is not what happens but how we respond to what happens that determines the quality of our lives.

PERSONAL CHARACTERISTICS

I have several personal characteristics that have supported me over the years. I am stubborn and persistent. When I applied to graduate school, I kept calling until they agreed to admit me on probational status, despite my undergraduate GPA of 2.6 and my poor Graduate Record Examination (GRE) scores. When I read my graduate school recommendations from my OB instructor at Indiana University and discovered she considered me a "terminal master's" student, I knew without a doubt that I would go for a PhD. All that is required to motivate me is someone telling me I can't do something or that something isn't possible. When I was developing the OB team system, one of the physicians said I would never get nurses to take call and come into work at 2 AM. I thought to myself, "Just watch me."

I am a high-energy person. I have always been willing to do whatever it takes to accomplish a goal. I would never ask nurses to do something that I was unwilling to do, so I scrubbed on cesareans and had a small caseload of patients whom I followed from clinic through delivery. I have never been afraid of long hours or hard work and have always believed that anything worth having is worth working for.

Persistence has been invaluable. If something I attempted did not work the first time, I went at it from a different angle. While mistakes were devastating at times, I usually succeeded in blocking out the pain and switching approaches. At an unconscious level, I viewed mistakes as my successfully learning what did not work.

I was a horrible writer. My first effort, an article for the *American Journal of Nursing* about the team system titled, "On-Call Staffing," was unrecognizable when it came back from the copy editors. Next, two colleagues and I wrote a manuscript on peer review. It was never published. I gradually learned that unless you are Ernest Hemingway, you learn to write by writing, rewriting, and practicing writing. Communicating ideas orally or in writing is essential to the progress of the profession. It is a learned behavior, just like leadership skills, and it requires an enormous amount of practice. Frequently, what differentiates excellence from mediocrity is practice.

I have consistently viewed myself as a champion of the underdogs, whether they were indigent care women or nurses. Some of this urge to help and protect may have come from my father. For years he was the safety officer for his region of the Nickle-Plate Railroad. He was always firing off letters to the home office when he found working conditions or equipment to be unsafe for the men. He took this responsibility very seriously, and I can remember him sitting at the dining room table late at night, pounding the keys of an old portable typewriter, his righteousness unleashed and his blood boiling. It was his mission to make the trains safe. It was my mission to improve health care for women and to support nurses to do it.

MY BURNING PASSION

One of my missions has been to work with parents experiencing pregnancy loss, stillbirths, and infant death. In the not-so-good old days, we used to put women with obstetrical complications to sleep for their deliveries. By the time they awoke from anesthesia, the dead infant had been taken to the morgue. We thought we were protecting and taking care of the mothers, when in reality we were protecting ourselves.

I learned about protecting myself the first time I took care of a fully conscious mother with a fetal demise. It was in my "permanent night shift" phase of life. She arrived on the unit with a 28-week double footling breech fetus already delivered to the umbilicus; the cord was not pulsating. I took her straight to the delivery room, yelling for the intern. The stillborn infant was delivered immediately—no lacerations and no episiotomy. The intern left the delivery room, and the patient climbed out of the stirrups and sat up in the middle of the delivery table, asking to see her baby. There had been no time to give her anesthesia or analgesia. I could not think of a reason to refuse her request, so I wrapped the baby in a blanket and gave it to the mother. She began to unwrap the baby, touching the fingertips, moving on to the trunk of the body, then stroking the baby's head (just as mothers do with liveborns). She began to cry and said to me, "I'm all alone here in Denver. My parents don't know I'm pregnant. I didn't want this baby, but I didn't want this baby to die." There she sat in the middle of the delivery table, rocking back and forth, clutching the baby to her body and crying.

No one had prepared me for that. I began to cry, and in 1969 it was unprofessional for nurses to cry in front of patients. I felt completely out of control. So many feelings came rushing to the surface. I walked out, leaving her alone. I struggled for control, tears splashing into the scrub sink. I could see all the faces of the men and boys that I took care of in Vietnam—the missing arms and legs, the blood-soaked stretchers, the body bags. It was like a nightmare in living color.

I do not remember how I got back to the delivery room, but for four years I never told a soul about abandoning that patient. It took most of that four years for me to gain insight into that experience: when professionals are confronted with death and bereavement, the feelings associated with the losses they have experienced in their lives surface, particularly repressed and unacknowledged losses. With the memories come the psychic pain and emotional responses, and the health care provider feels out of control. Few of us get up in the morning saying, "Today, I choose *pain*." Most often, we protect ourselves from this psychic stress.

The further revelation that refusing to let mothers see and hold dead infants was protecting ourselves, not the patient, came to me when two close friends (nurse colleagues) had babies who died on my unit in the summer of 1973. They told me the truth about the importance of seeing their babies. Within four months we changed our entire policy. The medical faculty thought I was crazy. However, Dr. Bowes and the physician who took care of my friends both supported me. Working with bereaved parents and changing the system to meet their needs became a burning passion—a mission. It led me to start the Bereavement Support Group for parents at Boulder County Hospice in 1980. I did my doctoral dissertation on bereaved parents, and I now work with the Bereaved Parents Group at my hospital in Denver. Prior to their discharge, I see most parents who have suffered a loss.

WILLINGNESS TO TAKE ACTION

Many people can have good ideas or feelings about something, but unless they are willing to act on those ideas, they might as well not have had them. It is admirable to believe that parents should be able to see and hold their dead babies, but until action is taken to change policies and to enlist the staff in those changes, it is just a good idea. Willingness to take action is more important than a high IQ or a host of other creative talents. Taking action is often equated with taking risks, with stretching our limits, going outside our comfort zone, and changing. My motto has most frequently been, "Act now and fine-tune later." It occasionally allows me to have major learning experiences, but I am always in motion creating programs and improving services to women.

BALANCE IN MY LIFE—RELATIONSHIPS

Making something work the way I want it to has been a driving force in my life. I do not bother with things or people or projects or ideas to which I am not committed. What keeps me sane and balanced is relationships. First there is Walt. We have been together for 20 years. We have worked hard on our relationship. There have been rocky times when I was unsure that we would survive, but commitment to the relationship and to our two sons pulled us through. We have grown and changed, and we value that process. Sometimes changes have been simultaneous, sometimes separate. Walt's love, support, and objectivity are invaluable. When I get upset with systems problems in my administrative role, he says calmly, "Remember, this is your laboratory. You are learning the health care business." Because of him, I remember that I can quit my job at any time. In order to do my job, I have to be willing each and every day to lose it.

In addition to my family, I have had wonderful women friends who have consistently expected more from me than I did from myself. Joanne, who was my assistant during my head nurse years and during my "rage phase," was the best labor and delivery nurse I have ever known. She was my team nurse when our oldest son was born and was his coach six years later when he was with us for the birth of his brother. I learned much from her in her living, as well as in her dying. She died of metastatic breast cancer at the age of 38, leaving a husband and two-year-old son. I miss her.

Betty Jennings is my nurse-midwife colleague. We were head nurses together at Colorado General Hospital. She joined me on the faculty of the School of Nursing when I became director of the Regional MCN Continuing Education Grant. We developed the curriculum of the Women's Health Care Nurse Practitioner Program. We wrote books together that weren't published (the peer review manuscript) and those that were, a three-volume series on women's health. We fought for legalization of nurse-midwifery together. Just as I believed I needed to deliver my first child on my unit, within the team system, I believed our second son should be delivered by a nurse-midwife, Betty. We jokingly talk about being burned at the stake together as witches/women healers in a former life.

Lois Sonstegard and I met in Kansas City as members of the joint American Nurses' Association/Nurses Association of the American College of Obstetrics and Gynecology Certification Examination Committee in 1987. At Lois's invitation, Betty and I joined her in the women's health book series. We wanted to write a book for graduate nurses— one that could also be used by students in women's health care nurse practitioner programs, nurse-midwifery programs, and maternity graduate student programs. While writing books together has caused other women to quit speaking to each other, all of our trials and tribulations seemed to pull us closer together. Lois and I have had wonderful adventures together. We were doctoral students at the same time, she in Minnesota and I in Colorado. We were inducted into the American Academy of Nursing together and ran for 45 minutes each morning of the meeting, creating no small amount of comment. Lois nurtured me when my last pregnancy terminated at 14 weeks, and I was with Lois in Minnesota teaching a bereavement seminar when Joanne called from Seattle to say good-bye—she died the following evening. Lois listened to my pain, felt my powerlessness, and didn't try to "fix it."

THE BUSINESS WORLD

Traditionally nurses have not been business oriented. Only in the last five years or so have nurse managers had more than token involvement in the unit budgeting process. I spent my first 15 years in nursing not wanting to be contaminated by the business aspects of health care. We could pretend, as not-for-profit institutions, that we were focused on patient care and not on money. The reality, of course, is that survival demands that each health care facility make a profit as well as provide patient care. The difference is in to whom the profits are distributed—shareholders, religious organizations, or the government.

My first exposure to business principles came in the form of instruction from Marshall Thurber. A lawyer, entrepreneur, and real estate developer, he has made and lost more money than is in the annual operating budgets of many large hospitals. He has not been a mentor to me as much as he has been a master teacher. He introduced me to the concept of win/win, that is, setting up planning, conflict resolution, and business arrangements in a way that allows all parties to achieve their goals. Nursing, medicine, and hospital administration have most often been involved in win/lose relationships, with nursing in the lose position. It is possible to create mutual gain situations.

We are all products of a dualistic society that tends to see situations in an either/or, black and white framework. It requires practice to visualize an entire range of possibilities. From Marshall, I learned about lateral thinking, or how to discover infinite possibilities. He also taught me to focus on what works and get away from what doesn't work. Time spent on negatives and "ain't it awful" is time wasted. My staff understand that when they come to me with a problem, they must also come with at least two realistic solutions. This stimulates them to think the problem through rather than expect me to have all the answers and rescue them.

From Marshall I learned how to build teams, to support them, and to teach them to work together synergistically. I learned about creating a vision and a corporate culture. I learned why the job satisfaction research has money at the bottom of the scale and working conditions or environment at the top. I learned as much from Marshall's mistakes as I did from his successes because he was willing to make his mistakes public.

I entered my doctoral program believing that I would take an academic position in teaching and doing research. What a surprise it was for me to discover at graduation that what I really wanted was to demonstrate that humanistic business principles could work, not just in entrepreneurial, privately owned business, but in bureaucratic structures and corporations and in health care.

Rather than return to the university, I chose the position of Director of Women's Hospital at AMI St. Luke's in Denver. It has been wonderful and agonizing. There have been days when the only reason I have come to work was knowing that I never learn less than when I don't go in. At Women's Hospital we do not have "failures," we have major learning experiences.

My leadership style has shifted from benevolent dictator at Colorado General Hospital to participative leader at AMI St. Luke's. One of my most important lessons from Marshall was that I cannot do it all. Consequently, I have to leverage myself by creating and teaching my program coordinators to be leaders. The more power I give away, the more I have. The emphasis is on learning and growing. If people are not making mistakes, they are not taking risks and they are not learning anything.

THE FUTURE OF THE HEALTH CARE BUSINESS

The only thing constant now is change. The geometric rate of change boggles the mind. We have entered Toffler's informational age. The quantity of available information is doubing every 28 months, and even that continues to shrink. The health care systems that will survive into the twenty-first century will be the ones that remain the most flexible, focus on high-quality service to clients, and value their employees. The American health care industry is in as much trouble as the automobile industry. It is reeling from DRGs and the increasing power of third-party payers. The most common approach is to focus on the bottom line for the current quarter rather than to plan effective strategies for 1995.

One key planning issue is the working environment and the treatment of personnel. The nursing shortage has reached staggering proportions in parts of the country, a situation that is predicted to become significantly worse before 1991. The chief problem is the work environment, with low salaries a secondary issue. An environment that supports and rewards creativity, self-determination, responsibility, and humanistic values would attract the best nurses, giving the sponsoring institution a competitive edge. The leadership to create such environments must be "new age." It is a style that has stereotypically been described as feminine.

Although over 90% of health care employees are female, there are very few women in the upper administrative positions other than directors or vice-presidents for nursing. Control of health care is monopolized by the old boys' network of administrators and physicians. It employs a hierarchical, authoritarian model reminiscent of the 1950s. This problem is a reflection of leadership problems in corporate America. The brightest and best female Harvard MBA graduates whose first jobs were in Fortune 500 companies are leaving and starting their own businesses. They have discovered that they do not like the politics and that they will probably never reach the top in corporate America.

Most women health care administrators are nurses who did not go to the same schools or pledge the same fraternities, use the same dressing rooms, or come from the same family backgrounds as the male executives. Consequently, they do not fit in and the men are not comfortable with them or with their leadership style. To some these obstacles seem insurmountable. Of course, I evaluate this information in much the same way that I viewed the assessment that I was a "terminal master's" candidate. It is a system ripe for change, and I intend to create some of those changes.

CHALLENGE→MASTERY

Life is a series of challenges that are mastered prior to moving on. One of the key challenges for nursing is to produce leaders with the courage to adapt to the fast-changing environment of health care while attracting men and women to the profession, rather than send them fleeing to "more money and better hours." Women's health services are now receiving considerable money in hopes of inducing women who make family health care decisions to use institutional services for their families in addition to women's services. Some people view this as a new form of exploitation of women. I view it as an opportunity—a new challenge to create women's health care in the way women want it, to provide an environment that supports nurses to be leaders, to be creative, responsible, always learning, flexible and growing—to travel the road from ordinariness to mastery.

Marlene F. Kramer

Marlene F. Kramer, PhD, RN, FAAN,
is Professor of Nursing at the
Orvis School of Nursing, University of
Nevada, Reno

Marlene Kramer is famed for her definitive work on reality shock—the situation facing new graduates who are steeped in idealism and anxious to practice what they have learned in the classroom when they go onto a ward with burned-out colleagues and too many patients and are expected to cope immediately. Kramer suggested biculturalism as a way of handling reality shock. In bicultural nursing the new graduate who learned to spend all day in the care of one patient is employed in a situation where she or he is expected to cope with caring for ten. This nurse learns to compromise without relinquishing the knowledge of what good nursing should be under differing circumstances.

I came from a family in which education was valued, but not readily available. Neither of my parents completed the eighth grade. They worked hard, and their goal in life was to provide their three daughters with a high school education. Book learning was not highly esteemed in my family, but experiencing life to its fullest was. A certain amount of schooling and visits to the public library were encouraged, as were solitary trips to downtown St. Louis on the bus when I was only eight or nine.

Teachers, classmates, and books stimulated my desire for a college education. Rather than nursing, going to college was my primary goal. I worked as a nurse's aide every summer from eighth grade on, and that is what stimulated me to want to be a nurse. I was happy the day I found out that it was possible to combine both of those aspirations. I won a scholarship to St. Louis University and entered its first class of baccalaureate students in 1953.

Three years after graduating from St. Louis University School of Nursing, I was working as a director of night nursing service at a 1,000-bed hospital in a large midwestern city. To staff that hospital at night, I had five registered nurses. I had one in the intensive care unit, one in delivery, one in the "premie" unit, one in the emergency room, and one on the polio ward. In addition to staffing their assigned units, those nurses also performed supervisory functions and watched over the practical nurses who were in charge of the individual patient care units.

I first became interested in the problems of transition from school to work when I watched what happened to the RNs I worked with. First of all, those five were not seasoned nurses; most of them were new graduates. Watching what happened to them night after night was almost as devastating for me as it was for them. They tried hard to put the theories and techniques that they had learned in school into operation in the work setting. However, with the responsibility of caring for 100 to 200 patients, that was an impossible task.

As I watched those new graduates, it became clear that they believed there were only two ways to go. About half of them tried to attend to everything. They tried to meet the needs of all of the patients for whom they were responsible, and they virtually killed themselves in the process. Either they became physically ill (diarrhea, tension headaches, upset stomachs), or else they became so edgy that if you happened to look at them a little too hard, they would immediately burst into tears. Sometimes they would cry even if you didn't look at them. In a way they wore their emotions on their sleeves. I never knew what state of mind they would be in at any given time.

The other half of the group adopted a different tactic. They would decide *a priori* that they could not attend to everything. So they put blinders on and drew a coat of armor around themselves and would not attend to more than they could handle. This group was efficient and seemed hard and cold.

Within one month the first group had left; the second group had earned seniority and therefore could work straight days. So, the following month would see another group of five RNs, and the process would start all over again. During the 12 months that I was director of night nursing service, I saw no fewer than 34 new graduates come on night duty, go through the process, then quit or transfer to days.

That experience had a profound impact on me and made me question what point there was in educating those beautiful young people and instilling them with high nursing values when they would face such situations when they graduated. That experience made me decide to go back to school and do research. There, I developed my theory on reality shock, a phenomenon with shocklike symptoms that results when workers who have spent years preparing for a particular vocation find that the theories they learned cannot be applied in practice. Reality shock hits the professional who finds that values acquired in educational settings are not always shared and go unrewarded in the workplace. As in culture shock and future shock, reality shock is often accompanied by disillusionment.

My research resulted in the book, *Reality Shock: Why Nurses Leave Nursing,* published in 1974 by The C.V. Mosby Company. The reality shock research and my interest in developing baccalaureate nursing that would be responsive to the needs of the profession, society, and the aspirant nurse proceeded simultaneously. I had the tremendous pleasure of working with Helen Nahm at the University of California, San Francisco (UCSF), who became my mentor.

In the early 1960s UCSF pioneered curriculum change and reform and was in the vanguard of implementing integrated nursing curricula and "process" curricula. It was a dynamic decade. Much of my writing and many of my curriculum consultations during the 1960s and early 1970s centered on my commitment to integrated, process-oriented nursing curricula. It was hard work, but during that period we implemented one of the most dynamic and sound integrated nursing curricula in the country. While I was dean of the undergraduate program at UCSF, I implemented and tested the Anticipatory Socialization Program designed to assist nursing students to cope with reality shock.

During the late 1970s and early 1980s I found that my speeches, writing, workshops, and teaching on integrated curricula gradually changed. Influenced to a large extent by my research on reality shock, I began to see that there were problems associated with "integrated curricula" that were perhaps unsolvable. By that time, my reality shock research had led me to develop the Bicultural Training Program, which was designed to train neophytes to use a type of conflict resolution to help bridge discrepancies between values learned in theory and values existing in reality.

While I was still deeply committed to the economy of learning and effort that integration and synthesis provide, I recognized certain facts that needed to be considered. The first was that integration was breeding generalization, and nursing is not generalized; it is specialized and becoming increasingly so as time passes. Second, nursing faculty did not and do not like to see themselves or to be seen as generalized. They are prepared in master's degree programs in a specialty area, and they like to be identified accordingly. Lastly, I discovered that lack of specialization in faculty breeds the clinical incompetence that new graduates often discussed and associated with their nursing faculty in the reality shock research.

In the late 1970s and early 1980s I saw myself making a marked career change. After many years in nursing service, teaching, and research, I decided to take a position as dean of a school of nursing. I wanted to be in a position where I would be able to implement my research findings on reality shock and biculturalism and where I would be able to influence faculty to make curriculum changes I felt were necessary for the future of nursing. To accomplish these goals, I wanted to be dean of a school of nursing that had a graduate program but was still small enough that I could associate with and influence all faculty. I chose the University of Connecticut School of Nursing, and in 1979 I became the school's third dean.

During my eight years as dean there the faculty and I accomplished many goals. We put into effect a summer internship program for junior students in nursing. Through my championing of faculty clinical competence and specialization, we implemented a Faculty Practice Program. Within five years more than one third of the faculty were actively engaged on a regular basis in clinical practice. I continued my research on biculturalism and reality shock and implemented a bicultural training program for experienced nurses. As dean I was able to influence and markedly develop faculty and faculty research. When I started at Connecticut, no faculty members were engaged in research. Within eight years, over half were doctorally prepared, and research productivity resulted in 10 to 15 publications per year. An international nursing experience was developed and implemented by the faculty, and one faculty member wrote a grant and received funding for a million-dollar international project through USAID. Several faculty received predoctoral fellowship grants; the school received a $400,000 contract grant from the Division of Nursing to establish a faculty-run wellness center for the elderly adjacent to the campus. Another faculty member had a project grant approved to establish and conduct an RN counseling center for diploma and associate degree RNs wishing to obtain a baccalaureate degree. When I resigned from my position as dean of the University of Connecticut School of Nursing, I had a tremendous feeling of accomplishment in achieving the goals I had established.

I have now returned to teaching research methods as a visiting professor at the University of Nevada, Reno, and am engaged in conducting research in the private sector. Currently I am completing a large-scale follow-up study on the magnet hospitals—the hospitals identified in an American Academy of Nursing study as places where nurses most like to work. I am also involved in looking at the factors that are instrumental in overcoming the nurse shortage.

Eleanor C. Lambertsen

Eleanor C. Lambertsen, EdD, RN, FAAN,
is engaged in health service research at
The New York Hospital–Cornell Medical Center
where she was Director of Nursing
before she retired from full-time
employment

Teacher, scholar, dean, director, administrator, and star spokesperson, Eleanor Lambertsen has been an effective mover and shaker in health care for half a century. As a historian she has traced the social, economic, and political forces influencing the education and practice of nurses, and she charges that the issues of the past persist. Her major work has been with the study and teaching of the organization and delivery of nursing services in hospitals, and she is associated in particular with the concepts of leadership and of team nursing.

"I learned early," she writes, "that you did not sit, wait, and wail because nurses were ignored in appointments to significant deliberative bodies. I have never been hesitant to offer my talents or the talents of others."

*I*n my publication *Education for Nursing Leadership,* I reviewed the nursing literature (1893-1958) in an attempt to trace the historical basis for persistent social, economic, and political forces influencing the education and practice of nurses. As I progressed in my study, I was tempted to title the review "Echoes from the Past" because the issues and questions expressed by nursing leaders of the past continue to be issues and questions today. The persistence of the issues and questions does not imply a lack of progress. It implies rather that nursing, as an essential social service, must continue to be examined critically within the context of other social phenomena.

The central concerns of nursing—care, comfort, guidance, and helping individuals to cope with health problems—have not changed. However, the dimension and scope of practice of the components of these concerns have continued to change along with social determinants for health care services. Issues and trends in the organization and delivery of nursing care services are a reflection of the nature and magnitude of changes in science and technology, in social structures, in intellectual concepts, and in economic and political establishments.

Nursing's evolution has been influenced by nursing leaders who, invested with a social conscience, have functioned as innovators in meeting the health care needs of the public. My career in nursing has been shaped by my associations with many of these courageous visionaries. They were interested in serving as mentors, and I developed contacts in the early days of my career that have been not only influential but lasting—people who opened many doors and provided opportunities.

A lasting impression that these associations left me with was my associates' effectiveness in multidisciplinary settings. Although the term "movers and shakers" was not in vogue when I developed these contacts, it is descriptive of the lives of many of my associates. I placed a priority throughout my career on seeking experiences or appointments in multidisciplinary deliberations and programs. I learned early not to sit, wait, and wail because nurses were ignored in appointments to significant deliberative bodies. I have never been hesitant to offer my talents or the talents of others, which has been a successful and rewarding strategy.

MY ENTRY INTO NURSING

I graduated from high school in 1934 during the depression and drifted into nursing. Two programs of study were available in high school at that time—the college preparatory track and the commercial track. I enrolled in the college preparatory track intent on becoming a teacher, but a brief ego-shattering experience as a substitute for the Latin teacher during my senior year had a greater influence on my career choice than the possibility of enlisting my father's support in financing college tuition.

The Latin teacher had planned to attend two state conferences during my senior year. A substitute teacher was not available within the immediate community, and when the principal approved my teacher's recommendation that I teach the class, my pride was boundless. That vanity, however, proved to be my downfall. I was enamored of the cognitive discipline associated with the study of Latin and was equally happy about being singled out to teach as a senior student.

The freshman and sophomore Latin students had anticipated that classes would be canceled, and so they treated me as an intruder upon their free time from a required course. Any attempt on my part to follow the lesson plan and proceed with translation was treated as a joke. I was baited with innocuous comments that were followed by gales of laughter. It was only after I threw an eraser at the primary heckler and let forth a stream of expletives that I gained some semblance of control. I was embarrassed; they were embarrassed; a truce was achieved.

To this day I prefer elective courses to required courses and mentally throw erasers at hecklers who denigrate the cognitive discipline of nursing.

Following graduation from high school I spent the summer (as usual) at the New Jersey shore with my grandfather. I met a nurse there and for the first time became interested in nursing. I wrote to schools of nursing in New Jersey and selected one that enrolled students in February because I didn't want to interrupt a long vacation period. Nursing was never mentioned as a career choice for those majoring in college preparatory programs, and the nurse I met at the shore only knew about hospital schools of nursing.

My only contact with nurses prior to that meeting was as a patient in a community hospital, where I was taken for surgery following an automobile accident. When I requested references (required by the school of nursing) from my principal, minister, and family physician, they all tried to dissuade me. Their perception was that nursing was a menial rather than intellectual vocation.

I did not accept this image of nursing then, nor do I accept it now. I hope that those nurses who find solace in continuing to deplore the negative image of the nurse may give way to those who have achieved public recognition and professional stature through innovation in education and practice.

In 1933 (two years prior to my enrollment in a school of nursing) the Department of Studies of the National League of Nursing Education published a *Study on the Use of the Graduate Nurse for Bedside Nursing in the Hospital*. In 1932, 63% of the hospitals did not employ staff nurses. The service was completely maintained by students. According to the study, the chief reasons offered by those who were not in favor of employing graduate nurses for patient care were that they lacked discipline, were extravagant in the use of supplies, lacked familiarity with the methods and routines of the particular hospital, were inclined to move from job to job, resented criticism, and increased the cost of hospitals. The graduate nurses (predominantly private duty nurses) objected to employment as general staff nurses because of the pressure of work, inability to plan and give patients the care they required, long and irregular hours, the lack of dignity with which the service was regarded, and living in the institution. However, as the depression continued, many private duty nurses turned to the hospital for employment. In some instances they worked for room and board and were forced into the existing nursing pattern that had been designed for students requiring supervision.

The appendix of the study listed activities of the bedside graduate nurse, the bedside student nurse, and the nurse's assistant. It also listed a schedule of work for ward helpers, kitchen maids, porters, and orderlies. This was the era before antibiotics, early ambulation, and advanced technology. Patients were captives in their beds, and nurses were captives of the patients. There was no question that nursing care made a difference in outcomes. In the current nursing scene, the practice of nurses in 1934 may be viewed as primitive. However, I was a product of the school of thought that held that a scientific base underlies the diagnosis and treatment of human ailments. I believed these ailments were expressed overtly as emotional and physical discomfort and as interference with normal life processes, and covert signs and symptoms primarily were dependent on human observations and nursing interventions rather than sophisticated diagnostic and therapeutic technology.

When I graduated in 1938, one classmate and I were offered employment, and we were both told that if we did not do well there would be others in the next graduating class to take our places. My first assignment was as a staff nurse on nights (12-hour duty and a six-day work week) on a medical-surgical unit. Within a year I became assistant night supervisor, and the following year I became night supervisor. The hospital did not have medical interns and residents but did employ one woman house physician. Since that position turned over frequently and because the house physicians were not familiar with the idiosyncrasies of the individual private practice physicians, house physicians were usually bypassed when information was relayed in the patient care network. The private physicians preferred to communicate directly with nurses in supervisory positions. My experience as night supervisor provided valuable continuing education experiences. I was primarily responsible for assessing the progress of patients, monitoring nursing care, intervening in complex or ambiguous patient care situations, and evaluating the need for alterations in patients' medical or nursing regimens.

That role demanded critical decisions that developed my cognitive skills and competence in nursing interventions. It was an environment where I was able to demonstrate that nursing care made a difference. At night no one was there except nurses and physicians, who made their rounds early in the evening. The only demands on nurses were patient care and recording data on the patients' charts. I hasten to add, before I am accused of hallucinating, that this was a 200-bed hospital, and a significant percentage of the patients there were convalescing. Patients routinely remained in the hospital for extensive periods. An average of 30 patients at any given time required intensive nursing care, including women in labor.

In 1942 I was told by the director of nursing that I was to be responsible for teaching nursing arts and medical-surgical nursing. I was also to serve as her assistant. That meant being the day supervisor. I had completed courses in premedical science at Rutgers University and in nursing at Seton Hall College, but I had never taught. The students had all had experiences on night duty and I was aware that they considered me a strict supervisor. As I arranged my lesson plan on the desk the first day of class, my hands were visibly shaking. Over the silence that greeted me, one student's whisper was clearly audible.

"Miss Lambertsen is nervous!" My thought flashed back to my experience as a Latin substitute. I thought, "I could lose control." However, my nursing experience came to my rescue, and I responded, "Yes, I am. This is my first class. It is normal to be nervous when one tries to do something the first time. Today's class is . . . ."

I am still anxious whenever I meet with a class for the first time. Call it stage fright. Until I sense an interactive response from students, I keep reaching out. I never experience this when presenting a paper to a large audience, but the teaching-learning process makes very different demands of the teacher. I am also aware of the financial investment the students have made for each course credit. I have always found teaching to be a very rewarding experience, and the longer I teach the more I am awed by the brilliance of students of nursing whom I have encountered in baccalaureate or higher degree programs.

On New Year's Eve in 1945, when I was dressing to go home for the holidays, I was called and asked to come to the hospital immediately. The president of the hospital's board of trustees and the hospital administrator told me that the director of nurses had been fired and that I was now principal of the school of nursing and director of nursing. I went home and wept. I had planned to resign and to continue my education in the fall. Early in 1946 the hospital administrator was dismissed, and I became acting hospital administrator with the president of the board of trustees functioning as president of the hospital.

I was aware of the community's opinion of the leadership of the president and former administrator. They had come from a major medical center in New York City and were insensitive to the cultural values held by a suburban community for its only hospital. The hospital was everybody's business. Shortly after they had come to the hospital, a citizen's committee was organized to address the problems of the hospital in the delivery of patient care and develop requirements for innovations. The committee members had direct access to physicians and nurses, but the hospital administration and the director of nurses considered the committee members interlopers. (Note the philosophy inherent in the job title "director of 'nurses'" at that time as compared with the change in title, in later years, to "director of 'nursing.'")

September 2, 1945, marked the end of World War II. The nation embarked on a rapid transition in sociopolitical structures from a prewar to postwar economy. Innovative programs in health, education, and welfare received a high priority. A nationally recognized medical administrator was appointed by the hospital board of trustees as a consultant. I soon found myself serving as his data collector and was intrigued with the nature of the issues and problems he addressed. However, I took issue with his emphasis on fiscal accountability of all services and programs. At one point, when he questioned the cost of meals for patients and staff, I compared his per diem rate with mine and suggested that he should allocate a portion of his compensation to me, since my services to him were in addition to my other responsibilities. It was my first experience in bargaining for remuneration because of an increase in responsibility in a position. (Incidentally, at his recommendation I received a significant increase in my salary.)

Later he offered to recommend me for a scholarship in hospital administration. I was not enticed. My nine. years at Overlook Hospital in Summit, New Jersey, as well as my involvement in nursing affairs at the state and national levels, convinced me that career opportunities in nursing were infinite. Leadership positions in either nursing service or nursing education were available. My concept of a hospital administrator was that the position was akin to being a business manager. At that stage of my career the concept of the triad of administration (director of nursing, chief medical officer, and hospital director) crystallized. The triad recognized the participation of the director of nursing in all deliberative sessions that directly or indirectly affected patient care programs and services.

In June 1947 appointments were made for the position of director of the hospital and director of nursing. My resignation took effect, and I enrolled in the Division of Nursing, Teachers College, Columbia University (TC). During the board of trustees meeting prior to the termination of my employment, I was presented with a check for $5,000 from the trustees and medical staff to cover the cost of my education. Tuition at TC was then $10 per credit, or $180 per semester.

When I enrolled as a student at TC in 1947, functional specialization was at the baccalaureate as well as the master's level. In 1950 a prespecialization program for registered nurses replaced specialization at the baccalaureate level. I elected to major in teaching and supervision of medical-surgical nursing on the baccalaureate level with clinical concentrations in chronic and long-term illness, rehabilitation, and geriatrics. On the master's level, I also completed all of the course requirements for a first-level position in public health nursing. I knew that faculty positions in collegiate programs required academic evidence of preparation for public health nursing practice.

During my experience at Overlook Hospital I had become interested in the role of nurses in the organization and delivery of patient care services and in the relationship of nurses and physicians as colleagues. The philosophy of the major in medical-surgical nursing at TC was patient care oriented, with an emphasis on the science and art underlying the practice of nursing. It was assumed that the teacher's or supervisor's functional area of specialization required scholarship and clinical competence in a defined area of nursing practice, as well as competence in the teaching-learning process.

On the master's level I majored in administration of collegiate schools of nursing, which included a concentration in curriculum development at the undergraduate level.

My mentors in the early stages of my career in nursing service and at TC were scholars of nursing, and my professional relationships with them fostered my need to study the role and function of the professional nurse in the delivery of patient care. When I graduated in 1950, I had several offers of employment and planned to accept a position as a faculty member in a baccalaureate program in nursing.

THE EVOLUTION OF THE NURSING TEAM CONCEPT

Social changes during and following World War II intensified problems confronting the nursing profession. The demand for professional nurses increased as a result of the expansion of health care services and because of the increasing complexity of modes of therapy within hospitals. Fewer practical nurses and nurses' aides were employed after the war. A major problem was the shortage of professional nurses and the consequence of this shortage on the quality of nursing and medical care. Nursing leaders faced a serious dilemma. Since the days of Florence Nightingale, leaders in the profession had insisted that nurses, and nurses alone, determine how to discharge their responsibilities to society. Although every profession has the ultimate responsibility for determining its distinctive role, the leadership in nursing was aware that many problems with which they had to grapple were only in part professional and were not subject to assessment or solution by nurses alone. Many of the critical issues were also affecting and being affected by medicine, administration of health services agencies, and educational institutions providing undergraduate and graduate programs in nursing, government, and economics.

In the fall of 1947, R. Louise McManus, the director of the Division of Nursing at TC, organized a multidisciplinary committee to study the problems confronting the nursing profession and to establish what the role of nursing should be in that period of rapid social change. The committee's report, *A Program for the Nursing Profession* (published in 1948), focused on the reasons for the shortage of nursing personnel, as well as on additional factors that appeared likely to intensify the shortage in the next decade. It recommended that the nursing function be divided between two groups—professional and practical nurses. The report also recommended that the relationship between the professional nurse and other members of the medical and health team be classified and improved, that similar suitable relationships be developed among the various groups of nursing personnel who together comprise the nursing team, and that the professional nurse complete a four-year course leading to a baccalaureate degree in a college- or university-affiliated school of nursing.

The faculty of the Division of Nursing prepared a blueprint for a comprehensive study of the function of nursing. Hypotheses were set up for study, and a plan for organizing hospital nursing service staffs to achieve patient-centered care was designed based on the use of all nursing personnel in the interests of economy and efficiency.

Previously the *Report of the President's Commission on Higher Education* (1946) had influenced the public and educators in general as well as leaders in nursing. The national commission had been organized to conduct a study of the functions of higher education and to recommend a means by which those functions could best be performed. That report reiterated many of the beliefs about and studies of nursing education that had been initiated by nurse leaders. (I have isolated from this report references made to nursing education.) The report advocated expansion of junior college education at the technical level.

The section of the report dealing with the role of the professional school stressed that shortages of professional personnel necessary to meet the health needs of the nation must be of concern to institutions of higher education, and that the expansion of physical facilities and their maximum use in medical, dental, nursing, and pharmaceutical education should not be delayed. The recommendations of the President's commission distinguished between a technical and a professional role in the occupation of nursing. (The report would well serve as political and professional clout in today's controversy surrounding entry into practice.)

THE TEAM NURSING PROJECT

On August 1, 1950, financial support from the W.K. Kellogg Foundation was received by TC's Division of Nursing for nursing service projects including the study of team nursing. A prior five-year study of the curriculum of the various majors led to the decision to discontinue specialization at the baccalaureate level. A prespecialization program was introduced in the fall of 1950 for registered nurses who had graduated from hospital schools of nursing. The purpose of the program was to prepare graduates for leadership roles as practitioners of nursing in hospitals and public health agencies.

I was recruited and appointed to the staff of the W.K. Kellogg project as an instructor in the major course—Team Nursing—and as project director for the organization of a hospital into a teaching demonstration center for educational programs leading to preparation for leadership positions in the hospital's nursing service department.

Contractual agreements between the New York City Department of Hospitals and the Division of Nursing of Teachers College provided for the development of the nursing service of a new hospital for the treatment of patients with cancer (Francis Delafield) affiliated with the medical college of Columbia University. The mutual concern of the educational institution and the service agency was the need for improvement of nursing care programs in general. It was envisioned that the projected study would provide an opportunity to set up a research field in which it would be possible to break away from traditional practice and seek ways of improving nursing care. February 1, 1951, was the date set for the admission of patients. In January I worked full time at the hospital with one other member of the project staff, participating in all phases of detailed planning with the medical, hospital administration, and nursing service staffs. (The director of nursing had been appointed to the project staff at a half-time salary.)

The advantage of organizing a new hospital was significant for it was understood and accepted that experimentation and ongoing evaluation were crucial to the evolution of the team concept. The plan included activation of one patient care unit at a time and allowed for orientation and training of nursing service staff. Full-time students, enrolled at the master's level in the nursing service administration major, led projects of significance to programs and services of the department of nursing service. Throughout the five years of the project, the resources of the TC clinical faculty were available to the project staff.

In two years the department of nursing service of Memorial Hospital for Cancer and Allied Diseases agreed to become the second teaching demonstration center. In 1952 I was appointed director of the entire W.K. Kellogg project, which encompassed responsibility for the majors on the master's level: supervision, in-service education, and administration of hospital departments of nursing services.

The basic premise underlying the organization of nursing service personnel at the delivery level of nursing service (the nursing team) was that the need of the individual patient for nursing care was the focus. The nature, scope, and standards for comprehensive nursing care were defined, and the supportive relationship of others in the nursing service hierarchy in the achievement of objectives for nursing care evolved. The traditional organization chart was reversed. The philosophy of the reversal is that the delivery of safe, effective, and efficient nursing care services is directly affected by the talents and competence of those providing the services within the various clinical patient care units.

My experiences in the study of nursing service administration with students in the major proved invaluable. During my tenure as director of nursing at The New York Hospital I followed the guidelines I had developed in revising the organization chart. In today's world of diagnosis-related groups (DRGs) this approach to organization is increasingly mandatory.

My study of team nursing extended to the totality of the nursing service organization and the critical nature of the role of the director of nursing. I have always been a student of the history of the evolution of nursing as a professional discipline within the context of the socioeconomic and political scene. It is because of this that I continue to be dismayed to the point of consternation by the current criticism that team nursing is limited to an organizational arrangement of nurses' aides, practical nurses, and registered nurses who happen to be employed on patient care units in a hospital. Reference should be made to my doctoral dissertation *Education for Nursing Leadership*, published in 1958 by J.B. Lippincott, for the comprehensive treatment of the projected role and functions of the team leader.

> The nature of the functions of the team leader requires education of a type and scope characteristic of preservice educational programs within university or colleges.... In-service education and on-the-job-training is an expedient approach....
>
> The principles and concepts of team leadership are at variance with some of the concepts of team nursing which stress only the management role of the team leader or merely a change in title of the general staff nurse.... The quality of nursing care is directly influenced by knowledge, judgment, skill and values of those participating in this care and they in turn are affected by the educational preparation and continued growth of competence in the experiences following their educational experiences.

TEAM NURSING REVISITED

The basic concepts and assumptions underlying the role and relationships of the team leader to supportive nursing service personnel and other health care providers have survived the test of time. The assumptions underlying nursing team leadership were the R. Louise McManus assumptions. The functions of nursing service personnel were perceived as a spectrum. Functions that encompassed involvements of techniques and cognitive skills varying in difficulty and complexity extended on a continuum, from the simplest to the most complex functions. The functions also demanded judgment ranging from that based on common knowledge to judgment that can be arrived at only by bringing to bear on professional problems pertinent knowledge from an extensive reservoir of scientific information derived from many fields of study. Unstructured and ambiguous patterns of practice confront the professional nurse practitioner at the team leader level, at the institutional level, and at the public health nurse level and often require the talents of clinical specialists. The process remains that of assessing, diagnosing, planning, providing, and evaluating outcomes of nursing care. This process is a scientific mode of inquiry—logical thinking involving the arrangement of assumptions, premises, and conclusions in arriving at anticipated outcomes.

THE SOCIAL AND PROFESSIONAL MILIEU—1950 TO 1987

I fully appreciate that today's graduates of preservice baccalaureate degree programs in nursing look at differentiation of the function of professional nurse practitioners and use such labels as *primary nurse* rather than *team leader*. I contend that the team leader's place on the nursing service staff is as the nurse with primary responsibility for the delivery and evaluation of nursing care services.

During my tenure at The New York Hospital, the nursing staff of the various patient care units were free to label their system for organizing the delivery of nursing care. I have long believed that commitment to a cause ensures positive outcomes. Therefore we had team nursing, primary nursing, district nursing, and a variety of mixes. Policies required senior staff nurses to hold baccalaureate degrees and clinical specialists to hold master's degrees. All were required to demonstrate clinical and leadership proficiency. During that period, recruitment of degreed nurses was not a major problem for medical centers in New York City. However, times have changed. The current problem with a decreasing number of graduates from baccalaureate nursing programs may result in proposals from vested-interest, fragmented groups of technicians, such as *medication distributors,* trained on the job to serve patients their medications. I am *not* hallucinating. Instant solutions to shortage problems are beginning to creep into deliberations at the same time that organized nursing is attempting to legitimize differentiation in the scope of practice of graduates of baccalaureate degree programs and associate degree programs for entry into practice. In 1958 in my publication *Education for Nursing Leadership,* I expressed my concern:

> Social changes, attitudes and changing roles within the occupation are jeopardizing the nurse's role in the practice of *nursing* . . . the churning within the occupation can be a motivating force or could terminate in a period which might be labeled "the great compromise." As long as groups of nurses continue to curtail progress in clearly defining nursing functions of a professional nature and impede progress through advances in education because "their status is showing," the quality of nursing care will remain at an elementary and superficial level. Tradition rightfully belongs to history; complacency must be replaced by vigorous effort.

During and following my involvement in experimentation with team nursing, I became involved at the national and state level as a member of committees and commissions focusing on the education and practice of nurses such as the Surgeon General's Consultant Group on Nursing, 1961; Education Committee of the American Nurses Association, 1963; National Commission for the Study of Nursing and Nursing Education, 1967; National Advisory Council of Nurse Training of the United States Public Health Service, 1969; Secretary's Committee to Study Extended Roles for Nurses, 1971; consultant to the New York State Nurses' Association Committee on Education, 1967; and consultant to the Committee to Study the Nurse Practice Act, 1969.

THE AMERICAN HOSPITAL ASSOCIATION, 1958 TO 1961

In 1957 I completed my doctorate and had been employed at Teachers College for seven years, studying and teaching the organization and delivery of nursing services in hospitals. My involvement in the study of the role of the nurse as team leader had influenced my decision to seek a faculty position in a generic baccalaureate degree program.

I was asked to apply for 16 positions. (At that time there was a limited supply of nurses with earned doctorates.) The offers included several dean positions and an appointment as general director of a large nursing organization. I knew that I was not ready to be a dean, and I knew that in good faith I could not accept a position with the National League for Nursing because I could not commit myself for the length of time an important position in organized nursing would incur. My career interest was education.

At the same time I was requested to apply for a position with the American Hospital Association (AHA). The administrative leadership of the AHA, with the endorsement of key leaders in nursing, planned to create a Division of Nursing and was seeking candidates. When an official of the AHA came to Teachers College to interview me about the position, I nominated several candidates. I was not interested in the position.

I was not aware that I had been recommended to the AHA by a number of nurses in strategic nursing positions, and since I had a healthy respect for the power they wielded in nursing, I succumbed to their subtle persuasion to accept the position. The women who had nominated me viewed it as being a strategic appointment. Their message was, "You are young enough at this stage to interrupt your plans for your career in education. It is important for a nurse with your background and interests to move into the AHA and help shape a program that could effectively relate to the goals and missions of nursing."

Prior to accepting the position as Director of the Division of Nursing and Assistant Secretary of the Council of Professional Practice of the AHA, I submitted my own job description. My major concern was that I be actively involved and have a voice in all activity and deliberations directly or indirectly concerned with nursing education or nursing service. I was not willing to take the risks implied in a general philosophical pronouncement of intent. I had had too much exposure to the limitations placed on directors of nursing in the deliberative process of hospitals.

Throughout my tenure at the AHA I had complete support from organized nursing and individual nurses in leadership positions as well as from the organization's administrative officers and trustees. Once I got to Chicago, I sought opportunities to meet with officials of the American Medical Association and numerous other medical organizations with offices there. As a result I was frequently sought out for information about nursing policies, positions, and practices. I was the acknowledged spokesperson for nursing as well as the liaison between the AHA, the ANA, the NLN, and other organized nursing groups. This does not imply that there were not organizational conflicts; there were, but I never felt that I had to compromise my positions.

My experience with the AHA was invaluable and resulted in my appointments to numerous multidisciplinary national commissions, councils, study groups, and conferences. I believe that my commitment to the philosophy and principles of the leadership role of the nurse in the organization and delivery of nursing care services fostered positive relationships with health service administrators and physicians, and it opened up a wealth of opportunities for me to represent nurses in a variety of situations when either the AHA or the ANA was requested to nominate a nurse to a deliberative body.

RETURN TO TEACHERS COLLEGE, 1961 TO 1970

I met my husband, Joseph R. Anderson, MD, when I first joined the AHA staff. When we decided to get married, I resigned my position. (Nepotism policies were in effect, and I wished to return to education.) We were married after I returned to TC, and my husband subsequently was transferred to the New York City office of the AHA. I retained the name of Lambertsen, although he hung the Anderson seal in the entry to our apartment. Our careers commingled, we had common interests, and our life together had overtones from our years at AHA. Frequently we had occasion to participate in the same meetings. However, in the 1960s, rooming together in a hotel as Dr. Lambertsen and Dr. Anderson was not without question at the registration desk.

Without any medical warning, Joseph died in our apartment in October 1965. After his death, I considered several dean positions but decided to work as Head of the Division of Nursing Education at TC, following the retirement of R. Louise McManus. I considered the opportunity a privilege.

The graduate programs in nursing under the leadership of Adelaide Nutting, Isabelle Stewart, and R. Louise McManus had achieved high esteem at the national and international levels. Faculty were visionaries and professional activists. TC alumni held strategic positions throughout the world and were a continuous source of inspiration for faculty. Throughout my years there, I found a network of alumni to be invaluable, and the graduate students were always challenging.

My nine years at TC (first as head of the Division of Nursing and later as director of the Division of Health Services, Sciences, and Research) can be classified as a case study in organizational relationships. That was an era in which TC as a graduate center of education, was appraising its mission and goals. There was also the 1968 student "rebellion" at Columbia and the resulting polarization of faculty. The social need for educators had extended beyond the traditional elementary school, secondary school, and college or university programs. The nursing faculty had established the precedent in 1950 by offering a master's degree program to prepare in-service educators for health service agencies providing nursing services.

In 1970 I accepted an appointment as dean of the Cornell University–New York Hospital School of Nursing. My interest and involvement was in the leadership role of the nurse in the emerging system of primary care, and I became active in the nurse practitioner movement at the national and international levels. My most significant appointment was to the Advisory Committee Nurse Faculty Fellowship Program in Primary Care of the Robert Wood Johnson Foundation from 1975 to 1982.

A CHANGE IN LIFE-STYLE: RETIREMENT FROM FULL-TIME EMPLOYMENT

I remain active in nursing organizations, governmental affairs, and multidisciplinary groups. For the last two years I have been engaged in health service research at the New York Hospital–Cornell Medical Center. It is a pilot study of access to care and of the changing nature of patients requiring acute, chronic, long-term, and primary care.

This year, however, I return once again to Teachers College to teach two courses in administration on the doctoral level. The pattern of my career has been one of alternating between nursing service and nursing education. Theorizing about what can be and having the opportunity to test my theories in practice can be challenging and rewarding.

Madeleine M. Leininger

Madeleine M. Leininger, RN, PhD, LhD, FAAN,
is Professor of Nursing and
Anthropology
at Wayne State University, Detroit

Madeleine Leininger was a pioneer in bringing forth a new and exciting body of transcultural nursing knowledge.

Working under Margaret Mead at the University of Cincinnati, she came to the understanding that cultural knowledge was a missing link in health care, and from her perspective, it was important to foster the use of that knowledge in nursing.

The rest is transcultural nursing history.

I discovered nursing as a teenager living in a midwestern agricultural community, and it was my aunt who influenced me to enter the profession. She had congenital heart disease and was often hospitalized. I remember her saying, "Nursing is the most wonderful profession. You can help people when they need you most." Aunt Margaret was a very special person; she died at an early age, leaving five sons. My mother, who was an exquisite caring person, not only cared for me and four brothers and sisters but took in Aunt Margaret's five boys after she died. Giving to others without expecting something in return and being willing to try something different were part of our family's philosophy of life. These values were reinforced by strong religious, family, and community ties.

In 1945 my sister and I dared to be different. We were the only people in the region to enter the nursing profession. Since this was the postdepression period and we had no money for nursing study, my sister and I entered the Cadet Nurse Corps and a diploma program in Colorado. This proved to be an important stepping stone to many other educational and service opportunities. I had already learned from my family, "If opportunities arise, take them. They may help you get to the next opportunity." I also was committed to the belief that if you value something or believe it to be good for humankind, you should never relinquish it.

My father's German-French background provided me with tenacity, purpose, and a hard work ethic; my mother's strong Irish heritage provided me with a sense of wit and humor and the ability to enjoy whatever I was doing and make the best of it. I believe that small-town country folks make good leaders because they usually have had to fend for themselves, work hard, set goals, and learn how to make the best of whatever resources they have in life.

While I was in my basic nursing program, I was elected president of my class. I was able to introduce changes that served the class well. That gave me confidence in my leadership abilities. Since 1948 the members of that class have continued to keep in touch with one another.

In 1950 I received my bachelor's degree (with a concentration in the humanities and the sciences) and opened a psychiatric nursing service and educational program in a new unit affiliated with Creighton University. I served in multiple roles as administrator, teacher, therapist, nursing service director, and multidisciplinary facilitator. Later I saw that I needed to obtain a master's degree in psychiatric nursing, and I fulfilled that goal in 1954.

In the mid-1950s I went to the University of Cincinnati, started a graduate program in child psychiatric nursing, and began to develop and study the role of the clinical specialist in that specialty area. While I was doing direct participant-observation experiences in a child guidance center, I observed that there were obvious differences in the way Jewish, German, Anglo-African, and Appalachian Americans wanted care. I found that the ways in which these children were eating, playing, sleeping, interacting, and responding to staff and family were clearly different. When I pointed this out to the director of the center (a physician who was a child psychiatry specialist) and suggested that the differences were cultural, she listened but believed she could explain them with psychoanalytical interpretations.

Shortly thereafter, anthropologist Margaret Mead was invited to the University of Cincinnati as a visiting professor. I found her female leadership and knowledge of people the world over inspiring, especially in the male-dominated medical world. Frequently she would challenge the psychiatric residents by saying, "On what basis are you making this diagnosis? What do you know about the cultural backgrounds of these children? How can you make an accurate diagnosis and attempt to help these children without cultural information?" Her comments seemed most relevant and were also of importance to nurses in their daily work. Dr. Mead showed me that the missing link in nursing and other health fields was cultural knowledge.

One day I asked her, "In what ways do you think anthropology would help nurses?" She replied, "Well, I don't know exactly, but anthropological insights are essential to an understanding of people—all people in the world. I wonder if nurses would really study cultures *in depth* so they could accurately interpret client behavior, sick or well." This was sufficient challenge to me, and it led me to study anthropology. I had never taken courses in that area and barely knew the content and goals of the field.

Ultimately I was led to the development of transcultural nursing as a new field of study and practice in nursing. I knew then that I had to be a strong risk taker to establish an entirely new line of thought and practice that would link nursing and anthropology together. There were no leaders to guide me on that path and no eager followers as I proceeded to carve out the trail.

In 1959 I entered the doctoral program in anthropology at the University of Washington. There were no students who had interests comparable to mine, so I had to hold fast to my nursing goals while learning. I was fascinated with the richness of the field, and I saw that anthropological knowledge was essential to help nurses provide reliable, complete, and meaningful care to people. Studying culture leads to an understanding of humans because culture includes people's religions, kinships, political beliefs, values, education, material technology, economics, and all other aspects that make people what they are in the world. It was shocking to think that "modern" nursing was nearly 100 years old and anthropological knowledge had never been a part of nursing curricula, let alone nursing practice.

I could see the marked ethnocentrism of Anglo content in nursing instruction and in the way nurses had imposed their values on clients in clinical settings. I envisioned that by 1980, clients of many different cultures would be asserting their cultural identities and that nurses would experience serious problems in caring for clients of different cultures.

My dream and action for preparing nurses in formal programs of study in transcultural nursing were real and imperative. Granted, nursing was not alone. Other health professions were equally ethnocentric and ignorant of different cultures.

My six years of study in anthropology were exceedingly valuable, and I was envisioning the theories and methodologies that had to be developed to make nursing a transcultural discipline. It was necessary to stimulate many other nurses to pursue graduate study in anthropology so there would be a core of well-prepared nurses to draw selected concepts and theories from anthropology and meld them with a nursing perspective. During the following decade I actively encouraged and influenced nearly 60 nurses to pursue master's or doctoral study in anthropology. (Since the field of transcultural nursing was established in the mid-1960s, I have helped to prepare nearly 5,000 nurses in the field through formal courses, workshops, and degree-based programs of study.)

I soon found myself being sought after by nurses who were working in foreign countries and experiencing culture shock and frustrations. They were concerned that they were not prepared to work with other cultures and believed that nursing education programs had failed to help them. Those communications gave more credence to our call for the need for transcultural nursing. Interestingly, there had been a few schools of nursing that had orientation sessions or courses for nurses from other countries who had come to work in hospitals in the United States. However, none of those nurses were prepared through formal and transculturally based educational programs of study, where the nurse's own culture could be taught and compared with American culture. In that way specific plans to use transcultural knowledge in American and worldwide nursing practices could have been developed. Indeed, it was a one-sided approach that offered no opportunity to learn the substantive content of transcultural nursing.

My first transcultural field experience was with the Gadsup people in the eastern highlands of New Guinea. This early field research was an impetus to the development of my theory of cultural care diversity and universality. It was clear that diversity of care and health could be identified, but at that point I wondered what commonalities existed in the differing human cultures that nurses served. I wanted a theory that could be used to explain, describe, interpret, and predict *all* cultures in nursing, not just a few.

Once I had completed my own doctoral program in anthropology in 1965, I began to establish courses, programs, and field studies in transcultural nursing. It took "New Guinea courage" and strong leadership to introduce transcultural nursing courses and programs into five major schools of nursing. Nursing majors were offered in the four traditional fields that had largely been in existence since almost the beginning of nursing and especially prevailed in twentieth-century nursing. The four majors of medical-surgical, maternal-child, psychiatric-mental health, and community nursing seemed to focus on the medical aspects of disease, with little content on human care and no content on transcultural care. I saw nursing as a discipline separate and different from medicine and felt that nursing needed to break its symbolic "umbilical cord" with medicine and become a separate discipline outside of medicine's paternalistic control. I had no objection to nursing having a complementary and cooperative relationship with medicine. However, I did not want medicine to engulf nursing.

The first transcultural nursing courses became part of the curriculum at the University of Colorado School of Nursing in 1966. Those courses opened the door that allowed nurses to develop a new way of thinking and making clinical decisions. Looking at problems from a cultural perspective helped to generate new ways of helping people. The content of the courses made the most sense to community health nurses and the least sense to psychiatric and medical-surgical nurses.

Many fascinating and frustrating incidents occurred as I worked to get transcultural content incorporated in baccalaureate and graduate programs. I remember presenting the first telelecture from Denver to nurses in the Western Rocky Mountain area and describing my "lived-through experiences" with two different cultures, the Mexican-Americans in Denver and the Gadsup in New Guinea. The telelectures and courses were highly successful. The nurses were left wanting more content and ideas on how they could help the people they were working with, particularly the Navajo Indians and Mexican-Americans. Getting nurses to talk about their own experiences with clients from other cultures was also a valuable way to learn transcultural nursing and to reach students, clinicians, and faculty of different cultural backgrounds.

I recall talking with Tahitian nurses via a Pacific Island satellite. The nurses had been suddenly faced with caring for a shipload of Russians who were stranded in Tahiti. The nurses were concerned because they could not communicate with the Russians, who were quiet and would not eat the local foods. (The nurses thought the Russians were starving to death.) I talked about the Soviets' culture, values, and their life-style back home and about what they must be experiencing on the island of Tahiti. Later the nurses wrote to tell me about the "magic of transcultural nursing" and how it had helped them to understand and care for the stranded Russians.

In many hospitals in the United States and overseas, I have served as a consultant on cultural problems, especially those relating to nurses' frustrations. The most common transcultural nursing problems have involved helping clients to eat unfamiliar hospital foods, gaining the cooperation of clients for medical and surgical procedures, working with mothers and fathers during pregnancy, getting consent forms signed, getting health instructions to make sense to families with differing cultural values, getting people to understand visiting regulations and other rules. Conflict and stress increase as clients from different cultures become assertive about their cultural rights and needs and begin to challenge professional staff expectations.

In recent years more nurses have been considering the meaning of culture-specific care and valuing ways in which transcultural nursing concepts and research findings aid in the care of the culturally different. The requests for transcultural courses, workshops, and conferences in this country and overseas have increased seven-fold since 1975. The demand for transcultural education far exceeds the resources.

Since academic nursing schools tend to espouse more steady-state norms than changing norms in their teachings, it has been difficult to get transcultural nursing courses and programs in place, unless one is in an influential leadership position as a dean or director. While I was a dean at the Universities of Washington and Utah, I was able to facilitate the establishment of transcultural nursing programs and departments with interested faculty and upon the request of many students. I have found that wherever there are many cultures in the area surrounding a school of nursing, there is more resistance; in areas with fewer different cultures, I have found greater interest and willingness to learn and practice transcultural nursing among faculty and students.

In 1974 the first national and international Transcultural Nursing Society was established, with approximately 90 members. Since then it has grown considerably and is the major organization of nurses prepared in transcultural nursing. Most transcultural nurses are involved in research, teaching, consultation, and clinical work. Recently we have established transcultural nursing councils in various countries to articulate with the parent organization. I have been able to stimulate organizations in the United States, Canada, South America, Australia, Africa, and Europe. It has been a most exciting development in transcultural nursing and provides for valuable exchanges in research, teaching, and consultation to advance the body of knowledge in the field.

The society has held annual transcultural nursing conferences for the past 15 years. The conferences have been a major source of help for nurses who are establishing transcultural nursing in schools of nursing, hospitals, and clinics. From the beginning the field of transcultural nursing was established with a comparative research focus, and research findings have been presented and discussed at these national meetings.

I have taught baccalaureate, master's, and doctoral students and have thoroughly enjoyed stimulating them to try new ideas and experiences and to investigate new lines of theory, research, and practice. There is much in this world to learn about human beings and their cultures from a nursing perspective. The more knowledgeable and skilled that nurses are in caring for people of different cultures, the greater the nurse and client satisfaction.

I return now after 50 years to Aunt Margaret's statement that, "Nursing is the most wonderful profession to help people." I would add that the combined nursing and anthropological perspective has provided me with special meanings and given me many challenges.

Carrie B. Lenburg

Carrie Lenburg, EdD, RN, FAAN, is
Coordinator of External Degrees in Nursing in the
Regents College Degrees Program in New York State

❖

> *Grandma Sally's admonition, "Screw yourself to the sticking place and you'll get it done," epitomizes Carrie Lenburg's stick-to-itiveness. Her hard work, determination, and strong spirit of independence have persevered from her early years. She was hospitalized as a child and recalls a Miss Cooper, the nurse who cared for her and influenced her to choose nursing as a career.*
>
> *Lenburg's firm belief in nontraditional education led her to readily accept the position of first coordinator of New York's External Degree Nursing Program (now known as the Regents College Degrees Program). After 14 years she continues to use every resource she has to overcome opposition to the Regents program. She continues to speak out, as has always been her wont, on those issues she feels keenly about. Opposition has honed rather than diminished her commitment to her beliefs, and although she feels that her individualism has been costly politically, mentally, and socially, she was pleased when someone once called her the Jane Fonda of nursing.*

I'm not sure where my strong spirit of independence and my sense of being a pioneer came from, but they have dominated my entire life and have led me to special leadership opportunities. I had no way of knowing that the difficult events of my childhood and early adult years would prepare me for an unusual and controversial national position for which I would receive simultaneous criticism and acclaim.

Undoubtedly, my maternal grandmother Sally Jernigan had a lot to do with that preparation. She was a small but strong woman with fine, gray hair that nearly reached the floor when she unwound it from the tight bun at the back of her head. She was the matriarch of a large family who lived and worked on a 100-acre farm in rural southeast Virginia. I was born in an unpainted farmhouse that had been built by my grandfather Charlie when he and Sally were married in 1893. My mother, Carrie, the youngest of eight children, had been born in the same room 22 years before my birth; all of her brothers and sisters were born there as well. I was profoundly influenced by my grandmother and my simple beginnings. Until I was five years old, I lived on the farm while my father served in the navy. I continued to spend summers and most holidays at the farm even after we moved in 1940 to Norfolk, Virginia, where my father completed 20 years of service and subsequently started his own contracting and carpentry business.

I have fond memories of those early years. I used to help my grandmother while my mother worked in the fields planting, cultivating, and harvesting crops of cotton, corn, and peanuts. Sally was an amazing woman. As I think of her now, I marvel at her emotional strength, endurance, capabilities, and caring spirit. As I worked with her, I learned to use available resources. She and the rest of the family lived virtually independent lives. The farm was an oasis in the woods, with the nearest neighbor about a mile away. I learned to split wood for the big iron cookstove and to make medicines from plants we grew. I made snuffsticks, brooms, and gourd dippers for the water bucket, canned vegetables and fruits, and helped slaughter animals and cure meat for the family. My father taught me to hunt. We made soap, butter, patchwork quilts, feather beds, clothes, toys, and items for our own entertainment. In the summer we occasionally made ice cream. That required a four-hour trip in a horsedrawn cart to get a chunk of ice, which we wrapped in sawdust and canvas for the return trip. We pumped water from the well, used kerosene lamps for light, and in the evening sometimes listened to Edward R. Murrow's newscast on the radio that had a battery the size of a car battery.

Early in my life I was held accountable for making a contribution, taking initiative, and being persistent. Those pioneer attitudes and expectations were nourished and strength-ened by subsequent experiences, when initiative and accountability were the expected norm. One of Grandma Sally's expressions that I remember and use often was, "Screw yourself to the sticking place and you'll get it done." That sounds like something from Shakespeare, but I don't know where she would have learned it.

We moved to Norfolk when I was six years old. My brother was a year older, and my sister was still a baby. As our family grew to include seven children, the economic and psychological demands and pressures mounted on my parents. My mother coped and kept us together with a strength that is seemingly reserved for women, while my father gradually succumbed to the numbing and addictive relief of alcohol. Our lives were characterized by endless work and growing tensions.

As the oldest girl I became a second mother to my brothers and sisters. When I was young, I was fully able and was expected to run the household and deal with issues that should have been reserved for someone more mature. I was forced to be resourceful, responsible, and resilient, and I was always in the company of difficulties. I had little time for play and never had the luxury of joining the Girl Scouts or other such groups. I always wanted to learn to play the piano.

During my childhood my mother saw to it that we attended church. She had grown up in a simple Christian religious faith and was uncomfortable with more formal ones. I sang in the choir, taught Sunday school classes, and led Bible-study groups. On many occasions I had to speak before the congregation. Those experiences provoked a sense of mission in me and also strengthened my concept of self and my ability to plan, organize, speak in public, and assume leadership in groups.

At 13, I had my first encounter with nursing when I was hospitalized with a serious infection for a four-week period in Portsmouth Naval Hospital. I was admitted to the adult ward instead of pediatrics, but because of my age I was put in a bed close to the nurse's station. It was an open 20-bed unit, and the nurses took special interest in me because I was young and vulnerable and surrounded by very ill adult women. As soon as my fever and pain were reduced, I began to help the nurses in routine tasks on the unit and started to collect the available artifacts of nursing: a syringe, empty medication bottles, a tourniquet, gauze, tape, and other such things. I kept them in a shoebox in my bedside stand and later took them home as my most prized possessions. I had decided to become a nurse.

One particular nurse encouraged me to work with her in dispensing medications, nourishments, and water. She even let me answer the telephone, which was an indication that I was her trusted assistant. During this month-long period I experienced the caring of some nurses and the insensitivity of others. Miss Cooper was my first role model. Not only did she help me through a painful and difficult period, but when I was discharged, she gave me her picture to take home and encouraged me to get strong, to study, and to become a nurse. I spent that summer at my grandparents' farm gaining back the 20 pounds I had lost. One of the highlights of that summer was when I received a letter from Miss Cooper. That made the mile-long walk through the woods to the mailbox worth the trip. She took the time to write a short note. It was an encouraging event in my young and troubled life.

During high school I excelled in sciences, English, and Latin, and I worked hard in the math courses. My grades qualified me for the honor society, and I earned the Pen and Scroll award for writing ability. I began to write poetry as a freshman, and one of my poems was published in the school's anthology. I have continued to write poems ever since then as one means of expression and caring.

I had a lead part in my senior play, but struggled to remember my lines. I did much better in writing and delivering one of the valedictory speeches at commencement. The topic of my speech related to the need for all people to work together for the good of others by using their talents constructively. As I think about it now, that theme has been woven throughout the speeches and projects that have occupied my attention and energies for the past 25 years.

When I was 14, I got my first real job at a department store. Until then I had earned money by babysitting, housecleaning, and doing yard work and other odd jobs. Over the following three years I worked in every department in the store, including the soda fountain, the stockroom, and the main office.

Through my work experience there I developed self-confidence and learned the important lesson of financial independence. My parents had little money so I learned to take care of my own needs, including saving for my education in nursing. I became fully self-supportive when I left home two weeks after graduating from high school, after a stream of heated arguments with my father. I needed independence. I lived with a friend and worked in the substation of the post office in her father's drugstore until I entered nursing school three months later.

God, fate, and good fortune often have been on my side. That certainly was true in 1952 when Norfolk General Hospital was recruiting nursing students by suspending fees and offering a small stipend to those who would enroll. I had only the money saved from my summer job; my parents had none to spare. I had not received much encouragement to enter nursing. In fact my father had told me it was hard menial work, that I would receive little pay, and that I would be better off doing something else. To this day I don't know what compelled me, but I enrolled at Norfolk in September of 1952 and moved into the dorm. I was soon active on student committees and the basketball team. I also sang in the chorus and participated in Bible-study groups while I worked part time. This was in addition to the 48 hours of work and classes required of students in the diploma program.

One of my early initiatives was to write the first history of the school of nursing and present it as the speech for the candlelight capping ceremony of my class. I found and interviewed graduates and others who recalled the early years of the school, which had been established in 1896. Among other things, I learned that Virginia Henderson taught there a few years before I enrolled. I didn't know how significant that was until many years later, but I am grateful for her influence on the educational quality of the program. Perhaps it was she who helped to arrange for the Norfolk students to earn college credits for the arts and sciences taught at William and Mary College during our first year of study. That policy later made it possible for me to apply 30 credits towards my BSN degree.

At the end of the first nine months of school I was assigned to work a month of nights. With one aide and one orderly, I was responsible for the nursing care of 48 patients on the male medical unit, some in the 20-bed ward and others in the tuberculosis isolation unit, the private rooms, and the solarium. I was 18 years old, had successfully survived my first year of independence and nursing school, and my inclinations for challenge, leadership, efficiency, and responsibility were being put to the serious test of real life. I completed the program with honors after three years and was voted most dependable in my class.

By the time I graduated, I believed that I could take on just about anything— fortunately I was also convinced that I had more to learn. The obstetrics instructor, who had earned a master's degree in nursing from Western Reserve University (now Case Western Reserve University) encouraged me to go there for a baccalaureate degree. Millie Bramble (a friend in the class ahead of me) and I decided to "go for it." I was compelled by a missionary vision to make that decision. Cleveland didn't seem too distant, even though the only long trips I had ever taken were to a Christian leadership camp in Ontario and to an Intervarsity Christian Fellowship missionary conference in Illinois. My personal sense of mission and service would later be converted from religion to education, but its beginnings were planted, watered, and nourished by the Christian spirit of helping others.

Mission or not, I needed all the money I could get as soon as possible if I was going to get to WRU. As a new hospital school graduate, I got a job in the operating room, where I earned $200 a month and saved half. On January 4, 1956, with $300 and a trunk filled with personal possessions, I boarded a Capital Airlines plane bound for Cleveland for my first flight.

I was the first member of my family to go to college. I was ready for a new challenge, even that of confronting cold and snow (which Virginians rarely experience) and the culture of the North, which Southerners historically find difficult to adjust to. My friend Millie was the only person I knew in Cleveland. She had preceded me by four months and had written back about the friends she had made and how much she was learning. I was ready.

The off-campus rooming house I moved into cost $7.00 a week, and at least half of those who lived there were international students. I shared a suite with a nurse from Thailand and a philosophy student from the Philippines, and later lived with a woman from India who was studying library science. Several of us decided to learn more about each other's cultures by cooking and eating together. It was a wonderful learning experience. My interest in international students and in broadening my knowledge and sensitivities to those from other cultures motivated me to organize monthly group activities to assist them. I helped arrange meetings and outings, and I lined up culture-sharing activities in family settings, especially at holiday times. During those years of shared daily living and study I learned about myself, my beliefs, and the common bonds between all people. I gained confidence in my interpersonal and leadership abilities, and I recognized that individuals learn and live in many different ways and that that's OK. I never knew there were so many different ways to cook rice.

During the first year at WRU I worked full time to earn enough money to pay tuition. During 1956 and 1957 I worked in Babies and Children's Hospital of University Hospitals. The following year I worked as one of the dorm nurses for Mather College, the undergraduate women's school of WRU. In that job I worked 36 hours and then was off for 36 hours, which left enough time for me to work private duty and take courses. In the winter of 1957-1958 an Asian flu epidemic hit both WRU and Case Institute of Technology, and all of us worked around the clock for many weeks until it was brought under control. I finished the requirements for the bachelor of science degree with a major in nursing in June 1958.

Courses with Val Prock and others in community nursing and interdisciplinary health care influenced me to change my major area of clinical emphasis to chronic illness and rehabilitation. During one semester I worked in the Benjamin Rose Hospital (a private facility) and in the large county facility, both of which provided comprehensive rehabilitation services to patients with chronic illnesses. That was a clinical turning point for me, where I chose a path from which I have not veered. I learned that I had the ability to set long-term goals for patients as well as for myself and that I had the patience to see small gains within a larger perspective. I did not need to have immediate validation that my efforts were influencing positive changes. After completing the BSN, I took a position at Benjamin Rose Hospital as assistant head nurse, determined to apply all that I had learned.

One year later, in 1959, I sought and was awarded a United States Public Health Service traineeship, which enabled me to complete a master's degree in nursing education with a specialization in medical-surgical nursing and an emphasis in rehabilitation. I returned to work full time at the hospital with renewed enthusiasm and the challenging assignment to convert the top floor of the building (then used as a storeroom) into a new patient-care unit. I was responsible for hiring and orienting staff, obtaining equipment and supplies, and initiating a successful unit. While doing this, I convinced the nursing administration and staff to allow me to use the team method of assignment. Using the few materials that were available at the time, I wrote a training manual for all levels of staff and used it for nurses throughout the hospital.

I learned much from my teachers at WRU, at both the BSN and MSN levels. Margene Faddis and Ruth Evans were my major professors in medical-surgical nursing; they insisted that we learn the comprehensive clinical content as well as how to teach it. Katherine Porter, the dean of the nursing school, was also president of the American Nurses' Association during the time she taught our courses related to curriculum development, principles of teaching, and issues and trends. Ida Streiter, Ruth Anderson, and Rosemary Ellis were others who influenced me at WRU.

My interest in research started early, even with the field study I conducted to obtain data when recording the history of my diploma school of nursing. After taking courses at WRU and conducting several ministudies, I was hooked. As an assistant head nurse at B. Rose Hospital, I initiated a study to determine the best methods to heal decubitus ulcers, which were a frequent problem for our patients. My enthusiasm and encouragement resulted in maximum participation by all levels of nursing staff. The physicians, with whom I had had a positive working relationship, were impressed with our efforts. The senior research physician even tried to persuade me to leave nursing and enter medical school. I told him no, that I thought my talents were being applied in the right place.

I remember with anger and frustration the meeting of all assistant head nurses when I presented my research project. In spite of the interest and excitement of staff nurses, LPNs, and aides, the assistant director of nursing summarily squelched the project by publicly announcing that the review of the literature was not complete. I was furious that she had such little insight into the value of getting staff involved in research on a daily clinical level. I was discouraged, but we continued the study anyway. It's interesting that

10 years later I earned a doctoral degree with a major in research. That might have occurred earlier with a little encouragement. Instead, I invested those ten years in nursing education, much to my benefit, as I later discovered.

During my years at B. Rose, I had many encounters with my head nurse or supervisor about my clinical behaviors, which deviated from established procedures. I had several "tub room conferences" in which I was questioned and criticized; I sided with the patients, their needs, and their requests instead of routines. Common sense and knowledge-based problem solving were less valued than established protocols, at least by some nurses. I seemed to stay in trouble, even though I was convinced that anyone should be able to see the merits in the changes I was implementing. Maybe that is why the administration made me a head nurse on my own unit—to try me. If that's the case, I won, and so did my patients and staff. As I think of it now, the characteristics required for working in chronic illness and rehabilitation are similar to those for nursing education. Both require persistent efforts toward long-term goals to alter chronic and debilitated conditions. Rapid progress is seldom seen, and often the behavior of those in charge is not only inappropriate and outmoded but harmful to those who supposedly are being served. Changes and improvements come slowly.

When I went to WRU in 1956, my objective was to become a teacher of nurses. Degree requirements changed that year, and teaching was offered only at the master's level. After earning an MSN, however, I made the conscious decision that teachers should be expert practitioners before presuming to teach students. Therefore I continued to work at Benjamin Rose from 1960, when I completed the MSN, until 1962, when I took my first teaching position at Cleveland Metropolitan Hospital School of Nursing (Cuyahoga County Medical Center). I taught medical nursing and had the wonderful experience of developing new course materials and approaches. I had little supervision or assistance and was physically isolated in an office in the basement of the hospital, unlike my fellow teachers who were in the school. I worked long hours and loved trying out different ways to help students learn. It didn't matter that other teachers were doing things differently. Fortunately the students were excited and learned, and so did I. The absence of direct supervision gave me the freedom to explore and expand the teaching-learning ideals I had been developing in nursing service. I loved it.

During my master's study, Dorothy Paulsen (now Dorothy P. Smith) from Illinois and I were classmates. We became good friends and have remained so ever since. She had taught at Frances Payne Bolton School of Nursing (WRU) and decided to enroll at Yale to earn a PhD in sociology. I decided to go with her and took a position at the University of Bridgeport, which offered another "first" opportunity. I joined Elsa Brown and Allison Bailey to initiate the first associate degree nursing program in Connecticut at a time when it was considered an experimental idea and was receiving considerable opposition from the state board of nursing and other educators. To satisfy the state's requirements, students had to earn 87 semester credits. Needless to say, they were exceptional students, and the program was demanding but successful.

Those four years at the University of Bridgeport proved to be crucial in preparing me for a lifetime of working against obstacles in nursing education. The curriculum and clinical components were designed to fit the philosophy of associate degree education, as well as to meet the requirements of the state and university authorities at a time when few models existed and when few people understood ADN education. We gained experience in explaining, defending, interpreting, persuading, and documenting our objectives and behaviors. I was active in the state nurses association and other public forums. Those activities gave the program visibility and helped me to learn statewide and regional concerns and to speak to the issues. Elsa was a caring and persistent leader who understood the politics of our innovative endeavor, and she had the wisdom to use the competence of the six-member faculty. Our sense of mission and the challenge helped us to become a cohesive team that cared about students and the quality of their learning. I taught in the BSN program during semesters when my teaching load was lighter in the ADN program, which gave me additional educational experience.

In 1967 I moved to Valparaiso, Indiana, with my friend Dorothy for yet another challenge. Once again, I assisted in establishing a new associate degree program, this time at the Westville campus of Purdue University. That new campus, with one building located in the middle of a cornfield, was a unique challenge with different problems to be solved. The student body was small (most were from surrounding farmlands), and the program was a satellite of the existing ADN program in Lafayette, some distance away. In spite of the differences in student needs, backgrounds, and resources, the curriculum and learning strategies of the main campus were imposed. I objected to those violations of principles and learning and once again found myself at odds with everyone and having "tub room conferences" with my superior. Inflexibility, a lack of responsiveness to creativity in problem solving, and the lack of resistance to an inappropriate system caused my departure after one year on the faculty. I decided to return to school for a doctoral degree to further develop my abilities. I was sure that I had more to offer but had not yet found my niche in nursing education.

I thought I would pursue clinical study related to rehabilitation, and therefore I sought to enter the University of Chicago's program in human development. I was extremely disappointed when I learned that I was not one of the 20 students selected from 200 applicants. I thought of it as a defeat—something I had not experienced before. Later I accepted it as evidence that I was headed for another and still unknown mission.

The only conference I was allowed to attend during the 1967-1968 school year was in Boston, where I talked with Mildred Schmidt, whom I had met in 1965 when she presented the concept of "credit by examination" at a New England nursing educators' conference in Stowe, Vermont. Her plan was a new college proficiency testing program developed by the New York State Education Department as a way to help adult learners earn college credit by taking standardized examinations. (That assessment service was the precurser of the Regents External Degree Program.) Little did I know how important both of those meetings would become.

I told Mildred my dilemma—the frustration with my teaching position, my desire to begin doctoral study, and the failure to gain admission to the University of Chicago. She told me of a new program at Teachers College that focused on research in nursing education and any other discipline of the student's choice. I was admitted and was the only student in the program. (One student was in the class ahead of me, and later Maggie

McClure became my little sister in the same major.) Now the problem was to obtain a USPHS fellowship.

On June 6, 1968, I left Valparaiso in my gold and black Falcon Future Sports Coupe pulling a U-Haul trailer with all of my possessions and headed back to Connecticut to work for the summer and get ready for a move to the big city. During the entire trip I listened to the shocking news that Robert Kennedy had been killed. It was a long, lonely, and mournful 850 miles; I had taken photos of him just a few weeks earlier when he had come to Valparaiso.

Fortunately, I was able to stay with friends and get a summer job in the nursing program at the University of Bridgeport. The first day I drove from Easton, Connecticut, into New York City for classes. It took me longer to find a parking space than the drive had. I registered for full-time study and waited to receive the all-important letter from Washington that I had been awarded the fellowship. On October 8, the day before the deadline for filing for tuition refunds, I went to see Helen Simmon, my advisor, and told her that if I did not receive the fellowship I would have to drop out. As fate would have it, Terry Christy shared the office next to hers and overheard my dilemma. She offered to help while she was in Washington the next day on business with Faye Abdellah, who then was responsible for the fellowship program. I was encouraged by her confidence in me and by her offer of assistance.

The following afternoon I got the good news, along with a note of caution, that I had received a fellowship. When I later saw Terry, she told me the full story. Faye had told her that there were enough funds for 15 fellowships; Carrie Byrd (my maiden name) was sixteenth on the list. Terry asked her to do something because, in her opinion, I had potential for the profession. Faye found the additional funds.

I felt compelled to excel. After commuting from Connecticut during that first semester, I found an apartment at 100th Street and Amsterdam Avenue. A fellow student, Muriel Poulin, sublet her apartment to me for the next year and a half. It was a godsend for both of us.

I also did something else that was unusual for Teachers College doctoral students— I got married. I had met Harold Lenburg at Valparaiso. He was well established in business there, and we decided we could survive a commuting marriage for four years, when I would be finished with school and when he planned to take an early retirement. I completed my EdD, but he did not retire, and we continued to travel back and forth for several years. It was another positive learning experience, but we grew in different directions and finally terminated the marriage in 1977.

As a doctoral student I learned content related to nursing, research, sociology, and survival in New York City. I took computer courses in the days when only whiz-kid computer majors had access to terminals. In one semester I had to write nine proposals, but that was easy in comparison to the year I worked in the Bureau of Social Research. Under Allen Barton's direction, I worked on a project to analyze and code more than 900 actual proposals in a study to determine the characteristics of institutions that received funding for research. I also had experience as the research assistant to Lois Davitz at Teachers College, which brought me into more contact with TC students; most of my contact was with sociology majors at Columbia. I was grateful for dear friends like Helen Burnside, who helped put caring and good humor into my disciplined study.

One of the most significant events of my TC years was meeting Nat Lefkowitz, a sociologist who became an important role model for me. I was taking a research methods course in field observation and elected to observe his course. We connected in our intellectual and research interests, and the following semester he and I designed and taught an experimental course on developing a counterculture in nursing. The course itself was a research project in which we studied change in the leaders and soon-to-be leaders in nursing. Together we explored two segments of the nursing culture, one that valued following rules and orders and one that valued using knowledge that motivated clinical behavior. It was an enriching experience for the students and for us, and it helped to reshape my thinking about nursing, myself, and my role and responsibility in creating change in nursing and nursing education. For the next decade I worked with Nat and others on funded projects to study and create a methodology for implementing change. Hundreds of nurses in the greater metropolitan area participated in our projects and were changed after experiencing the innovative programs we developed. Unfortunately, Nat did not live to see the projects finished. I have not yet forgiven him for departing so soon; he had much to give. Because he too was a rebel of sorts, he was often misunderstood. We had much in common. In the 20 years since we met, I have never had a more important mentor.

Others at TC and at Columbia who influenced me included Robert Merton, Paul Lazarsfeld, Amitai Etzioni, and Eleanor Lambertsen, who became the chairperson of my dissertation committee and helped me to bridge gaps between education and research, politics and philosophy—and the computer departments at TC and Columbia. My longitudinal, three-part panel analysis of change was a demanding and exciting opportunity to apply methods and content, nursing and sociology. All of this, as well as the anti-war demonstrations that occupied everyone's attention during those years, helped prepare me for future battles.

A significant though seemingly innocuous event in my final semester further set the course of my professional future. As a research major, I was invited to critique one of the studies presented at the annual Stewart Research Conference at TC. At the luncheon, I happened (fate again) to be seated next to Maggie Walsh, then executive director of the NLN. She told me of an opening on the research staff at NLN, and I agreed to come for an interview, even though I had already applied for a position at the Center for Nursing Research at Wayne State University. In another of a series of predestined events, my letter to Harriet Werley of Wayne State got lost in the TC mailroom. After a few weeks passed by and I had received no response, I changed my mind and decided, after a little pressure from Maggie, to take the position at the NLN as assistant director of the division of research. My primary responsibility was the Open Curriculum Project, under the direction of Walter Johnson. About three days after I accepted the NLN position I received the delayed letter from Harriet, but I told her that I had taken another position. This turn of events directed me to what was to become my most important contribution to nursing and nursing education: the New York Regents External Degree Nursing Program. Mildred Schmidt was to play yet another role in the chain of events that led to that end.

I plunged headlong into research at NLN, dividing my time between an annual survey of schools and faculties and the new open curriculum project. I revised and expanded the preliminary survey and conducted an extensive study of the curriculum practices being used in all types of programs related to flexible or alternative options. During that period I also read extensively and compiled the initial draft of the open curriculum bibliography, which the NLN later published. An advisory committee had been appointed just prior to my appointment, and we met twice a year to review progress and make project decisions. The project was designed to study the practices of diverse curriculum options among the types of preparatory programs in different regions and types of institutions. Fifty-one programs were selected to participate in the detailed study, and more than 250 others were involved in the conferences. One of the participating programs was the newly created and extremely controversial "Regents External Degree Program," located in the New York State Education Department.

For a period of time, Lucie Kelly assisted me by conducting field interviews at participating schools. After analyzing two national surveys, I created the first *Directory of Open Curriculum Opportunities in Nursing Education*. In spite of the 1970 decision of the NLN board of directors to support the open curriculum project, some senior members of the NLN staff rejected the philosophy of open curriculum, resisted the studies being conducted, and objected to the title of directory, claiming that such programs might not be real opportunities. As project director I encountered overt and covert hostility and obstruction both at the NLN headquarters and at the many professional meetings where I presented the project. That was early training for what was to follow two years later, when I decided to move out of New York City to an environment that included more space, quiet, clean air, and opportunity for professional growth.

Mildred Schmidt was a member of the advisory committee for the open curriculum project and also was a protagonist in the development of the Regents External Degree Nursing Program. When she learned that I wanted to leave the city and move to Albany, she urged me to wait to hear from someone about a position she was sure I would want to consider. A few days later the director of the Regents program, Donald J. Nolan, called and offered me the position of first coordinator of the external degree nursing program. Dolores Wozniac, the initial project director, whom I had studied with at TC and worked with on the open curriculum project, had decided to move to California. At that time I was completing a book on open learning and career mobility in nursing education, and I wanted to stay involved in nontraditional education.

I readily accepted the position, believing it would enable me to apply all of my previous experience, remain active at the national level, conduct seminal research on a new educational alternative approach, and be in the creative vanguard of nursing education. It fit my philosophy, life-style, and need for personal and professional development. My move to Albany in August 1973 was the beginning of the most challenging opportunity for creative work that I could imagine. It continues to be so now, 14 years later.

During these past 14 years I have had the unparalleled privilege of coordinating the development, implementation, and evaluation of the only national assessment program in nursing. This program is also the largest, most complex, and most innovative nursing program in the world. I also have had the opportunity to work with many nursing leaders who were willing to take the risk of being associated with it. In addition to radically different philosophies, conceptual bases, and curriculum designs, two creative and challenging aspects of this work have been the development and implementation of the four nursing performance examinations and the national network of the Regional Performance Assessment Centers. The first 10 years of development were funded by the W.K. Kellogg Foundation, based on the vision and support of Barbara Lee, Bob Kinsinger, and others at the Foundation.

The innovative nature of the program and the dispersion of its students throughout the United States and in countries abroad required that we secure approval from every state board of nursing and accreditation by each regional accrediting association and the NLN. We also had to gain acceptance from employers, the military, the Veterans Administration, undergraduate and graduate academic institutions and schools of nursing, nursing organizations, and the nursing and health care community at large. Scores of highly qualified faculty members at other institutions had to be persuaded to join with those of us on program staff to become essential long-term faculty consultants to various nursing committees, as well as for other activities. More than 600 nurse educators have contributed to some aspect of the program. Some of the original faculty still work with us, while many new faces appear each year.

My challenge has been to coordinate the multiple and complex aspects of the associate and baccalaureate degree nursing programs and the Regional Performance Assessment Centers located from coast to coast. The reward for the effort is knowing that more than 5,000 nurses have earned associate or baccalaureate degrees since 1975, and that 7,000 more currently are enrolled in this alternative program, which requires self-directed learning and objective documentation of the competencies essential to the practice of nursing. As I was helped to change my life circumstances and make a contribution to society and the profession, so am I motivated to create opportunities for others. My national and international experiences over the years have convinced me that a national assessment program is perfectly natural and responsive to the quality controls and academic standards essential for high-quality nursing education.

My personal philosophy, experience in educational mobility, commitment to improving the profession, and responsibilities in the Regents College Degrees Program (its new name as of 1985) also led to my deep involvement in the entry into practice issue at the state and national levels. These activities have heightened the controversy about whether I am helping or hindering the profession. I worked actively on the ANA Entry into Practice Committee from 1976 to 1980, and in other ways before and after that time. I have advocated that education is for those who want and need to change their knowledge and base of competence; that educators should embrace those who want to learn, not reject them because of their past; and that programs should be designed to meet the educational needs of students and society, not serve the needs and preferences of the faculty and the institution.

This mission, this professional commitment and life work of mine, has required hundreds of thousands of work hours and travel miles, as well as hundreds of speeches, letters, manuscripts, and other written documents. The efforts have been costly—physically, mentally, socially, and politically. For the past 16 years I have been regarded as the leader of the nontraditional vanguard and stalwart supporter of democratic opportunity for practicing nurses on one hand, and as the enemy of professional nursing as a scientific and knowledge-based discipline on the other. At one national meeting I was pleased when someone called me the Jane Fonda of nursing. Some have labeled me a "pied piper," able to persuade a multitude; other have called me anti-intellectual and anti-academic. I have lost many friends, mainly because I have spent my time working rather than socializing. Most of my family still do not understand my priorities. Often I have volunteered to serve on state and national committees, but rarely have I been nominated. I am considered too controversial—to some, a political liability. I was extremely pleased, but surprised, to be elected into the American Academy of Nursing in 1978. It was encouraging to think that some members of the profession value my contribution.

In my opinion, I am an enthusiastic Aquarian. I have a mission to change what has been and no longer works for a more rational approach to solving the needs of the profession and society. I am in a benevolent collusion with others of like mind to change outmoded traditional interpretations, customs, and practices of education for more relevent strategies and requirements for competence. I emulate the idea often expressed by John Kennedy: some people see things as they are and ask why; I see things that have never been and ask why not.

My entire life has been guided toward this purpose. Several times I tried to go in one direction and was diverted by circumstances or providence to take a different path. The attraction of the new and unchartered, the challenge of development and persuasion, the commitment to exploration and investigation, and the belief in a "Yes I can" philosophy have characterized my career. I have been slowed by progressive degenerative arthritis, but I feel internally rewarded. My vision and mission are renewed each time I talk with students or graduates of RCD, or with those who see it as their only alternative. I am thankful for having had a part in the evolving scheme of progress.

Throughout the years I have continued to write poetry, as well as professional manuscripts. One book, still in progress, combines my poems and nature photographs (another healing avocation) and follows a theme of triumph over difficulties; its title is *Out of the Hard Places*. Two of the verses illustrate my experience and feelings.

> *Out of the hard places*
> *I learn to be born again*
> *for part of me dies inside*
> *when I experience defeat and rejection.*

> *Out of the hard places*
> *I learn who I am,*
> *where I have been*
> *and where I yet can go.*

One of my favorite quotes, which is also my life's motto, was written by an anonymous poet. "Do not go where the path may lead; go instead where there is no path and leave a trail."

Lucile Petry Leone

Lucile Petry Leone, MPHN, RN, retired as
Chief Nurse Officer of the U.S. Public Health Service
and Assistant Surgeon General in the
PHS Commissioned Officer Corps

A lifetime of achievement started when a fellow Hopkins alumna who was in graduate school told Lucile Petry, then a new young head nurse, that nursing students were being exploited—that the value of their service to the hospital exceeded the value of the education they received.

From then on, Lucile Petry Leone was immersed in raising the quality of nursing education, in studying its costs, and in determining who should pay those costs. When this question of responsibility for cost arose in 1941, with the United States on the brink of entering World War II, the U.S. Cadet Corps, which provided nurses to serve both military and essential civilian needs, was born. Lucile Petry Leone was its first director.

Her story of the war years and of her later service as Chief Nurse Officer of the U.S. Public Health Service with the rank of Assistant Surgeon General offers a model for political and professional leadership.

*I*n college I could not choose between English and one of the sciences as a major, so I pursued both at a small college where even freshmen knew the department heads. I finally chose chemistry as my major because I admired the person and the intellect of the head of the department. The scientific niceties of chemistry, the breadth of my mentor's view of science in modern thinking and living, the chemist's search for the pieces of knowledge most needed, the weighing of values—all of these were the substance on which the foundations of my lifetime thinking were built.

When I studied physiological chemistry, I knew that I wanted my science to operate in human beings, not just in test tubes. Two years later I chose nursing because I thought it promised to meet that freshly formulated requirement and had social value as well.

English courses fascinated me because they led me to new perspectives and expressiveness. To this day, I long for the creativity to write the novel, poem, play, or essay that really tells what nursing is and what it means to people and to nurses themselves. I have always been on the alert for talent in writing among nurses and students in schools of nursing and have tried to give continuing encouragement.

During the Christmas holiday in my junior year at college, I discussed my inclination toward nursing with my parents. My father said, "You know nothing about nurses, doctors, or hospitals. You had better investigate." I became a nurse's aide in a Lower East Side hospital in New York the following summer, discovered that I could graduate with a bachelor's degree in February rather than June, and entered the School of Nursing at Johns Hopkins Hospital in February 1924.

The next three years were one big booming feast of science-in-people—clinical science, deepened knowledge, new research findings—all laid out for me to scrutinize and dig into. There were connections with social and behavioral sciences to pursue. Prevention of illness looked to the future. Tradition looked to the past. The lively halls were hallowed by history. For example, I studied under the "men who knew Osler." Adelaide Nutting, one of the founders of the school, smiled down on us from her portrait.

While a student, I spent several months as a head nurse—a common happening in most schools then—and it was exciting. A recent graduate of the school, who was then a student in the graduate program at Teachers College, came to Baltimore. She came to the hospital ward where I was working, and we sequestered ourselves in the linen room for a chat. She told me she was learning that student nurses were exploited. They supplied much of the nursing service in the hospitals where schools were located, she said. The value of the service exceeded the value of the education students received. Of course there were "good" schools—ours was one of them. It was something to ponder, we agreed.

Several years later I made small contributions to the cost study movement. A person who would now be called a health care economist and I wrote a manual on how to study the costs of education and the value of student services. In the years following, such studies helped clarify the role of hospitals and health agencies in the rapid growth of nursing, and they led to a more sound system. Education of higher quality meant higher costs. Questions arose about who should pay the costs of education of nurses. Federal and state governments? Private donors? Students themselves? These same questions have become urgent again in the 1980s as the shortage of nurses grows more acute and enrollments in schools of nursing are declining. The same problem—shortage of nurses—was very acute in 1940 when a role for the United States in World War II seemed certain. It gave rise to the U.S. Nurse Cadet Corps, a wartime answer to the question of who should pay for education of nurses. That story appears a bit later.

After I graduated from Hopkins, I spent six months in a postgraduate program in psychiatric nursing while serving as head nurse on a psychiatric ward at the same time. I moved to a communicable disease ward, then to a men's medical ward, and later to a women's surgical ward. I even had a few weeks of experience as the most junior night supervisor, all in little more than a year. The variety in my clinical experiences stood me in good stead in my first job away from Hopkins.

In September 1928 I went to Teachers College, where I received the Master of Arts degree in 1929. Adelaide Nutting (of the smiling portrait) was founder of that program.

The year of study at Teachers College stretched my horizons. I had already begun to think of nursing as a national force in health, and this idea was extended. Courses in philosophy of education and theories of teaching and learning, based on the philosophy of John Dewey, gave me an opportunity for hard thinking and development of my own philosophy and designs for action. Halfway through the year I accepted a position for the next fall at the School of Nursing at the University of Minnesota.

There I was supervisor of instruction in all clinical fields, and my varied background helped considerably. Twice when I had summers off in Minnesota I went back to Hopkins to be a head nurse and to feel again the direct responsibility for patient care. At Minnesota, as in most schools of nursing, physicians taught principles in each clinical field, and head nurses and supervisors in the hospitals taught practices. I was to coordinate and upgrade instruction. I taught principles of teaching and supervised students in practice teaching. Those were senior courses for students who had chosen that major.

Again my diversity in clinical background proved to be an advantage. I taught a course in experimental techniques in nursing. Each student did a small piece of research. Laboratories in the hospital and medical school opened their doors to us, and the collaboration was useful. Teachers and advanced students in the School of Nursing took courses in statistics in the School of Public Health. The School of Engineering shared projects on time and motion study with us. Valuable first steps were taken in laying the base on which recent, rapid developments in nursing research continue apace.

Katherine J. Densford became director of the School of Nursing in 1930 after the retirement of the beloved Marion L. Vannier. Qualified nurse specialists were employed to teach each of the major clinical specialties. All kinds of interconnections with other schools and departments of the university were developed. Students were encouraged to take electives from offerings throughout the university. Nursing faculty members established meaningful communications in other departments and were appointed to university-wide committees. The School of Nursing was acknowledged for its significant contribution to the university and to the state. These things can be found in all schools now, but their beginnings were made in the 1930s in places like Minnesota. And I was there to participate.

From Miss Densford we learned to reach beyond barriers of tradition but to hold on to pertinent old values. In human relations we were taught to look for strengths in people and not to pick on weaknesses. We also learned to examine our own practices to avoid letting prejudice color our decisions. Those were strengths she reinforced in all our staff. Miss Densford liked theater; she knew actors and authors. She loved painting; she knew painters. I credit her with inducing attitudes in me that readied me to work with public relations personnel (a novel experience for a nurse in that time) when I became director of the Cadet Nurse Corps in 1943. She opened many doors.

I was elected to the board of the National League of Nursing Education (NLNE) during my time at Minnesota. My platform, although I did not label it as such at the time, was to get a nurse from west of the Mississippi on every major committee of the League. I was meeting educators from around the country, and my close friendship with Margaret Arnstein in the School of Public Health at Minnesota gave me knowledge of outstanding nurses in community health. I had confidence in the nominations I made for committee membership.

One day in 1940 I received a phone call from Chicago. I was still a member of the School of Nursing faculty at the University of Minnesota. The call came from the dean of the North Central Accrediting Association, which accredited colleges and universities in that region. He asked me to do a study of baccalaureate degree programs in nursing in the colleges and universities in the region. I would be able to present a report of the study at the association's annual meeting, and it would be published in their quarterly, he said.

I was pleased to be asked, awed by the significance of the task, and frightened about undertaking it, so I said no to this first step outside the fold of nursing. He called Miss Densford and then phoned me again. He said that if I wouldn't do the study, he had no alternative but to ask a medical school dean, who was well known in the region, to do the study. I had been disagreeing with that dean's evaluation of nursing for some time. I changed my mind about doing the study. The report, quite a simple one, helped place nursing programs in universities in the region as credible and valuable university offerings, and it supported other universities that were considering the development of nursing programs. The report also strengthened the willingness of universities to approve the neophyte accreditation program of the NLNE.

What was then being called the "conflagration of war" was raging in Europe. The United States was not ready to take a stand on the issues of the war, but support for the war effort was growing and was soon to be a consuming passion that superseded all other activities. Hitler's armies pushed rapidly through Europe. Paris fell in June 1940. British troops had been evacuated in hundreds of small boats back to England from Dunkirk. The world seemed to hold its breath in suspense as to whether England, the last stronghold against Hitler, could hold on despite constant bombing until help came. It was not until Japan bombed Pearl Harbor that the United States declared war on Japan, Germany, and

Italy—more than a year after Paris and Dunkirk. It took almost another year to prepare for the invasion at Normandy and the offensives in the Pacific. That period of history was a time of heated discussion, large-scale planning, and detailed preparation here in the United States.

Isabel Stewart, director of nursing programs at Teachers College and president of the NLNE, had done yeoman service in making a plan for a government-supported program in nursing education, justifying it statistically, and presenting arguments favoring it. She and others rallied support within nursing organizations. The new Nursing Council for National Defense and the government committees related to nursing were active. With some revisions in the Stewart plan, a bill sponsored by Representative Frances Payne Bolton of Ohio was passed by Congress. However, the appropriation for it was $1.2 million, not the $15 million requested.

Dr. Thomas Parran, Surgeon General of the United States Public Health Service (PHS), who had helped push the bill through Congress, immediately placed the administration of the program under the supervision of Dr. J.W. Mountin and Pearl McIver of the States Relations Division of the PHS. Margaret Arnstein, Eugenia Spalding, and I were appointed members of that staff.

The program became operational on July 1, 1941. It turned out to be too small for the task, which seemed to grow by leaps and bounds. Pearl Harbor and the entrance of the United States into World War II came in December of 1941. During 1942, features of a new and much larger program were hammered out in a bill again sponsored by Frances Payne Bolton. The bill became law, authorizing the formation of the U.S. Cadet Corps with an appropriation of $65 million and an operating date of July 1, 1943. I was appointed director.

A splendid staff of nurses, public relations personnel, and auditors was put together in short order. The program was appealing to staff members. Six regional offices were set up around the country with staff members in those three categories.

Competition for womanpower was sharp throughout the entire labor market. There was pressure on all sides to shorten the education of nurses. Hospitals did not want to shorten the length of time spent in a school of nursing because they couldn't spare the nurse power, and many nurses thought the length of the training period should not be cut because state law required three years of training for licensure as a nurse. However, the curriculum had to be accelerated to get students into productive positions earlier. These were a few of the opposing points of view that had to be reconciled by legislation.

The bill was piloted through Congress and took effect July 1, 1943. Admission of 65,000 students in fiscal year 1943-1944 was the goal, with the greatest number to be admitted in September. Students would pledge themselves to give two years of nursing service in the military or in essential civilian services after graduation in return for their free education. Clinical facilities would have to be expanded. More housing would have to be found. Everyone would have to work very hard. Patriotism was at a high pitch.

Almost immediately, in the first weeks of July, Dr. Parran made two barnstorming trips around the country, half with me and half with Eugenia Spalding. School of nursing directors and hospital administrators came in large numbers to the conference nearest their homes. It was the quickest way to get the recruitment drive started.

The corps had to be organized rapidly if the major portion of the 65,000 quota for membership was to be admitted in September. A mammoth nationwide recruitment program was organized and set in motion with the J. Walter Thompson agency doing the public relations. Other employers were involved in recruitment of workers, and ours had to compete with the best of them. Our story of nursing was appealing. So too was the message that nursing education prepared one for a lifetime of continuing growth. Several leading designers competed to have their design for an outdoor uniform chosen. The winner, gray with small red epaulets and silver buttons with the PHS insignia pressed into them, was chosen at a fashion show held at the Waldorf in New York. Cadets loved them.

The three-year instructional program in the schools was condensed into two and a half years. The last six months of the 36-month program was spent in a military or other government hospital stateside, or in a selected essential civilian service. Targeting both military and civilian needs for nursing services had been a very sound feature of the program. The institution served paid a monthly allowance of at least $30 to the students, who were now Senior Cadets. Some paid more. All federal hospitals paid $60.

Travel to their assignments, though usually not far, was one of the program's attractions for students. The learning experience was well planned and supervised, and the Senior Cadets were enthusiastic about it.

Of the country's 1,320 schools of nursing, 1,150 participated in the program. That meant that not all were in the category of "good schools." Simple criteria had to be met, and some schools had to be approved temporarily. Nurse consultants from our staff worked with the schools to help them reach and surpass the minimum requirements. Our consultants urged the purchase of books for almost nonexistent libraries. Federal funds were made available for the purchase of classroom equipment. Courses had to be organized, and schedules of classes and clinical experience had to be adhered to, not left to haphazard arrangement as had been done previously. A budget had to be made. Accounting systems had to be set up. All of this accomplishment proved to be good when the war ended because schools became educational entities, not adjuncts to hospitals.

Statistical information drawn from school reports was the largest amount of information ever collected about nursing education. It fueled developments in accreditation and fed the planners' appetites for data.

VJ day ending World War II came in August 1945. The class to be admitted in September of that year had already been recruited. It was decided that it would be unfair not to allow those students the benefits they had been promised. Consequently, the last cadet graduated in 1948. Most cadets gave far more than two years of service. The pledges ended with the war, but the Cadet Corps nurses continued to supply nursing services for many years afterward.

There was talk about new role models for nursing that the Cadet Corps program had produced. The curriculum was improved though accelerated. Teachers now had to apply priorities when choosing one subject or experience over another for students, and teaching was fresher, observers said.

The program opened doors to government support of nursing education and of research in nursing. More than $2 billion has been allocated and spent in these areas since 1942. Nursing polished its image in the mainstream of progress in health care. Impacts have been lasting. More good students being taught by more excellent teachers about nursing—a discipline that has been analyzed and researched to higher effectiveness— became one vital factor in the improvement of health of the American people.

When the war ended, developments in medicine and health had reached a new peak. But this was only the beginning. Inside the PHS, programs for cancer, heart and lung diseases, mental health, and many others were developed. The new Clinical Center was built, then the largest research-only hospital in the world.

Every new front in the National Institutes of Health and in almost all parts of PHS had nurses on it. The expectation was that nurses employed in the central and regional office of the Cadet Corps would leave PHS at the end of the war. Almost all of them were offered and took positions in the new programs.

At the close of the Cadet Nurse Corps program, I was appointed Chief Nurse Officer of the U.S. Public Health Service and was given the rank of Assistant Surgeon General in the PHS Commissioned Officer Corps. I was the first woman to be given this rank in the commissioned corps of the United States. That sometimes made me conspicuous, which I tried to accept with equanimity.

I was already performing one function of a chief professional officer—to match capacities of officers and opportunities for service—without getting in the way of the personnel office. My responsibilities were stated in general terms with considerable leeway for interpretation. I often wished for more definitive guidance, but there was so much to do in the lively, expanding PHS that I was always more than busy.

I felt responsible for keeping informed of program developments throughout the PHS. Sometimes the inclusion of nurses on a staff had not been considered, and I worked at getting those opportunities to materialize. Often they did.

I believed that nurses should share general administrative duties—not only those that affected others as well as nurses, but sometimes those not affecting nurses at all. For example, an assistant director of personnel resigned and I suggested a very suitable nurse who was appointed and did a fine job. Several nurses thought nurses were too scarce to allow us to make that assignment, but everyone benefited from it. New insights were gained in many directions because of it.

I accepted the appointment to be the first fair employment practices officer of the PHS. My interest in civil and human rights was widely known. I was inexperienced, but I worked at learning the ways in which rights were protected. I was also chair of the Committee on Health of Migrant Workers. An excellent staff helped develop an action program in this field with staff, organization, and funds.

I believed that one of my functions was to keep aware of cutting-edge developments in nursing and related fields—to be alert to ways in which the PHS might be helpful. I traveled extensively throughout the country, usually with an invitation to make a speech to a group somewhere. I liked to speak to small groups in isolated places, but frequently the groups were large. I think I had a reputation for being a little ahead of the times. Always, I was interested in personalized, individualized nursing care—basic to primary care and to self-help.

I recall one instance vividly. I was invited to speak as the nurse on the program when the Mayo Building was opened at the University of Minnesota. I arrived, speech in hand, late in the evening before the dedication. When I read the paper again, I did not like it. I threw it in the wastebasket and spent the night writing a new speech. I remembered Albert Schweitzer's statement, "If you want to speak of a truth, speak in parable." So I told a story of a nurse who was to care for an 18-month-old boy who had had surgery on his trachea and would have to wear a tracheal tube for some months. The nurse found a rocking chair for herself and the boy and a table for the suction machine. She held the boy in her arms all night. When his tube needed suctioning, the boy would look toward the machine. She held his fingers on the switch and helped him turn it. He felt loved and secure. By morning, he was turning on the machine by himself. He never felt victimized by the tracheal tube; he controlled it. He would run in from play, suction the tube, then resume play.

The speaker before me was an eminent surgeon; we knew each other fairly well. I knew he did not have high expectations of nursing. When he took my hand after the conclusion of my story, he said, "Almost thou has persuaded me." My paper, "The Art of Nursing," was published in the *Journal of the American Medical Association*.

I once accepted an invitation to read a paper at a meeting of an association connected with ambulances without checking prior to my presentation to see who would be in the audience. My paper was entitled "Health on Wheels." The audience was composed entirely of funeral directors.

During my career, I was appointed to many committees and commissions outside the PHS—always in connection with the mission of the service. I worked with the Southern Regional Education Board and the Western Interstate Commission on Higher Education, both of which had nursing programs. Those were progressive groups that accomplished a great deal in their regions. I served on the Commission on Mental Illness and was an outside member of the curriculum committee of the School of Nursing at the University of Washington. I was on a committee composed of a professional and a concerned layman for each of the health-related schools at the University of Pennsylvania. Mary Rockefeller and I represented nursing. I was on the advisory committee of the Kellogg Foundation in the early years of its involvement in nursing, and I was a member of the Board on Medicine in the National Academy of Sciences. There were other national appointments, as well as many international meetings and conferences.

Of course, I worked with all of the professional associations in the health field. I was president of the National League for Nursing, chairman of the board of directors of the American Journal of Nursing Company, and a member of the board of the journal of the American Public Health Association, as well as its governing council.

International health has been one of my major interests, thanks to Dr. Parran. He had been chair of the committee that planned the organization of the World Health Organization (WHO, a specialized agency of the United Nations). He appointed me as a technical advisor to the U.S. delegation to the first assembly of the United Nations, which was held in Geneva in 1948. I was the only nurse on any delegation and had just been appointed Chief Nurse Officer of the PHS. Later I was a member of the Expert Committee in Nursing of WHO.

Through my many organization affiliations, I kept up on health issues of concern to nurses that related to PHS programs. I knew trends, experts, needs, and regional differences. However, most of all, in my lifetime I have learned that the same spirit engendered by a nation's expectations of nurses in times of crisis and the nurses' response in meeting these needs still prevails. Millions of people live in better health as a result.

Myra Levine

Myra Levine, MSN, RN, FAAN,
is Professor Emeritus
at the University of Illinois
College of Nursing

Myra Levine writes eloquently of her unusually close relationship with her family and of her accomplishments and disappointments that have influenced her, both personally and professionally. The charm of her open and honest writing is sharpened by the love that she and her husband share for language —a love that has led them both to high intellectual achievement. Her personal integrity and sense of justice are revealed in her standing up to the anti-Semitic discrimination she experienced in nursing.

One of nursing's best-known writers and speakers on ethical values and conservation principles, Myra expresses herself with clarity and conviction. This account of her poignant and bittersweet memories captures the spirit of her personality as a vibrant and sensitive human being.

All my life I have been a big sister, but I was the second-born sole survivor of twins. From my earliest memory, I was confronted with the challenge to be both myself and my lost sister—to be twice as good, twice as caring, twice as conscientious—so that in some way I could keep that baby alive. It took three years of psychoanalysis to end the burden. My brother Don was two and a half years younger than I, and when I was seven, my sister Golden was born. She came home to a large wicker laundry basket, set on a cedar chest in my parent's room. Once I heard her cry and went to see what was bothering her. I picked her up out of the basket and held her on my shoulder. I have never forgotten the soft warmth of her head against my neck, and the overwhelming love that flowed between us in that moment. It has never ceased.

MY MOTHER

She kept an old white mug on the windowsill in the kitchen. It was for the beggars who came, in those depression years, asking for food. She never turned them away. I remember how she would scurry around the kitchen making a sandwich out of any leftovers she could find, and filling the white mug with hot coffee.

She hosted birthday parties for me at the Martha Washington Home for Crippled Children. She baked cookies and brought oranges, ice cream, and party favors. My twenty-first birthday came when I was a student nurse. I was assigned to the orthopedic ward of Cook County Hospital, and she helped celebrate my birthday there, bringing cookies, ice cream, and a toy for each child. When the trays were served, we gave her a hospital gown. Together we visited each child, tears streaming down her face as the kids sang "Happy Birthday" to me.

She reached out as best she could, although her own life was never easy. She kept our home filled with love, even though my father's recurring illness led her to warn me often that we lived on the "edge of a volcano," waiting for catastrophe. It was never far away.

My father had suffered from gastric ulcers from his youth. Before I was 15, I was an expert on the therapies for ulcers. He was operated on repeatedly, and when I was 12 he was hospitalized for months, often critically ill. The household was disrupted because Mother never left his bedside. Goldy went to live with our aunt—not far away but a long walk, nevertheless. I was in charge of the house but the activities for each day depended on the report Mother brought every evening.

Mother was past 50 when, for the first time in her life, she went to work to help my father run his hardware store. She learned to cut keys and make windowshades, as well as the strange names of tools and nails and all the other mysteries in the store. After he died, she finally sold the business and got a job in a one-woman office. She was an expert typist and could put much younger women to shame. She was forced into retirement at 70 but only because the business was relocated in another city.

Mother was 83 when she died. Each of us had begged her to come and live with us, but she insisted on having her independence, and even though she finally lived in a retirement apartment building, she was impatient with the "old" people who were her neighbors. She hated growing old. Perhaps she never did.

MY FATHER

He had a red mustache and a crooked finger on his left hand. All his life, Father was confronted with the threat of serious illness. As children we knew we had to tiptoe around him. He was a hardware man and proprietor of a large store, but he was not gifted with his hands. We cherished him because he seemed so fragile to us. One child was always waiting to open the garage door when he came home in the evening, and another was quick to bring his slippers and the evening paper. "His" chair was empty when he was not in it.

The evening I finished nurses' training, my cousin Martin took me to see Father, who was then a patient at Passavant Hospital in Chicago. The following day I put on a white uniform for the first time and went on duty as his private nurse. He had been recently operated on and still had a nasogastric tube in place. The surgeon told me to keep it in if I could, but not to worry if it came out. Within 20 minutes after the private nurse who took over the next shift had arrived, the tube was out. When I returned the next day, he was furious with me because I had not allowed the tube to be removed while I was taking care of him. For years after that, he told that story and always announced how "tough" I was.

One morning he called me to tell me that he had bought his morning paper as usual and found that he could not understand the words. I knew at once that he had had a small stroke. We took him to a neurosurgeon who performed an angiogram on him. When Father's minor disability grew worse, we sought a neurologist.

Father struggled desperately to relearn speech, but he never did. Perhaps we loved him more because he did not have the strength to be strong for us, and the moments of joy became even more precious. There were rides on Sunday afternoons—everybody squeezed into the old blue Buick for a visit to the ice cream parlor at 95th Street and Stony Island Avenue. Each kid would get a rainbow ice-cream cone with chocolate sprinkles on top. In those rare times we had a hint of the happy, carefree, loving family we wanted to be.

MY EDUCATION BEFORE NURSING

I went, kicking and screaming, to kindergarten at the age of four. My protests were sufficiently annoying that the teacher instructed my mother to go home and then put me in the girls' bathroom to cool off. After I discovered what it was all about, I was never reluctant to go to school again. In my last year in grammar school we moved to a new neighborhood, and as an eighth-grader I had to begin a new school in which I was not only a stranger but also the only Jewish child. My classmates were as relentless and nasty as only self-assured 12-year-olds can be. I was lonely and hurt.

At graduation the eighth-graders were to participate in a gala musical comedy, and I won the leading role in a fair and square audition. The school newspaper recorded the fact that, "She [Myra] could sure take it." They had certainly dished it out. It was my triumph in the play that finally made me a happier child. I went off to high school still hearing applause in my ears and won a leading role in the high school musical comedy—the only freshman in the cast. That triumph set the stage for a very happy four years.

The school was unusual. The city-run junior colleges had closed because of a lack of money, and the faculty flocked to various senior high schools. We inherited a group of unusually well-educated teachers, and the result was an intellectual environment rare at that level of education in a city school system. I ranked in the top five of my class (well over 700 students) and won all sorts of contests. I was a member of the a capella choir that won a national award and was rewarded with a concert appearance in Orchestra Hall in Chicago. I won the George Washington Oratory contest, and I was selected by the school to receive the Citizenship Award of the Daughters of the American Revolution.

In perfect innocence my mother and I went to the DAR affair at a downtown hotel where the awards were to be distributed. As we listened to the speakers, we became aware that the woman at the microphone was delivering an anti-Semitic speech. We left the hotel at once. The following day the principal called me to his office to ask why I had not stayed to receive my gold medal. I explained to him why I could not do so, but he handed me the medal, saying, "You are our best citizen." I never took it out of the box. It was 1938.

I won an athletic letter and a field hockey bar, and the day before I was to pitch for the champion girls' baseball team, I had an emergency appendectomy. I underwent surgery on a Wednesday night and was sent home three days later. The three days in the hospital introduced me for the first time to student nurses. They wore old-fashioned striped aprons and black shoes and stockings, and I knew I wanted to do that, too. Ten days after my surgery, limping a little, I marched in the graduation processional.

A women's group gave me a full scholarship to attend the University of Chicago. The tuition was $100 a quarter, and I lived at home. In the wake of the great social change in the postdepression years, I had a job with the National Youth Administration and received $15 a month for a few hours per week working for the university. My assignment was to the senior kindergarten in the laboratory school of the University of Chicago, and I loved it. The teacher was Miss Adams, and the pupils were children of university faculty. I learned more about human relationships in that year than any time in my life.

On campus the excitement of intellectual pursuits was always present. The survey courses, a product of Robert Maynard Hutchins' prophetic view of education, opened worlds that have ever since remained wonderful and challenging. I spent two years at the University of Chicago and returned 13 years later to finish my baccalaureate.

In May of 1940 it had become clear that the turmoil in Europe would not remain apart from our lives. The news of the invasion of the Low Countries by the Germans confirmed what many had feared—that the Nazis would be contained only if the civilized world was strong enough to stop them. I had no more money for college and had applied for admission to the Michael Reese Hospital School of Nursing. Although it was funded by the Jewish Federation of Chicago, the director of nursing at the school maintained a careful quota of Jewish students. She did not admit me, although my grades at the university had been B or better. Later I was called by investigators of the Anti-Defamation League who had received so many complaints about her that they were finally trying to uncover the truth. She never held another job as a nursing director.

Cook County School of Nursing was my second choice. When I called and asked for an application, the nurse who answered the phone, an Illinois Training School graduate, completed her instructions to me by saying, "Don't buy white shoes until after you get here, because your feet will get bigger." In September of 1940, as America stood poised on the edge of World War II, I went to the Cook County School of Nursing to study.

NURSING EDUCATION

For the first time in my life I had a room of my own and I was living somewhere away from my family. It was a disciplined world I had entered, far different from the freedom of living at home. The schedule of our daily activities was rigid and the guardians of our virtue tireless. We were awarded "privileges" that permitted us to leave the premises of the nurses' home one night each week until midnight and once a month until 1 AM. Every other night the lights were out at 10:30 PM. We could sign up for a "late light" once a week if we planned to study past the witching hour, but that required that we remain in our own rooms. And we knew that Lydia Brickbauer—whom we came to dearly love—would be making her rounds to be certain that we were obeying the rules. No men were allowed above the second floor of the building.

We went to the wards on a dark afternoon in December of that first quarter, wearing for the first time the new blue uniforms we had been issued, with the starched white collar and cuffs and the black silk tie which we were told was worn in memory of Florence Nightingale. The wards of Cook County Hospital gathered all the heartache of the city streets and slums—the "lost and by the wind grieved" who came quite often in a police van when they were absolutely helpless from illness, trauma, and despair. Nothing in my life had prepared me for them. But I knew that when I had chosen nursing to help others, I had found a population that really needed me. I was terrified, but I loved it. We were "probies," and our future hung on the slim threads of our performance, both in the classroom and in the wards.

The day when the lists were posted naming those who would be allowed to continue into the clinical quarters was rocked with emotion. Several names were missing, but those of us who had succeeded were wild with joy. The capping ceremony was the high point of nurses' training. I remember yet the gentle touch of Edna Newman, the director of the school, as she placed the tiny organdy cap on my head. It was a moment in my life that never ended, because in that small cap was vested my life as a nurse. It was a harsh life—working eight hours on the wards, six days a week, and attending classes each day as well. The supervisors were not always kind, and while the instructors who followed us were often sources of strength, there was always a current of punitive and vindictive behavior. I had my share, and I wanted never to be that kind of nurse.

The United States was involved in the war by the time we returned to the nurses' home on December 7, 1941, and while we could not predict all of the changes that would come, as we gathered that evening we knew we would be important participants. On the vacant lot across from our quarters, the medical students, who had been inducted in the army, would perform their marching drills early each morning. We were lined up and marched to a nearby school to receive our ration books, which were then turned over to the school. The physicians left—many at once with the Michael Reese group. One by one the graduate nurses were gone. The responsibility for the care of the patients rested in large measure on the student nurses, and we were placed into positions of decision making that would have been impossible in a quieter time.

The Cadet Corps brought three times the number of students into the school of nursing, and Miss Newman arranged for me to act as an assistant teacher in the chemistry lab (under the wonderful guidance of Bernice Perdziak, who later became a physician). I spent my mornings as a teacher and my afternoons at the psychiatric hospital, completing my sequence in a tutorial with Lenore Kimball. That was an experience so precious that I cannot imagine what kind of nurse I would have been if I had not had her wisdom and gentle direction.

Nurse training in the frantic years of World War II may have had an intensity and purpose beyond its usual impact. There was a sense of importance and immediacy that followed us into the wards. The physical work required strong backs, and the drama and tragedy tested our spirits, perhaps in that institution beyond the experience in other kinds of hospitals. We came to have County "in our blood" and we carried our years there with us wherever we went.

We always had less equipment than we needed. There was rarely enough linen. The food served was wholesome but often inedible and day in and day out our devotion was tested by the difficulties confronting us in a population of deprived and desolate patients.

Years later at a graduation ceremony at the school, I was privileged to present a scholarship funded by the alumnae to one of the seniors. It had been a difficult year, with an unusual degree of political attack on the hospital and the school of nursing. The president of the Cook County Hospital Board of Directors, who was responsible for much of the clamor, was sitting in the front row. Frances Powell was standing beside me, and I was conscious of the lifetime of service she had given to Cook County. Before me were the graduating seniors. I said, "I am honored to stand here as a representative of the proudest nurses in the world." The audience erupted into a sustained standing cheer, and even the president of the board applauded weakly. Cook County School of Nursing will always mean that to me.

MY HUSBAND

I first met Ed on the steps of the Art Institute near the south lion, on a blind date arranged by his sister. I had just entered nursing school. Marriage was not allowed to student nurses, and I had a single aim—to become a nurse. Before New Year's Day he was gone, and it was three years before I heard from him again. I was on the threshold of completing nursing school, and he was in the army, stationed in Oklahoma. He wrote to me from Camp Gruber, saying he would be in Chicago and would like to see me. I barely remembered his name.

By the time Ed came on furlough in March of 1944, I was working at Bobs Robert Hospital on the University of Chicago campus. My shift was split from 7 to 11 AM and 3 to 7 PM, so when he called for a date I suggested he meet me at Billings at 11 AM. I rushed from the ward to the locker to change into a freshly starched uniform, but the sight of him in his army uniform was even more impressive. (He had to wait, then, while I returned to the locker room and put on my street clothes.) We bought a bag of sugar cookies on 57th St. and walked over to the Promontory on the lake. We sat on the rocks and watched the waves, and he kissed me for the first time. As I entered the hospital once more for my late afternoon shift, I watched him walking across the quadrangle in a misty rain, with the bag of cookies—untouched—in his hand. He called me later that evening to tell me of his love, and I offered mine. We were married six weeks later by the chaplain of the 24th Rainbow Division in a small cottage outside of Camp Gruber, Oklahoma, after sundown on a Sabbath evening.

We snatched whatever moments together we could during that summer, and by September he had his overseas orders and we began, after only four months of marriage, a separation of nearly two years. From the time he left the States in late September until the following March, I did not have a word from him. I went to New York to be nearer to him for a few months, but it was futile to try, and I was back in Chicago working for the Michael Reese Blood Bank when I first had word that he was safe. I was never certain of where he was—only that he was in Europe, and only later were the details of his experience there filled out. He came back six days before our second anniversary.

I was waiting for him in a downtown hotel, and we began then the life together that had been postponed by war. He applied for admission to the University of Chicago, but his admission was delayed by the tremendous number of GIs seeking a college education. Since he had been a student at the University of Minnesota, he was promptly readmitted there and we went to the Twin Cities to begin a new life.

The only housing we could find was in the Jewish ghetto of North Minneapolis, a city where Jews were not even allowed to join the AAA Motor Club. We had a desolate room in the home of a thoroughly psychotic woman, and I left the house each morning at 4:30 AM to take the long streetcar ride through Fort Snelling to St. Paul's Ancker Hospital. I was the "teaching supervisor"—administering all of the surgical wards and teaching all of the surgical nursing courses, being young and bold enough to be comfortable in knowing everything.

Ed spent a triumphant year in the classics department with the great Marbury Ogle and was rewarded with election to an honorary language fraternity, although he was only a freshman and the youngest student to be elected. He demonstrated from the beginning his tremendous talent as a philologist, and before the year was over, we learned that he had been admitted to the University of Chicago. We made plans to return to Chicago the following autumn.

My year in Minnesota was remarkable because as a member of 4th District, I could share with the other nurses the magic of Katherine Densford (later Dreves) who was then the dean of the College of Nursing and president of the American Nurses' Association. I still remember her in a multicolored skirt, virtually floating down the aisle of the meeting room. She retained into her old age the unusual beauty that so distinguished her, and she was bright, strong, and wonderful to be near. Many years later I was privileged to receive an award from Sigma Theta Tau (nursing's honor society) at the same time that she received one. The hotel was overcrowded, and I shall always remember how graciously and sincerely she offered to share her room with me. I took a course in nursing research at the University of Minnesota during the year in Minneapolis. The course was taught by a Professor Harris, the first nurse I ever met who loved to listen to Bach.

I earned my credit in that course by creating at Ancker Hospital the first recovery room and surgical intensive care unit in the State of Minnesota, fashioned on the one I knew from Cook County Hospital. And it was at Ancker that I witnessed the early effort of the Foley service and Dr. Charles Hodges to use peritoneal dialysis—initially on an alcoholic patient who had consumed wood alcohol. It was an exciting professional year for me because I saw some great physicians in action, including Dr. Owen Wangensteen, the inventor of suction-siphonage drainage of the gastrointestinal tract.

The director of nursing at Ancker had been Elizabeth Reynolds, but she retired shortly after I began my work. She was replaced by an old Ancker graduate who had a vigorously biased view of some ethnic groups and was especially harsh on Oriental students. I think of her still as representative of that group of embittered, unmarried women whose militaristic rule outdid anything a tough sergeant could ever achieve.

We came back to Chicago with relief, and Ed began the University of Chicago education that brought him his doctorate in 1953. This was a highlight of a distinguished scholarly career, which was financed through repeated fellowships. There had been a year during that time when his education had been delayed because I was pregnant, and he had accepted a teaching job at the University of Nebraska in Lincoln. We were terribly poor. He was paid barely $250 a month, and I was able to work only part time as a clinical instructor at Bryan Memorial Hospital, a school of nursing largely distinguished by the fact that it was in the former home of William Jennings Bryan and boasted the first bathtub in the state of Nebraska—oversized to fit Bryan's excessive girth.

THE CHILDREN

In March 1952, our son was born in Lincoln. And three days later, he died.

We named him Benjamin after Ed's father. He is the baby who will always be my baby. At first I thought, "I have to imagine him through infancy and childhood. I will have to create him as he grows and learns and comes to love us." However, I could only remember him as he was: so fragile, dressed to rest forever in the yellow sweater set and tiny visored cap that a friend had knit for him before he was born. We had to leave him behind, in the prairies of Nebraska.

A year later Bill was born. He was named for the wonderful physician who delivered him. He was a tiny baby, but he had the vigor he needed to grow strong and talk quickly.

When he was two and a half, Patricia came to us. She was born by my third cesarean section, and it was decided she would be the last. It was especially marvelous for me to have a daughter. She was, from the day of her birth, a source of constant motion and excitement for us. It was finally possible for me to look back at our first son—Benoni, the son of my sorrow—and to acknowledge the blessing that even his short three days of life had given us. During all the years as a PM "walking supervisor" at Henry Ford Hospital, I always went to the mothers whose babies had been lost, to sit with them in silence, to share their tears, to let them know they were not alone. In my own anguish I had been left alone by the nurses, and I promised myself I would never let that happen to anyone if I had it in my power to prevent it. Perhaps having Benoni made Bill and Patricia more precious, but I never wanted either of them to feel they had to compensate me because he had died.

Both of my children have grown into wonderful, mature adults. Bill was a Phi Beta Kappa in his junior year at the University of Chicago, and he is a thoughtful, gentle, caring man—much like his father. Patricia has my spirit—she is a warm and friendly companion, loyal and devoted and always the one who remembers birthdays and anniversaries or engages in a totally unexpected gift or greeting just for the joy of it. She once said she wanted to be a nurse, and I thanked her. It was compliment enough.

Bearing, nurturing, and growing with children creates the parent as a person. My children—all three—created me.

NURSING PRACTICE

I wanted to give nursing care to children, but events led me to other things. I once had a private duty case in Muskogee, Oklahoma, where I sat up all night with a young man who had a head injury from an auto accident. The rate was $5 for eight hours, but when his wife said the insurance would pay me, I retreated—and was never paid. That difficulty with demanding fair pay has been a consistent weakness. To the instant of retirement I have always been underpaid, and while I wanted to be able to do the things that needed to be done, money was rarely an issue in my professional life. I once asked a dean who was hiring me to offer me $1,000 less so that my husband would not feel demeaned by my salary. As an academic who worked almost without exception for tax-supported institutions, he was never fairly paid in his entire life of service. Facing the problems of living on retirement annuities, we know how shortsighted that view was, and still we seemed always to be caught in it.

As an academic, Ed had contracts that ended in June and began in September, and since nurses can find work more easily than classicists, when summer came, I went to work. When we first returned to Chicago from Minneapolis, I worked at the Cook County School of Nursing—Miss Newman was true to her word that she would always have a teaching position for me—and I became the chemistry teacher in the preclinical program. I introduced a course called "Physical Sciences in Nursing," in which I taught physics as well as chemistry. The McGraw-Hill representative who reviewed my syllabus for publication said I was 10 years ahead of my time. It was more like 30, but it indicates that from the outset I was never satisfied with the way things were. I never questioned the conviction I had that it was always possible to make a course better by allowing it to grow and change each time it was taught. I finished my BS at the University of Chicago, where the magic of Nellie X. Hawkinson and Sallie Mernin gave substance to my knowledge of nursing and myself. However, the fact that I had the degree (it was 1949) did nothing to improve the salary of $220 a month I was receiving, so when I was offered a post as the director of nursing at Drexel Home for $4,000 a year, I grabbed it.

I established the first all–registered nurse program in a home for the aged at Drexel Home and had the unique opportunity to learn about geriatrics from a true prophet, Ben Grossman. Working for him was a fast course in what geriatric nursing would be like 30 years later. In many ways the Drexel Home experience was a model for the evolution of care for the aged. My friend and colleague from Cook County School of Nursing, Zella von Gremp, had organized the first program for licensed practical nurses at the Manley Vocational School, and we arranged that the first class would have its clinical experience at Drexel Home. We soon were able to eliminate the unlicensed, self-styled "practicals" who worked there, and we replaced them with graduates of the Manley program. The registered nurses I hired for Drexel Home remained there from 1950 until the institution was closed in 1980. They were pioneers in the field of nursing the aged.

Ed's job move to Lincoln, Nebraska, in the fall of 1957 terminated my association with Drexel Home. I learned much there, including my determination to leave administration to others. I wanted to teach. Ed was teaching at Wayne State University in Detroit when Pat was born. I had been content to be home with my babies when Dean Katherine Faville of the Wayne State College of Nursing called and invited me over for lunch. She had heard of my work at Drexel and wanted to explore my interest in geriatrics. Even though I was in no position to pick up a career again, that call began a rare relationship with a truly great American nurse that eventually brought me back to graduate school and a full-time commitment to a teaching career.

In June 1955 we were facing three months without salary, so I went to Elizabeth Moran at Henry Ford Hospital and was hired as a clinical instructor for the summer. I continued on a part-time basis when the academic year began and, at my request, as a walking supervisor, since it seemed impossible to provide part-time instruction in a program I did not otherwise participate in. I continued in this role—with full-time summers— for seven years. Meanwhile, I entered Wayne State and earned a Master of Science degree in nursing.

The year at Wayne State was pure excitement. I had begun with much trepidation, but it was soon wiped away by a mentor of giant stature. It was my great fortune to have Irene Beland as a teacher and thesis advisor. Irene opened a view of nursing that made it not only a compassionate art, but open as well to rigid intellectual inspection. Mabel Wandelt and Mildred Gottdank were there also, as was Katherine Faville—the always towering presence—herself. My graduate experience was a time of great excitement for me, and I hoped that I could, in the future, make the experience live in the same way for my students.

We left Detroit in 1962 and went back to Chicago. I started at the University of Illinois College of Nursing, hired by Emily Cardew, who said I would have a blank slate on which to create a course in fundamentals of nursing. Before winter, Mary Kelly Mullane had been appointed dean. The year of creating the new course in concert with Doris Molbo (who later was designated the first American Cancer Society Professor of Nursing at the University of Washington) was a fantastic experience. Doris and I created a course that was a genuine departure from the usual pattern, and while the students thrived and grew in it, other faculty appeared threatened by it. At the end of the year it seemed wiser to move on than remain in combat with faculty members who yearned for "Nursing Arts" as it appeared in the old *NLN Curriculum Guide.*

I moved across the street—home—to Cook County as the coordinator of clinical nursing. Under Pauline Gesner, I had the freedom to produce a new, exciting, and enduring concept of nursing education. I was surrounded with gifted nurses who knew what nursing was all about: Ruby Roberts, Beulah Gingrich (both passed on much too soon), Laverne Lissy, DeeAnn Gillies, and a cadre of young instructors who were adventurous and zealous as nurses. The syllabus that ultimately became *An Introduction to Clinical Nursing* was written—chapter by chapter—every weekend in advance of the topic for the following week. All kinds of new material was added to the nursing curriculum. We taught research-based science and made the need for research in nursing a constant theme. We taught perception, distance behaviors, sleep (from its research bias), and periodicity as a factor in health and disease. We emphasized the wholeness of the individuals, and how every patient was a member of a family and every family shared in the individual's diagnosis.

The original syllabus discussed stress as Selye had described it and raised the issue of performing breast biopsies and radical mastectomies under the same anesthesia. The text was chosen an *AJN* "Book of the Year" in both its first and second editions. It introduced content into the nursing curriculum that became commonplace, and few people are even aware of where it came from. It was possible to create this program because Polly Gesner was the kind of director who not only spoke of confidence in her faculty but lived it, and under her guidance the mind could come alive. However, Irene Beland had told me before I left Wayne State that I should be teaching the teachers, and when I was offered a faculty position at Loyola University, I took it.

While many aspects of life at Loyola were difficult, the success of the master's program in the preparation of clinical specialists was remarkable. It was in large part because of the maturity of the nurses who entered the program. They made their educational effort into a reality, creating the true dimensions of the clinical specialist in their careers afterward. Margaret Stafford and Joyce Waterman Taylor set the pace from the first class, and distinguished clinicians followed each year. In 1973 I was invited to teach at Tel Aviv University in Israel. I was unable to get a sabbatical, so I left Loyola.

ISRAEL AND JUDAISM

My uncle had a cottage on Lake Geneva, and each summer we would visit there. As we drove down the country road that led to the house, we passed a fenced-in yard. On a tree near the road, there was a crudely printed sign that said, "No Jews Allowed." It was a sign seen frequently in the resort country of Wisconsin—and elsewhere—in those years, and while it was nothing compared with the events that were about to explode in Europe, it was a painful reminder to a Jewish child.

I remember wondering how it was possible that anyone would—sight unseen—hate me and my family. I could not understand how we were so different from "them." The facts of the Holocaust were distant from the subtle social stigma we wore wherever we went. Gentiles cannot understand that, but it was everywhere—in school and in all kinds of social situations where the slighting was so finely drawn that we could be accused of being oversensitive when we knew perfectly well that we had read the intention correctly. Some think it is a compliment to tell me that I don't "look Jewish." Real estate agents and college department chairmen often said, "You don't want to go where you are not wanted, do you?" And we were expected to be grateful for their thoughtfulness in our behalf.

Dr. Rebecca Bergman invited me to come to teach at Tel Aviv University. It took three years to arrange the six months of our visit, and we arrived in Israel on a warm, muggy evening in September 1973. Shoshanna Eckerling was waiting for us at the airport, and she took us to the Bergmans' lovely apartment, where we were to stay. There were several neighbors waiting for us. There were bouquets of fresh flowers, home-baked cookies, a large bowl of fruit, and the smiling faces of those strangers who were welcoming us like family. Standing in the dining room of that beautiful apartment, surrounded by those warm and wonderful people, I learned in an instant the importance of Israel. Since it was a hot evening, the women were wearing sleeveless dresses, and two of them had tattooed on their left arms the concentration camp numbers that were their heritage from Hitler.

Within two weeks the Israelis were trapped in another war. It was in those dangerous days that we learned the strength of their faith in themselves. I watched the mobilizing of the medical establishment and the selflessness of the nurses, working endless hours and always without complaint or murmur, although many were constantly fighting fatigue and heartache. Sharing that time with them speeded our relationships. We had come to Israel knowing no one and left in possession of a wide and loving family of friends and colleagues. My own religious education had been in Reform Judaism of a most extreme kind, and Ed's religious education had been completely neglected. However, we found in Israel a source of insight and feeling that had been dormant for many years and was now alive and thriving. We found synagogue life and a great rabbi, David Polish, to bring us into active participation. Our children have received the Jewish education we had not had. They know the pride of their heritage and wear it well. And even in an academic world where the undercurrent of polite anti-Semitism is still commonplace, we wear it, too—and proudly.

THEORY

I didn't plan to create a "nursing theory." I was trying to be a better teacher, and I was thoroughly imbued with the University of Chicago curriculum where the broad generalizations that tied knowledge into related categories had become a part of my own thinking process. The University of Chicago undergraduate curriculum was summarized in a course called "OII: Observation, Integration, Interpretation." My principal goal was to create an OII in nursing.

When Emily Cardew appointed me to the fundamentals program at the University of Illinois, I was determined to find a way to teach the beginning skills and knowledge of nursing at a collegiate level. That is how the "models"—outlined summaries of the basic science that was essential to intelligent use of nursing procedures—were created. I wanted students to learn the science principles *a priori* instead of in the traditional pattern in which they learned "how to" first and sought the applied science *a posteriori*. I was convinced then, as I have been throughout my career, that professional decision making rested on what the individual knew and that such knowledge had to be broad enough to serve well in a multiplicity of situations, both those that were predictable and those that were not.

The notion of conservation came from science, and it seemed eminently reasonable that a natural law that regulated all animate and inanimate matter in the universe must be included in the nursing curriculum. Four conservation principles evolved out of my thinking. They apply equally to living things, and the derivative meaning of "conservation" as a "keeping together" function seemed entirely appropriate as the essential goal of nursing care:

- *Conservation of energy* refers to balancing energy output and energy input to avoid excessive fatigue, that is, adequate rest, nutrition, and exercise.
- *Conservation of structural integrity* refers to maintaining or restoring the structure of the body, that is, preventing physical breakdown and promoting healing.
- *Conservation of personal integrity* refers to maintenance or restoration of the patient's sense of identity, self-worth, and acknowledgment of uniqueness.
- *Conservation of social integrity* refers to the acknowledgment of the patient as a social being. It involves the recognition and presentation of human interaction, particularly with the patient's significant others.

The development of the four conservation principles grew naturally out of my desire to organize nursing knowledge so that the student would have a strong organizing basis for interpreting all kinds of nursing situations. It was easy to work with, and in its simplicity it seemed to open many channels of thinking that had not been obvious before. It allowed me to produce courses in medical-surgical nursing that could be communicated both in the classroom and in the clinical area in very positive ways. I adopted it as the basis for a textbook in beginning nursing, *Introduction to Clinical Nursing*. I never dreamed that others would see in it a new nursing theory. I was certain it would educate good nurses. That is all I ever wanted to do.

FINALLY

People are defined by all of those who enter their life-space. Some are recalled, revered, and cherished in a multitude of conscious and unconscious ways. Even those who touched a life for a moment and went their way have left some remembrance, however impossible it may be to reconstruct and recognize. I have a treasure of those who did not seek to make me other than what I was, but left their gifts for me to celebrate through all my life afterward.

Sometimes I ask myself what it is I remember and what it is I have dreamed. The vision of my grandmother, tall and lovely, standing in a shaft of sunlight on an early morning, grinding the coffee in an old-fashioned mill—do I know it was thus, or only carry it in my mind as a source of protecting love all my life? I remember with abiding love—and I remember with still painful hurt—a parade of those who became part of me. Some I have named in these pages. Some I have forgotten to name. Some are so much the fiber of my being that I cannot truly separate them. One is remembered as the person touching other lives. Let the touch be gentle and caring, even if it seems a fantasy that was more imagined than real.

Ruth Watson Lubic

Ruth Watson Lubic, EdD, RN, CNM, FAAN,
is General Director of the Maternity Center Association
in New York City

❖

*As General Director of New York's famous Maternity Center
Association, Ruth Lubic established its Childbearing Center, where women
who choose not to go to hospitals have an alternative birthing place.
Her five-year struggle to get the center going taught her important
lessons about overt professional conflict, political leadership, and caring.
A scrapper all her life, Ruth Lubic has learned well the art of effecting
change and the true sources of strength. She offers here a set of principles
that she believes will ensure a successful professional life.*

*T*he year was 1933, and I was barely of school age. On the sliding doors of the glass cabinets that held the sundries in Watson's Drug Store in a small Pennsylvania town were posted stickers on which eagles and the legend "NRA We Do Our Part" were depicted.

It was in the heart of the depression, and the National Recovery Act had been put in place by President Roosevelt. Hopes were high in the nation, but in a small manufacturing town sitting on the edge of farmland everybody seemed to be poor. Because people couldn't afford a physician, they turned to my father, "Doc" Watson, for health care. They came with foreign bodies in their eyes; Doc would turn back their lids on a matchstick and remove the matter with a piece of gauze—no charge. They came with colds and were given small cardboard boxes of Watson's Cold Tablets; with boils, and were given tins of "black salve" (ichthyol ointment); with insect bites for stingers to be removed; with constipation, for citrate of magnesia or castor oil put in foaming root beer; and without periods, for Humphrey's Homeopathic #66 (as I recall) for delayed menses. And if they couldn't pay, Doc would put it on the tab. For an ice-cream cone you had to have a nickel, but if you were sick and needy, he tried to help. Father paid for his stock with money borrowed on my mother's jewelry, remnants of the halcyon days of the 1920s.

During those lean years, Aunt Alice, my mother's sister, would come from Philadelphia on occasional weekends to see my grandmother, whom she supported. Alice was, as she expressed it, "a graduate nurse," and had been trained at the Hospital of the University of Pennsylvania. At that point in her life, however, in order to support herself and her mother, she operated a School of Rhythm, for enhancing body mechanics and teaching stress reduction to any interested person. Her entrepreneurial nursing service (I didn't recognize it as such then) had been established to teach coordination to the neurologically impaired children of affluent families. Music was an important part of her program, and spiritual aspects of body movement and harmony were coordinated into her teaching. Years after her death, I read a newspaper interview of Aunt Alice. She was quoted regarding her concern about the overuse of machines in treating the sick. She instinctively felt they interfered with normal physiologic processes.

Without being aware of it at the time, I believe that I internalized her philosophy; the appropriate use of technology is one of my major concerns, and I see a tendency in physicians to be impressed by technology and assume a pathologic approach to human health problems. I believe that is a major alienating facet between nursing and medicine.

In 1942 my father died suddenly at age 48. He died at home, having been ill with "the flu" for just a day. I was awakened by the sounds of my mother calling to him. She had heard his last breath as he succumbed to a massive myocardial infarction. I well remember my mother telling me to call our family physician, George T. Fox, on the telephone. I remember, too, the doctor's quick arrival and his prayers over my father's body when he had confirmed the death.

Dr. Fox cared for our physical ills, but he also encouraged my sister's and my own intellectual and cultural growth. I recall reciting poetry to him for the reward of a fifty-cent piece. I remember visiting his office, which was in his home—the sunporch waiting room with its wicker furniture, his desk and interview room with a view of the Delaware River, and the examining room, with its odor of antiseptics and sight of fearsome instruments. How I hated the metal probes with cotton-wound tips he used to open sinuses and effect drainage—no antibiotics then! All the while he would sing or recite poetry to distract the patient's attention from the task at hand.

My father's death changed my life substantially. I was 14 at the time, and although our family life had always been constrained by the drugstore, now I had to assist my mother at every possible moment. She was unable to hire a pharmacist because none was available. Although the United States had just gotten into World War II officially, the war was three years old, and all able-bodied men were being pressed to serve in the military. My mother operated the business without a prescription department, as one could do then in Pennsylvania. The hours of business were 9 AM to 10 PM weekdays, 9 AM to 11 PM on Saturdays, and 9 AM to 1 PM and 6 PM to 10 PM on Sundays. Those five hours that we closed shop on Sunday were the only times we ever got together for a meal or just to relax as a family.

My only sister, who was five years older than I, was away at college, so it was up to me to help my mother stock shelves, sweep, run the soda fountain, and be a general clerk. I did my homework in the back of the store and took my evening meal at the local hotel. I always took home a platter of food for mother. It was at the hotel that I was befriended by a new general practitioner in town, Charles Sampsel. He understood the tragic aspects of my life. Often we would dine together and sometimes, when the store wasn't busy and my mother agreed to it, he would take me with him on house calls. He encouraged me to seek a career in nursing. The relationship was very meaningful for me but didn't last long. He was conscripted and later killed in the South Pacific. In those days people became used to disappointment, adversity, and the tragedy of the loss of family and friends. It was rigorous and difficult schooling, but I believe that that adversity prepared me well for the extraordinary difficulties I was to experience in later years in implementing a nursing model to change health care delivery to childbearing families.

At length I operated the store as principal for two years and there earned the money to put myself through nursing school. I entered my aunt's alma mater, the School of Nursing of the Hospital of the University of Pennsylvania, in June 1952 at the age of 25. I was the "old woman" of my class.

It wasn't long before I got into political difficulty. I was elected president of the student body. Students were depended on to provide much of the patient care. The burning issue for students of the school then was reducing the 44-hour duty week to 40 hours. Even the former was nearly half of what I was used to working, but I expressed the views of my constituency and attempted to have abolished the extra half day of service. I was taken to the senior hospital administrator (a nurse!) by the director of the school and there was scapegoated as the troublemaker. The issue was represented as entirely my own idea. My amazement at the accusation quickly turned to humiliation and frustration. The Hospital of the University of Pennsylvania (HUP) at that time had counseling available to nursing students, and I quickly made use of the service to pour out my feelings about being unfairly accused. The counselor sympathized and assured me that one day I would appreciate having had the experience. She was right, of course.

My student days at HUP were both exhilarating and frightening. As a "duster" (a student who had been at the hospital for six to eight months) I learned to be an evening charge nurse on a men's surgical ward. Most evenings a younger student and an aide worked with me; sometimes only the latter. There were no intensive care units. The recovery room closed each day, so you could count on the most serious surgical "cases" coming back to the ward on 15-minute signs. Radical neck dissections including mandibulectomies, thoracotomies on tuberculosis patients who had to be cared for in isolation— these occurred, often simultaneously. We students blessed the open ward because all patients were in sight, but I marvel that I didn't run in terror. I believe I was much more deeply affected by the magnitude of the responsibility than my younger classmates, but all of us managed to survive.

While at Penn I met my future husband, who had been a law school classmate of one of my high school chums. Just prior to my graduation in 1955, we married. I was the first known-to-be married student in the school. I still had to live in the dorm those few weeks, but with my bridegroom living in New York it wasn't too difficult.

I moved to New York as a new graduate and practiced in medicine and surgery while attending Hunter College part time in the evening to secure a bachelor's degree in nursing. My husband's support was and is crucial to my accomplishments. Often, I would fall asleep in class, and I resented the way assignments cut into my other responsibilities. In the middle of one semester I wanted to quit, but he insisted that I finish the semester. He knew, of course, that once I had completed my papers and taken my tests, there was no reason to quit. Bill not only encouraged me to achieve but did his share of the housework and other duties. As an attorney who went to school with dozens of other GIs returning from World War II, he was not making much money in the 1950s, when there was a glut of lawyers. When we were setting up housekeeping in New York, his weekly pay was $40; mine, as a beginning staff nurse, was $90.

In 1958 I was awarded a scholarship to Teachers College and transferred there for a year's full-time study to complete a bachelor's degree. During that period our son Douglas was conceived, and I gave birth two weeks after graduation.

I had not enjoyed my nursing school obstetrics rotation, especially after I was put in a room with four women whose labors were being induced when I had never even palpated a contraction. Those were the days when the use of "pit and caudal" anesthesia was in vogue and was administered almost routinely. Because of those student experiences, I knew I wanted Bill to be with me in labor. My obstetrician was a very sensitive man who believed in family-centered maternity care. He sent me to parents' classes, where I was exposed for the first time to a nurse-midwifery philosophy, although the instructors did not mention their midwifery preparation.

My doctor also *offered* to have Bill present in the delivery room if it seemed appropriate at the time, that is, if my labor and birth progressed normally and if the right people were on duty and the wrong people off. Much to our good fortune it all worked out. Douglas was born, and he was left with us in the delivery room for an hour or more. I was encouraged to nurse him immediately. We bonded, the three of us, and to this day we are close emotionally, even if not geographically.

Our early days of parenting were marred by Doug's "hospital staph" (*Staphylococcus aureus*) infection, which we discovered just after we arrived home five days after his birth. At first my milk was blamed and I had to bind my breasts, but even when the true cause was discovered I was not permitted to nurse him. It was a difficult time for all of us, but after a few days on medication he improved and began to thrive, although he was left with an impairment of coordination now outgrown.

I went back to medical-surgical nursing and studied with Frances Reiter at Teachers College for my master's in teaching, although I had begun to feel more and more strongly that I could make the best use of myself in maternity care. When I told all this to my obstetrician, he said, "Why don't you study midwifery?" "What's that?" I asked. In reply he sent me to the Maternity Center Association (MCA) to speak to Hazel Corbin, who was the general director at the time.

Not long thereafter I entered MCA's nurse-midwifery educational program, which had just moved from the renowned Lobenstine Clinic home birth setting into Kings County Hospital, Downstate Medical Center. Once again I was lucky; all the faculty had been prepared in home birth and with a strong noninterventionist philosophy. It was during that student experience that I learned one of my guiding principles—to always listen carefully to those we serve.

On one occasion I had provided prenatal care for a woman expecting her third baby. In discussing her past labors, she informed me that she would dilate to two fingers, and then the baby would come. I explained carefully how that was impossible and taught her all about cervical dilatation, using the finest teaching aids to support my information. I recall feeling quite satisfied that I had smitten the dragon of ignorance.

By coincidence, I was on intrapartum duty when she went into labor. She was deemed to be a candidate for nurse-midwifery management, and along with an instructor, I was assigned to her care. We got her settled into her labor bed (that was in 1961), and I examined her. While I was rearranging the sheets I smiled at her and said, "Well, you are two fingers now and you aren't having your baby, are you?" With that she gave a great groan, and there was the baby. Perhaps my being on duty that morning was no coincidence but part of a grand design for dispelling professional arrogance.

When I finished the program, I joined the maternity nursing faculty of a baccalaureate program. One of my responsibilities was to accompany students on obstetrical rounds each Monday. There was not much interest in family-centered care, but one of the younger attending physicians reported one day on his revolutionary but successful management of vaginal birth for a woman who had undergone a prior cesarean section. She actually was not his private patient but that of an older obstetrician whose practice the young physician had covered over the weekend. He described how he had stayed by the laboring woman's bedside, checking the fetal heart after each contraction. He also described the mother's joy at being able to give birth vaginally. At that point in the narrative the older man interrupted to say, "Well, you just did me out of a surgical fee!" It is just such blind self-interest among professionals that I denounce and feel compelled to resist on behalf of families.

In 1964 I became a parent educator for MCA. What a joy it was to welcome the apprehensive expectant couples and to see them change into confident families! I felt I should be paying for the privilege of working with them. More important, my conviction that maternity care offered nurses the best opportunity to break away from the pervasive illness orientation of the health care delivery system became more ingrained in me. However, I also realized that I had to become more aware of the belief systems and cultural heritage of the families who most needed personalized responsive care.

Back to school I went, this time to study applied anthropology. It was while I was completing my course work that I was asked to return to MCA as general director. Bill and I immediately went to visit Hazel Corbin, then retired, to get the benefit of her advice. I had and still have great respect for the work that she and her colleagues had done during her 46 years at MCA and wanted some assurance that she thought I might be a positive force in that unique agency. I was excited by the potential to effect change but concerned about the responsibility of maintaining the enviable reputation of the MCA.

On Friday, February 28, 1970, I took my doctoral certifying exam, and on Monday, March 3, 1970, I became the general director of MCA.

Another impressive event in my professional life occurred in 1973. I was fortunate in being selected the only woman and only nurse to be part of the first official medical delegation to the People's Republic of China. There I saw a system of care that convinced me that it is indeed possible to get health care to *all* the people of a nation. It further convinced me that it is part of my personal and professional responsibility to do what I can in that regard and to rid myself of the very subtle "victim-blaming" orientation that I have been exposed to along the way. The good medical friends I made among the delegation were of inestimable assistance in setting up the Childbearing Center. I learned to appreciate the importance of medical friends in implementing a nursing model.

It was not until 1979 that I completed my dissertation in applied anthropology. It is not, as I had originally planned, a work that sensitizes health professionals to the differing cultural needs of the people we serve. It is rather a political anthropological analysis of the problems encountered in attempting to change the health care delivery system. Entitled "Barriers and Conflict in Maternity Care Innovation," it is a success story of women and nurses committed to the improvement of care for childbearing families.

During the five-year struggle to establish and keep alive the Childbearing Center, I learned a very important lesson that can save countless hours when one is engaged in a battle for change: medical opposition is without exception voiced in terms of desire for clinical quality and safety. Because we nurses are often unsophisticated in overt professional conflict, our tendency is to rise to the bait and search diligently for proof of clinical safety, which early in innovation usually is not yet extant. If such proof *is* found and presented, one quickly learns that clinical safety is not the real—or at least not the main—reason for opposition.

When your position is challenged or refuted in public forums or before groups, carefully gauge the intensity of emotion displayed. The more strident the attack or argument, the greater the likelihood that self-interest, not concern for quality, is motivating the outburst. I lived through and still experience such attacks, although they have become less frequent. My years in the trenches have taught me that a nurse confronting medical opposition does best to remain calm, polite, and firm in presentation and affect. It does not help to respond in kind even when sorely tempted to do so.

Especially galling in such circumstances is the double standard that is sometimes used. In one instance, our service was accused of being responsible for a poor neonatal outcome that had occurred when an expectant mother had been transferred to the hospital, according to our criteria and in a timely fashion. When we were exonerated of any blame, the investigation was dropped abruptly. The intent of the investigation was not to determine the cause of the neonatal death but rather to discredit and eliminate our service. Remember that fear of change and confusion about receiving criticism from consumers may well be motivating the behavior being directed at you.

In conclusion, let me set down some guiding principles that I believe will ensure a successful professional life:

1. Begin with the needs of the people you serve.
2. Take care of all of the people of the nation.
3. Trust your caring instincts.
4. Choose colleagues for their caring philosophy rather than professional orientation.
5. Beware the limits of the medical model.
6. Avoid anger. It consumes energy and clouds vision.
7. Avoid bitterness against political opponents.
8. Base your design on the best science possible; then test your performance.
9. Overcome the fear associated with leadership.
10. Remember—the people you serve are your strength.
11. Nursing prepares you for excellence. Be proud you are a nurse.

Marie Manthey

Marie Manthey, MNA, RN, is President
of Creative Nursing Management,
a consulting firm based in Minneapolis

Marie Manthey writes about two major growth experiences that have had a profound impact on her life—the birth of primary nursing in 1968 and the beginning of her recovery from alcoholism in 1978. She believes that, in a peculiar way, they are similar. Primary nursing is an organizational adjustment that requires a nurse to take personal responsibility for his or her professional actions; recovery from alcoholism involves learning to accept responsibility for one's own acts. From both experiences, she learned that making choices creates energy and that seeing oneself as a victim is dispiriting.

Her story reflects no relationship between her self-image as a child and the decisions that led to her success. It does reflect the way her imaginative and creative talents moved her to welcome change and profit from it.

Growing up in Chicago—the city, not a suburb—embeds in a person's consciousness certain ethnic truths like "Irish live on the South Side, Germans live on the North Side, and Catholics live all over the place." My mom grew up on the South Side, and my father came from the North Side. As a young married couple striving to move up the economic and social ladder, their hopes for the future were brutally damaged by the depression. Economic security was a lost hope, and fear became a permanent part of the family experience.

No matter how unstable our family finances were, parochial schools were a must. In Chicago nearly all the kids on the block went to parochial school. Those who didn't were certainly not part of our gang. In fact school times were staggered so parochial and public school kids didn't walk the sidewalks at the same time.

Doctor/nurse sets were always my favorite Christmas toys, but I was never interested in the doctor side of the kit. Ever since I had been hospitalized at the age of five, I wanted to be a nurse. I had a nurse by the name of Florence Marie Fisher who cared for me during that hospitalization. Although I never saw her again, her personalized and very humane care became a model that I have followed throughout my life and professional career. I had a form of scarlet fever in the days before penicillin. One treatment consisted of withdrawing whole blood from one of my parents and injecting it directly into my gluteus maximus, which at that age wasn't very maximus! I remember excruciating pain. Miss Fisher's care was especially important in that context.

The family goal for my sister's and my own education was a high school diploma. That represented a significant improvement over the education of previous generations, some of whom didn't finish grade school.

Throughout my childhood I was an accepting, compliant, and obedient child. I look back now and wonder when I began to see myself as a person who should be involved in change. Even as a teenager I was neither angry nor rebellious. I enjoyed my family life, socialized moderately, and believed that at some point in time I would get married, have children, and wear housedresses. I'm not sure I ever reconciled being a nurse with being a homemaker, but if Sue Barton could alternate roles, so could I!

Career planning for me went something like this. In the spring of my senior year in high school my dad visited his general practitioner for some minor problem. In casual conversation the physician asked my dad what I intended to do after graduation. "She thinks she wants to be a nurse," Father replied. "Well, tell her to go to the tea next Sunday afternoon at St. Elizabeth's . . . it's a tea for high school senior girls who want to be nurses." As a basically obedient person I did just that, signed a form, and was notified several weeks later that I had been admitted.

The question of baccalaureate versus diploma education was never a real issue for me. I wanted to be the kind of nurse who took care of sick people, not the kind who taught school or sat at a desk. The program was typical for that era—a six-month probationary period, followed by a solemn capping ceremony, followed by two and a half years of intensive clinical work interspersed with relevant clinical classroom study. I think maybe I graduated because I was obedient. The ones who looked and acted smart didn't necessarily graduate; in fact, many didn't make it past the probationary period.

After graduation I stayed on at St. Elizabeth's until state board results were in. Shortly after I was registered to practice professional nursing in the state of Illinois, there was a family party. My mother's cousin, whom I didn't really know well, suggested that I apply at the University of Chicago for a job in the hospital. She worked in the university's personnel department and essentially told me that the University of Chicago was a good place to work. On the basis of that insider information I applied, was accepted, and began a four-year stint as staff nurse, assistant head nurse, and finally as head nurse of a postoperative surgical floor.

Since I felt that I was finished with school, suggestions from my supervisor that I get a bachelor's degree fell on deaf ears. However, when I was promoted to assistant head nurse, I reluctantly agreed to take a three-credit course entitled "Ward Administration" at Loyola University. Much to my surprise it was fun, and I embarked on a long period of full-time work and part-time school.

At one point I was head nurse of a 24-bed surgical unit at the University of Chicago while taking nine semester credits in night school. Fortunately I was living at home and my mother was enjoying the cooking, laundry, and shopping activities of adult living, thus freeing my time for work, school, and a little play. I was attending one school on Monday and Wednesday nights, another on Tuesdays and Thursdays, and was taking a for-credit course in freshman English on the educational television channel. In those days freshman English was mainly composition writing. The professor assigned one essay each week, which we sent to him in the mail. He corrected it and sent it back for rewrite. By the time I was six weeks into the semester I was so overextended that the situation seemed hopeless. I stopped watching television on Friday nights, forgetting that I needed to cancel out the course for which I was duly registered. The F thus earned is still on my transcripts.

Somewhere along the way someone convinced me that I should get my bachelor's degree. My attitude was one of ambivalence. The people I saw around me with baccalaureate degrees were old maids and I didn't know which happened first . . . whether they were single because they had a higher education or if they went to school because they weren't married.

I had many mentors at that time and throughout my career. At the University of Chicago, three people stand out as having influenced my career. Wanda Crouse, who was my first head nurse, Jo Sana, a supervisor, and Peg Sheehan, the director of nursing, were supportive and encouraging. They told me things like, "Yes, you are capable of earning a bachelor's degree," and they provided me with practical help and concrete advice. For example, Peg Sheehan not only suggested that I apply to the University of Minnesota School of Nursing (she had been director of nursing there) but also administered the tests required for admission in the conference room of my unit.

I credit Wanda Crouse with keeping me in nursing after I committed my first serious clinical mistake. I had been trained with the belief that in dealing with humans perfection is the only standard that can be tolerated. Therefore my first error was so devastating that I came very close to becoming a department store clerk. A combination of Wanda's support and six months of collecting innumerable plenary indulgences kept me in the profession long enough for the healing power of time to take effect.

In September 1960 I became a 26-year-old college freshman, living in a dorm with several other nurses returning for a bachelor's degree. We were not yet eligible for traineeships so we took advantage of the university's recruitment gimmick whereby we could work for 12 hours per week in exchange for our board and room in Powell Hall. When we were within 12 months of completion of the degree, we became eligible for a federal traineeship, which provided tuition, fees, and a monthly stipend on the theory that nurses should not have to work while getting their advanced education. The only return requested was two years of work (at full pay) in the field for which one had been educated. I was married within a year of coming to Minnesota and pregnant before graduation.

Part-time work in private duty, the Peace Corps, and teaching practical nurse students were my main professional activities from the spring of 1962 until the summer of 1963, when I worked full time as vacation relief for supervisors in nursing service. During that period I felt as though I was part of a relay system, being passed from nursing service to the school of nursing and back again. Miss Harris was associate dean and Miss Julian was director of nursing at the hospital. I have a feeling the two of them were in cahoots in providing me opportunities that fit my life situation and kept me moving forward in the profession. The school asked me to teach in the Peace Corps and in practical nursing. Then Miss Julian asked me to relieve the hospital supervisors for vacations. Then Miss Harris asked me to consider returning to school under another traineeship for a master's degree in nursing administration. By the time that program was completed, Miss Julian took me to lunch at the Campus Club and invited me to join her staff in the capacity of assistant director in charge of special projects.

That position marked a turning point in my career, but I didn't know it for a long time. The year was 1964, the organization was traditional, team nursing was embedded into the consciousness of the department, and there were serious problems with the quality of patient care and staff turnover. Patients were complaining about impersonal and fragmented care, and the turnover rate was outrageous. A 300% turnover rate was not uncommon, meaning that each position had been held by three individuals in a one-year period! My position was a radical departure from the norm because I was quite high in the organizational structure but had no operational responsibilities. My job was to do whatever the director of nursing didn't know who else to give something to, which often meant being a change agent.

After years of traditional leadership at the hospital administration level there was a change at the top. The old guard left and seven newcomers arrived, having been selected by an administrator who was young, energetic, and interested in doing things in a new and better way. Shortly thereafter we had approval to study the idea of unit management to determine whether that was a direction the University of Minnesota Hospital should take. This was like an answer to my prayers, since I had believed for several years that team nursing would work just fine if only nurses didn't have to do so many nonnursing tasks. However, now that we had permission to proceed, I had no idea what steps to take. My change experience went far beyond the boundaries of nursing into territory strange to me and my colleagues. Fortunately a friendly hospital administrator was also leading the project. A lifelong friendship began as we learned together on that project. We found that, when one is in doubt about how to proceed, it is best to appoint several committees and take a trip. Something is bound to turn up as an appropriate next step in your absence. Meanwhile the committees generate minutes, which makes it look as if something is happening.

Indeed many things were happening! In the following months every department and all individuals who worked in any capacity on Station 32 became part of Project 32, a far-reaching change experience that birthed primary nursing and other exciting new ideas about how hospitals should be organized.

To return to the discussion of the committees, there were three. One was interdisciplinary and consisted of top experts in health and other related fields (such as communications and industrial engineering), as well as the dean of the School of Nursing, a member of administration from the School of Medicine, and others. A second committee consisted of hospital department heads and nurses from a variety of positions, including several faculty members of the School of Nursing. Because there were faculty present, one of the first charges of this group was to identify objectives of nursing service. (Left to their own devices, nursing service people in those days avoided objectives whenever possible!) The objectives were like the flag and apple pie—nursing care should be comprehensive, coordinated, continuous, competent, personalized, and humane. This was at a time when most nurses didn't even know the names of the patients on their team and when patients heard themselves referred to in such terms as "the CVA in 356."

One member of the committee worked for a summer at the Loeb Center and came back to tell us how their delivery system worked. We learned that nurses, with the help of aides, did hands-on care for a certain group of patients. It sounded wonderful, but the nature and staffing patterns of Station 32 were so different that we knew that the Loeb model couldn't be duplicated in Station 32 and that the objective of continuity couldn't be ensured. What that report did do, however, was introduce the idea that there could be an alternative to team nursing.

The supervisor of the rehabilitation unit, Lorraine Delehanty, experimented with another concept—that of having a patient care coordinator assigned to each patient. We decided to try that idea but felt it needed to be done within the framework of team nursing. Each staff nurse was asked to take a single patient and to be the principal responsible nurse for that patient while functioning as a leader for the rest of the team. Needless to say we created a morale problem so serious that the entire staff threatened to resign unless drastic changes were made immediately. Supervisor Pat Robertson and I held a series of emergency meetings to prevent that disaster. We finally decided to have an open meeting of the staff at my house. In 1968 that was an earth-shaking event. Staff members were not usually invited to an assistant director's house for any reason—let alone because of a morale crisis.

At that meeting the staff asked for and was granted permission to not be team leaders and to work out a way to incorporate those objectives into their practice. Pat and I agreed to that but were not at all sure we had the authority to do so. We decided to go for "forgiveness" rather than "permission."

On the day following that meeting, primary nursing was born.

The nurses began to try to achieve those objectives as simply and directly as they could. As they worked together to do that, morale began to rise, the staff began to be excited about nursing again, and new ideas about how work should be done and who should be responsible for what job began to be formulated.

There is no question in my mind that what was going on in the world at the time primary nursing started had a profound impact on our project. Vietnam was dividing families, friends, and country. The civil rights marches had become civil rights challenges — women capitalized on the "joke" a lawmaker made in inserting the word sex into the civil rights law passed in 1964. I know those events were influencing my thinking about myself and about nursing. I also know that I happened to be in the right place at the right time to act on those thoughts. I don't think I would have forced a change in my environment under any condition. At that time and now, change was and is a real and acceptable part of my life, but I have never approached it from an angry or frustrated feeling.

The University of Minnesota campus was a hotbed of riotous challenges to the establishment. Thoughtful liberationists were deciding whether to support revolution or evolution, whether to work for change within the system or outside of it.

New hospital administrators brought with them the idea of decentralization. Miss Julian (the director of nursing) and I took a trip to Arizona Good Samaritan Hospital to see for ourselves how one director used this concept in structuring the nursing administrative staff. Rosamond Gabrielson is in my opinion one of nursing's pioneers for her successful implementation of this concept in the nursing department of Good Samaritan.

Another "happening" that prepared our environment for change was the publication of Sister Madeleine Vaillot's article, "Existentialism: A Philosophy of Commitment" (March 1966 *AJN*), in which she said that the essence of nursing is the therapeutic use of self in a relationship with the patient. That article vindicated those of us who had been unable to maintain a cool and aloof professional distance from our patients, and it paved the way in our thinking for the eventual establishment of a delivery system that centered on the therapeutic relationship between a nurse and a patient.

Shortly after the breakthrough meeting at my house, it was obvious that something dramatic had occurred. Change was evident in the way the unit operated, the way the nurses felt and acted, the way patients responded. The excitement was unbelievable! In several think-tank sessions with many friends and associates, we settled on the term *primary nursing* as an apt description of the new model.

We had the name, but not the understanding. We didn't know whether to write a job description, restaff all units, or have different people work on this unit. We weren't sure that what we had was not an unreplicable piece of magic. None of us associated with the project had a clear understanding of the concept of delivery systems, and we certainly had not set out to develop an alternative to team nursing.

Fortunately an administrative resident named Stan Williams, who was also a sociologist, was helping with the project. He taught me and the others about professional organizations and helped us think through the delivery system idea. As four major principles of organizations for unit level nursing work emerged, it became clear that the elements had been redefined by the staff of our unit, thus creating a new delivery system. Based on ancient truths about how sick people should be cared for, the system simply restructured work and the authority over it along the lines of total patient care and decentralized authority. As this became clear, we began to believe that replication was possible, but because the original development was such a serendipitous phenomenon, the best process for change was not at all clear to us.

Each time I finished an education program I said to myself, "Never again . . . I won't ever have to write a term paper or give a presentation once I'm in the work world." For that reason I wasn't particularly happy to be asked to share what was happening on the project. However, word began to spread in the nursing community, and requests for talks started dribbling in.

By the time the first article on primary nursing was published in Vol. I, No. 1 of *Nursing Forum,* 1970, I had already had several painful experiences trying to share with others what we were doing. The article itself was a painful experience. There were four authors of record, but many people were involved in other ways with the production of that piece. It was not easy writing. The publication resulted in a flow of interest at the national level causing ever more painful experiences for me as I reluctantly began to speak about it. I was so nervous as a public speaker that I suffered all the normal physiological symptoms of terror, including being unable to hear myself. The only way I could tell whether I was making sense was by watching the audience for signs of communication like smiles and nods. Eventually that problem of not hearing myself created an effective interactive speaking style that I am now comfortable with. For several years, however, I lived in almost constant dread of the next speaking date. A trick that helped was telling myself that I didn't really have to worry until the morning of the speech. On that day I would get up at 4:30 or 5 AM and pace the hotel room to put in a fair share of worry to ensure an effective presentation. There is no question in my mind that if I hadn't believed so strongly in primary nursing, I never could have sustained the prolonged learning curve I endured before public speaking became easy for me.

My first opportunity to be a director of nursing occurred in 1971 when Thelma Dodds retired from Miller Hospital in St. Paul and suggested I be considered a candidate for her position. I was not eager to leave my precious university, but I was ready to be a director. I had known that I was ready for a couple of years, ever since I realized administrators did not have "secret knowledge." Prior to that, whenever I disagreed with those in superior positions, I assumed they were smarter than I or somehow knew more about the issues than I did. Then one day I realized I knew more about the issues than they did and could therefore make better decisions. Somehow that insight opened my mind so that I could picture myself in an authoritative position. I was ready.

Miss Dodds had been director of nursing at Miller Hospital for 39 years and most of the head nurses there were her contemporaries. She had invited me to present primary nursing to the nursing supervisors the previous year and was very supportive of the idea. That support didn't automatically transfer to the old-guard head nurses. The unit most receptive to change was the one with the youngest head nurse, and primary nursing started on a pilot basis on that unit on the same day I started as the director. This auspicious introduction of the new director and her new ideas did not make the future implementation any easier, since the other units were able to identify many reasons why primary nursing wouldn't work, despite its success on that younger head nurse's unit.

The years at Miller were formative, challenging, exciting, and rewarding. I occasionally commented in public that being a director of nursing was not only fun but easy—a perspective I still maintain. For anyone who really wants to make a difference in the way patients are treated there is no position that offers a better opportunity. The rewards are dramatic, positive, and fulfilling. With a few simple management principles firmly adhered to and with a willingness to learn, a director can do all those things. Here are some principles directors should live by:

1. Do nothing that violates your common sense.
2. The staff knows more about their business than you do.
3. Your boss knows less about your business than you do; therefore you must find opportunities to enlighten the boss without preaching.
4. The best decisions are made at the action level.
5. As director of nursing, you must treat everyone in the department equally. Registered nurses are not more important than nurse's aides.
6. Your first priority is to provide the best patient care possible; then your decisions can support the advancement of professional nursing.

Two months after my appointment the merger of Miller Hospital and St. Luke's was executed, and two years later I became assistant administrator over both departments. The task of merging two departments into one proved to be a crucible for fast-track learning of new management techniques. The people issues of mergers are phenomenal. To be successful, one's good decisions have to be acceptable to the staff on both sides of every issue.

After two years of that challenge I was beginning to feel a restlessness on two counts. My marriage had ended about the time I became a director (an unrelated issue, I believe). *Future Shock* by Alvin Toffler taught me not to make three major changes simultaneously, so I remained in the house we had bought several years earlier. In 1975 Chuck Womer of Yale–New Haven Hospital called to see if I could be enticed to become a candidate for the replacement of their director, who had left after 27 years in the position. My restlessness had prepared me for a move, and the idea of leaving the Twin Cities appealed to me.

Although I loved being a director and felt that I was managing raising my two children alone quite well, I had discovered that a couple of martinis after work was a good way to make the transition from career woman to homemaker. Ignorant of the disease dynamics of alcoholism, I didn't understand its hereditary tendencies and moved through the early stages of addiction during those years. Wise friends confronted me during that time, and I sought help—more to appease them than out of any conviction that I had a serious problem.

The "help" was successful in that I was comfortable not drinking for several months prior to the first visit to Yale–New Haven. My interest in getting the job conquered my earlier skepticism. At the end of the first day of interviews, my future boss had a cocktail party for me, which was attended by the greats and near-greats. I had picked up on the fact that he liked his martinis, and since I didn't really understand the nature of the disease of alcoholism I felt that just one wouldn't hurt. By the time I moved the household (Claire was 13 then and Mark was 9), I was back to daily drinking—never while on duty and never in the morning. However, the before-dinner martini soon expanded to all-evening, and of course I needed a nightcap to sleep well. For a while the effects were not noticeable, but after two and a half years my behavior became a work performance problem.

One evening the president of the hospital and the chief of the medical staff invited the vice-president of patient services to dinner at a private club in New Haven. That is where I had my last martini. After dinner I was confronted by those two men and was told I had to enter inpatient treatment to save my job. (At least that is what I heard.) My response was primarily one of relief because I was really sick and full of fears. What would happen to my job? Who would care for my children?

After they assured me that my job would be waiting for me and arrangements were made for someone to stay in my home for the inpatient treatment period, I entered a facility in Connecticut. Four weeks later I was visited by those same two men and was told that my job was no longer available to me—that my behavior had made it necessary for "bridges to be burned." The devastation of my life at that time seemed complete. I didn't know what to do nor even how to decide what to do.

After eliminating every other option through a painful thought process, I concluded that independent consultation was the most logical way for me to earn a living. My work in primary nursing up to that time involved some informal consultations, some sponsored seminars, and the writing of three articles. Immediately after I completed treatment and before beginning any consultation activities, I started writing the book, *The Practice of Primary Nursing*. At that time I also figured out how to package my knowledge about primary nursing so it could be made available through consultations.

I decided to be open about my problem with alcoholism, and when I was discharged from the treatment facility, I called three national leaders in nursing and told them the truth about why I left Yale. I felt that rumors could in some ways be worse than the truth. I also realized that recovery is a long-term process, and I became involved with a self-help group. That involvement continues to be an important part of my life.

I stayed in New Haven for three more years, building an independent consultation service, going to meetings, and taking care of my family. Professional contacts in New Haven during that period were limited to a few friends from the hospital with whom I maintained contact.

In 1982 I returned to Minneapolis. During a visit with my daughter, who had entered the University of Minnesota in 1980, I toured the city with a friend, became reacquainted with some professional associates, and decided the time was right to leave New Haven.

The return was logistically and financially challenging. Yale had paid my way to Connecticut, but I was responsible for financing the move back. Finding and buying a home, selling the one in New Haven (during a period of high interest rates), and the simple logistics of managing everything were squeezed into a period of five months of continuous weekly travel necessary to earn enough to finance the move. Thanks to the life-style changes I had made through practicing the principles taught in the self-help group, the challenge of those events was not a terribly stressful experience.

The idea of developing a training program for first-line managers of primary nurses was hatched in February 1982 at the home of a friend, who was also my real estate agent. I got up early one morning and drafted the curriculum on a yellow pad.

In planning the move, I persuaded a hospital consultant friend who also needed to make a change to move to the midwest with me, and he became a staff support person for my consultation service, Creative Nursing Management. This freed me of some of the support activities that otherwise took up my off-the-road time thus freeing me to develop the program. Three months after we moved, the first course was offered and a manual had been written. I believe this course was the first management training program for head nurses with a curriculum designed by and content taught by experienced nurse administrators.

Creative Nursing Management continues to grow and expand one step at a time. The staff now consists of five people who work the equivalent of full time and about 25 to 30 faculty and consultants who have been trained to function in the programs and services designed and marketed by CNM. These professionals are employed on a per diem basis. The company mission is to get nursing services to sick people now. We are doing this within a belief system that says we can be financially successful without compromising the highest professional values we can identify. It is wonderful to be able to report this.

My story is about choices. The life I lived in no way matches the self-image I had as a little girl. I believed then that the whole world was like Paulina Street and that someday I would be like the women I knew—wearing housedresses, putting newspapers on the floor after scrubbing it, and worrying about whether to have my husband paint the house or to replace the worn carpeting. As I look back I realize how little that picture matches my reality. I have done things for which there had been no role modeling nor even any anticipatory thinking. Life has been full of surprises for me, and I wouldn't give back a single moment. All of it—the pain and the joy—has been part of my journey, and I am grateful for it all.

Ida M. Martinson

Ida M. Martinson, PhD, RN, FAAN,
is Professor and Chair of the
Department of Family Health Care Nursing
in the School of Nursing
at the University of California,
San Francisco

For Ida Martinson, during the depression it was a challenge to scrape together enough money for tuition for nursing school. With the help of scholarships and the loving encouragement of her husband, she went on to earn a doctorate. Much of her early nursing experience was in Hong Kong, where her interest in Oriental culture and in the care of children began. Her recounting here of her experience with a project on home care for the dying child is poignant and cogent. That project became well known and a national model, funded for four years by the National Cancer Institute, with its basic approach replicated in many places.

Now Ida Martinson is president of Children's Hospice International. Her hope is that funds will make it possible for all terminally ill children and their families to have the option of home care.

*M*y family was poor, having lost the homestead farm during the depression. My father said the $50 he had to pay the physician for my delivery in 1936 was very tough to come by. The farm was lost soon after my birth. Because of numerous family difficulties, I was placed in a foster home in a strange town, but the foster home setting and the townspeople gave me support that enabled me to have confidence in the future.

An English teacher encouraged me to consider nursing as a career. At the time I was taking all the courses needed to become a secretary after high school graduation. The American Legion gave me a scholarship to the St. Luke's Hospital School of Nursing in Duluth, Minnesota, and advanced education became possible. During my three years there, my father sent me $10 a month for expenses. I certainly enjoyed nursing; we took all our prerequisites at the Duluth campus of the University of Minnesota and were given a rich background in the sciences.

Following graduation I taught tuberculosis nursing for one year at a sanatorium and then enrolled at the University of Minnesota to obtain a bachelor's degree in nursing education. I received a scholarship under Student Project for Amity among Nations (SPAN) and studied tuberculosis in Japan for six weeks. That trip had both a personal and a professional long-term effect on me. The Orient fascinated me, and my interest in things Oriental has continued over these many years. Furthermore, Hong Kong is where I met the parents of my future husband.

If I had to name one person who has influenced and supported me most, my husband Paul would be that individual. We recently celebrated our twenty-fifth wedding anniversary, so I have now spent more years married to him than being single. His influence and support can be measured in many ways more than in time.

Following our wedding, we drove straight to Yale, where I attended the Yale Intensive Chinese Program along with the handpicked language whiz kids of the Air Force. Perhaps what I learned more than anything in that program was how to study intensively, something that proved useful when I entered a PhD program in physiology in 1969. Paul was supportive of my doctoral studies. He thought it was important for me to have a professional role in Hong Kong.

Possibly my first interest in home care developed in that period of my life. We began making home visits to people in the huts in Hong Kong. I learned that an individual could make a difference. For example, I found a child of five who had been chained since she was two and a half years old. We succeeded in getting her off that chain and into school by collaborating with social workers. Another child who had been taken to a hospital for abdominal pain and had been turned away was admitted to the hospital when I went with the family. The child needed an appendectomy. Those events were good for me to experience early in my career. I returned to the United States greatly impressed with the resources of this country and with the belief that we could do more with our resources.

The history behind the development of the home care for dying children project includes a personal experience, a chance incident with a neighbor, and the experiences of the first and third families to participate in the program.

The personal family experience was with my father-in-law, who was found to have inoperable cancer of the pancreas. My in-laws had returned to the United States from Hong Kong and were up at their summer cabin in northern Minnesota when my father-in-law was admitted to the local hospital for treatment of bleeding. My mother-in-law called for Paul and me to come directly to the hospital, and we set out for Minnesota from Chicago, where both of us were doctoral students.

After the eight-hour trip, when we entered my father-in-law's hospital room, he looked at me and said, "Ida, I want to go home." I said OK, but inwardly I was wondering if we could possibly provide the necessary care for him. I believed it was important to honor his request, and after all, there were three registered nurses in the family—his sister and the two of us who were daughters-in-law. We provided the care for him, and he died in the cabin with all the family members around him.

About 14 months later we had moved to Minnesota, and I took a position as the director of nursing research at the University of Minnesota. I was planning my own research program as well as facilitating the school's renewed emphasis on research. One night I noticed that my next-door neighbor, John Kersey, a pediatric oncologist, looked sad. I asked him what was the matter and he said, "I have to admit a child to the hospital tomorrow because he is dying."

Because of the way he said that, the idea of home care for the dying child flashed through my mind as I recalled the experience with my father-in-law. My neighbor agreed with me that the hospital was no place for the boy, Eric, to die. While I had intended to develop a longitudinal clinical trial research study in the area, John called me the following night and said Eric's mother wanted to see me to talk with me about home care. From a research point of view, I had to design a case study approach. Therefore I requested the mother to keep a record of what I did and indicate what was helpful and what was not.

Eric's mother kept a diary and later wrote for publication. Here is an excerpt from her log:

> During one of the initial visits, Dr. Martinson brought up the possibility of our "making it all the way," something we had not even considered. At first we were rather repelled by the notion. We had heard that the manner of death in leukemics was never predictable and that sometimes their deaths were violent. How could we be prepared? Would we be continually plagued with the thought of a nightmarish happening? What if Betsy, Eric's six-year-old sister, whom we didn't feel could be forewarned, were around to witness such an event? Those close to us who knew what we were considering felt it would be too difficult for us physically and emotionally. Del wondered how much more I could take; Eric and I had been especially close and Del felt I wouldn't be able to bear his death, much less be an active participant helping Eric through it. The doctors had said, "When you can no longer manage caring for Eric at home, bring him to the hospital." From this we assumed there would be a time when we would

no longer be able to handle the situation. We considered it seriously, but tried not to think about what tomorrow would bring . . . .

When I entered Eric's room, I had the distinct feeling that he would die very soon as his breathing was labored. Dr. Martinson had said she thought his breathing might get very erratic near the end.

I sat by Eric's bed and he held my hand. I asked if he needed anything and he replied, "No." How I longed to be able to talk with him, to find out how he really felt, to tell him more of my own feelings. But conversation was very limited; except for simple words he wasn't able to communicate.

An hour later, I thought he was finally resting more peacefully as the difficult breathing was no longer evident. I lay on the floor to get some rest. Lying there, I automatically listened for his breathing but heard nothing. I got up to check. There was no more breathing or heartbeat. Eric had died while holding my hand, at peace at last.

For the last time I held my son, told him how very much I have loved him, and that "Jesus will take care of you now." I spent several minutes alone with him before wakening Del. We returned to Eric's room. I gently wiped the side of Eric's mouth, which led Del to comment, "Thank God he no longer hurts when he's touched."

I had never seen anyone die nor had I ever experienced the loss of someone I had dearly loved. It was extremely important to me to have been with Eric during the actual transition from life to death, to really know firsthand that it went smoothly for him. The dreaded fear, death, wasn't ugly as I had thought it would be—Eric was at peace.

We, too, had a feeling of peace. Eric's problems were over and we did not have to bear the guilt of not having done all we could for our son. To bear his loss was in itself a great enough burden.

If that first family had recommended that I discontinue the project, I would have stopped right then. However, they were highly supportive and urged me to continue to make the home care option available for others.

The second family was cared for by a nurse who lived 250 miles away from me. That time I served as a backup consultant. The approach worked well, and the family, which included eight children, was equally appreciative of the opportunity.

The following is an excerpt from the journal of the father of Meri, whose family was the third to participate in the home care program:

After sending our friend to bed, Jodi and I sat with Meri and opened the last of her birthday gifts, which had been ignored during the hectic days of the past week. Ida had told us that hearing was thought to be the last body sense to fail so even though Meri did not respond to us and stared inquiringly at nothing, we spoke to her and described the gifts she had gotten and read the birthday cards. Periodically we checked her vital signs, particularly her respiration. Though her breathing was shallow, it remained steady. The momentary air hunger that she suffered earlier had apparently passed; she was unalarmed, relaxed, and motionless.

Then her breathing changed again, so slightly as to be undetectable any other time. We listened carefully and noticed that while her respiration rate was steady, she seemed to be taking in less air with each breath. Jodi went immediately to the phone and called Ida, who said she would be over right away. Now Meri was dropping fast. Her eyes were fixed and calm and still faintly quizzical, but she was not gasping for air. By the time Jodi entered the room and came to her side, Meri was dead.

Together we held her for the last time and cried over her. Soon Ida arrived and sat with us while we talked about Meri, about what had suddenly seemed like a distant life, and shared the grief we had for her. When the mortician came, he thoughtfully waited for us to say goodbye a last time to Meri and accepted my offer to help him remove the body. This was important to me—it seemed to make our participation in her dying and death a finished one. Then, after informing our relatives and friends of her death, we walked to Emil and Marie's to bring Richard home and tell him, too.

After this third experience I was a little more confident regarding the capacities and capabilities of parents and nurses. I began to talk about the project and submitted various proposals for research to further investigate the feasibility and desirability of home care for the dying child.

During the development of home care, Isabell Harris, who was then the dean at the University of Minnesota School of Nursing, would listen to me and at times would shed the tears that I could not. Her support was invaluable. Dr. Barbara Redman, who was the associate dean, was the first to make me see that the program could be a national model— that there was a need. When I had doubts and worries about lawsuits, my husband was the person who kept me focused. He put up with my absentmindedness during those 17 days when I assisted Eric's family in caring for him at home and at times when I would become involved with other families, including Meri's.

The home care project has become well known. It was funded by the National Cancer Institute for four years, and has been replicated in several places. Mary Laur, of the Pediatric Cancer Center in Milwaukee, went right ahead and provided care for numerous families, and the program is ongoing today. Belinda Martin is at present nurse-coordinator of the program at Los Angeles Children's Hospital, where home care for the terminally ill child has been successful for a good many years. Here at UCSF the program is offered as an option for all the children. Throughout the nation more concern is being shown and commitment being made to allow children the option of home care. Recently Children's Hospice International was established, and this national and international clearinghouse is making a difference on the federal scene. I am currently serving as president of this organization, and fund-raising is under way. It is our hope that funds will be available in the future to enable all children and their families to have the option of home care.

Ingeborg Grosser Mauksch

Ingeborg Grosser Mauksch, PhD, RN, FAAN, is
Associate Executive Director of Redi-Care, Inc.,
Fort Meyers, Florida

❖

Ingeborg Grosser Mauksch knew she had to learn to speak English quickly and have an answer when the boat bringing her from Germany docked and the U.S. immigration officer asked, "How will you earn your daily bread?" "I will be a nurse," she thought. To her brother's surprise, as well as her own, she had the answer, learned English, stuck to her decision, and is glad she did. An avid reader and good student, she was always goal oriented and moved deliberately and satisfactorily up the educational and experiential ladders. She honed her writing and speaking skills, became involved in nursing organizations, and fought consistently to support social justice, civil rights, and women's issues.

Whatever her position, Inge has been able to bring about change and pioneer new roles for nurses. Whether she was functioning from a national, international, or local vantage point, she was outspoken in her beliefs and her love for the profession. Her story here reflects the wide range of people who have been significant in her life and her bold challenge to those who would put down nursing and its practice.

I came to this country just before the beginning of World War II as a refugee from Nazism. Jews were severely persecuted by Hitler in my native Austria, and thus it was fortunate that my brother and I could leave our homeland and come to the United States, where my aunt and uncle made a wonderful home for us.

My first task in the country, of course, was to learn to speak English. To this purpose I attended Radcliffe College for a year. At the end of that time I had a basic understanding of the language. I was able to comprehend what was being said on the radio, and I had overcome the tremendous anxiety that I initially experienced when having to talk on the telephone.

The trip from Europe to America, which my brother and I made on a small Belgian freighter, was an extremely important time in my life. The topic of conversation at the dining table with the captain every night centered on our arrival in New York Harbor. He told us that we would be privileged to see the Statue of Liberty, how we would start life in a country where freedom prevails and where the dignity of the human being is of prime significance, and finally, that we would be expected to make our own way. For my brother and myself, the youngest passengers on the boat and the only teenagers, that presented a definite problem. We needed to be ready to state an occupation that would be acceptable to the immigration officer. My brother decided to be a printer, and the captain agreed with his choice of vocation. Turning to me, the captain said, "What about you? What will you be?" "I really don't know," I said. "All I ever wanted to be was a mother." "That won't do," replied the captain. "Don't forget, the immigration officer will ask you how you plan to earn your daily bread."

That conversation gave me much to think about. I never told the captain what I planned to do with my life. In fact, I was surprised when on that cold December morning, as we slid into Brooklyn Harbor and the immigration officers had boarded the ship, I answered the question, "And how will you earn your daily bread?" with "I think I will be a nurse." My brother looked at me in great surprise. I smiled. I had made my decision, I said it, and I knew then that I would stick to it.

Two weeks later, my uncle took me to the Massachusetts General Hospital to be interviewed by Miss Sally Johnson, the superintendent of nursing. Miss Johnson pronounced me unacceptable because my English was too limited! Thus my trip to the admissions office at Radcliffe College. By the end of my first year at Radcliffe, the war had started. The dean encouraged me to stay, but I knew that it was time for me to become a nurse.

There is much to tell about the three years I spent as a nursing student at the Massachusetts General Hospital School of Nursing in Boston. In the interest of brevity let me just say that they were probably the most productive and generative, as well as the happiest, years of my life. The satisfaction I derived from school blunted the pain I felt because of the war—the events in Europe that I knew meant certain death for a large number of my extended family and left me uncertain about my parents' welfare.

Learning to become a nurse gave me a new life. I had awesome role models: Sally Johnson, who taught us ethics and professional adjustment; Ruth Sleeper, who was our history teacher and a role model in the sense that she was already nationally involved in nursing matters and would tell us about national meetings and the issues discussed; and my main instructor, Sylvia Perkins, who had an inexhaustible ability to bring joy to learning.

In my senior year I was honored to be appointed assistant instructor, a role that readied me to move into teaching immediately after graduation. While most of my class-mates went into the military, I remained at the Massachusetts General Hospital. I was classified 4E (frozen on the job) for the duration of the war.

Teaching nursing gave me extensive opportunities to explore the roots of nursing care as they were then understood. I appreciated the needs of our patients because of my study of psychology and sociology. I found that the most interesting component of nursing practice and pursued it within the resources of our extensive library. There was much talk about continuing one's formal education among the school's teachers. Ruth Sleeper frequently encouraged me to get a baccalaureate degree. I applied to Teachers College, Columbia University, and spent three summers of my career studying toward my bac-calaureate degree.

At the end of the war I left Massachusetts General and went to TC full time. Earning the baccalaureate degree gave me a great sense of accomplishment. At the same time I acquired humility as I learned at TC that nursing was an infinitely more complex and sophisticated occupation than I had ever realized. As I met nurses from all over the country and from overseas, I learned much about the different ways in which nursing was viewed, what nursing had to offer, and what its demands were in clinical areas that I had yet to explore. TC also put me in contact with some of nursing's greats: Virginia Henderson, Frances Reiter, Isabel Stewart, and Dr. R. Louise McManus. All of these women—experts in their fields, authors, and women of national prominence—touched my life deeply. They gave me a vision of a future in nursing that I could not have acquired otherwise. Gradually it occurred to me that nursing was a field in which I could rise to the top— that in nursing it was possible for me to make a contribution of significance. Nursing would give me the opportunity to apply myself completely.

After receiving my baccalaureate, I married and moved to Chicago. In my first job I became clinical instructor at the Michael Reese Hospital School of Nursing. That was a significant first for me, but even more significant was the 1948 convention of the American Nurses' Association in Chicago, the first national convention that I was able to attend. The experience was overwhelming—listening to the debates at the House of Delegates, trying to understand the issues, and observing the differences of opinion expressed by nursing leaders. Some of the issues debated at that convention were the 40-hour work week, licensure of practical nurses, health insurance and retirement plans for nurses. Collective bargaining was one of the most controversial issues on the floor. I understood very little but found myself spending hours thereafter in the library at Michael Reese Hospital reading and learning. Subsequently we discussed collective bargaining at the First District meetings of the Illinois Nurses Association.

As I learned more about nursing, I became convinced that I needed a master's degree. A master's program in nursing was available at the University of Chicago so I enrolled there.

While taking graduate classes, I accepted a position as a nursing instructor at St. Luke's Hospital, where I was deeply disturbed that the major share of nursing care was not delivered by professional nurses but principally by nurse's aides. My hospital school students were surprised by that, and I could not explain why the professionals were not more involved in providing care because I did not understand myself. Thus in the early 1950s I started to read about professionalism. The faculty at the University of Chicago were magnificent teachers in the field—Nellie Hawkinson, Frances Thieldbar, and Rose-mary Ellis. They understood the importance of scholarship in nursing and worked diligently to instill in us a sense of inquiry and professionalism. Most important, they taught us how to seek out information that would further nursing as an academic discipline.

At that point, I found myself existing in two separate worlds. At St. Luke's Hospital and later at Presbyterian–St. Luke's Hospital the world of nursing was principally technical, highly independent, unaccountable, and nondifferentiating. It seems to me that we taught our students in the late 1950s that nursing was a series of procedures, most of which were ordered by the physician or prescribed by the routine of the floor, the policy book of the hospital, and the procedure book of the nursing department. However, at the university I was being exposed to thinking on a truly professional level. We were taught that nurses would become autonomous and that they could expect one day to initiate interventions based on their understanding of patients' needs. It was a difficult time because the teacher's perspective I was gaining was convincing, yet the reality of what went on in the hospital contradicted it.

Rosemary Ellis had a wise way of explaining the transition from what goes on in the real world to what needs to underlie the decision-making process in the academic world. It was difficult for me to understand, but by the time I had completed my master's degree, I had learned how to move from the abstract to the concrete and from the complex to the simple. It was then that I became a much better teacher because I finally understood that the practice of nursing was more than a sum of technical skills and that nursing care could not be delivered by on-the-job trained personnel. It required the competencies of a professional.

I published my first article in the *American Journal of Nursing* in 1951. It dealt with the nursing care study, a much-advocated tool among nurse educators that helped learners to see the patient as a whole and to explore all possible avenues in assisting patients to achieve their highest level of wellness.

Through my first publishing venture I also learned the importance of respecting the quality of my thoughts. When my manuscript was accepted by the *American Journal of Nursing,* I was elated beyond description, only to be extremely deflated a few weeks later when I received the edited copy—a sea of red. Virtually every sentence had been changed. I remember talking to my husband (we were later divorced) about the incredibly humiliating experience of seeing my beautiful manuscript thus desecrated. He encouraged me to express this to the editor, and after much reflection and soul-searching I did just that. I wrote a letter to Ruth McGrorey, my editor, and explained to her that I wanted my manuscript to be published as I had submitted it. I listed a few changes that I found acceptable; all others were to be deleted.

After having sent off that letter, I was quite convinced that I would not see the article in print. I was surprised when I received a letter indicating that the article would be published as I had specified. Years later I had a wonderful experience. I met Miss McGrorey, who was then retired, at an ANA convention. I would never have known her, but she came up to me and said, "Aren't you Ingeborg Mauksch?" When I acknowledged this, she said, "I hope you know that you taught me one of the most important lessons a young editor needs to learn." That is when the light went on and I remembered my letter. "You see," she continued, "I had done you a great disservice. I had indeed destroyed your prose. I respected you immensely for rejecting my work and insisting that the article be printed as you had originally submitted it." That was one of the most enjoyable moments of the convention, and I have always held Miss McGrorey in high esteem because of her honest remarks.

The end of the 1950s saw me become the assistant director of a large diploma school of nursing, the Presbyterian–St. Luke's School in Chicago. It was a challenging task, and yet it occurred to me that I should move from the diploma school to an academic setting. It was during that period that I encountered yet another magnificent role model, Mary Kelly Mullane.

Dr. Mullane was the chair of the Council of Baccalaureate and Higher Degrees of the National League for Nursing. At an NLN convention, I heard her talking about the need to move nursing education into academe. Although her speech was exciting and, at the same time, scary, she was persuasive and thought provoking. I questioned whether I could measure up to the rigors of academe and whether I was ready to commit myself to doing research. Could one truly become an academician without having a doctorate? How difficult would it be to teach academically advanced students?

Those thoughts and many more were almost constant companions as I went about the business of running the school on a day-to-day basis. As I perused the research literature, which had certainly begun to attract my attention, I learned about innovation and issues of professional practice. It was difficult then to find a circle of people who were committed to nursing in academe, but one existed in Chicago, and I found it.

Within the ANA the concern was with standards of nursing practice, with economic welfare, and with those legislative issues that were at least tangential, if not focal, to nursing. It was the NLN and its state leagues that dealt with education issues then. I became active in the Illinois League for Nursing. In fact I was its president in subsequent years. Yet my attraction to the Illinois Nurses Association was always strong. Looking back, it is obvious to me why that was so. It was the persona of Anne Zimmerman, who was then the executive director of the INA, that attracted me. Her perspective of nursing engaged my imagination, and she gradually convinced me that the core of nursing's growth was dependent on improving the welfare, self-respect, and sense of self-worth of the individual nurse.

In 1962 I took the big step. I left the diploma school without having decided how to make the transition to academe but being very sure that the time had come when I had to be true to my thinking. An unexpected opportunity that provided the right transition arose when the Chicago Council on Community Nursing invited me to direct its study of nursing activities in hospital outpatient departments—a funded study that had to be completed within a year.

In the course of my work I had frequent contact with D. Ann Sparmacher, the executive director of the council, who had a clear vision of the nature, purpose, and impact of the study. As director of an independent study, I had to be self-directing, self-reliant, creative, and properly communicative. I succeeded in enlisting a fairly large number of volunteers at each of four study sites and was able to collect all of the data I needed. It was a year of tremendous personal growth, and in the end I completed my task—the report was satisfactory and was well accepted by the nursing community.

Opportunities for presenting my findings gave me good public speaking practice. I had never known how much I would like public speaking. I critiqued my presentations and at the same time enjoyed working on improving my style and manner of delivery. To my surprise and joy I was soon lauded as a dynamic speaker, one who could get her audience motivated to participate in discussion and to pursue new ideas and perspectives. Soon I was much in demand and had numerous opportunities to talk about my research, and later, to give talks on topics of my choice.

After completing the outpatient study, I was invited by the dean of the School of Nursing of Loyola University, Gladys Kiniery, to join the nursing faculty as chair of the Department of General Nursing (set up for RN students pursuing a baccalaureate).

The experience of participating on a university faculty proved to be infinitely more fateful than I had anticipated. I remember attending the first all–university faculty meeting. It was an impressive ceremonial event. After the meeting I went home and told my family, "One thing is clear. If you want to be effective on the university faculty, you have to have a doctorate." At that time my children were in elementary school and the idea of their mother going back to school, which I am sure evoked their memories of me as a student in the master's program, appealed to them greatly. They thought it was wonderful that they would not be the only ones having to study, carry books, and prepare assignments.

The following two years I taught at Loyola University. It was a productive and significant period in terms of career building. While the idea of obtaining a doctorate was frightening, I was realistic about that goal. When I applied for the doctoral program at Northwestern University, I was rejected because of my age. The University of Chicago, however, informed me that I could register in its doctoral program, since I was a master's graduate of that institution. There were no requirements for me to meet. All I had to do was fill out the application in person, then visit with the academic dean of the Division of Social Sciences to discuss program decisions. At the same time I decided to try for a USPHS research fellowship. When that came through, it was as if the fates had divined my course of action.

I decided to pursue a PhD in educational administration, an area that promised to afford me the opportunity to pursue my research interests. It was obvious to me that no one on the faculty would be able to assist me in a clinical study, yet I knew that I had to deal with some component of nursing practice in my dissertation to satisfy my commitment to the core of my profession. I took a leave of absence from my job and started work at the University of Chicago. Shortly thereafter I attended the ANA convention in San Francisco and, while there, witnessed the first significant strike by nurses. Many of us at the convention marched in the picket line. The strike and the issues surrounding it were the most significant topics of conversation there. On the trip back to Chicago I decided to discuss the study of collective bargaining in nursing with my chairman. He was enthusiastic because a number of teachers' strikes had taken place prior to that time, and he was interested in comparing studies of those strikes with a study of a nurses' strike.

He had heard about the difficulties nurses encountered at Chicago's Cook County Hospital and said he would not be surprised if nurses at that institution organized some form of collective action. In the summer of 1967 the nurses at Cook County Hospital staged a number of demonstrations after forming a collective bargaining unit that was represented by the state nurses' association. My contact with the leaders of that group, specifically Margaret Stafford and Joyce Waterman Taylor, led to the formation of lasting friendships, and the topic for my dissertation research was determined.

During the 1960s everything fell into place for me. I was interested and supportive of the civil rights, student rights, and women's rights movements. It wasn't quite clear to me then what role I was to play, but I was conscious of the fact that all of those movements had a valuable bearing on the future of nursing. As a woman to whom nursing was an academic career as well as a significant practice, I knew that the changes advocated by the liberation movements were most applicable to my profession.

It was also during the 1960s that the issues of nonpractice in nursing emerged. One could hardly open a journal without finding articles on the plight of patients in hospitals who were neglected by physicians and "never saw a nurse." These were what I consider to be nursing's darkest days because professionals nursed desks, telephones, and charts and allowed nurses' aides to care for patients. The voices in the wilderness arose—Frances Reiter, Virginia Henderson, Dorothy Smith, to mention only a few. My interests were truly focused on their pronouncements. I avidly read all that was written by these advocates of nursing practice concerning what they believed nursing schools had to teach.

Near the end of the 1960s my family and I moved to Columbia, Missouri, and my then husband and I became faculty members in the School of Medicine at the University of Missouri. The School of Nursing there was not interested in doctoral faculty and was not committed to looking at the education of nurses from the perspective of inquiry and scholarship. The School of Medicine, on the other hand, had developed some novel ideas about the education of medical students. I thus had a chance to teach in a program called Human Ecology and Behavioral Science. I also worked in an interdisciplinary research department and taught in the public health programs of the medical school.

Teaching medical students showed me how much more autonomous they were than nursing students. As a result of that experience I became interested in finding means of intensifying nurses' sense of identity and self-worth. I knew that the route that would see these goals attained was through the practice of nursing. By coincidence I was invited to a conference sponsored by the Massachusetts General Hospital that dealt with the "expanded role of the nurse." There I met Loretta Ford. It was a case of instant "sympatico" and the beginning of a wonderful friendship. We discussed the role of the nurse practitioner and the new relationship this role would foster between the nurse and the physician.

So many things happened in the nursing profession between 1968 and 1972 that I can mention only a couple—the development of the role of the nurse practitioner and the idea of joint practice as enunciated in Jerome Lysaught's report *From Abstract to Action*. I became more active in the ANA, first as a member of the Commission on Nursing Research, as chair of the Congress on Nursing Practice, and later as chair of the Interdivisional Council on Certification.

During that time my marriage ended. The children were off to college, and I found myself eager to devote all my time to professional activities. In the medical school I was invited to participate in the founding of a primary care center and was also encouraged to demonstrate the role of the nurse practitioner. That was one of the most challenging periods of my professional career. I designed my own educational program, selected my teachers (mainly physicians), and became a family nurse practitioner. The relationship of equity between my physician colleagues and myself was demanding, stimulating, and exhilarating. We developed protocols, wrote grants for residency programs, and ultimately wrote a grant for a nurse practitioner training program that was funded by the Kellogg Foundation.

In the 1970s I had many public speaking engagements. One of my colleagues at ANA revealed to me one night, over a glass of wine, that I was considered by many to be nursing's "cheerleader" because I frequently spoke analytically about nursing. As a means of pursuing one of my interests I had joined the World Future Society in the late 1960s and had become an avid reader of materials and research on the future. No wonder, then, that in the late 1970s I started to incorporate future-oriented material into my speeches and to develop a course on the topic.

My opportunities were unlimited. I was offered a number of deanships, but a chance to become the Valere Potter Distinguished Professor of Nursing at Vanderbilt University School of Nursing was irresistible. It allowed me to participate in a highly respected academic setting on a level that virtually had no boundaries. Simultaneous to my acceptance of that position, the Robert Wood Johnson Foundation invited me to direct its first national nursing fellowship program—the Nurse Faculty Fellowship Program in Primary Care. Thus it became possible for me to combine those activities in nursing that I felt I did best with those that I enjoyed the most. I had a chance to teach, to administer a major national program with a sizable budget, and to deal with crucial issues of practice in primary care. The program's advisory committee, comprising 12 distinguished nurses and physicians, gave me the kind of peer relationships and intellectual exchanges that I loved. At the same time I was able to practice primary health care with a resident in the newly created Primary Care Center at Vanderbilt University. I truly had it all.

Also during that time, through my participation at the leadership level of the American Nurses' Association, I had many first-hand opportunities to study and understand the significant issues of the profession. I worked hard on developing logical arguments to sharpen nursing's focus on practice, and I spoke to as many audiences as I could about nursing's future as a significant practice profession.

Throughout that period I experienced the joy and privilege of being honored by nurses. I received a number of awards, but the most important ones to me were those that represented peer acclamation—the Centennial Education Award of the Alumni Association of the Massachusetts General Hospital of Nursing, a similar award from the TC nursing alumnae association, and the Special Membership Award bestowed on me in 1980 by the American Nurses' Association.

In 1977 President Jimmy Carter appointed me to HEW Secretary Califano's Advisory Committee on National Health Insurance. That was my first experience on a highly visible national committee whose doings and whereabouts were reported in the press and whose reports ultimately wound up in a safe repository on some backroom shelf in the White House without ever having been introduced to Congress, as had been the original intent. Thus my learning from that appointment was multifaceted. I learned what it was like to be in the public eye and how to respond to unexpected questions from reporters who seemed to appear out of nowhere at airports and hotels. I also learned to appreciate the fact that not everything that is governmentally initiated, supported, and acclaimed terminates in as logical a fashion as one might expect. The entire National Health Insurance initiative fizzled before our eyes in a matter of months. By the time our reports were ready, much had changed; Congress was not only unsupportive but quite averse to the notion of entertaining legislation that would have turned the nation toward a much needed health policy.

My second call from the White House came three years later when President Carter appointed me to the United States Holocaust Memorial Council. This council was legislatively established to memorialize the Holocaust annually, to establish a museum as a permanent memorial, and to develop educational materials about the Holocaust for students of all ages. My appointment to this council, on which I still serve, means a great deal to me. The Holocaust has now been recognized as an event of universal significance. For me, a victim who carries the pain of that travesty in my heart every day of my life, it has been gratifying to play a part in attempting to achieve the goals that President Carter had in mind when he established the council.

It is also appropriate here to raise the issue of being Jewish in a predominantly non-Jewish occupation. There are relatively few Jewish nurses in the United States—certainly in fewer numbers than to be representative of the United States' Jewish population, which comprises three percent of the overall population. However, I feel that I have always had the respect of my peers and colleagues regarding my observance of Jewish holidays and my perspective on world politics, which obviously reflects my Jewish point of view. I am always identified as a Jew and feel that I have been respected as such. Likewise, that feeling enhances the respect I have for my professional colleagues and my profession. Nurses have always proclaimed to be blind to ethnic differences but have not always been reputed to act that way. I am glad to say that my experiences as a minority in virtually every position that I have had on the local, state, and national levels in nursing have been positive.

Over the years I have had the pleasure of traveling to Israel on a number of occasions, each time teaching at the Hadassah-Hebrew University School of Nursing, consulting with faculties in some of the other schools in the country, and visiting many of the hospitals, lecturing to nursing staffs. Twice, I have participated in the International Congress on

Nursing Law and Ethics in Israel, and I have been named chair of the International Advisory Committee for the Third International Congress on Nursing Law and Ethics, to meet in Jerusalem in November 1988.

The end of the 1970s and the beginning of the 1980s found me moving into the status of elder statesperson and extending my career into home health. This field is very important for nursing and will become increasingly prominent in the future. It's my first business venture and has been both difficult and gratifying.

Mentoring also became a task of this final career stage. I not only enjoy it but spend more and more time doing it. Erickson's stage of "generativity" describes my current perspective extremely well. Now is a time in my life when I enjoy being the support behind the action, the person who serves on the board but does not chair, the person who promotes those who seek leadership roles. This is a time when it is most enjoyable to be contacted by former students, fellows, and colleagues who happen to visit in Florida. It is exciting to be able to reminisce with them and to hear of their goals, dreams, and successes. To say that nursing has been good to me is a great understatement. It has been a source of joy and growth, of maturation and valued achievement. It has been a wellspring of gratification and contentment, but it has also allowed me to realize my limitations and shortcomings. Most of my friends are my colleagues and peers in nursing. The majority of people who are significant in my life are professional peers. When I look to the future and think of the exciting opportunities that I envision for those in the profession who are younger than I am, I have a sense of joy and a certain feeling of ownership. This is a wonderful profession, it's mine, and I'd like to pass it on to those who will value and cherish it as I have.

Angela Barron McBride

Angela Barron McBride, PhD, RN, FAAN, is Professor and
Associate Dean for Research, Development and Resources at the
University of Indiana School of Nursing in Indianapolis

❖

> Angela McBride was the first person in her grammar school
> class to go to an academic high school. She knew she wanted to be a
> nurse, but she also wanted a university education. From the beginning,
> she was attracted to psychiatric nursing as a way to better understand
> human behavior—including her own.
>
> She is a feminist, and her marriage to a professor of philosophy
> has provided her "with a license to take my own ruminations seriously."
> She wrote The Growth and Development of Mothers, the first
> critically acclaimed book to look at motherhood in light of the Women's
> Movement. Finding herself with the discomfort of being "alone out front,"
> she decided that taking the lead was well worth the risk.
>
> Creatively and thoughtfully she ponders certain themes in her
> professional life that are echoed time and again. Those themes include,
> "The best way to improve the image of nursing is for all nurses to become
> image makers. . . . Leaders must develop a talent for optimism. . . . Cre-
> ativity means taking one's own key thoughts and strong feelings as the
> starting-off point for pursuing new ideas."

My police lieutenant father thought highly of nurses as a result of all his experience taking battered people to the emergency rooms of Baltimore hospitals. His uncle, the patriarch of Baltimore's Polish-Catholic community, introduced me to his nun friend, the director of nursing at Bon Secours Hospital, because he thought we should get to know each other in case I had a calling to religious life. By the age of 13 I was putting in long hours as a nurse's aide working on one of her medical-surgical services. I eventually worked for a couple of years in the newborn nursery and on the postpartum floor, then went back to a medical-surgical service for another summer of experience. I started working as a nurse's aide not convinced that I wanted to become a professional nurse, but I finished those years believing that I had a talent for making people feel comfortable: I could make an anxious new mother feel better about breast-feeding; I could give backrubs that some patients preferred to sleeping pills; I could talk to some unconscious patients and see their breathing shift in time to the rhythm of my sentences.

East Baltimore, where I grew up, was very traditional. In high school you were either on the commercial track preparing to become a secretary or on the academic track aiming to become a grammar school teacher, a nurse, or a nun—in which case you became either a grammar school teacher or a nurse. Everyone assumed that the ultimate goal of girls who did not enter the convent was to get married and raise children. There were less conventional themes, but you had to listen hard to hear them. The grandmother with whom we lived had been gutsy enough to arrange her own passage from Poland to the United States when she was 13. My father was maverick enough to believe that his daughters should go to college, even if all they did eventually was to get married. My mother talked wistfully of having wanted to become a professional, but the depression had killed that dream.

I went into my teenage years not unlike I am today, feeling very committed to certain traditions—religiously based values of contemplation and generosity—but a risk taker, too. I was the only one from my grammar school class to go to an academically oriented high school (Institute of Notre Dame) and the only one from my high school to attend Georgetown University School of Nursing. By 1958 I was sure that I wanted to become a nurse, but I also wanted the benefits of university education. I felt drawn to psychiatric nursing because I saw it as the specialty that would most help me understand human behavior, including my own. My semester-long psychiatric rotation at Walter Reed Army Hospital, a summer fellowship between my junior and senior years at St. Elizabeths Hospital (a federal psychiatric facility), and some staff experience at Phipps Clinic at Johns Hopkins Hospital set me in that direction.

Although I knew generally what I wanted, it was during my years at Yale (1962 to

1973) that my unfocused inclinations and talents came into sharp relief. Yale took the attitude that only the bright were admitted and that once in place they should be encouraged to think the unthinkable and do the impossible. First as a graduate student and later as a faculty member, I had the opportunity to work with women and men who were on the cutting edge of clinical scholarship. They took nursing and themselves very seriously. Those were wonderful years for being able to have extended conversations with individuals who either were already leaders in the field (Virginia Henderson, Ernestine Wiedenbach, Jean Barrett, Lucy Conant, Florence Wald) or were about to become widely known for their contributions to the profession (Rhetaugh Dumas, Jean Johnson, Donna Diers, Ruth Elder, Robert Leonard, Bill Dickoff, Pat James).

Yale's Department of Psychiatry and Department of Psychiatric–Mental Health Nursing were steeped in the psychoanalytic tradition, so reading Simone de Beauvoir's *The Second Sex* (1952) and Betty Friedan's *The Feminine Mystique* (1963) in the first years I was there constituted major events. Those books, and others that I read in quick succession, challenged some Freudian assumptions and seemed to give me permission to question ideas that had until then seemed beyond question. It is difficult to understand in the late 1980s how much those books in the early 1960s pointed to a different way of conceptualizing women's experience, but they had a profound effect on me. They gave me permission to take my own experience seriously and not to assume that male writers were invariably correct in their formulations.

I was a feminist even before I realized that I was one. I had long resented the special privileges automatically conferred on sons when I was growing up, for example, that they were entitled to go to college while it was believed to be something of a waste of money to educate daughters. I had already bristled, even though I also preened, at the compliment, "You think like a man." I had been the first woman officer of Georgetown University's dramatic society, Mask and Bauble. What reading Simone de Beauvoir and Betty Friedan did was to provide me with a framework for organizing my thoughts. My personal musings were part of some larger whole that questioned stereotypes and existing paradigms. Why, for example, should man be head of the family and woman be the heart, when every family needs at least two heads and two hearts?

In 1965 one other thing happened that moved me in a feminist direction. I married William Leon McBride, a philosopher. Bill's mother had been admitted to Phi Beta Kappa at Hunter College in New York during World War I, when few women went to college. She then gave up a 20-year career as a high school teacher to devote herself to motherhood when he was born. Unbeknownst to me, Bill came into our marriage convinced that he never wanted a wife who would ever say to him, "After all I gave up for you . . . ." He regularly asked me, "What do you want to do next?" even when I thought it was an unseemly question to ask a new mother. The surprising thing is that I always had (and continue to have) an answer to that question. There was something about the fact that I always had answers that made me realize the extent of my own ambition and that I could hope to be anything I wanted to be. Being married to a professor of philosophy also provided me with a license to take my own ruminations seriously.

By 1970, when our second daughter was born, I realized that there was an entire area of existing thought with which I did not agree, that is, what had been written on motherhood from the psychoanalytic perspective. None of the literature seemed to speak to my own experience. I thought that traditional role descriptions stifled women (and men), but the Women's Movement had completely ignored the situation of woman as mother. It seemed to me that the editors of *Ms.* magazine, as it was then, would be much more likely to run an article on lesbian nurturing than they would be to discuss the frustrations of women with preschool children. I started to write down my thoughts with a view to handing my daughters a copy of the manuscript on their twenty-first birthdays. It would explain why I had been the way I had been! Those thoughts eventually became *The Growth and Development of Mothers* (1973a), the first critically acclaimed book to look at motherhood in light of the Women's Movement.

Publishing that book was a watershed experience. Getting a glowing review in the *New York Times* was one of life's peak moments. Old fears that I was only "smart for a nurse" gave way to a conviction that I was wholly smart . . . that nurses are smart. In writing the book, I had been seized by crazy thoughts—if this is so original and perceptive, then why hasn't anyone written it before? Intellectually, I understood that something cannot be both original and widely accepted, but practically, I wanted to take the lead yet not endure the doubts you have when you are alone out front. To this day I remain uncomfortable alone out front, but success does make the risk seem well worth taking.

Since 1973 I have continued to take my own experience as the starting point for explorations of important issues in women's lives. This is in keeping with what has been written about feminist methods. The personal may suggest something about important patterns. You do not reify your own ideas, but you explore them systematically for what they suggest about the larger questions that concern others as well. Since so much of women's experience has been either ignored or misinterpreted by male professionals, it is important for women scientists to explore commonplace thoughts and feelings for over-arching themes. The techniques for doing this build on those used generally by nurses in doing process recordings. One analyzes behavior in terms of underlying thoughts and feelings.

I have explored what it means for women to find traditional values, as well as feminist ones, appealing (1976a, 1984a), the theoretical underpinnings for women's health (McBride & McBride, 1981), obesity (1982), and the experience of parents when their children are teenagers (1987). I obtained a doctorate at Purdue University in 1978 in order to develop my analytic skills further. Much of my work since then has made use of attribution theory (1983, 1985a), which assumes that there are patterns to how people explain themselves and that these patterns have affective and behavioral consequences. That model is compatible with nursing's assumption that one builds care on people's perceptions of their own situation (1980b) and with the feminist notion that consciousness raising involves one in deliberately choosing to reframe situations so they do not reinforce helplessness.

Over time I have developed a strong sense that nursing process and feminist methods have much in common (1984b). Both are concerned with reflecting on everyday experiences and relationships. It is in analyzing the activities of daily living that knotted expectations are unraveled. Care should not be geared to helping women simply adjust to their lot in life but to their seeing that they have options. The emphasis is on self-help; women want to learn how to take care of themselves (1985c). They demand self-determination in matters of health care, not only when it comes to understanding their bodies better but in the larger sense of always being informed about what is happening to them, so they can be prepared to make informed choices. The professional mandate of nursing has long been expressed in terms of helping the patient gain independence as rapidly as possible.

Since I joined the faculty of Indiana University School of Nursing in 1978, there have been several involvements that have further shaped my professional life. As a National Kellogg Fellow between 1981 and 1984, I had the opportunity to take part in a series of interdisciplinary seminars that gave me a sense of just how generic some issues are. For example, those in the practice professions (nursing, medicine, clinical psychology, drama, law, and others) have more in common than they may realize unless they talk with each other over time. The aim of the fellowship program was to get individuals who were already accomplished in their own fields to think more broadly about current issues, in the belief that leaders have to be visionary and think interdisciplinarily to be effective. As uncomfortable as many of us felt when described as leaders, the experience had the effect of making me think more about social policy, career development, and strategic planning.

I thought more and more about the progress one makes over a career from learning what to do, to developing one's competence, then to using one's skills to further the development of one's setting, field, and the public good. These interests led to a four-year involvement on the Social Policy Committee of the Society for Research in Child Development (1983 to 1987) and to six years on the Governing Council of nursing's honor society, Sigma Theta Tau (1983 to 1989), where I helped make the association one that prepares nurses for life after graduation. The many presentations I have given in recent years on orchestrating a career (1985b) and helping nurses become image makers are very much connected with the feminist themes of my other writings. They emphasize understanding one's experience and taking control of one's life—at least to the extent that one sees that there are always options.

In the 25 years since I graduated from college certain themes have been echoed in my professional life time and again. Those themes include the following: in decoding personal experiences, one begins to discern patterns of behavior. . . . Creativity means taking one's own key thoughts and strong feelings as the starting point for pursuing new ideas. . . . Nurses are the professionals ideally suited to meet the growing consumer demand for self-determination in health care. . . . The best way to improve the image of nursing is for all nurses to become image makers. . . . In terms of a career, one must progress from proving one's own abilities to taking responsibility for facilitating the development of colleagues. . . . Leaders must develop a talent for optimism (that is, good-news sharing, transforming problems into challenges). . . . Nurses must share their knowledge with the general public (1973b, 1976b, 1978, 1980a).

Nursing is a profession about which I can be very enthusiastic. It is featured on most lists of growth opportunities in the decades ahead. Many of the difficulties practitioners have stem from the tension they experience between meeting the needs of others and at the same time meeting their own needs. Indeed, this is the central dilemma that caring women and men have in the last years of the twentieth century.

Since nursing requires one to be both instrumental and expressive, to combine the principles of communion and agency (heart and head), it is a profession that can play *the* leadership role in enabling individuals and society to deal with these issues. As Reverby has said: "If nursing can achieve the power to practice altruism with autonomy, all of us have much to gain. Nursing has always been a much conflicted metaphor in our culture, reflecting all the ambivalences we give to the meaning of womanhood. Perhaps in the future it can give this metaphor and, ultimately, caring, new value in all our lives" (1987, p. 10).

REFERENCES

DeBeauvoir, S. (1952). *The second sex.* New York: Bantam Books.

Friedan, B. (1963). *The feminine mystique.* New York: Dell Publishing.

McBride, A.B. (1973a). *The growth and development of mothers.* New York: Harper & Row.

McBride, A.B. (1973b, October). Why do you really want a baby? *Glamour,* pp. 180-181; 253; 256-258; 262-265.

McBride, A.B. (1976a). *Living with contradictions: a married feminist.* New York: Harper & Row.

McBride, A.B. (1976b, July). You are why you cook. *Ms.* magazine, pp. 26-28.

McBride, A.B. (1978, December). Nursing: let's turn around the image. *New Woman,* pp. 95; 100.

McBride, A.B. (1980a, September). Coming to terms with your body. *Women's Day Diet and Exercise Guide,* pp. 14; 109.

McBride, A.B. (1980b). How attribution theory can shape therapeutic goal-setting. In *New directions for nursing in the 80's* (pp. 73-82). Kansas City, Mo.: American Nurses' Association.

McBride, A.B. (1982). Obesity of women during the childbearing years: psychosocial and physiologic aspects. *Nursing Clinics of North America,* **17**(2), 29-38.

McBride, A.B. (1983). Differences in parents' and their grown children's perceptions of parenting. *Developmental Psychology,* **19,** 686-693.

McBride, A.B. (1984a). Living with contradictions: a married feminist. In R.F. Hettlinger & G. Worth (Eds.), *Self-discovery through the humanities: exploring values* (pp. 167-170). Washington, D.C.: the National Council on Aging, Inc.

McBride, A.B. (1984b). Nursing and the women's movement. Editorial in *Image: The Journal of Nursing Scholarship,* **16,** 66.

McBride, A.B. (1985a). Differences in women's and men's thinking about parent-child interactions. *Research in Nursing and Health,* **8,** 389-396.

McBride, A.B. (1985b). Orchestrating a career. *Nursing Outlook,* **33,** 244-247.

McBride, A.B. (1985c). Women's health: research for the future. In B.S. Raff and N.W. Paul (Eds.), *NAACOG Invitational Research Conference* (pp. 17-28). White Plains, N.Y.: March of Dimes Birth Defects Foundation.

McBride, A.B. (1987). *The secret of a good life with your teenager.* New York: Times Books.

McBride, A.B., and McBride, W.L. (1981). Theoretical underpinnings for women's health. *Women and Health,* **6**(1/2), 37-55.

Reverby, S. (1987). A caring dilemma: womanhood and nursing in historical perspective. *Nursing Research,* **36,** 5-11.

Margo McCaffery

Margo McCaffery, MS, RN, FAAN, is a consultant
in the nursing care of people with pain
and is based in Santa Monica, California

❖

Margo McCaffery was an impatient child. She graduated from high school at 16 and went into a baccalaureate program for which she had a generous scholarship. Armed with her degree and little experience, she became an instructor teaching on a floor where there were a number of patients with burns. Their excruciating pain made her feel very helpless.

Motivated toward a master's degree, which she thought would ensure a job with a decent income and acceptable working conditions, she chose the closest and shortest program. However, at Vanderbilt she learned more than she ever imagined possible. No longer looking for a shortcut, she wrote her first graduate paper on pain and found herself committed to nursing's role in the care of patients with pain. Her commitment led her to teach pain control to baccalaureate nursing students, and her first book on the subject prompted so many requests for appearances that she became a self-employed lecturer. She continues to present information about pain so that others are able to learn about it.

*E*arly motivations and plans that eventually led to my present professional activity are not very admirable. I ended up in nursing without really knowing what it was all about and without much dedication. Here is how it began.

One summer day in my fifteenth year, my father had a motorcycle accident that left him with severe brain damage. He was admitted to a large hospital where I would, some five years later, be teaching surgical nursing. However, at the time of his accident I had no desire to be a nurse. My fury at the neurosurgeon who said he could do nothing to reverse my father's brain damage motivated me to declare that I would become a neurosurgeon. Because of an educational system that permitted acceleration, I graduated from high school the following year at the age of 16.

Since my grades were quite good (mostly A's), it was fairly certain that I would be awarded one of the generous college scholarships available to graduates of my high school. I thought it would be a waste not to use it. However, when I looked at the curriculum for becoming a neurosurgeon, I found it was too long to suit me. I considered attending the local junior college practical nurse program, but faced with a scholarship and acceptance into Baylor University (thanks to my mother completing the application), I enrolled in the nursing program there in the fall of 1955.

My choice of nursing was naive. I thought a nurse was like a junior doctor. I tried to persuade my mother to let me take the three-year diploma course, since that was much shorter than the five-year baccalaureate program. We struck a bargain—I would attend college for one year, and then I could do as I pleased. After that year it was apparent to me that I would gain no time by transferring to the diploma program, so I continued at Baylor. Once again the educational system allowed me to accelerate, and I finished the program requirements by December 1958, officially graduating in January 1959 at the age of 20.

I returned to my hometown of Corsicana, Texas, and worked as an assistant head nurse on a surgical floor for about eight months. I recall that we worked five-and-a-half-day weeks, which meant five days one week and six days the next. It was possible and common to work 10 or 11 days without any time off. Because I was an assistant head nurse, I rarely worked evenings or nights and the pay was less than $300 a month. As a result, I was motivated to continue to work only days—no weekends—and to make more money.

Because baccalaureate degrees with a major in nursing were fairly rare in those days, I managed to become an instructor in nursing in the baccalaureate program at Texas Woman's University (TWU) in Denton, Texas. The primary clinical facility was Parkland Hospital in Dallas, where my father had been admitted following his accident in 1955.

My job at Parkland began just before I turned 21. I was hardly experienced enough to handle those teaching responsibilities, and they took their toll. During that time two things occurred that caused me to become forever interested in the problem of pain. I experienced a sharp increase in the severity and frequency of migraines (there is a history of this problem in my family), and I was teaching on a surgical floor that winter where there was a fairly large number of patients with burns. That was before the days of burn units, when such patients were still being placed on a general surgical unit along with patients who had chronic infections. The burned patients were often debrided without anesthesia or analgesia. I felt terribly helpless because I could do little to assist those patients with their pain. My own experience with migraines not only made me more aware of the pain of others but brought into sharp focus the fact that the existence and character of pain cannot be proved. I realized that I was very lucky to be believed about my headaches and to receive pain relief so readily from my physicians. I became afraid of pain, and I suppose that is one important reason for my interest in the subject. The chief resident on the surgical unit that year is one of the few people I remember from that time—Charlie Baxter. I had great respect for him then and was astounded to learn some 20 years later that he had become a famous specialist in burn care. Sometimes I wonder if the year that we cared for those particular burned patients was a determining factor in his career, as it was in mine.

Once again some of my lesser motivations surfaced. I was determined to get a job for myself that would provide a decent income, acceptable working conditions (weekdays only), and a possibility of advancement. I was told that a master's degree would do that.

After working at Parkland for a little over a year, I left for Vanderbilt University in Nashville, Tennessee, to obtain that master's degree. I chose Vanderbilt because it was closer to home than some other universities and had the shortest program—one year. Thanks to Lee Gilmer, one of my nursing professors, I learned more at Vanderbilt than I had ever imagined possible. Lee Gilmer taught me to think (she taught the "nursing process" long before it was called that) and to accept that some answers to patient problems had yet to be found. I learned problem solving and how to live with uncertainty. For some reason, that made nursing much more interesting to me.

In the fall of 1960, in one of my first graduate courses in nursing, we addressed the major issues of that era . . . Is there a science *of* nursing or is there science *in* nursing? (Naturally, the safest position was that both existed.) Does nursing meet the criteria for being called a profession? It seemed unfortunate to me that of equal importance were questions like, "Is it necessary for nurses to wear white caps?" and "Is it acceptable for a nurse to wear flesh-colored hose as opposed to white?" . . . Nursing was trying to decide what nursing was, and that got mixed up with what nurses should look like. Of course, given the choice, I chose nude stockings and no cap. The year before, I had given up starched uniforms in favor of the softer cotton and synthetic fibers for which I was severely (but unofficially) criticized by the assistant dean at TWU. She also said unofficially that I was too young and immature to recognize, much less handle, issues faced daily by bedside nurses—I suspected she was right about the immaturity, but I wasn't sure that age had anything to do with it.

In my graduate course "Science of Nursing" (thus titled despite controversy), my nursing professor told us to choose a topic related to nursing care and document the scientific principles being applied. I selected pain, since the question of what nurses could do for patients during their pain experience had already appealed to me. Now it seemed that my interest coincided with the current academic focus. It was clear to me that most patients had some difficulty with discomfort or pain—brief to prolonged, mild to severe—and that nurses spent more time with patients who were in pain than did any other member of the health team.

Although I wanted to address the issue of pain in my paper, my nursing professor called me into her office and told me that I could not write on that topic because not enough was known about it. I did not argue the point, since my motivation was to complete the requirements for the degree. I then chose to focus on catheterization of the female patient, not because I had any interest in this, but because it involved scientific principles that could be easily documented from the basic sciences.

Much to the credit of that professor, she called me back into her office a week later to tell me that I could write about pain. She had two reasons for changing her mind—UCLA was already investigating the topic (UCLA was then challenging Vanderbilt's position on the list of top-ranked schools of nursing), and she believed that one of the purposes of graduate education was to investigate the unknown. I may be mistaken, but I recall that she warned me that she did not think I could produce a paper on pain but felt that she had the responsibility to allow me to try. I proceeded to write a paper on pain.

That was before the days of duplicating machines, abstract services, and computer literature searches, so I went to Vanderbilt's medical library. Now, every time I enter UCLA's biomedical library, I can't help but remember the small library I used at Vanderbilt—so small that it took me only one day to pull off the shelves every book and journal with any potential for information about pain. Indeed, there was little that had been written about pain. I did find John Bonica's book on the management of pain and the classic *Signs and Symptoms*. However, those did not address what nursing's unique contribution to the care of a patient with pain might be.

Given my motivational history, one might expect that I would have abandoned that project in favor of something easier, but I was hooked on two things. For reasons I can never explain, I had become irrevocably committed to nursing's role in the care of patients with pain. I believed that nursing could make a unique contribution there. I also had acquired a belief about nursing as a profession. I believed that if nursing did become a profession—if nurses were to identify their unique and significant contributions to patient care—then helping the patient with pain would play a major part. It astounds me to this day that nursing has not yet made pain control a basic part of the curriculum. I believed then as I believe now that patients experience many problems and devastating losses that nurses cannot eliminate; they can only assist patients to accept and integrate them.

As lacking as my original motivations for being a nurse were, I always cared about the people called patients. I wanted to help, but I was acutely aware of some of the things I could not do. There are irrevocable physical and emotional losses that will not go away; they require time and grieving if they are to be dealt with. There may be denial, but to some extent these problems must be felt if they are to be handled. Except for some patients with chronic idiopathic physical pain that is uncontrollable, pain rarely requires handling—it can be eliminated or significantly reduced. Scarring, loss of a limb, brain damage—these we cannot as easily dispense with. However, in the vast majority of cases we can at least minimize the physical pain and suffering. It makes no sense to me that we fail to devote our attention to pain in everyday nursing practice. Compared to the myriad problems faced by a patient, it is one problem we can do something about.

Once I narrowed down my topic, I focused on anticipation of pain. The library had nothing whatsoever to offer. In 1960, if there was research related to this, I could not find it. I began to use what I suspected would be considered unorthodox and unscientific techniques. I asked people whom I knew (mostly fellow graduate students) what help they would want from a nurse if they knew pain was impending. I constructed a theoretical approach based on their responses. That was over 25 years ago, and what they told me is still much of what is known today. Then I went out and tried to find documentation and research to support what they said. I found only a few studies that could be stretched to cover the ideas that evolved from my interviews.

When I presented my paper, my nursing professor was impressed. The usual course of events was for a paper in that class to be developed into the field study for thesis. I wrote an exhaustive, detailed approach to nursing care of the patient anticipating pain. The Tennessee Nurses Association published a synopsis of this—my first publication. Then the American Nurses' Association invited me to present my study at the national meeting in 1962, which I did.

For personal reasons I wanted to stay at Vanderbilt for a year after graduation, and I was willing to take any offer. That resulted in my becoming chair of the Department of Nursing of Children. Never had I considered involvement with pediatric nursing. I remember reading a textbook on pediatric nursing while on a flight from Nashville to Dallas, where I went to visit my family before the academic year began. I read the chapters on child development with great interest because I knew little about young children. What I did understand, however, was that basic principles applied but were altered to fit the child's method of dealing with life.

I had already comprehended that with adults it was helpful to explain (patient teaching) what was happening and what would occur. So when I noticed that children were afraid of injections, I assumed that they would more easily understand this experience if they could handle the equipment. That was my first attempt to help young children deal with a painful experience. It seemed logical to me to give the child the syringe and needle and allow him to perform injections on dolls and talk about them. I was surprised to find this was not acceptable to many of my colleagues, who suggested that the idea was dangerous. A child might stab me with the needle. They did not understand that the most angry or fearful child was the most unlikely to strike out because he feared retribution. In fact the most frightened children would not touch the needle. To me the most amazing thing I was told was that letting young children play with needles would lead to drug addiction.

During the year I spent teaching at Vanderbilt I was dating an exceptional physician who encouraged and supported me almost as much as Lee Gilmer had. He was an emotional oasis for me and made me believe that I was valuable and different. The first article I ever submitted and had published in a national nursing journal was written because of his suggestion that I should find something to do while he read his medical journals, in particular the *New England Journal of Medicine,* which he read from cover to cover the day it arrived. One evening he was reading, and I was disturbing him. He suggested that I write an article while he finished his journal. I went to the kitchen table, where my typewriter resided, and wrote a rough draft about helping young children through illness and hospitalization experiences. I wrote what I considered a detailed outline and asked the *American Journal of Nursing* if they were interested in this type of article. They said yes and published, with few changes, what I had submitted as an outline and rough draft. That left me with the erroneous impression that it was easy to write an article and get it published.

As I was making plans to leave Vanderbilt at the end of that academic year (1961-1962), my physician friend suggested I apply to teach at the best school of nursing in the country. Again Lee Gilmer had an influence on my decision. She suggested I apply to UCLA, since many of the people she respected were there. I applied, was accepted, and began as a research nurse in the summer of 1962.

When I took my faculty assignment in the fall of 1962, I was introduced to the newly revised nursing curriculum. There was much talk of scientific theory, a scientific basis for nursing, and theoretical models of nursing. But the specifics of the revised curriculum boiled down to a number of topics that needed lecturers. It reminded me of a poker game. They dealt out topics as a dealer deals cards, except that I could request a particular card. When pain was dealt, I said I would take it—an unchallenged position, since no one else knew more about it than I knew. (My other two topics were sensory restriction and cognitive processes.) I taught pain control to students in the baccalaureate program three times a year until I left in 1970.

It is important to me to note that in the history of nursing, that was the time we decided to teach science. For example, nursing instructors had to go beyond knowing the required nursing textbook—they had to know theory from other professional disciplines. During those years I heard a lot of theory that I found hard to apply to the care of patients. I remember hearing discussions about body image disturbance but no suggestions about what the nurse could to do to help with this.

Anyway, I wanted to teach my topics as well as possible—especially pain. Instead of distributing long lists of journals and books for required reading, I began to excerpt the material I thought was applicable in nursing. I distributed handouts of this along with guides for application in the clinical setting. My handouts became so voluminous that the secretaries complained of the burden. Finally the dean suggested that I have the university publish the handouts and sell them to the students. The 207-page syllabus for my course was sold in the bookstore (54 pages were devoted to pain).

During my eighth and last year at UCLA, 1969-1970, I became pregnant with my first and only child, Melissa. I wanted to stay home with her, but I wondered how I could continue to do something intellectually stimulating. Therefore I was glad to have several representatives of publishing companies ask me about the possibility of publishing my course syllabus. The person most interested in this idea was a representative from J.B. Lippincott. He took a copy of my syllabus and said he would present it to his company and get back to me. Months passed with no word, and I assumed that the company was not interested. Then one day I received a letter from David Miller, nursing editor at Lippincott. Dave told me that the representative had been killed in an automobile accident several months before and that only recently had my syllabus been forwarded to him by someone who was sorting out the representative's belongings. Before Melissa was born, I had signed a contract to write a book on pain for nurses, and I spent the first year of her life typing whenever she was sleeping. The book was published in 1972.

What happened after that was truly a surprise to me. I had intended to begin working again on a part-time basis, but before I had a chance to think much about how I would do this, I began to get phone calls asking me to speak to practicing nurses about pain. Two things occurred at just the right time to make it possible for me to become self-employed lecturing and leading workshops about the nursing care of patients with pain. First, professional interest in pain was rising after the founding of the International Association for the Study of Pain in 1973. Pain management was becoming a popular topic in newspapers and magazines. Second, the importance of continuing education for graduate nurses was beginning to be recognized. Some states were considering making it mandatory for continuing licensure.

Requests for me to present lectures and all-day programs on pain slowly increased at an ideal rate for me. As my daughter got older and needed my presence less, the requests increased.

Now I get more invitations than I can accept. That is encouraging to me simply because it indicates that nursing is pursuing its role in the care of the patient with pain. Someday we will have a clear idea of our unique contribution to this area. In the meantime, I will continue to talk about pain as much and as fast as I can. Occasionally people ask me why I never suffered burnout. I don't know. The subject of pain and the many misconceptions we all have about it continue to fascinate me. I enjoy developing better ways of presenting information about pain so others are better able to learn about it.

Mildred Montag

Mildred Montag, EdD, RN, FAAN,
is Professor Emerita, Teachers College,
Columbia University, New York City

❖

Mildred Montag may be best known for her pioneering work with the associate degree nursing program. For her doctoral dissertation at Teachers College, she studied the concept of preparing nursing technicians in a two-year program in community colleges. Once her dissertation was published, however, it took on a life of its own. The stir it caused—the strong pros and cons—continues to this day. Following the book's publication, a project was funded to test the program in seven junior colleges; Mildred Montag was project director. By the time the project was completed, there were more programs outside the project than in it, and the tide could not be stopped. At Teachers College, R. Louise McManus, who had originally proposed that nursing functions be differentiated on a continuum, was not surprised at the mushrooming of the programs. "It was," she said, "an idea whose time had come."

Although she has been associated with AD education since its advent, Mildred Montag has been a teacher all her life, and most of her years at TC have been devoted to teaching and advising doctoral students.

*T*he year I entered nursing school, 1930, was the year of the Great Depression—hardly a time to embark on a new venture. In June of that year I had received a bachelor of arts degree with a major in history from Hamline University in St. Paul. When I went to Hamline, I had no intention of being a nurse. It was not until my senior year that I began to wonder what I wanted to do. It was assumed that I would probably be a teacher, and I, along with many others, took the requisite courses in education. Midway through my senior year there, I began to think seriously about a career in nursing. Quite incidentally, I heard about the University of Minnesota School of Nursing from an alumna of Hamline who was a librarian. Hamline had just hired an occupational counselor, so I went to see her. She responded to my question about going into nursing with the statement, "Why do you want to go backward?" Her attitude remains clear in my memory. She tried to persuade me to go into social work, which was her profession. I left that conference dismayed but convinced that I did not want to be a social worker.

Soon after that I went to the University of Minnesota, where I talked with Phoebe Gordon, a psychometrist. She received me graciously and explained that she was not a nurse but was employed in the school of nursing and was able to give me the information I needed. I maintained a friendship with her through the years. Much later, when she was in the nurse testing division of the Psychological Corporation, I worked there part time while doing doctoral work.

My years in the school of nursing were very pleasant. The courses were challenging, and in the science courses I was privileged to have had Dr. Greisheimer for physiology and Dr. Harold N. Wright—with whom I later collaborated on a book—for pharmacology. There were not many students entering nursing schools then who had a baccalaureate, so I was treated as a "five-year student," of whom there was a sizeable number. I was able to choose the hospital in which I would have my major clinical experience, and my choice was Minneapolis General Hospital, now the Hennepin County Medical Center. That choice proved to be a good one because of the high quality of nursing care given there. The exceptional consideration given patients of all ages, socioeconomic conditions, social status, color, and creed has colored my attitude about nursing care more than anything else.

While I do not know how I would have reacted to nursing without my liberal arts background, I believe that it made a great difference. It has certainly influenced my long-standing belief that nursing should be taught in educational institutions. I know it influenced my work at Adelphi University (then College) as that program began. I think I knew something about colleges and universities after being a student at both. I knew what liberal education would mean to students because it had meant so much to me. The longer I live, the more I appreciate my liberal education, and the more I want it for every nurse.

The year I entered the School of Nursing at the University of Minnesota, Katherine J. Densford (Dreves) began her first year as director of the school. The school was often in the forefront of curriculum innovations. I think that is where I got my belief that one should change as situations and conditions change rather than fall back on the comment, "it has always been done this way." At Minnesota we had the first ward instructor in the United States, Myrtle Hodgkins (Coe), and she was followed by others. Our instruction kept pace with experience.

The five-year curriculum allowed for specialization in the senior year, with a choice between public health nursing and nursing education. The courses included appropriate field work in either of the chosen majors. While I had rejected teaching preparation at Hamline, I chose nursing education at the university. My introduction to John Dewey was in courses taught by Lucile Petry (Leone). Because of my Hamline courses, I was allowed to take courses in the graduate school, chiefly in psychology and sociology. Thus I was able to have advanced courses in areas that would provide a greater understanding of individuals and of society.

Long before "mentor" and "mentoring" were in common use, Miss Densford was just that for me. It was she who invited me to teach at the university—it was she who prodded me almost daily with the question, "When are you going on?" I have often said that my decision to pursue a master's degree was in self-defense. There was no getting around her question, although I attempted to dissuade her by saying I couldn't afford to go to school. Her response was, "Sell your car." I said I couldn't do that, but I did—to Lucile Petry. It proved to be no great sacrifice.

At Lucile's advice, I applied for an Isabel Hampton Robb Scholarship, which I got, and almost simultaneously I was admitted to Columbia University for graduate work. At first I intended to major in sociology while taking some courses at TC. However, after taking several courses, I decided to transfer to TC—a decision I have never regretted. My experience at Teachers College is in no small measure responsible for my conviction that teachers of nursing need broad preparation, including courses in nursing and in the philosophy of education, as well as knowledge about educational practices. The contacts I had with the faculty in and out of the nursing education department have been invaluable. I am indebted to Professor Hamden L. Forkner for much of my philosophy of education. While his courses were in the area of vocational education, his approach was broad, covering education in general. Isabel Stewart was my advisor. She too had a broad view of education, and the courses she approved for me covered a wide range of subjects.

Isabel Stewart became another mentor. It had been my intention to remain in New York only the one year that it would take to get my master's degree. I knew from catalogs and experience that a master's degree in other disciplines required one year, and I assumed that nursing was no different. With Miss Stewart's help I had my degree in one year. It was Miss Stewart who suggested that I consider going on for a doctorate, an idea that hadn't occurred to me. She told me that Harold Laski, the noted British writer and teacher from the London School of Economics, would be giving a course on American democracy the following fall. She thought I might be interested, and I took the course, which was my first step toward the doctorate.

I studied for my doctorate part time because making a living was a necessity. I taught at St. Luke's Hospital School of Nursing what was then called "Nursing Arts." That was an interesting experience. I was the first teacher of nursing arts who had not been a St. Luke's graduate. The usual pattern in many hospitals and schools of nursing was that only their own graduates were employed. I found to my surprise that nursing had been taught in a way specific to that hospital, not as generic nursing that is the same wherever it is carried out.

Again wondering whether teaching was the right choice, I decided to seek employment at the Henry Street Visiting Nurse Service, now the New York Visiting Nurse Service. I was accepted and assigned to the Kips Bay Office, which was on the east side of New York City. I was a senior advisor there, and I began to learn what visiting nursing was about. My district was an interesting one and included some of the worst housing in New York, as well as some of the most expensive. At that time all newborn babies were visited once by a visiting nurse—birth certificate visits they were called. I learned there what a difference it makes to teach the mother of a newborn how to cope after the return home. There were several hospitals in the district and it didn't take long to be able to tell at which hospital the baby had been born. Some mothers were well taught, and others groped for ways to cope. I learned many other things while at Kips Bay, and I still have distinct recollections of the patients I cared for there. I was having interesting experiences, but I was not satisfied that my future lay in public health nursing. Accordingly, I resigned and returned to part-time study and part-time employment at the Psychological Corporation. I had finally decided that education was the right choice for me.

Crises have a way of changing one's plans. By that time, World War II was in progress, and a nurse shortage was just beginning. Several colleges in New York had been requested by the State Education Department to establish nursing programs rather than have hospital schools reopen. Adelphi was one, and following a feasibility study, I became the director of the nursing program. The Cadet Nurse Corps came into being during that period, and we were able to recruit excellent students the whole time I was there. Adelphi had been largely a commuter college, but the nursing program attracted students from a wide geographical area. That fact prompted the building of dormitories, which brought about considerable change. I was able to make the nursing program an integral part of the college. I believed strongly in the need for nursing education to be comparable to other educational experiences. Recent conversations with graduates of that period have convinced me that my efforts were not in vain—that what they experienced in that program has influenced their lives. Another satisfaction is that most of those graduates have remained in nursing and nursing education. Until nurses make a lifelong commitment to nursing, professional status is not a reality.

Completion of doctoral work was a necessity, and I turned to TC as a part-time student, part-time instructor. Within a semester I became a full-time instructor and remained so until my doctoral degree was awarded.

My choice of a dissertation topic was influenced by a number of factors. Among these was the proposition put forth by Mrs. R. Louise McManus that nursing functions were too broad and too complex to be encompassed by a single worker in nursing and therefore should be differentiated. She proposed three categories on a continuum— complex (professional), intermediate (technical), and simple (assisting). Another factor was the idea of vocational education being on a continuum, gleaned from Professor Forkner's courses. Still another was my doubts about practical nursing. Underlying all of these was my conviction that education for nursing belonged in educational institutions. The dissertation I developed made a proposal to prepare nursing technicians in a two-year program in community colleges, which were then developing at a rapid rate.

I thought that my dissertation had accomplished its purpose—I had the degree. I do not recall whose idea it was to submit it to a publisher, but it was submitted. Asa Elliot, an editor at G.P. Putnam & Sons, felt that a publisher had an obligation to occasionally publish a book that would not have wide circulation but was worthy. So my dissertation was published and it caused quite a stir. It was released just prior to the National League of Nursing Education convention in Boston in 1950. While not on the official program, it was much discussed, pro and con, but mostly con. The term nursing "technician" was rejected by almost everyone.

The book generated discussion but it would not have gone any further had not Mrs. McManus translated the idea into a grant proposal and had not a donor given the money to implement the proposal. Announcement of the grant to carry out a research project to "develop and test a new program to prepare young men and women for those functions commonly associated with the registered nurse" appeared in the *New York Times* in January 1952. I was appointed director of the program while maintaining my teaching responsibilities at TC.

We were deluged with requests from community colleges wishing to participate in the project. The colleges were selected on the basis of data received from questionnaires and on advice of the project's advisory committee and the accreditation districts of the American Association of Junior Colleges (now American Association of Community and Junior Colleges). Seven colleges were chosen, and it was expected that that number would not be exceeded until the research was completed in the five years of the project. Such was not to be, for when those five years were up, there were more programs outside the project than within. The idea caught on, as Mrs. McManus said, because "it was an idea whose time had come."

That is not to say there were not many who opposed the idea. I remember well a time when a noted nurse educator announced at a meeting in Atlantic City that I had "set nursing back 25 years." I remember well, too, a meeting in Cleveland where a member of a panel on which I also served berated me so that the chair of the panel had to call for silence. Fortunately I was able to keep from speaking out. Close to home, some of my colleagues at Teachers College were also skeptical. They said to me, "Just wait until they take State Boards. Then you'll see." Fortunately, all who took the licensure examinations in the first class of the first two junior colleges passed. Then the skeptics said, "Just wait until they go to work. The State Boards don't tell you anything." The skeptics were quieted somewhat when our evaluation studies showed that 75% to 80% of the graduates were rated as "better than" or "as good as" graduates from other programs with the same length of experience.

The programs developed through the Cooperative Research Project, now known as associate degree nursing programs, have had phenomenal growth. There was a tremendous surge in the beginning, and new programs have been added annually. At present there are close to 800. This is gratifying not only to me but to all who have devoted years to AD education. Most of all, it has meant so much to so many individuals who would not have been able to be nurses were it not for these programs. I have talked to hundreds and have had letters from many who credit these programs with changing their lives. To think one has helped someone achieve a goal makes it all worthwhile. Not only has the program helped students, it has given many nurses a career in teaching and administration of these programs. I have been told by many people that they believe in AD education and will fight for it.

Certain things stand out in the success of the associate degree programs. An important one is the acceptance of the program by college administrators and the AACJC. Another is the willingness of those first administrators and teachers who braved the unknown and charted new programs, even when they were "committing professional suicide." To them I am indebted.

During all my years on the faculty at Teachers College I carried out teaching assignments and advised students. I taught in the prespecialization program and in the master's program, but most of my years at TC were devoted to doctoral students. That was a most gratifying experience. To see students grow, to see the results of their intellectual and research activities, and then to see them accept leadership positions in nursing across the country can only be described as exhilarating. It has been my privilege to have kept up with a substantial number of these students through meetings, visits, and correspondence. They have sent me their publications and reports of their involvement in meetings, conferences, and conventions. Foremost, I count them as friends.

I take satisfaction when I am identified with associate degree programs, but I take no less satisfaction from my teaching. I believe whatever influence I have had in nursing has been through my contact with students as a teacher and advisor as much as it has been through my work with the associate degree program. I consider myself an educator who is interested in all aspects of nursing education.

My years at Teachers College were rewarding, but when it was time to retire I did so without resistance. I expected my retirement to be one of leisure. Such was not to be. Some few months before retirement, I was invited to be a member of the New York State Regents Committee, which was developing an external associate degree program in nursing. When the idea of an external degree in nursing was proposed by Ewald Nyquist in his inaugural address as New York State Commissioner of Education, I thought that nursing was just being used. With some encouragement from Dolores Wozniak, a former student and then coordinator of the proposed external degree program, I agreed to accept the appointment. The experience of helping to develop this program, which operated differently from any other educational system in which I had been involved, was one of the most rewarding experiences I have had. To develop an assessment program that did not involve teaching students directly was a real challenge. I learned much about testing, and I found the experiences I had had at the Psychological Corporation very helpful. The AD External Degree Program was developed, launched, and in due course accredited. While there were some doubts about the desirability and feasibility of such a program, its advent was not seriously challenged.

When the external baccalaureate degree program was developed, there was much more resistance from those involved with baccalaureate programs. My belief is that they did not understand the program or the clientele it was designed to serve. I believe they saw it as competition for colleges and universities. Both the associate and baccalaureate external degree programs are targeted at a different group of students—those who cannot attend a campus-based program. I am convinced that anyone succeeding in either of these external programs is well equipped to provide quality nursing care, and there is evidence to support this belief.

I have continued to give consultations, workshops, and speeches. Perhaps the most interesting invitation I have received was to give the annual Oration at the College of Nursing, New South Wales, Australia, in 1973. I am sure that Ruth White, an Australian doctoral student at Teachers College then, was responsible for that invitation. After that visit I was invited back to give seminars two years in succession.

In 1975 I was named an Honorary Fellow of the College of Nursing, the third in the college's history and the only American to be so honored. I made many friends in Australia with whom I have traded visits.

Lest anyone think that my life has been limited to work, let me say that such is not the case. I have traveled widely—to Russia (three times), England, the Scandinavian countries, nearly all the countries of western Europe, Turkey, Greece, Israel, Morocco, Tunisia, and the Balkans. I have been in every state except Alaska and have not given up hope of going there.

I have been a member of Zonta International, a service organization for executive women, for over 25 years. I have served as president of the Long Island Zonta Club and am currently secretary. I am chair of the board of trustees of my church and a member of the Garden City–Hempstead Community Club, the American Association of University Women, and the Long Island University Club. I also serve on the local advisory committee of the nursing program at State University Agricultural and Technical College at Farmingdale, New York. I have served on the board of Nurses Educational Funds for more than 40 years, having been president and serving now as vice-president.

My retirement years have been active, both personally and professionally. They have been influenced by my professional life and by my educational experiences. What has led me to do the things I have, I cannot explain. I have enjoyed what I have done. Who could ask for more?

Virginia M. Ohlson

Virginia M. Ohlson, PhD, RN, FAAN,
is Professor Emerita,
University of Illinois College of Nursing

❖

Virginia Ohlson was one of four American nurses assigned to the Public Health and Welfare section of the Supreme Command of Allied Powers, General Douglas MacArthur's central headquarters during the Occupation of Japan in 1947. As chief nurse of the section, she and her staff worked closely with their Japanese nurse counterparts to rebuild Japan's shattered educational and health care systems. She returned to the United States in 1951 and six months later joined the staff of the Atomic Bomb Casualty Commission in an educational and research center in Hiroshima.

In her third assignment in the Orient, she was invited by the government of Japan to serve as a consultant to Japanese nurses in the Institute of Public Health in Tokyo. Enriched by all she had learned and taught, she returned to the United States and in 1963 joined the faculty at the University of Illinois College of Nursing as head of the Department of Public Health Nursing. Famous for her efforts in promoting cross-cultural understanding, she became assistant Dean for International Studies at the university. She has continued to work with international studies part time since her retirement.

*F*rom my early life, my church (the Evangelical Covenant Church) has been very important to me. It has always had a strong emphasis on missions, and I remember from my childhood that a number of our missionaries would come home on furlough and tell stories about their experiences in places like China, Africa, and Alaska. Their children became my friends, and I thought those were lucky kids to live in such fascinating places in the world.

I was always tall for my age, and I used to think that that was the reason my teachers "scooted" me through the elementary school grades. I was quite young when I started high school at North Park College Academy (a Covenant school) in Chicago, and I finished the program in three and a half years. I then went on to junior college at North Park. Those were difficult times. My father was a painter and decorator who did a great deal of work for the college. My two sisters and I used to say that he "painted us through college."

I had initially enrolled in courses in junior college to prepare for teaching. I later realized that I would need to contribute to my own support, so I changed my program and took some secretarial courses. All the while, I had a nagging interest in nursing. My aunt was a nurse. My dad thought she always had to work very hard, and therefore he wasn't enthusiastic about my interest. However, my aunt used to tell me stories about nursing, and eventually I convinced my family that nursing was what I wanted to do. I decided to enroll at the Swedish Covenant Hospital School of Nursing.

I finished junior college in June 1933, worked as a waitress at the Chicago World's Fair that summer and in a neighborhood restaurant for a few months that fall, and then entered nursing school in February 1934.

While in nursing school, I definitely had a leadership role, mostly owing to luck. We had a strange system in our school. The person who reported in *first* on admission day of the entering class in September became the president of the class, on assignment from the director of the school. I was the first person to check in on the day the February class was admitted and therefore became vice-president of the class.

All our assignments to the clinical areas were changed on the first day of every month and were made according to the order of admittance. Since I was number one of the February class of 1934, I was always the first to get new assignments. That meant I was moved quickly through clinical experiences while my classmates at the end of the list were often reassigned to areas and responsibilities they had had previously. That method of assignment moved me quickly into charge nurse positions as a student and into all of the required clinical, functional, and leadership roles. I got along well with my classmates, and they did not resent my good fortune. Others who had enrolled early on that first day were also moved along quickly. It was the latecomers who suffered under that rigid system.

After I received my nursing diploma, I was employed for one year in the operating room at the Swedish Covenant Hospital in Chicago. I was the surgical nurse assistant to Dr. O.T. Roberg, Sr., who was chief of the Department of Surgery. Although I enjoyed assisting Dr. Roberg at the "Mayo stand," I kept looking around in my off-duty hours for a position in public health nursing. That was my goal! I had been strongly influenced when I was about 14 by a public health nurse, Ruth Nordlund. She used to tell me about her work with families—about how she was able to care for persons in their homes and to teach members of the family to care for them. That appealed to me as a young girl. I never forgot Ruth Nordlund, and as I grew older I continued to think about public health nursing.

Because I couldn't find a position in the Chicago area, I contacted the nursing director at the Illinois Department of Health in Springfield and asked her to keep me in mind if a position in public health nursing became available, or if she saw a way to help me apply for an Illinois Public Health Nursing Traineeship. I told her that I hoped to enroll in some public health nursing courses at the University of Chicago. She helped me obtain the traineeship and recommended me for an open position in public health nursing at the Evanston Health Department in Evanston, Illinois, where I worked for seven years.

When I first went to Evanston in 1938, I was employed as a public health nurse. I was in charge of immunization clinics and the health supervision of children in four elementary schools—three Catholic and one Lutheran. I was appointed director of nursing of the health department within three years.

In 1943 I began to think seriously about China and about my commitment to the Christian missions there. I enrolled at the University of Chicago, attended as a part-time student (evenings and summers) for approximately three years, and earned a bachelor of science degree with a major in nursing in 1946.

I then left Evanston to take a position I had been offered in Japan, thinking at that time that an experience there might prepare me for service in China someday. Although I was enjoying my work in the health department, I felt *keenly* that the door had been opened for me to go to Japan and that God was leading me in that direction.

JOURNEY TO THE ORIENT

When I first went to Japan, it was with the U.S. Occupation Army. World War II had ended in the fall of 1945; I went to Japan in 1947 as one of ten American nurses initially employed in the Army of Occupation under the Department of the Army. We were civilian, not army, nurses. Eventually our number was increased to about 30.

My first impressions of Japan came as I was being transported in a U.S. Army bus from the Haneda (Tokyo) Airport to the hotel that was to be my first home in Japan. It was evening. The rain that had been falling earlier in the day had given way to a still, warm twilight. As our bus wound its way through narrow streets of small villages that surrounded the airport, I could see through the windows of all the storefront homes— small, dim homes. I saw families sitting on floors near open doorways, cooling off in the fresh, rain-washed breeze of that warm spring evening. I remember so very well my prayer that evening as I looked at those scenes. "God, be with me in this new country. Help me to know and understand the Japanese people and help them to know and understand me. Like the open doors of these little homes, may the Japanese open their minds and their hearts to me—and may I find the way to open my mind and my heart to them."

I was assigned to the Public Health and Welfare Section of the General Headquarters of the Supreme Command of Allied Powers (SCAP), which was General Douglas Mac-Arthur's central headquarters. We were four American nurses in that section who worked primarily, but not exclusively, with Japanese nurses who held positions in government offices similar to the positions we held in SCAP.

The Japanese Ministry of Health and Welfare was the counterpart organization to SCAP's Public Health and Welfare Section. I was initially employed as a public health nursing consultant, and my counterpart was the chief public health nurse of the Japanese Ministry of Health and Welfare.

We American nurses of the Occupation were responsible for laying groundwork and working with the Japanese nurses, physicians, and government officials to reestablish organized nursing education and practice in Japan. In the early days of the Occupation, American and Japanese nurses surveyed hospitals and existing nursing schools. Over the course of the war, nursing standards had dropped considerably; Japan had been at war in the Pacific for many years before being at war with us. As a result, nurses were being educated in short courses that emphasized emergency measures to care for the wounded on battlefields and in hospitals in various parts of the country.

The civilian population was not able to use major hospital facilities when the war became intense. Those facilities were reserved for the military.

Civilians who needed care went to ambulatory centers or to small neighborhood hospitals. Nurses were working and studying under very poor conditions. They were malnourished; many had no shoes, and their feet and hands were covered with chilblains. All metal in public and private buildings had been stripped and used to make weapons and other implements of war. There were no glass panes left in any windows, no central heating or cooking facilities—no big rice vats that had been a common sight in large Japanese institutions.

When patients were admitted to the hospital, their families had to bring in supplies such as bedding, cooking utensils, and personal care items. They also had to provide someone to care for the patient, to prepare meals, and to bring in charcoal to make small fires for cooking. Running water was not available in the patient care areas because water pipes had been removed. Nurses walked long distances to carry water for the patients. It was a pitiful, difficult situation. I often felt helpless after spending a morning or afternoon at a hospital.

In an effort to reestablish nursing education, demonstration schools of nursing were set up and staffed by Japanese and American nurses. Two were located in Tokyo and one in the south-central city of Okayama. A program was established at the Institute of Public Health in Tokyo that provided a four-month course of study for leadership positions in public health nursing. The faculty for that program included both Japanese and American nurses. A model health center was established in Tokyo where public health personnel were trained to staff other health centers that were being set up throughout the country.

In establishing the model schools and centers, our goal was to set patterns of education and services that could be duplicated in the redeveloping nursing schools, health centers, and teaching centers. The reestablishment of nursing education and practice in Japan that occurred in the years of the United States' occupation could not have happened had it not been for the core of Japanese nurses who had been prepared through the educational programs that their own schools provided prior to the war. Many of the nurses with whom we Americans worked had studied in the United States and Canada on fellowships provided by the Rockefeller Foundation. Japan therefore had a core of nurse leaders who, with our help, set a course for the future of nursing education and practice in the country.

Many of those nurse leaders were graduates of the St. Luke's Hospital School of Nursing in Tokyo, which was established by the Episcopal Church, USA. At the close of World War II, the hospital was occupied by the U.S. Army for use by American military personnel and their families; it was then staffed by U.S. Army nurses. The Japanese St. Luke's nurses were sent to various places in the country where schools of nursing and health care facilities were being reinstituted.

The Japanese nurses knew what they wanted for nursing in their country. They simply needed people to help in the accomplishment of those goals. As members of the U.S. Occupation we had the power to help them break through barriers that were hindering the progress of nursing in Japan. The status of nursing was low. The status of women was low. During the years of the Occupation a nurse practice act was enacted to establish regulations for nursing, midwifery, and public health nursing. Minimum standards for nursing education and the accreditation of schools were established, and an examination system was set up as the basis for licensure for practice.

A very intricate series of so-called refresher courses was initiated for nursing leaders. These courses were offered at the national, regional, state, and local levels. Japanese nurses were the course teachers. Lectures by American nurses were translated by the Japanese.

We American nurses worked closely with the Japanese nurses for the reorganization of the Japanese Nursing Association (JNA). The JNA had lost its status with the International Council of Nurses (ICN) during World War II. In 1949 in Stockholm, the newly reorganized JNA was readmitted into membership in the ICN. Because of an ICN policy that requires a country being admitted to be represented at the meeting, and because in 1949 the JNA could not send a Japanese representative owing to the travel restrictions of the Occupation, I was selected to represent the JNA. It was a privilege to witness for the Japanese their readmission to the ICN.

Also in 1949, Grace Alt, who was the first Chief Nurse of the U.S. Occupation, went back to the United States to attend graduate school on a Rockefeller Foundation fellowship. I was then appointed Chief Nurse of the U.S. Occupation. By that time we had quite a corps of American nurses stationed in each of the eight regions of Japan.

BIBLE STUDY IN JAPAN

One of the unique opportunities I had during my years in Japan was teaching the Bible to young Japanese girls and nurses. Often in my travels, nurses in the cities where I stayed would ask me to teach the Bible to a group in their hospital. I would meet with them in the evenings apart from working hours, so as not to conflict with their or my own work schedules.

In 1949 when the Communists assumed power in China, most Americans and people of other countries had to leave that country. The Evangelical Covenant Church had many missionaries there, and when they were forced out, a number of them went to Japan to help establish Covenant missions. Three nurses were assigned by the Covenant Missionary Council in Japan to teach English Bible classes to interested student nurses. Those three nurses and I worked together with the Japanese nurses to establish the Nurses' Christian Fellowship in Japan. Bible classes were offered weekly in a number of nursing schools in Tokyo and other areas. With approval of the planning committees for the annual meetings of the JNA, New Testaments written in Japanese, which were provided by Gideons International, were distributed through an NCF booth in the exhibits section.

The Occupation was over in 1951, and by July of that year all of us American nurses of the U.S. Army of Occupation had left Japan. I returned to the United States. Six months later, I accepted an invitation to go again to Japan, this time to Hiroshima on the staff of the Atomic Bomb Casualty Commission. The ABCC was a research and educational organization of the U.S. Energy Commission that had been established to determine the effects of radiation on the populations of Hiroshima and Nagasaki. I went to the ABCC as a public health nursing consultant and two months later was appointed director of nursing.

By the time I arrived at ABCC in Hiroshima, the nurses there knew I was a Christian. They asked me to teach a Bible class. I had to be very careful not to make the nurses feel that their attendance at my classes was expected, since to them I held an esteemed position in the Occupation and at the ABCC in Hiroshima. The Japanese have a high respect for authority, and they behave accordingly.

Teaching Bible classes was a good opportunity for me and was helpful in establishing a nurses' home-visit program for very ill A-bomb victims and their troubled family members. A Japanese nurse arranged for our group to meet in a small church close to the ABCC center. Everyone knew that attendance was voluntary. However, in time more than three fourths of the nurses on staff came to those weekly Bible classes.

WORKING WITH THE ABCC

I was not the first American nurse at the ABCC. Others had preceded me, had set up the clinics, and had worked with the Japanese nurses to establish policies and programs. I was, however, the only American nurse on the Hiroshima staff. Another American nurse was on the staff in Nagasaki.

There were about 25 to 30 Japanese nurses on the staff in Hiroshima. I had a Japanese counterpart who was the director of nursing, and we worked together closely.

On our staff were American physicians who also had their Japanese counterparts. Whenever a patient was seen in our clinics, that patient's Japanese physician was notified and invited to be present to assist with the examination and discuss the patient's treatment plan. Recommendations for treatment were arrived at jointly by the Japanese and the American doctors, but treatments were carried out by the Japanese.

We saw a lot of pitiful conditions in those days, just six years after the bomb had been dropped. There had been many birth anomalies in the earlier years—children born anencephalic or with other abnormalities. Women who were in the first trimester of pregnancy at the time the bomb was dropped delivered stillborn or malformed infants. There were many severely burned patients and persons with cataracts or blindness caused by the intense flash of the bomb.

When I went to work for the ABCC, we were still seeing many stillborn babies because of poor prenatal care, malnutrition, or tuberculosis in the mothers. I saw a lot of severely crippled and handicapped persons and many people of all ages with varying stages of leukemia. Sometimes when the ABCC van would go to a home to pick up a patient for an appointment at the clinic, the driver would learn that the patient had died and that the death had not yet been reported because the home was so far from the clinic and telephones were unavailable.

One of the first things I had to do when I went to Hiroshima was to help set up a visiting system for patients who were no longer able to keep clinic appointments. The nurses were to go to the homes of those patients to make assessments and do tests and measurements important to the research studies of the effect of the A-bomb on the patient's condition. Those tests and assessments could best be made by persons familiar with the patient and with clinic procedures—by someone the families could trust. The nurses had developed rapport with patients and family members by that time.

My role was to get this program under way and to help the nurses work with families who were being asked to bring their stillborn babies into the clinic for examination before burial. This was hard on the nurses—very hard. It was extremely difficult for me, too. At times I felt so useless, embarrassed, and guilty—although I can honestly say that it was *never* the nurses or the patients who made me feel that way. The Japanese are a stoic people; they have a unique capacity to accept things as they are when things can't be changed. No doubt they hid a lot of their feelings. The composure they maintained while dealing with fear, pain, and suffering was always difficult for me—one of another culture—to comprehend. My years in Japan gave me a whole new insight into the complexities of cultural differences.

THE ROCKEFELLER FOUNDATION YEARS

I remained in Hiroshima for approximately one year. When the peace treaty between Japan and the United States was signed, I was invited by the Japanese government to return to the Tokyo area to accept a unique position under the employ of the Rockefeller Foundation.

One of the nicest compliments I have been given in my professional life was to be invited back by the Japanese government after I had been a part of the United States Occupation force in their country. During the Occupation years the devastated conditions of their health care facilities had become known to us American nurses. None of the unpleasant conditions could be covered. I had often felt the humiliation and pain of the Japanese, who remembered and frequently tried to share with us their memories of better times. I was gratified to know that the Japanese nurses trusted me enough to invite me back again to work with them at a national level, so I returned to Japan in 1952 for two more years.

My office on that assignment was in the Institute of Public Health in Tokyo, which in prewar years had been built and subsidized by the Rockefeller Foundation. I functioned as a consultant to the Japanese nurses in programs or projects for which they requested my time and participation. I continued to travel a great deal with nurses in visiting schools of nursing, hospitals, and health centers, and in participating in professional conferences and meetings. I was involved in many of the activities that were being initiated as a result of the new nursing legislation—the establishment of an accreditation system for nursing schools, the initiation and refinement of the examination system for licensure and practice, and the development of baccalaureate programs in nursing. I also worked closely with the Japanese Nursing Association in those years, particularly in their publication and continuing education programs.

I returned to the United States in December 1954; seven years and eight months had passed since I first embarked on that challenging, life-changing experience.

Whenever I think back now to that May evening in 1947 when I first arrived in Japan, I remember the prayer I said, and I am mindful of how fully God answered that prayer through the years.

NURSING EDUCATION AT THE UNIVERSITY OF ILLINOIS

I joined the faculty of the College of Nursing, University of Illinois, in 1963. At that time the baccalaureate curriculum of the college had been accredited by the National League for Nursing, but it had not received the credential for recognition as an approved program in public health nursing.

I was appointed chair of Public Health Nursing in the college in 1963 with prime responsibility for the preparation of courses and learning experiences to enable the curriculum of the college to be recognized by the National League for Nursing as an approved program in public health nursing.

In 1970 the organization of the College of Nursing was changed, and instead of chairing programs, we were appointed as heads of departments, similar to the organization of the medical school. Thus I was named head of the Department of Public Health Nursing. These departments are autonomous; each is largely responsible for the generation and control of its own budget, the employment of faculty, and review of curriculum that is relevant to that department's specialty area.

Concurrent with my appointment as department head in 1970, the master's program in public health nursing was initiated. This graduate program grew rapidly; the curriculum was organized to provide specialty nursing preparation in community, family, school, and occupational health. We had federal government support for all of these programs. Through the department, we also offered integrated courses in international health nursing.

An emphasis in international nursing has been continuous since its inauguration at the university. Courses relating to international health nursing have been an option to students in the graduate program every quarter of the academic year.

FURTHER TRAVELS IN JAPAN

In 1968 I returned to Japan after 14 years in the states. In that interim I had earned a master's degree in nursing education from the University of Chicago, had taught for four years in the nursing master's program there, and had nearly completed my dissertation for a doctorate there. By then I had also spent several years on the faculty at the University of Illinois.

My good friend and colleague Rosemary Ellis went with me on that return trip. It was a return trip for her as well, since she had been a nurse with the U.S. Army in Japan in 1945 at the close of World War II.

For both of us, Japan had changed tremendously. I looked hard for many of the old buildings where I formerly had worked and lived. All had changed. The old buildings had been replaced or renovated into modern establishments. New schools of nursing were being built in all the major cities of Japan. Nursing education and nursing care had progressed significantly.

In 1974 I again traveled to Japan and stayed for seven months while on sabbatical from the University of Illinois. That was a tremendously interesting time for me. I asked the JNA for their assistance in a project to study the extent to which the nursing education system established during the years of the U.S. Occupation had been sustained or changed since the 1940s. I wanted to know if the Western influence on education and nursing had withstood the test of time in Japanese society.

I visited Japan again in 1977 to attend the ICN Congress hosted by the JNA and in 1981 when the JNA awarded me honorary membership. Also in 1981, Japan's Minister of Health and Welfare presented me with the Award of Merit for my contributions to nursing during the Occupation.

Baccalaureate education in nursing got a slow start in Japan. Even at the present time there are only about 12 BSN programs in the entire country, although there are many associate degree programs. Those AD programs are three-year programs and are quite solid clinically and in the liberal arts. Japan now has two master's degree nursing programs, and two doctoral programs are just under way. The Japanese nurses have not been able to move as quickly as they would like in developing graduate programs in nursing, mostly because it has been difficult to move nursing education into the universities. As a result, preparation for teachers for university schools of nursing has lagged, which has hindered the development of both undergraduate and graduate education.

In 1986 the JNA passed a resolution supporting the goal of baccalaureate education as a requirement for entry into practice by the year 2000. The difficulty of achieving this goal is clearly recognized. The Japanese Nursing Practice and Education Act is a national legislative document. To change the law will require much patience, wisdom, perseverance, and careful planning.

AN ATTEMPT TO RETIRE

I officially retired from the College of Nursing at the University of Illinois in August 1984. After 60 days of leisure, I was reemployed on a 40% appointment, which means that I am at the College two or three days a week. I do a considerable amount of traveling to represent the college in international matters. I continue to teach, advise students, and serve on thesis and dissertation committees.

I had resigned from my position as head of the Department of Public Health Nursing in 1980 and at that time was appointed assistant dean for the Office for International Studies within the college. Since that time we have made a forward thrust in international nursing. We have given high priority to our international students and have developed programs geared to their needs. Although these students follow the same graduate program as our regular students, faculty members try to meet the differing needs of these students just as they do with the international undergraduate students at the university.

In August 1986 the College of Nursing was designated as the first global World Health Organization Collaborating Center for Nursing. As a WHO Collaborating Center, the college will cooperate with WHO in advancing the goal of "Health for All by the Year 2000 through Primary Health Care."

The biggest change in nursing students that I have noticed over the years has been a matter of age. In undergraduate programs students used to enter directly from high school. Now a number of entering students in BSN programs already have a master's or even a doctoral degree in a discipline other than nursing. Others are registered nurses who have worked a number of years in nursing or other fields. Some of the RNs have been at home with their children and are returning to school.

Students today are different from those of the 1960s. They are more independent, and they know what they want. They are goal directed.

Until recently, when college enrollments dropped in many areas, we have not needed to advertise much or recruit. Many of our students are part-time students who work and care for a family in addition to their studies. Relationships between students and faculty are more informal than they were when I began my teaching career.

For me one thing about students has remained constant over the years—they are interesting and challenging. They continue to be the motivation that brings me back to the university, even though I am officially retired.

I have been fortunate to receive many awards and citations over the years. Each one has been very special to me. Receiving the Pearl McIver Award from the American Nurses' Association was very meaningful because it is granted as a public health nursing award in memory of an outstanding public health nursing leader, Pearl McIver.

An award I received from the Japanese Nursing Association in the 1980s is also one I prize highly. It was presented to me when I was named an honorary member of the Japanese Nursing Association, in recognition of the work I was privileged to do in Japan from 1947 to 1954. It has also been my privilege to receive a Doctor of Humane Letters (honora causa) from North Park College.

I have accepted each of these awards with humility and gratitude, and always my thoughts have gone in many directions. With thankfulness, I have thought about the many opportunities I have known in my lifetime—the education I have been privileged to enjoy, the world where I have worked, and especially the people who have shared my goals and helped me to reach them.

These experiences and friendships have been my greatest award.

Sister Callista Roy

Sister Callista Roy, PhD, RN, FAAN, is Professor
in the School of Nursing and Nurse Theorist
for the PhD Program at Boston College

Highly respected as a nurse-theorist, researcher, writer, and lecturer, Sister Callista Roy says her greatest interest is in nursing knowledge development. Her work with her own Roy Adaptation Model for Nursing Practice is ongoing, as the model, first conceptualized in the 1960s, continues to evolve.

*I*n my professional career I am a nurse-theorist, writer, lecturer, researcher, and teacher. These multiple roles are very much integrated in who I am and in what I believe about nursing and my hopes for the future.

The development of the Roy Adaptation Model for Nursing Practice has been pivotal in my contribution to nursing. Knowledge development—including a broad perspective on nursing as a practice discipline, theory development, and programs of research—is a significant part of the work that I am doing. All the major turning points in my career have been influenced by the same basic factors. My family, my religious commitment, my teachers, and my mentors have shaped my personal and professional life.

I was born at Los Angeles County General Hospital on October 14, 1939, the second child and first daughter of a young couple, Mr. and Mrs. Fabien W. Roy. My birth was on the Feast of Saint Callistus, Pope and martyr of the Roman Catholic Church, and thus I was named Lorraine Callista.

As a child I attended parochial school and was impressed with the teaching of religion. The sisters were good teachers. I acquired good study habits and was delighted with learning. Our family grew, and when I was in the sixth grade, my mother went to work as a nurse's aide. My father was a punch-press operator who sometimes also took on evening maintenance jobs. My mother went to evening school and worked nights, eventually getting her vocational nurse's license. I remember my mother having a large book she called "The Doctor Book," which she used with great care and reverence. As the oldest girl, I took over much of the care responsibilities of my brothers and sisters. My parents taught me about selflessness and hard work.

My high school days were those of a normal adolescent and were filled with games, dances, parties, and studies. I was still interested in religion but became much more involved with friends, both boys and girls. At the end of my freshman year I started to work as a pantry girl at a large general hospital. Within a year I was "promoted" to maid, and later to nurse's aide. I liked working at the hospital very much, even though my contact with patients was limited because I was still only 14 years old.

As I was mopping the floor or changing water in patients' flower vases, I tried to be observant about what was happening with individual patients, and sometimes I had the chance to talk with them and with the nurses about what was happening. I carried a spirit of awe and inquisitiveness with me in my early days at the hospital.

At the end of high school I applied to both a diploma and a baccalaureate nursing program. At the same time I was struggling with the difficult decision of whether to enter a religious community. My motivation in that direction had been strong in childhood, but at age 17 it was a much more difficult situation. The conflict was most poignant because of the steady boyfriend I had at that time. I tend to maintain friendships and, in fact, Manuel and I are still friends today.

A very deep faith and a commitment to God was central in my family. This involved working hard for others and personal prayer. In my struggle to deal with the possibility of a religious commitment, I was struck by the simple words of our catechism of the day, "God made me to know Him, to love Him, and to serve Him in this life, and be happy with Him in the next." I became convinced that the best way to fulfill my purpose in life was through a religious commitment. That conviction has never changed throughout 30 years as a member of the Sisters of Saint Joseph of Carondelet.

I spent the first few years in religious life taking general college classes at Mount St. Mary's College in Los Angeles and studying religion there. After making first vows on March 19, 1960, some of my classmates began to select majors in college. The process was that you were called in by your religious superiors or the director of studies, and these arrangements were made then.

As a high school student, I had very much wanted to be a nurse. However, I began to think that perhaps as a sister, I could be more effective as a teacher. As I saw my classmates entering other majors, however, I became more and more convinced that I really did want to be a nurse. The opportunity came, and I entered the nursing major at the college and graduated with a bachelor of arts degree in 1963. The program satisfied my initial interest in nursing and sparked another interest in nursing research. I can remember looking for relationships between patient behavior and other variables in the environment.

One instructor encouraged me to try to publish one of my senior papers. I was greatly disappointed when it was rejected, however, she said that I had perhaps just submitted it to the wrong journal. So I sent it elsewhere, it was accepted, and I had my first publication. In college I was also interested in liberal arts and took as many extra courses as I could in English and history. I was eager to pursue graduate study and was encouraged by many of my teachers to do so. However, I felt that I really needed clinical practice in addition to what I had had each summer as a student.

As a young sister nurse, I had good experience in several hospitals run by the Sisters of St. Joseph in Idaho and Arizona. I worked in pediatrics and loved the experience with the children. When I had the opportunity to enroll in the master's program in nursing at the University of California at Los Angeles in September 1964, I chose to study pediatrics. That was a most fortunate choice, since it put me in close contact with Dorothy E. Johnson, who became very influential in my professional life.

I loved graduate school and the climate of the UCLA campus, as well as the wonderful leaders in nursing who were on faculty at that time. Dr. Burton Meyer taught research and gave me a firm grounding in both inductive and deductive processes for developing a framework, as well as in the meticulous steps of design, data collection, and analysis. My master's thesis was an intervention nursing study that was published in *Nursing Research* in 1967. It was the seminars in pediatric nursing with Dorothy Johnson, however, that set the direction for the next 20 years of my work.

In 1959 Dorothy Johnson had begun to write of the need for nurses to define the nature of their practice. In a significant article nine years later (Johnson, 1968), she described the nature of the knowledge required for practice in nursing. I am forever grateful that I had the opportunity to catch the enthusiasm and commitment to defining the nature of nursing so early in my career. That initial conviction grew stronger through my later work with other disciplines including my work toward a doctoral degree in sociology, post-doctoral studies in neuroscience nursing, and clinical research in neurotrauma with a department of neurosurgery.

In my graduate courses at UCLA I had begun to describe the beginning of the Roy Adaptation Model of Nursing. I had outlined a research proposal for testing my model of nursing and was urged to seek funding to do so. I was able to test that design a few years later through a training grant received at Mount St. Mary's College. When I joined that faculty in the summer of 1966, we were discussing a concept of nursing in preparation for a major curriculum change. Cautiously, I began to introduce some of my ideas about adaptation. There were about a dozen faculty members, all but one of whom had taught me as an undergraduate. There was some mild interest in the adaptation concept but not enthusiastic support.

By the end of that year, I had become ill, suffering what was then called enceph-alomyelitis, and I had to be in bed the greater part of a year and a half. When I came back to work in the fall of 1968, the faculty began asking me more about my concept of nursing. Soon I was chairperson of the committee charged with writing the philosophy for the new curriculum. On one dramatic day, a vote was taken on whether to adopt the adaptation framework as the basis for the new curriculum. The vote was unanimous in favor of adoption. The new curriculum was set for implementation in the spring of 1970.

Meanwhile, under pressure from Dorothy Johnson, I had begun to publish articles about the Roy Adaptation Model. As a result I began to get requests to give workshops on the use of the model in curriculum development. I traveled throughout the United States and Canada and continued to teach and to be coordinator for the new curriculum. The major concepts of the model grew quickly as we worked with students to implement it in clinical practice. The model views the person as a whole being, constantly interacting with his or her environment, adapting to change through four adaptive modes: physiological needs, self-concept, role function, and interdependence.

In 1971, I was made chair of the nursing department and continued in that position while studying for a doctorate in sociology at UCLA. I thoroughly enjoyed those years of rapid growth and development of both the department and the adaptation model. My greatest joy in administration was helping young faculty grow, develop, and find new ways to articulate nursing and nursing practice.

With an educational leave from Mount St. Mary's College, I completed my PhD in 1977. My clinical research at that time was done in six health care institutions across the United States, including the Loeb Center at Montefiore Hospital in the Bronx and Rush–Presbyterian Medical Center in Chicago. That was my first introduction to winter outside of Southern California and Arizona.

I returned to Mount St. Mary's College as chair of the Department of Nursing and encouraged both faculty and student research projects. I initiated a grant program in which two grants of $500 each were given every summer for faculty to work on projects related to the implementation and teaching of the Roy model. Our first textbook on the subject,

Introduction to Nursing: An Adaptation Model, was published in 1976 and revised in 1984. Many faculty contributed to the literature reviews and clarifications of the four adaptive modes in each of these volumes.

The symptoms that I had suffered in 1967 and 1968 recurred for the next 12 years, but intermittently. In 1979 I was diagnosed as having an acoustic neuroma, which was successfully removed in October of that year. It took some time for me to "adapt" to right-sided hearing loss, tinnitus, and residual balance problems. I took a year's sabbatical leave and was able to complete a number of writing assignments, including the Roy and Roberts 1981 text *Theory Construction in Nursing: An Adaptation Model.* I continued to speak frequently, and increasingly my role in presentations was to set direction for the profession and to articulate the issues of the day.

The implementation of the Roy Adaptation Model in nursing education was wide-spread, and now hundreds of schools are using this approach to undergraduate curricula, as well as in teaching nurses at the graduate level. Several schools have awarded me honorary doctorates because of the contribution the model has made to their own programs and nursing in their regions. Recently I was reading a section of a doctoral dissertation in which the author surveyed a small group of schools who use the Roy Adaptation Model in preparation for designing an educational research project. It was an overwhelming experience for me to read the statistic that, in this representative group of 26 schools, already approximately 6,500 graduates have passed through the Roy Model programs.

In 1980 I began to speak in other countries. In January of that year, just three months after my craniotomy, I was the keynote speaker each day at the first French-speaking conference on nursing theory in Geneva, Switzerland. On the same trip I traveled to Paris for a one-day conference. My mother traveled with me, and we had the opportunity to also visit Florence, Assisi, and Rome. Other significant travels have been to South America, where I gave a short conference in Lima, Peru, and taught in the graduate program in nursing in Concepcion, Chile.

I had the unique opportunity to know the kindness of the people in Concepcion through an unusual experience. My traveling companion was Dr. Rose McKay, a professor at the University of Colorado. Dr. McKay was on sabbatical leave and wanted to do some international travel, and thus I had invited her to help me with an unusually heavy schedule. Dr. McKay died of a heart attack on the first day we were to start teaching in Concepcion.

Although I had known Rose for about 15 years and worked with her on the Western Interstate Commission for Higher Education in Nursing, I knew her best as we traveled in the last 10 days of her life. She thoroughly enjoyed the adventures and experiences of the trip. In Cusco, Peru, Rose had taken care of me when I had a severe headache from the altitude.

The nursing faculty from the University of Concepcion, particularly Maria Figuroa, were extremely helpful and wonderfully sensitive throughout the ordeal of arranging for Rose's funeral in Chile and then sending her home to the United States to her sister in Washington, D.C. Lifelong friendships were formed then. I also found that I was able to handle the rigors of the teaching, conference, and consultation assignments while grieving for Rose. That convinced me that I had finally mastered the neurological deficits and aftereffects of acoustic neuroma surgery.

Since that time, I have also traveled in the Scandinavian countries, giving an eight-day conference in Malmo, Sweden, for nurse leaders of Denmark, Norway, Sweden, and Finland. I have also spent time at the Royal College of Nursing in London, at the University of Ulster in Northern Ireland, and at the University of Edinburgh in Scotland. My inter-national travels have been a rich experience in all ways. I continue to marvel at what our colleagues overseas are able to do.

Another highlight of my foreign travels was a trip to the Holy Land for the Inter-national Council of Nurses meeting in the summer of 1985. There I talked with nurses who said their most difficult job was to help young children sit quietly for long hours in a bomb shelter in a kibbutz located near the Lebanese border. The most profound ex-periences for me there were being in a boat on the Sea of Galilee and standing in the River Jordan.

An important experience in my growth in nursing education was serving on faculty at the University of Portland in Oregon from 1977 to 1983. During that time we established a master of science program in nursing with a strong basis in advanced practice in the community—both in primary care and in care of the community as aggregate. It was during this time that the idea of clinical comparisons of nursing models in advanced practice was developed. This work, initially implemented in San Francisco and Portland, Oregon, compared three nursing models—the Orem, the Roy, and the Rogers—in four areas of advanced practice: critical care, care of the elderly, primary care, and community. This will become a multistate project and will include the northeastern, midwestern, and southern regions of the country.

My graduate classes at the University of Portland served as the testing ground for some of those initial ideas, and my colleagues took part in the process of developing them.

In the spring of 1983 I was selected as one of the first Robert Wood Johnson Clinical Nurse Scholars and did postdoctoral work in neuroscience nursing in the Department of Physiological Nursing at the University of California at San Francisco. I had become convinced of the need for postdoctoral studies in nursing. When the RWJ program was announced, I applied immediately, since a clinical and research focus seemed most ap-propriate in furthering the work I had pursued throughout my years in nursing education. The competition for the first nine fellowships was high, but I saw the experience as an opportunity to raise my work to a whole new level. The national advisory board members who selected the fellows apparently were convinced of this, too. In retrospect, I can say that .t the time I did not fully realize those implications.

I selected neuroscience as my field of study, since I felt that this rapidly developing science would provide for knowledge development of the holistic person, or in terms of the Roy Adaptation Model, the interrelationship of cognator and regulator activity. My familiarity with this clinical area had increased throughout the 15 years of my own neurological difficulties and surgical treatment.

The next two years were exciting—at times exhausting. I was immersed in the world of basic and clinical neurosciences under the mentorship of Dr. Connie Robinson. Again, as in my master's work at UCLA with Dorothy Johnson, I was extremely fortunate in the selection of my advisor. Dr. Robinson is a PhD-prepared neurophysiologist, an expert clinician in advanced neuroscience nursing, and a keen scientist. She had herself done postdoctoral work at MIT and at the University of Alabama. Quickly I focused my work on the cognitive recovery of head injury patients. I completed a descriptive study of 50 such patients over a six-month span. My clinical practice was in neurosurgery, neurotrauma critical care, and outpatient neuro-oncology. Being an advanced practitioner in neuroscience nursing has greatly enriched my writing and speaking on theory and research.

At the end of my postdoctoral studies I remained in San Francisco to conduct a pilot study of interventions for cognitive recovery in minor head injury, funded by the American Nurses' Foundation. I maintained a part-time academic appointment in the Department of Physiological Nursing and taught in all departments of the school as a guest lecturer. Concurrently I taught nursing theory courses in the graduate programs at the University of San Francisco and at Boston College.

I have enjoyed living in San Francisco with all its cultural richness. The weather has been generally cooler than in Southern California and my time for outdoor activities more limited. However, on a clear day I can enjoy beautiful sunsets over the Pacific Ocean through the back window of the house where I live. My ties to my religious community remain important to me, and I value greatly sharing with my sister friends and attending regional and province-wide activities as often as I can.

In July 1986 I accepted a full-time clinical research appointment in the Department of Neurosurgery, University of California at San Francisco. I have worked with the chief of neurosurgery at San Francisco General Hospital, Dr. Lawrence Pitts, have been involved in an outcome-of-coma study with patients who have had severe head injury, and have also worked on an experimental drug trial for spinal cord injury. This position provided me the opportunity to explore the interface of science and ethics as well as to enhance my advanced clinical and research skills with neuro patients.

Those last four years of clinical research were invaluable, and I thoroughly enjoyed them. However, I became convinced that I needed to share my convictions about the integration of theory, practice, and research with new nurse scholars. I had been acting as a consultant on a project for a new doctoral program at Boston College for three or four years. The program is one that I very much believe in because of its focus on clinical judgment, ethics, and human life patterns and processes. Therefore I accepted a full-time faculty position as professor in nursing theory for the new PhD program at Boston College in the fall of 1987. The new program is now under way, and I have great hopes for continuing the direction of developing nursing knowledge based on my particular conceptual approach to nursing.

The academic and clinical resources of the Boston area are rich for continuing my clinical research in cognitive processing. Since I believe there is more work yet to be done in nursing knowledge development with the Roy Adaptation Model in particular, I expect that the next 20 years will be full and rewarding. This is, in my opinion, the greatest growth period in the history of nursing. I am privileged to be a part of that, and I look forward to encouraging many other nurse scholars to do the same.

REFERENCE

Johnson, D.E.: Symposium on theory development
in nursing. Theory in nursing: borrowed and
unique. *Nursing Research* **17**:206-9, May-June
1968.

Rozella M. Schlotfeldt

Rozella M. Schlotfeldt, PhD, RN, FAAN,
is Professor and Dean Emerita,
Case Western Reserve University, Cleveland, Ohio

❖

Rozella Schlotfeldt's early life was arduous, but to her it was full and happy as well. Her experience with the Army Nurse Corps in World War II taught her how to set strategy, organize, and communicate promptly and efficiently. Her respect for the human spirit and the will to survive were deepened through the care of victims of war.

After graduate school under the GI Bill, she went to Colorado and helped turn the oldest diploma program west of the Mississippi into a unit of the University of Colorado's School of Nursing.

She earned her doctorate at the University of Chicago and then returned to Wayne State University. One is taken through her personal and professional experiences to her appointment as dean at the Frances Payne Bolton School of Nursing, Western Reserve University. There she developed the collaboration model by combining clinical teaching, practice, and research, the ND (nursing doctorate) as the first professional degree, and the paradigm she believes offers an approach to identifying the human needs nurses must be concerned with.

*B*eing a future-oriented person, I find it difficult to write a treatise that requires a backward look to recount influences on my development and to assess my professional contributions. Therefore I will provide an apt and currently accurate characterization of myself and engage in introspection to identify antecedents to that characterization.

I consider myself to be an able, idealistic, impatient, courageous, conservative visionary who has enjoyed a rewarding personal life and nursing career. In some ways advantaged and in some ways deprived as a child, I was born and reared in a small Iowa town (2,000 population) and was influenced by the values espoused in my home and community— ambition, hard work, self-reliance, integrity, and the love of nature and learning.

My father, a business college graduate, owned a prosperous business. His career abruptly ended at age 38 when he died of influenza and pneumonia for which there was then no known effective treatment. My mother was widowed at age 34. I was just past four and my sister was six.

My mother had enrolled in a hospital school of nursing following graduation (with honors) from high school and had almost completed her training when she developed typhoid fever. She had a long convalescence, following which she married and was thus not permitted to complete her program of study. However, private duty nursing afforded her the opportunity to support her family while my sister and I were cared for primarily by our maternal grandmother.

The maternal figures influential in my life were models of intelligent, ambitious, courageous, multitalented women. Both my mother and grandmother conveyed the unmistakable message in deed and word that learning was highly valued and that anything could be attained if one worked hard enough. My mother had a magnificent ability to show her pride and to praise our accomplishments, whether mundane or quite important. Simultaneously, she gave us the clear message that, with greater application of our talents and capabilities, we could have accomplished more. I have been guided by her philosophy that anything worthwhile can be achieved and also by my grandmother's oft-repeated, colloquial expression of values, "Right will out!"

Throughout my career, my midwestern conservatism has led me to envision futures for my profession and for myself and to test them thoroughly through discussion and thought prior to embarking on approaches to their attainment. Some of my ideas were likely quite visionary, but to me they were simply possible and right, even though sometimes they were neither timely nor in line with prevailing thought.

Whatever contributions I have made to nursing's future have been guided by the firm conviction that nursing is an essential human service that must become a uniformly beneficial, consequential, and respected profession whose practitioners have mastered vast amounts of professional knowledge that they wisely, skillfully, humanely, and ethically apply. Sound programs of professional education, led by scholars who teach, model exemplary practice, and engage in significant, systematic inquiry to advance professional knowledge, provide the means for achieving that end. My professional career has been devoted to testing and demonstrating approaches that promised to see my goals reached. I have been involved in practice, teaching, research, and other scholarly endeavors and in giving leadership designed to create climates in which creative teaching, contemplative and skillful practice, and scholarship are valued, exemplified, and rewarded. Most of my career has been devoted to work associated with responsibilities of a faculty member (and administrator) in nursing schools operating under the aegis of major research universities. However, my work in direct patient care and in leadership positions in a university and in a U.S. Veterans Administration hospital, and as a member of the Army Nurse Corps during World War II, remarkably influenced my ideas and later work. So did my family, friends, and associates.

CHILDHOOD EXPERIENCES

My early life was happy and full. I recall, with pleasure, learning to cook, bake, clean, sew, crochet, assist with gardening, and gather and assist with preserving fruits and vegetables, even as a small child. My sister and I regularly did chores so that we could enjoy particular outings and rewards. We spent one summer sightseeing in Colorado and then several weeks on a ranch. Most summers my sister and I had long "vacations" on a farm with a childless couple, friends of my parents, whom we called uncle and aunt. There we learned the multiple joys of farm life and helped cook and serve sumptuous meals to large groups of farmhands and neighbors who assembled to assist in threshing grain and picking corn during abundant harvests. "Uncle Jack" taught us to dance to the music of a fiddle, organ, and horn while we enjoyed the farmhouse parties that were then often held in the rural midwest. I also recall helping to bottle and cap the "home brew" (much to my mother's consternation) that provided libation for those parties and for huge Independence Day picnics.

School provided a series of great experiences. I was an eager learner and a good student. My mother arranged for my sister and me to have piano lessons, but those lessons were wasted on me. When I was asked to select a different instrument, I chose drums. From sixth grade through high school, I played drums in the school's orchestra and band. I also sat in occasionally with a pickup dance band, but I preferred dancing to drumming. Encouraged as I was to partake of all opportunities for extracurricular activities, I sang in the glee club, was active in class plays, and competed in public speaking contests.

I was expected to work while I was in high school in order to earn spending money and pay for some of my clothing. I worked in a local store and sweetshop, cared for children, and "sat" quite regularly with a handicapped woman when her caretaker sister was on vacation or needed relief for evenings away from her home. I also earned prize money in baking, preserving, crocheting, and embroidery contests at the county fair. I learned to value working, saving, and investing during my childhood. I was graduated from high school prior to my seventeenth birthday and was eager to prepare for a career.

GETTING READY

I never seriously considered any career except nursing, although I completed typing, shorthand, and bookkeeping classes in high school in addition to college preparatory courses. By virtue of having been named class valedictorian, I was offered a scholarship to a liberal arts college that had recently launched a program leading to an undergraduate degree in nursing. The superintendent of our school suggested that I not accept the proffered scholarship until I had investigated the five-year baccalaureate program offered by the State University of Iowa. I shall be forever grateful to that kind and wise educator who took me to Iowa City so I could investigate that nursing program. Being sensitive to the uncertain economic circumstances in 1931 (our local banks closed a few weeks after I began my program of university study), he advised that I investigate opportunities to become a student live-in helper. The university-approved homes provided room and board for students in exchange for 21 hours of work each week.

It was my good fortune to live in the home of a young, growing family while I pursued the liberal arts portion of a first-rate education. There I had magnificent opportunities to learn much about child development and rearing from a well-educated, wise mother of twin boys. It was also my privilege to observe the twins' younger brother who was born after my arrival in Iowa City and to experience life with a complete family. With them I established treasured friendships that were sustained for many years. In 1973 the parents served as my surrogate family during the several events scheduled for those honored by the University of Iowa's Distinguished Service Award. In 1984 I visited the mother and one of the middle-aged twins who came to see her while I was visiting. Experiences I had while living with that family had a very positive influence on my development as a professional.

The University of Iowa's five-year, combined liberal arts and nursing program required completion of a minimum of 90 semester hours of liberal education and a two-year, in-residence nursing program. By carrying a heavy academic schedule, I was able to complete additional liberal arts courses in two academic years and two summer terms and graduated (magna cum laude) after completing a program of study that extended over four calendar years. I have since been a devotee of flexibility of regulations governing students' combining work and study. In my view, it is inappropriate to curtail ambition.

I enjoyed the nursing major as much as I had enjoyed classes taught by the university's distinguished scientists and humanists in the liberal arts. Preclinical science courses were taught by science professors from the medical school, and some of those classes were shared by medical students. Teaching responsibilities for clinical courses were shared by medical and nursing professors, with medical department heads frequently assuming major teaching assignments. All nursing professors held dual responsibilities—for nursing education and for leadership in their respective specialty departments in the university hospitals. Each clinical service provided a series of exciting learning opportunities, with my assessment of the one I enjoyed most changing regularly to the one I was currently experiencing.

The nursing school and hospital initiated several studies and many innovations that I later learned were then not standard operations elsewhere. In maternity nursing, for example, soap and water cleansing had supplanted the ritualistic breast and perineal care (quite common elsewhere) when bacterial studies provided evidence that the former was efficacious and other studies documented time and money savings. Empirical evidence concerning reduction in the incidence of postpartal thrombophlebitis, following the institution of graduated, required exercises for mothers, led to a nursing routine that was the forerunner of what is now called "early ambulation." I think I grew to appreciate and value documented evidence and the decentralization of responsibility and authority for operation of a clinical nursing department during my student experiences at Iowa.

BEGINNING A LONG CAREER

Immediately after graduation I became a maternity staff nurse at the University of Iowa Hospitals. In 1935 such opportunities were not abundant, both because nursing students were still relied on for service (one-half day off duty per week, after the probationary period) and because the economic plight of hospitals persisted after the Great Depression of 1929. Staff nursing was a relatively new phenomenon, and salaries for nurses were low ($60 per month, with board and a dormitory room provided).

Within a few months a former classmate and I, attracted by the advertised $90 per month salary (room and board in addition) and burdened by financial obligations for our education, completed a civil service examination to compete for staff nurse positions in the U.S. Veterans Administration system of hospitals. When my letter of appointment came, I readily accepted the available position in Des Moines. There I had a series of rewarding experiences, including working with nurse-veterans from World War I. My horizons were widened remarkably by their accounts of war experiences, by working in a federal hospital system, and through extensive travels that were made possible by the relatively liberal vacation policy of the VA.

I recall vividly the first experimental use of antibiotics and the cautious introduction of early ambulation for postsurgical patients. I recall also, with revulsion, my experiences with implanting maggots into traumatized, infected extremities of veterans. I had to comfort them while changing their dressings, removing the thriving maggots, and irrigating the wounds following periods of such debridement with live insects. That was in 1936 and 1937. I enjoyed my work at the VA hospital and learned a great deal from varied experiences, although I missed caring for mothers and infants and the stimulation of a university environment.

After practicing two and one half years in the VA hospital, I was invited to return to the University of Iowa School of Nursing and University Hospitals as instructor-supervisor of maternity nursing, contingent on my completion of a postgraduate program of study offered by the New York Hospital. (The medical chiefs of obstetrics at Iowa and the New York Hospital had been trained at Johns Hopkins; I am confident that the former influenced the choice of institution in which I was asked to study.) At that time (1938), the only available "advanced" programs in clinical nursing were offered under the aegis of hospitals, sometimes affiliated with nursing and medical schools. The New York Hospital then provided clinical learning opportunities for Cornell University nursing and medical students.

It was indeed my good fortune to have lived and studied in New York in the late 1930s. The New York Hospital provided myriad learning opportunities. In addition to a plethora of clinical phenomena, the hospital clientele represented a wide variety of ethnic and social backgrounds, providing new experiences for someone from the rural Midwest. I also had my first community nursing experiences in New York, some with home health nurses from the Visiting Nurse Service, the Maternity Center, and the Margaret Sanger Clinic. In 1938 New York City was quite safe for solo exploration, and its wonders were abundant. Bus and subway transportation was cheap, as were Broadway and off-Broadway productions, performances of the ballet, and a host of events at Madison Square Garden An endless variety of restaurants offered strange and wonderful culinary delights from around the world. Anticipating a further stimulating, rewarding, and varied nursing career, I returned to Iowa City in 1939. I recall the railway agent's response when I sought to purchase a one-way ticket to Iowa City. He looked at me over the rims of his glasses and asked, with wonder, "A one-way ticket, young lady?"

Serving as an instructor-supervisor in an active maternity unit within a university medical center that served as a referral hospital for the entire state and accommodated the learning needs of 25 to 30 basic nursing students each 12 weeks provided tremendous challenges and opportunities. The dual appointment responsibilities included both classroom and clinical instruction, in-service education for the nursing staff, and periodic orientation to the department for new groups of medical students and residents. It also included planning for and managing equipment, supplies, and records, as well as making staff schedules for the department (prenatal, postpartal, labor, delivery, nurseries, and offices where senior staff physicians cared for private patients). Since there were few registered nurses to whom responsibilities could be delegated, the dual appointment responsibilities were truly demanding in a busy service whose client care needs were quite unpredictable, were frequently of an emergency nature, and were in widely diverse and separated locales. Personal experience with dual appointment responsibilities undoubtedly initiated my thinking about better ways to combine teaching and practice while experimenting with creative approaches that held promise for improving nursing care.

My plans for graduate study, which would prepare me more adequately for a leadership position, were delayed by the advent of World War II. Soon after the war began, nurses holding teaching positions were declared "essential" for preparing enhanced numbers of nurses for both military and civilian service. Although I had sought to be released from teaching responsibilities earlier, that opportunity did not come until the departmental census dropped remarkably when the military dependents' program became fully operative. I entered military service in the Army Nurse Corps in early 1944 and quickly learned that one who had specialized in maternity nursing would not cease to be a generalist practitioner. New adventures awaited.

After completing basic training and a brief period of service in a stateside hospital for the usual staging preparation, our general hospital unit was mobilized and sailed to England en route to the European mainland. There was something ludicrous about going ashore in PT boats and being transported in army trucks to the Grand Hotel of Paris, where we set up our first temporary hospital. When we arrived, the music of Glenn Miller's band emanated from the Winter Garden Ballroom, where some weary soldiers were enjoying relaxation and rehabilitation, while others who were injured but ambulatory (the hotel lifts would not accommodate litters) were cared for by health professionals in hotel rooms transformed into minor surgery and treatment suites. They subsequently recuperated in beautifully appointed rooms and rested on beds covered with satin puffs. Our stay in Paris was short lived but busy. We soon moved to Soissons, where our general hospital was operative in a partially destroyed French Army barracks, which had been restored by U.S. troops and was quite functional.

Volunteering for service in the China-Burma-India theater took me to Marseilles on the first leg of that journey; while I awaited moving orders, VJ Day ended the war. The remainder of my military service was spent in a station hospital near Salzburg, Austria, as a member of the Army of Occupation.

As I reminisce about the influence of military service on my subsequent career, I think of the respect I gained for the military's ability to strategize, organize, and execute with a predetermined plan of operation that was communicated promptly and efficiently to all who had need to know it in order to make it operative. The unfailing cooperation of all those who knew and subscribed to an agreed-upon, immediate purpose or long-range goal was largely responsible for the demonstrated excellence of operation of all parts of the whole, even under extreme danger and hardship. I have ever since tried to be an effective communicator.

Under the stress of caring for the war's ill and wounded, I gave little conscious thought to the development of theoretical notions about nursing. I vividly recall, however, the deepened respect I gained for the inherent abilities of human beings to survive and become restored. I also respected the need for nurses to learn more about those human assets in order to develop strategies that would be reliable and useful in helping people to achieve those ends they so fervently sought. I pondered over the human spirit, which manifests itself among ill and injured people as evidence of an innate spirituality and is exemplified as verve, determination, resolve, and courage. It is the will to survive, heal, win, and overcome with which human beings are so magnificently endowed.

PREPARING FOR LEADERSHIP

Following discharge from military service and a brief general duty nursing assignment, I took advantage of the GI Bill and enrolled for graduate study in nursing at the University of Chicago. A planned career in nursing education and administration caused me to select that major program of study, following which I accepted an appointment as assistant professor of nursing at the University of Colorado. There, I discovered an unusual set of opportunities.

Shortly after my arrival, plans were completed to shut down the oldest hospital-operated school of nursing west of the Mississippi River, the Denver General Hospital School of Nursing, which was under the aegis of the municipal hospital. That school was to be replaced by a unit of the University of Colorado's School of Nursing, operative at the Denver General Hospital and school sites. Henrietta Laughran, then dean of the University of Colorado school, asked me to serve as her deputy to effect that change. I learned more that year about the human relationships aspect of administration than I shall ever again. I have been grateful to Dean Laughran for providing that experience, as well as for sharing her enlightened leadership prowess.

A plan was carefully drawn to make it possible for first- and second-year students in the diploma program to enroll in the university and to be graduated after completing requirements for the baccalaureate. Alternatively, they could complete the diploma program, with elimination of the university option, after two years. We also made it possible for faculty teaching in the diploma program to be granted, or to qualify for and subsequently receive, university appointments. I recall endless meetings with students, alumni representatives, faculty, nursing service staff, secretarial and library personnel, and numerous university and hospital administrators to effect a smooth transition in a situation that was not accepted by many of those most affected by it.

My respect for, and interest in, administration deepened remarkably as a consequence of my experiences at the University of Colorado. Those experiences were, I suspect, largely responsible for my differentiating administration from management, a distinction that is frequently blurred or denied. I perceive administration to be ministering to people in an operating enterprise—supporting and assisting them to achieve their own goals while maximizing the particular contributions that each makes or can make to the organization. Management, I believe, is being accountable for control of inanimate things—facilities, supplies, equipment, budgets, and the like. Both, of course, are responsibilities of those holding leadership positions in operative organizations. Successful administrators are skilled as administrators and also good as managers, and they know and respect the differences between those responsibilities.

It was possible for me to teach baccalaureate and master's candidates at the University of Colorado, which I had originally planned to do, but the administrative responsibilities precluded my fulfilling that goal. Thus with mixed emotions, I resigned at Colorado to accept an assistant professorship at the College of Nursing, Wayne University, Detroit.

The college was one of only a few whose dean and faculty were demonstrating that it was not necessary for a university to own and operate a hospital in order to offer first-rate programs of nursing education. That was a time when educators were critical of the exploitation of students and faculty that allegedly occurred in some settings, and the slogan of leaders in education was to "separate nursing education from nursing service."

At Wayne, nursing students were provided clinical learning opportunities in several hospitals and community health nursing agencies, in all of which agency nursing staffs were responsible for nursing care. I recall some of the strengths of that system, as well as the laments of the faculty about their inability to influence the clinical environments in which students learned to practice. The Wayne faculty responded to that discontent when Professor Irene Beland and her associates developed a "Wayne unit," wherein faculty and students demonstrated exemplary nursing care in one of the cooperating hospitals. Empirical evidence of the success of that demonstration was provided by attending physicians who, in increasing numbers, competed for beds to accommodate their patients on that Wayne unit. I became convinced that, whereas dual appointments were fraught with problems, faculty and students could not and should not become substitute agency personnel; neither was it satisfactory to deny faculty members' responsibility for the effectiveness of the environments in which students learned to practice and to engage in systematic inquiry. I began to think about models for relating an educational institution and the multiple-service agencies essential for preparing professionals.

My primary responsibilities at Wayne included teaching students enrolled in courses in teaching, curriculum development, evaluation, administration, and research design and methods. In the early 1950s nursing research was in its infancy. Only a few nurses had completed doctoral study, and even fewer were active investigators. Women were then not abundantly represented as students in programs of doctoral study; indeed, they were usually not welcomed in the basic sciences. Most nurses who sought doctoral study selected programs in education. At Wayne a plan was developed for several interested faculty members to have educational leaves of absence (without salary) on a rotation basis.

In the summer of 1952 I began my program of PhD study in education at the University of Chicago. I completed five quarters of course work, the preliminary examinations, and the language examinations before returning to Wayne. I remained there until 1955, when I resigned to complete requirements for the PhD. I was graduated in December 1956. My dissertation, "The Educational Leadership Role of Nursing School Executives and Faculty Satisfaction," was undoubtedly an expression of my own career aspirations. I returned to Wayne (then Wayne State University) to a newly created position—associate dean for research and development.

Credit for that appointment is surely due Dean Katharine Faville, who sanctioned a program of research development for faculty, strengthened the research component of the master's program, and initiated clinical research by interested faculty members. Dean Faville miraculously found funding to support several college-sponsored investigations that were completed by my colleagues and me and were reported in nursing's research literature.

During the middle and late 1950s the nursing profession made a strong commitment to research. Grants from both private and public sources increasingly became available for research training for nurses and for nursing research. At that time many leadership positions were available to nurses who had completed doctoral study. The opportunity that seemed uniquely suited to my own career aspirations came in early 1960, when I was invited by President John S. Millis to accept the position of dean and professor of nursing at the Frances Payne Bolton School of Nursing at Western Reserve University. I had some ideas concerning needed changes in nursing education that I wanted to share and test. I made several return visits to the Western Reserve campus to ascertain the readiness of the school's faculty, the leaders in other components of the Health Sciences Center, and the university to support the experimentation I envisioned. When I became convinced that a unique opportunity in leadership could be mine with the support of President Millis, I accepted the proffered position and joined another higher education institution that was destined to undergo a remarkable restructuring within a few years.*

---

*In 1967, Western Reserve University and Case Institute of Technology became a federated institution known as Case Western Reserve University, after completion of a long and detailed study reported in the publication *Vision for the Future.*

From 1960 through June 1972 I served as dean and professor of nursing, during which time a detailed "Plan for Progress" was developed and was given positive sanction by the school's faculty, by President Millis, and by administrators in other units of the Health Sciences Center. The plan was implemented, and evidence was gained concerning its efficacy. The components of that plan were at several stages of development and implementation simultaneously and thus were inexorably interrelated. Each component deserves brief comment, for I suspect they are judged to represent my contributions to nursing. To me, they were appropriate, promising changes that needed to be made in the educational system of an emerging profession. They were challenges to me, and I was eager to give leadership through which the profession could make needed progress.

THE COLLABORATION MODEL

I designed the collaboration model as a promising, rational approach to relating a nursing school with any and all health care agencies required for fulfilling the clinical teaching, research, and practice responsibilities of faculty. It was my response to the shortcomings of the dual appointment phenomenon for clinical nursing leaders in a system that denied faculty opportunities to have direct influence on the quality of clinical learning and research environments required for fulfilling their responsibilities.

The model recognizes the *interdependence* of university schools preparing health professionals and agencies providing health care; it also respects and safeguards their inherent differences in priorities (education/service), in orientation (future/present), and in primary modes of operation (contemplative/immediate action). It recognizes also the goals the two types of institutions share—excellence of learning opportunities for students and staff, exemplary programs of care, and systematic inquiry that provides knowledge for improvements in the practice of professionals. Details of the collaboration model and its discovered merits are discussed elsewhere. Suffice it to say here that experience demonstrated that it was sound, workable, and efficacious. Implementation of the model facilitated the attainment of goals shared by pairs of institutions. Several major programs of clinical nursing research were developed while faculty and staff members (several jointly appointed) demonstrated excellent nursing care and offered fine programs of professional nursing education.

A NURSING PARADIGM

The programs of nursing education—professional, clinical specialties, and research (PhD)—were influenced by my conceptual model of nursing that was initially published as a paradigm for guiding nursing research. That paradigm is this: nursing is the appraisal and enhancement of the health status, health assets, and health potential of human beings and the preservation of the dignity appropriate to their humanity.

Although it is not yet widely influential, I believe that nurses will eventually come to accept the succinct definition of nursing that I present and will recognize that the paradigm offers an approach to identifying the human phenomena that are of particular concern to nurses, about which theories should be propounded and tested as an approach to advancing nursing's body of knowledge. I continue to think and write about my definition and paradigm with the intent of capturing the critical interest of increasing numbers of colleagues.

A NEW APPROACH TO PREPARING PROFESSIONALS

Throughout the last half of my career I have been concerned that professionals do not control the system of nursing education. As a consequence, programs of education whose faculties claim they are preparing professionals are widely disparate. No representative group has effective control over requirements such as a base of subject matter that *all* aspiring nursing professionals must master and be able to use selectively, wisely, humanely, and ethically before being recommended for licensure. Influential nurses and others have been successful in mandating *minimal* amounts of disparate subject matter (both liberal and professional) that nursing candidates must master, even though the complexities of nursing practice grow ever more apparent, and relevant knowledge becomes more abundant.

A prevailing notion is that nursing is a set of simple tasks whose accomplishment requires minimal knowledge, skills, and judgment. It seemed imperative to me that a recognized leadership school had to take the initiative to demonstrate that nursing is a complex, demanding, rewarding profession that can attract liberally educated intellectuals who are willing to master vast amounts of professional knowledge and skills and to internalize professional values unique to nursing in order to serve fellow human beings.

If indeed nursing is a profession (it is) and a recognized academic discipline (it is), then the preparation of professionals known as nurses requires professional education comparable to that provided for other health professionals. That thinking, coupled with experience, led me to share my ideas concerning preservice nursing education for professionals with large numbers of actual and potential nursing students and colleagues in several nursing schools and nursing practice agencies. I then suggested that my Case Western Reserve University faculty colleagues design and implement a preservice program of nursing education that would merit the award of the professional doctorate, the ND degree. After several years of study, that recommendation to the school's faculty was approved, and the existing baccalaureate in nursing program was supplanted by the ND program beginning in the fall of 1978 under the leadership of Dean Jannetta MacPhail. National forums providing opportunities for other faculties to study the program and to explore the concept have been initiated by the current dean of the school, Joyce J. Fitzpatrick.

I was gratified when my Case Western Reserve University colleagues perceived the significance of the proposal that the ND program be first offered by the school with which I had so long been associated and which had become recognized for its several innovations. I truly believe that the corporate profession's leaders will come to recognize the ND as the appropriate symbol of accomplishment for the first professional degree in nursing.

I resigned the deanship in 1972 and continued to be an active professor through 1982. During three years of that time I led a feasibility study that culminated in the incorporation and continued functioning of the nation's first multistate consortium of all types of existing nursing education institutions and nursing departments of a wide variety of health care agencies—the Midwest Alliance in Nursing (MAIN). I served as MAIN's interim director for its first year of operation. Credit for that idea must be given to a small group of midwestern deans of nursing schools who conjointly designed the study. I was privileged to be a part of that innovation—an idea that has influenced the development of other such regional nursing agencies in the United States.

In 1982 I retired from Case Western Reserve University. Since then, I have served as a visiting professor in several of the nation's prestigious universities and as a consultant, speaker, and author. In 1985 I returned to the University of Iowa to celebrate the fiftieth anniversary of my graduation from that great institution. I have enjoyed and continue to enjoy a most exciting and rewarding profession. In fact, I seem not to be able to relinquish my involvement. One of my high school classmates calls me the consummate careerist. His characterization is as apt as my own.

Doris R. Schwartz

Doris R. Schwartz, MA, RN, FAAN is Senior Fellow,
University of Pennsylvania School of Nursing

❖

Doris Schwartz learned in nursing school to keep records and to set goals, and excerpts from daily entries in her journals make this journey through her nursing career absorbing. This habit, which she learned early and well and carried out meticulously, elicits envy from those of us who did not discipline ourselves to write each day to document growth and achievement.

Her World War II experiences from the front are vividly recorded, and they influenced her later career in public health nursing. She loved working in Red Hook, a work site which grew out of combining "the district of Brooklyn's great Visiting Nurse Association with New York City's outstanding Department of Health." Her work as a geriatric nurse practitioner in what she calls a wonderful amalgam of gerontological nursing and public health has continued in the life care community where she now makes her home.

Included here is Doris's charming poem first published in the **American Journal of Nursing** *in 1979. It is the only reference she makes to her early ambitions and career choice.*

At about the time that I entered nursing school in the late 1930s, I became aware of the work and the writing of that extraordinary philosopher, Dr. Albert Schweitzer, who had just returned to his jungle hospital in Africa after a long, enforced stay in Europe. My thinking about humanistic values has been influenced by Schweitzer throughout the whole of my career, and I want to write about the subject of this book against a background of three short quotations from his writings.

First (and remember that these were written many decades ago):

The spirit of this age dislikes what is simple. It no longer believes that the simple can be profound. It loves the complicated and regards it as profound.

Second:

Just as a tree bears, year after year, the same fruit which is each year new, so must all permanently valuable ideas be continually born again in our thought.

And third:

To the question whether I am a pessimist or an optimist, I answer that my knowledge is pessimistic but my will and my hope are optimistic.

Over the past two years I have been reviewing journals I kept during my 40-year career in active nursing. I have found treasures therein that reflect the interaction among patients, families, and nursing staff in a great variety of settings: within hospitals and patients' homes, in war and in peace, in urban areas and remotely rural ones, in the United States and in several other countries. Patients have been my greatest teachers throughout the years.

Why did I keep these journals? As student nurses, I and my classmates were taught to articulate our goals for each patient and for each clinical semester, noting the use of old concepts with which we were already familiar and the acquisition and use of new concepts that were built on the foundations of the old ones. Initially these journals were incorporated into case studies and something labeled "thought books." In practice they were a forerunner of what were later called "process records," and when reviewed over time they add up to a sort of personal growth chart—a chance to look at the personal and professional development of the nurse who kept one.

This assignment to record goals and priorities became a habit. For 40 years in every setting in which I have worked as a nurse, I have kept a journal. Some of my entries are considerably detailed, while others are rather sparse. The developmental record is there, however, and it clearly documents one fact: whatever the setting and however varied the job title or the sophistication of the technology involved, I never relinquished the humanistic values in nursing that I learned as a student. Each entry documents a new undertaking and better integration and expansion of priorities chosen in a previous experience. The values at the end of a long career are clearly imprinted with the influence of the earlier concepts. Perhaps that in itself is a useful thing for teachers to know about a student.

Those early concepts were not labeled "humanistic," of course, although they were sometimes called "comprehensive" goals. I think nurses simply thought of those values as "good nursing care."

No period in history has seen the technology of health care change as rapidly as it did in the 40 years between my student days and my retirement from active clinical nursing. Yet the habit of setting down goals and the priorities for attaining them can be as useful today as it was in the late 1930s. We nursing students of that era defended our options orally in what were then known as "bedside clinics" (antecedents of the clinical seminars of today), and we documented them in writing.

One concept we learned early was that patients were to be listened to and recognized as teachers. A memorable documentation of this is taken from a later portion of the journal, written when I was serving in the Army Nurse Corps.

While working nights in a busy, wartime barracks hospital with soldiers recently out of combat, I heard the padding of bare feet in the hall as a rather confused patient with combat fatigue walked sleepily toward the office. "Lieutenant," he said in a troubled voice, "could you get the goat out from under my bed?"

"The what?" I asked.

"Please, lieutenant. Get the goat out from under my bed."

None of my suggestions about shadows or dreams shook his certainty. "It looks like a goat, and it smells like a goat. And it's under my bed."

I brought him into the office, got him a glass of milk, and talked with him for a couple of minutes. "Would you feel better, Corporal, if I walked down to your bed with my flashlight so you can see there's nothing there?"

He thought that would be fine. We crept softly down the ward so as not to waken the others. Whispering a heartening, "See, Chavez, there isn't any goat," I threw the flashlight's beam beneath his bed. Two bright eyes looking up at us with interest from beneath a pair of well-shaped horns, not to mention a distinctly goatish odor, fortified my patient's claim. Mumbling, "Didn't think I could go crazy that quick," the soldier collapsed onto his bed and immediately fell asleep, leaving me in a ward full of snoring patients with a flashlight in one hand and a fistful of goat hair in the other.

Experience does help you to set priorities. Never say a patient's complaint is untrue until you've checked it out!

One of my most memorable teachers was the first dying patient I ever cared for. Under the supervision of my instructor, whose clinical skills were outstanding, I gave morning care to this fevered, dehydrated, dry-skinned old man in this last hour of life. I heard him say gratefully, "How did you know that could feel so good? Why didn't somebody do it sooner?" My instructor told me to stay with him—he was restlessly pulling at the bedclothes and was going to die very soon. She said that he needed to know that someone who cared was with him. That old man taught me a great deal in his last 60 minutes of life as I sat by his bedside. Sometimes we talked quietly; sometimes we were just there together without speaking.

By graduation time, I emerged with three convictions—three top priorities in nursing:

1. Patient care must be planned.
2. Patient care must be individualized.
3. Patient care must have continuity (around the clock and through calendar time). Though the personnel change, the patient needs to feel that he or she is the focus of one concerned, caring person.

By graduation, too, I had learned from Virginia Henderson's early writing that the nurse did for a patient, or taught him to do for himself, or taught a helping person to do for him those things which he would manage on his own if he was not a patient and had the knowledge of what was needed. And if death was inevitable, the nurse could help him die as he would want to die if he could control the situation. Virginia had not yet written her splendid booklet on basic nursing care that would be published by the International Council of Nurses, but her early textbooks were full of that empathic thinking.

In those long ago days, the pronoun *he* in a nursing text meant the patient and *she* meant the nurse. Some things were simpler, then.

At nursing school we were taught that from the time of the Old Testament or from the period of the ancient Greeks, it was not the prolongation of life but the prevention of untimely death and needless suffering that was the goal of health care. Only the technology—the know-how—had changed over the centuries, and all the know-how was useless without that concern for preventing untimely death and needless suffering. It was our job to do that.

It was called to our attention that patients who got better did a great service for the doctors and nurses responsible for their care. So the idea that caring personnel were human, too, was carefully inculcated. All of this was accomplished in a hospital school, at a time when there were few degree-granting basic programs of nursing in the entire country.

I don't remember hearing the term "professionalism" used very often while I was in nursing school. There wasn't much stress on it. We did learn Mary Follett's definition of a profession: "A profession requires a foundation of science and a motive of service." Our foundation of science may have been a little shaky, but Lordy, as undergraduates we did have a motive of service!

In the years 1943 to 1946, most of my classmates and I were exposed to a war. Spread across half the globe, we added to our earlier goals and priorities the concept: "Rehabilitation starts on day one." We learned new approaches to mass care, including the concept of "triage." We also learned to keep big situations small and personal. I quote from the journal, in wartime:

> This morning, as we walked from our quarters to the hospital, long lines of ambulances started rolling in (from the Overseas Air Evacuation planes). Painted with red crosses, they crept at a snail's pace along the rough dirt road to avoid jouncing. To be ready with an empty ward and watch them bring in the litters, forty-five at a time, provides one of the most dramatic sensations you could imagine. You expect almost anything to turn up, you never know what is coming

next. You can always count on the next hectic thirty minutes being absolutely packed with such an assortment of emotions as one would ordinarily experience in a whole lifetime. Pain, humor, courage, happiness, all appear at once and rather than merging into one big scene, they stand out as a dozen or more clear, distinct pictures flashing a whole story before you in an instant and then fading into the routine of a busy, hospital ward. . . .

You learn to size up situations so quickly, almost intuitively. One part of you says coolly, "Put that next patient into bed 3." He looks pathetically small on the stretcher, and you realize, suddenly, that both his legs are gone. The realization and the sharp stab of pain that it brings and the grin and the kidding remark that you toss at him are all separate thoughts and emotions. Yet all told, they don't occupy thirty seconds. Then you turn to the next stretcher and begin again.

While I carried out backbreaking wartime schedules, the early learning held. "Document your goals and plans in writing." I started to write for publication. Articles came straight out of the journals: "Nursing Care Can Be Measured," "Nursing Aboard a Hospital Ship," "Today, I Saw What a War Leaves in its Wake," "An Open Letter From the Army Nurse Corps," "For These, The War Is Not Over."

I emerged from that experience with new priorities and lived by two purposeful mottoes:

1. Let there be no more wars!
2. Let there be peace, and let it begin with me!

At long last, back home again, I could pursue my life's goal: to work in public health nursing in a combined nursing agency.

A combined nursing agency was the exciting postwar concept of melding what we think of today as public health nursing with the work of the traditional visiting nurse who gave hands-on care, as well as health teaching, within the patient's home—usually the homes of the poor.

From 1947 to 1951, I worked in one of those early amalgamations—the Red Hook Experiment. In that experiment, a district of Brooklyn's great Visiting Nurse Association joined forces with New York City's outstanding Department of Health in the Red Hook area along the waterfront. Just to name it makes me homesick for the project—for that missed opportunity in American nursing when, for a moment in time, it looked as if public health nurses in both official and voluntary agencies were going to become true primary practitioners of public health to an underserved population and offer a new kind of nurse to America.

Red Hook was the work site that influenced me more than any other, and it gave me my most joyous years in nursing. It was surely the program that most effectively met the needs of the families of the inner city and offered the richest experiences to the staff. Other cities copied it and found it good, but when money was scarce, society chose to do away with it and nursing let it go, almost without complaint. Red Hook was where I learned to transfer all my priorities from the patient to the family setting, from the family setting to the community. That was where I really came to understand that *the community was the patient* and learned to appreciate the public health engineers' insistence that every problem represents a watershed, that even when a problem is superficially similar in two districts, if one looked at all sides of the problem, one would be led to different solutions for it because in the natural or human ecology of the districts there would be significant differences.

It was Marion Sheehan (Bailey) who taught me the importance of that watershed concept, although I first heard it from Red Hook's sanitation officers. Marion, now 95 and almost blind, still writes to me occasionally, and I learn new ideas from her every letter.

It was in Red Hook that I learned to apply epidemiological concepts in clinical nursing during home visiting in Brooklyn's last polio epidemic.

Following the Red Hook experiment, I took my first teaching job in a clinical setting, with a joint appointment in public health, at the university's medical and nursing schools.

My goals and concepts kept expanding. I focused on teaching students to wonder and on developing interdisciplinary planning for patients, which I believed would lead to better patient care. I also became involved in small research projects—preresearch activities such as observing a series of cases to create a hypothesis for study. And there came more publications straight out of my journal: "Medication Errors Made by Older Patients" and "The Use of Health Literature for Clinic Patients."

After publication of the above articles, I received a grant that led to my first experience in independent research, which culminated in the book *The Elderly Ambulatory Patient: Nursing and Psychosocial Needs.*

My appointment to the nursing studies section of the National Institutes of Health after the publication of that book was a mind-stretching adventure. I was asked to conduct a 10-year follow-up study of the NIH's faculty research development grants at 17 universities. That study put me in contact for the first time with Rozella Schlotfeldt, then dean of the School of Nursing at Western Reserve. In that school of nursing, interdisciplinary goals were being set, not only with the physicians, but with sociologists and medical anthropologists as well.

It was also during that follow-up study that I was introduced to Cornell University's wonderful home care program on the Navajo Indian Reservation in Arizona. Here was a chance again to set goals and priorities through the case study method. I developed a comparative study of terminal care in two of Cornell's home care programs, focusing on two families from disparate cultures—one lived in an East Harlem tenement, the other in a Navajo hogan.

In both families the patients were old, dying of cancer, and being cared for by a family member and a public health nurse. The nursing help offered each family was for the most part accepted; however, in each situation at least one suggested treatment was omitted because it ran counter to the family's cultural beliefs.

Here is my journal account of the family situations:

> Culture played a part, although only a part, in the behavior of both these families, in a time of terminal illness. One common factor was the extent to which the two families, low on the economic scale by any standards, strapped themselves financially to provide handsomely for the deceased. The Italian family went heavily into debt to provide an elaborate funeral for the father. Two carloads of flowers led the procession to the church and cemetery and this, plus the expense of a richly finished coffin, gave great solace to the daughter who had accepted

responsibility for the father's care, and to her sick mother for whom the daughter was still caring, although their own living expenses were sharply curtailed by it during the final months of the mother's life.

The Navajo family provided a satin comforter and new, woolen blankets for their patient to be buried in, although their use was prohibited to warm and comfort her while she was dying, cold and shivering in the chilled night air. After her death, the husband asked the nurse to place his red purse with all his ready cash on the body, as she prepared the body for burial. The patient's turquoise and silver jewelry, which represented most of the family's possessions, were buried with her.

Charon, the boatman, was a familiar figure in ancient Greek mythology, the one who ferried souls across the river Styx to the underworld of Hades. The common custom was to place coins in the mouth of the deceased so that he could pay his fare across.

Neither our Arizona Navajo nor our East Harlem Italian family had ever heard of Charon the boatman, yet both in the way of their culture followed a similar custom, at the cost of providing for the living.

Conversation with an anthropologist and a doctor, who like ourselves rotated from one Cornell teaching home care program to the other, made all of us realize that one of the greatest problems in bringing health care services to such families is the refusal of some professionals, either through ignorance or scorn, to recognize the peculiar conditions under which care must operate. Persons from one culture tend to view another culture in terms of their own. Variations are seen as oddities to be ignored or reserved for conversational anecdotes and the whole complex of custom and behavior is put out of consciousness. In the end, ignorance of the customs results in confusion, inactivity or frustration, and the care plan breaks down because of blocked communication, lack of response, or antagonism.

The concepts gained through this experience are quoted directly from the journal:

When a nurse is giving care to a family whose lifestyle is molded by a different culture, the underlying beliefs which influence behavior can often be identified either by the care-giver or the recipient of care. But sometimes they cannot, or at least cannot at the time when nursing is required.

We believe ["we" means Jean French and myself—the two nurses who gave the care in these two family situations] that even when the explanation cannot be surfaced and validated, respect for the personhood of patient and family makes it possible to establish and continue a relationship that permits the nurse to give effective care while continuing to search for the cause of behavior. That respect for personhood we believe to be among the patient's and the family's rights.

At the start of the 1970s there came another new concept (or was it—as some nurses believed—only a new technology?). Within 10 years of retirement, I learned to be a nurse practitioner—first a family nurse practitioner and then, because the need seemed greater in the older population, a geriatric nurse practitioner.

What a wonderful amalgam of gerontological nursing and public health this geriatric nurse practitioner preparation was!

My goals and priorities then centered on achieving simpler yet more sophisticated relationships among patients, nurse practitioners, and physicians. I also entered into a new phase of research and writing, producing "The Clinical Nurse Practitioner in an Ambulatory Care Service," which described my students at New York Hospital.

On a sabbatical in Scotland, as a Fogarty Fellow on Sir Ferguson Anderson's Geriatric

Assessment Service, there was ample opportunity for me to return to basics—the simplicity and goals of my nursing school days. Practitioners in the Scottish health care system were well acquainted with high technology, but they knew how to use it sparingly—how to be selective in their care of the aged while hewing to strong professional standards. They met the needs of elderly patients and elderly client groups without jeopardizing care.

There I became involved in the miracle of day hospitals for older persons who were in need of rehabilitation and maintenance. I was impressed by the Scottish sensitivity to the problems of the geriatric patient, specifically failure of confidence and bereavement depression, which is brought on by multiple losses that cannot be fully grieved over because they happen during a short time span.

Another highlight of my career came with my participation on the first expert committee on the planning and organization of geriatric services of the World Health Organization. That work gave me international insights in both health care and family life. Setting goals and priorities for developing, and for already technologically developed countries, was enormously thought provoking, especially as all of them were facing fast-growing proportions of older citizens. I hope the reader will look at that 1974 report. It is full of humanistic goals and priorities despite its brevity.

After retirement, I was slowed by a stroke, which resulted in a major loss of useful vision. The stroke did not keep me from a second career as a part-time teacher or from working as a volunteer in the care of the elderly.

Writing publishable, professional material, which I hope can provide some guidelines for humanistic, geriatric thinking, has become my priority as I search for a nursing alternative to restraints.

Let me close with some advice. Take heart from the elderly, from the geriatric self-help groups that are everywhere taking root and growing fast. As a very old, fragile, and chronically ill resident in the life care community where I now make my home once said to me:

> You hear many people say that the world only values *material things* today. I don't think that is true. Both *people* and *things* are important if you want to grow old well. If you *use people* and you *care about things,* old age is going to be heavy, overwhelming. But if you *use things* and *care about people,* you can take the losses of chronic illness and aging and still stay strong, still reach out and be reached.

Fruit, on the Tree of an Early Ambition

As a child I was especially fascinated
By two trades.
Sailors, it seemed to me,
Were the luckiest people in the world.
To live aboard a ship. To travel.
To speak from personal knowledge
Of strange lands.
That was the perfect life.
I wanted to be a sailor
But was told, "Girls can't." It sounded stupid
But there was no use
Arguing with adults. They always won.

The other calling on which I looked
With envy,
Was that of the man
Who read the gas meters
On our block.
What a job he had.
Fuller Brush men, insurance agents,
And even peddlers
With their fine mysterious wares
Were turned away from many doors
But the man who read
The gas meters
Got into every single house.

To get into people's houses
And discover how they lived
Seemed to me,
At the age of ten,
More exciting than any other pastime possible.
Adults, always discouraging,
Assured me
That I could not become
A reader of gas meters.
"Girls don't go
Into anyone's house
Like that."

So I became a nurse.
In that capacity I sailed the Pacific
On a war-time hospital ship.
I visited foreign lands
And spoke with personal knowledge
Of a great assortment of colorful, friendly people.
Later, as a visiting nurse
I climbed unknown house steps
Rang unknown bells and
Was welcomed into other people's houses
In a New York tenement district
All day long.

Sometimes adults are not
So smart. They don't know
That in nursing
You find the adventure
Of people caring for people.
Why a colleague of mine
In the World Health Organization
Was the nursing consultant
To Outer Mongolia.
Imagine that! Adventure and happiness
To be found in nursing.
"Happiness adds and multiplies
As we divide it with others."

—*Doris Schwartz, R.N., New York, N.Y.*

Gloria R. Smith

Gloria R. Smith, PhD, MPH, RN, FAAN,
is Director of the Department of Public Health
for the state of Michigan

❖

Gloria Smith has a strong belief in fate and also believes she has led a charmed life. Her ability to make the most of very limited resources spurred her to take every opportunity that came her way. Her mother expressed a strong wish for her to be an influential woman leader in nursing, holding up Florence Nightingale, Dorothea Dix, and Clara Barton as role models. Gloria's scholarship, her dream of one day being on a college campus, and encouragement from her family and from Katharine Faville at Wayne State University all helped her get through nursing school and into public health nursing. She credits her early mentors with crystallizing her love for this field and, though she has had several successful ventures into other areas of nursing, it is clear that her deep commitment is to public health. She quotes Katharine Faville who reminded her students continually that combining marriage, family, and career must work because nurses made a commitment and "our communities are depending on us."

The quest for complete understanding of what creates leadership is continuous. There is a small body of literature that addresses what leadership ought to be and surprisingly little of what it is. It has been observed that the work that exists in this area tends to be prescriptive rather than descriptive (Kellerman 1984). When I think of leadership in nursing, I am struck by the rich traditions that have given rise to mechanisms for the selection, nurturance, and mentoring of future leaders. My own career offers some insights into how such mechanisms have worked.

I am a strong believer in fate and often think that I have lived a charmed life. One of my brothers has his own interpretation—he says that I see the world through rose-colored glasses. In any analysis of my professional career so far, I can always see the positive side.

I say that my life has been charmed. What else can you call a chain of events that begins with an immature, excited student losing her unmarked change purse in a telephone booth in the administration building on campus during registration—the purse containing her tuition, which had been borrowed from an elderly neighbor? My immediate response to that crisis was normal for a 16-year-old—tears and not-so-gentle sobbing. I was quickly taken in hand by an understanding male student who dried my tears, got the garbled story out of me, and decided to help. Although I had always been taught to be honest and to turn in items I found that did not belong to me, I did not expect to retrieve from the lost and found department my purple flannel change purse containing the borrowed $66 for tuition and $2 for extras. I have never known the name of the student who was so kind to me that day nor the honest person who had no way of knowing how much that money meant to me.

That important experience was not an isolated one. Many people helped me get through the four and a half years of the undergraduate program. The academic challenges were exciting and wonderful. I never had academic problems. The problems I had were related to resources. Looking back, I would say that I was very fortunate. My parents made sacrifices. My aunts and uncles could be counted on for frequent gifts. We had no family car, so clinical rotations that were inaccessible by public transportation were a real problem. Neighbors, classmates, and once even a sympathetic cab driver ferried me to distant clinical sites.

When one talks to graduates from the early university schools of nursing, one always gets the impression that their leaders were larger than life. Katharine Faville, the dean of the College of Nursing at Wayne (State) University from 1945 to 1965, was such a person. Miss Faville was not only a dominant figure in the university but also an outstanding leader in nursing and health care in the city and state. Among the persons she sought to influence were nursing service and nursing education administrators, hospital and health care administrators, and corporate and political leaders.

In my mind, Wayne University College of Nursing circa 1951 will always be the ideal professional school. Of course, I didn't think it was ideal until after I graduated, and the further I get away from the experience the more ideal it becomes. In the utopian environment that I remember, the dean knew every student by name, status, and potential. She determined that she would personally invest in selected students beyond graduation so that they would actualize their potential and contribute fully to society.

Nursing was the career choice of my mother's dreams. It was she, not I, who wanted to be a strong woman leader making decisions that would have an impact on the quality of life for whole communities. My mother's role models were the nurse reformers—Florence Nightingale, Clara Barton, and Dorothea Dix. I delayed making a specific career choice until faced with the college enrollment application forms. I knew that I wanted a career in the sciences. There was something appealing and glamorous about being a professional in a white coat, helping humanity through the discovery of new therapeutics. However, it was the nursing profession's recruiting apparatus that helped me to narrow my decision to nursing, which has been fulfilling personally and professionally ever since I entered it.

I grew up in Detroit, where during my formative years I lived with my family in the neighborhoods near the city's cultural center, which included Wayne University, the Detroit Institute of Art, the Detroit Public Library, and the Detroit Historical Museum. Those neighborhoods were also clustered around the institutions that evolved into the Detroit Medical Center. While the university was not a major factor in my life as I was growing up, the art institute and the public library were significant and influential. With younger siblings and friends, I spent many Saturday afternoons in one or both institutions. I was never curious about the university, which was just one block away. When I thought about universities, the image that popped into my mind was that of Southern University in Baton Rouge, Louisiana. On one of many family vacations in the South while I was growing up, I had been on the campus at Southern University. I was left with an indelible impression of the university from that visit.

If anyone were to ask what it is that I remember most about seeing a university campus as a young girl, I would say that I was impressed by the orderliness, the architecture, and the physical layout of the campus, which seemed so different from the uneven, dusty, concrete city blocks. I was struck by the green lawns and the large trees covered with moss. It was peaceful and spacious. The students seemed to be moving with some purpose in mind, and I remember promising myself that I would be like them.

What possible significance can there be in exposing a ghetto youngster to a campus experience? That may well be a question to which community leaders and educators are or should be seeking answers. I can say that in my own situation, while television was a limited medium in my neighborhood, I was an avid reader and moviegoer. Neither movies nor books made me feel certain that I would someday go to the university, but those informal walks on a college campus with my grandparents did. Through those limited exposures I somehow knew that I belonged in such places and spaces and that, yes, I could aspire to a college education.

I'm not really sure of the precise moment when I recognized that I had a special relationship with Katharine Faville. I do know that the kind of confident, self-assured, assertive, risk-taking professional that I've become was molded and honed at Wayne University. I had been fortunate to grow up in a nurturing environment where my parents and neighbors took pride in my accomplishments and in my potential. The environment at the college of nursing was also a nurturing one. Administration, faculty, and staff took a personal interest in students. In fact the students felt that there were mind readers among the faculty and that the dean had omnipotent powers. She knew everyone and everything.

During the 1950s the college of nursing was small. It was possible for the dean not only to know individual students, but also to know their parents. She knew a great deal about the needs of individuals and had a plan of action to see that each student was supported.

I lived on a direct bus line to the college of nursing. The ride was short, 10 to 15 minutes, and in the 1950s the service was reliable. The dean, however, observed that I was missing a big part of the college experience by being a commuter. I was thrilled when she arranged the support for me to move into the dormitory at the beginning of my sophomore year. To a 17-year-old, the exposure to college life as an on-campus student was a wondrous opportunity.

The dean believed that she had to produce in four and a half years a graduate who had not only intellectual and professional skills but also social grace and skills that would enable the graduate to move in any social circle. When we were students, some of those strategies confounded and baffled us, but there is no question that they made a lasting impact. On occasion, when some of my black friends and I get together, we can sit and laugh for hours about the dean's methods. I was required to take several speech courses, including noncredit speech laboratories on Saturday morning, to correct my lisp and my southern inflection. Because I was born in Chicago and had lived in Detroit since I was six months old, I would have had to acquire the southern inflection in Michigan. Another friend was considered an inelegant person who needed to achieve a refined look. She was sent on weekly tutorials to the posh home of one of Detroit's leading society doyennes, who had agreed to attempt the transformation. Although my friend, like me, can *demonstrate on demand* how to walk, stand, pivot, slide gracefully into a chair, rise out of a chair, glide off, slip white gloves on and off, and descend a spiral staircase to make a grand entrance, she was not turned into a swan, nor was I. We laugh about these and other similar experiences and have come to appreciate the many sincere, highly committed people who invested in our development. I can talk at length on a subject if need be. I can manage my own anxieties about speaking before audiences, meeting new people, or just presenting myself. These are important abilities for professional persons—particularly for those seeking leadership roles.

I am a product of the total gestalt created by the Wayne University College of Nursing in the 1950s. More than half of the graduates of that period chose to practice in public health because that setting came closest to supporting professional practice as idealized by the profession. The criteria for appointment were based on educational credentials. The practice itself was challenging, and there was a high degree of autonomy.

I had loved public health nursing from my first day of field practice as a junior student. We had a 14-week block assignment in which I spent two weeks of observation at the Detroit Health Department and 12 weeks of practice at the Detroit Visiting Nurses Association. At the VNA I carried my own caseload of 12 to 15 families within my agency field teacher's district. I loved the independence and the expectation that I would be able to assess the needs of my patients and their families, that I would be using my knowledge and judgment, and that on the basis of my analysis I would be putting forth written plans. I was heady from the knowledge that my clinical skills were sufficient for my responsibilities. More important, within a 12-week period I was able to see the results of some of my work. There is nothing to compare to the exhilaration and satisfaction one feels when one can see positive outcomes from a specific set of nursing interventions. I enjoyed working with other community advocates and agency workers like myself to identify community problems and to develop strategies for mobilizing the community.

My agency field teacher was the assistant district office supervisor. She was a mature nurse who had a great compassion for people and believed in the mission of her agency. She offered me weekend employment when I completed my field practice. On one of the many Saturdays that we worked together she turned to me and said, "Of course you will come to work for us." I don't know what it feels like to be knighted, but it couldn't excite me any more than having been offered a position with the most fantastic organization in the world—an organization headed by a nurse who was an extraordinarily tough executive and that was filled with the brightest, most clever, and most competent independent nurses. Each was treated as an individual, and together they made a wonderful team. And I was going to join them. Whoopee!

The Detroit Visiting Nurses Association fulfilled my dreams. I have looked back on my first practice experience as the second major milestone in my career. Choosing the Wayne University College of Nursing or being chosen by them was the first. The dean had a set of principles about first jobs, as she had about everything else. She expected that we would work for two years or more in an environment that would allow us to function as generalists, where qualified and appropriate supervision would be available on a consistent basis. She expected us to season as beginning practitioners before we moved on to advanced responsibility or specialty practice. The VNA filled this bill for me, and it was a place where I could grow as a practitioner and fledgling leader.

In the past 30 years I have been employed in various roles at academic and health care agencies in five states. I have been a staff nurse supervisor, agency field teacher, team leader, consultant, university professor, academic administrator, dean of a college of nursing, and a political appointee heading a state public health department, which is my current position. All along, it has been clear to me that the foundation for my career was crafted in my undergraduate program and firmed in my first work experience. I was exposed to some of nursing's finest leaders from 1955 to 1963 in the college of nursing and at the Detroit Visiting Nurses Association—Katharine Faville, Emilie G. Sargent, Kay Robeson, Ann Conley, Irene Beland, Esther Reed, Mildred Gottdank, Mary K. Mullane, Cathryn Kurtagh, and Cora Lloyd.

I remained one of Katharine Faville's mentees until she was no longer physically able to maintain the relationship. She truly was a remarkable person. She had such strength, integrity, and compassion for humanity. She had a vision for the contribution of nursing and women to society, and she worked with discipline and vigor to transform vision into reality.

Miss Faville influenced everyone with whom she came in contact. Wayne State graduates, faculty, and former faculty all have their favorite Katharine Faville stories to tell. There is one theme that has been often repeated, for it was a lesson that she wanted Wayne graduates to remember always. She told us through several dean's messages to the class that no matter what our families paid for our education or how many sacrifices they had made, those contributions were small compared to the huge investment the community was making in our education and preparation as professionals. She told us that we were obligated to work in our profession and to give the community a return on its investment. She demanded that we plan our lives around that obligation.

Although she herself never married, she was strong and clear in urging us that a combination of marriage, family, and career could work; that indeed it *must* work for we, as nursing graduates, had made a commitment, and our communities were depending on us.

REFERENCE

Kellerman, Barbara (Ed.). *Leadership: multidisciplinary perspectives,* Prentice-Hall, Inc., Englewood Cliffs, New Jersey, p. ix-xiii.

Margaret Stafford

Margaret Stafford, MSN, RN, FAAN,
is Clinical Nurse Specialist,
Hines Veterans Administration Hospital,
Northlake, Illinois

A deeply religious person, Margaret (Peg) Stafford tells of her early childhood in the hard times of the 1930s. She graduated from the Cook County School of Nursing, where her experiences with short-staffing, limited supplies, and an unenlightened administration collided with her ethical and moral values as she felt that the dignity and worth of the patients was being violated. She believed in unionization, however, she was uncertain about organizing professional nurses. She vividly recounts the organizing struggle at Cook County and its eventual success.

Peg is a widely known and highly respected master's-prepared clinical nurse specialist in cardiac nursing, and she has not worked outside a local unit since her Cook County experience. Her fundamental belief is that "the collective bargaining process is a rightful and ethical means to achieve a rightful and ethical twofold goal: the provision of quality care for the patient and the maintenance of the professional integrity of the nurse."

I was born October 4, 1922, the second of three girls. My behavior during infancy and early adolescence, from all reliable reports, was what one would expect from a middle child. I was aggressive, busy, and bossy—always trying to catch up with (and secretly trying to outdo) my older sister Beverly. Bev was a unique person. She died of pneumonia at the young age of 18, but, actually, Bev never seemed young. She was a humanist and a social activist. A case in point—as a senior in high school she was elected by her classmates and teachers (Providence Sisters) to participate in one of the first antisegregation movements in Washington, D.C.

My younger sister (by six years) Pat and I had some stormy times when Bev died. We were very angry about her death and initially directed our anger at each other. Ultimately we developed a strong bond of love, friendship, and reciprocal protection, as well as a nasty habit of inflicting guilt when either one of us does not live up to the standards or expectations of the other.

It is strange the way God works. He not only took Bev without much warning but my mother (three months prior) and my father (a little over a year later) as well. Those losses over a short time span influenced the course of my life—spiritually and professionally.

My mother was a stern taskmaster. We did not "sass her," nor did we "talk back." I remember an incident in which I decided to test the waters—to tell her that I disagreed with one of her unilateral decisions. (I was about six or seven.) When she asked me, "Who do you think you're talking to, young lady?" I replied, "The wall," because she had often said that talking to me was like talking to a wall. Although she gave me a couple of swats on the seat for my impertinence, she laughed as she did it. She was a great lady and a great nurse. She did not know a stranger, and the word prejudice really was alien to her.

My mother's mother, my beloved Mammaw, was a feisty lady who was probably among the first equal rights proponents. When my mother left home at the age of 18 to join the Red Cross Army Nurse Corps, Mammaw was sad to lose her, but she was very proud that her daughter had been accepted into nurses' "training." Mammaw was the only midwife in her small town. Delivering babies was her specialty, but she considered herself a generalist and loved to tell of her experiences in caring for all the children in town during a diphtheria outbreak (which was called the Black Death) and of how she nursed them back to health.

At the same time that Mom entered the Army Nurse Corps my father, a registered pharmacist, entered the medical corps of the infantry. When they met, it was love at first sight, and in spite of their many differences, they were married. I talk of their differences because my mother, though very independent, was a small-town, teetotaling Protestant and the fifth generation in America, while my father was an Irish Catholic whose grandparents and uncles had been born in Ireland. He was from the big city of Chicago and his family considered drinking alcohol to be a way of life. He was so Catholic that he had determined to be a Jesuit until he joined the service and met my mother.

My father was a scholar who excelled in Latin and Greek, as well as in mathematics. My mother felt he was a frustrated intellectual with a potential he never realized. Mom was good at diagnosing behavior but had a difficult time with Dad's method of coping—drinking.

They weathered some hard times and endured many sorrows. The depression took its toll on my family, as my paternal grandfather, my uncle, and my father all lost their drugstores.

Pa, my paternal grandfather, was a strict disciplinarian who was intellectually gifted but lacked his son's sensitivity. He was a self-made man—initially a successful salesman. At the age of 40 he became a pharmacist, bought a drugstore, patented a cough mixture, and helped two of his sons buy drugstores.

They used to say of Pa, "There are two ways to do things—Pa's way and the wrong way." After my family moved into "the house" (my grandparents' home), I used to love the conversations we had at dinner. Actually, we weren't supposed to talk during dinner, but Pa always broke his own rule. He would get excited about the political scene and quiz us about local news. He was a staunch supporter of the union movement, as was my grandmother. It was one of the few things on which they agreed. We all knew to read the daily paper and to listen to the news because Pa had a way of making you feel fat, dumb, and ugly if you didn't have the right answers.

With the advent of the depression, my mother returned to work as a nurse. Bev and I were in high school and both worked part time, she in a department store and I as a dentist's assistant. I loved it!

It was at this time that my mother's uterine cancer was diagnosed. As a veteran, she was admitted to the local Veterans Administration hospital. My dad, an incurable alcoholic, developed diabetes and a heart condition. He too was admitted. While hospitalized, they spent as much time together as possible. I remember visiting them; the three of us would take walks together. Though I was saddened with the reality of their illnesses, I felt and shared in their deep love for each other. It was at this time that Mom decided to take instruction in the Catholic faith. We girls moved in with our paternal grandparents.

My grandmother, Ma, was truly the matriarch of this extended family, even though Pa made noises like the boss. Ma held us together, and when she died (five years after my father), the family disintegrated.

In recalling my days at "the house," I think of my Aunt Alice. She helped me through some pretty critical times by stimulating my intellectual and spiritual growth, which otherwise might have been neglected. I wanted desperately to become a nurse, but my father's family discouraged this. And so I got a job at the telephone company, made good money for the times, and supported Pat. When she graduated from high school, she too took a job at the telephone company. Shortly after World War II began, we moved into our own apartment.

This was a particularly difficult time for Pat. She was struggling not only with Ma's death, but also with the separation from our family members. My way of coping with her unhappiness and with my felt rejection took many forms—too much partying, too much work, and too many hours as a volunteer "Gray Lady" at Cook County Hospital.

Let me tell you a little about County at that time. Because of the nursing shortage during the war, other health care providers such as nursing aides and volunteers emerged en masse. To nursing's discredit, caregiving was delegated, and the nurse became the delegator.

I vividly recall that as a volunteer Gray Lady at County, I felt for those sick, sick patients—for their extreme poverty, aloneness, and apparent isolation from others, which seemed to be the real illness.

I had to take a three-month course to work as a volunteer—two evenings a week with some few classes in the school of nursing—but most of what I learned came through on-the-job training. My instructor, a County graduate, often bemoaned the good old days before the war, when there had been enough nurses. I remember her as dynamic, knowledgeable, and skillful, and I respected her.

After I graduated as a volunteer, I became quite an independent practitioner on those wards on my two (and sometimes three) evenings a week. I changed dressings on the most awful draining wounds, emptied colostomy bags (at the time, I wasn't sure what they were), and fed and bathed patients.

And so my life at that time was a mixed bag. When the war ended, I divided my free time between County and my AT&T union activities, burning the candle at both ends. I had moved up rapidly in the telephone company and was being groomed for an assistant chief operator position. I'm not sure to this day whether my upward mobility was related to my managerial skills or was just a concerted effort to move me not up but out of union involvement. The postwar slump increased our union activities, and as a steward I was becoming an effective bargaining agent on behalf of the telephone operators.

I was a puzzlement to Pat—giving so much of myself to the patients at County on the one hand and to the union cause (for which I often worked into the late hours of the night) on the other. Pat summed up her feelings one day: "You and your telephone friends," she said. "Women aren't supposed to stop after work for a drink and forget to go home. Men do that, not women." In retrospect, I am sure that my strong commitment to protecting the rights of women in the workplace was at that time little understood by me, much less by Pat. Our common bond—a deep faith in God and our love for and trust in each other—was understood, however. And so we tolerated what we did not understand.

Just the other day, I heard someone say, "All's well that ends!" So too did my in-limbo existence end. I was in an automobile accident that pushed my face right into the mirror of reality. My prognosis was grim. I wasn't expected to live, but if I did, there was a strong possibility that I would have brain damage and would be confined to a wheelchair. Recuperation was a slow, two-year process. I had a good hospitalization insurance plan, and the telephone company contract provided me a generous sick leave. Money was not an issue.

My primary nurse took me on as a real challenge. I wish I could relate adequately her excellence. She did not use the term, but her caring was holistic in the true Levine spirit.

On the other side of the ledger, I must tell you about the part-time night nurse who agreed, after my sister's tearful persuasion, to take care of me *only* if I promised not to use the bedpan during her shift. In a way I could understand the nurse's anxiety. I was in neck traction, both of my legs were in casts, and I had a body cast that was cut out to allow me to use a bedpan. The bed I was on, which could separate to allow for this important aspect of daily living, had broken. This meant that she would have to help me turn, and believe me, if you could have seen her you would know she could not assist anyone. Well, I promised not to use the bedpan, she gave me my morphine on time, and I obediently slept most of the night.

Suffice it to say that through the grace of God, excellent care, and good friends, I recovered. I developed a slight foot drop, no bed sores, and some nasty scars on both legs. I promised myself that I would become a "real nurse," as Mammaw would say.

During the healing process I walked with crutches, wore a neck brace, and signed up at the local high school for chemistry courses. I did well with the healing, as well as with the schooling, and decided it was time to apply to a school of nursing. Of course, I applied to the school at Cook County Hospital. Knowing how badly they needed nurses, I believed they would greet me with open arms. I soon found out that having been a Gray Lady and being a prospective nursing student had little in common. The entrance exam, which I anticipated would be a breeze (especially since I had taken my dreaded courses in chemistry), proved to be a rude awakening. However, my interview went well enough to compensate for my low score, and so, with a few cautions regarding study habits, I was accepted. I sold my stock in the telephone company to pay for my schooling and my meager needs.

The day I actually moved into the Cook County School of Nursing dormitory, I cried myself to sleep. I wondered what I was doing there, a 29-year-old woman starting a new career with teenagers. I soon found out "what I was doing there," and I have never regretted it. I studied, probably harder than most, and it paid off. Shortly after I graduated, I realized I needed to do more. I went on to get my BSN at Loyola, and as usual, working full time and going to school part time was not enough—I became involved in the movement to improve the care that was being offered to our patients. We were good nurses; there just were not enough of us.

I reminded myself many times that the reason I chose County as a place to learn and practice was the image I had of the suffering patients there during my Gray Lady days. That image, though from a different perspective, was still very real.

In 1965 at Cook County Hospital, I was carrying the medicine keys for seven floors of patients (approximately 70 to 80 patients per floor). They were on open wards in an area referred to as "Male Medicine." My title was evening supervisor; my responsibility was to accommodate, to fill in, and to do the best I could in this untenable situation. I walked continuously from floor to floor. Three or four of the floors had no nurses, only nursing attendants. I would hang or discontinue intravenous solutions and give those medicines—narcotics, antibiotics, or whatever—that I determined were priorities and that could be given within the time I had.

My tour of duty was 3 PM to 11 PM, but actually I seldom left the hospital before 1 or 2 in the morning. It took me a long time to realize that this was not professional commitment but rather social injustice to patients and the profession of nursing. My experiences were part of the status quo; inadequate staffing as well as substandard supplies and equipment were the rule of the day. The excellence of the prewar Cook County Hospital was not to be found. Care was deteriorating, salaries were noncompetitive, and graduating students were going elsewhere to work. The nursing budget was meager, and any attempts to modify this situation by individual appeals to the administration—the governing bodies of the hospital and the school—resulted in a sympathetic response but no action.

I knew something had to be done. I was of the opinion that "organizing" was all right for telephone operators, but for the nursing profession? Nurses should not have to organize, I believed. In retrospect, I wonder how Anne Zimmerman, then the executive administrator of the Illinois Nurses' Association, put up with the lot of us, repeatedly asking for INA's help, as we did, and then rejecting it. I remember the day she told us flatly, "Don't call me and I won't call you," or words to that effect.

I believe the turning point was the 1966 American Nurses' Association convention in San Francisco. The keynote speaker reminded us eloquently not only of our professional responsibility to our patients, but also of the responsibility we owed ourselves, our personhood, and our integrity. The association took a stand on minimum salaries and adopted a new organizational structure with clinical divisions, which underscored the importance of clinical practice. We went home ready to move professional nursing and nurses from what Kant would describe as our "dogmatic slumber." Successful organization of the nurses at Cook County Hospital in 1966 through the Illinois Nurses' Association resulted in competitive salaries, improved working conditions, and ultimately effective recruitment and retention of nurses. Those changes did not happen overnight but were managed in good time. Care for patients was not only safe, in many areas of the hospital it also reached and maintained a new peak of excellence. An equitable nurse/patient ratio was achieved, and when necessary, wards were closed to admissions because of inadequate staffing.

A significant provision in that first Cook County contract was the implementation of a Patient Care Review Committee, in which representative nurses at all levels of administration and practice could gather to study and resolve problems that interfered with patient care.

The agenda for that first meeting of the committee, as presented by the local unit nurse members, reflects their many concerns:

1. Lack of visiting hours in obstetrics
2. Linen shortages
3. Middle rows of patients (indicating overcrowding)
4. Poor RN staffing

The committee's activities resulted in numerous improvements, including the establishment of visiting privileges for husbands or significant others of obstetrical patients with the provision of adequate privacy, a properly equipped and staffed playroom for children in the pediatrics department, nonnursing duties being reassigned appropriately, rehabilitation therapy for the chronically ill patients, and consent forms in various languages that were representative of the patient population. Those changes are documented, not hearsay. They emphasize the fact that, by joining together and supporting each other, nurses can achieve for patients and themselves what no individual nurse can achieve alone. I appreciate and believe to this day that collective action of and for nurses and their patients is one of the most professional activities in which I have been involved.

The story is incomplete without recognizing the many nurse leaders who made the difference—Alice Braisher, Mary Ann Mejdrick, Jerry Fessler, Myra Levine, LaVerne Lissy, Jeannette Logan, Francis L.A. Powell, Joyce Waterman Taylor (who cochaired the unit with me), and many, many more. Most significantly, it was Anne Zimmerman and Kathleen Radicke Hoover, Associate Director of the Economic & General Welfare Program on Anne's staff at that time, and Jack Frye, consultant economist, who provided what was needed to bring this about. Their insightful expertise, their ability (in Lissy's words) "to cajole, encourage and inspire the nurses at Cook County School of Nursing," resulted in our organizing the effective local economic security unit under the aegis of the Illinois Nurses' Association. That local unit is alive and well today and fulfilling its intent.

Shortly after our first contract, I worked part time to secure my master's degree as a clinical nurse specialist in cardiac nursing. Prior to this decision and throughout the County crisis, I was taking graduate classes in philosophy at Loyola University. My search for a more comprehensive understanding of man and his behavior was stimulated, I'm sure, by the myriad interactions I was experiencing, as well as by my own need for certitude. It did indeed give credibility to my spiritual beliefs, and I hope someday to return to that pursuit of knowledge for the sake of knowledge.

When I was offered the opportunity to pursue graduate study in a clinical specialty and toward the emerging role of clinical nurse specialist, I transferred back to the school of nursing. I knew that this was a unique opportunity to continue my commitment not only to nursing, but to nurses. It was at this time that I was introduced to Levine's concept of holism in nursing practice, a philosophy that complemented my recent studies and gave a new meaning to nursing.

Following graduate school I returned to work full time, assisting in the establishment of the Cook County Hospital cardiac care unit. At that same time Joyce Waterman Taylor, clinical nurse specialist in neurological disorders, opened the first neurology unit at County. Although we were both covered by our local unit contract, there was no contract language that could accommodate to the inadequate nursing administration we faced. I'm afraid that when we returned to County with our newly acquired armamentarium, we were viewed as suspect and threatening to the status quo. Recognizing this lack of administrative support, which is so vital for the success of a clinical nurse specialist, I resigned just a few months after Joyce did. I might have left County, but not completely. Have you ever felt a bit of you in someplace else?

If I have learned nothing else from life's experiences, I have learned how to pick up, move on, and adapt. In an interim position I accepted the role as coordinator for a continuing education–media technology project that was federally funded by the Department of Health, Education and Welfare. The grant agency was Video Nursing, Inc. Harriett Koch—author, lecturer, excellent nurse, and friend—was the president of the company, and she hired me. Harriett's management style offered me the opportunity to be creative and self-directed and to fall on my face more than once. I learned to appreciate a side of nursing other than clinical practice. I also witnessed enlightened management.

In this milieu I added considerably to my knowledge of continuing education and technology, and I developed good personal communication skills. I acquired an understanding, at a different dimension, of behavior in general.

At the close of the project, I was itching to return to what I did and liked best — clinical practice. Most of the medical staff with whom I worked at County had moved to what was jokingly being called Suburban Cook County but in reality was Hines Veterans Administration Hospital. My medical colleagues convinced Chief Nurse Beatrice Murray, another great lady, to interview me. And so another chapter in my life began.

As I am convinced that no man is an island and that we all do very little in isolation, it is important to mention that through all of my transitions, Pat, her husband Bob, and their seven beautiful children always supported me. One last word about Mammaw — she was one of the first people I knew to write a living will. Her physician honored it, and she died a dignified death without extraordinary measures being taken to extend her 95 years.

As I moved into my clinical specialist role at Hines, I was less than enthusiastic about starting a local unit. Within two years, however, it was evident that the patients were not getting the care they needed. And, as is always the case in that kind of environment, the nurses and their nursing practice were being compromised.

The local nonprofessional union, capitalizing on the dissatisfaction of the nurses, was actively recruiting. This and the expressed concern and commitment to change of many of the nurses rekindled my enthusiasm. We formed a local unit, and once again the nurses voted to have INA represent them.

In 1976 our first Hines/INA Local Unit contract was signed by members of the unit's bargaining team under the capable leadership of Martha Garcia, INA's associate director for economic and general welfare. The purpose of the contract was stated without equivocation:

> ... to promote sound and mutually beneficial relationships between the hospital and the Association. These relationships should provide opportunity to develop and implement standards of nursing practice resulting in improved patient care. Such relationships include the recognition that employees covered herein have responsibilities in their practice, both to the hospital and to their patients, to base actions and decisions on sound professional judgment and adhere to the code and standards of their profession.

Because of the collective bargaining process and that contract, the nurses are now reassigned from their usual ward only in emergencies — after a thorough evaluation of the need to reassign is completed and a rationale offered to the reassigned nurse by her or his immediate supervisor. In addition, the staff nurse or nurses who are reassigned are given as thorough an orientation to the new environment as possible. This includes an orientation not only to the unique needs of the patients but also to the operation of specialized equipment and procedures. Being respected as an integral part of this necessary emergency measure considerably alters the nurse's attitude and response to a reassignment; the in-depth orientation ensures the patient of at least safe and continuous care.

As outlined in the contract, each nursing unit works out a pattern of time that provides for safe practice and a fair and equitable staffing pattern. No nurse works more than six consecutive days or more than two overtime tours of duty in one week except by the mutual agreement of the nurse and the supervisor. This provides a safety factor for patients by limiting the fatigue level and stress of the staff.

Also, the contract specifies that the following nonnursing tasks are not intended to be a normal part of the RN's activities:

1. Stripping, cleaning, and remaking discharge units
2. Preparing, passing, and collecting food trays
3. General housekeeping
4. Transportation of patients and patient-related data such as x-rays, medical records, and specimens
5. Secretarial duties during routine absence of a secretary

These might appear to some to be mundane, hardly worthy of contract language. Nevertheless, those of us who work within the hospital structure are aware that many nurses are still doing many of these "go-for" tasks that create barriers to better use of the professional nurses' time, knowledge, and skill—tasks that interfere with high-quality patient care.

The contract allows for adjustment of the nurses' work schedules to accommodate those who are furthering their academic preparation, and a professional nurse advisory committee has been established that provides for a monthly meeting between nurses from the local unit and top nursing management representatives. Discussions concerning inappropriate use of LPNs in professional nurse positions and implementation of clinical privileges are examples of points on their agenda. The hospital also provides for local unit employees to be represented on the Professional Standards Board. This board deals with promotions and recognition awards for all professional nurses. The contract provides that local unit nurses are considered for selection on all hospital committees that affect their practice.

An addendum to the contract is a statement of commitment by the local unit nurses and nursing management to a peer review process. Staff nurses monitor and evaluate their practice to improve the quality of care and enhance their own knowledge, skills, and professional conscience.

It is worthy to note that through INA's persistence, an arbitration ruling was upheld and a nurse who was dismissed for refusing to wash a bed was given the right to be rehired and was awarded back pay amounting to close to $30,000.

A serendipitous occurrence that I have noticed through my years of collective action is the emergence of nurse leaders who start as grievance representatives and members of negotiating teams, as well as officers in local bargaining units. The unit activities have provided them an avenue to pursue their commitment to clinical practice and to each other.

At the 1987 ANA House of Delegates meeting in Kansas City, Missouri, the ANA served notice to the health care community that unless some tangible changes are made for professional nurses—improved working conditions and nurse/patient ratios, increased salaries, and better fringe benefits—other efforts toward the recruitment and retention of nurses will not be effective.

I concur with ANA's dictum, but there is no magic formula. Nurses have basic needs as well as higher needs for self-actualization, and the barriers to achieving these are simple—lack of money, power, and recognition of their integral role in the care of sick people and the prevention of their illnesses. I believe, without equivocation, that health care systems cannot survive without us, and we must represent ourselves in the practice arena. I have long been of the opinion that local units have not been given their rightful place in the organization. They serve to accomplish tangible changes, but also they provide a legal process by which nurses themselves are involved in making the critical decisions related to those changes. Local units offer a forum for practicing nurses in the clinical areas to talk together as peers, to help each other grow professionally, and to enhance their professional conscience. Local units provide a forum for practicing nurses to talk with nursing management from a position of authority and respect and to identify what is needed to provide what practitioners market best—high-quality patient care.

I view the collective bargaining process as a means of making things better and not an end unto itself. I feel strongly that it is a rightful and ethical means to accomplish a rightful and ethical goal, a goal that is twofold—the provision of high-quality care for the patient and the achievement and maintenance of the professional integrity of the nurse. One is contingent upon the other.

Jean E. Steel

Jean E. Steel, MS, RN, is Assistant Professor
and Consultant in the Graduate Program
of the Boston University School of Nursing

❖

*Although her mother was a nurse and her father a physician,
Jean Steel's first career choice after completing a community college
course was secretarial. She was unsatisfied, however, and decided that
she wanted to be a nurse. She was accepted at Cornell and spent two
of her next three years on academic probation, but she acquired the
knowledge and skill she needed to experience "the joy of nursing practice."*

*Jean is compelling in her description of the respect and caring
for people that she gained as a public health nurse. The hands-on "tasks"
of nursing care, she believes, provide quiet time for conversation, observation, and teaching of patients.*

*Choosing to try private practice was not without its hazards,
but eventually her collaboration in a joint practice with a believing
physician became a model for others. It took boldness and determination
to push the private practice idea into a college curriculum. Jean's inner
resources that allow her to "appreciate the magnitude of the gift of
nature in the world around us" provide her times of reflective loneness
by which she is comforted and refreshed.*

*T*he fabric of one's life is woven by people and experience. People enrich the self and form the spirit, guide one's everyday development, and mold one's future. Experiences build, intertwine, and promote the self. The whole of any individual is a collection of all those people and experiences. The conscious and subconscious do not always permit one to know the source of these experiences, nor the special contributions of people along the way. The beginning is always different from the end, but the end is better because of the beginning.

What one becomes is a combination of what others have given. Who are those people, and what particular gifts do they give?

So many have influenced my professional life that I find it hard to be inclusive and yet not exclusive. Here are some of those people and their contributions:

1. Mom and Dad—their undying love
2. Mark Twain—his true humor
3. Gretta Styles—her vision
4. Hildegard Peplau and Maria Phaneuf—infinite wisdom
5. Students—challenge
6. Patients—the test and opportunities
7. Friends—loyal support and faith
8. Charles Dickens—his ability to understand people
9. The Lord—hope

My folks thought they had produced a tomboy. I was far more interested in climbing a tree, running in a track meet, or playing field hockey than pursuing the usual activities of little girls. My earliest recollection is my wanting to sail a toy boat in the Shaker Lakes.

While the Cleveland area was my permanent home, for many summers my joys were boosted by the waters of Cape Cod, where I moved from that wish for a toy boat to a real boat. Those many Cape summers of my youth formed a bond to New England and my subsequent career.

The folks managed to survive my childhood and gave me the greatest gift of roots and wings—roots of family tradition, love for others, and untold advantages. Mother gave me a love for life, the creativity to dream, and the imagination of a free spirit. Dad showed me how to laugh, and gave me the will to succeed and the means to give to others. They let me fly, picked me up when I fell, dusted me off, and urged me to try again.

Schooling was not my favorite experience. Never at the top of anything, except a tree or as class president, I managed to graduate from Laurel School—but not before I had struggled with academics. Latin was a required course, but it became impossible for me so they waived the requirements. My Latin teacher, Miss Andrews, would climb under her desk and stay there until Jean conjugated the verbs correctly. For all I know she is still there. The glee club, the speakers' panel, all athletics, and the school government were my favorite activities.

When Miss Lake, the headmistress, told my parents that I was "not college material," it was a like a call to war! My parents and I took that statement, agonized over it, fought it, and in later years laughed at it. If only Miss Lake were alive today . . . .

Unaware that Laurel had laid the groundwork for later scholarly pursuits, I managed to succeed at Endicott Junior College in my beloved New England. After graduation and certain that my career was to be launched as a professional secretary, I moved to Boston, rented a small apartment on Commonwealth Avenue, and began my job at the New England Deaconess Hospital. My daily challenge there was to type the operating room schedule and order the hospital supplies for my boss, a nurse. Every day the medical terminology floored me, and I soon became restless to be something more than a secretary.

Believing that my future was somewhere in the business world, I returned to college a year later. It was in that year, 1956, that I began to think nursing should be my future. It was neither Mom's nursing background nor Dad's medical practice that influenced my decision but rather the love of a medical student at Columbia.

Chuck had been a longtime friend at the Cape, and as our relationship matured, I thought I was in love with him. I recall the summers he worked as a busboy at Quisett Harbor House. He was often able to borrow a guest's car for nights we went to the movies. One of those unique loans was the use of Benjamin Spock's car. The only requirement was that Chuck had to feed the test mice in the car's trunk at specific times. How romantic to be at a drive-in with Chuck having to feed mice as part of the evening!

I was not very discriminating about my choice of nursing school. I knew I wanted to be in New York City, and I was accepted at both Columbia and Cornell. Columbia students were required to wear black stockings, and Cornell students were not. I moved into the Cornell residence for three years, spent two of those years on academic probation, but acquired sound knowledge and the skills needed to begin practice. My gratitude for that Cornell education is beyond description. My terror in obstetrics was calmed by Vera Keane's comfort of the normal process, Marge Millar's loyalty and presence as a Cornell mentor, Virginia Derick's knowledge of nursing practice as a skill, and most important, Doris Schwartz's infinite understanding of community and health care.

Test-taking was not one of my strengths, but I could change a dressing, comfort the dying, and counsel the troubled well enough to receive a bachelor's degree in 1960. What pride I felt the day I graduated! All along the way, my parents kept the faith, supported my decisions, and loved me as a daughter. Both Dad and Mark Twain gave me the gift of understanding the humor in ourselves. Their dry, descriptive ready wit has helped to describe the real, the ridiculous, and the best in people.

Through my practice as a visiting nurse, staff nurse, supervisor, and director, I was able to achieve a deep commitment and love for the joy of nursing practice. Patients from all walks of life, at all ages, and with a variety of health problems have taught me the many lessons of life. They have given me the opportunity to learn to accept people as they are. The poor have taught me dignity, humility, and how to cope in the face of great odds. The elderly have shown me the importance and value of history as a predictor for tomorrow. The confused person awaiting permanent placement, the substance-abused soul who finds life unbearable without a pint a day, the non-English speaker trying to understand, the newborn struggling for life, and the terminally ill of all ages—all have helped draw the parts of the picture and have guided me in the direction that my nursing care would take. While I have not always agreed with patients' choices, I have tried to redesign plans of care to support their decisions. The valiant independence of patients sends strong messages that I have paid close attention to over and over again.

There have been patients whom I will never forget. Many were "difficult," but they all had individual characteristics that I tried to understand and incorporate in my treatment plans. When others rejected bag ladies or drunks as dirty, irresponsible, and unacceptable, I felt challenged by their problems, to find some solutions to ease their days. While my plan was not always within the expected protocol, I persisted to implement it, often despite great criticism and the misunderstanding of other health care providers. I have tried to be flexible, generous, firm, committed, and caring.

And what of the tasks of nursing care? I have always enjoyed making a bed—more the challenge to have someone in it. This activity alone has provided quiet time for conversation, observation, and even teaching. It is truly one of the hallmarks of the professional's care of people. The direct laying-on-of-hands has always been for me a unique opportunity to render care.

When I decided to strike out into a private practice in 1973, it was with fear and doubt and at great personal risk. Although I believed the nursing care I had to sell was worth the adventure, I was really not sure anyone would pay to see a nurse. When I completed my first health assessment, I was nervous that the rate I set was too high. What joy I had when the patient paid $20 for that visit. Over the next few years I grew confident that the public would pay to see a nurse. The opportunity to establish my joint practice with Rob Funkhouser, M.D., was a challenge for us both. We grew to understand each other's skills, comforts, and peculiarities. Our chance to complement patient care through collaboration was a strong marketing piece for our patients. It saddened me to watch the medical profession punish Rob for "needing to share his practice with a nurse." His vision and openness reassured me that collaboration could occur. Many nurses asked me where they could find a Rob!

Because of the success of our practice and the belief that this system of providing care in hospital, home, and office could provide new opportunities for nurses, I began to formalize my thoughts and dreams into an academic curriculum. It seemed so right that I wondered why other nurses didn't seize the opportunity. Through the establishment of the primary care program at the Boston University School of Nursing and in Boston City Hospital's ambulatory care center, the chance to do just that became a reality. Over the next ten years, with superb contributions from our faculty, we were able to make those dreams realities. Although we defended our beliefs about this expanding role, there were times of despair and near defeat. We believers often thought, "If only nursing colleagues would accept that our vision is within the domain of nursing." The criticisms seemed to cluster in large numbers.

Despite the rhetoric of physicians, they too mounted huge obstacles to our success.

There were annual negotiations for space to practice. The priority for examination rooms in the ambulatory care center put the nurse faculty and students at the bottom. It was hard to always be last. It was not encouraging to have to constantly petition physicians to collaborate with nurses. My participation with the National Joint Practice Commission only seemed to escalate local problems up to the national scene. However, that participation did provide a larger arena to promote the benefits, joys, and outcomes of nurses and doctors in joint collaborative practice.

During the 10-year implementation of the primary care program, I believed strongly in the practice of the nurse faculty and each week devoted the equivalent of two days of practice to the hospital without pay. I saw this opportunity as a unique chance to demonstrate care to graduate students and to continue to find solutions to the problems of patients, yet maintain a constant involvement in contemporary practice. Again the criticism of colleagues was harsh and without cause. Nursing administrators in the school were critical of my schedules, my expectations with other program faculty, and the entire direction of a joint practice model. While it was not a perfect model, it did contribute to newer schemes that have emerged.

There were many great moments during that last 10 years of practice. The staff at the ambulatory care center, my community of patients, and the challenges of the graduate students all built a solid belief in the practice and the unique contributions of professional nurses. I believe my greatest contribution was through the demonstration of patient care to others. I genuinely treasure the opportunities I had to care, to teach, and to learn.

By 1985 I knew it was time to pursue my doctoral education on a full-time basis. After intense soul-searching and with deep regret I terminated my practice, holding fast to the hope of rebuilding it one day. I had provided direct patient care for 25 years in one capacity or another. I worried that I would lose my gift of providing care and the recognition I had with colleagues as a contemporary practitioner. I knew I would miss the patients and hoped that they would miss me. I have been touched by their persistence, faith, and loyalty.

The works of Charles Dickens have given me insight to people of the past and the present. His descriptions of the poor, the unfortunate, and the haughty have permitted me to understand the people I have met. His "best of times and worst of times" theme has been so applicable. I felt close to him as I entered the Old Curiosity Shop in London many years ago. I have met the Scrooges and the Sairey Gamps of this life. I think I have understood them better because of Dickens' work.

The greats in nursing are present in my thinking, my writing, and in my beliefs. The imparted wisdom of Hildegard Peplau and Maria Phaneuf was a personal and professional privilege to receive. Throughout the development of the ANA Social Policy Statement, they encouraged, debated, and shaped many of my beliefs and hopes for the profession.

Through my intense ANA activities over the past eight years I have come to appreciate the precious attributes of nurses in all specialties. The nurses that I have met throughout the country and around the world have freely given me their criticisms, their visions, and their support.

At the untimely death of a close friend in 1983 the significance and meaning of friendship was poignantly realized. How assuming we are of loyal friendships, and how desperately we must strive for constant expression of our appreciation. Her heavenly star shines brighter on my life as I have included this lesson in each of my days.

My spirit has been refreshed and renewed by free expression. Whether playing a Bach fugue or "Bill Bailey" on my organ, the creation of sounds has released me from stress. Camping under a pine tree or beating upwind on a starboard tack has helped me appreciate the magnitude and the gift of nature in the world. Times of reflective silence and loneness have cured my sometimes aching heart and have helped me to modify expectations for others and myself. This world abounds with lessons of humility, the love of beauty, the joys of closeness, and the hope for peace.

In my search for professional autonomy I have won and lost. Everything that has happened has contributed to my being and has stylized the beliefs and values that are a part of me. Unjustified criticism has been hard to bear but has served to strengthen my hope for the next day.

In my own practice and in the practice of others, I have come to know the benefits and pleasures of the work we do. To heal the sick, counsel the afflicted, and support the dying are unique opportunities that our profession offers. Nurses are our most valuable resource.

We can achieve through creative designs, application of knowledge, collaborative efforts, and the love of people. We must be the best we can be. Nurses and nursing *do* make a difference. I believe this with all my heart.

My participation in a documentary movie about my practice was either to be a bust or a success. Through long days and nights of filming, I wondered if it would contribute to the public's general knowledge of nursing practice. I was acutely conscious that my actions should be truly representative of professional nursing practice; "Portrait of a Nurse" reached well beyond my expectations.

As we strive for excellence we must temper our power and strength with tenderness, love, and understanding. We must use vision and creativity wisely. We must see how things could be, dream effectively, and then mold fantasy into reality. We must learn to strike a balance between the internal and external debates, how to understand competition and assertiveness, and when to collaborate. We should focus on the profession's future.

As Maria Phaneuf once said, "Learn to emphasize commonalities and glory in differences."

The ability nurses have to understand people seems to be a divine gift. Caring, listening, compromising, and encouraging are essential qualities and practices to me. When we temper the overstated, tighten what is possible, and then promote what is useful, we have a chance. The more we learn from each other and the more we build beliefs in ourselves, the more hopeful and proud I am to be among the members of this great profession.

Virginia Stone

Virginia Stone, PhD, RN, FAAN,
is a consultant in gerontology

❖

As a latchkey child happily reared by a wonderful single parent, Virginia Stone made the most of all her experiences. She learned early the meaning of responsibility, volunteerism, and leadership. Like many people, she credits having been in the right place at the right time as pivotal in her career. Throughout her nursing school program and her entire career, she sought additional education and cherished every chance she had for new encounters. Always setting goals for herself, she plotted her way through a doctoral program that emphasized sociology, drew out public health as her first program choice, and moved her right into gerontology—a field in which she has become widely recognized. She has shared generously her knowledge and skill with professional nursing organizations—from local to international levels. At present, she is pursuing both her dream of improved nursing care for the aging and her lively and productive career in continuing education in gerontological nursing.

*W*hat in life determines one's destiny? Some believe much is set in our childhood, so this is where I shall begin. When I was two years old, my father died, leaving three children. My mother went to work in a tobacco factory to support us. As latchkey children of a single parent, we were each given responsibilities and boundaries about behavior. I learned to accept responsibility early. When I was eight, we moved to a new neighborhood right across the street from the Instructive Visiting Nurses Association (IVNA). The nurses lived in a beautiful old house. When I had typhoid fever a year later, I was cared for by the IVNA nurses. Soon I became a mascot and was allowed to make home visits with the nurses who were on call on Sundays. When I was 12 there was an epidemic, which increased the workload. I was taught to file and help as a volunteer in the office.

I have always been a leader. I don't know why I was, but I remember as a teenager being president of my Sunday School class and of the Baptist Youth Union. I was also active in the Girl Scouts.

When I was ready to graduate from high school, I knew I wanted to be a nurse. That was during the Great Depression, so my mother could not afford to support my education. The director of nurses and two other nurses sponsored me as a student at Stuart Circle Hospital. I had wanted to go to the Boston Floating Hospital for children, but my mother preferred keeping her children at home.

Throughout much of my life I have been in the right place at the right time. As a first-year student in nursing, I went to the Medical College of Virginia for some classes, one being taught by a well-starched nurse, Lulu K. Wolf (Hassenplug). She sometimes put the fear of God in me, and she talked about research, of which I was ignorant. Through her teaching, my life and way of thinking expanded. A few years after I had studied with Lulu Wolf, I was privileged to attend an affair to celebrate her being honored with the Florence Nightingale International Foundation Award from the Red Cross. She was one of my early role models.

I knew when I graduated that I had a position waiting for me as a staff nurse at the IVNA at $99 a month. Most of my classmates had trouble finding work because of the depression. However, that had been a fortunate time to be a student. Hospital census was low, so we were not rushed during patient care. Head nurses had time to arrange special demonstrations for us. We were responsible for total patient care. I have never been involved in functional nursing.

Soon after becoming a staff nurse I knew I wanted to continue my education, so I enrolled in late afternoon and evening classes to obtain a certificate in public health nursing. I had a yen for the big city and thought I would try a summer school stint at Teachers

College, Columbia University—but I needed money. The Virginia Nurses Association had a scholarship fund that had been used only for nurses in the field of education. I argued, "Why not other fields?" and came out with my first scholarship. At TC one of my professors was Mary Ella Chayer, who became another role model. For an extended period I kept taking classes toward a bachelor's degree. After ten years I received one of those "bastard" bachelor's degrees in nursing. I like to laugh about that and call myself a slow learner.

All during that time I continued in public health nursing in several locations. Being a public health nurse in a rural county was most exciting. As a staff nurse at the IVNA, I was always challenged to see how early I could locate expectant mothers. But in the county my challenge was tuberculosis case-finding. I also established the first maternity clinic in the county. You should have seen it—pretty curtains and colored walls. Later I found I had made a big mistake by leaving out the midwives in planning the clinic. Also during that 10-year period, I became interested in Red Cross disaster nursing. What fun to volunteer and to use all the creativity possible to improvise care. My first disaster experience was in a flood in 1937, the second was after a tornado in Mississippi, and then as I finished college, I was engaged in polio nursing. All my activities had been geared to practice.

When I was ready to receive my degree, my sociology professor interested me in going for a master's degree in sociology. I really hadn't given advanced education much thought. She was a great professor who had lived in Russia. Her PhD was from the University of North Carolina. In some ways she was a maverick who enjoyed making one analyze her values. She was sure she could get me accepted, along with a research scholarship of $250. I think that was a turning point in my professional career—moving into higher education.

At the end of nine months I completed work for my master's degree. While at the University, I met a number of students working toward PhD's. Until then I had erroneous ideas about a PhD and thought I could never obtain one. However, after meeting some of the candidates, I decided if they could do it so could I, and so I started planning. My plan was to attend summer school sessions—courses off campus with university approval. However, I had to work to save money. I had advanced to several supervisory positions in public health nursing. Because of my previous disaster nursing with the Red Cross, I decided I would join the staff. Having been in public health previously, I naturally had read a great deal about the Henry Street Settlement, so what a pleasure it was to work with Marguerite Wales at the Red Cross and later with Ruth Freeman. All during my career I have been thrown in with the earlier leaders. I'm sure some of this rubbed off. After a period with the Red Cross, I moved into administrative positions. I really didn't like those roles because much of my time was taken up with personnel problems. However, I did learn a great deal. One staff I was with had been accustomed to laissez-faire administration. Being a graduate of sociology I was determined to move them into a democratic setting. I soon learned there were steps between such processes.

I started to work toward a PhD with another 10-year goal. During my first summer session my roommate, who was in public health nursing, told me I just had to come to one of her classes taught by a nurse who was different from the run of the mill—who even wore high heels while lecturing. This was my introduction to Lydia Hall, who taught me about specialization in nursing and the importance of learning everything possible in that specialty. I looked around for night classes in the Washington area that I thought the University of North Carolina would allow for credit toward my PhD. I found a course in social gerontology taught by Dr. Clark Tibbitts, one of the founders of American social gerontology. This proved to be my introduction to gerontological nursing. I came away from his course knowing I would develop a dissertation on a three-generation family— which I did not do.

I have always watched for opportunities and sought them out. In 1956 I learned that public health research scholarships were available, so I applied for one. I became a full-time student who would major in sociology and minor in public health. I realized that even though I was interested in sociology, public health was of greater interest to me. I became acquainted with the chairman of the Health Education Department at the University of North Carolina, Dr. Lucy S. Morgan, who informed me that she thought at one time the university had approved the program for a major in public health and a minor in sociology. That was on the books but had never been used. After a great deal of investigation, I switched. Dr. Morgan was a leader in the study of aging who had developed a high-power committee in the community to study the needs of older people and develop plans to meet those needs. She moved me right into the committee, as well as the field of aging. Just before completing my doctorate, I read about a five-week course in social gerontology for prospective leaders in the field. Again I applied, knowing that the course was limited to 40 participants and that in the first course no nurses were selected. In 1959 two nurses received scholarships, Laurie Gunter and myself. In that course we became acquainted with many leaders whom we continue to work with. After completing my degree, I was invited to remain on the faculty to develop a gerontology program.

During my two years in health education I developed some of the early continuing education courses. My dissertation was in demand, as it was one of the early studies on aging. I was becoming known in the field because there were few people with my background. (Again, that was a matter of being in the right place at the right time.) It was a time when few people were working in the field of gerontology. I was still being sought by multidisciplinary groups, but I wanted to be more closely identified with nursing. The opportunity to direct graduate education in the school of nursing arose, so I transferred. While there I read about World Health Organization fellowships. My nature being what it was, I applied. I spent six weeks abroad looking at health care programs for the aged. That was also an opportunity to become acquainted with gerontological nurses in other countries. For some reason, I missed colleague relationships in gerontology. I knew that Duke University had the oldest center for aging in the country, and I transferred into Duke's School of Nursing as chairman of graduate education, a department in which I would also have contact with gerontologists conducting research. I understood that in revamping the graduate program, I could develop a specialty in gerontological nursing. The first master's program in the country with a major in gerontology was launched. Soon after that, a post-master's program in geropsychiatric nursing was developed but never really got off the ground, although one student did complete the program.

Before proceeding with my further exploits at Duke, I must discuss my involvement with professional nursing organizations. I feel strongly that one should become involved with her or his profession. I have always been interested and involved in the American Nurses' Association, holding various offices at the district level. At the state level I've been president, board member, and chair of a conference group on gerontological nursing. This prepared me for leadership at the national level. In 1962 I was part of the first national conference group on geriatric practice called by the ANA. In the early 1960s ANA was going through a change in structure. Geriatric nursing became recognized as a specialty by the professional organization. I was right there when the Division on Gerontological Nursing was established. Over an extended period, I had a leadership role in that division. Being in the right place at the right time provided me the opportunity to serve on the Interim Committee on Certification and to assist in the formation of the first standards on gerontological nursing. The ANA received a grant to develop a prototype for continuing education. This was done and was conducted by the Duke School of Nursing. Representatives from each state were charged with the responsibility to return home and establish continuing education programs, using the prototype as a guide.

Also during the time I was active in ANA, we called the first national conference for directors of nursing of nursing homes to learn their needs and to develop plans for meeting them.

One must get satisfaction out of her or his work. I think the greatest reward is when one's peers recognize one's achievements, such as when I was awarded the ANA Honorary Award for Leadership in gerontological nursing. The opportunity for leadership was there because gerontological nursing development was new. It was easy to be a part of establishing the "first" in so many areas.

Nursing seems always to have problems within academic spheres. Graduates of the master's program were increasing when the powers that be decided to discontinue the graduate program at Duke. One of the satisfactions, though, is that most of the graduates have become leaders in gerontological nursing. Even though the graduate program closed, I continued at Duke, where I offered multidisciplinary courses for undergraduates. I was also busy with committees and lecturing. With so few nurses prepared in gerontology, I found myself on many committees as the only nurse. I had an opportunity to interpret and present gerontological nursing to committees representing other disciplines. The White House Conferences on Aging in 1971 and again in 1981 provided such opportunity.

My lectures have carried me throughout the United States and Canada. The major thrust of my talks has been to promote understanding of the process of aging and its relationship to nursing behavior. Because of my continuing practice, I had developed many illustrations and case studies that helped my audiences to view me as not only an academician, but as a practitioner. Continuing education became my love, because I saw it as a way of sharing gerontological nursing to improve care. I took early retirement from Duke so that I could devote more time to continuing education. That is where I am now.

However, in the interim I had the honor of being the first nurse to occupy the first gerontological nursing chair in the United States, the Florence Cellar Professorship at Frances Payne Bolton School of Nursing, Case Western Reserve University.

I've always been able to evaluate situations to determine needs. Since I'm partly maverick, I don't always accept the status quo on regulations. I tend to question. For example, I think we have tried so hard in nursing to establish professional recognition that we went overboard in experimental designs for research. We have tried to learn too much about the elderly through structured questionnaires. At present, although we have more contact with those 85 years and older, we have little knowledge of this group. There is an opportunity now for good case study method research. I am so convinced of the need for case studies in this area that I am engaged in private research of some 90-year-olds using the case study approach. I also happen to think that some research can be done without grant money. It would certainly allow for more flexibility.

I can't describe my pattern of leadership because I don't fit any mold. I am a highly independent individual who was brought up from childhood to accept responsibility. At times I'm impatient with others, especially if they do not perform at a high level. Some think of me as "bossy" and autocratic. I wouldn't be where I am today in my profession if I hadn't had support from others, such as the women who opened doors to me. Because they did, I always felt a great responsibility to them to succeed. I was also fortunate in having such good role models in the early years of my profession.

I still have a need for continued learning. I regret my lack of publications, but I resorted to the spoken word. Writing has never been easy for me. Being in the right place at the right time probably had as much to do with my life-style as any other single factor.

Margretta M. Styles

Margretta M. Styles, EdD, RN, FAAN,
is Professor and Livingston Chair in Nursing at the
School of Nursing, University of California, San Francisco

❖

Deliberatively and with classic charm, Margretta Styles tells her story: into the world; into nursing; into credentialing. In describing the influence of her Irish heritage on her love of the sound of words, Gretta feels that being able to laugh at herself and the foibles of others is her most comfortable interpersonal device. Her journey through a childhood hospitalization, an undergraduate degree in biology and chemistry, a brush with the idea of a religious vocation, and finally into nursing is told exquisitely. There is a richness in her various teaching and administrative experiences, but it was and is her affinity for care for patients that keeps her rooted in nursing. In discussing her leadership style she says "From the speaker's platform I have attempted to excite a tide of rising expectations; to describe what nursing might be ... I have sat around countless tables negotiating for a consensus position so that nursing might move forward on major issues." Her clear explanation of credentialing and how she came to be so connected with it is instructive, and her dream for nursing leads one to cheer.

INTO THE WORLD

*B*irth order has always held great meaning to me. I am the youngest of eight children, born and raised in Pennsylvania. Siblings were older, bigger, stronger— I always felt like a runt scrambling for my share of attention. From this I learned two lifelong lessons—to be self-sufficient and to reach way beyond my grasp.

Maternal influence was also powerful. I loved my mother intensely but quietly, and I studied her every move. My values were shaped from the reflections in her eyes more than from her words, which were never harsh and seldom direct. Even today I can feel her every pleasure and disappointment. I remember her pain when she found a cigarette in my sister's jacket pocket, so I have never smoked. I saw the pain she felt when an alcoholic sibling stumbled into the house, and thus I have never been able to tolerate spirits. I also saw my mother's pride when a report card with straight A's appeared in the hand of my big sister. I have seldom missed the mark and didn't stop until I had earned the highest degree academia had to offer. Maybe it was only imagined, but my mother seemed secretly pleased at small acts of rebellion.

Today, at 56, I still measure myself against those reflections.

I am also proud of my Irish O'Madden heritage, although those traits were greatly diluted as they passed through previous generations. I fancy that my love of the sound of words, even more than their meaning, can be traced to those origins and has enriched my career in public speaking. The Black Irish belief that the worst must be expected if the best is to be achieved has influenced my cautious administrative style, and laughing at myself and the foibles of others is my most comfortable interpersonal device.

INTO NURSING

Several events conspired to lead me into nursing.

As a teenager I developed a scoliosis requiring periodic hospitalizations for application of a body cast. During those long, mortifying days and nights, some of my mother-watching shifted to nurse- and patient-watching. Hospitals, which I came to view as medieval torture chambers because of a number of unspeakable experiences, held a macabre fascination for me. During my undergraduate years I would circle hospitals in the dark of night, spellbound by the glimpses of activity to be seen through the lighted windows. Today the most intimate hospital scenes are displayed promiscuously on TV in our living rooms; in 1950 we had to settle for distant and infrequent exposures to the real thing. I often wonder ... does such intimacy make the heart grow fonder—of nursing?

College brought two absorbing interests—biology and religion. As a child I had halfheartedly but regularly attended the middle-of-the-road Methodist church with my family. The small liberal arts college I attended near my hometown was affiliated with the Church of the Brethren, a plain, joyless, narrow sect as it seemed to me in those days. In reaching out for a more colorful, more personal religion, I discovered the Episcopal church, for which I felt an immediate affinity—actually a calling. I loved—and still love—its embracing liturgy. It drew me to a commitment to service.

An interest in natural phenomena led me to major in biology and minor in chemistry. However, at graduation I still had not made a decision as to what career to pursue. So I followed my religious leanings to the convent of the Episcopal Community of the Trans-figuration in Ponce, Puerto Rico, where I had been offered a summer job in a recreation center for boys. Then I became a sister-watcher.

Nursing reappeared. Because of my background in biology, the sisters asked me to stay on for the school year to teach microbiology to the nursing students enrolled in the church's hospital diploma program located near the convent. The students knew little English, and I knew less Spanish and nothing about teaching and nursing. It can only be said that we struggled and survived. However, I was fascinated once again with the clinical vignettes.

My career choice was made. I would become a religious sister. I prepared to try my vocation at the novitiate in Glendale, Ohio. When I announced this decision to my parents, once again I saw and could not withstand the pain in my mother's eyes. Hence, I became a nurse.

Yale University School of Nursing was at that time one of only two in the country tailoring its program to the college graduate. I entered in 1951 and graduated three years later with a master of nursing degree.

The intervening years are a blur of long hours of study, longer hours of staffing the hospital, slipping and sliding over the wintery streets of New Haven as a visiting nurse, summer exile to a psychiatric warehouse for a three-month rotation, and lots and lots of dating Yalies.

The question of role models often comes up. I must admit that, with a few shining exceptions, I found the faculty to be uninspiring. However, I was immensely drawn to the head nurses who were both swift of foot and fleet of mind. They were magnificent in managing personnel and patient care on large, crowded, understaffed, and poorly equipped units. While we were students, the young head nurse we all admired most died of polio on the very unit she had managed with such competence and compassion.

It was, however, the patients from whom I learned the most. I can close my eyes today and review case after case, face after face, despair after despair, and hope after hope. Those ancient memories constitute my clinical roots because I have been in teaching and administration since leaving Yale.

Thirty years ago a master's degree in nursing was a rarity. Repeatedly I applied for staff positions and was offered teaching or management posts despite my inexperience as a graduate nurse. The Veterans Administration hired me, right out of school, at their entry level and chose to make me a roving charge nurse, circulating from unit to unit replacing head nurses who were doing their required stints on night duty. I was also a new bride, having married an Episcopal seminarian who was finishing his last year at Yale.

Following my husband's career moves, and later my own as his cardiac problems restricted his activities, I served on the faculty of a diploma program in Brooklyn, as an associate director of nursing in a community hospital, as a founding director of an associate degree program in Florida, as assistant dean for undergraduate studies at Duke University in North Carolina, as founding dean of the School of Nursing at the University of Texas Medical Center in San Antonio, as dean at Wayne State University in Detroit, and finally as professor, dean, and associate director of nursing service at the University of California, San Francisco. Three children and a doctorate in education from the University of Florida enhanced this zigzag course across the United States. I became increasingly active in organized nursing with each move and reached the American Nurses' Association (ANA) presidency in 1986.

Nursing is my identity, in fact, my obsession. Administration has been my role. What has been my leadership style in that role?

From the vast literature on leadership philosophy, traits, and practices, I find most meaningful political scientist–philosopher James McGregor Burns' descriptions of trans-actional and transforming leadership. Transactional leadership operates on exchange theory, trading one thing for another to achieve goals. Transforming leadership looks for potential motivations, seeks to satisfy higher needs, and engages the full person of the follower, resulting in a relationship of mutual stimulation and elevation (Burns, 1978). I have aspired to provide both. On the one hand, from the speaker's platform I have attempted to excite a tide of rising expectations—to describe what nursing might be. On the other hand, I have sat around countless tables negotiating for a consensus position so that nursing might move forward on major issues. "Negotiating progress," the sociological concept of main-taining order while major changes occur within a social system, has been the personal theme of my ANA presidency.

While I was dean at UCSF the school totally revised its mission and pioneered several innovative programs and projects. My attempts throughout this process were to have faculty and students believe in the possibility of their dreams and to support them in their pursuit.

INTO CREDENTIALING

Often I am asked what is my specialty, my area of expertise. The field of credentialing*— an ugly word with serious implications—is my closest claim to fame and infamy. It was not a choice but a series of invitations.

In 1974 the ANA House of Delegates demanded a greater role in the accreditation of nursing education, which was historically the purview of the National League for Nursing (NLN). The board of directors chose to convene a small conference group to develop an

---

Regulation may be defined quite simply as the *forms and processes whereby order, consistency, and control are brought to an occupation and its practice.* Nothing inherent in the word specifies the various means by which this order, consistency and control are accomplished. *Credentialing* refers to particular forms and processes, such as licensure, registration, certification, and accred-itation, whereby qualified agents designate various persons, programs, or practices as having met specified standards (Styles, 1986a, p. 7).

approach to the mandate. I was invited to be keynote speaker at the conference and spoke with some force about nursing's divided house and about the interrelationships among licensure, accreditation, and certification. I appealed for careful, comprehensive consideration of the appropriate role of all elements of organized nursing in all forms of credentialing (Styles and Gottdank, 1976).

As a result the ANA funded a large project on credentialing. I was invited to chair the study committee, which included nursing leaders and nonnurse experts in the field. Also involved were a fine staff headed by Inez Hinsvark and representatives from a large number of cooperating organizations, including the ANA, NLN, and nursing specialty groups. A full report containing a series of definitions and recommendations on standard-setting and the conduct of licensure, accreditation of nursing education and nursing service, and the certification of specialists, as well as a volume of background papers, was published in 1979 (American Nurses' Association, Vols. I and II, 1979). Many of the recommendations were opposed, others were ignored—none were implemented. Strangely, the study is now being revisited, its proposals reviewed after nearly a decade. An ANA monograph, *The 1979 Study of Credentialing in Nursing Recommendations: Where Are We Now?*, has been released (Carter, 1986). Nursing's house has remained divided, though perhaps more at peace, on these issues. And proving the Peter Principle, one might think, I was invited into a wider scope of influence on the subject.

In 1983 the International Council of Nurses (ICN) determined that it was time for a worldwide study of the standards and mechanisms whereby nursing is regulated and how such regulation facilitates or impedes the development of the profession. Having chaired a national study, I was chosen to conduct the project, under the auspices of the ICN Professional Services Committee (PSC). This provided a wonderful opportunity to broaden my perspective and to serve essentially as a one-person researcher and think tank. The project report, *The Regulation of Nursing* (Styles, 1986a), after undergoing review and modification by the PSC and the ICN Board of Directors, was approved by unanimous vote of the ICN Council of National Representatives meeting in Israel in June 1985. Its recommendations, in the form of principles, policy objectives, and national guidelines, constitute the position paper of the ICN on credentialing matters and is serving as the blueprint for many nations in assessing and developing their own regulatory systems (ICN, 1986). In December 1986 the ANA published my invited monograph measuring nursing in the United States against these international goals (Styles, 1986b).

The World Health Organization (WHO) has a natural interest in developing health manpower to achieve its goal of "Health for All by the Year 2000" (HFA/2000) through primary health care (PHC). Thus in 1985 a study committee was commissioned to determine how regulatory standards were affecting the role of nurses as PHC providers. Because of my earlier work I was asked to chair this committee made up of nurses from all regions of the world. Our findings and recommendations were released in 1986 (WHO, 1986). As a consequence, a plan has been proposed by WHO for removing unreasonable scope of practice restrictions and for improving educational standards to unleash and enhance nursing's contribution to PHC and HFA/2000.

Having come full circle, as an American Nurses' Foundation Distinguished Scholar, I am completing a study of specialization in nursing, including the standards and processes for certifying specialists. I now serve on the ICN Professional Services Committee, having formerly served as the committee's consultant and project director on the regulation study. Our agenda continues to address matters of credentialing. Locally I am a member of the California Board of Registered Nursing, a position that keeps me rooted in reality at the operations level in licensure and program accreditation.

That I have step-by-step been drawn externally to a deeper and wider involvement in credentialing does not indicate any reluctance or reticence about the field on my part. Quite the contrary, I am increasingly convinced of the criticality and pervasiveness of its influence.

Regulatory means, including forms of credentialing, can significantly strengthen or weaken nursing's future. Consider these realities:

- Regulation, in the form of standards of education, selects us for nursing and shapes our capabilities.
- Regulation, in the form of legal definitions of practice and employment and reimbursement policies, enables or deters our full use of those capabilities, as well as determines where we may practice those capabilities and how we shall be compensated for those capabilities.
- Regulation, in the form of licensing and registration, defines us and names us and identifies us and certifies us to the public.
- Regulation, in the form of licensing laws and health care policies, sets up the hierarchy among the health professions.
- Regulation, in all of the above forms, helps or hinders the WHO goal of health for all and the strategies of primary health care.

With respect to the actual and potential influence of regulatory standards and means, I have encouraged nurses everywhere to

- Think of a world in which nurses are a strong, vital, and dynamic social force.
- Think of a world in which nursing is at the forefront of health care.
- Think of a world in which the word "nurse" has a singular, positive meaning and the image of nursing is sharp and distinct in the eyes of the public.
- Think of a world in which nursing speaks with one voice.
- Think of a world in which nurses bring honor and reward to themselves, to all women, and to all people.
- Think of a world in which the words of Florence Nightingale, "No system can endure that does not march," resound throughout our daily lives.
- Think of a world in which the Director-General of the World Health Organization is a nurse (Styles, 1985).

This, by the way, is my dream for nursing.

REFERENCES

American Nurses' Association (1979). *The study of credentialing in nursing: a new approach* (Vols. I & II). Kansas City, MO: Author.

Burns, J.M. (1978). *Leadership.* New York: Harper and Row.

Carter, E.W. (1986). *Credentialing in nursing: contemporary developments and trends: the 1979 study of credentialing in nursing recommendations: where are we now?* Kansas City, MO: American Nurses' Association.

Styles, M.M. (1986b). *Credentialing in nursing: contemporary developments and trends: U.S.A. within a world view.* Kansas City, MO: American Nurses' Association.

Styles, M.M. (1986a). *Report on the regulation of nursing.* Geneva: International Council of Nurses.

Styles, M.M. (1985). *Think of a world.* Presentation made at the General Session, 18th Quadrennial Congress, International Congress of Nurses, Tel Aviv, Israel, June 19, 1985.

Styles, M.M., and Gottdank, M. (1976). Nursing's vulnerability. *American Journal of Nursing, 76*(12), 1978-1980.

World Health Organization (1986). *Regulatory mechanisms for nursing training and practice: meeting primary health care needs* (WHO Technical Report Series No. 739). Geneva: Author.

Joy K. Ufema

Joy K. Ufema, RN, is a thanatologist
based in Airville, Pennsylvania

❖

Joy Ufema had a rocky beginning in nursing school, failing a drugs and solutions course. Being asked to leave was devastating, embarrassing, and confusing, but she dusted herself off, got herself tutored, and entered another hospital school—only to leave again after two years to get married. Four years later she was divorced, still hungry for knowledge, and wanting to be a nurse. On her third try, at a community college in Harrisburg, Pennsylvania, she completed a two-year nursing program.

Her outspokenness didn't help her career much, but she remembered learning from her study of Maslow's work that self-actualized people simply find out what they do right and do it. Her affinity for death and dying prompted her to sign up for a seminar with Elisabeth Kübler-Ross, and she was off and running. She approached the director of nursing at the hospital where she was employed to ask for a job working exclusively with dying patients throughout the hospital. She got it, and a newspaper reporter became interested in what she was doing. Then she was featured on 60 Minutes and, after that, Linda Lavin made a TV movie about Joy's life and work.

*I*t was a toss-up. At age seven I couldn't decide between being a nurse or a cowboy. (I've done both.)

I wasn't one of those little girls who was always bandaging the dog or pretending to be a Red Cross nurse while my boy chums played soldier. Nah! Not me! I'd stand with my hands on my hips, feet apart, and defiantly order the smallest kid in the neighborhood, Eddie, to be the nurse. Of course I would frequently offer my services as a consultant, whether Eddie had requested them or not.

I was a heck of a tomboy—the best tree climber in the neighborhood. I had a great imagination and plenty of raw materials around that I could use to express my creativity. I once built a fantastic stagecoach (sans wheels) and organized and directed the passengers through marvelous summer afternoons filled with adventure.

I've always been a lively person, and I believe that quality—to bring life to situations—had a large influence on my choosing to specialize in death and dying.

My twelfth summer was spent at the school playground perfecting my skills as a shortstop. The young lady who was the playground director that summer told all of us about her plans to enter Altoona Hospital's School of Nursing.

I thought that was wonderful.

Although I preferred Nancy Drew to Cherry Ames, I began fervently reading about nurses.

By the time I was 16, I decided that I would not go to Texas to be a cattle baron, as earlier planned (a decision that was applauded by my relieved parents). I announced that I would go to the Altoona Hospital School of Nursing and from there on to Japan to become a medical missionary.

That summer I volunteered at the hospital. It was nice, and I found intrinsic rewards almost daily.

I was an enthusiastic worker and sighed with admiration when I saw the nursing students in their crisp, blue- and white-striped uniforms.

I had found my niche.

My senior year in high school was eventful. Eagerly I studied the required microbiology course. I achieved and excelled—it all felt so right.

Working as a "Yellow Jacket" (candy striper) during that year was a healthy experience. I fit in with my peers and was even requested by a *real* nurse to help her with a difficult patient.

Rather smugly, I left the towels and sheets I was placing on the linen cart and strolled behind the nurse as we entered a four-bed ward. I believe I even stole a glance over my shoulder to smile at my fellow Yellow Jackets as they continued with their mundane folding.

"Come over here, Joy, to Mrs. Duncan's bed." the nurse cooed.

Innocent and unsuspecting, I was totally unprepared for what was to greet me from behind the curtain.

Mrs. Ducan was lying with her face to the wall, with her back and buttocks exposed to a heat lamp. At her coccyx was a bedsore so deep I could see into her spinal column. Necrotic and purulent tissue gave off a foul odor.

I felt my ears getting hot and my hands getting cold.

"Mrs. Duncan," said the nurse, "I've brought a new helper with me today. She's thinking about becoming a nurse, aren't you, Joy, and I thought maybe she should see what real nursing is like." Smiling sardonically, she added, "Don't you think that would be a good idea, Mrs. Duncan?"

No response.

Afraid I was going to faint, I knelt to fake tying a shoelace of my new white Clinics.

Taking a few deep breaths, I slowly rose and walked to the opposite side of the bed.

Drawing from deep in my marrow, I bent close to Mrs. Duncan's face and said, "Thank you for allowing me to be with you. I'll help hold you over while we get this dressing changed."

I held her hand tightly—more for myself than for her. I was able to transcend, in the name of dignity, the sight and the smell.

Six months later I was proudly marching through those same hospital corridors as an official student nurse.

Perhaps it was because of my immaturity, or that things usually came easy for me, or that I just made wrong choices (play instead of study), but I failed the drugs and solutions course and was asked to leave the Altoona Hospital School of Nursing.

Devastated, embarrassed, and confused, I went home.

My parents encouraged me to get a job. Skill-less, the only work I could find was slinging hash at the lunch counter of McCrory's Five and Ten. My uniform was not crisp, nor did it have white and blue stripes. It was an awful yellow and green thing with a dippy apron.

As a gentle form of rebellion, I would conveniently "forget" to wear the stupid fringed hat that went with the uniform. I silently vowed to wear only a nurse's cap and sustained myself with the thought that this waitress job was temporary.

My hopes frequently got dampened when five or six of my ex-fellow students would arrive at the counter and sit at my station.

With snickers and whispers, they would coolly order me to prepare exotic ice cream sundaes. Giggling and chatting, they continued to act out the scene using well-rehearsed and painful lines.

"I'm assigned 4 West this week. Oh! I'm so glad to be working there!"

"Did you sign up for the Big Sister's picnic? We're gonna have a ball!"

I fought back. I got myself tutored in drugs and solutions and I got accepted at another hospital—out of town.

Things went well for two years. Then I got involved with a handsome Russian and left school to marry.

Immature and inexperienced in relationships, I divorced after four years.

I moved to New York State to just plain forget and start fresh. I worked odd jobs—from picking grapes for Welch's to painting fences to being a psychiatric aide at Warren State Hospital.

The work at that hospital wasn't especially physically hard (as it had been before phenothiazines), but it took a toll on my spirit. I had a moral dilemma about the way some of the patients were treated—cold showers and verbal abuse, not to mention the almost total lack of helpful psychiatric intervention. Coworkers reminded me of my low status and said to do as I was told and keep my mouth shut.

"Perhaps the third time will be the charm," I said as I enrolled at the off-campus class of Edinborough College. "I need to get some education so I have some clout in helping patients with their rights."

I took Psychology 101.

I aced the class.

I wanted more, but Edinborough was offering a four-year BSN program and had decided against the ADN idea. The same week that I heard this bad news my apartment house caught fire. I received $1,000 from a small insurance policy and decided to move to Harrisburg, where the community college had a two-year nursing program.

I was accepted within a week.

Eager and grateful, I walked the lovely campus at dusk. "This time," I mused, "this time I'm going to be successful!"

And I was.

I was hungry for knowledge. I worked part time as an LPN. I studied all of the time, except for a few Friday night parties.

I was hot. I was employed before I graduated, passed state boards, and started to work 3 to 11 on the urology ward.

It didn't go well. I remember a conversation I had with the head nurse.

"Ufema, what were you doing last evening? Honestly, you were late counting narcotics and you failed to record if Mr. DeFranco had a bowel movement."

"I'm sorry about the count. As for my patient's bowels, neither he nor I give a damn. He was given the results of his prostate biopsy and was very upset about it being positive. I spent some time talking with him."

"Well, you're not here to talk. You can talk all you want after the work is done, and the way you're going at it, it doesn't look to me like you have enough time to do that."

"I don't feel OK about giving someone 50 mg of Demerol for fear. He just needed to talk. I see that as my job just as much as irrigating his catheter."

Things weren't any better after that little altercation. My three-month evaluation said I was not a speedy worker, that I wasn't picking up fast enough, and that I wasn't learning to cut corners. (I guess not.) I've always trusted my intuition. It was obvious to me that my place in nursing was not 20 years on the urology floor. It just didn't feel right.

Abraham Maslow said the self-actualized person simply finds out what he does right and does it.

My affinity to dying patients led me to read and study. I signed up to go to a seminar conducted by Elisabeth Kübler-Ross.

Sitting among 2,000 participants, I suddenly saw myself standing at a podium, lecturing to hundreds of people about *my* experiences of working with dying patients and their families.

This imagery and self-fulfilling prophecy would soon serve me quite successfully.

I attended workshops and seminars, read lots of books, studied theories, and then sorted out for myself what I felt was good and valuable.

I spent more time with terminally ill patients—listening. I visited before and after my regular shift. Within a few weeks, I realized this work was tenfold more rewarding for me than regular nursing.

Never having been the kind of person to sit back and wait for opportunity to knock, I decided to *make* something happen. I approached Jean Deeter, the director of nursing, and asked if I could have a job working exclusively with the dying patients throughout the hospital.

She said yes. She had also heard the challenge of Kübler-Ross, and, after all, not many young nurses were bombarding her with this request.

One of the most difficult adjustments for me was to learn to sit down and stop "fussing" over the patients.

I recall the first morning that I worked as a "nurse-specialist in death and dying." I had worked ten days in a row on the urology floor and had five more days to put in before my first weekend off in a long time. Yet, I had energy to spare!

My patient was a 19-year-old with cancer of the testicle. It had metastasized to his lung. His night nurse had given him a bath and changed his linens. He was resting.

At 8 AM I introduced myself.

"Tom, my name is Joy, and I'm working with the patients here who are seriously ill. Do you feel like talking about anything?"

"Not right this minute, but you could hang around if you don't have anybody else who needs you right now."

After 20 minutes of "hanging around" his bedside, I felt terribly uncomfortable— not with death, but with my need to do something. I had fluffed his pillow, examined his IV site, gotten fresh juice, and done several other busy things.

Wearily, Tom took my hand and said, "Look, Joy, I don't really need any nurse stuff right now, but it sure would feel good just to have you sit here beside me."

I got his message.

I sat.

He dozed.

The nurses stared.

I felt comfortable.

I learned a profound lesson from Tom: dying persons know exactly what is best for themselves. If they don't come right out and tell you, you have to ask.

"What do you want?"

"What can I do that will help?"

"What are we doing that isn't helping?"

The days turned into years—good, hard-working years.

One afternoon I received a phone call from a reporter from the *Washington Post*. He said he was doing a piece on death and dying, and someone in Maryland had referred him to me.

He spent several days at the hospital, visiting me and talking with a few special patients. Both the reporter and the photographer were respectful of the message I wanted to give—that dying is an experience that is different for each individual and that most people die the way they live.

Simple but true.

Following the article, I received hundreds of letters. It was quite an event, and I'm glad the story was told.

About a year later I was contacted by Susanne St. Pierre, one of the producers of *60 Minutes*. What impressed me most about her was that she pronounced my name correctly.

"I was just calling to see if you're still riding roughshod over some of the doctors," she said.

"Occasionally," I replied. "But for the most part, I think I've trained them quite well."

She was interested in doing a story about me. I would be interviewed by Morley Safer, she said. I heaved a sigh of relief that it wasn't Mike Wallace!

Could she come to Harrisburg and spend some time getting a feel for things?

"Sure," I said, "What's the worst thing that could happen?"

They filmed for one week to get 14 minutes of film for the show. It was exhausting. I wasn't convinced it was all worth it. I had to trust that this producer would not distort my story in the "name of journalism." She came through like a true professional, and I was thrilled and honored.

A week after the show ran, I found myself struggling with and swearing at my tractor. Eleven inches of snow had piled up on my driveway, and I needed to plow myself out to get to work the next day.

The machine would not start, despite all my wrestling, yanking, and pulling.

With snow packed down my neck and pants, I had gone into the house to get warm and dry and to find my pistol so I could shoot the tractor—then the telephone rang.

The caller said she was Linda Lavin. She told me she had been impressed with the *60 Minutes* piece and wanted to produce a made-for-television movie about my life and work. I didn't know if it was really Linda Lavin, nor did I know if hers was a legitimate offer.

"Prove it," I said.

The contract arrived in three days.

More than a year later, the project was aired on CBS. Although I was the script consultant, Hollywood did their thing. They fictionalized and combined characters for the sake of brevity. It wasn't great, but it was good, and a lot of people were touched—and taught.

On the night that the movie aired, I received a terribly moving phone call from a woman who had earlier that day delivered tiny twins. One of the infants had died shortly after birth. The mother was crying and grieving during my movie.

An OB nurse having difficulty with her own pain had lashed out at the young mother, "I don't know why you're so upset. You have one live baby."

Enraged, the bereaved woman pointed to the television and screamed, "Why can't you be like *that* nurse!"

When I began my work, my goal was simple—to function as an advocate for the terminally ill patient. In fact, Jean Deeter had predicted that I would work myself out of a job because other nurses would see me as a role model. I felt a cognitive dissonance about that possibility. On one hand I was highly motivated to teach and be an example. I certainly couldn't do it all, and I wanted many nurses to feel the rewards I was receiving. On the other hand, I didn't want to not be needed by the patients. I loved the work, and I was good at it. I liked being unique.

I realize now that I had nothing to fear. Death affects us all differently. Some nurses will always have trouble with it no matter how many workshops they attend.

And that's OK.

What is not acceptable is when those same nurses act in a subversive way to prevent those of us who are comfortable with death from offering our services. One of the greatest obstacles I've faced in my career has not been burnout from too many deaths, but the problem of threatened nurses who resent all the publicity I've received, or the fact that I work mostly days and have weekends off. (Of course they never take my offer to spend one of those "days" making rounds with me.)

There is much displacement in the hospital setting. Administrators dictate to admitting physicians; physicians dictate to female nurses; nurses dictate to patients or other nurses. Patients rarely rebel because they fear receiving unsafe care. Physicians may exhibit clout by threatening to admit all of their patients to another hospital. However, nurses have been their own worst enemy. They seem to have lost sight of that original vision that called them to nursing. (And I hope that vision wasn't to be handmaidens!)

Professional nurses have to take a harder stand in asserting themselves as valuable, contributing members of the health care team. They have to be better educated through continuing education to feel more secure in being assertive in their pursuit of high-quality care for patients.

I've always gotten much out of my work because I've put a lot into it. I found the energy for such enthusiasm by listening to the "still, small voice" inside me. It is my spiritual belief that each one of us has that voice within. It was divinely given. It is universal.

I believe I chose to come to Earth at this time (one of my many reincarnations) and that I was spiritually educated and trained to do specific work in thanatology.

I agreed to this eons ago, and all of the people in this "play" agreed, too.

There are no coincidences. We all know our assignments, and we have free choice whether to carry those assignments through to completion.

I believe we have everything we need to carry out our agreed-upon tasks. We brought all the tools with us from past lives and we have constant, spiritual awareness.

We may ask for help to use these tools more effectively, and we will be reminded of our wondrous abilities to do anything we want to do.

We have the incredible power of self-fulfilling prophecy. If we see ourselves as getting cancer, we will. If we see ourselves marrying and having three children, we will. We create our own reality, and every minute is filled with the power to choose how we want to feel and act.

It doesn't really matter what happens to me externally. What matters is how I *choose* to be affected by the event.

Throughout my 14 years as a specialist, I have been sustained by the belief that people choose when and how they will die.

Every nurse can tell of patients who were close to death but held on for days or weeks for a special reason, or about those sweet folks who asked not to be disturbed because they were going to die that day, which indeed they did.

When I work with terminally ill people, I understand from the start that I am a brief companion—that these people are the captains of their fate and that I play a rather minor role.

I advocate for them so this final event will be relatively pain free and dignified. However, I know they will choose, ultimately, how to cope with the experience—whether I am there or not.

I offer what I have learned as helpful hints for making worth out of dying, but the individual chooses whether or not to use that information, as I too must do someday.

I will take to my own deathbed all of the memories of my life, and I know that the TV shows and the awards are not going to be of value to me then. My dying will take care of itself if I have simply lived within my beliefs—if I have listened well and learned from my patients . . . that big houses, big boats, and big bucks don't "do it" . . . that it is senseless to work to get "there" because "there" does not exist. There is only the joy to be found in each moment.

Of my hundreds of patients, I have never heard one say, "I wish I would have spent more time at the office."

I know that death is not the enemy; inhumanity is.

I will die well, knowing that whenever I had doubt, I risked it!

Harriet H. Werley

Harriet H. Werley, PhD, RN, FAAN,
is Distinguished Professor at the
University of Wisconsin–Milwaukee
School of Nursing

Following an extensive and illustrious military career, Harriet Werley expanded in civilian life the passionate interest in research she had developed as a high-ranking officer in the Army Nurse Corps. As teacher, consultant, administrator, editor, and inspirational role model, she has encouraged the commitment to research in hundreds of productive nurse researchers. Now she is involved in developing a nursing minimum data set that will hasten information processing and will help nurses develop computerized systems through which they can justify their stands in decision making. Those systems will also allow nurses to compare data for research across clinical settings, populations, geographical areas, and time.

I grew up during the depression of the 1930s and attended a one-room country school in Berks County, Pennsylvania. My father died when I was 12 years old. In fact, the township eighth-grade examination was scheduled for the day before my father was to be buried. I can still recall the school officials calling on my mother to ask about how they should handle my examination. They were willing to give me a special examination after the burial, but they also were concerned about whether that might affect my examination adversely, more so than if I were to take it with the other students as scheduled. It was left up to me and my mother. I decided to go with my fellow students and take the examination on the scheduled day.

As I look back on my life, I guess one of the things that always sustained me was the fact that people believed in me and expected me to do well, and I was treated accordingly.

As a child during the depression years, I was never certain that I would be able to finish high school because after my father died, we did not have the resources to pay for my room and board and travel expenses. Somehow we worked out the finances with all of us working odd jobs and through the generosity of one of my teachers and a neighbor for whom I delivered newspapers.

After I graduated from high school I found employment and at times was the sole employed individual of our family. My brother found full-time employment when he was old enough to work. I worked a number of years and saved some of my meager pay for tuition to enter nursing school. I was motivated to become a nurse because of my father's death.

FROM NURSING SCHOOL TO A CAREER IN THE ARMY NURSE CORPS

With my graduation from the Jefferson Medical College Hospital School of Nursing in Philadelphia in 1941, I soon was among those who served their country during World War II. I started my military career in the Army Nurse Corps (ANC) at the famous Walter Reed Army Hospital and then served 37 continuous months overseas in the Mediterranean theater. My experiences were broadening in terms of both personal growth and nursing. On my return from overseas, I had enough accumulated leave to negotiate a delay so that I could attend an accelerated semester at the University of Pennsylvania before reporting to Brooke Army Hospital, Fort Sam Houston, Texas. There I functioned as a staff nurse, a supervisor, and later an assistant chief nurse. I was asked to apply to three university schools of nursing. If I was accepted, I would be sent to complete my baccalaureate degree under army sponsorship. As it turned out, the turnover in those educational assignment slots was delayed. However, I had been accepted at the University of California School of Nursing at Berkeley, and so I decided to resign from the army and go on to complete my bachelor's degree under the GI Bill of Rights.

As I neared completion of the bachelor's degree, with a major in nursing education, I applied and was accepted for return to active duty. I was assigned to the U.S. Army Hospital, Camp Stoneman, Pittsburg, California, and was appointed assistant chief nurse. Within a year, I became chief nurse. I also was invited to apply for an army educational assignment to obtain a master's degree. Thus I attended Teachers College, Columbia University, from 1950 to 1951 under army sponsorship and completed an MA degree with a major in nursing administration.

During the year at Columbia I was the student representative on the faculty administration committee, which met frequently. I appreciated working with Thelma Ryan and Eugenia Spaulding. Subsequently, I was assigned to the Department of the Army, Office of the Surgeon General (OTSG), Personnel Division, which stabilized as a four-year tour of duty for me in Washington, D.C.

ASSIGNMENT TO THE OFFICE OF THE SURGEON GENERAL

After learning the work of an Army Nurse Corps assignment officer, I was approached about my growing interest in the career guidance and planning program in the OTSG. I had noted that the Army Nurse Corps had not yet formally developed its program and that there was no ANC officer representative in the career guidance and planning section working on ANC matters. Col. Ruby F. Bryant was chief of the ANC then, and Lt. Col. Inez Haynes was chief of the ANC section in the personnel division. They agreed the ANC should move in this direction, and eventually I became a member of the career guidance and planning section of the ANC.

Chief Anne Carey welcomed me and served as my mentor. She was a remarkable woman who spearheaded a career development program after the war to accord U.S. Army physicians the advanced training they had missed by having to go on to wartime leadership positions, many of which were administrative in nature. It was through her efforts that Army Medical Corps officers became board certified in the various specialties of their choice. She is 95 years old now, but she is still my good friend and counselor.

This work in the area of career guidance and planning was very satisfying. Some of the principles of the Department of the Army career planning program pertained to identifying outstanding young officers early and according them additional education or training opportunities, which were to be followed by planned developmental assignments in which they could use their newly acquired knowledge. Thus I was personally dealing with excellent ANC officers, helping them look for alternating educational and developmental duty assignment opportunities that would lead to positions of increased responsibility.

In working with ANC officers on a worldwide basis, I became familiar with records of many fine nurses and worked with them in terms of their desires and commitment to the ANC and the Army. I helped them present their applications for civilian schooling to the OTSG Education and Training Committee, recommended officers for assignment to the service courses, and recommended types of duty assignments following their educational assignments. While much of this was done by mail and telephone, it was gratifying to meet many of these fine individuals later at American Nurses' Association or National League for Nursing conventions and learn how they were progressing (Werley 1954a, 1954b).

Through a balanced assessment of corps needs and officer requests, we were able to increase the types of programs (both service and civilian) available to ANC officers, as well as to increase the number of slots in some of the courses. For example, we were able to have the nursing administration course given at the Army Medical Service (AMedS) School in Texas twice a year instead of only once. This meant a great deal in terms of the graduates being able to influence change when assigned to new facilities, for it made possible the assignment of two newly educated officers from this program to the same station as they were sent on assignments around the world. They then could be more effective working as colleague change agents. It was around that time that the Baccalaureate Degree Completion Program was initiated for the ANC, and spaces were increased for study at the master's and doctoral levels.

We made a concerted effort to inform the ANC officers and chief nurses that the corps was moving toward having the bachelor's degree as the minimum level of education for nurses, the same as for other army officers. Chief nurses were urged to encourage their staffs to pursue part-time study at their respective army posts, so the ANC officers could accumulate college credits and become eligible for an educational assignment to complete the last year's requirements for the bachelor's degree. Progress reports were always given at the army chief nurses' conferences to inform them of the increasing percentage of the ANC officers who had completed the bachelor's degree. It is ironic that in civilian life there is still opposition to the baccalaureate requirement for professional nurses, when in the 1950s we were moving along successfully with this idea as a matter of ANC career guidance and planning.

While on duty in the OTSG, I also attended and participated in numerous activities at the Walter Reed Army Institute of Research (WRAIR). I became a member of a panel of health professionals who participated in a series of short courses on medical management of mass casualties, which were given a number of times a year. This was an effort on the part of the WRAIR personnel to help medical schools integrate concepts of disaster medicine in the curricula so that in a war or conflict there would never again be an initially higher than average soldier death rate because physicians sent to the battlefields were not trained in disaster medicine. This effort was part of the Medical Education in National Defense (MEND) Program—developed by the joint services and the Veterans Administration, with the Army Medical Service initially given administrative responsibility for the program.

At that time the WRAIR and AMedS officials were reexamining the role of the WRAIR and of the AMedS in national defense. Among their many recommendations was that opportunities for wider nurse participation be provided in research, education, and publication activities of the Army Medical Service Graduate School, as it was once called, or the Institute. They also recommended that an ANC officer be assigned to the school in a consultant or advisory role to help implement the necessary nursing activities (Werley 1962a).

About six months before I completed my stabilized tour in the OTSG, the director of the WRAIR called the chief of the career guidance and planning branch to ask if I might be assigned at the WRAIR. I would be assigned to a position to be developed at the recommendation of the study group that had assessed the roles of the WRAIR and AMedS in national defense. I believed that this was an opportunity for nursing research development and nurse participation in various ways. I knew that this opportunity could mean a great deal for the Army Nurse Corps and for all of nursing. I was torn between believing the officer assigned as a consultant to the school must be a nurse with a PhD and wanting to give it a try. I respected the physicians and scientists at the WRAIR, some of whom knew me, and I knew that I would learn a great deal. Hoping I could contribute appropriately, I accepted the challenge.

THE WALTER REED ARMY INSTITUTE OF RESEARCH ASSIGNMENT

At the WRAIR I was placed in the Department of Atomic Casualties Studies, but I also was appointed coordinator of nursing activities. I was kept very busy with planning the series of mass casualties courses and becoming oriented to plans for projects at one of the Nevada test site bomb explosions. I participated in one of these projects and, properly garbed in protective clothes, was in the first vehicle that entered the site after the explosion to help record the trauma and burn results on the research animals.

I became acquainted with the contributions of the physicists, trauma and nuclear medicine specialists, and other scientists. Most of them had been consultants in battlefield surgery during wartime, had studied radiation and trauma effects after the bomb explosions in Japan, had been present at various test explosions, and were familiar with the structural and human damage that results.

Since I was involved in the medical management of mass casualties series of short courses, I was able to influence the allocation of some of the spaces for nurses. These included ANC officers, civilian nurse faculty in schools of nursing, and nurses in disaster planning positions with the Red Cross and the Civil Defense. However, I soon realized that the few spaces that could be obtained for nurses in these courses were not sufficient to acquaint nurses generally with the importance and the need for comparable disaster preparedness for nursing, medicine, dentistry, and other fields. Consequently I worked toward finding other ways nurses could share in this disaster preparedness training (Goldstein and Werley, 1956; Werley and Goldstein, 1959).

When civilian nurses became more interested in expanding the work on disaster preparedness, I served on the advisory committee of an Office of Defense Mobilization–National League for Nursing (ODM-NLN) project to integrate disaster nursing and mass casualties into the curricula of schools of nursing. The army provided ANC project directors on temporary duty for a year at the WRAIR Department of Nursing with assignment to three of the four participating schools of nursing (Teachers College, the University of Minnesota, and Massachusetts General Hospital School of Nursing) to work with faculty on this project. At the other school (Skidmore College), a faculty member active in the U.S. Army Reserve filled that position.

In addition to my work on the mass casualties courses, I participated on a team of specialists sent to speak and consult at the military bases throughout Europe. Wearing my WRAIR Coordinator of Nursing Activities hat and at the request of Col. Inez Haynes from the OTSG, I also began to schedule some clinical nursing short courses at the WRAIR for ANC officers. These were led by appropriate clinical nursing course directors. I assisted when I could and made sure the WRAIR facilities were at the course directors' disposal. These course directors requested presentations on care of mass casualties, nursing research projects, and overviews of nursing research at the WRAIR. We welcomed the opportunity to have WRAIR participation in these short courses, for it not only helped to spread the word about the needs for disaster preparedness, but also brought supportive attitudes toward the movement of developing nursing research.

As I became more involved in the WRAIR activities, I found that I had many questions. Why had nurses not been involved in particular studies? Why were no nurses on research teams that were sent out to study unusual diseases and the care of patients with those diseases or the care of trauma patients? Why were nurses not studying their practice as systematically as members of other disciplines were doing? Why had it taken 62 years to establish the Institute (in 1893 as the Army Medical School) before an Army Nurse Corps officer was assigned to full-time duty, not only to carry out her assigned departmental duty, but also to view possibilities of planning and developing nursing's role in this well-recognized research-education-service institution?

In an attempt to answer some of those questions, I wrote a staff study report on establishing a department of nursing within WRAIR and in November 1956 submitted it to Col. Richard Mason, then the director of the Institute of Research. This resulted in the establishment of a department of nursing on February 25, 1957, and I was named chief of the department. Since this new department was organizationally a special activity, I was responsible to the WRAIR director through the deputy director (Kalish, 1977; Werley, 1962a).

Both the director and deputy director were physicians who had devoted most of their professional lives to research, and so they were aware of the problems of new disciplines struggling to secure a role in a research-education situation. They supported the planning and actions deemed necessary to move along a group they believed would play a vital part in medical progress. Nursing, like other professions at the WRAIR, used the services of consultants, and Dr. R. Louise McManus was appointed as the first nursing consultant in December 1956.

Here then in the middle 1950s was a unique and challenging opportunity for nurses to develop a research-education-practice program located in the mainstream of the Army Medical Service research enterprise. We had the support of medical and allied scientists at the Institute of Research, and we had close relationships with the staff at the Walter Reed Army Hospital.

We identified several potential research nurses, and in April 1958 they were brought together as a unit. I assumed full-time responsibility for the department of nursing. Provision had been made for an assistant chief of research (Capt. Phyllis J. Verhonick) and an assistant chief for education (Maj. Ruth Greenfield). Maj. Clara M. Duley served as a surgical nursing investigator, and Capt. Miriam K. Ginsberg was a medical nursing investigator.

In developing the department of nursing's mission and program, we parelleled the broad mission of the WRAIR, stated our objectives, set our goals, and planned our approaches. Since the stated mission of the Institute stressed the sciences and professional practice, we were fortunate to be a part of an institution where the emphasis could be placed on evolving a nursing research-education-practice program that was patient care oriented.

The goals that had been stated initially in the fall of 1956 were reaffirmed: to continue conducting required clinical nursing short courses, improving them yearly in terms of clinical depth so that the experiences from these courses might contribute to the long-term development of the department; to initiate a series of research projects with emphasis on patient care; to conduct a nursing research conference in fiscal year 1959; and to initiate in fiscal year 1960 a professional program designed to prepare a small number of U.S. Army nurse officers in accordance with the statement of the department mission. It was hoped that these prepared nurse officers might then be assigned to research positions in one of the Army Medical Service research and development command units, or in a hospital with excellent opportunities for investigative clinical nursing practice.

Some of the nursing research projects initiated then were these:

1. Nursing measures of oral and nasal hygiene related to renal failure cases
2. An animal study on nursing therapy and procedures in the treatment of induced oral lesions and manifestations
3. Nursing measures that contribute to prevention, care, and treatment of pressure areas and decubiti
4. Identification of principles of nursing care underlying taking oral temperatures

In our initial efforts we encouraged the development of projects of a nursing or patient care nature. We stressed the necessity of looking at the military importance of the problem. Thinking one of the best ways to evolve a program of research might be to ask the ANC officers what they considered to be problem areas, we conducted such a survey on a worldwide basis in 1957. The response was small, but that was understandable because in those days most nurses had not been educated to think in terms of research. The responses to the survey were interesting, and we referred to them, using some of the material in exercise sessions for the two-week research conference that we conducted in 1959, thus attaining our third goal. The conference was designed primarily for ANC officers assigned to the Army Medical Service research and development command units. We again stressed the philosophy of nurse participation in medical and nursing research and emphasized research methods and techniques and their application to problems of military health care importance. The proceedings of this research conference were published (Werley, 1962b), and the table of contents reflected a virtual who's who of presenters. The publication was much in demand by university personnel across the country, for there was little research in civilian nursing in those days.

The fourth goal for the department of nursing, that of initiating in 1960 an educational program to develop a small number of practitioner-research nurses for the U.S. Army, had to be deferred for a year because of personnel reasons. In the interim the idea gained strength, and support was growing among members of the other disciplines in the Institute of Research as we acquainted them with our plans. This 40-week program of instruction was developed fully and reviewed by consultants. Additionally, it was coordinated with similar ongoing programs in the Institute for medical and dental officers, so that some of the research methods, statistics, and design portions could be shared. It was initiated in fall 1961 and was continued for seven classes, with 33 army nurses completing it (Kalish, 1977; Verhonick and Werley 1963; Werley, 1962a; Werley 1963a, 1963b). The program was discontinued in part because more ANC officers were being sent to universities to acquire graduate degrees.

While at the WRAIR, I also was active in nursing organization activities. One of those endeavors in which I was engaged, as a member of the ANA Committee on Research and Studies (1962), was the writing of a "Blueprint for Nursing Research." It was published in the *American Journal of Nursing* so it would be readily accessible to all as "a guide for the shaping of a research program." It was a forward-looking document for its time, and in a recent examination (Werley and Westlake, 1985) it was pointed out that communication and decision making in nursing is still a far-reaching area for research. Nursing is still behind the times in developing nursing information systems and in the management of information processing, even though computer technology has been available for years. As a result, nursing does not have adequate ongoing systems of data collection that would make available to nurses appropriate data to back up various stands pertinent to health care delivery systems and health policy making.

While I was assigned at the WRAIR, the nursing research study section was established at the National Institutes of Health (NIH), and I was invited to serve as a member. This was a valuable learning experience for me, but having been involved as I was at the WRAIR, I also had something to contribute during the review process. I served from 1957 to 1962, when I resigned because of my overseas assignment that fall.

CHIEF NURSE, U.S. EIGHTH ARMY, KOREA

In September 1962 I became chief nurse of the U.S. Eighth Army and was stationed in Seoul, Korea. I made my rounds by helicopter to the respective army medical facilities. Dr. R. Louise McManus visited me as a consultant then and was well received throughout the total command structure—U.S. Eighth Army, Armed Forces Korea, and the United Nations Command.

I was able to plan a week's trip for Dr. McManus to visit Japan and tour medical research laboratories—the U.S. Army ones and several Japanese ones—as well as the Japanese Department of Health. The Japanese knew Dr. Richard Mason, director of the WRAIR, for he had served several tours of duty in Japan. As director of the WRAIR, he also hosted many foreign nationals on visits to the United States or on various types of study fellowships. Dr. McManus and I were received graciously by the Japanese, as well as by the American physicians and scientists, both military and civilian, in the army research laboratories. We explored possible opportunities for placement of some of the ANC officers in the laboratories where they could serve with research mentors as they initiated and pursued nursing research projects.

My rich experiences at the WRAIR and the value I saw in the research going on around me stimulated me to explore the possibility of enrolling in a doctoral program upon my return from Korea.

In 1964 when I was accepted as a doctoral student in psychology at the University of Utah, I decided to end my army career and start my studies.

I was pleased to be a doctoral student in psychology, a science in which I believed I would gain much in the way of content appropriate to research in nursing, as well as knowledge of research methods, statistics, and research design. I was approved for a U.S. Public Health Service predoctoral fellowship and completed the doctorate in June 1969. I thoroughly enjoyed being a student.

RESEARCH CENTER DIRECTOR, WAYNE STATE UNIVERSITY

In September 1969 I took a position as the first director of the Center for Nursing Research at Wayne State University (WSU) College of Nursing. A short time later, when a proposal was funded, I administered a grant from the U.S. Department of Health, Education and Welfare (USDHEW) Division of Nursing to develop the center. The proposal had been written by WSU faculty who were committed to following the center route; among them were Mabel Wandelt and Virginia Cleland. I generally credit Virginia Cleland for influencing me to come to WSU. She knew of my background at the WRAIR and believed I was suited to develop and direct the WSU center.

After several experiences of being turned down by funding groups, we changed the name to the Center for Health Research. Before the center proposal was funded, I worked with volunteers. Suzanne Feetham was my first volunteer, and today she is a well-known researcher.

I appointed a distinguished, nationally known scientific advisory board for the center, and at their first orientation meeting, faculty shared with them the various types of research that were ongoing in the college. The faculty investigators received reactions and advice. My colleague psychologist, Dr. Joel Ager, and I initiated a program of research in the population and family planning area, one of the first in the college of nursing. The researchers who participated in this program became recognized both nationally and internationally.

We kept submitting research proposals to the USDHEW, and soon the college was awarded a biomedical research support grant. It was a mark of prestige for the college to so qualify, as it still is today. Researchers were functioning well, and the center mechanism was effective in helping potential researchers develop their research and seek external funds. In addition, we were involved in researcher networking, mostly because of an informative nursing research newsletter in which we shared what research and research-related activities were taking place in the center and the college (Werley and Shea, 1973). This newsletter was distributed nationally and internationally. We received requests weekly from individuals who wished to be added to the mailing list.

Shortly after I had moved to Wayne State, Joan Guy, then executive director of the Michigan Nurses' Association (MNA), asked how she could help me promote research development. We met several times and then decided to meet informally with the Michigan nurses to gauge their interest in doing something as a group about research development. This led to the formation of a state Council of Nurse Researchers, the first one of that kind, I believe. Eventually a research proposal was prepared by a task force of university and MNA personnel, and a grant was awarded to MNA by the USDHEW Division of Nursing for a project on research implementation to be carried out jointly by MNA and the University of Michigan School of Nursing personnel.

While at Wayne State University, I was one of 36 nurses selected as charter fellows of the American Academy of Nursing. Of that group, Rheba De Tornyay and I were invited to the ANA headquarters to work with ANA officials in preparing for the initial academy meeting that Rheba chaired, and at which she was elected the first president. I served on the governing council from 1977 to 1979.

Also at Wayne State I began to advise graduate students that when they were interviewing for jobs they should be certain to inquire about how much time they could expect to have for research. I suggested that if they did not negotiate for research time before accepting the position, they should not expect that they could arrange for it later. Far too much lip service was being given to research. I also stressed that nurses should be sure that what they negotiate was included in their letter of appointment.

ASSOCIATE DEAN FOR RESEARCH, UNIVERSITY OF ILLINOIS, CHICAGO

On April 1, 1974, I took a position at the University of Illinois College of Nursing as the first associate dean for research. While we did not establish a nursing research center per se, I had considerable space on a floor of the college, and we did a lot to facilitate faculty research development there—guiding the faculty research potential, directing it toward research development, proposal writing, gathering data, and publishing results in refereed journals.

While at the University of Illinois I obtained a large grant from the USDHEW Division of Nursing designed to foster and facilitate research through unleashing the research potential at the university. Through this grant we employed student research assistants, who were a valuable resource to faculty. One of the unique features of this proposal was a provision for each department to have its own faculty relief person.

In this way research-interested faculty within the departments could in turn be provided up to six months' leave from teaching duties while developing research proposals for external funds. The department head could manage the situation by hiring a full-time person and rotating the relief tasks or hiring a specific person for each occasion to relieve the faculty member who was ready to write a research proposal. There were varying reactions among the department heads concerning the use of, or even the willingness to use, these resources for research development. This unevenness corresponded to whether the department heads themselves had been brought up professionally to value and conduct research.

Dr. Gladys Courtney, for example, was a bona fide researcher herself (a nurse physiologist) and was research productive in her area of expertise before she became a department head. Thus it was her philosophy that research-qualified and productive faculty needed at least 50% time for research, as is frequently the case in some of the hard sciences.

Within the Midwest, the deans of schools of nursing in those universities that participate in the Committee on Interinstitutional Cooperation (the Big Ten plus Northwestern and the University of Chicago) meet occasionally, and at one time they urged joint research proposal development. This led to the project "Midwest Resources for Graduate Education in Nursing," which was headed by Dr. Helen Grace (with co-directors Dr. Beverly McElmurray and Dr. Nola Pender) and was ongoing when I arrived at the University of Illinois College of Nursing.

As that initial project was coming to an end, I was in on the proposal development for two other projects that followed. These were "Midwest Nursing Data Base" and "Nurse Faculty Research Development in the Midwest." By the time these projects were approved and about to be funded, Dr. Grace had gone on to become dean, so I assumed the program director position on both grants.

Dr. Beverly McElmurry was project director for the data base project, and I recruited Dr. Barbara Minckley to become project director of the faculty research development program. That project involved an effort to facilitate faculty research development in 33 university schools of nursing in the Midwest that had master's programs in nursing. Among other things that were done as part of this effort was the formation of research interest groups, in which personnel could work together in developing research projects and writing proposals for external funding. These research interest groups later became sections of the Midwest Nursing Research Society when it was being formed.

Around that time there was a mushrooming of doctoral nursing programs being planned throughout the country. Because I knew that many nurse faculty members lacked research experience, I objected to the initiation of nursing doctoral programs if there was no evidence of research-productive, doctorally prepared faculty already in place. I did not hesitate to speak up on this matter at conventions and conferences where doctoral programs were discussed. I believed strongly that the doctoral students were being cheated in situations where there were not sufficient faculty with research experience and ongoing research programs who could serve as research mentors for students.

I next turned to advising prospective nursing doctoral students that they should not select a doctoral program without examining the credentials of the faculty. Pursuing doctoral study is an investment in one's future, and students should be assured that the faculty are research prepared, productive, and available to guide them in their research learning experiences.

At the University of Illinois College of Nursing, I became aware of the inordinate time some faculty were waiting to have their research published. I concluded that *Nursing Research* could no longer handle all of the nurses' research publications, so I began to talk about the need for a second research journal. Thus I became the founding editor of *Research in Nursing and Health,* published by John Wiley & Sons, with the first issue in April 1978. I served as editor for about five years and then turned it over to Dr. Margaret R. Grier, whom I had invited to join me initially as associate editor. I was ready to devote more time to developing an *Annual Review of Nursing Research* (ARNR) series.

ASSOCIATE DEAN (RESEARCH), UNIVERSITY OF MISSOURI–COLUMBIA

In 1980 Dr. Gladys Courtney was trying to convince me I ought to join her at the University of Missouri–Columbia School of Nursing, where she was then dean, to help that faculty move with research development. Being a researcher herself and prepared as a physiologist, she knew what it took to be a productive scholar. In January 1980 I assumed the newly established position as associate dean (research) at the University of Missouri–Columbia School of Nursing, and shortly after arrival became principal investigator of a newly awarded biomedical research development grant (BRDG) from the NIH Division of Research Resources.

I appointed an excellent multidisciplinary advisory board for the BRDG and invited Dr. Hans Mauksch to serve as chairperson. In that situation the board members functioned as a review panel for research proposals solicited periodically from faculty for research support from the BRDG funds, and they sometimes served as research consultants to the faculty. We conducted some of the proposal review business much like NIH research study sections, except that nurse faculty members were allowed to be present to profit from seeing the reviewers in operation and hearing the discussion of proposals. As principal investigator of a proposal under review for BRDG funds, a faculty member also could present a summary statement of his or her research, and if needed could offer additional information.

For final decision making the board went into executive session, but faculty members could wait for the board's decisions if they wished. Thus they could have immediate feedback, as well as a written explanation of the board's action. This way of dealing with faculty worked well, and with their observation of various board members in action, they saw which ones might be appropriate for them to consult. Having those meetings open gave less experienced faculty a good opportunity to learn how they could proceed with research projects.

About that time, Roma Lee Taunton, then a doctoral student at the University of Kansas–Lawrence who was majoring in educational psychology and research, joined me for a year to get research experience. I was just beginning my work on establishing the *Annual Review of Nursing Research* and was in the throes of implementing a funded BRDG project to help the UMC School of Nursing faculty move forward with their research development.

I had by that time invited Dr. Joyce J. Fitzpatrick to join me as coeditor of the *ARNR* series and had settled on Springer as the publisher for this important nursing research tool. I gave Roma Lee the notes of reactions and suggestions I had accumulated over the years as I explored with nurses the idea of developing an *ARNR*. Roma Lee was present for the first meeting of the coeditors of the *ARNR* and was a valuable contributor as we worked through blending our thoughts, the essence of the suggestions from the field, and the guidelines provided by Springer Publishing Co., Inc. Dr. Ursula Springer had encouraged me during those earlier years before the time was right to move ahead with the *ARNR*. Roma Lee Taunton worked with us on the *ARNR*, even after she concluded her year's research experience. Today she is one of the coeditors of that series. The first volume became available in December 1983 (Werley and Fitzpatrick, 1984). The fourth volume won an *American Journal of Nursing* book award, and volume five became available in 1987.

The UMC faculty progressed with their research development work, but Dr. Courtney, who was credited with having moved the UMC School of Nursing toward becoming more of an academic unit of the university, left early in my stay there. Some of the physicians of the medical school and hospital believed that this movement for the school of nursing was too rapid and they undermined her; they were not interested in educated nurses. Some of them even talked of starting a short technical training program to prepare women to nurse patients. I met with the chancellor to see whether I would have support in continuing to work with faculty to promote research development, and she assured me that I would. She remained faithful to that commitment.

Whenever I was in a research development position, I saw to it that we had a schedule of active researchers visit the school of nursing throughout the academic year to present their research. This exposed faculty to interactions with distinguished researchers that were stimulating to both groups.

During the time I was at the University of Illinois and at the University of Missouri–Columbia I also served on several USDHHS committees that reviewed research proposals. This service was important because there were few nurse researchers on any of the different research study sections. As a nurse reviewer I felt that I had to do a particularly good job among all the other scientists, so that as my term ended another nurse researcher would be appointed.

DISTINGUISHED PROFESSOR, UNIVERSITY OF WISCONSIN–MILWAUKEE

With a change in deans at the UMC School of Nursing I believed it was time for me to move on to a situation where there would be a nursing doctoral program. Thus, in April, I moved to the University of Wisconsin–Milwaukee School of Nursing as a distinguished professor. With this move I was not going to be responsible administratively for research development but would be in a position where my own work could influence scholarship and research productivity in the school in general. I explored the situation in advance to be certain I would have the resources and staff support necessary to conduct research. I had learned from both my military and university experiences that research productivity required appropriate support, and I was assured that it would be arranged.

At the UWM I participated in meetings regarding the nursing doctoral program before it was approved by the board of regents, and since its approval, I have continued to meet with the doctoral faculty who are bringing the program to fruition. I have conducted sessions on writing for publication, stressing the need to publish in refereed journals. This is essential if faculty are to be viewed as qualified for research grants and for promotion and tenure. I review manuscripts for numerous faculty and meet frequently with them to discuss writing for publication. I often consult with faculty whose manuscripts have been rejected. Since my arrival at the UWM, five volumes of the *ARNR* have become available. After Volume 6, the editorship went to Joyce J. Fitzpatrick and Roma Lee Taunton, but I continue to sit on the advisory board.

In 1984 I initiated follow-through work on an idea I had tried out earlier at the University of Illinois during the 1977 Nursing Information Systems conference (Werley and Grier, 1981). We had assigned the problem of developing a basic nursing data set to one of the smaller groups at the conference. The group did quite well, but the time was not right for a comprehensive study and no one followed through on this work. When I arrived at the UWM, I elicited interest in the idea of developing a Nursing Minimum Data Set similar to others that had been developed through the National Center for Health Statistics. With the dean's help we identified a small group of interested researchers who eventually planned the 1985 NMDS conference, where the conferees determined by consensus a data set that was pilot-tested under the direction of Dr. Elizabeth C. Devine in four types of settings—a hospital, a nursing home, a home health care agency, and two hospital-based ambulatory clinics (Devine and Werley, 1987). This preliminary work showed that the data could be collected reliably, that the NMDS elements generally were available in the health care record, and that the data collection instruments and study approaches were suitable. Only slight revisions were necessary prior to conducting a field study for which we are hoping to prepare a research proposal.

The NMDS has appeal to many nurse groups because through its use nursing diagnoses and care can be described, and nursing resource use can be assessed. Different nurse groups across the country are including the NMDS elements as they develop nursing information systems. The NMDS also can be introduced into the ongoing data collection systems at the local and state levels. Thus the regular health data reports can reflect nursing data for assessing quality of care and for research that can be conducted with the NMDS elements and may be adopted for use in some of the federal health care programs.

In summary, I have shared some experiences that have made it possible for me to help influence nursing research in a variety of ways. As a result of my moving around both in the military and in civilian life, I have encountered many individuals who fostered my professional growth, and I like to think that I have likewise helped others grow professionally. Generally I have been in newly created positions. My main efforts were directed toward research and research development, concern about quality nursing doctoral programs, concern about scholarly publication, and information processing, especially as it pertains to nurses developing computerized nursing information systems so that necessary data may be retrieved readily. These data are needed to justify stands on matters pertaining to health care delivery and health policy making and to enable nurses to have comparable data for research purposes and for assessing care across clinical settings, populations, geographical areas, and time.

REFERENCES

ANA Committee on Research and Studies (H.H. Werley, a member). (1962). ANA blueprint for research in nursing. *American Journal of Nursing,* **62**(8), 69-71.

Devine, E.C., and Werley, H.H. (1987). *Test of the Nursing Minimum Data Set: Availability of data and reliability.* Manuscript submitted for publication.

Goldstein, J.D., and Werley, H.H. (1956). Care of casualties caused by nuclear weapons: 1. Problems of medical care (Goldstein); 2. The nurse's role in nuclear disaster (Werley). *American Journal of Nursing,* **56,** 1576-1582.

Kalisch, P.A. (1977). Weavers of scientific patient care: development of nursing research in the U.S. Armed Forces. *Nursing Research,* **26,** 253-271.

National Academy of Sciences (1978). *Personnel needs and training for biomedical research. Washington, D.C.: Author.*

Verhonick, P.J., and Werley, H.H. (1963). Experimentation in nursing practice in the army. *Nursing Outlook,* **11,** 204-206.

Werley, H.H. (1954a). Career planning for the army nurse. *U.S.Armed Forces Medical Journal,* **5,**108-111.

Werley, H.H. (1954b). Shared responsibilities for career planning for Army Nurse Corps officers. *The Military Surgeon,* **115,** 436-441.

Werley, H.H. (1956). The role of the nurse in the care of nuclear weapons casualties. In American Nurses' Association, *Report of work conference on disaster nursing, February 20-24, 1956, Washington, D.C.* (pp. 21-25). New York: American Nurses' Association.

Werley, H.H. (1962a). Promoting the research dimension in the practice of nursing through the establishment and development of a department of nursing in an institute of research. *Military Medicine,* **127,** 219-231.

Werley, H.H. (Ed.). (1962b). *Report on nursing research conference, 24 February-7 March 1959* (held at Walter Reed Army Institute of Research). Washington, D.C.: U.S. Government Printing Office.

Werley, H.H. (1963a). Army nurse participation in and contribution to research. *Nursing Outlook,* **11,** 52-55.

Werley, H.H. (1963b). The different research roles in army nursing. *Nursing Outlook,* **11,** 134-136.

Werley, H.H., and Fitzpatrick, J.J. (Eds.). (1984). *Annual review of nursing research* (Vol. 1). New York: Springer Publishing.

Werley, H.H., and Goldstein, J.D. (1959). Nursing in disaster: are you prepared? In M.C. Cowan (Ed.), *The yearbook of modern nursing, 1958-1959* (pp. 182-192). New York: Putnam.

Werley, H.H., and Grier, M.R. (Eds). *Nursing information systems.* New York: Springer Publishing.

Werley, H.H., and Lang, N.M. (Eds.). (in press). *Identification of the nursing minimum data set.* New York: Springer Publishing.

Werley, H.H., and Shea, F.P. (1973). The first center for research in nursing: its development, accomplishments, and problems. *Nursing Research,* **22,** 217-231.

Werley, H.H., and Westlake, S.K. (1985). Impact of nursing research on public policy: an examination of ANA research priority statements. *Journal of Professional Nursing,* **2,** 148-156.

Werley, H.H., Lang, N.M., and Westlake, S.K. (1986a). Brief summary of the nursing minimum data set conference. *Nursing Management,* **17**(7), 42-45.

Werley, H.H., Lang, N.M., and Westlake, S.K. (1986b). The nursing minimum data set conference: executive summary. *Journal of Professional Nursing,* **2,** 217-224.

Werley, H.H., Murphy, P.A., Gosch, S.M., Gottesman, H., and Newcomb, B.J. (1981). Research publication credit assignment: nurses' views. *Research in Nursing and Health,* **4,** 261-279.

Werley, H.H., Murphy, P.A., and Newcomb, B.J. (1981). Student research assistant: tomorrow's nurse researcher. In S. Krampitz & N. Pavlovich (Eds.), *Readings for nursing research* (pp. 180-192). New York: the C. V. Mosby Company.

June Werner

June Werner, MSN, RN,
is Chairman, Department of Nursing,
Evanston Hospital Corporation, Evanston, Illinois

❖

June Werner writes affectionately about the support she received from her family through an early childhood illness and candidly about her career choice and her adult life. Her strong sense of advocacy for patients surfaced early in her career, and her religious conviction strengthened her respect for all human beings. She believes her ascendency in nursing was often a matter of being the person "on site" who was best prepared for the job rather than being prepared as she felt she should have been. Her wide-ranging experiences led her to pursue higher education, and she credits her mentors through that period as being responsible for a good deal of her success.

Her husband's ethnographic explorations on the Navajo Indian Reservation in Arizona have been a significant part of family life for June, who put her nursing skills to work there.

It is easy to see how her consummate respect for nursing, as well as for those with whom she works, has challenged her to champion nurse autonomy and to advance primary nursing for patients.

I was the first of two daughters born into a loving and protective family. My father was the eldest son of a large and close-knit family, while my mother was the sole survivor of nine children. She describes her upbringing as being "under glass." Though overprotected, I realize that I was influenced by both my grandmothers.

When I was born, my maternal grandmother was thrilled. She had protected my mother for all those years and found it hard to believe that my mother could go through a difficult pregnancy and deliver a healthy youngster. I had a great deal of exposure to my grandmother during the 12 years that she lived after my birth. She was a religious woman whose convictions were manifest in her service to humanity. I remember her as a strong, caring woman who was soft spoken but resolute.

The summer I was eight I had pneumonia. I remember being very sick. According to family lore I was not supposed to have survived, but my grandmother resolved that I would. I remember lying in her big bed, looking at the cabbage roses on the wallpaper. A nurse appeared in her standard white uniform and cap. She was the spirit of efficiency. I didn't like her. My grandmother also hovered about me. The nurse was brought in as respite for grandmother, who seemed ever present. My little sister was five at that time, and my mother was frequently busy with her—my mother was somehow in the background, and my grandmother was in charge. I did not know that the doctor had said I wouldn't live and that my grandmother decided otherwise. Everyone said that it was my grandmother's prayers and skills that made me recover. I remember the dichotomy between the brisk and brusque nurse and my calm, gentle, caring grandmother, who seemed so much more effective.

Grandmother invested a lot of time in preparing me for life, as well as for her death. She instilled in me philosophy and values while she was alive. She convinced me early that, like her, I was an instrument put on earth to act in behalf of a wise and caring God. I wasn't sure what that meant, but as I watched and helped grandmother attend to neighbors and others who needed her, extending kindness to everyone, I learned. In a convincing but understated way, she assured me that "the Lord fits the back to the burden." She lived quietly, making a difference to any life she touched, particularly to those who had need of her.

My father's mother also was a remarkable woman. His family lived in a small town in Massachusetts in a rambling New England farmhouse on land where my grandfather grew huge and beautiful flowers, seedless watermelons, and the biggest strawberries anyone ever saw. My grandfather loved the land, and when he died in his garden, everyone was saddened but understood that the garden was where he'd wanted to die. He loved children and was very patient with us.

Grandma Travers was a quiet, staunch, and benevolent matriarch. Her house was never empty. Family, friends, and neighbors came and went constantly. She never prepared just enough food for the present company—she always prepared extra in case someone dropped in. For a while, my sister and I attended school in Massachusetts. We passed her house on our way home from school. Whenever she was home, my sister and I and the four or five children who came home from school with us would stop at Grandma Travers's for a snack. She gave us hot chocolate and cookies in winter and lemonade and cupcakes when it was warm. She really did enjoy those visits with us. Her home was affectionately known as "the house of the Good Shepherd." She validated that title. People who needed a place to stay for an hour or a month went to her door. She taught me how to live with ambiguity. A strong yet gentle woman, she loved her family and the world.

My memories of my nuclear family are that we led comfortably pleasant lives together prior to 1929, followed by lean times after the stock market crashed. My father was terribly dispirited by that event. My mother, the fairy princess who had been raised under glass, emerged as a strong advocate for her entire family—particularly for her children.

My mother tells tales of when she was pregnant with my sister, recalling a three-year-old daughter June who presumed to take care of her. The pregnancy was difficult; Mother was constantly nauseated and lacked the energy to deal with me. I tried to be very much involved in caring for her. My sister's birth was a special event in my life. The love and closeness that we feel for each other at this stage of our lives (now we are both grandmothers) had its genesis in those early years.

My mother has reminded me of a significant incident that occurred when I was about 11. We were living in a lovely little town in Massachusetts. A pageant was being held in a nearby city, and there was a lot of excitement about it. My sister and I were very happy to be going until we found out that not all of our playmates could go. Travel and tickets made it an expensive adventure. Distressed that several children would be left out, I remembered that my mother, as president of the PTA a year or so before, had been involved in a benefit raffle. I thought that sounded like a great idea. At that early age, I had a reputation of being a very good, fledgling cook. I went through the neighborhood selling raffle tickets for a cake that I promised to deliver to the winner. I was exhilarated by this effort since it would make it possible for all of us to go to the pageant. It worked. On the appointed day, I delivered a cake baked from scratch to the neighbor who had won it. That was probably the beginning of my conviction that even seemingly impossible goals can be achieved, given equal parts of creativity and tenacity.

By the time I went to high school I knew I wanted to be a nurse. When my father realized that nursing might be my career choice, he let me know in no uncertain terms that no daughter of his would do such a thing. My mother's reaction to this was, "We'll see." I suspect that my mother hoped I would change my mind. By the time I was a junior, my mother knew that I had my heart set on nursing. It was she who asked my uncle Mac, a prominent Presbyterian minister, to talk to my father in my behalf. Uncle Mac probably felt that my choice of career was a genetic endowment. I believe he envisioned me spending my life in the service of humankind. My mother and my uncle Mac devised a plan to convince my father that nursing was an appropriate choice for me. I was never a part of those discussions. It was a matter for adults to work out. Finally (I learned later) my uncle Mac convinced my father that if I was able to get into the Columbia Presbyterian Hospital School of Nursing, I would come out the same "sweet" girl who went in. My guess is that he meant "chaste" when he said "sweet." My application to Columbia Presbyterian marked the beginning of my character-building experience in nursing.

We learned that Columbia was going to select one of thirteen applicants. I had taken a concentrated academic preparatory course in high school, and high achiever that I am, I received very good grades. The letter finally came that said my application was being considered. The next step was an interview. I remember my mother lecturing me at length about what I was going to wear for the interview. I must "look healthy." I had a wonderful lightweight natural wool dress that I wanted to wear. My mother would not hear of it; I needed something more colorful. In the end I wore a soft, aqua wool shirtwaist, which was entirely appropriate. My mother and I spent the entire day in the school of nursing during the interview. While at luncheon, I was well aware of the scrutiny of the faculty who screened my social development and table manners.

I endured all kinds of interviews and examinations that day, including one that presumed to test my mechanical aptitude. This was administered by a somber, authoritative nurse educator in a long-sleeved white Presbyterian uniform, complete with cap. Her no-nonsense presence offered no comfort to this somewhat apprehensive prospective student. I took the entire test and knew I was doing very badly. At the end of the examination, my examiner assured me that I "certainly had no mechanical ability!" I left the room and went to rejoin my mother, telling her I was not going to get into the school, that I had just failed my mechanical aptitude test, which was very important for a nurse. I wanted her to be prepared and not to be too disappointed. After some analysis of my record, it was decided that since my other scores were so high I might be considered. I improved my mechanical skills and ultimately entered the school of nursing at the Columbia Presbyterian Hospital in the fall of 1942. Having graduated from high school with honors, I had learned to balance the business of school with extracurricular activities. My involvement in high school politics was responsible for my appointment as prom chairman. This inclination to balance my life has benefited me throughout my career.

Our family physician was a lovely man who thought my mother and father were making a mistake in sending me to Columbia Presbyterian. He said, "She will not come out of the school a nurse. She is going to be trained like a medical student. It is the wrong school for this girl." That was never a consideration, since this was the only school my father would have allowed me to attend. I didn't even understand the argument.

As prescribed, I arrived at Maxwell Hall complete with trunk and an overnight case. The school of nursing was a 12-story building on Fort Washington Avenue in New York City and seemed very, very large. It was the most formal atmosphere I had ever experienced. There were times in those early months when I didn't feel a part of it, and my fellow students did commiserate with me. There was a relentless expectation that we be ladies and students, as well as fledgling nurses. The faculty seemed awesome, all in full Presbyterian uniform with buttons across the shoulders, down the arms, and below the waist. We met every morning—the entire student body and faculty—for prayers and proceeded to the unit. Intellectual, professional, and personal rigor predominated. It stands out in my mind that the instructor who taught us pharmacology was perhaps the only friendly faculty we knew. Our advisor smiled but wasn't as accessible as we'd hoped. I perceived the probationary garb, the gray uniforms, the white stiff collars, the black stockings and shoes, and the hairnets as part of the culture. I had no objection. They were not attractive, but that seemed appropriate.

At mid-year, we had the most beautiful capping service I have ever witnessed. It was inspiring and reaffirming. I knew deep within that this was the right road. In my second year I moved to the eighth floor of Maxwell Hall, having lived my first year on the sixth. I liked my new corridor mates very much. We enjoyed a shared spirit of support and frivolity, nicely balanced. Early in that year, we named ourselves "Harmony Hall." I was closest to Denny Baldwin, who continues to be very significant in my life. Having grown up in a reserved household that valued strict observance of decorum, I found in Denny a new experience. Her candor almost shocked me. She said exactly what she thought. Her observations were acute, insightful. I was awed by her ability to speak her mind without regard for consequences. This is not to say that Denny Baldwin was inappropriate. She was warm and caring, but I could depend on her for a truthful answer to anything. She was credibility epitomized. With her I could discuss how I felt about a patient or a faculty member, anyone or anything.

I look back to my student days with mixed emotions. The curriculum was demanding; the clinical experience component was always reinforcing. Dozens of incidents in those years were significant to me. I remember two worth noting. Mr. C. was a patient who was in and out of the hospital several times while I was in school. He had been my first case study on his initial admission, and I came to know him and his precious wife very well. Once after he was readmitted, I incited the event that almost ended my life as a student nurse.

Mr. C. was debilitated and discouraged. In preparation for the intern doing his history and physical, I alerted the doctor that Mr. C. was deaf in his right ear and partially deaf in his left. I advised him to stand at Mr. C.'s left ear rather than in his usual position (draped over the bed table as was the conventional way that medical students and interns took histories at that time). The young intern ignored my suggestion, and sprawling over the bedside table smoking a cigarette, he proceeded to ask Mr. C. the questions related to his health history. The intern barked out the questions; Mr. C. did his best to be attentive. He repeatedly asked, "What did you say, son?" After several minutes, the exasperated intern growled at him, "Damn it, man, you listen to me!" I was between Mr. C. and the intern. I was shocked because profanity was not part of my life. I had not heard it at home, and it seemed particularly inappropriate to me. My reflex was to kick the intern in the shins. In a steely voice, I advised him, "Mr. C. cannot hear you this far from his good ear."

Within the hour I was "on the carpet." The head nurse sat in judgment of me. The incident had been reported to the teaching supervisor, who was responsible for the delivery of care and the education of students in the service area. I did not end up in the school office, as I thought I might. Both the head nurse and the supervisor made it quite clear that my behavior had been inappropriate and unbecoming of a nursing student. I tried to explain my overwhelming sense of advocacy for Mr. C., but I realized I had gone beyond the limits of acceptable behavior. (The director of the school removed that incident from my permanent record the day that I finished school.)

The other incident that stands out in my mind involved a woman I had cared for several times. She was a diabetic with serious circulatory problems. On this admission, her physicians had determined that she would need her leg amputated. She refused to sign the permit allowing the procedure. A lot of consultation went on. The intern tried, the resident physician tried, the medical student working with her tried. One day the senior attending surgeon, a distinguished, authoritative, well-known medical scholar, arrived on the unit. When the dilemma was explained to him, he said in a booming voice, "Who is this patient's nurse?" I will never forget the consequences of that question. He asked to see Miss Travers. I stood before him, and in a very kindly but indisputable way he said, "Miss Travers, if you are any kind of a nurse you will convince your patient that this amputation is in her best interest." I talked to Mrs. G., and she agreed to the surgery, but I was burdened with anxiety, thinking that she finally signed that permit because she felt that I might get in trouble if she did not.

Mrs. G. was a wise and philosophical elder stateswoman, and the trust and confidence she and I had developed won out. During her recovery she crocheted. She told me one day that she was making a potholder for my hope chest. She was very pleased about it. I couldn't find the words to tell her that I wouldn't be able to accept the potholder because it was an absolute dictum of the system that we were never, under any circumstances, to take gifts from patients. It was unprofessional. I didn't feel comfortable discussing this with the faculty. When she was ready to go home, she said good-bye to me and we were both just a little tearful. She handed me a little tissue paper package with the potholder inside of it. The guilt that I felt in accepting that potholder was overwhelming, but no more so than my ambivalence. I knew it was important for her to be able to give me something, since she felt I had given her so much. However, I also knew I was breaking the rules of the system. It took me a long time to come to terms with that little event, but I learned that it is sometimes more professional to break the rules than it is to observe them.

On my twenty-first birthday, I was having a clinical experience that was new in the system. I had been asked to help develop a role for a "night float." This was to be an experience in which I would be able to respond to units where they had a clinical problem and needed assistance. I would report directly to the night supervisor, who would be a resource for any problems I might have. That was an exciting experience. I enjoyed it and learned a lot. I was working 11 PM to 7 AM the night before my birthday. I was sent to Babies Hospital to special (as a private duty nurse) a two-year-old who had acute tracheitis. The child was very ill and lay in a room with steam going full tilt. The intern was worried and told me not to be surprised if the child didn't live through the night. He tossed a remark over his shoulder as he was going out the door that I will never forget. "If he lives, it will be nursing care that saved him."

That challenge was an awesome burden. It proved to be a long night. I remember attending carefully to every changing symptom as I rocked that little boy. He seemed to become more comfortable as dawn came. I said every prayer I knew. When I wrote to my mother that morning, I told her about that significant night in my life—the beginning of my adulthood—noting that I had done all the worrying while God had done all the work.

The first time I ever witnessed childbirth was also at night. I was awed by the event. The metaphysical mysteries of life reflected in that event were made manifest for me. At dawn the night supervisor took me up on the roof of the hospital. I had explained to her my perception of this monumental experience, the beginning of this life, and what it had meant to me. She was a wise and wonderful counselor. She said, "Come along with me. We won't be gone long. Come with me and see another metaphysical event." It was under these conditions that I saw the sunrise on that very special morning.

During the spring of my senior year I had an elevated sedimentation rate. I was put to bed in the infirmary and cared for as a patient. I learned a lot being on the other side of the sheets. I was not acutely ill, nor did I experience anything but excellent care. However, since I knew that my symptoms might have serious implications, I recognized the need for counseling, support, and rational concern.

My years as a student nurse were significant insofar as I became very introspective about my commitment to a religious philosophy. I read the New Testament every day. I was chair of devotions during my junior and senior years. That meant that I chose the biblical selection and hymn for prayers every morning. I tried to invite other students to make recommendations, and although that was a good idea, it wasn't successful. The students seemed satisfied to have devotions related to whatever June Travers thought was acceptable.

In my senior year I became aware that my hero, my uncle Mac, the prominent Presbyterian minister who had been very important in my childhood, was not the man I thought he was in terms of his values. I concluded on the basis of unequivocal documentation that although he saw himself as an ardent practicing Christian, he was capable of racism and bigotry. During that time of skepticism, I discussed with him the nature of conscientious objection and the concept of pacifism. I became interested in this because Columbia Presbyterian had a large number of pacifist men who were doing their alternate service in the institution. My disappointment and disillusionment regarding this flaw in my beloved uncle hurt me deeply. I began to look at other religious groups who were committed to pacifism. My baseline was that everything I knew about Christianity said, "Thou shalt not kill," and "Do unto others as you would have them do unto you." I found myself desperately seeking religious groups who lived by those principles. It was then that I had my first experience in a Quaker meeting. It moved me philosophically, and I was impressed with the work the Quakers were doing in the world. I became convinced that there really was something of God in *every* person—color, race, or creed notwithstanding. This conviction has formed the core of my life.

After I graduated, I moved to a small town in rural Connecticut. I had been advised not to work for at least six months to see what would happen to my elevated sedimentation rate. I felt fine and was annoyed that I couldn't get on with my career but accepted the medical recommendation reluctantly. I worked with children in the Sunday school and with the Girl Scouts. Since everyone knew I was a nurse, I was called on in emergencies ranging from fishbones lodged in a child's throat, to someone who died in the middle of the night, to a little girl who got her arm caught in her mother's washing machine wringer. The local physician was then practicing in two towns. If he had a baby to deliver, he had to travel 17 miles to the hospital. He and I became good friends. Sometimes he or his wife would call me to ask if I would see somebody or respond to some need that he simply could not attend to.

The following fall, a representative from the town's selectmen came to see me. (I was now well enough to function normally.) They had spoken with my friend the physician and asked me if I would become the town nurse. I knew I did not have enough experience to fill the position. My public health work had been at Henry Street in New York City. I loved that experience but also realized I would need supervision. Dr. Walker assured me that he would be available and that I would always be able to reach him. I knew that would be true so I spent most of the next year being the town nurse. I stayed with patients during the night when they were dying. I attended to patients at home who were critically ill. I provided health maintenance for a hermit who lived on a back road. I loved the work, but as time passed it became clear to me that I couldn't continue to do it without more experience in an acute care setting. Since it was my first experience in collaboration with a physician, it raised my expectations for the rest of my life. The quality of that relationship made me realize that a patient's care is maximized to the extent that the patient's physician and the patient's nurse have a collaborative relationship.

My first experience in a hospital was at Mary Fletcher Hospital in Burlington, Vermont, where I worked as a staff nurse in pediatrics. I loved it. The medical school was the center for the crippled children's division of the state of Vermont. We had children in the pediatrics unit from all over the state who were separated from their parents and far from home. They were often lonely, and part of caring for those children involved improving the quality of their lives. I had not been on that unit six months when I was asked to replace the head nurse, who was pregnant and leaving. I remember feeling that I wasn't prepared to be the head nurse, that I was too inexperienced. I had two conditions for taking the position. One was that they remove the wooden top that covered the bathtub in the utility room so we could submerge the children when bathing them. That was not a problem. My other request was that rocking chairs be put on the unit for these many little tykes who needed rocking. Eventually, both conditions were met. I became head nurse the following year, with no more preparation than a confident message from the supervisor who said, "I'm sure you can do this."

The medical director of the crippled children's division went to the director of nursing six months later and asked that I replace a person who was leaving in ambulatory services. This was a supervisory position in which I would run the emergency room and all the clinics, of which there were many. I would also teach the social and health aspects of nursing in the diploma school. Additionally, I would provide clinical experience for the baccalaureate students at the University of Vermont. Once again I felt ambivalence. However, I was reinforced by Dr. Bell's request that I take the position (even though I knew perfectly well that I wasn't prepared for it) because I respected him.

I went to see Dean Crabbe at the University of Vermont to explain my dilemma. She was a wise and wonderful mentor who assured me I was right, that I wasn't prepared to take the position but was the most prepared person on site. I remember she then turned the tables on me and asked me for advice. She had before her a pile of student applications. On the top was one that seemed to be troubling her. Her question was, "June, do you think we should admit a student whose name is Sara Sloppey? Can you imagine her going into a room to say to a patient, 'Good morning, I am your nurse, Miss Sloppey.'" I told Dean Crabbe that I felt students should not be kept out of nursing because of a name—maybe she could change it?

In 1949 my first child was born, a precious, long-awaited daughter, Debbie. During her early years, at the insistence and encouragement of Dr. Bell, I became a volunteer for the National Foundation for Infantile Paralysis. I had been one of the few people who could administer on-site care to children with polio on respirators. He wanted me to help NFIP develop courses to teach nurses in Vermont to care for polio patients so that the patients wouldn't have to leave the state and their families in order to get care. I did that and ended up doing some fund raising to support the activity. As a result I was appointed state advisor on women's activities of the National Foundation in the state of Vermont, the youngest state advisor in the country. I knew I was going to need help.

I went to New York to a meeting of all the state advisors. Helen Hayes was the national chair that year. Someone had told her that I was the youngest state advisor in the country. I was surrounded by mature, seasoned women who had been doing volunteer work for years. I felt there was a gap, and I also felt my own deficiencies.

Helen Hayes asked to see me. I thought my heart would stop. She took my right hand in both of hers and said, "I just want to thank you. I understand that you have a little girl at home, and I want to thank you for being willing to spend some time away from her so that people like me will not have to give up our little girls forever." Every molecule in my soul responded to that remark. I did not give up my volunteer work with the National Foundation for Infantile Paralysis until there was a vaccine and until I had been all over the state of Vermont to make sure that children had access to it.

I taught one year in a diploma program before I left the state. That experience propelled me back into school. I chose Syracuse University because of Jean Barrett's reputation. My days at Syracuse were memorable. I finished my baccalaureate degree and received the USPHS Research Fellowship to complete a master's program.

I sat in classes in graduate school where my fellow classmates seemed almost contemptuous of my idealistic philosophy of nursing. They believed I was setting myself up to fail in the real world. They groaned and told me I was being unrealistic. Jean Barrett sat in class and listened to this, and then in counseling sessions advised me unequivocally that there was nothing wrong with being an idealist. My job, she said, was to make those idealistic conditions happen. My profound gratitude to the nursing staff at Evanston and Glenbrook has much to do with the fact that they have helped me to convert my ideals into reality.

Ida MacDonald was my academic advisor. When my idealism got in Ida's way, she would gently growl at me, "Oh, June, you are so eastern." Ida was from Montana and found my eastern ways too stilted. She and I had a wonderful relationship. We respected each other's differences, and our bond of affection grew stronger over the years. Both Ida MacDonald and Jean Barrett became mentors for me.

There were two other people at that time who became extremely important to me.

When I entered graduate school, there were two other people in the class—Louise Hapeman and Barbara Narrow. We constituted that entire graduate class. Barbara and Louise majored in nursing education, and I majored in nursing administration. We were an inveterate threesome. Our triumvirate exploded the myth that three women can never get along. Our relationship was rich on so many personal and professional levels. It has lasted over the years. We were employed by the school of nursing after graduation.

Prior to that time, the bachelor's degree had been available only in nursing education. It was now to be available in nursing. My job was to help students apply everything they had learned in physical, biological, and social sciences to the care of the patient. The only way I knew how to achieve this was to take students back to the hospital to care for patients. The students strongly resisted having to return to providing direct patient care. The other side of the problem was that it was difficult at first to get physicians to give us permission to care for their patients. Students were known as the Syracuse University field students.

I arranged to have all the patients that the students were going to care for on one unit. The university paid a night nurse to care for those patients, and at all other times, from 7 AM to 11 PM, the field students assumed responsibility for the care of the patients. Although the students were tentative at first, they soon affirmed their nursing skills. We assessed the needs of every single patient and made plans to meet those needs. By the end of the first semester, the students had learned a great deal. The physicians were pleased with the care of their patients, and the field students built an excellent reputation for their nursing skills.

In my three years at Syracuse I learned that it was possible to deliver high-quality nursing care to patients on a sustained basis. I was, however, disheartened by communication from students who had graduated. Each Christmas I would get cards from past students who would say, "Dear June Werner, Merry Christmas. It was sure nice to be a student— the real world is not like that." My reaction fell somewhere between anger and despair. I often thought, "So much for the real world!"

I left Syracuse on the verge of acquiring tenure when my husband was given the opportunity to write his dissertation under the finest scholar in his field at Indiana University. It was the end of an era for me—an absolutely spectacular era. In Indiana I did some consulting, and miraculously the Werners' fertility problem was solved. We had been alerted to the magical cures of the water in Bloomington, Indiana. In November 1961, Derek Whitney Werner was born. I did not go back to work until he was a year old, when I returned to Bloomington Hospital part time to continue my role as consultant in the department of nursing. During our final months in Bloomington I acted as director of volunteers to facilitate their role in patient care.

From the summer of 1959 to the present the Werners have spent every summer on the Navajo Reservation in Arizona. My husband's interest in meanings across cultures was the central core of his scholarly work. He attached his theoretical notions to the health care of the Navajo so that this wife, who felt Burlington, Vermont, was the center of the universe, would get hooked on the Southwest. Every summer the Werners— mother, father, and children—packed off to the reservation, in the early days to do dissertation research and in later years to do continuing research funded by the National

Institutes of Health. During those summers we lived in a remote area where the post office was farthest from a railhead in the United States, on the edge of Monument Valley in Kayenta, Arizona. We were about 12 miles from the local USPHS clinic. These clinics were staffed by an Anglo physician (usually from the East) and Navajo auxiliary staff. Sometimes there was an Anglo nurse, but usually Navajo nurses staffed the clinics.

The Navajo learned early that if they went to the Werners, they would be cared for or directed to appropriate care. They assumed they were bringing the ill or injured to "Dr. Werner" for care, but soon found out that Dr. Werner was really Professor Werner and that it was Mrs. Werner, the nurse, who provided the care. Sometimes we gave first aid on the spot—sometimes we sent for an ambulance. Sometimes we took the patient to the clinic or 60 miles in the other direction to Tuba City Hospital. The consequence of these activities was a sense of trust and confidence in our family on the part of the Navajo.

In 1967, when my husband had a sabbatical and we were out West for 15 months, I was invited by the local physician to build a health program for the 900 Navajo children from kindergarten through twelfth grade who attended the local school system. I knew the Navajo—I had lived with them for almost 10 summers—and they knew me. The first thing I did in my role as school nurse was a needs assessment of the system. I interviewed everybody—the children, their families, the teachers, and the staff at the clinic. Clearly the biggest problem was impetigo.

Children with impetigo filled Dr. Kompare's clinic every day. I developed an educational program for the various age groups. I had negotiated to have an extremely intelligent Navajo woman, Mrs. Nez, to be my assistant. Mable Nez and I went from classroom to classroom with our educational program, teaching the children what caused impetigo and how it could be prevented. I shared with them all kinds of apparatuses our family had used during our summers camping in remote areas of the Navajo Reservation to find a way to shower every day. These children and their families were so inventive they far outdistanced us when it came to innovation. By the first week in October, the school had almost no impetigo. My office had cartons of soap with hexachlorophene. The children knew they could come anytime and get some.

Although the staff in the clinic was delighted that we had solved the problem, it was the children now free from the discomfort and embarrassment who made the project worthwhile. During that year we taught nutrition to the junior high school students, and we developed a sex education program for the community. When developing this kind of a program in an outlying area, you must have at least a year's lead time to win the confidence of the community before you start teaching their children anything in the area of sex education. Ed Kompare and I had gained that trust over the years. That was one more time in my life when superb collaboration with a physician made health care for a patient population possible. Ed Kompare is one of the finest physicians I have known. Trained at the University of Illinois, he remains in Tuba City Hospital, serving the Navajo well. One of the joys of my life is to be godmother to his first daughter by special dispensation from the Pope, since I am not a Catholic.

The children for whom I provided services in 1967 have become men and women with children of their own. Nothing delights me more than to be out in the Southwest and have a grown man approach me and say "Aren't you Mrs. Werner? You were my nurse." I treasure my connections with those families.

Let me return to the discussion of our leaving Bloomington, Indiana. My husband was a seasoned scholar and had many teaching offers. The one that excited him most was at Northwestern University. I had sent for materials from the Chamber of Commerce there when he showed interest in going. When he came home the day the information arrived, I said, "Do you really have to go to Evanston, Illinois? It's the home of the WCTU and the Funeral Directors of America." My husband's answer was, "Northwestern is the Harvard of the Midwest." My answer was, "We'll go."

We arrived in fall 1963, and I was four months pregnant. Debbie was to start high school in Evanston that year, and Derek was not quite two years old. Rickard West Werner was born January 24, 1964, in Evanston Hospital. We affectionately call that time "June's diaper-folding era." My good husband was aware that, although I was enjoying the children and loved being with them, I *missed* my professional life. He saw to it that I had my journals. Every other Friday (a day when he didn't teach), it was my day to go do something that interested me in the realm of nursing. I would spend the day in the library. I became friends with Ingeborg Mauksch. She and I had differing views about nursing, each of us passionate about her own perspective. Occasional luncheon meetings were stimulating, and I am grateful to Ingeborg for that. It was she who informed Harriett Koch in 1966 that I was not working and that I might be useful to Harriett in her Video Nursing project. When Harriett first called me, I told her I could not do anything until my youngest son went to nursery school. I didn't believe he would be going in the fall of 1967. However, even then Rick had strong opinions of his own. His best friend Erica was going to nursery school in the fall of 1966, and Rick was adamant that he would accompany her. He passed his nursery school readiness evaluation with flying colors. I stood on the porch waving as he went off to school, shattered because he never looked back. He was ready to go.

I called Harriett Koch, and Halloween 1966 was the start of our wonderful experience with Video Nursing. We developed, delivered, and performed programs designed to share the talents of well-prepared faculty in the Chicago area. Harriett Koch was then and remains a visionary. Together we developed a course called "Trends in Nursing." Luther Christman did a 44-minute program for us. It took two days to produce that segment. I was involved in developing that program, and although I had met Luther Christman before, I had never gotten to know him. In those two days we came to know each other well. It was Luther Christman who suggested to Dorothy Johnson, the first chairman of the department of nursing at Evanston, that she hire me as a consultant. He said, "June Werner is all about patient care. Why don't you steal her from Harriett?" I was much too committed to Video Nursing and to Harriett Koch to make any immediate move, but our sabbatical the following year interrupted my experience with Video Nursing, and when I returned I went to the department of nursing as a consultant. There I had the responsibility for education and research within the department. I developed a course for head nurses called "The Management of Care," in which I tried to help them see that it wasn't the unit they needed to manage but the care of the patients in the unit.

In 1970 I resigned from that position. I started looking for a doctoral program that spoke to my condition. By that time I realized that if I was going to make changes in nursing (I felt I knew what changes needed to be made), I was going to have to learn to be a good coach. I would need to know a great deal more about the dynamics of human behavior and about systems. I could not find a doctoral program that would have prepared me to be anything but a dean or a researcher—possibly a professor of nursing.

At the suggestion of a respected colleague, I started to investigate psychiatric nursing programs. I ended up at St. Xavier College in Chicago because the director, Frank Shea, recognized that I was a mature student who came with articulated needs and a specialized goal. At St. Xavier I tested out of many courses and took classes in guidance and counseling with Dr. Dorothy Binder. Dorothy helped unravel all my preconceived notions about nursing. She also inspired a lot of confidence by assuring me I had the skills to accomplish my goals. I have cherished my relationship with her.

By mid-fall of 1970, I was well into my program at St. Xavier. I received a call from the vice-president for patient care at Evanston, who asked me if I would come to see him. Prior to my departure from Evanston, I had assured them that I would be glad to help recruit a replacement for the departing chairman. I was advised that they were considering someone, and they wanted to talk to me about it. I was shocked to learn that I was the candidate. The staff who had come to know me at Evanston had gone to the administration to suggest that they recruit me to fill the chairmanship. I assured the vice-president that I was committed to the program in which I was studying, that I had an obligation to the traineeship, and that I would not withdraw. He asked me what it would take for me to stay in the program and accept this position. That query seemed so ridiculous that I laughed. The vice-president knew my husband and knew the character of our relationship and our marriage and suggested that I go home and talk things over with Ossy.

That was one of the hardest decisions I have ever had to face. I had enjoyed a nine-month appointment for years. The chairmanship at Evanston is a year-round position. I wouldn't be able to go to the Navajo Reservation every summer. Debbie was away at college, and the boys were almost 8 and 10. My husband was remarkably supportive in helping me make a decision. One of the things he pointed out went back to that time in Syracuse when the students wrote Christmas cards telling me it was great to be a student, but that the real world wasn't like that. My husband thought perhaps it was a great temptation for me to become "the real world."

It was at that point that I looked seriously at how I could arrange my life—my very busy life—to do both these things. Ossy assured me that the children would be fine. They would go with him every summer, and we would employ a mother's helper to live in the house during the academic year. We had purchased a house the year before very near the hospital, so I avoided the hassle of commuting. I agreed to take the position effective January 4, 1971. I spent most of my Christmas vacation in the office familiarizing myself with the records and the environment. I had written 11 conditions of employment— most of them related to the freedom to redevelop the department in terms of objectives that related to the provision of clinically competent, humane care for every patient and his family. Those conditions included protection for myself as a student and assurance that I could balance the three sides of my life—professional, graduate school, and personal.

By September 1971 I had a serious, committed group of nurse leaders in nursing administration at Evanston. We conducted a small-scale study in preparation for improving the delivery system for nursing, with excellent support from the University of Illinois. A group survey of the literature resulted in a major interest in Marie Manthey's work on primary nursing in Minnesota. On Valentine's Day 1972, we initiated a demonstration project on primary nursing on our most challenging unit, feeling that if it could work there it would work in other areas. As the project unfolded, tremendous excitement was generated by the outcomes. Patients, families, nurses, and physicians reinforced our hypotheses. In three months we were convinced that primary nursing was a genesis of high-quality nursing care and a viable professional practice climate in the Evanston setting. We never looked back. Carefully we nurtured the model on every unit where the clinical coordinator felt the staff was ready. By 1975 we could say to patients being admitted, "Let us tell you about your primary nurse." Nurses experienced great pride in their autonomy and the related accountability.

At the same time a healthy interdependence developed between the patient's primary nurse and the patient's primary physician. Increasing competence of the nursing staff spawned an interest in professional development and resulted in the development of our levels of practice program. Outside consultants assured us that the system provided impressive productivity. In a collaborative manner we contained costs, setting prudent priorities that protected patient care. In 1983 consultants from the Meidinger Company conducted an attitude survey of employees and stated they had never before seen such high levels of satisfaction in nursing. Patient satisfaction in the area of nursing increased to well above 90% and has never declined.

Evanston's strength in nursing has been in its leaders and their ability to facilitate and nurture staff nurses in their quest to become professionals capable of delivering clinically competent, humane care to every patient and family. I'm convinced that a primary function of leadership is to generate emotional glue—it supports the members in good times and bad, sustains morale, and builds human bridges that ultimately create a network of caring. We learned that if we expect nurses to provide high-quality care to patients, nursing leaders must take care of the nurses. We turned the table of organization upside down and put the caregivers at the top, responding to the community of patients. The rest of us assumed supportive roles to make it possible for those caregivers, the patient's nurses, to provide quality care. We learned together and took seriously the obligation of keeping communications open between us. We reached the conclusion early that in recruiting to fill positions, it was necessary not only to find a competent professional, but also to find a person capable of being a colleague to the rest of us—especially in times of trouble.

The nurses with whom I've worked at Evanston are the finest group of professionals I've ever experienced in one system. They will forever have my respect, my affection, and my gratitude. In developing the high quality of nursing care we have known at Evanston, my colleagues have earned the confidence of the community and also have made my dream for nursing and patients come true.

In the Evanston experience, it must be noted that we could not have accomplished nursing's goal for high-quality nursing care without sustained support from Bernard Lachner, the president of the corporation, and from the board of trustees. Their confidence in our pursuit made the outcomes possible. Evanston was not really Camelot, contrary to the myth. The only time we have experienced anything but a low turnover rate was when our salaries dropped in the marketplace. We accomplished every change and aspiration with data and copious pages of justification.

The practice climate was responsible for our recognition as a Magnet Hospital, which was a source of great gratification for us. We developed a climate of support for nurses returning to school and a scholars program to support them beyond tuition rebate. In 1987 we felt our evaluation of the primary nursing model indicated a response to differentiated practice and the fast-changing health care scene. The one thing that will not change is the accountability of the nurse that is inherent in the primary nursing model.

Reviewing my life has reinforced those values at the core of it. Clearly that core is composed of my basic assumption that I am an instrument and that there truly is something of God in every person. The direct result is my inherent respect for all humans and my concern for their condition. My unequivocal value for family life, my passion for nursing as it responds to the vulnerable or the potentially vulnerable, and my sense of mission to fulfill the calling that nursing has provided are the central components of my world.

I continue to feel blessed and challenged. I could not have met the challenges that have prevailed without a well-developed value system, the support of loved ones, and courage. Embedded in my memory is Amelia Earhart's poem, "Courage," which has given regular support to me:

> *Courage is the price which life exacts for granting peace.*
> *The soul which knows it not, knows no release from little things—*
> *Knows not the livid loneliness of fear nor mountain heights where*
> *   bitter joy can hear the sounds of wings.*
> *How can life grant us boon of living—*
> *Compensate for dull gray ugliness and pregnant hate*
> *   unless we have the soul's dominion?*
> *Each time we make a choice we pay with courage to behold*
> *   resistless day and count it fair.*

Virginia T. Williams

Virginia T. Williams, MS, RN,
owns her own business—an independent nursing
practice called Family Nursing

❖

   Though Virginia Williams worked in various institutions for over 30 years, she always yearned for more independence for herself and for nursing. Finally, she broke out on her own and set up an independent nursing practice.

   Wellness *became Ginny's watchword, and against great odds she persisted in her determination to provide services that members of her community wanted and were willing to pay for. Her father was sure she'd starve, but her business has done well. Her admirable philosophy, "I feel I am a guest in my clients' homes," has endeared her to everyone she serves.*

I was born the third of four children. My father grew up on a farm, married my mother, who was from McHenry, Illinois, (a neighboring town) and worked there as a truck driver for 40 years. It was hard work with few or no benefits— except that he could come home for lunch—but he did work through the depression. During those years he and Mama kept four of us in parochial school on an $18 a week salary.

My mother's parents were German immigrants who enjoyed art, music, and teaching, which was a benefit to all of us. Convent life attracted a maternal and a paternal aunt. Religion was very important to us and has remained so.

Being in a class of 36 in a small-town high school allowed me many privileges in athletics and academics. A nurse friend of mine introduced me to another nurse, who hired me to do housework and child care. Each of them helped direct my choice of vocation. Both influenced my career goal and my enrollment at St. Anne's Hospital School of Nursing in Chicago.

Hospital life, in retrospect, was confining. My choice to apply to affiliations rather than stay in the routine three-year program allowed me two months in a state psychiatric hospital, followed by a six-month tour as a Senior Cadet nurse in an Indiana service hospital. It seemed there was always more to see, more to do, and more places to go.

Shortly after graduation, I decided to travel again. The staff nursing position I held at a 50-bed hospital was costing me a 12-hour day without benefit of much free time. Some friends in California who lived near San Diego beckoned me and two friends to visit. We found jobs at a county hospital there, and three months of work permitted lots of pleasure and served me well professionally. However, home ties were strong. The Hines Veterans Administration Hospital back in Chicago had staff nurse positions that sounded attractive, so I went back and remained for 14 years. Home and family were close, just 50 miles away, and friendships were strong. Life was good until night duty took its toll. Only then, 10 years after graduation, did I consider a return to school. It took me seven years of part-time study to complete a BSN degree at Loyola University, where I graduated cum laude.

My final clinical experiences there demanded full-time, five-day weeks for study, so I could no longer work at the VA. I worked instead at a local public health agency. It may well have been time for a change because my parents were growing old and were not well. I moved home in 1961 and commuted. Mama died in 1964. My two sisters lived in town, and both of them have large families—ten and seven children. We were all close.

I belonged to the Illinois Nurses Association and became involved in its legislative activities. Anne Zimmerman invited me to coordinate a project funded by the Department of Health, Education and Welfare to attract inactive nurses back to practice. We worked together on it for four years and found out that those 20,000 "inactive" nurses were very active, very smart, and very busy doing all kinds of family nursing. It was not until the project was completed and I had enrolled in graduate school for community health nursing at Northern Illinois University that my real concern for family, wellness, strength, and normalcy began to outweigh the medical model of patient, pathology, illness, and abnormalities. In curriculum development the term "wellness" was coined, and on that philosophical note I planned a continuing career.

Throughout my life, people have allowed me to do what I have shown potential for. I have always been blessed with good health. In 1973, after 30 years in nursing, I realized that nurses should be working independently of the medical model. That was when, as a substitute for a thesis, I chose the practicum of working with a pediatrician— he in the care of sick children, I for the wellness potential of the family. From that lead I found the freedom to hang a shingle:

> V. T. WILLIAMS, RN, FAMILY NURSING

There could have been other avenues for my practice to take, but they were closed by a rigid health care system.

The concept of continuity of care was attractive enough that I attempted to work in that setting at our local 135-bed hospital. But I could not convince the administrator that all the discharged, so-called cured, healed, abandoned, or terminally ill needed someone to care for them or have home care arranged for them.

Neither could I influence the medical specialists that they needed someone to assess or evaluate those who petitioned them for care—those who were usually worried and whose reception into the health care system was jumbled, delayed, or inappropriate. Those who were rejected for care because the physicians' practices were full had little recourse but to get sicker and use the emergency room.

My third option was private practice, which I had explored during graduate school. A public relations course I took had prompted me to survey the community of physicians, nurses, and the public to see how they felt about this kind of practice. Physicians did not seem to mind, believing it could not hurt them. Nurses did not see any future in it— many in fact thought it a "cop-out" of nursing. However, it turned out that the lay public, many of whom had requested and received care for years as neighbors, friends, and relatives, would be pleased to purchase such services. That was how, why, and when I started my independent nursing practice.

The time was ripe because the teaching position called not for my community or generalist experience but for a new medical-surgical expertise. I declined that position, although it paid $14,000 per year—more than I had ever made. I chose instead a situation that to my conservative father looked like surefire starvation. He said I was "the only one in our family who had ever been to college, then on to grad school, and then to quit work." It took a few years before I reached that income level again, but I did not starve. I did enjoy some eggs and other barter products as pay, but that was OK. It helped me to develop a fee schedule.

Competition, if there was any, was from a county health department whose bylaws I helped review in an advisory capacity. They demanded physicians' orders for nursing care, and they still do. Medicare and Medicaid require that, and it is the system that dominates.

By that time in my life, I was used to having my freedom. Never having married, I took advantage of much travel during long government benefit vacations. Once I even quit the VA for a four-month trip to Europe without a reservation or a return ticket. I took advantage of having friends in South Africa to visit by way of Belgium and Spain, and I came back through the south of France and Paris with my old French and Latin language teacher. Later, she became a client and completed her life in my care.

We talked a lot during our travels but could never pinpoint exactly why I wandered off the main streets. We decided that I felt the "real people" were families in the community, not individuals at work or where the tourists traveled. To this day, I feel it is a real privilege to be a guest in my clients' homes. That is where people are the strongest—in their own castle. Years ago one of my friends suggested that I should do work that allowed me to go visiting all the time. How little we realized then that I was headed that way. While I have often referred to my work as "going off to play," it almost seems profane to enjoy work as much as I do and to treat the practice that casually. One of my sisters thought it inappropriate to speak of work that way. My other sister once described my work to someone as "riding around all day in the country."

Simplicity rules my practice. Clients' records are treated as their property, and we do paperwork together at their kitchen table. Referrals come from clients. In their own words: " . . . Will you help us? . . . I want to get my husband/wife out of a nursing home. . . . Take me to the hospital/doctor. . . . See if my child needs stitches. . . . Find us someone to take care of _____." All such statements of need are invitations for nursing care.

Simple accounting is my byword. It is accomplished with two separate checking accounts—one is for business, the other is personal. The business account pays me a salary as the cash flow builds up, and it does.

My independent and solo practice has been reviewed by many of my peers on field trips or in independent study courses and by others who consider it a potential nursing goal.

Recently, a doctoral candidate prepared the following description of my practice, with which I humbly and gratefully concur.

Family Nursing: A Model of Independent Nursing Practice

Family Nursing is an independent nursing practice model conceived, developed and practiced by its sole owner, Virginia T. Williams. This model of private practice nursing is based on a philosophy of nursing surrounding such concepts as caring, coping, and contracting, as well as autonomy, accountability and availability.

Virginia Williams has been in business for herself in the town of McHenry for nearly 13 years. Today, the practice thrives with financial stability. Often there is too much work for one person. Grossing around $40,000 annually, Virginia manages her work with a solid personal business sense, referring some work to other nurses in the community when she is overloaded.

The concept of family nursing was conceived by Virginia while she was still employed in nursing institutions where she began to feel constrained by bureaucratic orderliness. Her beliefs about nursing needs of people in a community setting, as well as her growing discontent with traditional medical model 'health' programs, encouraged her own strong sense of independence. With an experienced nursing background and a completed master's degree in nursing, Virginia decided that her own skills and knowledge could best be used by making herself available to those who wanted her.

Family Nursing became the title of her business as well as her philosophy of nursing. Virginia believes that in many primary care situations, families should be, and, as social research supports today, are the primary care givers in the community. Focusing her interest as a nurse on helping family members to care for their own at home, Virginia went to work in her home town. Today Virginia maintains her basic philosophy. She contracts directly with individual clients or with individual family members to provide, or help them provide, short- and long-term nursing care in the home. Her clients are all ages and she practices as a generalist.

Basing the practice on legal limits of nursing within the guidelines of the Illinois Nurse Practice Act, Virginia seldom finds herself in situations where she needs to refer to a physician. The reasons for this are undoubtedly the reputation she has in the community, where people understand what she does, and also the fact that she develops contracts with clients.

Contracting is done by a simple process of assessment and decision making. Using a 24-hour answering service should she be out of her office, new potential clients call to seek her help. They have seen her advertising in the church bulletin or know of her from word of mouth. Virginia's initial approach, depending on the inquiry, is to ask the caller if they would like her to make a home visit to assess the situation.

Because she keeps her own appointment book in an informal yet particular manner, Virginia believes she can and must be available at irregular hours. This allows her the freedom to make those assessment visits at times of convenience to clients and herself. If Virginia finds at the first visit that she can help the family or the person, she seeks verbal agreement from the client and/or the family member to work *with* them.

These contracts vary depending on individual needs. They may include direct ongoing nursing care such as bowel and bladder care for a bedfast person, a program of rehabilitation care which is also taught to family members, respite care for primary carers, medication organization programs for the visually handicapped, hygiene care of all kinds, blood pressure monitoring, to name but a few. Teaching and supporting family caregivers becomes a high priority in the practice and Virginia believes strongly in the need to care for the carers, especially in long-term-care situations.

Helping an individual learn to cope with his limitations, such as functional weakness, by focusing that person's attention on building onto what he can do, is a major part of the work, especially for elderly clients and handicapped persons. Virginia helps individuals to become creative in their own learning of how to manage problems, with a sense of dignity and independence. She believes that people—clients and families—can always continue to make their own choices about health care matters if they are provided with alternatives and assistance.

Occasionally those alternatives will include suggesting ongoing 24-hour assistance which she cannot provide, but she can help the family find the right assistance and does so, if they wish her to.

In any one day, Virginia travels many miles or stays in local neighborhoods to see her clients, depending on where the needs are. With a strong faith, nursing knowledge, her hands, her eyes and ears, her keen sensitivity and her belief in people making decisions about their own needs, Virginia practices without fear of litigation. While covered by insurance, she is committed to a nursing practice philosophy which prescribes clear boundaries of autonomy and accountability and she never attempts to work without the contract. For this reason she has no fear about the independent practice role for nurses. Neither, it seems, do the residents, as she is known by the local community as "the angel of McHenry."

Family Nursing as a business is a simple though efficient one. Virginia works out of her own home, having separate business and private telephones, and uses the 24-hour answering service to keep track of her calls. She charges flat fees of $20 to $40 per visit, depending on the time and work required, and maintains her own billing system. Monthly, she sends out invoices on printed stationery to those clients who prefer to be billed. Some pay cash at visits, others pay in installments. Some of her work contracts come from other health agencies, for example, Veterans Affairs, which pays her directly.

Virginia encourages her clients to claim against their insurance policies for her care, and in some cases they are successful. For Medicare coverage, Virginia can sometimes obtain a physician's referral to her to cover costs. Inability to pay does not stop her service to an individual. Occasional losses are part of her public relations and her commitment to community service. Virginia maintains a viable practice.

Virginia does not concern herself with lots of expensive equipment and instruments. She uses an accountant to keep her books appropriately audited and for tax purposes. Taxes are paid quarterly in advance, based on the previous year's income. Virginia has good relations with local pharmacists and can assist her clients in filling prescriptions and obtaining appropriate information as the need arises. In her home office area, she maintains a closet with nursing supplies, mostly disposable. Because of her influence in the community, she can always find that extra wheelchair or walker someone needs to borrow for a while. Lots of sharing and caring seems to go on in McHenry.

Although Virginia Williams appears to be a one-man band, she is by no means an isolationist within the nursing profession or in community affairs. Virginia has frequent requests for nursing students and peers to precept nursing experiences and she gets a steady stream of inquiries about independent practice from nurse researchers and faculty. Virginia takes on all these activities with serious professional concern and interest in helping others learn.

Occasionally Virginia is asked to speak at nursing seminars and she tries to attend as many professional development programs for her own learning needs as she can. She subscribes to a wide variety of multidisciplinary journals.

Family Nursing as a nursing practice model has great potential for any community. All it seems to need is one nurse who has the courage to go out and nurse!

Barbara Oudt, Rush University College of Nursing

Index

A

Abdellah, Faye, 201
Accreditation, 353
Adams, Ansel, 161
Adelphi University, 96, 275, 277
Adirondack Community College, 90
Administration, nursing; *see* Nursing administration
Adolescents, working with, 99
Advance of American Nursing, 133
Advanced Nurse Training Grant Program, 134
Advisory Committee on National Health Insurance, 259
Ager, Joel, 372
Aging, studies in, 346
Aiken, Linda H., 1-6
Alcoholism, 243-244
Alpha Kappa Delta, 52
Alpha Omega Alpha, 52
Alt, Grace, 285
Alta Bates Hospital, 17
Altoona Hospital School of Nursing, 357, 358
Ambulatory nursing, 108, 109
American Academy of Nursing, 40, 49, 75, 167, 174, 205, 373
American Association for the Advancement of Science, 52
American Association of Critical Care Nurses, 154, 157, 158
A.N. Brady Maternity Hospital, 87, 89
American Association of Junior Colleges, 278
American Cancer Society Professor of Nursing, 225
American Civil Liberties Union, 18
American Educational Research Association, 89
American Hospital Association, 184-185
American Journal of Nursing, 39, 165, 254, 272
American Journal of Nursing Company, 213
American Medical Association, 21, 185
American Nurses' Association, 13, 19, 21, 35, 49, 50, 75, 112, 118, 119, 121, 140, 144, 158, 164, 198, 222, 253, 258, 271, 290, 332, 347, 352, 353, 367, 373

American Nurses' Association—cont'd
black nurses and, 30
Commission on Nursing Education, 75
Entry into Practice Committee on, 204
House of Delegates meeting of, 335
legislative work of, 120
Minority Fellowship Programs of, 26
Social Policy Statement of, 341
American Nurses' Association/Nurses Association of the American College of Obstetrics and Gynecology Certification Examination Committee, 167
American Nurses' Foundation, 81, 297
American Public Health Association, 5, 213
American Sociological Association, 52
American University, 132
Ancker Hospital, 221, 222
Anderson, Ferguson, 317
Anderson, Joseph R., 185
Anderson, Ruth, 198
Annual Review of Nursing Research, 374, 375
Anstey, Olive, 121
Anthropology, nursing and, 189, 234, 317
Anticipatory Socialization Program, 173
Arizona Good Samaritan Hospital, 241
Army Medical Service Graduate School, 367
Army Medical Service School, 367
Army Nurse Corps; *see* U.S. Army Nurse Corps
Arnstein, Margaret, 10, 12, 82, 210
Associate degree nursing, 199-200, 274
early days of, 278
external degree in, 279
programs in, 278-279
Association of Collegiate Schools of Nursing, 35
Atomic Bomb Casualty Commission, 281, 286-287
Attribution theory, 264
Aydelotte, Myrtle K., 7-14

B

Babies Hospital, Columbia Presbyterian Medical Center, 63

Baccalaureate nursing
  external degree, 279
  in Japan, 289
Baez, Joan, 22
Bailey, Allison, 199
Baldwin, Denny, 383
Baltimore City Hospital, 112
Barrett, Jean, 263, 387
"Barriers and Conflict in Maternity Care Innovation," 234
Barton, Allen, 201
Barton, Clara, 323
Bauknecht, Ginny, 120
Baxter, Charlie, 269
Baylor University, 268
Baziak, Anna T. (Dugan), 79
Beck, Patricia, 89
Becker, Diane, 114
Beeby, Nell, 39
Beland, Irene, 10, 224, 225, 306, 325
Bellevue Hospital, 98, 100
Benchmark School, 112
Benjamin Rose Hospital, 198, 199
Benoliel, Jeanne Quint, 15-22, 81
Bergman, Rebecca, 121, 226
Bessent, Hattie, 12, 23-26
Bicultural Training Program, 173
Biculturalism, 171, 174
Binder, Dorothy, 391
Blendon, Robert, 5
Blood pressure, high; *see* Hypertension
"Blueprint for Nursing Research," 371
Blueprint of Examinations Committee of ANA
      Council of State Boards of Nursing, 91
Bobs Robert Hospital, 221
Bolton, Frances Payne, 210
Bolton Bill, 32
Bon Secours Hospital, 262
Bonica, John, 270
Boston City Hospital, 340
Boston College, 84, 88, 297
Boston College School of Nursing, 87
Boston Floating Hospital, 344
Boston University, 64
Boston University School of Nursing, 340
Bowes, Watson, 164, 166
Braisher, Alice, 333
Bramble, Millie, 197
Breckenridge, Mary, 161
Brewster, Kingman, 82, 83
Brickbauer, Lydia, 219

Bridgman, Margaret, 12
Bridgman, Percy, 18
Brooke Army Hospital, 365
Brown, Elsa, 199
Bryan, William Jennings, 222
Bryan Memorial Hospital, 222
Bryant, Ruby F., 366
Bryson, Lyman, 100
Burns, treatment of, 269
Burns, James McGregor, 352
Burnside, Helen, 202
Burr, Mary, 96

C

Cadet Nurse Corps, 132, 139, 188, 277
California Nurses' Association, 75
California State College, Los Angeles, 142
Camp White, Oregon, 17
Camus, Albert, 18
Cantor, Marjorie, 12
Cardew, Emily, 224
Cardiac nursing, 333
Cardiovascular disorders, behavioral aspects of, 113
Carey, Anne, 366
Carnegie, Bernice, 33
Carnegie, M. Elizabeth, 27-42
Carnegie Scholarship, 41
Carney Hospital, Dorchester, Massachusetts, 86
Carroll, Margaret, 12
Carter, Jimmy, 119, 259
Case Institute of Technology, 197
Case study method, 316
Case Western Reserve University, 134, 309, 310, 347
Casualties, mass, management of, 367, 368, 369
Catholic University, 118
Center for Health Research, 372
Center of Excellence in Nursing, 51
Changing Image of the Nurse, 134
Charles T. Miller Hospital, 11
Chayer, Mary Ella, 345
Chicago Council on Community Nursing, 256
Chicago Institute of Medicine, 52
Childbearing Center, 234
Children
  dying, home care for, 248-250
  pain management and, 271
  psychiatric nursing and, 101, 102
Children's Hospice International, 250
Children's Hospital, Chicago, 86

Children's Hospital, Washington, D.C., 101

Christman, Luther, 43-52, 390

Christman's Laws of Behavior, 49-50

Christy, Terry, 201

City University of New York, 97, 103

Clarke, Alice, 47

Cleland, Virginia, 372

Cleveland Metropolitan Hospital School of Nursing, 199

Clinical nurse specialist, 3, 333, 334

Coalition for Health Funding, 121

Coe, Myrtle, 10

Collaboration model of nursing, 308

Collective bargaining, 257, 333, 334, 335, 336

College of St. Rose, 86, 90

Collins, Margaret, 90, 91

Colorado General Hospital, 163, 167, 168

Colorado Nurses' Association, 164

Colorado State Hospital, 79

Columbia Presbyterian Hospital School of Nursing, 382

Columbia University, 339

Columbia University School of Public Health, 143

Commission on Human Medicine and Health Care of the Southern Regional Education Board, 38

Committee on Interinstitutional Cooperation, 374

Committee to Study the Nurse Practice Act, 184

Community as patient, 315-316

Community health nursing, 108, 296

Community medicine, 143

Community nursing service, 51

Conant, Lucy, 263

Conflict resolution, 173

Conley, Ann, 325

Conservation, principles of, 227

Cook County Hospital, 216, 222, 257, 330, 331

Cook County School of Nursing, 218, 223, 224, 327, 331

Cooper Hospital School of Nursing, 47

Corbin, Hazel, 233, 234

Cornell University, 304, 316, 339

Cornell University–New York Hospital School of Nursing, 186

Coronary care, 156

Coston, Harriet, 19

Council of Nurse Researchers, 373

Courtney, Gladys, 373-374, 375, 376

Courtney, Margaret, 106, 107, 113

Covenant Missionary Council, 286

Creative Nursing Management, 245

Credentialing, 352

Credit by examination, 200

Creedmoor State Hospital, 98

Creighton University, 188

Critical care nursing, 157-158

Crouse, Wanda, 238, 239

Culture
  health and, 189
  nursing and, 316-317

Culture shock, 190

Cunningham, Susanna, 112

Curriculum and Instruction in Nursing, 150, 152

Cushing, Maureen, 53-60

D

Davis, Anne, 61-69

Davis, Harvey, 12

Davitz, Lois, 201

de Beauvoir, Simone, 263

de Tornyay, Rheba, 70-76, 373

Death and dying, 16, 81, 356, 361
  nurse specialist in, 360

Decubitus ulcers, 198

Deeter, Jean, 360, 362

Delafield, Francis, 182

Delehanty, Lorraine, 240

Delta Sigma Theta sorority, 38, 40

Demography, nursing and, 3

Densford, Katherine J., 10-11, 208, 209, 222, 276

Denver General Hospital School of Nursing, 305

Department of Atomic Casualties Studies, 368

Department of Health, Education and Welfare, 118, 142

Derick, Virginia, 339

Detroit Medical Center, 323

Detroit Visiting Nurses Association, 325

Developmental disability, court case involving, 57

Devine, Elizabeth C., 377

Dewey, John, 208, 276

Diagnosis-related groups (DRGs), 183

Dickens, Charles, 338, 341

Dickoff, Bill, 80, 263

Diers, Donna, 77-84, 263

Dillard University, 32

Dimensions of Professional Nursing, 143, 144

Dinesen, Isak, 66

Directory of Open Curriculum Opportunities in Nursing Education, 203

Disability, developmental, court case involving, 57

Disadvantaged Students in RN Programs, 40

Disaster nursing, 345, 368

Ditchfield, Alda, 32
Dix, Dorothea, 161, 323
Dodds, Thelma, 11, 242
Downs, Florence, 104
Drexel Home, 224
Duke University, 352
  center for aging of, 346
Duke University School of Nursing, 346
Duley, Clara M., 370
Dumas, Rhetaugh, 80, 263
Duquesne University, 46
Duval Medical Center, 34, 35
Dvorak, Eileen McQuaid, 85-93

E

Earhart, Amelia, 393
East African Women's International Seminar, 40
Eckerling, Shoshanna, 226
Eckert, Ruth, 11, 12
Economic security unit of Illinois Nurses' Association, 333, 334
Education Committee of the American Nurses' Association, 184
Education for Nursing Leadership, 176, 183, 184
Educational administration, 256
Elder, Ruth, 263
Elderly, nursing care of, 318
Elderly Ambulatory Patient: Nursing and Psychosocial Needs, 316
Elliott, Jo Eleanor, 19
Ellis, Rosemary, 198, 254, 289
Emergency medicine, court case involving, 57-58
Emory University, 63
Engleman, Karl, 109
Erickson, Florence, 12
Ethics, study of, 67-69
Ethnocentrism in nursing care, 189-190
Etzioni, Amitai, 202
Evans, Ruth, 198
"Existentialism: A Philosophy of Commitment," 241

F

Faculty Practice Program, 174
Faddis, Margene, 198
Fagin, Claire, 94-104, 112
Fagin, Sam, 101
Fahey, George, 141
Family nurse practitioner, 317
Family nursing, 396
  model of, 397-400

Faville, Katharine, 224, 307, 321, 322, 324, 325, 326
Federal Career Teacher's Grant, 25
Federation of Specialty Nursing Organizations, 158
Feetham, Suzanne, 372
Feminine Mystique, 263
Feminism, 263
Fessler, Jerry, 333
Figuroa, Maria, 295
Fitzpatrick, Joyce J., 309, 376
Florida A&M College, 33, 38, 39
Florida A&M University, 25
Florida Association of Colored Graduate Nurses, 35
Florida League for Nursing, 38
Florida State League of Nursing Education, 35, 38
Florida State Nurses Association, 35, 36, 37, 38, 39
Florida State University, Tallahassee, 36, 38
Focus on Critical Care, 158
Foley, Hugh, 89
Follett, Mary, 314
Ford, Loretta, 127, 257
Forkner, Hamden L., 276
Frances Payne Bolton School of Nursing, 199, 307, 347
Freedmen's Hospital, 31
Freedmen's Nursing School, 30
Freeman, Ruth, 345
French, Jean, 317
Fresno General Hospital School of Nursing, 18, 19
Friedan, Betty, 263
From Abstract to Action, 258
Frost, David, 75
Frye, Jack, 333
Fundamentals of nursing, 224-225
Funkhouser, Rob, 340
Future Nurses of America, 130

G

Gadsup people, 190, 191
Garcia, Martha, 334
Garfinkel, Harold, 20
Garrison, Esther, 100
Georgetown University, 107, 263
Georgetown University School of Nursing, 262
Georgopoulos, Basil, 49
Geriatric nurse practitioner, 311, 317

Geriatric patient, 318
Geriatrics, 180
Gerontological nursing, 346, 347
Gerontology, social, 346
Geropsychiatric nursing, 346
Gesner, Pauline, 225
Ghana, 40
Gillies, DeeAnn, 225
Gilmer, Lee, 269, 272
Gingrich, Beulah, 225
Ginsberg, Miriam K., 370
Goal attainment, theory of, 150
Gordon, Ira, 25
Gordon, Phoebe, 275
Gottdank, Mildred, 98, 99, 100, 224, 325
Grace, Helen, 374
Gray, Carol, 113
Gray, William H., 34
Green, Chad, 57
Greenfield, Ruth, 370
Grier, Margaret R., 374
Grossman, Ben, 224
Growth and Development of Mothers, 264
Gunter, Laurie, 346
Guy, Joan, 372

H

Hadassah–Hebrew University School of Nursing,
    259
Hall, Lydia, 345
Hamline University, 275
Hampton Institute, 32
Hampton University, 33, 41
Hapeman, Louise, 388
Harlem Hospital, 30
Harrington, Ruth, 10
Harris, Isabell, 250
Hartman, Sylvia, 19
Harvard University, 68
Hassenplug, Lulu Wolf, 18, 19, 20
Hauge, Cecilia, 11
Hawkinson, Nellie X., 224, 254
Hayes, Helen, 387
Haynes, Inez, 369
Health
    international, nursing courses in, 288
    women's, theoretical basis of, 264
Health care
    business aspects of, 168
    cultural differences and, 189
    future of, 169

"Health for All by the Year 2000," 353
Health PACT, 126
Health Professions Institute, 103
Heart & Lung, 157
"Helping the Hypertensive Patient Control So-
    dium Intake," 111
Henderson, Virginia, 81, 82, 253, 257, 263, 314
Hennepin County Medical Center, 275
Henry Ford Hospital, 223, 224
Henry Street Settlement, 345
Henry Street Visiting Nurse Service, 30, 277
Herbert H. Lehman College, 102-103
Higgs, Grace, 36
High Blood Pressure Information Center, 111
Hill, Gary, 107
Hill, Martha H., 105-114
Hines Veterans Administration Hospital, 334
Hinsvark, Inez, 353
Hiroshima, injuries caused by bombing of, 286-
    287
Hodges, Charles, 222
Hodgkins, Myrtle (Coe), 276
Holleran, Constance, 115-122
Home care, 316
    for dying child, 248-250
Homer G. Phillips Hospital, 31, 32
Hoover, Kathleen Radicke, 333
Hopkins High Blood Pressure Conference Series,
    114
Horney, Karen, 18
Hospital of the University of Pennsylvania, 110,
    111, 232
Howard University, 31
Hudson, Wellborn, 12
Hudson Valley Community College, 88
Human ecology, 257
Hunter College, 95, 232, 263
Hypertension
    behavioral aspects of, 113
    incidence of, among black patients, 111
    nursing program for care of patients with, 110
    uncontrolled, 109
Hypertension outreach program, 110, 111

I

Igoe, Judith Bellaire, 123-128
Illinois League for Nursing, 255
Illinois Nurse Practice Act, 398
Illinois Nurses' Association, 254, 332, 295-296
    collective bargaining by, 335
    economic security unit of, 333, 334

Images of Nurses on Television, 134

Indiana University, 162, 388

Indiana University School of Nursing, 265

Indiana University—Bloomington, 25

Institute of Medicine, National Academy of Sciences, 75

Institute of Public Health (Tokyo), 288

Instructive Visiting Nurses Association, 344, 345

International Association for the Study of Pain, 273

International Congress of Nurses, 36

International Congress on Nursing Law and Ethics, 259-260

International Council of Nurses, 118, 121, 285, 289, 296, 314, 353

International health, nursing courses in, 288

International Labor Organization, 122

International nursing, 290

Introduction to Clinical Nursing, 225, 227

Introduction to Nursing: An Adaptation Model, 295

J

Jacobi, Eileen, 119, 121

Jacobson, Barbara, 111

James, Pat, 80, 263

Japanese Department of Health, 371

Japanese Ministry of Health and Welfare, 284

Japanese Nursing Association, 285, 288, 289, 290

Japanese Nursing Practice and Education Act, 289

Jaspen, Nathan, 88

Jefferson Medical College Hospital School of Nursing, 365

Jefferson University, 52

Jennings, Betty, 167

Jernigan, Sally, 194

Jewish Federation of Chicago, 218

Johns Hopkins Hospital, 108, 207

Johns Hopkins University, 106

Johns Hopkins University School of Hygiene and Public Health, 106, 113

Johns Hopkins University School of Nursing, 113

Johnson, Dorothy E., 19, 293, 294, 390

Johnson, Jean, 263

Johnson, Sally, 252, 253

Johnson, Walter, 202

Jourard, Sidney, 22

Journal of Nursing Education, 74-75

Journal of the American Medical Association, 213

K

Kalisch, Beatrice, 129-135

Kalisch, Philip, 129, 131, 132, 135

Kalkman, Marion, 65

Kane, Michael, 91

Kaplan, Abraham, 22

Keane, Anne, 111

Keane, Vera, 339

Kellen, Mona Marie Badgerow Bellaire, 127

Kellogg, Helen, 51

Kellogg, John, 51

Kelly, Lucie S., 136-145, 203

Kennedy, John F., 67, 81, 205

Kennedy, Robert, 201

Kennedy Foundation, 67

Kersey, John, 248

Kesey, Ken, 22

Keuhn, Ruth, 48

Kimball, Lenore, 220

King, Coretta Scott, 26

King, Imogene M., 146-153

King, Martin Luther, Jr., 26, 81

Kiniery, Gladys, 256

Kinney, Marguerite, R., 154-159

Kinsinger, Bob, 204

Koch, Harriett, 333, 390

Kompare, Ed, 389

Kowalski, Karren, 160-170

Kramer, Marlene F., 171-174

Kübler-Ross, Elisabeth, 356, 360

Kuehn, Ruth, 141, 142

Kurtagh, Cathryn, 325

L

Lachner, Bernard, 392

Lambertsen, Eleanor C., 175-186, 202

Langfitt, Thomas, 103

Langley Porter Neuropsychiatric Hospital, 72

Langley Porter Psychiatric Institute, 65

Laskevich, Lee, 91

Laski, Harold, 276

Laughran, Henrietta, 306

Laur, Mary, 250

Lavin, Linda, 356, 361

Lazarsfeld, Paul, 202

Leadership

  components of, 322

  transactional, 352

Leavel, Lutie, 12

Lee, Barbara, 204
Lefkowitz, Nat, 202
Legislative issues, 120, 121
Leininger, Madeleine M., 187-192
Lenburg, Carrie B., 90, 193-205
Lenburg, Harold, 201
Leonard, Robert, 80, 263
Leone, Lucile Petry, 206-214
Lettus, Marianne, 90
Levine, David, 113
Levine, Myra, 215-228, 333
Liberia, 40
Licensed practical nurse, inappropriate use of, 335
Licensure, 353
Lincoln Hospital, 30, 31
Lincoln School for Nurses, 29
Lissy, LaVerne, 225, 333
Lloyd, Cora, 325
Lobenstine Clinic, 233
Logan, Jeannette, 333
London School of Economics, 276
Loretto Heights College, 125
Los Angeles Children's Hospital, 250
Lourie, Reginald, 101
Love, Elise, 112
Lowery, Barbara, 103, 114
Loyola University, 225, 238, 256, 331
Lubic, Ruth Watson, 229-235
Lysaught, Jerome, 258

M

MacArthur, Douglas, 281, 284
MacDonald, Ida, 387
MacDowell, Mac, 89
MacPhail, Jannetta, 309
Maglacas, Amelia, 122
Magnussen, Ann, 126
Mahoney, Mary, 41
Manley Vocational School, 224
Mannock, Helen, 84
Mansfield, Mike, 121
Manthey, Marie, 236-245, 392
Margaret Sanger Clinic, 304
Martha Washington Home for Crippled Children, 216
Martin, Belinda, 250
Martinson, Ida M., 246-250
Mary Fletcher Hospital, 386
Maryville College, 148
Maslow, Abraham, 22, 360
Mason, Richard, 369, 371

Massachusetts General Hospital, 106, 116, 117, 252, 253, 257
Massachusetts General Hospital School of Nursing, 252, 368
Massachusetts Institute of Technology, 297
Massey, Frank, 20
Mastectomy, women's adaptations after, 20, 21
Maternal–Child Nursing Conference Group, 164
Maternity Center, 304
Maternity Center Association, 233, 234
Maternity clinic, establishment of first, 345
Maternity nursing, 303
Mather College, 197
Mauksch, Hans, 3, 375
Mauksch, Ingeborg Grosser, 3, 163, 251-260, 390
McBride, Angela Barron, 261-266
McBride, William Leon, 263
McCaffery, Margo, 267-273
McClure, Maggie, 200-201
McDonald, Fred, 73
McDonald, Ida, 10
McElmurry, Beverly, 374
McGivern, Diane, 104
McGrorey, Ruth, 255
McIver, Pearl, 210
McKay, Rose, 295
McKeesport Hospital, 140, 142
McKeesport Hospital School of Nursing, 141
McKewen, Anne Hewitt, 107
McLean Hospital, 64
McManus, R. Louise, 181, 183, 186, 253, 274, 277, 371
Mead, Margaret, 189
Mechanic, David, 4
Medical College of Virginia, 31, 344
Medical Education in National Defense (MEND) Program, 367
Medical sociology, 4
Medical-surgical nursing, 108, 151, 178, 198, 233
Megatrends, 134
Mejdrick, Mary Ann, 333
Memorial Hospital for Cancer and Allied Diseases, 182
Mentors, 13, 96
Mercy Nursing School, 30
Mereness, Dorothy, 102
Mernin, Sallie, 224
Merton, Robert, 202
Mexican-Americans, 191
Meyer, Burton, 293
Michael Reese Blood Bank, 221

Michael Reese Hospital, 254
Michael Reese Hospital School of Nursing, 219, 253
Michigan Nurses' Association, 49, 373
Michigan State University, 49
Microteaching, 73-74
Mid-Atlantic Regional Nursing Association, 144
Midwest Alliance in Nursing (MAIN), 309
"Midwest Nursing Data Base," 374
Midwest Nursing Research Society, 374
"Midwest Resources for Graduate Education in Nursing," 374
Midwifery, 233; *see also* Nurse-midwifery
Millar, Marge, 339
Miller, David, 273
Miller, Rita, 32
Miller Hospital, 242
Millis, John S., 307, 308
Minckley, Barbara, 374
Minneapolis General Hospital, 275
Minority Fellowship Programs, 26
Mobile Army Surgical Hospital (MASH) unit, 162
Molbo, Doris, 225
Montag, Mildred, 150, 274-280
Montefiore Hospital, 103, 294
Moore, Mike, 109
Moore, Phyllis, 17
Moran, Elizabeth, 224
Morgan, Lucy S., 346
Morgan, Tirzah, 101
Motherhood, women's movement and, 264
Mount St. Mary's College, 293, 294
Mount Zion Hospital School of Nursing, 71
Mountin, J.W., 210
Ms. magazine, 264
Mullane, Mary Kelly, 120, 224-225, 255, 325
Mulqueen, Father T. Gerald, 87
Murray, Beatrice, 334
Mylander, Jane 107

N

Nahm, Helen, 65, 73, 173
Naisbitt, John, 134
Nakagawa, Helen, 19
Narrow, Barbara, 388
National Academies of Practice, 52
National Academy of Sciences, 213
National Advisory Council of Nurse Training, 118
National Advisory Council of Nurse Training of the United States Public Health Service, 184

National Association for the Advancement of Colored People, 38
National Association of Colored Graduate Nurses (NACGN), 29, 30, 37, 41
National Cancer Institute, 250
National Center for Health Statistics, 377
National Commission for the Study of Nursing and Nursing Education, 184
National Council of Negro Women, 38
National Council of State Boards of Nursing, 91, 92
National Foundation for Infantile Paralysis, 387
National Health Insurance Initiative, 259
National High Blood Pressure Education Program of National Institutes of Health, 111, 112
National Institute of Medicine, 52
National Institute of Mental Health, 20, 25, 40, 64, 100
National Institutes of Health, 212, 388-389
   Clinical Center, 101
   National High Blood Pressure Education Program of, 112
National Joint Practice Commission, 341
National League for Nursing, 38, 39, 48, 49, 63, 82, 92, 100, 185, 202, 203, 213, 353, 367
   Council of Baccalaureate and Higher Degrees of, 255
   Department of Test Construction of, 91
National League of Nursing Education, 19, 177, 278
National Nursing Council for War Service, 32
National Recovery Act, 230
National Teaching Institute, 157
National Youth Administration, 31, 218
Navajo Indian Reservation, 388-389
Neale, Melvin, 11
Neuroscience nursing, 296, 297
New England Deaconess Hospital, 339
New England Journal of Medicine, 272
New Jersey State Nurses' Association, 143
New York City Nursing Council for War Service, 95
New York Hospital, 182, 184, 304, 317
New York State Board of Nursing, 87
New York State Education Department, 87, 89
New York State Nurses' Association Committee on Education, 184
New York Times, 264, 278
New York University, 30, 40, 89, 102
New York Visiting Nurse Service, 277
Newman, Edna, 219, 220

Nez, Mable, 389

Nichols, Barbara, 37

Nigeria, 40

Nightingale, Florence, 162, 180, 219, 323, 354

1979 Study of Credential in Nursing Recommendations: Where Are We Now?, 353

Nixon, Richard, 119, 120

Nolan, Donald, J., 203

Norfolk General Hospital, 196

North Central Accrediting Association, 209

Northern Illinois University, 396

Northern Rhodesia, 40

Northwestern University, 256, 390

Nurse attorneys, 54, 56

Nurse Cadet Corps, 71, 95, 132, 139, 208, 209, 211, 212, 220

Nurse Faculty Fellowship Program in Primary Care, 258

"Nurse Faculty Research Development in the Midwest," 374

Nurse practitioners, 109, 163, 317

Nurse Training Act of 1964, 118

Nurse-midwifery, 80, 82, 163, 233

Nurse-physician team management, 48

Nurses, images of, 133

Nurses' Christian Fellowship, 286

Nurses' Coalition for Action in Politics (N-CAP), 119-120

"Nurses Do Make a Difference" program, 111-112

Nurses' Educational Funds, 41

Nursing

anthropology and, 189, 317

baccalaureate; *see* Baccalaureate nursing

cardiac, 333

case study approach to, 316

collaboration model of, 308

cross cultural, 316

disaster, 345, 368

family, 396

model of, 397-400

gerontological, 346, 347

geropsychiatric, 346

international, 290

international health, 288

maternity, 345

models of

compared, 296

Roy, 292, 294, 295, 296

neuroscience, 296, 297

private practice in, 340

Nursing—cont'd

psychiatric, 391

scientific principles of, 270

transcultural, 190

visiting, 277

during war, 314-315

Nursing administration, 11, 149, 306, 366, 392

Nursing arts, 178, 277

Nursing at the Midcentury, 149

Nursing care, continuity of, 396

Nursing Council for National Defense, 210

Nursing education, 72

accreditation of, 353

consortium in, 309

continuum of, 277-278

doctoral, 309

professional control of, 309

Nursing Experience: Trends, Challenges and Transitions, 144

Nursing Forum, 242

Nursing functions, categories of, 277-278

Nursing Involvement in Health Planning, 134

Nursing Minimum Data Set, 377

Nursing organizations, building, 12

Nursing Outlook, 39, 40, 141, 144

Nursing process, feminism and, 264

Nursing research, 3, 4, 5, 10, 20, 80, 88, 174, 198, 248, 293, 307

in critical care, 158

paradigm for, 308-309

projects in, at WRAIR, 370

and study of elderly, 347-348

at University of Chicago School of Nursing, 373-374

at University of Missouri—Columbia School of Nursing, 375

and Walter Reed Army Institute of Research, 369

at Wayne State University, 372

Nursing Research, 3, 39, 40, 41, 293, 374

Nursing Studies Index, 81

Nursing theory, 81, 226, 297

Nutting, Adelaide, 186, 207, 208

Nyquist, Ewald, 279

O

Obstetrics, 163

Office of Consumer Health Education, 143

Office of Defense Mobilization—National League for Nursing, 368

Office of the Surgeon General, 366, 367, 368

Ogle, Marbury, 221

Ohlson, Virginia M., 281-290
Omen, Dorothea, 118
Open Curriculum Project, 202
Open-heart surgery, 155, 156
Oregon State University, 17
Orlando, Ida, 78, 80
Osborne, Estelle Massey, 41
Osler wards, 106, 107
Oudt, Barbara, 400
Out of the Hard Places, 205
Overlook Hospital, 179, 180

P

Pain
    anticipation of, 271
    in children, 271
    management of, 270-273
Pain control, 267
Parent-child nursing, 134
Parkland Hospital, 268, 269
Parran, Thomas, 210, 213
Passavant Hospital, 217
The Path We Tread: Blacks in Nursing, 1854–1984,
    41, 42
Patient Care Review Committee, 332
Patient, geriatric, 318
Patient plans, interdisciplinary, 316
Paulsen, Dorothy (Smith), 199
Paulson, Virginia Ward, 164
Peace Corps, 239
Pederson, Evelyn, 72
Pediatric Cancer Center, 250
Pediatric nurse practitioner, 127
Pediatric Nurse Practitioner School, 128
Pediatric nursing, 19, 293
    pain management and, 271
Pediatrics, 126
Pennsylvania Department of Health, 112
Pennsylvania Hospital School of Nursing for Men,
    45
Pennsylvania Hospital School of Nursing for
    Women, 45
Pennsylvania Nurses' Association, 112, 141
Pennsylvania State University, 41
People's Republic of China, health care in, 234
Peplau, Hildegard, 12, 99, 119, 121, 338, 341
Peralta Hospital, 71
Perdziak, Bernice, 220
Perkins, Hugh, 132, 135
Perkins, Sylvia, 253
Peterson, Margaret, 130

Peterson, Peter, 130
Petry, Lucile (Leone), 10, 19, 276
Phaneuf, Maria, 338, 341
Phipps Clinic, 262
Physiology, 19, 20
Pitts, Lawrence, 297
The Plague, 18
Polish, David, 226
Politics of Nursing, 134
Porter, Katherine, 198
"Portrait of a Nurse," 342
Poulin, Muriel, 201
Powell, Francis L.A., 220, 333
Practice of Primary Nursing, 244
Practitioner-teacher model, 50
Preoperative teaching, 156-157
Presbyterian–St. Luke's Hospital, 254
Presbyterian–St. Luke's School, 255
Primary care, 258
Primary Care Center, 258
Primary care nursing, 340, 341, 392
Primary healthcare and WHO healthcare goals,
    353
Primary nurse, 184
Primary nursing, 48, 51, 241, 242, 244
Prock, Val, 198
Professional Standards Board, 335
Program for the Nursing Profession, 181
Provident Hospital, 33
Psychiatric nursing, 25, 63-67, 79, 80, 98, 99,
    100, 140, 188, 208, 391
    child, 101, 102, 189
Psychiatry, adolescent, 98
Psychoanalytic Institute, San Francisco, 65
Psychometrics, 89
Public health nursing, 95, 126, 180, 277, 283,
    315, 344, 345, 346
    at University of Illinois, 288
Publication, tips about, 5
Purdue University, 200

Q

Queen's Hospital, 125

R

Radcliffe College, 252
Radiation, effects of, 368
Reagan, Ronald, 142
Reality shock, 171, 173, 174
Reality Shock: Why Nurses Leave Nursing, 173

Red Cross, 345
Red Cross Army Nurse Corps, 328
Red Hook Experiment, 311, 315, 316
Redman, Barbara, 250
Reed, Ann, 91
Reed, Esther, 325
Reed, Frank, 91
Regents External Degree Nursing Program, 90,
    200, 202, 203, 204
Regional Performance Assessment Centers, 204
Regulation
    defined, 352
    and future of nursing, 354
Regulation of Nursing, 353
Rehabilitation, 180, 198
Reichgott, Mike, 111
Reiter, Frances, 233, 253, 257
Report of the President's Commission on Higher Edu-
    cation, 181
Research, nursing; *see* Nursing research
Research in Nursing and Health, 374
Reynolds, Elizabeth, 222
Richards, Linda, 161
Riddle, Estelle Massey, 32
Riverside Hospital, 30
Roberg, O.T., Sr., 283
Robert Wood Johnson Clinical Nurse Scholar,
    114
Robert Wood Johnson Foundation, 4-5, 258
Roberts, Ruby, 225
Robertson, Pat, 240
Robeson, Kay, 325
Robinson, Connie, 296
Rockefeller, Mary, 213
Rockefeller Foundation, 33, 287-288
Rogers, David, 5
Rogers, Martha, 21, 102
Roy, Sister Callista, 291-298
Roy Adaptation Model of Nursing, 292, 294, 295,
    296
Royal College of Nursing, 296
Rush Medical College, 51
Rush Model of Nursing, 51
Rush University, 51
Rush University College of Nursing, 400
Rush–Presbyterian Medical Center, 294
Rutgers Medical School, 143
Rutgers University, 178
Ryan, Thelma, 366

S

Safer, Morley, 361
St. Anne's Hospital School of Nursing, 395
St. Elizabeth's Hospital, 262
St. Elizabeth's School of Nursing, 237, 238
St. John's Hospital School of Nursing, 148, 149
St. Louis University, 148, 149, 172
St. Luke's Hospital, 254
St. Luke's Hospital School of Nursing, 17, 277
St. Luke's Hospital School of Nursing (Tokyo),
    285
St. Mary's Hospital, Troy, New York, 86
St. Peter's Hospital School of Nursing, 89
St. Philip Hospital, 32
St. Philip Nursing School, 30, 33
St. Pierre, Susanne, 361
St. Xavier College, 391
Sampsel, Charles, 231
San Diego County Hospital, 17
San Francisco State University, 72, 73
Sana, Jo, 238
Sargent, Emilie G., 325
Saturday Review of Literature, 49
Schindel, Alice, 19
Schlotfeldt, Rozella M., 297-310, 316
Schmidt, Mildred S., 87, 91, 92, 200, 202, 203
Schorr, Thelma, 147
Schwartz, Doris R., 311-320, 339
Schweitzer, Albert, 312
Scott, Jessie, 118, 121
Seaview Hospital, 30, 98
The Second Sex, 263
Secretary's Committee to Study Extended Roles
    for Nurses, 184
Self-determination, 265
Self-help, 264
Selye, Hans, 225
Seton Hall College, 178
Sex education, 389
Shea, Frank, 391
Sheahan, Marian, 38
Sheehan, Marion, 316
Sheehan, Peg, 238
Sheldon, Eleanor, 19
Shirley Titus Distinguished Professor of Nursing,
    134
Showalter, Ray, 92
Sigma Theta Tau, 52, 144, 222, 265
Sills, Grayce, 12
Silver, Henry, 127

Simmon, Helen, 201
Simmons, Leo, 81
60 Minutes, 361
Skidmore College, 96, 369
Skipper, Jim, 81
Sleeper, Ruth, 117, 118, 253
Slusher, Margaret, 19
Smith, Dorothy, 2, 3, 5, 257
Smith, Gloria R., 321-326
Smith College School of Social Work, 99
Social gerontology, 346
Social work, 99
Society for Research in Child Development, 265
Sociology, 21, 202
  medical, 4
  nursing and, 3, 4
Somers, Anne, 143
Sonstegard, Lois, 167
Southern Regional Education Board, 213
Southern Rhodesia, 40
Southern University, 323
Spaney, Emma, 100
Sparmacher, Ann, 256
Spaulding, Eugenia, 210, 366
Spock, Benjamin, 339
Springer, Ursula, 375
Stafford, Margaret, 225, 257, 327-336
Stanford Research Institute, 68
Stanford University, 73
Statistics, 19
Staupers, Mabel K., 29, 30, 41
Steel, Jean E., 337-342
Stemmler, Edward, 103
Stephenson, Ellen, 19
Stewart, Isabel, 186, 210, 253, 276
Stewart Research Conference, 202
Stokes, Gertrude, 99
Stone, Virginia, 343-348
Stonesby, Ella, 47
Strategies for Teaching Nursing, 74
Strauss, Anselm, 20, 21
Streiter, Ida, 198
Stress, physical and biochemical responses to, 20
Stuart Circle Hospital, 344
Student Project for Amity among Nations (SPAN), 247
Studies in Nursing Management, 134
Study on the Use of the Graduate Nurse for Bedside Nursing in the Hospital, 177

Styles, Margretta M., 338, 349-355
Supreme Command of Allied Powers (SCAP), 284
Surgeon General's Consultant Group on Nursing, 184
Swedish Covenant Hospital, 283
Swedish Covenant Hospital School of Nursing, 282
Symbolic interactionism, 20
Syracuse University, 38, 387

T

Tannenbaum, Bob, 18
Taunton, Roma Lee, 375, 376
Taylor, Charles, 82
Taylor, Joyce Waterman, 225, 257, 333
Teachers College, Columbia University, 32, 64, 99, 100, 102, 117, 143, 150, 180, 181, 182, 184, 185, 200, 201, 202, 207, 208, 210, 232, 233, 253, 274, 276, 279, 344-345, 366, 368
Teaching, preoperative, 156-157
Team leader, 184
Team leadership, 183
Team nursing, 239
  concept of, 180-181
  Kellogg study of, 181-183
Tel Aviv University, 225, 226
Temple University, 47
Tennessee Nurses Association, 271
Texas Woman's University, 268
Thanatology, 362; *see also* Death and dying
Theory Construction in Nursing: An Adaptation Model, 295
Thieldbar, Frances, 254
Thompson, John, 80
Thompson, Julia, 119
Thurber, Marshall, 168
Tibbitts, Clark, 346
Tierney, Ann, 88
Tillich, Paul, 22
Toward a Theory for Nursing, 151
Transactional leadership, 352
Transactional theory, 147
Transcultural nursing, 190
Transcultural Nursing Society, 192
Tuba City Hospital, 389
Tubman, William, 40
Tudor, Gwen, 101
Tuskegee Institute, 31
Twain, Mark, 338, 339

U

Ufema, Joy K., 356-363
United Nations, 121, 213
U.S. Army Medical Corps, 36
U.S. Army Nurse Corps, 17, 32, 162, 297, 304, 313, 364, 366, 368
    Baccalaureate Degree Completion Program of, 367
U.S. Army of Occupation, 283, 285, 286, 305
U.S. Cadet Nurse Corps, 132, 139, 188, 277
U.S. Department of Health, Education and Welfare, 372
U.S. Energy Commission, 286
U.S. Holocaust Memorial Council, 259
U.S. Navy Nurse Corps, 32
U.S. Nurse Cadet Corps, 71, 95, 132, 139, 208, 209, 211, 212, 220
U.S. Public Health Service, 118
    Division of Nursing, 132
University of Alabama, 197
University of Bridgeport, 199, 201
University of California—Berkeley, 17, 67, 71, 366
University of California—Los Angeles, 18, 74, 270, 272, 293
    School of Public Health, 20
University of California—San Francisco, 20, 65, 67, 71, 73, 173, 296, 297, 352
University of Chicago, 89, 200, 218, 221, 226, 238, 254, 256, 257, 283, 289, 305
University of Cincinnati, 189
University of Colorado, 127, 128, 163, 190-191, 295, 305
University of Colorado School of Nursing, 305, 306
University of Concepcion, 295
University of Connecticut, 188
University of Connecticut School of Nursing, 174
University of Denver School of Nursing, 79
University of Edinburgh, 296
University of Florida, 25, 36, 352
    Institute of Human Resources, 25
University of Florida College of Nursing, 2
University of Illinois, 120, 289, 376, 389
University of Illinois College of Nursing, 224, 289, 374
    development of baccalaureate program at, 288-289
University of Illinois—Chicago, 376
University of Iowa, 302, 310

University of Iowa College of Nursing, 12, 13, 125
University of Iowa Hospitals, 303
University of Iowa School of Nursing and University Hospitals, 303
University of Kansas, 375
University of Maryland, 132, 151
University of Michigan, 41, 132
University of Michigan School of Nursing, 373
University of Minnesota, 9, 208, 209, 213, 221, 241, 244, 248, 368
    nursing faculty of, 10
University of Minnesota—Duluth, 247
University of Minnesota Hospital, 239
University of Minnesota School of Nursing, 238, 250, 275, 276
University of Minnesota School of Public Health, 127
University of Missouri, 257, 376
University of Missouri—Columbia School of Nursing, 375, 376
University of Nebraska, 131, 222
University of Nevada—Reno, 174
University of North Carolina, 345, 346
University of North Carolina—Greensboro, 41
University of Pennsylvania, 47, 97, 102, 103, 104, 109, 111, 213, 365
    Hospital of, 110, 111, 232
University of Pittsburgh, 48, 138
University of Portland, 296
University of San Francisco, 297
University of Southern Mississippi, 132
University of Texas, 3
University of Texas Medical Center School of Nursing, 352
University of Toronto, 33
University of Ulster, 296
University of Utah, 191, 372
University of Vermont, 386
University of Washington, 74, 101, 189, 191, 225
University of Washington School of Nursing, 112
University of Wisconsin, 4
University of Wisconsin—Milwaukee, 376, 377

V

Vaillot, Sister Madeleine, 241
Valere Potter Distinguished Professor of Nursing, 258
Vanderbilt University, 50, 258, 269
Vannier, Marion L., 208
Verhonick, Phyllis J., 369

Veterans Administration, 9, 204, 351

Veterans Administration hospitals, 303

Veterans Administration—Pittsburgh, 112

Veterans Hospital, black nurses and, 30

Video Nursing, Inc., 333

Virginia Nurses Association, 345

Visiting Nurse Association, 311, 315

Visiting Nurse Service, 304

Visiting Nurses Association, 325

Visiting nursing, 277

von Gremp, Zella, 224

W

W.K. Kellogg Foundation, 143, 204
  team nursing study of, 181-183

Wagner College, 96, 97

Wald, Florence, 80, 263

Wallace, Mike, 361

Walsh, Maggie, 202

Walter Reed Army Hospital, 262, 365, 369

Walter Reed Army Institute of Research, 367, 368, 369, 370, 371

Wandelt, Mabel, 224, 372

Wangensteen, Owen, 222

War
  and medical management of mass casualties, 367
  nursing during, 314-315

Washington, Booker T., 31

Watson, Goodwin, 100

The Way Things Are, 18

Wayne State University, 202, 224, 225, 321, 322, 324, 352, 372, 373

Wayne State University College of Nursing, 224, 306

Wayne unit, 306

Wayne University College of Nursing, 323, 324, 325

Werley, Harriet H., 202, 364-378

Werner, June, 379-393

West Philadelphia Local Coordinating Council, 111

West Texas State University, 132

West Virginia State College, 31

Western Interstate Commission for Higher Education in Nursing, 295

Western Interstate Commission on Higher Education, 213

Western Reserve University, 197, 199, 307

"What Can Go Wrong When You Measure Blood Pressure," 111

Wheeler, Dorothy, 95

Whelton, Paul, 114

White, Ruth, 280

White House Conferences on Aging, 347

Wiedenbach, Ernestine, 80, 263

Will, Gwen Tudor, 100

William and Mary College, 196

Williams, Dorothy Rogers, 35

Williams, Stan, 241

Williams, Virginia T., 394-400

Wolf, Lulu K., 344

Women's Africa Committee of the African-American Institute, 40

Women's health, theoretical basis of, 264

Women's Health Care Nurse Practitioner Program, 167

Women's Hospital, 168

Women's Hospital, Spanish Harlem, 65

Women's Movement, 264

Womer, Chuck, 243

Wooldridge, Powhatan, 81

World Future Society, 258

World Health Organization, 121, 122, 213, 353

World Health Organization Collaborating Center for Nursing, 290

World War II
  casualities of, 17
  nursing during, 304-305

Wozniak, Dolores, 90, 203, 279

Wright, Benjamin, 89

Wright, Harold N., 275

Y

Yale Intensive Chinese Program, 247

Yale Psychiatric Institute, 79, 80

Yale University, 80, 199, 262-263

Yale University School of Nursing, 82, 351

Yale–New Haven Hospital, 243

Yankton State Hospital, 48

Z

Zimmering, Paul, 99

Zimmerman, Anne, xi, 12, 121, 255, 332, 333, 396

Zonta International, 280